Essential Research Methods for Social Work

Cengage Learning Empowerment Series

Fourth Edition

ALLEN RUBIN
University of Houston

EARL BABBIE
Chapman University

CENGAGE
Learning·

Australia • Brazil • Mexico • Singapore • United Kingdom • United States

CENGAGE
Learning

Cengage Learning Empowerment Series:
Essential Research Methods for
Social Work, **Fourth Edition**
Allen Rubin and Earl Babbie

Product Director: Jon-David Hague

Product Manager: Gordon Lee

Content Developer: Christopher Santos

Product Assistant: Stephen Lagos

Media Developer: John Chell

Marketing Manager: Jennifer levanduski

Art and Cover Direction, Production
Management, and Composition: Lumina
Datamatics, Inc.

Manufacturing Planner: Judy Inouye

Cover Image: Stephanie Horrocks/E+/
Getty Images

For product information and technology assistance, contact us at
Cengage Learning Customer & Sales Support, 1-800-354-9706.

For permission to use material from this text or product,
submit all requests online at **www.cengage.com/permissions**.
Further permissions questions can be e-mailed to
permissionrequest@cengage.com.

Library of Congress Control Number: 2014949462

ISBN: 978-1-305-10168-5

Cengage Learning
20 Channel Center Street
Boston, MA 02210
USA

Cengage Learning is a leading provider of customized learning solutions with office locations around the globe, including Singapore, the
United Kingdom, Australia, Mexico, Brazil, and Japan. Locate your local
office at **www.cengage.com/global**.

Cengage Learning products are represented in Canada by
Nelson Education, Ltd.

To learn more about Cengage Learning Solutions,
visit **www.cengage.com**.

Purchase any of our products at your local college store or at our
preferred online store **www.cengagebrain.com**.

Printed in the United States of America
Print Number: 03   Print Year: 2017

To our wives, Christina Rubin and Suzanne Babbie

Contents

Preface

More than 25 years ago we wrote the text *Research Methods for Social Work*, which is now in its eighth edition. Although that text was an immediate success and continues to be widely adopted, some colleagues who really like that text suggested that we create a less advanced version. At the same time, these colleagues expressed dissatisfaction with the existing less advanced texts, which they characterized as too sketchy and simplistic. What they wanted was a sort of middle-ground text—one that is less advanced than our other text but that still provides *essential* research methods content in sufficient depth and breadth, with social work illustrations and applications throughout, and with a constant focus on the utility of social work research in social work practice.

We wrote the first three editions of this text, *Essential Research Methods for Social Work*, to meet that need. Those editions retained most of the content of the more advanced version, but presented it in a simplified fashion and organized into fewer and shorter chapters. The success of those editions suggests that we met the needs of instructors who deemed the original content to be too advanced for students at the BSW level (and perhaps some at the MSW level).

Although we presented the material in a more simplified fashion, we attempted to maintain the strengths of the more advanced text. For example, we integrated quantitative and qualitative methods and showed how using both can enhance a research study. We attempted to balance the attention we give to both types of inquiry and to their respective advantages and limitations. At times we discussed the strengths and weaknesses of quantitative and qualitative methods in general. At other times we discussed the strengths and weaknesses of specific types of quantitative or qualitative methods. We attempted to do this without implying that either of these two complementary approaches to inquiry has more strengths or weaknesses than the other.

Despite the success of the previous editions of this text, we appreciated the excellent suggestions made to improve them by colleagues who used or reviewed them. This fourth edition contains most of their suggested improvements as well as some that we envisioned ourselves.

EPAS CORE COMPETENCIES

In this edition we continue to show how its contents pertain to the core competencies delineated in the Council on Social Work Education's (CSWE) Educational Policy and Accreditation Standards (EPAS). Each chapter has icons indicating which of the core competencies and recommended practice behaviors apply to the material in that chapter. Some of the icons match a particular chapter section with its corresponding core competency or practice behavior. Others indicate that the entire chapter pertains to several competencies and practice behaviors.

At the end of each chapter, we added competency notes to elaborate upon the core competencies and practice behaviors addressed in the chapter. For example, Chapter 2, on Evidence-Based Practice, contains icons pertaining to seven of the ten EPAS core competencies. One of those seven competency icons in Chapter 2 pertains to engaging in career-long learning. In the competency notes at the end of that chapter, we explain how content in that chapter pertains to each core competency icon. For the icon pertaining to engaging in career-long learning, we explain that evidence-based practitioners recognize that practice-related knowledge can change as newer and better research emerges, and that therefore they must engage in career-long learning to stay abreast of those changes and incorporate them into their practice.

MIXED METHODS

One of the significant additions to our previous edition was its increased attention to mixed methods research. We have expanded that coverage in Chapter 3 of this edition in several ways. We have added a case example box summarizing a published mixed methods study regarding engaging child welfare clients in working relationships. We added a major section describing Creswell's (2014) three basic mixed methods designs. Each of the three designs is described in subsections that include examples of each. Another new section summarizes Creswell's three advanced mixed methods designs.

SIGNIFICANT ADDITIONS AND MODIFICATIONS IN OTHER CHAPTERS

The philosophical section in Chapter 1 on objectivity and paradigms has been removed from that chapter in keeping with suggestions that it is too advanced to appear so soon in the book. Content on that topic already appeared in Chapter 4, so we expanded it somewhat in that chapter. We added a box providing a case example of a social worker exposing the pseudoscientific aspects of thought field therapy and how they weaken critical thinking. We also added a brief discussion of Karl Popper's principle of falsifiability in science.

In the section of Chapter 2 on formulating an evidence-based practice (EBP) question we added a box that illustrates examples of EBP questions about effectiveness, predictors of desirable and undesirable consequences, understanding client experiences, and assessment tools. We also expanded our coverage of systematic reviews and meta-analyses to make searching for evidence more feasible. In another box we expanded our list of Internet sites for reviews and practice guidelines.

In Chapter 4, in addition to the increased coverage regarding objectivity and paradigms we significantly expanded our coverage of longitudinal studies, including more attention to panel attrition as well as a new figure that compares cross-sectional studies to the three types of longitudinal studies.

In response to requests from reviewers, we have moved the section on ethical and cultural issues in social work research up from Part 7 to Part 2. Those areas are now covered in Chapters 5 and 6.

This edition has one fewer chapter because we merged the chapter on reviewing the literature and developing research questions with the chapter on conceptualization. The merged chapter (now Chapter 7) is titled *Problem Formulation*, as it combines those aspects of problem formulation that were previously covered in two separate chapters. The merger involved moving the section on using the library to a new appendix on that topic. The section on writing the literature review overlapped with coverage of that in the appendixes on writing research proposals and reports, so we moved that coverage to those appendixes.

In Chapter 8 on measurement (previously Chapter 7) we added a box near the end of the chapter to further illustrate the difference between reliability and validity. In Chapter 10 on surveys (previously Chapter 9) we added a new section on emerging developments in online surveys to address various technological advances such as the use of tablets and smartphones. We also referred readers to sources for keeping abreast of these developments. Also in this chapter is expanded attention to issues regarding cell phones in telephone surveys.

In Chapter 12 (previously Chapter 11) we elaborated the section on attrition in experiments and quasi-experiments by discussing the use of intent-to-treat analysis. We also added a box clarifying the difference between random assignment in experiments versus random selection in surveys.

Significant revisions were made in Chapter 14 on program evaluation (previously Chapter 13). The chapter has been reorganized so that coverage of the purposes and types of program evaluation and how to plan one follow immediately after the historical overview section. We think that this will give readers a better grasp of the basics of program evaluation before getting into issues regarding its politics and practical pitfalls. The historical overview section is expanded to include more content on accountability and the importance of demonstrating that programs are effective and not harmful, and the connection of accountability to our professional ethics. Also added to the historical coverage is a section on evidence-based practice and the utility of meta-analyses and effect-size statistics. A section on the utility of preexperimental designs in program evaluation that appears later in the chapter returns to those two concepts to show how they can enhance the value of preexperimental designs. That later section also discusses why preexperimental designs are commonly used in program evaluation and why their limitations are less problematic in a program evaluation context. Another significant addition is a section on logic models.

In the quantitative data analysis chapter we expanded the coverage of effect sizes to include odds ratios and risk ratios along with *Cohen's d*. We also added a figure to illustrate how distributions with different degrees of dispersion can have the same central tendency and how reports of descriptive findings that rely exclusively on central tendency can be incomplete and possibly misleading. Also regarding effect sizes, a new Appendix (E) has been added that discusses a novel approach being advanced by one of us (Rubin) for calculating within group effect sizes which might enhance the value of preexperimental designs in program evaluation and reduce the gap between research and practice in a way that aims to advance evidence-based practice to a new level.

We hope you'll find that the above additions and modifications have improved the usefulness of this book. We would like to know what you think of this edition and to receive any suggestions you might have for improving it. Please e-mail us at arubin@mail.utexas.edu.

ANCILLARY PACKAGE

Book Companion Website

For students, the Book Companion Website at www.cengagebrain.com offers practice quizzes and web links.

Instructor's Manual

Also, as with our other text, an *Instructor's Manual* mirrors the organization of this text, offering our recommended teaching methods. Each chapter of the online manual provides an outline of relevant discussion, behavioral objectives, teaching suggestions and resources, and test items. This *Instructor's Manual* is set up to allow instructors the freedom and flexibility needed to teach research methods courses.

The test questions for each chapter include multiple-choice and true–false items and several essay questions that may be used for exams or to stimulate class discussion. Page references to the text are given for the multiple-choice and true–false questions.

ACKNOWLEDGMENTS

We owe special thanks to the following colleagues who reviewed an earlier draft of this text and made valuable suggestions for improving it: Mary Beth Hyatt, Limestone College; Chris Lloyd, University of Arkansas at Little Rock; Paul Lanier, UNC Chapel Hill; Jeannine Rowe, University of Wisconsin-Whitewater; Yong Li, SUNY Plattsburgh; Stephanie Warren, Limestone College; Min Zhan, University of Illinois at Urbana-Champaign.

Thanks also to the following staff members at Cengage Learning for their help in improving this new edition: Gordon Lee, Product Manager; Stephen Lagos, Product Assistant; Ruth Sakata Corley, Production Manager; Deanna Ettinger, IP Analyst; Kristina Mose-Libon, Art Director; Brenda Ginty, Managing Editor, Production; John Chell, Media Editor; and Judy Inoue, Manufacturing Planner

Allen Rubin
Earl Babbie

An Introduction to Scientific Inquiry in Social Work

Part 1 of this text lays the groundwork for the rest of the book by examining the value and fundamental characteristics of scientific inquiry in social work. In Chapter 1 we will begin by discussing the relevance of research to social work practice. We will also explore the use of the scientific method as a basis for how social workers come to know things, and how it helps safeguard against some of the risks inherent in unscientific sources of practice knowledge. Chapter 2 will extend the ideas discussed in Chapter 1 by delving into the evidence-based practice process, which is the primary way that research can be used by social work practitioners.

Why Study Research?

1.1 INTRODUCTION

You may be wondering why social work students are required to take a research course. Part of the answer is that social work research aims to provide the practical knowledge that social workers need to solve everyday practice problems.

You are likely to encounter numerous situations in your career in which you'll use your research expertise and perhaps wish you had more of it. For example, you may administer a substance abuse program whose continued funding requires you to conduct a scientific evaluation of its effectiveness in preventing or alleviating substance abuse. You may provide direct services and want to evaluate scientifically your own effectiveness or the effects certain interventions are having on your clients. You may be involved in community organizing or planning and want to conduct a scientific survey to assess a community's greatest needs. You may be engaged in social reform efforts and need scientific data to expose the harmful effects of current welfare policies and thus persuade legislators to enact more humanitarian welfare legislation.

Even if you never do any research, you'll need to understand it and use it to guide your practice. That's because our profession remains quite uncertain about what really works in many practice situations. Some agencies provide interventions that research has found to be ineffective. Someday you may even work in such an agency and may be expected to provide such interventions yourself. By understanding research and then reading studies that provide new evidence on what is and is not effective, you can increase your own practice effectiveness. By doing so, you will have taken a major step toward establishing an *evidence-based practice*.

The evidence-based practice process (which we will examine in depth in Chapter 2) involves using the best scientific evidence available in deciding how to intervene with individuals, families, groups, or communities. Despite recent advances in identifying evidence-based interventions, social workers today continue to use some interventions and procedures that have not yet received adequate testing. In fact, new interventions continually emerge and are promoted without adequate scientific evidence as to their effectiveness. Some will have received no scientific testing whatsoever. Others will have been "tested" in a scientifically unsound manner in which the research design or measurement procedures were biased to produce desired results. Some will have been tested with certain ethnic groups but not with others. Professional social workers are often bombarded with fliers promoting expensive continuing education training workshops for new interventions. These interventions, of course, are touted as being effective, but such claims may not be warranted. In the face of this reality, understanding scientific inquiry and research methods becomes practice knowledge, too. Learning how to critically appraise whether adequate scientific evidence supports particular interventions in certain practice situations becomes at least as important as learning how to apply interventions in general.

Why can't we just let the researchers produce the needed studies and then tell practitioners the results? First of all, there is a vast range in the quality of the social work research produced and published. Some of it is excellent, and some of it probably should never have been published. It is not hard to find studies that violate some of the fundamental principles that you will learn in this book. If social work practitioners are going to rely on the findings of social work research studies for guidance, then they must understand social work research methods well enough to distinguish strong studies from weak ones. Moreover, the quality of social work research ultimately depends not just on the researchers' methodological expertise but also on their practice knowledge and the practitioners' research knowledge. Without a partnership between practice-oriented researchers and methodologically informed practitioners, there is not likely to be a climate of support in agencies for the type of research our field desperately needs—research that is responsive to the real needs of agency practitioners under conditions that permit an adequate level of methodological rigor. Even if you never produce any research, an understanding of research methods will help you critically appraise and use research produced by others, communicate with researchers to help ensure that their work is responsive to the needs of practice, and ultimately help foster an agency environment conducive to carrying out cogent, relevant studies.

Being professional involves striving to make sure we provide our clients with the most effective services available. How do we do that? Do we just ask our supervisors what they think is best? Such a tactic may be a starting point, but practitioners who conform only to ongoing practices without keeping abreast of the latest research in their fields are not doing everything they can to provide clients with the best possible service.

Given how frequently social work services have been found to be ineffective, and the recent emergence of studies identifying new and apparently effective interventions, failure to keep abreast of the research in the field is a serious shortcoming. We cannot justify disregarding research with the rationalization that we are too busy helping people. If our services have not been tested for their effects on clients, then chances are we are not really helping anyone. In that case, who benefits from our blind faith in conventional but untested practice wisdom? Not our clients. Not those who pay for our services. Not society. Do we? In one sense, perhaps. It is less work for us if we unquestioningly perpetuate ongoing practices. That way, we do not make waves. We do not have to think as much. There is one less task—reading research reports— in our daily grind. In the long run, however, practitioners who keep up on the research and know they are doing all they can to provide the best possible services to their clients might experience more job satisfaction and be less vulnerable to burnout.

The main reason to use research, however, is compassion for our clients. We care about helping them; thus we seek scientific evidence about the effects of the services we are providing and of alternative services that might help them more. If the services we provide are not effective and others are, then we are harming our clients by perpetuating our current services. We are wasting their time (and perhaps money) by allowing their problems to go on without the best possible treatment. Because we are inattentive to the literature, we deny our clients a service opportunity that might better help them.

Thus, understanding research methods and using research discriminately have much to do with basic social work values such as caring and compassion. The practitioner who understands and uses research shows more concern for the welfare of his or her clients, and ultimately is more helpful to them, than the one who does not take that trouble, perhaps misguided by erroneous assumptions about research.

However, studies on the effects of social work interventions are just one prominent example of useful social work research. A long list of other examples of completed research studies would also convey the value of research to social work, and why students preparing to become practitioners should know research methods so they can use and contribute to such research. Many of these studies will be cited as illustrations of the methodological concepts addressed throughout this text.

We also could cite countless examples of additional topics on which you might someday want to see research findings. Only a few will be cited here. For example, why do so many of your agency's clients terminate treatment prematurely? What types of clients stay with or drop out of treatment? What reasons do they give? What services did they receive? How satisfied were they with those services? In what part of your target community or region should you locate your outreach efforts? Where are you most likely to engage hard-to-reach individuals such as the homeless or recent immigrants? What proportion of your target population does not understand English? Why are so few ethnic minorities being served by your agency? What does your agency mean to them? What is the agency atmosphere like from their viewpoint? We could go on and on, but you get the idea: The possibilities are endless.

Ethics is one of the most important concerns of social workers as they consider research and appears as a recurring topic of discussion throughout this book. The Code of Ethics of the National Association of Social Work-

EP 2.1.2b

ers specifically requires social workers to keep current with and critically appraise practice-related research in the professional literature, and to include evidence-based knowledge as part of the knowledge base for their practice. When we use research discriminatingly, we uphold and advance the values and mission of the profession, and thus are more ethical in our practice. Still, social work students quite commonly approach research methodology with skepticism about the ethics of many research studies. We will address those ethical concerns in various chapters of the book, not just in the chapter devoted to ethics. We hope that by the time you finish reading this book, you will have a better understanding not only of the ethical dilemmas involved in social work research, but also of the reasons why our professional code of ethics comes to bear on our responsibility to understand, use, and contribute to research.

Perhaps more than ever before, social work research offers all social workers an opportunity to make a difference in the problems they confront. Whether you become a direct service practitioner seeking to maximize the effectiveness of your services, or a social activist seeking to promote more humane social welfare legislation (or perhaps both), the success of your efforts to help people will likely be enhanced by your use of scientific inquiry and research. In the hope that this introduction has whetted your appetite for what you are about to learn in this book, let's now examine the various ways social workers seek to know things.

1.2 HOW DO SOCIAL WORKERS KNOW THINGS?

Social work students study various theories about human behavior and alternative perspectives on social welfare policies and social work intervention. Sometimes these theories and perspectives seem compatible. Sometimes they do not. How will you decide which of them should guide your future practice? Will you base your decision on which author or professor is most esteemed? Will you just take your field supervisor's word for things, or accept without question long-standing agency traditions? To what extent will you rely on your own direct social work experience as the basis of your practice wisdom? This book aims to help you develop a scientific approach for answering questions like these now and throughout your career as a social worker.

Let's begin by examining a few things you probably know already. You know that the world is round and that people speak Japanese in Japan. You probably also know it's cold on the planet Mars. How do you know? Unless you've been to Mars lately, you know it's cold there because somebody told you, and you believed what you were told. Perhaps your physics or astronomy instructor told you it was cold on Mars, or maybe you read it in *Newsweek*. You may have read in *National Geographic* that people speak Japanese in Japan, and that made sense to you, so you didn't question it.

Some of the things you know seem absolutely obvious to you. If someone asked how you know

the world is round, you'd probably say, "Everybody knows that." There are a lot of things everybody knows. Of course, at one time, everyone "knew" the world was flat.

Most of what we know is a matter of agreement and belief. But we also can know things through direct experience and observation. If you sleep outside like a homeless person on a cold winter night, you won't need anyone to tell you it's cold—you notice that all by yourself. When your experience conflicts with what everyone else knows, though, there's a good chance you will surrender your experience in favor of the agreement.

Let's take an example to illustrate this: Imagine you're at a party. It's a high-class affair, and the drinks and food are excellent. You are particularly taken by one type of appetizer the host brings around on a tray. It's breaded, deep-fried, and especially tasty. You have a couple, and they are delicious! You have more. Soon you are subtly moving around the room to be wherever the host arrives with a tray of these nibblies. Finally, you can't contain yourself anymore. "What are they?" you ask. "How can I get the recipe?" The host lets you in on the secret: "You've been eating breaded, deep-fried worms!" Your response is dramatic: Your stomach rebels, and you promptly throw up all over the living room rug. Awful! What a terrible thing to serve guests!

The point of the story is that both feelings about the appetizer would be real. Your initial liking for them, based on your own direct experience, was certainly real, but so was the feeling of disgust you had when you found out that you had been eating worms. It should be evident, however, that the feeling of disgust was strictly a product of the agreements you have with those around you that worms aren't fit to eat. That's an agreement you entered into the first time your parents found you sitting in a pile of dirt with half a wriggling worm dangling from your lips. When they pried your mouth open and reached down your throat to find the other half, you learned that worms are not acceptable food in our society.

Aside from the agreements we have, what's wrong with worms? They're probably high in protein and low in calories. Bite-sized and easily packaged, they're a distributor's dream. They are also a delicacy for some people who live in societies that lack our agreement that worms are disgusting.

We learn some things by experience, others by agreement. This young man seems to be into personal experience.
SOURCE: Allen Rubin

Other people might love the worms but be turned off by the deep-fried breadcrumb crust.

Reality, then, is a tricky business. You probably already suspect that some of the things you "know" may not be true, but how can you really know what's real? People have grappled with that question for thousands of years. Science is one of the strategies that has arisen from that grappling.

1.3 THE SCIENTIFIC METHOD

Science offers an approach to both agreement reality and experiential reality. That approach is called the **scientific method**. One key feature of the scientific method is that *everything is open to question.* That means that in our quest to understand things, we should strive to keep an open mind about everything we think we know or that we want to believe. In other words, we should consider the things we call "knowledge" to be *tentative and subject to refutation.* This feature has no exceptions. No matter how long a particular tradition has been practiced, no matter how much power or esteem a particular authority figure may have, no matter how noble a cause may be, we can question any belief—no matter how cherished it may be.

Another key feature of the scientific method is the search for *evidence based on observation* as the basis for knowledge. The term *empirical* refers to this valuing of observation-based evidence. As we will see later, one can be empirical in different ways, depending on the nature of the evidence and the way we search for and observe it. For now, remember that the scientific method seeks truth through

---

scientific method An approach to inquiry that attempts to safeguard against errors commonly made in casual human inquiry. Chief features include viewing all knowledge as provisional and subject to refutation, searching for evidence based on systematic and comprehensive observation, pursuing objectivity in observation, and replicating studies.

Key Features of the Scientific Method

A mnemonic for remembering some of the key features of the scientific method is the word *trout*. Think of catching or eating a delicious trout,* and it will help you remember the following key features:

T	**Tentative:**	Everything we think we know today is open to question and subject to reassessment, modification, or refutation.
R	**Replication:**	Even the best studies are open to question and need to be replicated.
O	**Observation:**	Knowledge is grounded in orderly and comprehensive observations.
U	**Unbiased:**	Observations should be unbiased.
T	**Transparent:**	All procedural details are openly specified for review and evaluation and to show the basis of conclusions that were reached.

*If you are a vegetarian, you might want to just picture how beautiful these fish are and imagine how many of their lives you are saving.

observed evidence—not through authority, tradition, or dogma—no matter how much social pressure or political correctness may be connected to particular beliefs, and no matter how many people embrace those beliefs or how long they have been proclaimed to be true. It took courage long ago to question fiercely held beliefs that the earth is flat. Scientifically minded social workers today should find the same courage to ask whether adequate evidence supports interventions or policies that they have been told or taught to believe in.

They should also examine the nature of that evidence. To be truly scientific, the observations that have accumulated that evidence should have been *orderly* and *comprehensive*. The *sample* of observations should have been *large* and *diverse*. The observational *procedures should be specified* so that we can see the *basis for the conclusions* that were reached, and be able to judge whether the conclusions are indeed warranted in light of the evidence and the ways in which it was observed.

The specified procedures should also be scrutinized for potential bias. The scientific method recognizes that we all have biases that can distort how we look for or perceive evidence. It therefore emphasizes the *pursuit of objectivity* in the way we seek and observe evidence. None of us may ever be purely objective, no matter how strongly committed we are to the scientific method. No matter how scientifically pure their research may be, researchers want to discover something important—that is, to have findings that will make a significant contribution to improving human well-being or (less nobly) enhancing their professional stature. The scientific method does not require that researchers deceive themselves into thinking they lack these biases. Instead, recognizing that they may have these biases, they must find ways to gather observations that are not influenced by their biases.

Suppose, for example, you devise a new intervention to prevent child abuse. Naturally, you will be biased in wanting your intervention to be effective. It's okay to have that bias and still scientifically inquire whether your intervention really does prevent child abuse. You would not want to base your inquiry solely on your own subjective clinical impressions. That approach would engender a great deal of skepticism about the objectivity of your judgments with regard to the intervention's effects. Thus, instead of relying exclusively on your clinical impressions, you would devise an observation procedure that was not influenced by your own biases. Perhaps you would see if the parents receiving your intervention had fewer child abuse incidents reported to the child welfare department than parents who received a different intervention. Or perhaps you would administer an existing paper-and-pencil test that social scientists regard as a valid measure of parental child-raising knowledge and attitudes. Although neither alternative can guarantee complete objectivity, each would be more scientific than your subjective judgments, reflecting your effort to pursue objectivity.

Because there are no foolproof ways for social science to guarantee that evidence is purely objective, accurate, and generalizable, the scientific method also calls for the *replication* of studies. This is in keeping with the notion that all knowledge is tentative and refutable.

EP 2.1.6b

Replication means duplicating a study to see if the same evidence and conclusions are produced. It also refers to modified replications in which the procedures are changed in certain ways that improve on previous studies, or determine if findings hold up with different target populations or under different circumstances. The need to replicate implies that scientifically minded social workers should have the courage to question not only cherished beliefs that were not derived from scientific evidence but also the conclusions of scientific studies and the way those studies were carried out. The box "Key Features of the Scientific Method" summarizes these features and provides a handy mnemonic for remembering them.

1.4 OTHER WAYS OF KNOWING

The scientific method is not the only way to learn about the world. We also can learn from personal experience, tradition, authority, common sense, and the popular media. Let's now examine each of these ways of acquiring knowledge and compare them to the scientific method. As you will see, some of the things people believe from these alternative sources of learning may not be true. When thinking critically and with a scientific orientation, people would want to consider observations that might contradict or disprove some of the things they "learn" from these other ways of "knowing." Some conclusions people reach from these other sources may well be true, but no matter how much they cherish a belief, unless it is possible to state observations that would contradict or disprove, it no conclusion can be considered to be "scientific." Karl Popper (1934) described this as the principle of *falsifiability* in science. This is what distinguishes scientific conclusions from religious, political, or philosophical *beliefs*.

1.4a Personal Experience

As mentioned earlier, we all discover things through our personal experiences from birth on, and from the agreed-on knowledge that others give us. Sometimes this knowledge can profoundly influence our lives. We learn that getting an education will affect how much money we earn later in life and that studying hard will result in better examination grades. The term *practice wisdom*, also as noted

earlier, refers to social workers learning things about social work practice via their personal practice experience. Despite the value of such experience, it is important to recognize its limitations and the ways in which the scientific method can augment it and safeguard against some common errors. Sometimes information that we believe to be knowledge acquired through our practice experience actually comes from observations that are casual and unsystematic or influenced by our predilections. We will examine these errors more closely later in this chapter. For now, you should remember that the scientific method safeguards against these errors through observations that are systematic, comprehensive, and unbiased.

1.4b Tradition

One important secondhand way to attempt to learn things is through tradition. Each of us inherits a culture made up in part of firmly accepted knowledge about the workings of the world. We may learn from others that planting corn in the spring will gain the greatest assistance from the gods, that sugar from too much candy will cause tooth decay, or that the circumference of a circle is approximately twenty-two sevenths of its diameter. We may test a few of these "truths" on our own, but we simply accept the great majority of them. These are the things that "everybody knows."

Tradition, in this sense of the term, has some clear advantages for human inquiry. By accepting what everybody knows, you are spared the overwhelming task of starting from scratch in your search for regularities and understanding. At the same time, tradition may be detrimental to human inquiry. If you seek a fresh and different understanding of something that everybody already understands and has always understood, you may be seen as a fool. More to the point, it will probably never occur to you to seek a different understanding of something that is already understood and obvious.

When you enter your first job as a professional social worker, you may learn about your agency's preferred intervention approaches. Chances are you will feel good about receiving instructions about "how we do things in this agency." You may be anxious about beginning to work with real cases and relieved that you won't have to choose between competing theories to guide what you do with clients. In conforming to agency traditions, you may feel that you have a head start, benefiting from the accumulated "practice wisdom" of previous generations of practitioners in your new work setting. Indeed you do. After all, how many recently graduated social workers are in a better position than experienced agency staff to determine the best intervention approaches in their agency?

But the downside of conforming to traditional practice wisdom is that you can become too comfortable doing it. You may never think to look for evidence that the traditional approaches are (or are not) as effective as everyone believes, or for evidence concerning whether alternative approaches are more effective. And if you do seek and find such evidence, you may find that agency traditions make your colleagues unreceptive to the new information.

1.4c Authority

Despite the power of tradition, new knowledge appears every day. Aside from your personal inquiries, you will benefit from others' new discoveries and understandings throughout your life. Often, acceptance of these new acquisitions will depend on the status of the discoverer. You're more likely, for example, to believe a physician who says that the common cold can be transmitted through kissing than to believe your landlord who says the same thing.

Like tradition, authority can both assist and hinder human inquiry. Inquiry is hindered when we depend on the authority of experts speaking outside their realm of expertise. The advertising industry plays heavily on this misuse of authority by having popular athletes discuss the nutritional value of breakfast cereals or movie actors evaluate the performance of automobiles, among similar tactics. It is better to trust the judgment of the person who has special training, expertise, and credentials in the matter, especially in the face of contradictory positions on a given question. At the same time, inquiry can be greatly hindered by the legitimate authority who errs within his or her own special province. Biologists, after all, can and do make mistakes in the field of biology. Biological knowledge changes over time; so does social work knowledge.

Several decades ago, authorities in psychoanalysis and family therapy blamed faulty parenting as a prime cause of schizophrenia. They commonly portrayed the mothers of individuals who became afflicted with schizophrenia as "schizophrenigenic mothers" with cold, domineering, and overprotective behavior that did not permit their children to develop individual identities. No compelling research evidence supported these concepts, but they were nonetheless widely accepted by mental health practitioners. As a result, social workers and other mental health professionals often dealt with the family as a cause of the problem rather than developing treatment alliances with them. Many parents consequently reported feelings of self-recrimination for the illnesses of their offspring. As you can imagine, this was painful for many parents. Current scientific evidence, however, indicates that treating schizophrenia as a result of bad parenting can be harmful both for family members and for their ill relative. Consequently, mental health professionals have designed new treatment approaches—usually called psycho educational approaches—that seek to build alliances with families and be more supportive of them.

Our point is that knowledge accepted on the authority of legitimate and highly regarded experts can be incorrect, even harmful. It is therefore important for social work practitioners to be open to new discoveries that might challenge the cherished beliefs of their respected supervisors or favorite theorists. They must also keep an open mind about the new knowledge that displaces the old. It, too, may be flawed, no matter how prestigious its founders.

Both tradition and authority, then, are two-edged swords in the search for knowledge about the world. They provide us with a starting point for our own inquiry, but they also may lead us to start at the wrong point or push us in the wrong direction.

1.4d Common Sense

Common sense is often cited as another way to know about the world, such as when we reason that it makes no sense to think that rainbows cause rainfall, because rainbows appear only after the rain starts falling and only when the sun shines during the storm. However, sometimes what we think of as being "common sense" is actually received wisdom, knowledge that because of its association with tradition or authority has come to be accepted as self-evident and commonsensical.

The problem with this sort of common sense is that what "everyone knows" can be wrong. Long ago everyone "knew" that the earth was flat. It was just plain common sense, because you could see no curvature to the earth's surface, and because hell was below the surface. At one point in our history, a great many people thought that slavery made common sense. Terrorists think terrorism makes common sense. Many people think that laws against gays and lesbians marrying or allowing them to raise children make common sense. Most social workers think such laws make no sense whatsoever. Although common sense can be rational and accurate, it is an insufficient and highly risky alternative to science as a source of knowledge.

1.4e Popular Media

Much of what we know about the world we learn from articles and reports in newspapers and magazines, on television, and on the Internet. We all know about the 9/11 attack on the World Trade Center from watching coverage of that tragic event on television and reading about it in newspapers, in magazines, and on the Internet. The same sources informed us of the victims and heroes in New York City, Pennsylvania, and Washington, D.C. They provided information on the perpetrators of the attack, and many related issues and events. We did not have to conduct a scientific study to know about the attack or have strong feelings about it. Neither did we need tradition or authority. We did not have to experience the attack firsthand (although we really did experience it—and probably were at least somewhat traumatized by it—through what we saw and heard on our television sets).

Although we can learn a lot from the popular media, we can also be misled by them. Witness, for example, disagreements between cable news networks such as CNN, MSNBC, and the more politically conservative FOX as to which news network is really more trustworthy, fair, and balanced. Although most journalists might strive for accuracy and objectivity, some may be influenced by their own political biases. Some might also seek out the most sensationalist aspects of events and then report them in a biased manner, to garner reader interest or to appeal to their prejudices. (Media ratings affect corporate profits.) In addition, there are some journalists whose job is to deliver editorials and opinion pieces, not to report stories factually. What we learn from them is colored by their viewpoints.

Even when journalists strive for accuracy in their reportage, the nature of their business can impede their efforts. For example, they have deadlines to meet and word limits on how much they can write. Thus, when covering testimony at city hall by residents of an African American neighborhood, some of whom support a proposed plan for economic development in their neighborhood and some of whom oppose it, journalists might not be influenced by a group such as the majority of residents, who may not be outspoken. Instead, journalists might unintentionally rely on the least representative, but most outspoken and demonstrative, supporters or opponents of the proposed development.

The popular media also include fictional movies and television shows that can influence what we think we know about the world. Some fictional accounts of history are indeed educational; perhaps informing us for the first time about African Americans who fought for the Union during the American Civil War or sensitizing us to the horrors of the Holocaust or of slavery. Others, however, can be misleading, such as when most mentally ill people are portrayed as violent or when most welfare recipients are portrayed as African Americans.

More and more these days, many folks—especially college students and other young adults—get much of their information from the Internet. Despite the wonders of the Internet and the immediate availability of a tremendous array of useful information therein, information available on unscientific sites is not risk-free. Perhaps most noteworthy in this regard is the Wikipedia website. Wikipedia is a free online encyclopedia that anyone can edit. A humorous illustration of the risks inherent in allowing anyone to edit the information available at that site was reported by Eve Fairbanks (2008, p. 5). In February 2008, during the heat of the battle between Hillary Clinton and Barack Obama for the Democratic Party's presidential nomination, somebody accessed Hillary's Wikipedia page and replaced her photo with a picture of a walrus. Perhaps in retaliation, the next month a Hillary supporter altered Barack's bio so that it called him "a Kenyan-American politician." Also that month, somebody replaced Hillary's whole page with "It has been reported that Hillary Rodham Clinton has contracted genital herpes due to sexual intercourse with an orangutan."

EP 2.1.3a

Obviously, the above Wikipedia example is extreme, and unless readers despised Hillary or were imbibing something peculiar when accessing the above website, they would not believe that the walrus was really Hillary or that she'd had intercourse with an orangutan. But it does illustrate that despite the tremendous value of the Internet, and the fact that we can learn many valuable things from popular media, they do not provide an adequate alternative to scientific sources of knowledge.

1.5 RECOGNIZING FLAWS IN UNSCIENTIFIC SOURCES OF SOCIAL WORK PRACTICE KNOWLEDGE

As discussed previously, scientific inquiry helps safeguard against the dangers of relying exclusively on tradition, authority, common sense, and popular media as the sources of knowledge to guide social work practice. It also helps safeguard against errors we might make in attempting to build wisdom primarily through our own practice experiences and unsystematic observations. Scientific inquiry also involves critical thinking so that we can spot fallacies in what others may tell us about their practice wisdom or the interventions they are touting. Let's now look at some common errors and fallacies you should watch out for, and some of the ways that science guards against those mistakes.

1.5a Inaccurate Observation

Imagine that you are providing play therapy to a group of eight hyperactive children with various emotional and behavioral problems. At the end of each one-hour group session, you write up your progress notes. It is unlikely that you will have observed every clinically meaningful thing that transpired for each child in the session. Even if you did notice something meaningful in one child, you may not have realized it was meaningful at the time, especially if it happened just as two children across the room went out of control and began fighting.

Moreover, you may not remember certain observations later when it is time to record your progress notes—especially if something happens that keeps you from recording your observations until later that day. Recall, for example, the last person you talked to today. What kind of shoes was that person wearing? Are you even certain the person was wearing shoes? On the whole, we are pretty casual in observing things; as a result, we make mistakes. We fail to observe things right in front of us, and mistakenly observe things that are not so.

In contrast to casual human inquiry, scientific observation is a conscious activity. Simply making observation more deliberate helps to reduce error. You probably don't recall, for example, what your instructor was wearing the first day of this class. If you had to guess now, you'd probably make a mistake. But if you had gone to the first class meeting with a conscious plan to observe and record what your instructor was wearing, then you would be more accurate.

Both simple and complex measurement devices help guard against inaccurate observations. Moreover, they add a degree of precision that is well beyond the capacity of the unassisted human senses. Suppose, for example, that you had taken color photographs of your instructor that first day. If you consulted that photograph when recalling your instructor's clothes, you'd be hard-pressed to make a mistake!

1.5b Overgeneralization

When we look for patterns among the specific things we observe around us, we often assume that a few similar events are evidence of a general pattern. The term for this is *overgeneralization*. Imagine you are a community organizer and you just found out that a riot has started in your community. You have a meeting in two hours that you cannot miss, and you need to let others at the meeting know why citizens are rioting. Rushing to the scene, you start interviewing rioters, asking them about their motivations. If the first two rioters tell you they are doing it just to loot some stores, you would probably be wrong in assuming that the other 300 are rioting only for that reason.

Scientists guard against overgeneralization by committing themselves in advance to a sufficiently large sample of observations (see Chapter 10). The *replication* of inquiry provides another safeguard. As we mentioned earlier, replication basically means repeating a study and checking to see if the same results are produced each time. Then the study may be repeated under slightly varied conditions. Thus, when a social work researcher discovers that a particular program of service in a particular setting is effective, that conclusion is only the beginning. Is the program equally effective for all types of clients? For both men and women? For both old and young? Among all ethnic groups? Would it be just as effective in other agency settings? This extension of the inquiry seeks to find the breadth and the limits of the generalization about the program's effectiveness.

Independent replications by other researchers extend the safeguards. Suppose you read a study that shows an intervention to be effective. Later, you might conduct your own study of different clients, perhaps measuring effectiveness somewhat differently. If your independent study produced exactly the same conclusion as the one you first read, then you would feel more confident in the generalizability of the findings. If you obtained somewhat different results or found a subgroup of clients among whom the findings didn't hold at all, you would have helped to save us from overgeneralizing.

1.5c Selective Observation

One danger of overgeneralization is that it may lead to *selective observation*. Once you have concluded that a particular pattern exists and developed a general understanding of why, then you will be tempted to pay attention to future events and situations that correspond with the pattern. You will most likely ignore those that don't correspond. Figure 1.1 illustrates the circular fashion in which overgeneralization can lead to selective observation, and selective observation can lead to overgeneralization.

Racial and ethnic prejudices depend heavily on selective observation for their persistence. However, selective observation occurs among all of us, not just people with distasteful prejudices. Social work practitioners who have great compassion for their clients and who do the best they can to help their clients, for example, commonly engage in selective observation in ways that may limit their effectiveness. The practitioner trained to interpret problems

FIGURE 1.1 An Illustration of Overgeneralization and Selective Observation

OVERGENERALIZATION

Ann is Dr. Donald Dork's first recipient of dorkotherapy (his new treatment for depression). She seems happy afterward, so he claims that dorkotherapy is an effective treatment for depression and encourages others to use it.

SELECTIVE OBSERVATION

Dr. Dork next provides dorkotherapy to four more clients: Jan, Dan, Nan, and Van. Three of them remain unhappy, but Dork fails to notice that, only being impressed by Nan's apparent happiness.

OVERGENERALIZATION & SELECTIVE OBSERVATION

Dr. Dork guest lectures in a direct practice elective on the treatment of depression. His lecture discusses only the cases of Ann and Nan, as he extols the wonders of dorkotherapy.

in terms of family communication dynamics is apt to look vigilantly for signs of potential communication problems, and then magnify the role those problems play in explaining the presenting problem. At the same time, that practitioner is likely to overlook other dynamics, or perhaps to underestimate their impact.

Usually, a research design will specify in advance the number and kind of observations to be made as a basis for reaching a conclusion. If we wanted to learn whether women were more likely than men to support the pro-choice position on abortion, we would commit ourselves to making a specified number of observations on that question in a research project. We might decide to interview a thousand people on the issue. Even if the first 10 women supported the pro-choice position and the first 10 men opposed it, we would interview everyone selected for the study and recognize and record each observation. Then we would base our conclusion on an analysis of all the observations.

1.5d Ex Post Facto Hypothesizing

Suppose you run an outreach program for battered women still living with the batterer, and you have the idea that if your program is successful, soon after entering treatment the battered women should start feeling more positive about themselves as individuals and about their capacity to be less dependent on the batterer. You might test the program's effectiveness by conducting a brief structured interview with clients several times before and after they enter treatment. In the interview, you would find out (1) how good they feel about themselves, and (2) how capable they feel they are of living independently away from the batterer. You would then examine whether they feel better or more capable after entering treatment than before entering it. But suppose their answers are the opposite of what you expected—that is, suppose they express worse feelings after entering treatment than before. What a disappointment. "Aha!" you might say. "The reason for the negative findings is that before entering treatment the women were unconsciously protecting themselves with the psychological defense mechanism of denial. They expressed better feelings before treatment because they were refusing to face the dangerous and deplorable situation they were in. Our treatment helped overcome some of this denial, and helped them get more in touch with an unpleasant reality they need to face in order to begin trying to change. Therefore, the more 'negative' responses recorded after entering

treatment are really more 'positive'! It is good that they are beginning to recognize what bad shape they were in; that's the first step in trying to improve it."

The example we have just described is sometimes called *ex post facto hypothesizing*, and it is perfectly acceptable in science if it doesn't stop there. The argument you proposed clearly suggests that you need to test your hypothesis about the program's effectiveness in new ways and among a broader spectrum of people. The line of reasoning doesn't prove your hypothesis is correct, only that there's still some hope for it. Later observations may prove its accuracy. Thus, scientists often engage in deducing information, and they follow up on their deductions by looking at the facts again.

1.5e Ego Involvement in Understanding

The search for knowledge is not a trivial intellectual exercise: It can affect our personal lives and have psychological significance to us. If you lose your job or fail to get a promotion, you may be tempted to conclude that your boss wants to get you out of the way to promote a personal friend. That explanation would save you from examining your own abilities and worth. Consequently, any challenge to that explanation is also a challenge to your abilities and worth.

In countless ways, we link our understandings of how things are to the image of ourselves we present to others. Because of this linkage, any disproof of these understandings tends to make us feel stupid, gullible, and generally not okay. So we commit ourselves all the more unshakably to our understanding of how things are, and create a formidable barrier to further inquiry and more accurate understanding. This *ego involvement in understanding* is commonly encountered in social work practice. Naturally, practitioners see it in some of their clients, who may blame others or external circumstances beyond their control for their difficulties, rather than accepting responsibility and facing up to the way their own behavior contributes to their problems. Practitioners are less likely to see the way their own ego involvement may impede practice. Rather than scientifically reexamining the effectiveness of our approaches to practice (which we may like because we are used to them and have special expertise in them), we may tenaciously engage in selective observation, ex post facto hypothesizing, and other efforts to explain away evidence that suggests our approaches may be ineffective.

Social workers who conduct evaluation research frequently confront this form of ego involvement when their evaluations fail to support the effectiveness of the programs they are evaluating. The same people who initially express disinterest and lack of expertise in evaluation can become fanatical critics and challenge the methodology of any study whose findings question the efficacy of their program, no matter how rigorous that study might be. Influenced by their ego involvement and vested interests in the program under fire, administrators and practitioners may grasp at any straw or magnify any trivial methodological imperfection in a study in order to undermine the study's methodological credibility. Similarly, they may not notice even glaring methodological imperfections in studies whose results they like; they are apt to tout those studies as proving the value of their programs. (Chapter 14, which explains program evaluation, will examine this phenomenon in more depth.)

Administrators and practitioners aren't the only social workers who are vulnerable to ego involvement in understanding. Program evaluators and other social work researchers are just as human. They also run the risk of becoming personally involved in and committed to the conclusions they reach in scientific inquiry. Sometimes it's worse than in nonscientific life. Imagine, for example, that you have discovered an apparent cure for cancer and have been awarded the Nobel Prize. How do you suppose you'd feel when somebody else published an article that argued your cure didn't really work? You might not be totally objective.

1.5f Other Forms of Illogical Reasoning

Social workers need to use critical thinking and be vigilant in examining the reasoning of individuals whose ego involvement or vested interests lead them to make fallacious claims or arguments. Gibbs and Gambrill (1999) have identified some common fallacies that you are likely to encounter, in addition to the ones we've already mentioned. One is called the *straw person argument*, in which someone attacks a particular position by distorting it in a way that makes it easier to attack. For example, opponents of proposed health care reforms—such as

national health insurance or a patients' bill of rights with managed-care companies—might exaggerate the extent to which the proposed reforms contain features that will inflate costs or increase delays in obtaining medical care.

Another fallacy is the *ad hominem attack*, which tries to discredit the person making an argument rather than addressing the argument itself. In a debate between two psychologists who had vested interests in competing forms of psychotherapy, for example, one ridiculed the legitimacy of the school from which the other had obtained her professional degree.

Sometimes new interventions are promoted based merely on their *newness or promise*. A related fallacy is the bandwagon appeal, in which a relatively new intervention is touted on the basis of its growing popularity. The implicit assumption is that the sheer weight of the number of your professional colleagues jumping on the bandwagon must mean that the intervention is effective. When you encounter colleagues promoting an intervention in this way, you might want to remind them that a lobotomy was once considered to be a new and promising treatment for mental illness.

We do not wish to imply that interventions or policies that are promoted with fallacious appeals are necessarily ineffective or undesirable. Some might eventually be supported, or may have already been supported, by sound scientific studies, despite the unfortunate ways their proponents have chosen to promote them. The point is not to be swayed one way or the other by appeals based on illogical reasoning. Instead, you should look for and critically appraise the scientific evidence for them (and this book aims to give you the tools you'll need to do that).

1.5g The Premature Closure of Inquiry

Overgeneralization, selective observation, and the defensive use of illogical reasoning all conspire to close inquiry prematurely. This discussion began with our desire to understand the world around us, and the various errors we have detailed often lead us to stop inquiry too soon. The bigot who says, "I already understand Mexicans, so don't confuse me with facts," has achieved a personal closure on the subject. Sometimes this closure of inquiry is a social rather than individual act. For example, the private foundation or government agency that refuses to support further research on an "already understood" topic effects closure as a social act, as does the denominational college that prohibits scholarship and research that might challenge traditional religious beliefs. Social workers may do this by refusing to consider evidence that their favored interventions, programs, or policies are not as effective as they believe they are. The danger of premature closure of inquiry is obvious. It halts attempts to understand things before understanding is complete. If you review the history of human knowledge, you will reach a startling conclusion: We keep changing the things we know—even the things we know for certain. In an important sense, then, any closure of inquiry is premature.

At its base, science is an open-ended enterprise in which conclusions are constantly being modified—that is an explicit norm of science. Experienced scientists accept it as a fact of life, and expect established theories to be overturned eventually. Even if one scientist considers a line of inquiry to be completed forever, others will not. Even if a whole generation of scientists closes inquiry on a given topic, a later generation is likely to set about testing the old ideas and changing many of them. In part, the reward structure of science supports this openness. Although you may have to overcome a great deal of initial resistance and disparagement, imagine how famous you would be if you could demonstrate persuasively that something people have always believed simply isn't true. What if you could prove that carbon monoxide was really good for people? The potential rewards for astounding discoveries keep everything fair game for inquiry in science.

1.5h Pseudoscience

EP 2.1.3

In your social work career, you will probably learn about some practice methods or interventions that are based on the solid foundation of a replicated string of strong research studies. But you'll probably also encounter many claims about the wonders of other interventions based on sloppy and biased research studies, or on unscientific sources of knowledge. Some of these claims will be expressed in the form of fliers advertising expensive continuing education training workshops in some "miracle cure." Sometimes these claims will seem to contain some of the

elements of scientific inquiry and thus have the surface appearance of being scientific, but upon careful inspection will be seen to violate one or more principles of the scientific method or contain fallacies against which the scientific method attempts to guard. Such claims are *pseudoscientific*.

The prefix "pseudo-" means "fake"; thus, *pseudoscience* is fake science. Some figureheads may espouse an intervention based on pseudoscience because they have a vested interest in the intervention—perhaps gaining fame and fortune from marketing books and workshops on it. Chances are, they really believe in what they are touting. Their followers might also be true believers, and might be so ego-invested in the intervention they swear by that they won't let facts get in the way of their cherished beliefs.

It's not hard to recognize some purveyors of pseudoscience, such as those peddling miracle cures for obesity or other woes on late-night TV infomercials based on the testimonials of a few individuals, some of whom might be celebrities. But other pseudoscientific claims can be harder to recognize, especially when they are based on some weak studies that managed to slip by reviewers and get printed in professional journals. Figure 1.2 displays some common warning signs that should arouse your suspicions as to whether an intervention might be based more on pseudoscience than on science. Most of the signs pertain to flawed ways of knowing that have been discussed earlier in this chapter. The presence of one or more of these signs does not *necessarily* mean that an intervention is based on pseudoscience. The flaws might be in the inappropriate way some are touting the intervention, not in the quality of the research being cited. For example, solid scientific research might find an intervention to be moderately effective with certain problems under certain conditions, while purveyors of the intervention make it sound like a more universal cure-all. Still, if you recognize these signs, you should at least be aware of the possibility that pseudoscience is in play, and the more warning signs you detect, the more skeptical you should become. At the bottom of Figure 1.2 are features of the scientific method that we discussed earlier and that contrast with pseudoscience.

Although it is important to recognize purveyors of pseudoscience, not everything that some people call pseudoscience is fake or without value. Likewise,

FIGURE 1.2 Common Warning Signs for Detecting the Possibility of Pseudoscience

---

Pseudoscientific proponents of an intervention will:

- *Make extreme claims about its wonders*
- *Overgeneralize regarding whom it benefits*
- *Concoct unusual, speculative explanations for its effectiveness*
- *Concoct pretentious jargon for aspects of their intervention that sounds scientific but really is not*
- *Base their claims on:*
  - *Testimonials and anecdotes*
  - *Authorities or gurus*
  - *Tradition*
  - *Sloppy or biased research*
  - *The popularity of their intervention*
  - *Selective observation of a few cases*
  - *Portrayals of their intervention in popular media (such as movies or TV shows)*
- *React to disconfirming evidence by:*
  - *Ignoring it, citing only those sources that support their intervention*
  - *Explaining it away through ex post facto hypothesizing*
  - *Engaging in ad hominem attacks on those who cite the disconfirming evidence*
  - *Exaggerating the importance of minor flaws in the source of the disconfirming evidence*
  - *Exaggerating the rigor and superiority of the studies that support their intervention*
  - *Engaging in a straw person argument in which they distort the arguments of those who question them so as to make those arguments easier to attack*
  - *Citing a historical scientist (such as Galileo or Freud) whose contemporaries were wrong in questioning them (thus implicitly comparing themselves to the historical luminary)*
  - *Attributing it to the vested interests of those who are threatened by their intervention and thus engaged in a conspiracy to discredit it*
- *Pursue a premature closure of inquiry by pressuring their followers to refrain from:*
  - *Subjecting their claims to rigorous, unbiased research*
  - *Publishing studies that produce disconfirming findings (pointing out flaws in the studies or arguing that publication will prevent those in need of their intervention from benefiting from it)*

In contrast, those employing the scientific method will:

- *Encourage and welcome the pursuit of disconfirming evidence because all knowledge is provisional and subject to refutation*
- *Be cautious in making claims*
- *Avoid overgeneralization*
- *Base their conclusions on:*
  - *Observations that are comprehensive, systematic, and unbiased*
  - *Rigorous studies*
  - *Replication, not ignoring or dismissing disconfirming evidence produced by sound research*

---

just because purveyors of a new intervention have a vested interest in it, that does not necessarily mean that the new intervention is worthless or harmful—even if the research they report or cite is shoddy and biased. Moreover, as noted above, some pseudoscience involves interventions that have value and are based on solid scientific research but have their effects exaggerated by purveyors of pseudoscience who have vested interests in them. Some things that are now seen as scientifically acceptable were

portrayed as pseudoscientific when first introduced. Eye movement desensitization and reprocessing (EMDR), for example, was once decried as pseudoscience by its various critics, who cited the weaknesses in its early research and some of the pseudoscientific ways that its proponents were touting it. However, after its effectiveness was replicated by many studies with scientifically rigorous designs, it became widely accepted among scientifically oriented experts on psychotherapy research as one of

Case Example: A Former Insider Exposes the Pseudoscientific Aspects of Thought Field Therapy and How They Weaken Critical Thinking

This case example is based on an article written by Monica Pignotti (2007) about her own experience. Early in Monica's career as an MSW level social worker she read an online posting claiming that a new intervention called thought field therapy (TFT) cured a wide range of psychological problems relevant to her caseload. Although Monica was skeptical about the claims as well as TFT's unusual techniques—such as finger taps on certain body parts while the client focused on a psychological problem or physical symptoms—her dialogue with the psychologist who invented TFT eventually convinced her to try the technique on herself. She did so, and it seemed to relieve the job-related anxiety she had been experiencing at the time. As Monica later reported, she "stopped thinking critically about TFT and openly embraced it" (Pignotti, 2007, p. 395). She paid a large amount of money to obtain training in TFT, more than the combined cost of her college and graduate education. After the training, Monica's enthusiastic commitment to TFT increased, and she began practicing it and collaborating with its inventor, Roger Callahan, in writing about TFT. She became known as Callahan's most outspoken and fanatical supporter, defending TFT against criticism that it was pseudoscience. Over time, however, Monica developed ethical concerns about how TFT was being misrepresented by Callahan. Realizing that no scientific research existed supporting the effectiveness of this controversial therapy, she told Callahan that she wanted to test some of the TFT claims with several TFT practitioners. He reacted negatively, and their relationship deteriorated. Nevertheless, she eventually did test it out in a small scientific experiment with results that defied the claimed benefits of TFT. During the ensuing years, Monica's doubts accumulated as she observed Callahan trying to explain away failures of clients not benefitting from TFT, his tolerance of unscientific endorsements of TFT, and the increasingly grandiose claims being made for TFT. After reading the book *Science and Pseudoscience in Clinical Psychology* (by Lilienfeld et al., 2003—listed as an additional reading at the end of this chapter), Monica realized that she had spent seven years of her career supporting a pseudoscientific therapy. Nevertheless, she told Callahan that she would continue to support him if he would drop the unsupported claims and scientifically test the effectiveness of TFT. Callahan refused and soon ceased responding to her emails. Eventually, Monica published a retraction to an earlier article she had written in support of TFT and decided to obtain her PhD in social work at Florida State University so she could educate people about evidence-based practice, the dangers of pseudoscience, and the importance of research in social work.

Source: Pignotti, M. (2007). "Thought Field Therapy: A Former Insider's Experience." "*Research on Social Work Practice*, Vol. 17, No. 3, May 2007, 392–407.

the three most effective treatments for acute posttraumatic stress disorder (PTSD). In contrast to EMDR is an intervention called thought-field therapy. The case example box at the top of this page describes how a social worker exposed the pseudoscientific aspects of that intervention and how those aspects weaken critical thinking.

1.6 MAIN POINTS

- Social work research seeks to provide the practical knowledge that social workers need to solve the problems they confront.
- Social work research seeks to give the field the information it needs to alleviate human suffering and promote social welfare.
- Social work research seeks to accomplish the same humanistic goals as social work practice.

Like practice, social work research is a compassionate, problem-solving, and practical endeavor.
- Social work practitioners should understand social work research methods well enough to be able to distinguish strong studies from weak studies.
- Compassion for our clients is the main reason for us to use research.
- Social workers have an ethical responsibility to utilize research and contribute to the development of the profession's knowledge base.
- Much of what we know is by agreement rather than by experience.
- Personal experience, tradition, and authority are important sources of understanding, but relying on them exclusively can be risky.
- In day-to-day inquiry, we often make mistakes. Science offers protection against such mistakes.

- When we use the scientific method, everything is open to question, and we should keep an open mind about everything we think we know or want to believe.
- When we use the scientific method, we should consider the things we call "knowledge" to be provisional and subject to refutation.
- When we use the scientific method, we should search for evidence that is based on observation as the basis for knowledge.
- Scientific observations should be systematic, comprehensive, and as objective as possible.
- Scientific observations should be specified in ways that show the basis for the conclusions that were reached, and that allow others to judge whether the evidence warrants those conclusions.
- The scientific method calls for the replication of studies.
- People often observe inaccurately, but such errors are avoided in science by making observation a careful and deliberate activity.
- Sometimes we jump to general conclusions on the basis of only a few observations. Researchers and scientific practitioners avoid overgeneralization through replication, or the repeating of studies.
- Once a conclusion has been reached, we sometimes ignore evidence that contradicts that conclusion, only paying attention to evidence that confirms it. Researchers and scientific practitioners commit themselves in advance to a set of observations to be made regardless of whether a pattern seems to be emerging early.
- When confronted with contradictory evidence, all of us make up explanations to dismiss the contradictions, often making assumptions about facts not actually observed. Researchers and scientific practitioners, however, make further observations to test those assumptions.
- Our ego involvement can influence us to disregard evidence that contradicts our beliefs.
- Sometimes people simply reason illogically. Researchers and scientific practitioners avoid this by being as careful and deliberate in their reasoning as in their observations. Moreover, the public nature of science means that scientists have colleagues looking over their shoulders.
- Whereas people often decide they understand something and stop looking for new answers,

researchers and scientific practitioners—as a group—ultimately regard all issues as open.
- Pseudoscience has the surface appearance of being scientific, but upon careful inspection can be seen to violate one or more principles of the scientific method, or to contain fallacies against which the scientific method attempts to guard.

1.7 PRACTICE-RELATED EXERCISES

1. Interview a social work practitioner. Ask her about whether she uses research to guide her practice, and why or why not. Take notes on her answers and bring your notes to class for discussion.
2. Examine a few recent issues of the journals *Research on Social Work Practice* and *Social Work Research* Find an article that reports evidence about the effectiveness of an intervention and thus illustrates the value of research in guiding social work practice. Discuss how a social worker who wants her practice to be evidence-based might be guided by that article.
3. Interview a social work practitioner or a social work student who has been doing her field placement for a while. Ask her about the interventions or practice techniques she most strongly believes in. Ask her how she came to develop these beliefs. What does she base those beliefs on? Is it her experience? Research findings? Authority? Tradition? Something else?
4. Suppose you were recently hired as a social worker in a nursing home. During your first week on the job, you notice that some direct care aides routinely humiliate residents who complain or request extra help. You'd like to change this unfortunate situation, but it's only your first week on the job. Discuss how you would use tradition and authority to guide what you should do. Discuss the pros and cons of relying *exclusively* on tradition and authority to guide you. How might you examine whether research can guide your decision about how to handle this dilemma?
5. Review the common errors of human inquiry discussed in this chapter in the section "Recognizing Flaws in Unscientific Sources of Social Work Practice Knowledge." Find a magazine or newspaper article, or perhaps a letter to the editor,

that illustrates one of those errors. Discuss how a scientist would avoid making the error.

6. Think about a social work practice approach or a social justice issue or cause to which you are strongly committed and about which you fiercely hold certain beliefs. Rate yourself on a scale from 1 to 10 on how scientific you are willing to be about those beliefs. How willing are you to allow them to be questioned and refuted by scientific evidence? How much do you seek scientific evidence as a basis for maintaining or changing those beliefs? Find a classmate whose beliefs differ from yours. Discuss your contrasting views. Then rate each other on the same 10-point scale. Compare and discuss the degree to which your self-rating matches the rating your classmate gave you. If you are not willing to be scientific about any of those beliefs, discuss your reasons in class and encourage your classmates to share their reactions to your point of view.

1.8 INTERNET EXERCISES

1. Find an article that discusses the scientific method by entering the search term "scientific method." Read an article that sounds useful. Write down the bibliographic reference information for the article and summarize the article in a few sentences.

2. Find an example of a research study that offers useful implications for social work practice. Write down the bibliographic reference information for the report and briefly describe the report's implications for practice. For example, if you are interested in treatment for individuals suffering from mental disorders and substance abuse, then you might want to read "Analysis of Postdischarge Change in a Dual Diagnosis Population" by Carol T. Mowbray and colleagues, which appeared in Health and Social Work (May 1999). Toward the end of the article appears a section with the subheading "Implications for Practice."

3. Search the Internet for controversial interventions that have been depicted as pseudoscientific. (You can enter one of the following search terms: *pseudoscientific interventions thought field therapy,* or *EMDR.*) Summarize the arguments and counterarguments you find regarding whether a particular intervention is or is not pseudoscientific. Write down which side has the more

persuasive argument and why, or why you are uncertain about the issue.

1.9 ADDITIONAL READINGS

Brekke, J. (2012). "Shaping a science of social work." *Research on social work practice,* 22(5), 455–464. In this article John Brekke proposes a way to shape social work into a scientific discipline. He argues that its domains of inquiry involve seeking to understand and foster change regarding people who are poor, marginalized, or disenfranchised and seeking to understand social factors associated with disease and health. Brekke also proposes core constructs and goals for a science of social work. This article appears in a special issue of the journal, *Research on Social Work Practice,* which includes additional articles on the theme of shaping a science of social work.

Gibbs, L., & Gambrill, E. (1999). *Critical thinking for social workers: Exercises for the helping professions.* Thousand Oaks, CA: Pine Forge Press. This enjoyable workbook is filled with useful exercises to help you reason more effectively about social work practice decisions, as well as other decisions that you will encounter in life. By teaching you to recognize propaganda in human services advertising and to recognize and avoid fallacies and pitfalls in professional decision making, the exercises will help you think like an evidence-based practitioner.

Kirk, S. A., & Reid, W. J. (2002). *Science and social work.* New York: Columbia University Press. This book presents a critical appraisal of past and present efforts to develop scientific knowledge for social work practice and to make social work practice more scientific. It identifies the conceptual and practical impediments these efforts have encountered, offers lessons to improve future efforts, and is optimistic about the progress being made. It is a must-read for students and others who want to learn about the enduring struggle to improve the scientific base of social work practice.

Lilienfeld, S. O., Lynn, S. J., & Lohr, J. M. (2003). *Science and pseudoscience in clinical psychology.* New York: Guilford Press. Although the title of this provocative text refers to psychology, it is highly relevant to social work. Reading it will enhance your understanding of the scientific method and help you recognize warning signs of pseudoscientific claims touting the effectiveness of certain interventions. Such claims contain some elements of scientific inquiry and thus have the surface appearance of being scientific, but upon careful inspection they can be seen to violate one or more principles of the scientific method or to contain fallacies against which the scientific method attempts to guard.

1.9a Competency Notes

EP 2.1.2b: Make ethical decisions by applying standards of the National Association of Social Workers Code of Ethics (p. 5): Social workers apply the NASW code of ethics as part of conducting ethical research as well as appraising whether the research completed or proposed by others is ethical.

EP 2.1.3: Apply critical thinking to inform professional judgments (p. 16): Social workers apply critical thinking when recognizing fallacies in unscientific pseudoscience and other unscientific sources of practice knowledge.

EP 2.1.3a: Distinguish, appraise, and integrate multiple sources of knowledge, including research-based knowledge and practice wisdom (p. 12): The scientific method is not the only way to learn about the world. We all discover things through our personal experiences from birth on, and from the agreed-on knowledge that others give us. Critically thinking social workers will understand how different paradigms can influence research-based knowledge.

EP 2.1.6b: Use research evidence to inform practice (p. 8): Social workers should apply the scientific method when ascertaining which policies, programs, or interventions are the most effective.

Evidence-Based Prac

2.1 INTRODUCTION

Throughout the history
practice models have
practitioners synthe
views when dec
practice situa
example,
ory an
mo

- Be willing to test their own beliefs or conclusions and then alter them on the basis of new experiences and evidence
- Formulate appropriate questions and then gather and appraise evidence as a basis for making decisions

2.3 EVIDENCE-BASED PRACTICE IMPLIES CAREER-LONG LEARNING

Before evidence-based, critical thinking practitioners can consider the best scientific evidence as a basis for their practice decisions, they first need to find such evidence. They cannot be passive in this process, hoping or assuming that the evidence will somehow find its way to them. They need to know how to find relevant evidence and to understand research designs and methods so that they can "critically appraise" the validity of the evidence they find. Finally, they need to use research methods to evaluate whether the evidence-based actions they take actually result in the outcomes they seek to achieve (Gambrill, 2001).

In recognizing that even evidence-based knowledge is subject to change as newer and perhaps better studies might refute it with better evidence, being an evidence-based practitioner implies engaging in career-long learning. It means recognizing the need to search for and appraise new evidence as an ongoing, "lifelong" part of one's practice.

EP 2.1.1e

The evidence-based practitioner will not always find evidence that automatically determines what actions to take. Sometimes the evidence will be inconclusive, with some valid studies implying one course of action, and other valid studies implying a different way to intervene. Sometimes the evidence will indicate what actions *not* to take, such as when studies show certain interventions or policies to be *ineffective*. Although evidence-based practitioners will not always find a clear answer on how best to proceed, the important thing is to look for those answers. You would not want to miss them if they exist. And even when the evidence is mixed, it will often indicate possibilities you had not considered that are supported by more evidence than another action you were considering. Moreover, you can test one possibility out, and if that doesn't appear to be working, you can try one of the other evidence-based alternatives.

Sometimes the evidence will point toward taking an action that the client does not want. One key step in the evidence-based practice process is considering the values and expectations of clients and involving them as informed participants in the decision-making process. Gambrill (2001) reminds us that evidence-based practice is primarily a compassionate, client-centered approach to practice. We care about finding the best evidence because we care about maximizing our helpfulness to the client. We should not, therefore, disregard the values and concerns of clients when deciding whether the evidence we find fits the particular client with whom we are working.

Also, even interventions supported by the best evidence are not necessarily effective with every client or situation. An intervention that works with clients of one ethnic group may be less effective with clients of a different ethnicity. An intervention that is effective in treating male batterers may not work with female batterers, or vice versa. The evidence-based practitioner needs to consider whether the client or situation in question really matches the context in which the evidence-based intervention was tested. And even if things match, one should remember that evidence-based interventions are not guaranteed to work. Studies providing valid evidence that an intervention is effective typically find that the intervention is *more likely* to be effective than some alternative, not that it is effective with every case. These considerations underscore the importance of the client-centered nature of evidence-based practice and of taking the final step in the evidence-based practice process: using research methods to evaluate whether the evidence-based actions you take with a particular case result in the outcomes you seek. Much of what you learn in this book will help you through this and other steps in the evidence-based practice process—such as finding relevant studies and critically appraising them—and doing so throughout your career.

2.4 FLEXIBILITY IN EVIDENCE-BASED PRACTICE

As implied above, although the *evidence-based practice* process involves making practice decisions in light of the best research evidence available, it

FIGURE 2.1 Integrative Model of Evidence-Based Practice (EBP)

does not rigidly constrict practitioner options. Instead, it encourages practitioners to integrate scientific evidence with their practice expertise and knowledge of the idiosyncratic circumstances bearing on specific practice decisions. The diagram that appears in Figure 2.1 illustrates this integrative model of evidence-based practice. The diagram indicates that practice decisions should be made by skillfully blending the three elements (the best research evidence, practitioner expertise, and client attributes) at the intersection of the circles in the shaded area. Shlonsky and Gibbs (2004) discuss this model as follows:

> *None of the three core elements can stand alone; they work in concert by using practitioner skills to develop a client-sensitive case plan that utilizes interventions with a history of effectiveness. In the absence of relevant evidence, the other two elements are weighted more heavily, whereas in the presence of overwhelming evidence the best-evidence component might be weighted more heavily. (p. 138)*

Although the evidence-based practice process is most commonly discussed in regard to decisions about what interventions to provide clients, it also applies to decisions about how best to assess the practice problems and decisions practitioners make at other levels of practice—such as decisions about social policies, communities, and so on. For example,

a clinical practitioner employing the evidence-based practice process with a newly referred client will attempt to find and use the most scientifically validated diagnostic tools in assessing client problems and treatment needs, and then develop a treatment plan in light of the best research evidence available as to what interventions are most likely to be effective in light of that assessment, the practitioner's clinical expertise regarding the client, and the client's idiosyncratic attributes and circumstances.

At the level of social policy, evidence-based practitioners will attempt to formulate and advocate policies that the best research available suggests are most likely to achieve their desired aims. Likewise, evidence-based practitioners working at the community level will make practice decisions at that level in light of community-level practice research. Moreover, evidence-based practitioners at each level will utilize research methods to evaluate the outcomes of their practice decisions to see if the chosen course of action is achieving its desired aim. If it is not, then the evidence-based practitioner will choose an alternative course of action—again in light of the best research evidence available and again evaluating its outcome.

2.5 STEPS IN THE EVIDENCE-BASED PRACTICE PROCESS

Now that we've explored the nature of evidence-based practice, let's examine more closely the steps that have been recommended in the evidence-based practice process. As we do, you may notice the need for practitioners to understand research methods throughout the process.

2.5a Step 1. Formulate a Question to Answer Practice Needs

In the first step, the practitioner formulates a question based on what is known; the question will be relevant to the practice decision that must be made and to what additional information is needed to best inform that decision. Although much of the literature on evidence-based practice focuses on questions about the effectiveness of programs, policies, or interventions, there are other types of evidence-based practice questions. According to Rubin

(2008), four common types of evidence-based practice questions are as follows:

1. What intervention, program, or policy has the best effects?
2. What factors best predict desirable or undesirable consequences?
3. What's it like to have had my client's experiences?
4. What assessment tool should be used? (p. 43)

The box "Examples of EBP Questions" illustrates some specific types of EBP questions that can be asked at different levels of social work practice for each of the above four general types of EBP questions. In that questions about effectiveness are the most common ones, let's focus on them as we consider the process of formulating an EBP question.

Suppose, for example, you reside in Alaska and work in a residential treatment facility for girls with emotional and behavioral problems, most of whom are Native Alaskans who have been victims of physical or sexual abuse. Your first question might be, "What interventions have the best research evidence supporting their effectiveness with abused girls with emotional and behavioral problems who reside in residential treatment facilities?" As you search the literature for the answer to that question, you may quickly discover the need to incorporate into your question information about variations in the girls' characteristics.

Interventions that are effective in treating posttraumatic stress disorder (PTSD) may not be effective with borderline personality disorder. A particular intervention might be very effective with girls who have had a single trauma but ineffective with girls who have had multiple traumas. That same intervention might even be potentially harmful for girls with dissociative disorders. You might find that some interventions have been found to be effective with older girls but not younger ones. Consequently, you may have to revise your question and perhaps formulate a series of questions. Instead of just asking about abused girls with emotional and behavioral problems, you may need separate questions about the most effective interventions for girls with different diagnoses, different problem histories, different ages, and so on.

You'll also want to incorporate the Native Alaskan ethnicity of the girls into your question. If you do not, you are likely to find many studies relevant to your question, but perhaps none that included Native Alaskan participants. Consequently, the

---

Examples of EBP Questions

Questions About Effectiveness

- Is trauma-focused cognitive-behavioral therapy more effective than nondirective play therapy in reducing the trauma symptoms of children who have been sexually abused?
- Is the Housing and Urban Development VA-Supported Housing Program effective in decreasing homelessness among chronically homeless military veterans?

Questions About Predictors of Desirable or Undesirable Consequences

- Are child welfare direct service practitioners with social work degrees less likely to turn over or burn out than their counterparts who do not have social work degrees?
- What characteristics of foster parent–child matches are most and least likely to result in successful and unsuccessful foster care placements?

Questions About Understanding Client Experiences

- What is it like for homeless females to stay in an emergency shelter?
- How do multiple overseas deployments of military service members affect the service member's family in regard to family roles, the quality of the marital relationship, and the well-being of their children?

Questions About Assessment Tools

- What standardized measure of symptoms of posttraumatic stress disorder (PTSD) is most accurate in assessing for possible PTSD among combat veterans returning from Iraq or Afghanistan?
- What measure of children's self-esteem is best able to detect small changes in self-esteem among children who are being treated for low self-esteem and thus will be the best choice for monitoring treatment progress among such children?

interventions you find that were effective with girls of other ethnicities might not be effective with the girls with whom you work. If you do incorporate the Native Alaskan ethnicity of the girls into your question, you will find numerous studies dealing with traumatized youths with substance abuse problems in combination with their other trauma-related disorders and few, if any, studies that focus exclusively on singular disorders that do not include substance abuse. You'll also find studies whose findings indicate that Native Alaskan youths with PTSD may not have a diagnosis of PTSD because cultural factors may influence them to mask their PTSD symptoms. Learning this might lead you to reconsider the diagnoses some of the girls have received and to consider evidence-based interventions for PTSD for some girls who had not previously had that diagnosis in their case record. Thus, including ethnicity in your question can make a huge difference in the evidence you find and the implications of that evidence for your practice.*

The questions we've discussed so far did not specify an intervention in advance. We took an open-ended approach in looking for evidence about whatever interventions have been studied and supported by the best scientific evidence. Sometimes, however, you'll have a good reason to narrow your question to one or more interventions that you specify in advance. Suppose, for example, the traumatized girls you work with are very young, and your agency tradition is to provide nondirective play therapy as the prime intervention for every girl. As a critically thinking, evidence-based practitioner, you might inquire as to the scientific evidence base for this tradition. Suppose that esteemed consultants or supervisors ask you to just trust their authority— or "practice wisdom"—on the matter. As a truly evidence-based practitioner, you'll need the courage to proceed with a search for evidence anyway. If you do, you'd have good reason to formulate a question that specifies play therapy, such as the

following: "Will nondirective play therapy be effective in reducing the trauma symptoms of sexually abused Native Alaskan girls aged 8 or less?"

Sometimes it is reasonable to specify one or more alternative interventions in your question, as well. Suppose, for example, a colleague who works in a similar setting, and with similar clients, informs you that in her agency they prefer directive play therapy approaches that incorporate components of exposure therapy, and that a debate rages among play therapy luminaries as to which of the two agencies' approaches makes more sense on theoretical grounds. Seeking scientific evidence to guide your practice in light of this new information, you might formulate an evidence-based question that specifies both alternative interventions, such as: "If sexually abused Native Alaskan girls aged 8 or less receive nondirective play therapy or directive play therapy, which will result in fewer trauma symptoms?" You might also want to expand the question to include exposure therapy.

The following acronym might come in handy when you want to formulate a question that specifies one or more interventions in advance: CIAO. To help you remember this acronym, in Italy "ciao" means goodbye, so long, hasta la vista baby, or later, dude. Here's what the acronym stands for:

- Client characteristics
- Intervention being considered
- Alternative intervention (if any)
- Outcome

Applying the acronym to our question illustrated above, we get:

- **C:** If sexually abused Native Alaskan girls aged 8 or less
- **I:** Receive nondirective play therapy
- **A:** Or directive play therapy incorporating exposure therapy techniques
- **O:** Which will result in fewer trauma symptoms?

2.5b Step 2. Search for the Evidence

In Chapter 7 and Appendix B we will examine how to conduct literature reviews to guide research projects. The same principles that we will examine later apply to practitioners searching for evidence to guide their practice decisions. However, practitioners

---

*We hope you are thinking critically and thus wondering what the evidence is for the assertions made in this paragraph on what you'll find if you incorporate the Native Alaskan ethnicity of the girls into your question. The assertions are based on what one of us (Rubin) found when he conducted a literature search on this question in preparation for a talk on evidence-based practice delivered on April 29, 2006, at the University of Alaska Anchorage School of Social Work.

rarely have nearly as much time and other resources for conducting exhaustive literature reviews as researchers are likely to have. One option likely to appeal to busy practitioners is the use of computerized library searches or searches of professional literature databases.

To help you search for literature online, your libraries may provide a variety of Internet professional literature database services, such as Social Services Abstracts, PsycINFO, and many others. There is considerable overlap in what you'll find across different databases in related areas. For example, if you are looking for literature on child abuse, many of the references you'll find using Social Services Abstracts can also be found using PsycINFO. You can scan your library's list of online abstracting or indexing databases to find one (or perhaps a few) that seems most relevant to your topic.

After you enter some search terms, these databases will instantly provide you with a list of relevant books, journal articles, dissertations, and other publications related to your search terms. You can click on the ones that seem most pertinent to view the abstract for that reference. You may even be able to download the entire journal article, book, or dissertation.

What search terms you enter will depend on what you are looking for. If you're interested in a particular book or journal, for example, you can click on *title* and then enter the title of that book or journal. To find the published works of a particular author, you can click on *author* and then enter the name of that author. To find references related to a particular subject area, you would follow the same procedure, typing in a search term connected to your subject of interest. Search terms that can be used in a search for evidence about the effectiveness of interventions include *treatment outcome, effectiveness, evaluation, intervention*, and similar terms. These terms can be used in conjunction with those that are descriptive of the client and situation, such as *residential treatment facility, post-traumatic stress disorder (PTSD), dissociative disorders, borderline personality disorder, sexual abuse*, and *child abuse* for the example mentioned in Step 1.

Suppose, for example, you want to find literature on support groups for battered women. Then you might enter such search terms as *battered women, spouse abuse, domestic violence*, or *support groups*. You will have options as to how broad or narrow you'd like the search to be. If you want the search to be limited to evaluations of the effectiveness of support groups for battered women, then you could ask for only those references pertaining to an entire set of keywords, such as *battered women and evaluation*. You might also be able to limit the search according to other criteria, such as certain years of publication or the English language. If you want a broader search, then you can enter more keywords or more broadly worded keywords (*domestic violence* will yield more references than *battered wives*), and you would ask for references pertaining to any of your keywords instead of the entire set.

If you do not have online access to the professional literature through a specific library, an alternative is to access the Internet directly through your own personal computer's search engine. There are various websites through which you can search for the literature you need. One site is provided by the National Library of Medicine at www.nlm.nih.gov. There you can obtain free usage of MEDLINE, a database containing many references relevant to social work and allied fields.

Perhaps the most expedient option, however, is to use a popular search engine, such as Google. Finding sources and links to relevant websites on Google has become so popular that many folks now use the word *google* as a verb. You might be amazed at how many things you can "google." Google our names, for example, and you can find links to websites about our books and other things, including our photos. Google also provides a website called Google Scholar. The difference between the two sites is that Google is more likely to provide you with a list of links to websites pertinent to your search term, whereas Google Scholar is geared to providing you with links to specific published scholarly articles and books on the topic.

Systematic Reviews and Meta-Analyses

Another way to expedite your search is to look for systematic reviews and meta-analyses. A **systematic review** will report comprehensive searches for unpublished as well as published studies that address a particular research question. For example, it may examine which interventions have been found to be most (and least) effective in alleviating a specific problem. A good, trustworthy systematic review will indicate whether its authors have a vested interest in the intervention or other focus of the review. It also will critically appraise the rigor of the included studies and will give more weight to the most rigorous studies in developing conclusions and implications for practice. A **meta-analysis** is a type of systematic review that pools the statistical results across studies of particular interventions and generates conclusions about which interventions have the strongest impacts on treatment outcome. Understandably, busy practitioners with limited time to search for literature might rely exclusively on the systematic reviews or meta-analyses that they find. However, there are risks in relying exclusively on the *top-down* search approach, as we will discuss in the next section.

Top-Down and Bottom-Up Searches

Two major approaches to searching for evidence have been defined by Mullen (2006) as the *top-down* and *bottom-up* strategies. Using the bottom-up strategy, you would search the literature looking for any and all sources that provide evidence pertaining to the practice question you formulated. You would then read and critically appraise the quality of the evidence in each source, judge whether it is applicable to your unique practice decision, and ultimately choose a course of action based on what you deem to be the best applicable evidence available. Using the top-down strategy, instead of starting from scratch to find and appraise all the relevant studies yourself, you would rely on the results of evidence-based searches that others have done. You can find these reports in such sources as books providing practice guidelines for intervening in specific problem areas or diagnostic categories, systematic reviews of the research in particular areas, or meta-analyses.

Both approaches have advantages as well as disadvantages, and therefore relying exclusively on either one is problematic. The prime advantage of the top-down approach is its feasibility. The social work agency where you work may have limited computer access to Internet literature databases, which can be expensive. Universities typically provide their students and faculty with free access to Internet databases that save much time in searching the literature. If you have already used such databases to search the literature for term papers or other course assignments, you can imagine how much more time it would have taken to go to the library to look for the sources manually. Moreover, even with access to Internet databases, the bottom-up approach can be very time-consuming if your search yields a large number of studies that need to be appraised as to the scientific quality of the evidence they provide and the applicability of that evidence to your unique practice decision. Some search terms—such as those looking for effective interventions for child maltreatment, domestic violence, or trauma—can yield more than a hundred studies that you'll need to examine. Reading and appraising those studies, even when you can download them electronically, can take a lot more time than is feasible for busy practitioners with large caseloads. How much easier it is to rely on others with advanced expertise in appraising research evidence in particular areas of practice.

The top-down approach, however, has one serious disadvantage—the fallibility of the experts who have conducted the reviews, appraised the evidence, and derived practice guidelines from them. To a certain extent, relying exclusively on a top-down search as an evidence-based way to answer your practice question requires relying on the authority of those experts. Because reliance on authority is inconsistent with the scientific method, using *only* a top-down approach is therefore paradoxical. Just as you may miss some relevant studies in your bottom-up search, perhaps the "experts" missed some relevant studies in their search. Perhaps other experts with higher methodological standards would disagree with their appraisals as to the scientific quality of the evidence in particular studies and as to which interventions appear to be supported by the best evidence. Some "experts" may even be biased in their appraisals—especially if they have a vested interest in the intervention they claim has the best evidentiary support. If you conduct a top-down search for effective interventions for posttraumatic stress disorder (PTSD), for example, you likely will find experts in exposure therapy and experts in eye movement desensitization and reprocessing (EMDR) therapy arguing over whose reviews are more biased and whose favored treatment approach has the better evidentiary support.

If feasibility obstacles to using the bottom-up approach require practitioners to rely solely on a top-down approach, therefore, they should do so as critical thinkers. They should not rely on just one or a few top-down sources that have been recommended to them or that they find at first. They should try to find and appraise all the top-down sources relevant to their practice decision and look for possible disagreements among them. They should try to ascertain whether the authors of the sources have a vested interest in the particular practice approach recommended. Finally, they should examine the evidentiary standards used in the appraisals of studies. Did the studies have to meet certain minimal methodological criteria to qualify for inclusion in the review? What methodological criteria were used to distinguish studies offering the best evidence from those offering weaker evidence? Were those criteria appropriate in light of the information in the rest of this book and in your research courses?

Fortunately, the top-down and bottom-up approaches are not mutually exclusive. Time and access permitting, you can search for and appraise individual studies as well as top-down sources that have already appraised individual studies and developed practice guidelines from them. In fact, a thorough bottom-up search would implicitly find and appraise top-down sources as well as individual studies. It can't hurt to augment your own review of individual studies with the reviews others have provided, as long as you critically appraise each source as recommended previously. Likewise, you should augment a top-down approach by searching for studies that may have been published after the top-down sources were published. The more recent studies might disagree with or imply modifications of the conclusions and implications of the top-down sources. With that in mind, let's now look at two top-down resources that are regarded highly by researchers in social work and allied fields. The box titled "Some Useful Internet Sites for Reviews and Practice Guidelines" lists the websites for these two sources as well as some others that you might find useful.

The Cochrane Collaboration and the Campbell Collaboration

The Cochrane Collaboration is an international nonprofit organization that recruits researchers, practitioners, and consumers into review groups that provide systematic reviews and meta-analyses of research on the effects of health care interventions. If you visit the Cochrane Collaboration's website at www.cochrane.org, you will find a link to its library, which contains its reviews, comments and criticisms, abstracts of other reviews, bibliographies of studies, reviews regarding methodology, and links that can help you conduct your own review. The Cochrane website also has information that will help you judge the quality of the Cochrane review system.

In 2000, shortly after the emergence of the Cochrane Collaboration, a sibling international nonprofit organization—the Campbell Collaboration—was formally established. Its mission and operations mirror those of its sibling but focus on social welfare, education, and criminal justice. Its systematic reviews and meta-analyses are written for use by practitioners, the public, policy makers, students, and researchers. If you go to its website at www.campbellcollaboration.org, you can find links that are like those of the Cochrane Collaboration but with a focus on topics not limited to health care. For example, you can find reviews of the effectiveness of interventions for domestic violence, sexual abuse, parent training, criminal offenders, juvenile delinquency, personality disorders, conduct disorders among youths, serious mental illness, substance abuse, welfare reform, housing, foster parent training, eating disorders, and many others.

2.5c Step 3. Critically Appraise the Relevant Studies You Find

As we noted in Chapter 1, there is a vast range in the quality of published studies evaluating the effectiveness of various interventions. Many are excellent, but many others violate some of the fundamental principles that you will learn in this book. It would be silly to attempt at this point to explain in depth all the research methods and research design concepts you'll need to know to critically appraise the various individual studies you will find. That's what the rest of this book is for. Moreover, as we mentioned earlier, a good systematic review or meta-analysis (such as those found at the Cochrane Collaboration and Campbell Collaboration sites) will critically appraise the rigor of its included studies and will give more weight to the

Some Useful Internet Sites for Reviews and Practice Guidelines

- Campbell Collaboration: http://www.campbellcollaboration.org/index.html
- Cochrane Collaboration: http://www.cochrane.org
- American Psychological Association's website on empirically supported treatments: http://www.apa.org/divisions/div12/rev_es
- Child Welfare: California Evidence-Based Clearinghouse for Child Welfare: www.cachildwelfareclearinghouse.org/
- Crisis Intervention and Domestic Violence National Resource: http://www.crisisinterventionnetwork.com
- Substance Abuse: http://nrepp.samhsa.gov/
- Crisis Intervention and Domestic Violence National Resource: http://www.crisisinterventionnetwork.com

- Expert Consensus Guidelines series: http://www.psychguides.com/
- National Guideline Clearinghouse: http://www.guidelines.gov/
- National Institute on Drug Abuse: http://www.nida.nih.gov/
- Substance Abuse and Mental Health Services Administration: http://www.samhsa.gov/index.aspx
- BMG Clinical Evidence: www.clinicalevidence.com/ceweb/conditions/index.jsp
- Oregon Evidence-Based Practice Center: www.ohsu.edu/epc/
- Additional sites for top-down reviews can be found by entering search terms into a search engine such as Google, Yahoo, or others.

most rigorous studies in developing conclusions and implications for practice. However, not all systematic reviews and meta-analyses are equally trustworthy. Therefore, Figure 2.2 lists criteria that can guide you in critically appraising the quality of systematic reviews and meta-analyses.

2.5d Step 4. Determine Which Evidence-Based Intervention Is Most Appropriate for Your Particular Client(s)

Even interventions supported by the best evidence are not necessarily effective with every client or situation. Strong studies providing valid evidence that an intervention is effective typically find that the intervention is *more likely* to be effective than some alternative, not that it is effective with every case. Interventions found to be effective with members of one ethnic group might not be effective with clients with other ethnicities. The intervention supported by the strongest studies might involve procedures that conflict with the values of certain cultures or individual clients. As illustrated in Figure 2.1 (see p. 26) you should use your practice expertise, your knowledge of the client, client feedback, and your cultural competence in making a judgment call.

Determining which of the interventions you find is the best fit for your particular client or group of clients involves several considerations. One consideration, of course, is the quality of the evidence that

you appraise in Step 3. Students commonly ask, "How many good studies do I need to find that support a particular intervention before I can consider it evidence-based?" There is no precise answer to that question. One or two strong studies supporting a particular intervention will probably suffice. An intervention supported by one very strong study probably has better evidence than an intervention supported only by many very weak studies. Ideally, you might find a rigorous systematic review that synthesizes and critically appraises all of the prior studies that merit guiding your decision.

More important, asking which intervention is evidence-based is not the right question. It has a ring of finality to it that is not consistent with the provisional nature and refutability of knowledge in the scientific method. Rather than ask whether to consider an intervention to be evidence-based, it's better to think in terms of which intervention has the best evidence for the time being. And if the evidence supporting that intervention emerged from research with clients unlike yours in meaningful ways, it may not be as good as evidence from a study using a somewhat weaker design, but with clients who are just like yours.

But what if you find no intervention supported by any study involving clients just like yours, even as you find an intervention supported by a strong study involving clients that are like yours in some important ways but unlike yours in other important

FIGURE 2.2 Criteria for Critically Appraising Systematic Reviews and Meta-Analyses

- Did the author of the review, or those who sponsored or funded it, have a vested interest at stake in its conclusions?
- Did the study even reveal whether the author of the review, or those who funded or sponsored it, have a conflict of interest regarding any vested interest?
- Are the criteria used for including or excluding studies in the review identified?
- Are those criteria too narrow or restrictive?
- Did the author search for unpublished studies (which may be less likely to have findings supporting the effectiveness of interventions than are published studies)?
- Did the author search for studies written in languages other than English?
- Did the author search multiple literature databases instead of relying on just one or two?
- Did the author examine studies cited in studies already found?
- Did the author search websites related to the research question?
- Did the author contact authors of any studies being reviewed to get further clarification regarding the methodological rigor of the study or the meaning of its findings?
- Does the review critically appraise the methodological rigor of the included studies?
- Does the review sort the evidence from the reviewed studies according to differences in the methodological rigor of studies with contrasting findings?
- Does the review sort the evidence from the reviewed studies according to differences in the types and characteristics of research participants in studies with contrasting findings?
- Did the review use at least two researchers to independently extract findings from the studies and rate their methodological rigor, and did their conclusions agree?
- Does the review report steps that were taken to prevent bias in the review process?

ways? Unless the latter intervention is unacceptable for some clinical reason, it might be worth trying with your client. For example, suppose you found no intervention that appears to be effective with 12- and 13-year-old girls in a residential treatment facility who are diagnosed with borderline personality disorder. But maybe you found strong evidence supporting the effectiveness of an intervention for 14- to 16-year-old girls with that disorder but not in a residential facility. Because you've found no better alternative, you might employ the latter intervention on a trial basis and evaluate (in Step 6) what happens.

EP 2.1.3a

If it is appropriate and possible to do so before finalizing the selection of any intervention and applying it, you should consider the values and expectations of your client and involve the client in the decision. This means informing the client about the intervention and the evidence about its potential effectiveness and any possible undesirable side effects, and obtaining the client's informed consent to participate in the intervention. You'll probably want to avoid a lot of detail when you do this and thus merely say something like, "This has the most evidence of effectiveness to date," "This has had a few promising results," or "We have some beginning evidence that this treatment may work well for people who have your kinds of concerns." That way, the client can make an informed decision regarding the treatment in terms of both what fits best (in terms of culture, personality, and other factors) and what is most likely to have positive outcomes. Beyond the ethical reasons for obtaining the client's informed consent regarding the choice of intervention, doing so might help the client feel a sense of ownership and responsibility in the treatment process. As a consequence, the client might be more likely to achieve a successful outcome.

2.5e Step 5. Apply the Evidence-Based Intervention

Once the selection of the intervention is finalized, several steps may be needed before applying it. To begin, you may need to obtain training in the intervention through a continuing education workshop or professional conference. Perhaps an elective course on the intervention is offered at a nearby school of social work. You should also obtain readings on how to implement the intervention, including any treatment manuals for it. Try to locate a colleague who has experience providing the intervention and arrange for consultation or supervision. For some relatively new interventions, you may find a support group of professional colleagues who meet regularly to provide each other peer feedback about how they are implementing the new intervention with various cases. If you are unable to obtain sufficient training or supervision, you should try to refer the client to other practitioners who have the requisite training and experience in the intervention.

EP 2.1.10g

If you provide the intervention yourself, or if you continue working with the clients after you've referred them for it, one more step should be taken before the intervention is introduced. As an evidence-based practitioner, you should formulate, in collaboration with the client, treatment goals that can be measured in evaluating whether the selected intervention really helps the client. Chapter 5 of this text will help you define treatment goals in measurable terms. Some of the studies you appraise in Step 2 might also identify useful ways to define and measure treatment goals.

2.5f Step 6. Evaluation and Feedback

During this phase, you and the client will measure and evaluate progress in achieving the treatment goals you have set. Several later chapters of this text will help you design the methods for doing that. You might, for example, have the client self-monitor certain behaviors, emotions, or cognitions daily for a while before you apply the intervention, during the course of treatment with the intervention, and perhaps during a follow-up period after you have completed the intervention protocol.

To assess whether the intervention appears to be effective for that particular client, you might graph the daily data and look for the pattern of the graphed data to improve significantly after intervention begins. You and the client should discuss the data in an ongoing fashion, including perhaps the need to modify the treatment plan if the intervention does not appear to be helpful or if treatment goals are achieved. Some clients may really like this process—seeing their progress and discussing why

symptoms are getting worse or better. (Sometimes extraneous important events come up in their lives that affect their progress and inform the treatment process.)

Once your work with the client has finished, you should communicate your findings to relevant colleagues. You might even want to write your work up as a single-case evaluation study for publication. (If you choose to do that, Chapter 13 and Appendix C of this text can help you.) Cournoyer and Powers (2002) even suggest that you might communicate your findings to the researchers whose studies provided the evidence base for choosing the intervention you applied and evaluated.

But perhaps you are wondering why Step 6 is needed in the first place. Why evaluate an intervention with your one client if published studies have already provided credible evidence of its effectiveness? Evaluating it is necessary because studies supporting the effectiveness of interventions typically do not find that the tested interventions are guaranteed to work with every client or situation. Instead, they merely find that an intervention is more likely to be effective than some alternative. Your client may be one of the cases for whom the intervention does not work.

EP 2.1.10d
EP 2.1.10m

2.6 DISTINGUISHING THE EVIDENCE-BASED PRACTICE PROCESS FROM EVIDENCE-BASED PRACTICES

Many scholars and practitioners commonly use the term *evidence-based practice* (EBP) when referring to the EBP process. However, others commonly use the same term when referring not to the process, but rather to specific interventions that have been supported by research. Thus, a particular program, policy, or intervention that has received consistent research support might be called evidence-based and might appear on a list with a plural heading such as *evidence-based practices*. Because both the singular and plural headings can have the same EBP acronym, this often leads to confusion in discussions and debates about EBP. For example, if you probe as to why some clinical practitioners have negative attitudes about EBP, you might find that their attitudes are in reference not to the process definition of EBP, but rather to the notion that insurance companies or government agencies will not pay for their services unless they mechanistically provide one of the interventions that appear on the company's list of interventions deemed to be evidence-based, regardless of practitioner judgment or client attributes. Keeping in mind the distinction between the singular concept of the EBP process and the plural concept of evidence-based practices, let's now examine some commonly expressed problems in and objections to EBP.

2.7 PROBLEMS IN AND OBJECTIONS TO EVIDENCE-BASED PRACTICE

Although most social work educators and practitioners appear to support the evidence-based practice process, not all of them do (Rubin & Parrish, 2007, 2011). Some of the arguments against EBP are based on real world feasibility obstacles to it. Other arguments are based on methodological or philosophical grounds or on misconceptions of EBP, especially misconceptions that conflate the EBP *process* with evidence-based *interventions*. Let's begin our examination of problems in and objections to EBP with some common misconceptions.

EBP is an overly restrictive cookbook approach that denigrates professional expertise and ignores client values and preferences. This portrayal misconstrues the EBP *process*, which recognizes the role of practitioner judgment and client attributes in that process (as displayed in Figure 2.1), with the plural concept of *evidence-based practices*.

It is merely a cost-cutting tool. Some critics of evidence-based practice have portrayed it as merely a cost-cutting tool that can be exploited by government agencies and managed care companies that pay for services. Their criticism is based on the notion that these third-party payers will pay only for the provision of interventions that have been supported by research, and only for the number of sessions that the research results indicate are needed. Proponents of evidence-based practice counter that this would not be a criticism of evidence-based practice, but rather a criticism of the way managed care companies might distort it. Moreover, it is based on the plural concept of evidence-based interventions rather than on the

process definition. Also, they argue that some interventions supported by the best research evidence are more costly than the less supported alternatives (Gibbs & Gambrill, 2002; Mullen & Streiner, 2004). The aim of evidence-based practice is to find the most *effective* interventions, not to find the cheapest.

EBP is based on studies of clients unlike those typically encountered in everyday social work practice. One objection concerns the characteristics of clients that have participated in the most scientifically rigorous experiments that provide some of the best evidence in support of the effectiveness of interventions deemed to be evidence-based. For example, many such experiments have excluded clients with more than one diagnosis. Also, racial or ethnic minority clients have been underrepresented in many of the experiments (Messer, 2006; Westen, 2006). This objection is particularly germane to social work, since social workers commonly work with ethnic minority clients and clients with multiple disorders, or with unique concerns that don't fit the formal diagnostic categories required for participation in many experimental evaluations. In light of the discrepancies between the kinds of clients participating in these evaluations of interventions and the kinds of clients practitioners are most likely to encounter in everyday practice, the perception of evidence-based practice as requiring practitioners to rigidly follow treatment manuals has been criticized as not allowing them the flexibility to use their expertise to respond to unique client attributes and circumstances. Again, however, this objection pertains more to the *plural* concept of evidence-based interventions than to the *singular* concept of the EBP *process*.

Evidence is in short supply. Another criticism of evidence-based practice is that there are not enough quality research studies to guide practice in many social work treatment areas and for many populations. Although there is some truth to that assertion, the number of such studies is growing. Moreover, evidence-based practice proponents counter this criticism by asserting that a shortage of quality outcome studies is less of an argument against evidence-based practice than an argument for the EBP *process*. If practitioners are making decisions based on little or no evidence, all the more reason to "exercise caution and perhaps be even more vigilant in monitoring outcomes" (Mullen & Streiner, 2004, p. 115) in the final stage of the process.

Another counterargument to this objection is the peace of mind you can have knowing that you left no stone unturned in trying to find the most effective way to help your client, even if the evidence you seek does not exist. Imagine the alternative; that is, proceeding to intervene with a client without first thoroughly checking to see whether the way you plan to proceed is or is not the best way to help your client. Imagine being treated by a physician who tells you that she hasn't bothered to check to see if the medication she is prescribing is the best thing for you because she does not want to waste her time looking for evidence that *might* not exist.

Furthermore, some interventions that might seem theoretically sound and perhaps might even be in vogue, are actually harmful (as discussed in Chapter 1). Imagine how you would feel if you provided a harmful intervention, only to discover that had you examined the research on that intervention, you could have avoided harming your client.

 The evidence-based practice process inappropriately devalues qualitative research and alternative philosophies. As we noted earlier in this chapter, the quality of the evidence reported in practice effectiveness studies is based largely on the following two questions: (1) Was treatment outcome measured in a reliable, valid, and unbiased manner? (2) Was the research design strong enough to indicate conclusively whether the intervention or something else most plausibly explains the variations in client outcome?

EP 2.1.6b

Rigorous experiments (to be discussed in Chapter 11) are considered the strongest designs for obtaining affirmative answers to these questions. In contrast, studies that rely on qualitative research methods are usually depicted as offering much weaker evidence for conclusively verifying what factor or factors really cause what particular outcomes. As you will see in Chapter 3 as well as in later chapters, qualitative studies tend to have different priorities than experiments, and put more value on subjectively probing for deeper meanings than on trying to logically rule out alternative plausible explanations for treatment outcomes.

Though their value is widely recognized by scholars in social work and allied fields, many scholars who prefer qualitative methods feel that those methods are inappropriately devalued in evidence-based practice. Although that perception is understandable

in light of the emphasis on experiments in trying to ascertain causality, not all evidence-based practice questions pertain to verifying causality. As noted earlier in this chapter, some questions ask: "What's it like to have had my client's experiences?" For questions like that, qualitative studies should get more emphasis than experimental studies. For example, if you seek to understand what it's like to be homeless, or why so many homeless people refuse to sleep in shelters, your best bet for gaining new or deeper insights is from studies that employ qualitative methods such as conducting open-ended and in-depth interviews with homeless people or hanging out with them and observing and subjectively experiencing the phenomenon of homelessness.

Also objecting to evidence-based practice are some scholars who—on philosophical grounds—reject the emphasis on objectivity in the traditional scientific method that guides evidence-based practice. Some scholars argue that everything is subjective, that all we have are our subjective realities, and that therefore no point of view about practice is superior to any other. Proponents of evidence-based practice counter that if this is so, how can professionals claim to have special knowledge, and how do we avoid having elite authorities dictate what is and is not true (Gibbs & Gambrill, 2002)?

We will delve into these methodological and philosophical debates in more depth in the next two chapters. Moreover, throughout the rest of this text, you will be learning what you need to know about research methods in order to become an effective evidence-based practitioner.

The therapeutic alliance will be hindered. Another objection is based on research that has supported the notion that the quality of the practitioner–client relationship might be the most important aspect of effective treatment regardless of what type of intervention the practitioner employs. Some argue that rigid adherence to treatment manuals on how to provide evidence-based interventions can inhibit practitioner flexibility in using professional experience and expertise in relationship building, which may harm the therapeutic alliance and result in poorer treatment outcomes (Messer, 2006; Reed, 2006; Westen, 2006; Zlotnik & Galambos, 2004). Again, however, this objection is based on the plural concept of evidence-based interventions, and ignores the part of the evidence-based process that involves the integration of professional expertise. Furthermore, it overlooks the fact that treatment manuals typically emphasize the importance of the therapeutic relationship as part of the intervention and warn readers that for the intervention to be effective, it must be provided in the context of a strong therapeutic alliance. (In fact, every evidence-based treatment manual that we have seen has had that emphasis.)

Real-world obstacles prevent implementing evidence-based practice in everyday practice. Perhaps the most problematic controversy about evidence-based practice has nothing to do with its desirability. It has to do with obstacles to implementing it in real-world, everyday practice, which even its proponents find daunting. Social workers commonly work in settings where superiors do not understand or appreciate evidence-based practice and do not give practitioners enough time to carry out the evidence-based practice process—especially if they follow the bottom-up approach in searching for evidence (as discussed earlier in this chapter). Even in settings where evidence-based practice is valued, resources may be insufficient to provide staff with the time, training, publications, and access to Internet databases and search engines needed to carry out the evidence-based practice process efficiently and appropriately.

Although some leaders in evidence-based practice are formulating and pilot-testing strategies for overcoming these obstacles in agencies, the going is rough. For example, even when it is feasible to find and appraise research—that is, to carry out the evidence-based practice *process*—agencies might not be able to afford the costs of the training and supervision that practitioners need to effectively provide the *intervention* that has the best research support.

2.8 ALLEVIATING FEASIBILITY OBSTACLES TO EVIDENCE-BASED PRACTICE

Acknowledging that feasibility concerns perhaps pose the most daunting challenge facing EBP, proponents of EBP have suggested ways to make the EBP process more feasible (Rubin, 2010). One way is to divide the tasks of the EBP process up among a team of practitioners in an agency. The team would focus on one EBP question at a time,

with each question addressing a common type of agency client or problem. Each team member would execute one phase of the process. After completing the process for one EBP question of significance to the agency, the team could move on to another. This task could be made even more feasible in agencies that have student field-placement interns. Those interns could complete the process above as part of their fieldwork assignments, thus sparing agency staff members of the burden while learning more about EBP themselves. Furthermore, the students probably would have access to Internet literature databases through their university library. If that access were not available to the students or to agency practitioners, another option would be to use free governmental literature database sites such as Medline. Also, especially for agencies in urban areas, students or practitioners might be able to get free access to Internet literature databases through their local public library system.

Mullen et al. (2007) suggested that the burden on practitioners might also be eased by including EBP training in existing agency in-service training sessions or meetings. They also urged schools of social work to train EBP teams within agencies and to provide EBP training to field practicum instructors. Offering continuing education credits for such training would be a good incentive.

2.9 COMMON FACTORS AND THE DODO BIRD

If your EBP question pertains to choosing an intervention that has the best effects, you should keep in mind that treatment outcome will be influenced by other treatment factors, as well, not just selecting the best intervention modality. For example, we noted previously the importance of the therapeutic relationship and acknowledged that for any evidence based intervention to be effective it must be provided in the context of a strong therapeutic alliance. Research has consistently identified some common practitioner and treatment characteristics that are likely to influence the strength of the therapeutic alliance and treatment outcome across the gamut of intervention modalities (Hubble, Duncan, & Miller, 2009). Although the empirical literature on such common factors is still evolving, here are some of the practitioner and treatment characteristics that have been supported by rigorous research as having a key influence on treatment outcome:

- Accurate empathy
- Warmth
- Positive regard
- Cultivating hope
- Adapting treatment to the client's stage of change

The research supporting the importance of these common factors should be viewed as an essential part of what should guide practitioners seeking to engage in evidence-based practice. That is, if you want to maximize your practice effectiveness in light of research evidence, you will not only consider evidence about intervention modalities; you will also consider evidence about common treatment factors. Moreover, you will seek to maximize your skills in the common factors that have the best evidence. Therefore, developing and improving your skills in these common factors is an essential part of learning to intervene effectively with a diverse range of people who have diverse problems, and thus of learning to engage in evidence-based practice.

Some critics of EBP, however, see the importance of these common factors as diminishing the importance of EBP. Citing research studies that found the quality of the therapeutic relationship to have a much greater impact on treatment outcome than does the specific intervention provided, they have deemed the choice of intervention to be irrelevant, arguing that all interventions are equally effective when they are provided by practitioners with good relationship skills (Wampold, 2001). That argument is known as the "dodo bird verdict," because in *Alice in Wonderland* the dodo bird declares after a race that "Everyone has won, and all must have prizes" (Luborsky, 1975).

Others, however, have argued against the dodo bird verdict, citing methodological flaws in the studies that support that verdict as well as other studies that found the choice of intervention to have the greater impact (Beutler, 2002; Craighead, Sheets, & Bjornsson, 2005; Lilienfeld, 2007). They have also noted that even if relationship factors have a greater impact on outcome than does the choice of intervention, that does not mean that the choice of intervention is unimportant. Why not emphasize both, they reason. Moreover, the EBP process does emphasize both, as do the treatment manuals for many evidence-based interventions.

We do not intend to take sides in the debate over whether intervention choice or relationship factors have the greater impact on treatment outcome. We do, however, suggest that unless and until the controversy becomes resolved in a way that shows that the choice of intervention has no meaningful impact on outcome, then the dodo bird verdict is a false dichotomy. That is, as long as intervention choice can add to the impact of relationship factors in a meaningful way, then even if relationship factors have the greater impact, that is not a compelling argument against engaging in the EBP process. Furthermore, if practitioners base their decision to emphasize relationship factors on the research supporting the dodo bird verdict, then ironically they are in fact engaging in evidence-based practice because they are basing their practice decision on their appraisal of the research evidence!

2.10 MAIN POINTS

- In the evidence-based practice process, practitioners make practice decisions in light of the best research evidence available.
- The evidence-based practice process encourages practitioners to integrate scientific evidence with their practice expertise and knowledge of the idiosyncratic circumstances bearing on specific practice decisions.
- Although evidence-based practice is most commonly discussed in regard to decisions about what interventions to provide clients, it also applies to decisions about how best to assess the practice problems and decisions practitioners make at other levels of practice.
- Evidence-based practice involves critical thinking, questioning, recognizing unfounded beliefs and assumptions, and using the best scientific evidence available in deciding how to intervene with individuals, families, groups, or communities.
- Evidence-based practitioners need to track down evidence as an ongoing part of their practice. They need to know how to find relevant studies and understand research designs and methods so that they can critically appraise the validity of the studies they find. They need to base the actions they take on the best evidence they find

and use research methods to evaluate whether their evidence-based actions result in the outcomes they seek to achieve.

- In recognizing that even evidence-based knowledge is subject to change as newer and perhaps better studies might refute it with better evidence, being an evidence-based practitioner implies engaging in career-long learning. It means recognizing the need to search for and appraise new evidence as an ongoing, "lifelong" part of one's practice.

- Steps in the evidence-based practice process include formulating a question, searching for evidence, critically appraising the studies you find, determining which evidence-based intervention is most appropriate for your particular client(s), applying the evidence-based intervention, and evaluating progress and providing feedback.

- Evidence-based practice questions may be open-ended regarding interventions or may specify one or more interventions in advance.

- Searching for evidence can employ *top-down* and *bottom-up* strategies.

- Using the bottom-up strategy, you would search the literature looking for any and all sources that provide evidence pertaining to the practice question you formulated. You would then read and critically appraise the quality of the evidence in each source, judge whether it is applicable to your unique practice decision, and ultimately choose a course of action based on what you deem to be the best applicable evidence available.

- Using the top-down strategy, instead of starting from scratch to find and appraise all the relevant studies yourself, you would rely on the results of evidence-based searches that others have done, as reported in such sources as systematic reviews, meta-analyses, or books providing practice guidelines.

- Even interventions supported by the best evidence are not necessarily effective with every client or situation. Interventions found to be effective with members of one ethnic group might not be effective with clients of other ethnicities. Interventions supported by the strongest studies might involve procedures that conflict with the values of certain cultures or individual clients.

- Although most social work educators and practitioners appear to support the evidence-based

practice process, not all of them do. Some of the arguments against EBP are based on real-world feasibility obstacles to it. Other arguments are based on methodological or philosophical grounds or on misconceptions of EBP, especially misconceptions that conflate the EBP *process* with evidence-based *interventions*.

- Social workers commonly work in settings that might not be able to afford to provide staff with the time, training, publications, and access to Internet databases and search engines needed to carry out the evidence-based practice process efficiently and appropriately. However, various ways have been suggested to alleviate feasibility obstacles to the EBP process in such settings.

- Some common treatment factors have been supported by research as influencing treatment outcome across the gamut of intervention modalities. Although some have cited the importance of those common factors as an argument against EBP, proponents of EBP can cite various counterpoints to that argument.

2.11 PRACTICE-RELATED EXERCISES

1. Formulate an evidence-based practice question to guide your decision about the most effective intervention to employ in the case of a 6-year-old African American boy who witnessed his father severely battering his mother, and whose diagnosis includes both conduct disorder and posttraumatic stress disorder.

2. Suppose your search for evidence to answer your question in Exercise 1 yielded no study in which the characteristics of the participants matched those of your client. Discuss the various considerations that would guide your decision about which of several different empirically supported interventions is most likely to be effective for your client.

3. Discuss how your answer to Exercise 2 bears on several objections raised by critics of evidence-based practice.

4. Identify what you deem the most important generic relationship skills that you are learning in your practice courses, and discuss how they are part of becoming an evidence-based practitioner.

2.12 INTERNET EXERCISES

1. To help you engage in the first two steps of the evidence-based practice (EBP) process and to find links to many other EBP-related sites, go to the following website: www.lib.umich.edu/socwork/rescue/ebsw.html. Discuss how what you found there can help you complete the first two steps of the EBP process.

2. Briefly describe how at least two of the links to additional EBP sites that you found at the website in Internet Exercise 1 can facilitate the EBP process.

3. Using an Internet search engine such as Google, enter a search term for a policy or intervention that interests you. In the search results, click on several links that look most interesting. Briefly describe what you find at those links and how helpful they appear to be in facilitating a search for evidence to guide practice decisions about the intervention or policy you specified in your search term.

4. If you have access to Google Scholar or one of the alternative database services specified in this chapter, go to that service and enter a search term for a policy or intervention that interests you. In the search results, click on several literature sources that look most relevant. Briefly summarize the type of evidence at each of those sources and how they would bear on practice decisions about the intervention or policy you specified in your search term.

5. Visit the Campbell Collaboration's website at www.campbellcollaboration.org. Find a review of the effectiveness of interventions for a problem that interests you. Discuss how relying on reviews such as that one represents a top-down search strategy, and why using such a strategy would be more expedient than using a bottom-up search strategy. (If you are more interested in health or mental health care interventions, you can use the Cochrane Collaboration's website at www.cochrane.org.)

6. Enter the search terms *dodo bird verdict* and *common factors psychotherapy*. Go to several sources that discuss the common factors and several sites that argue for or against the dodo bird verdict. Briefly summarize how what you read is likely to influence your outlook regarding EBP.

2.13 ADDITIONAL READINGS

Littell, J. H., Corcoran, J., & Pillai, V. (2008). *Systematic reviews and meta-analysis*. New York: Oxford University Press. This handy, user-friendly pocket guide shows how to read and appraise systematic reviews and meta-analyses. It also provides some basics that can help you to embark on conducting your own systematic review or meta-analysis. If you want to conduct a meta-analysis using advanced statistical formulas, you will need to examine other, more statistically oriented, references that the authors identify.

Roberts, A. R., & Yeager, K. R. (Eds.). (2006). *Foundations of evidence-based social work practice*. New York: Oxford University Press. The chapters in this compendium cover a wide range of topics on evidence-based practice, with a focus on social work.

Rubin, A. (2008). *Practitioner's guide to using research for evidence-based practice*. Hoboken, NJ: John Wiley & Sons. This book provides a practitioner-oriented guide to appraising and using research as part of the EBP process.

Rubin, A., & Springer, D. W. (Eds.) (2010). *The clinician's guide to evidence-based practice*. Hoboken, NJ: John Wiley & Sons. This series of volumes attempts to help clinicians learn how to implement empirically supported interventions in such areas as PTSD, substance abuse, schizophrenia, depression, and child welfare.

2.13a Competency Notes

EP 2.1.1e: Engage in career-long learning (p. 25): In recognizing that knowledge is subject to change as newer and perhaps better studies emerge, being an evidence-based practitioner implies engaging in career-long learning.

EP 2.1.3: Apply critical thinking to inform and communicate professional judgments (p. 24): The EBP process requires that social workers be critical thinkers regarding practice knowledge.

EP 2.1.3a: Distinguish, appraise, and integrate multiple sources of knowledge, including research-based knowledge and practice wisdom (p. 33): Social workers engaged in the evidence-based practice process will know how to find and critically appraise research-based knowledge and integrate it with other sources of practice knowledge in determining the best course of action that fits their idiosyncratic practice context.

EP 2.1.6b: Use research evidence to inform practice (p. 36): Understanding qualitative, quantitative, and mixed methods of assessment evaluation—and understanding the research process—enhances social workers' ability to use research evidence to inform their practice.

EP 2.1.10d: Collect, organize, and interpret client data (p. 34): The final phase of the EBP process involves collecting and interpreting client data to assess whether the chosen intervention appears to be achieving its aims.

EP 2.1.10g: Select appropriate intervention strategies (p. 34): The EBP process involves selecting appropriate intervention strategies in light of the integration of scientific evidence with other sources of practice knowledge.

EP 2.1.10m: Critically analyze, monitor, and evaluate interventions (p. 34): The phases of the EBP process involve selecting an intervention based on a critical analysis of alternatives and then monitoring client data to evaluate whether the chosen intervention may or may not be the best fit for the client.

The Research Process

Having examined in Part 1 the value and uses of scientific inquiry and research in social work practice, let's now begin to examine the process of conducting research. We'll continue that examination throughout the rest of this text. As we do so, we'll be looking at many different types of research. The two chapters in Part 2 will provide an overview of those different types of research and the factors that influence which type of research is conducted in any particular inquiry. They will also examine how some studies can combine more than one type of research process.

Chapter 3 will provide an overview of two contrasting and overarching types of research processes: quantitative and qualitative methods of inquiry. Each of these approaches to scientific inquiry will be reflected in the remaining chapters of this book. In addition to describing each of these categories of inquiry and contrasting them, Chapter 3 will discuss how they are compatible and can be combined in the same study. In fact, increased appreciation of the compatibility of these approaches has resulted in the development of a category of inquiry called *mixed methods inquiry*, which combines qualitative and qualitative approaches and will also be discussed in Chapter 3.

Chapter 4 will look at how different studies can have different research purposes and will discuss how alternative purposes and various other factors can influence the research process in social work. Among those other factors are two—ethical and multicultural considerations—that merit their own separate chapters in Part 3 of this book.

Quantitative, Qualitative, and Mixed Methods of Inquiry

3.1 INTRODUCTION

We ended Chapter 2 by noting that scholars disagree about some methodological and philosophical issues that can influence how research is conducted, and about the value of the evidence produced by different kinds of research. In the past, one of the major areas of disagreement concerned the comparative value of qualitative versus quantitative research methods. In fact, it was not uncommon to hear some referred to as quantitative researchers (or more briefly as *quants*), and others referred to as qualitative researchers (or *quals*). Each side would argue for the superiority of its approach to inquiry. During the latter decades of the twentieth century, advocates of qualitative methods occasionally objected to what they perceived as the prominence of quantitative methods in the social work research literature, while extolling the advantages of qualitative methods. At the same time, and perhaps owing in part to the arguments made by advocates of qualitative research, the notion that these two approaches to inquiry were incompatible became less prevalent, and researchers began to see the approaches as complementary and to use them in conjunction with each other within individual studies. Eventually, this recognition led to the development of a third approach—mixed methods research—which emphasized the importance of combining qualitative and quantitative research methods within the same studies and included a framework for the different ways of combining them.

This chapter will provide an overview of each of these three approaches of inquiry. It will identify the distinguishing features of qualitative and quantitative methods, their advantages and disadvantages,

---

Quantitative research methods Research methods that typically seek to produce precise and generalizable findings. Studies using quantitative methods typically attempt to formulate all or most of their research procedures in advance and then try to adhere precisely to those procedures with maximum objectivity as data are collected.

Qualitative research methods Research methods that are more flexible than quantitative methods, that allow research procedures to evolve as more observations are gathered, and that typically permit the use of subjectivity to generate deeper understandings of the meanings of human experiences.

and the benefits of combining them in mixed methods research. This overview should facilitate your reading of the remaining chapters of this book, in which various qualitative and quantitative research methods are described in depth. The advantages and disadvantages and the complementarity of specific quantitative and qualitative methods will continue to reappear throughout this book.

3.2 A COMPARISON OF QUANTITATIVE AND QUALITATIVE METHODS OF INQUIRY

Quantitative research methods emphasize the production of precise and generalizable statistical findings. When we want to verify whether a cause produces an effect in general, we are likely to use quantitative methods. Quantitative research studies typically attempt to formulate all or most of their research procedures in advance, and then try to adhere precisely to those procedures with maximum objectivity as data are collected.

EP 2.1.3a
EP 2.1.3b
EP 2.1.6b

Qualitative research methods are more likely to tap the deeper meanings of particular human experiences and generate theoretically richer observations that are not easily reduced to numbers. Qualitative research studies typically begin with a more flexible plan, one that allows the research procedures to evolve as more observations are gathered.

Whereas quantitative studies are more likely to seek to generalize precise and objective findings to a larger population, qualitative studies typically permit the use of subjectivity to generate deeper understandings of the meanings of human experiences. This does not imply that quantitative studies are completely inflexible or that qualitative studies have no advanced planned procedures. It's more a matter of emphasis, and some studies combine quantitative and qualitative research procedures.

Here is an example of the distinction between the two methods. Suppose a medical social worker wants to assess the psychosocial aspects of hospice care versus standard hospital care for terminally ill patients. Put simply, standard hospital care emphasizes using medical technology to fight disease at all costs, even if the technology entails undesirable costs in quality of life and patient discomfort. Hospice care emphasizes minimizing patients' discomfort and maximizing their quality of life during their final days, even if that means eschewing certain technologies that prolong life but hinder its quality.

Suppose the social worker's prime focus in the study is whether and how quality of life differs for patients depending on the form of care they receive. In a quantitative study, the social worker might ask the closest family member of each patient to complete a standardized list of interview questions about the degree of pain the patient expressed feeling, the frequency of undesirable side effects associated with medical technology (loss of hair because of chemotherapy, for example), the patient's mood, the patient's activities, and so on. An effort would probably be made to find an instrument that scored each question—scores that could be summed to produce an overall quality-of-life score. Ideally, it would be an instrument that had been tested elsewhere and seemed to produce consistent data over repeated administrations and with different interviewers. Thus, it would appear to be a measure that seems unaffected by the investigator's predilections or vested interests. If the scores of the hospice-treated patients turn out to be higher than the scores for patients receiving standard medical care, then the social worker might conclude that hospice care better affects quality of life than does standard medical care.

Perhaps, however, the social worker is skeptical about whether the instrument really taps all of the complex dimensions of quality of life. The instrument gives only a numerical score; perhaps this is superficial—it tells us little about the ways the two forms of care may differentially affect quality of life, and it provides little understanding of what patients experience and what those experiences mean to them.

As an alternative, the social worker may choose to take a qualitative approach to the inquiry. This might entail spending a great deal of time on the standard and hospice wards that care for terminally ill patients in the hospital. There the social worker might simply observe what goes on and keep a detailed log of the observations. The information in the logs can be analyzed to see what patterns emerge. In Chapter 5 we will examine in depth a study that took this approach (Buckingham et al., 1976), one in which the investigator actually posed as a terminally ill patient and observed how he was treated differently in the two wards and how this made him feel.

Rather than rely on indirect quantitative measures, he decided to experience the phenomenon directly. Based on the investigator's direct observations and subjective experiences, he was able to discuss in depth how the medical staff members on the hospice ward seemed much more sensitive and empathic than those on the other ward, how family members seemed encouraged to be more involved on the hospice ward and the implications this had for personalized care, and how all of this made the patient feel. By subjectively entering the role of the patient, the investigator was able to propose a deep, empathic understanding of how the two forms of care had different implications for quality of life.

But what are the potential pitfalls of the preceding approach? Some might question whether the investigator's previous ties to hospice care, his predilections, and his desire to obtain important findings may have predisposed him to make observations that would reflect favorably on the relative advantages of hospice care. In short, they would be concerned about whether his observations were sufficiently objective. Which of the two studies is preferable, the quantitative or qualitative? Actually, both are valuable. Each provides useful information, and each has its own set of advantages and disadvantages in its quest for truth and understanding. Consequently, some of the best social work research studies combine both qualitative and quantitative research methods.

Whether we should emphasize qualitative or quantitative research methods in a particular study—or use both—will depend on the conditions and purposes of our inquiry. Qualitative methods may be more suitable when flexibility is required to study a new phenomenon about which we know very little, or when we seek to gain insight into the subjective meanings of complex phenomena to advance our conceptualization of them and build a theory that can be tested in future studies. Qualitative research thus can sometimes pave the way for quantitative studies of the same subject. Other times, qualitative methods produce results that are sufficient in themselves. Each approach is useful and legitimate. Each makes its unique contribution to inquiry. Each has its own advantages and disadvantages. Each is a set of tools, not a dogma. Researchers need to match the tools they use with the research questions and conditions they face—using quantitative methods for some studies, qualitative methods for others, and both methods in combination for still others. Although qualitative and quantitative methods are compatible, many studies use one or the other approach exclusively or predominantly, and which one they use or emphasize will significantly influence the nature of the research process.

We will be mentioning the terms *qualitative* and *quantitative* research methods throughout this book. At times, we will focus more on qualitative methods; at other times, the focus will be on quantitative methods. Whenever we discuss the strengths or weaknesses of either type of method, you should bear in mind that we are not implying that that particular type is stronger or weaker than the other type. Figure 3.1 lists various attributes of quantitative and qualitative methods of inquiry that tend to differ in emphasis. We have discussed some of the contrasting attributes above. Others may be unfamiliar to you at this point, but will be discussed later in this chapter and in subsequent chapters. As you examine Figure 3.1, therefore, don't worry if you notice terms that are unfamiliar to you. Also keep in mind that, despite their contrasting emphases, qualitative and quantitative methods are compatible (as discussed earlier). Moreover, although some attributes are more *likely* to apply to one method of inquiry than the other, that doesn't mean they cannot apply to both. For example, some quantitative studies can be inductive, involve small samples, or be conducted early in an investigation for exploratory purposes. Likewise, some qualitative studies might be conducted in an agency instead of the natural environment of the participants. Also, some qualitative studies might be conducted later in an investigation to try to generate a better understanding of quantitative findings from earlier research.

3.3   MIXED METHODS

Many social work research studies use more than one research method. A strictly quantitative evaluation of the effectiveness of a child welfare program, for example, might examine whether rates of child maltreatment in official records decline after the program's onset while also examining whether the program's clients score better after treatment on a test of knowledge of positive parenting. A strictly qualitative inquiry into the experience of being

homeless might combine conducting unstructured, open-ended interviews of homeless people with having the researchers live homeless themselves to observe the behaviors of other homeless people with whom they hang out and to get a subjective sense of how it feels to live on the streets.

Although some might describe the above examples as having used mixed methods because one study used more than one quantitative method and the other used more than one qualitative method, the term *mixed methods research* more commonly has referred to the combination of quantitative and qualitative research methods within the same study. However, as **mixed methods research** has become increasingly popular since the turn of the century, it has come to be defined as more than just research that happens to use both qualitative and quantitative methods in a particular study. Instead, it is now seen as a stand-alone type of research design in which a single study not only collects both qualitative and quantitative data, but also integrates both sources of data at one or more stages of the research process so as to improve the understanding of the phenomenon being investigated (Hanson et al., 2005).

For example, Creswell (2014a) cautions that mixed methods research is not merely gathering both qualitative and quantitative data. In addition to gathering both forms, it must integrate them in a way that strengthens the study. Likewise, one should not label their study as *mixed methods* research simply because both forms of data were collected. It is also a mistake to use that label if the different forms of data collected were all quantitative or all qualitative. Both qualitative and quantitative data need to be collected and integrated to merit the *mixed methods* label. Creswell (2104a) also cautions that mixed methods research does not imply that the scope or rigor of the qualitative or quantitative approach can be reduced.

---

mixed methods research   A stand-alone research design in which a single study not only collects both qualitative and quantitative data, but also integrates both sources of data at one or more stages of the research process so as to improve the understanding of the phenomenon being investigated.

FIGURE 3.1 Contrasting Emphases in Quantitative and Qualitative Methods of Inquiry

Attribute	Quantitative	Qualitative
Aims	Precision Generalizability Testing hypotheses	Deeper understandings Describing contexts Generating hypotheses Discovery
Structure	Research procedures specified in advance	Flexible procedures evolve as data are gathered
Setting for data gathering	Office, agency, or via mail or Internet	Natural environment of research participants
Theoretical approach most commonly employed	Deductive	Inductive
Sample size likely or preferred	Larger	Smaller
Most likely timing in investigating phenomena	Later, after familiarity with phenomenon has been established	Early, to gain familiarity with phenomenon
Emphasis on objectivity or subjectivity	Objectivity	Subjectivity
Nature of data emphasized	Numbers	Words
Depth and generalizability of findings	More superficial, but more generalizable	Deeper, but less generalizable
Richness of detail and context	Less contextual detail	Rich descriptions with more contextual detail
Nature of data-gathering methods emphasized	Various, but highly structured	Lengthier and less structured observations and interviews
Types of designs and methods commonly used	Experiments Quasi-experiments Single-case designs Surveys	Ethnography Case studies Life history Focus groups Participatory action research Grounded theory
Data-gathering instruments emphasized	Closed-ended items in questionnaires and scales	Open-ended items and interviews with probes
Labor intensiveness of data collection for researchers	Less time-consuming	More time-consuming
Labor intensiveness of data analysis	Less time-consuming	More time-consuming
Data analysis process	Calculate statistics that describe a population or assess the probability of error in inferences about hypotheses	Search for patterns and meanings in narratives, not numbers
Paradigms emphasized in appraising rigor	Contemporary positivist standards for minimizing bias, maximizing objectivity, and statistically controlling for alternative explanations	Contemporary positivist standards might be used, but standards based on interpretivist, social constructivist, critical social science, and feminist paradigms are commonly used
Ease of replication by other researchers	Easier	Harder

3.3a Types of Mixed Methods Designs

Various ways have been suggested for classifying the types of mixed methods research designs. One way identifies nine types of designs according to whether qualitative or quantitative methods are emphasized and according to the time sequence in which each set of methods is implemented. According to this way of classifying, there are three possibilities regarding emphasis, as follows:

- Qualitative emphasized
- Quantitative emphasized
- Equal emphasis

There are also three possibilities regarding sequencing:

- Qualitative first
- Quantitative first
- Concurrent (qualitative and quantitative methods implemented at the same time)

The resulting nine possible types of design are displayed in Figure 3.2. In that figure, the type of method that is capitalized is the one that gets priority. Let's now consider some hypothetical illustrations of each of the nine types of mixed methods designs listed in Figure 3.2.

QUALITATIVE → quantitative. The first design on the list might involve a study that begins with in-depth, open-ended qualitative interviews of military combat veterans who have returned home from the wars in Iraq and Afghanistan. The priority would be on gaining an in-depth understanding of the challenges they experience in returning and adjusting to civilian life. After collecting and analyzing the data using qualitative data-analysis techniques, quantitative methods could be used to examine how many respondents fell into what types of categories generated by the qualitative analysis. The emphasis in the study and its reportage would be on the qualitative analysis, and the numbers generated in the quantitative analysis, although not unimportant, would not be the study's priority.

quantitative → QUALITATIVE. The second design on the list might begin with a quantitative, structured interview survey of a random sample of military combat veterans in which the veterans complete a checklist indicating what posttraumatic stress symptoms they are experiencing. The data from the survey results would *not* be the study's priority. Instead they would be used as the basis for the ensuing qualitative inquiry, in which in-depth, open-ended probing interviews would be conducted with a subsample of vets with the most symptoms and a subsample with the least symptoms to try to understand why some vets have worse trauma symptoms than others and to describe what it is like to walk in their shoes.

FIGURE 3.2 Nine Types of Mixed Methods Designs: Emphasis by Sequence

QUALITATIVE EMPHASIS	
QUALITATIVE → quantitative	(Qualitative Emphasized with Qualitative Implemented First)
quantitative → QUALITATIVE	(Qualitative Emphasized with Quantitative Implemented First)
QUALITATIVE Emphasized with Concurrent Implementation	
QUANTITATIVE EMPHASIS	
QUANTITATIVE → qualitative	(Quantitative Emphasized with Quantitative Implemented First)
qualitative → QUANTITATIVE	(Quantitative Emphasized with Qualitative Implemented First)
QUANTITATIVE Emphasized with Concurrent Implementation	
EQUAL EMPHASIS	
Qualitative → Quantitative	(Equal Emphasis with Qualitative Implemented First)
Quantitative → Qualitative	(Equal Emphasis with Quantitative Implemented First)
Equal Emphasis with Concurrent Implementation	

QUALITATIVE Emphasized with Concurrent Implementation. The third design on the list might administer the above qualitative interviews and quantitative checklists to the same vets during the same data collection session. (Perhaps half the vets would respond to the qualitative part first, whereas the other half responded to the quantitative part first.) The priority would be on gaining an in-depth understanding of what it's like for the vets to try to readjust to civilian life, and the quantitative data would be used for two secondary purposes: (1) to see if they corroborate the qualitative part of the analysis for each vet, and (2) to enumerate how many vets are experiencing the various in-depth depictions of the qualitative analysis.

QUANTITATIVE → Qualitative. The fourth design on the list might have as its priority answering the research question of whether male and female vets differ in the impact of combat on their emotional well-being or in their level of psychosocial readjustment to civilian life. The male and female vets could complete quantitative scales that measure their trauma symptoms and their psychosocial adjustment. Although the priority of the study would be to test whether there were statistically significant differences between the genders in their scores on the above measures, after the quantitative data were analyzed, qualitative interviews would be conducted with those vets whose scores indicated the worst symptoms and adjustment levels.

The aim of the qualitative interviews would be to supplement the quantitative findings with illustrations that bring the quantitative findings to life and to exemplify how those findings apply in particular cases.

qualitative → QUANTITATIVE. The fifth design on the list might begin with qualitative interviews conducted as part of a pilot study to generate ideas for developing a quantitative instrument to measure psychosocial adjustment to civilian life. Based on the results of the qualitative interviews, for example, the researchers might develop items that will go on the quantitative instrument. The pilot study might also be used to generate hypotheses that could then be tested in a quantitative study. The priority of the mixed methods study would *not* be on the results of the qualitative analysis. Instead, it would be on the subsequent use of the instrument in a quantitative study to test the hypotheses generated in the qualitative study. One such hypothesis might postulate that male and female vets differ in their level of psychosocial readjustment to civilian life.

QUANTITATIVE Emphasized with Concurrent Implementation. The sixth design on the list might also seek to answer the question of whether male and female vets differ in their level of psychosocial readjustment to civilian life. But instead of administering the qualitative interviews after the quantitative data are analyzed, the vets would be divided into two groups. Male and female vets in the larger of the two groups would complete the quantitative scales while their counterparts in the smaller group responded to the in-depth qualitative interviews. The priority would be on the quantitative findings, and the qualitative findings would just be used to illustrate some of the ways that male and female vets encounter different problems in readjusting to civilian life.

Qualitative → Quantitative. The seventh design on the list might place an equal emphasis on answering the question of whether male and female vets differ in their level of psychosocial readjustment to civilian life and on gaining an in-depth understanding of the different kinds of problems they experience and how they try to cope with them during the readjustment process. One group of male and female vets might respond to the qualitative interviews; based on the analysis of those interviews, quantitative instruments would developed and then implemented with another group of male and female vets. In the report of the study findings, both sets of findings would be given equal emphasis.

Quantitative → Qualitative. The eighth design on the list also would place an equal emphasis on answering the question of whether male and female vets differ in their level of psychosocial readjustment to civilian life and on gaining an in-depth understanding of the different kinds of problems they experience and how they try to cope with them during the readjustment process. However, this design would implement the quantitative part of the study first, and then later conduct qualitative interviews with small subsamples of respondents who represented vets with the best, worst, and average adjustment scores. In the report of the study findings, both sets of findings would be given equal emphasis.

Equal Emphasized with Concurrent Implementation. The ninth design on the list might also seek to

Case Example: Mixed-Methods Study of Engaging Nonvoluntary Child Welfare Clients in Working Relationships

Many parents entering the child welfare system have a severely limited capacity to engage in healthy relationships. Given this limited capacity, compounded by the fact that their participation in child welfare services is not voluntary, one of the key challenges faced by child welfare practitioners is developing a healthy relationship with the client and enhancing their investment and commitment toward working on resolving the problems that led to their being referred. In light of this problem, Julie Cooper Altman (2008) conducted a mixed-methods study to examine the processes involved in client engagement and whether those processes are related to service outcomes. She collected qualitative and quantitative data concurrently, with both components receiving equal emphasis. The qualitative component of her phenomenological investigation involved interviews with parents and workers in a neighborhood-based family service center provided by a child welfare agency in New York City. The analysis of the qualitative data from those interviews yielded seven main themes perceived to be key in engaging clients. These themes pertained to the need to set mutual goals; to maintain a sense of hopefulness throughout the change process; to have parents acknowledge understanding of their situation; to remain motivated for change; to respect cultural differences; to have respectful and honest communication; and to maintain persistent and diligent work by all parties in a timely fashion. In the quantitative components of the study, workers and clients completed self-report scales that measured the quality of the worker–client alliance and their degree of satisfaction with the service they were receiving or providing. Quantitative data also were collected from case records to assess whether the case outcome was successful. Unfortunately, however, there was no relationship between the quality of engagement and improved case outcomes. Nevertheless, Altman's findings have value for guiding child welfare practice. Noting that conventional wisdom may be overrating the degree to which the quality of the worker–client relationship impacts case outcomes in child welfare, Altman suggested alternative ways of considering and investigating this service delivery problem.

Source: Altman, J. C. (2008). A study of engagement in neighborhood-based child welfare services. *Research on Social Work Practice*, 18, 6, 555–564.

answer the question of whether male and female vets differ in their level of psychosocial readjustment to civilian life. But instead of administering the qualitative and quantitative components sequentially, the vets would divide into two groups. Male and female vets in the larger of the two groups would complete the quantitative scales, whereas their counterparts in the smaller group responded to the qualitative interviews. In the report of the study findings, both sets of findings would be given equal emphasis. The box providing a case example of a mixed methods study of child welfare clients offers an illustration of this ninth design.

Three Basic Mixed Methods Designs

More recently, Creswell (2014a,b) suggested three basic mixed methods designs, as illustrated in Figure 3.3. These are the convergent mixed methods design, the exploratory sequential mixed methods design, and the explanatory sequential mixed methods design. We'll now discuss each of those designs, in that order.

Convergent mixed methods design

With this design, quantitative and qualitative data are collected concurrently and then analyzed separately. The results of the separate analyses are then merged for comparison purposes to see if they confirm each other. If they do, then there can be more confidence in the veracity of the set of conclusions derived from the joint findings. For example, suppose a study is undertaken to assess whether there is a difference in the quality of the practitioner–client relationship depending upon whether the practitioner follows an evidence-based model of practice. The quantitative data could be collected by having clients complete a written self-report scale regarding the quality of the relationship they have with their practitioner. The qualitative data could delve into the same issue using nondirective, probing interviews with the clients. Both

FIGURE 3.3 Three Basic Mixed Methods Designs

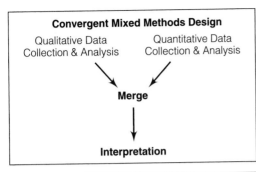

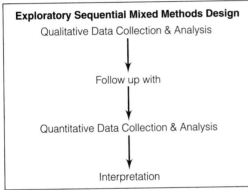

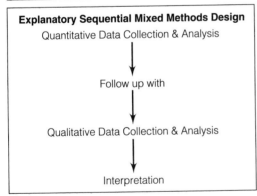

Sources: Creswell, 2014a, pp. 37–41; Creswell, 2014b, p. 220.

types of data collection would be used because there is uncertainty as to whether either type, alone, would yield accurate, unbiased results. Suppose that after the data are collected and analyzed separately they both agree that there is no difference in the quality of the relationship between those practitioners who do and do not follow an evidence-based model of practice. There would be more confidence in the accuracy of that conclusion than if it had been derived from only quantitative data or only qualitative data.

Even if the results agree for the most part, the qualitative data might shed additional light on the nature of the relationships that the more narrow and structured quantitative data are unable to uncover. For example, they might show that although the clients of both sets of practitioners are on average equally pleased with the quality of the relationship, maybe the clients of the practitioners using the evidence-based model will comment that their practitioners gave them more information about the type of intervention to be provided and were more likely to seek their consent to provide the intervention. Likewise, perhaps the clients of the other practitioners will comment that their practitioners were more flexible from session to session regarding the session focus.

Exploratory sequential mixed methods design

With this design the qualitative data are collected first, to provide a basis for formulating the quantitative phase. According to Creswell (2014), one aim of this design could be to see if the insights generated from a small sample of people in the qualitative phase can be generalized to a larger, more representative sample of the population in the quantitative phase. Another aim might be to use the qualitative data as a basis for developing a good quantitative data collection instrument. For example, let's return to the fictitious study (discussed above) undertaken to assess whether there is a difference in the quality of the practitioner–client relationship depending on whether the practitioner follows an evidence-based model of practice. If the qualitative phase were conducted first, the researchers might learn to include items in their quantitative scale pertaining to whether the client felt that the practitioner made an adequate effort to explain potential interventions to them and secure their informed consent. They might also learn to include an item or two regarding whether the client felt that the practitioner was too rigid about the focus of each session.

Explanatory sequential mixed methods design

According to Creswell, this design is thought to appeal to researchers who are more quantitatively oriented. The quantitative data are collected first, followed by qualitative data collection aimed at developing a better understanding of the quantitative data. For example, consider a program that brings juvenile offenders into prisons where convicts attempt to scare the youths away from criminal behavior by portraying the sordid nature of prison life. Such a program, known as *Scared Straight*, was implemented in the 1970s and had unexpected, harmful results based on the quantitative crime record data. The juvenile offenders who participated in the program later engaged in much more crime than did a comparable group of offenders who did not participate. Why did this happen? One author speculated that the "tough" juveniles who participated in the program perhaps wanted to prove that they were not scared (Finckenauer, 1979). Although this speculation seems reasonable, following the quantitative data collection with a qualitative approach using in-depth interviews with the juveniles might have made this interpretation less speculative and perhaps would have suggested other explanations for the unexpected findings. (We will return to the *Scared Straight* example in Chapter 14, on program evaluation.)

Three Advanced Mixed Methods Designs

In addition to the foregoing three *basic* mixed-methods designs, Creswell (2014a) describes three *advanced* ones. The main basis for calling these designs advanced is that a particular research purpose or overarching framework is added to the basic design. For example, the **intervention mixed methods** design involves merging a qualitative inquiry with a quantitative evaluation of an intervention's outcome to get a better handle on the meaning of the results. For example, during a large experiment to test the effectiveness of a clinical intervention, a researcher might come to realize that qualitative interviews need to be implemented with clinicians to see if they are enthusiastic and committed to the new intervention.

The second advanced design is the **social justice mixed methods** design. What makes this design distinct is not the degree of emphasis or the sequencing of the qualitative and quantitative methods, but rather that its various methods are based on a social justice theory and aimed at collecting data that will yield a call for action to improve the plight of vulnerable, marginalized or oppressed groups. (In the next chapter you will see how this design is akin to what others call the *critical social science* paradigm.)

The third advanced design is **the multiphase mixed methods** design, which also is not distinguished by the sequence or emphasis of the various methods. Instead, it is distinguished by the use of several mixed methods projects that are implemented in multiple phases over time in a longitudinal study in which the multiple projects focus on a common objective. (We will examine longitudinal studies in the next chapter.)

3.3b Reasons for Using Mixed Methods

As you might surmise from the above illustrations, there are various reasons for choosing to combine qualitative and quantitative methods of inquiry. Three broad types of reasons for doing so are as follows: (1) to use one set of methods to illustrate cases or provide numbers for the findings of the other set, (2) to use one set to initiate ideas or techniques that subsequently can be pursued by the other set, and (3) to see if the two sets of findings corroborate each other. These reasons are illustrated in Figure 3.4, with the emphasized type of method in capital letters and with each type abbreviated (*qual* for qualitative and *quant* for quantitative).

For example, in some studies the methods are combined so that the qualitative data can provide descriptions of how the quantitative data apply in particular cases. Likewise, some studies might

---

intervention mixed methods design A qualitative inquiry is merged with a quantitative evaluation of an intervention's outcome to get a better handle on the meaning of the results.

social justice mixed methods design This design is distinguished by the use of various methods that are based on a social justice theory and aimed at collecting data that will yield a call for action to improve the plight of vulnerable, marginalized, or oppressed groups.

multiphase mixed methods design This design is distinguished by the use of several mixed methods projects that are implemented in multiple phases over time in a longitudinal study in which the multiple projects focus on a common objective.

FIGURE 3.4 Reasons for Using Mixed Methods*

Reason	Sequence	Example
Extend main findings	QUANT → qual QUAL → quant	Qual illustrates how QUANT applies in particular cases Quant indicates the number of cases in the QUAL categories
Generate research questions or techniques	qual → QUANT	Qual identifies research questions to assess using QUANT or facilitates the development of QUANT measurement instruments
Corroborate findings	QUANT → qual QUAL → quant Concurrent	Qual used to support the validity of the QUANT findings Quant used to support the validity of the QUAL findings Either of the above corroborations, with both qual and quant findings having an equal emphasis

*The emphasized type of method is in capital letters, and each type is abbreviated (qual = qualitative and quant = quantitative)

combine them so that the quantitative data can indicate the numbers of cases that fall within the qualitative categories. Those two studies would exemplify the first reason. The second reason would be exemplified by a study in which the qualitative part is used to generate hypotheses to be tested in the quantitative part, or a study in which the quantitative part yields perplexing findings that need to be explained by the qualitative part. To illustrate the third reason, we can imagine findings in which qualitative interviews show that male and female vets are experiencing differences in the types of problems they encounter in trying to readjust to civilian life and differences in their level of adjustment; those data would corroborate quantitative findings that point to such differences. Alternatively, if the two sets of data contradict each other, then the validity of the findings are in doubt, and the contradictions might have value in implying the need for new avenues of research that might illuminate the meaning of—or resolve—the contradiction.

EP 2.1.3a
EP 2.1.3b
EP 2.1.6b

At this point we surmise that you might be feeling somewhat overwhelmed with this discussion of qualitative, quantitative, and mixed methods because we have not yet covered the various specific kinds of qualitative and quantitative research methods. If you are feeling that way, we encourage you not to worry. Most of your peers are probably feeling the same way. Never fear, the rest of this book will delve into those specific methods in depth. But before we leave this chapter, we'll present an overview of the phases of the research process—phases that apply regardless of the type of research method chosen or emphasized.

3.4 PHASES IN THE RESEARCH PROCESS IN QUANTITATIVE, QUALITATIVE, AND MIXED METHODS STUDIES

Despite the differences between qualitative and quantitative methods, the studies that employ them either separately or in combination tend to follow the same general research phases. Let's now look at some phases in the research process that are common across quantitative, qualitative, and mixed methods approaches to inquiry.

- **Phase 1: Problem Formulation** In the first phase, a difficulty is recognized for which more knowledge is needed. A question—the research question—is posed. The question and its inherent concepts are progressively sharpened to become more specific, relevant, and meaningful to the field. As this is done, the question of feasibility of implementation is always considered. Ultimately, the purpose of the research is determined and the elements of the research are explicated. The literature review is one critical step in this phase. In addition, deductive quantitative studies will specify hypotheses and variables during this phase, and will define the variables in observable terms called *operational definitions* (which we'll discuss in Chapter 7). Inductive qualitative studies, on the other hand, are more likely to wait and let hypotheses emerge later, after observations have been conducted. As mentioned above, mixed methods studies will vary as to the order and emphasis of the quantitative or qualitative approach to problem formulation.

Some mixed methods studies will start with the qualitative approach. Others will start with the quantitative approach. However, the approach they start with may or may not be the one that gets the greater priority in the study. Likewise, the approaches might get equal priority regardless of the sequencing. Others will embark on both simultaneously, perhaps—but not necessarily—with an equal emphasis on each. As we will discuss in the next chapter, two factors that can influence the entire research process are paradigms and theories. According to Hanson et al. (2005), those factors are particularly important in the problem-formulation phase of mixed methods research because the theory or paradigm chosen to guide one's study will guide decisions about what type of methods to emphasize in the study.

- **Phase 2: Designing the Study** The second phase considers alternative logical arrangements and data collection methods. The arrangements and methods selected will depend on the issues addressed during the problem-formulation phase. Feasibility is one such issue; the purpose of the research is another. Studies that inquire about causation will require logical arrangements that meet the three criteria for establishing causality, which we will discuss in Chapter 12. Other arrangements might suffice for studies that seek to explore or describe certain phenomena.

- **Phase 3: Data Collection** In Phase 3, the study designed in the second phase is implemented. The study's purpose and design direct to what degree this implementation either is rigidly structured in advance, or is more flexible and open to modification as new insights are discovered. Quantitative explanatory studies that seek to verify hypotheses or quantitative descriptive studies that emphasize accuracy and objectivity will require more rigidly structured data collection procedures than will studies that use qualitative methods to better understand the meanings of certain phenomena or to generate hypotheses about them.

- **Phase 4: Data Processing** Depending on the research methods chosen, a volume of observations will have been amassed in a form that is probably difficult to interpret. Whether the data are quantitative or qualitative, or both,

the data processing in the fourth phase typically involves the classification, or coding, of observations to make them more interpretable.

- **Phase 5: Data Analysis** In this phase, the processed data are manipulated to help answer the research question. Conceivably, the analysis will also yield unanticipated findings that reflect on the research problem but go beyond the specific question that guided the research. The results of the analysis will feed back into the initial problem formulation and may initiate another cycle of inquiry.

- **Phase 6: Interpreting the Findings** It will become apparent throughout the rest of this book that there is no one correct way to plan a study, and no way to ensure that the outcome of the data analysis will provide the correct answer to the research question. With quantitative data, certain statistical procedures may be essential to provide the best possible interpretation of the data, but no mathematical formula or computer will remove the need to make some judgments about the meaning of the findings. Inevitably, we encounter rival explanations of the findings and must consider various methodological limitations that influence the degree to which the findings can be generalized. Consequently, research reports do not end with a presentation of the data analysis results. Instead, the results are followed by or included in a thorough discussion of alternative ways to interpret those results, of what generalizations can and cannot be made based on them, and of methodological limitations bearing on the meaning and validity of the results. Finally, implications are drawn for social welfare policy and program development, social work practice and theory, and future research.

- **Phase 7: Writing the Research Report** Although writing up our research logically comes in the last phase of the research process, in practice we write pieces about it as we go along. The components of the research report follow in large part the above phases of the research process. Although the specific terminology of the headings will vary from study to study, typically the report begins with an *introduction* that provides a background to the research problem, informs the reader of the rationale and significance of the study, and reviews relevant theory and research. This introduction is followed by an explication of the conceptual elements of the study. A *methodology* section delineates the design of the study, including quantitative or qualitative data collection methods used and any logical arrangements. Next come the *results* of the data analysis, which identify the quantitative or qualitative analytic procedures employed; display data in tables, graphs, or other visual devices; and provide a narrative that reports in a technical, factual sense what specific data mean. This is followed by a *discussion* section, which includes the issues identified in Phase 6. Depending on the length of the report or its discussion section (or both) and whether an abstract was developed, the report might end with a brief summary of the foregoing components that highlights the major findings and conclusions. Appendix C of this book provides further information on writing research reports and describes the differences between the reports of qualitative and quantitative studies.

EP 2.1.3a
EP 2.1.3b
EP 2.1.6b

Now that you have a broad view of the above three approaches to inquiry and the phases of the research process, the next chapter will examine the various factors that can influence the way in which the various phases of research process are carried out in qualitative, quantitative, and mixed methods studies.

3.5 MAIN POINTS

- Quantitative research methods attempt to produce findings that are precise and generalizable.
- Qualitative research methods emphasize depth of understanding, attempt to subjectively tap the deeper meanings of human experiences, and are intended to generate theoretically rich observations.
- Mixed methods research studies collect both qualitative and quantitative data, and integrate both sources of data at one or more stages of the research process so as to improve the understanding of the phenomenon being investigated.
- Nine subtypes of mixed methods designs can be classified according to whether qualitative or quantitative methods are emphasized and according to the time sequence in which each set of methods is implemented.
- Three basic mixed methods designs are the convergent parallel mixed methods design, the exploratory sequential mixed methods design, and explanatory sequential mixed methods design.
- Three advanced mixed methods designs are the embedded mixed methods design, the transformative mixed methods design, and the multiphase mixed methods design.
- Reasons for choosing to combine qualitative and quantitative methods include: 1) to use one set of methods to illustrate cases or provide numbers for the findings of the other set; 2) to use one set to initiate ideas or techniques that subsequently can be pursued by the other set; and 3) to see if the two sets of findings corroborate each other.
- The phases of research include: problem formulation, designing the study, data collection, data processing, data analysis, interpreting the findings, and writing the research report.

3.6 PRACTICE-RELATED EXERCISES

1. Examine several recent issues of a social work research journal (such as *Research on Social Work Practice* or *Social Work Research*). Find one article that emphasizes quantitative methods and one emphasizing qualitative methods. Discuss the value of each and how they illustrate the contrasting methods.

2. In the same journal, find a recent study that has the term mixed methods in the title or abstract and that emphasizes its use of mixed methods. Identify which of the nine mixed methods designs described in this chapter best matches the approach used in that study and why.

3. Suppose you have been asked to design a research study that evaluates the degree of success of a family preservation program that seeks to prevent out-of-home placements of children who are at risk of child abuse or neglect by providing intensive in-home social work services. Under what conditions might you opt to emphasize quantitative methods or qualitative methods

in your design? What would be the advantages and disadvantages of each approach?

4. Using the family preservation study example in exercise 3 above, how and why might you choose to combine both types of methods in a mixed methods design? Provide an example of two alternative mixed methods designs you might use for that study and their rationale.

3.7   INTERNET EXERCISES

1. Go to the website for the online Journal of Mixed-Methods Research (http://mmr.sagepub.com/content/8/2.toc). Click on the prompts for the tables of contents for previous issues until you find the issues published in 2013. Click on the abstracts for each of the articles in those issues to find two articles that report studies that used one or more of the mixed methods designs discussed in this chapter. For each of the articles write down the article citation, identify and describe the type of mixed method design used.

2. At the same site and for the same year, find two articles that illustrate the applicability of mixed methods research to problems of concern to social workers. For each of the articles, write down the article citation briefly summarize the article, and discuss its applicability to social work.

3.8   ADDITIONAL READINGS

Creswell, J. (2014). *A Concise Introduction to Mixed Methods Research*. Thousand Oaks, CA: Sage. This book covers the features of mixed methods research, skills needed to conduct it, its basic and advanced designs, how to conduct and report it, and how to evaluate its quality.

Creswell, J. (2014). *Research Design: Qualitative, Quantitative, and Mixed Methods Approaches*. Thousand Oaks, CA: Sage. In addition to discussing the various aspects of mixed methods research, this book provides overviews of quantitative and qualitative approaches to inquiry, compares and contrasts the two approaches, and discusses considerations influencing whether to use either or both approaches.

Creswell, J., & Plano Clark, V. (2010). *Designing and conducting mixed methods research* (2nd ed.) Thousand Oaks, CA: Sage. This book provides 10 chapters on understanding mixed methods research, how to conduct it, how to analyze and report mixed methods findings, illustrations of real mixed methods studies, and critical questions often raised about mixed methods research.

Tashakkori, A., & Teddlie, C. (Eds.). 2010. *Sage handbook of mixed methods research in social and behavioral research* (2nd ed.). Thousand Oaks, CA: Sage. This handbook, edited by two pioneers in mixed methods research, includes 31 chapters on mixed methods research that are divided into the following sections: conceptual issues, methodological issues, and contemporary applications.

3.8a   Competency Notes

EP 2.1.3a: Distinguish, appraise, and integrate multiple sources of knowledge, including research-based knowledge (pp. 46, 55, 57): Social workers distinguish qualitative, quantitative, and mixed methods sources of knowledge.

EP 2.1.3b: Analyze models of assessment, prevention, intervention, and evaluation (pp. 46, 55, 57): Social workers understand qualitative, quantitative, and mixed methods of assessment and evaluation.

EP 2.1.6b: Use research evidence to inform practice (pp. 46, 55, 57): Understanding qualitative, quantitative, and mixed methods of assessment evaluation—and understanding the research process—enhances social workers' ability to use research evidence to inform their practice.

chapter
4

Factors Influencing the Research Process

4.1   INTRODUCTION

We ended Chapter 2 by noting that scholars disagree about some methodological and philosophical issues that can influence how research is conducted, and about the value of the evidence produced by different kinds of research. This chapter will delve into some of those methodological and philosophical issues. But as we do, you should keep in mind that regardless of one's stance on those issues, there is agreement that both social work research and social work practice seek to resolve social welfare problems. They also share the same problem-solving process. Both practice and research begin with the formulation of a problem, which includes recognizing a difficulty, defining it, and specifying it. Researchers and practitioners then generate, explore, and select alternative strategies for solving the problem. Finally, they implement the chosen approach, evaluate it, and disseminate their findings. In both practice and research, these phases are contingent on one another. Although the logical order is to go from one phase to the next, insurmountable obstacles encountered in any particular phase can prevent researchers from moving to the next phase, and require them to return to a previous one. Various factors can influence how these phases are carried out in different research studies. Let's begin by examining one such factor: the purpose of the research.

4.2   RESEARCH PURPOSES IN QUALITATIVE AND QUANTITATIVE STUDIES

If you glance through the abstracts contained in virtually any issue of a journal that reports research studies you will quickly notice that the studies vary in purpose. They might have aimed to generate tentative new insights about some phenomenon, to provide a more conclusive description of a phenomenon, or to verify some postulated explanation of a phenomenon. Some studies might have aimed to evaluate a policy, program, or intervention. Other studies might have developed and tested a new assessment instrument.

If you read some of those studies, you might also see how their different aims are connected to different research processes. For example, a study with the purpose of generating insights about a new phenomenon is more likely to employ flexible *qualitative* research methods and be more open to subjective observations and interpretations. In contrast, a study testing whether an intervention is truly as effective as some say it is will be more likely to employ *quantitative* research procedures that are highly structured and specified in advance. We compared qualitative and quantitative methods in Chapter 3 and will continue to do so throughout the rest of this book. This section will provide a glimpse of what is to come by giving quantitative and qualitative examples of some different research purposes. There are various ways to categorize the different purposes of social work research studies. Although a given study can have more than one purpose—and most do—we will examine them separately because each has different implications for other aspects of research design.

4.2a   Exploration

Much of social work research is conducted to explore a topic—to provide a beginning familiarity with it. This purpose is typical when a researcher is examining a new interest, when the subject of study is relatively new and unstudied, or when a researcher seeks to test the feasibility of undertaking a more careful study or wants to refine the methods to be used in a more careful study. For example, suppose your first job as a social worker is to develop services for the frail elderly in a predominantly ethnic-minority community about which you know very little. You want to conduct a community-wide survey to assess the need for and likely utilization of alternative services that you are contemplating developing. Before mounting a large-scale study geared to producing precise, conclusive findings, you'd be well advised to begin with a smaller, more flexible exploratory study that will help you plan a larger and more careful study in a culturally sensitive manner.

Exploratory studies can employ various qualitative or quantitative methods, or, in mixed methods studies, both in combination. Occasionally we will hear a colleague or student equate exploratory research with qualitative research. Although that is incorrect, it is an understandable mistake because many (but not all) qualitative studies are exploratory. However, it is not uncommon to see exploratory quantitative studies. For example, researchers seeking to obtain federal grants for large-scale quantitative, experimental evaluations of the effectiveness of certain interventions often carry out small, exploratory, pilot versions of the experiments to address feasibility issues and obtain some preliminary data that will help support their grant proposals. Also, small-sample quantitative surveys might be used to get preliminary data regarding a new area of inquiry; depending on their findings, more conclusive surveys might ensue. The chief shortcoming of such exploratory studies—regardless of which methods they employ—is that they seldom provide conclusive answers to research questions. They can only hint at the answers and give insights into the research methods that could provide definitive answers. One reason exploratory studies are seldom definitive in themselves is the issue of representativeness, which is discussed at length in Chapter 10 in connection with sampling. Once you understand sampling and representativeness, you will be able to determine whether a given exploratory study actually answered its research question or merely pointed the way toward an answer.

4.2b Description

Many social work studies seek a second purpose: to describe situations and events. The researcher observes and then describes what was observed. Because scientific observation is careful and deliberate, scientific descriptions are typically more accurate and precise than casual descriptions.

Descriptive studies can follow a quantitative or qualitative research process, or combine both processes in mixed methods studies. A quantitative descriptive study, for example, might assess community needs by conducting a careful, large-scale survey of a representative sample of residents in the community. The sampling would be conducted to describe the precise proportion of different types of residents who have the need for each service specified. The U.S. census is an excellent example of a descriptive social scientific research project. Its goal is to describe accurately and precisely a wide variety of characteristics of the U.S. population, as well as the populations of smaller areas such as states and counties.

The term *description* is used differently in qualitative and quantitative studies. In quantitative studies, *description* typically refers to the characteristics of a population; it is based on data obtained from a sample of people that is thought to be representative of that population. The data being described in quantitative studies are likely to refer to surface attributes that can be easily quantified, such as age, income, size of family, and so on. In quantitative descriptive studies, the objectivity, precision, and generalizability of the description are paramount concerns.

In qualitative studies, *description* is more likely to refer to a thicker examination of phenomena and their deeper meanings. Qualitative descriptions tend to be more concerned with conveying a sense of what it's like to walk in the shoes of the people being described—providing rich details about their environments, interactions, meanings, and everyday lives—than with generalizing with precision to a larger population. A qualitative descriptive study of mothers receiving welfare in states where the levels of such support are lowest, for example, might describe the effects that the inadequate payments have on the daily lives of a small sample of mothers and their children, how they struggle to survive, how neighbors and welfare workers interact with them, how that makes them feel, and what things they must do to provide for their families. A quantitative descriptive study of mothers receiving welfare, in contrast, would be likely to select a large, representative sample of these mothers and assess things like how long they require public assistance, their ages and educational levels, and so on.

4.2c Explanation

The third general purpose of social work research is to explain things. Simply reporting that some cities have higher child abuse rates than others is a case of description, but analyzing why the child abuse rates differ is explanation. A researcher has an explanatory purpose if he or she wishes to know why battered women repeatedly return to live with their batterers, rather than simply describing how often they do.

Like exploratory and descriptive studies, *explanatory* studies can follow a quantitative or qualitative research process, or combine both processes in mixed methods studies. Suppose, for example, we want to explain why some battered women repeatedly return to live with their batterers, whereas others do not. A qualitative explanatory study might conduct in-depth, probing, and relatively unstructured interviews with battered women to ascertain the reasons. A quantitative explanatory study might start out with a hypothesis about some factor (or factors) that helps explain the phenomenon, and then test that hypothesis. For example, it might hypothesize that battered women who participate in a support group for battered women are less likely to return to the batterer than women who do not participate.

4.2d Evaluation

EP 2.1.3a
EP 2.1.6b

A fourth purpose of social work research is to evaluate social policies, programs, and interventions. The *evaluative* purpose of social work research actually encompasses all three of the preceding purposes: exploration, description, and explanation. For example, we might conduct qualitative open-ended exploratory interviews with community residents as a first step toward evaluating what services they need. We might conduct a quantitative descriptive community survey to evaluate the problems residents report having and the services they say they need. A descriptive study might also evaluate whether services are being implemented as intended. We might conduct an explanatory analysis to evaluate whether factors such as ethnicity explain why some residents are more likely than others to utilize services.

Evaluative studies also might ask whether social policies, programs, or services are effective in achieving their stated goals. Evaluations of goal achievement can be done in an exploratory, descriptive, or explanatory way. For example, if we simply asked practitioners in a qualitative, open-ended fashion to recall techniques they have employed that seemed to be the most or least effective in achieving treatment goals, we would be conducting an exploratory evaluation to generate tentative insights as to what ways of intervening might be worth evaluating further. Suppose we evaluated the proportion of service recipients who achieve treatment goals, such as whether they graduate

from high school as opposed to dropping out. That would be a quantitative descriptive evaluation. We should not call it *explanatory* unless our study design enabled us to determine whether it was really our service, and not some other factor, that explained why the goal was achieved. Perhaps the students who were the most motivated to succeed were more likely to seek our services than those who were least motivated. If we did assess such alternative factors, then we would have an explanatory evaluation—one that enabled us to determine whether it was really our services that caused the desired outcome. Part 5 of this text will cover the evaluation of program and practice effectiveness in much greater depth.

4.2e Constructing Measurement Instruments

EP 2.1.3b

Some quantitative studies aim to develop and test out measurement instruments that can be used by other researchers or by practitioners as part of the assessment or evaluation aspects of their practice. The research questions implicit in these studies contrast with the types of research questions we've discussed so far. Rather than attempt to develop implications for practice, they ask whether a particular measurement instrument is a useful and valid tool that can be applied in practice or research. Thus, they may assess whether a 40-item family risk scale accurately predicts whether parents in treatment for child abuse or neglect are likely to be abusive or neglectful again in the future. Or they may assess whether such an instrument that has been accurate with clients from a dominant culture in one country is valid when used with clients of minority ethnicity in that country or with clients residing in other countries. Chapters 7 and 8 of this text will examine the key concepts and methods pertaining to studies that develop and test out measurement instruments.

The foregoing are just a few examples of how research purposes can influence the social work research process. Some additional examples are provided in Figure 4.1, which shows how different research purposes might influence research about an effort to provide culturally competent substance abuse services in a border town.

FIGURE 4.1 How Might an Effort to Provide Culturally Competent Substance Abuse Services in a Border Town Be Researched Differently in Light of Different Research Purposes?

Research Purpose	Research Question	Research Design
Exploration	How do residents—especially those for whom English is not their main language—perceive current substance abuse services, and how do they react to a description of the new services being considered?	Conduct in-depth, qualitative interviews by bilingual and culturally competent interviewers, probing into the perceptions of the residents.
Description	What are the extent and nature of the substance abuse problems in the town—especially among those for whom English is not their main language?	Survey a large representative sample of community residents regarding their substance abuse behaviors, making sure that an adequate proportion of the sample is composed of residents for whom English is not their main language, and using culturally sensitive data collection procedures (as discussed in Chapter 7).
Explanation	What factors are most and least predictive of successful treatment outcomes in current substance abuse services?	Analyze the records of agencies providing the current services, using multivariate statistical procedures to ascertain what client attributes and service provision characteristics are most highly correlated with the degree of treatment outcome success.
Evaluation	Is the new, culturally competent service program more effective than the older approach in reducing the extent and severity of substance abuse?	Conduct an experiment that compares the outcomes of the two approaches when provided to similar groups of service recipients.
Construct a measurement instrument	Is a new self-report paper-and-pencil measurement instrument that attempts to be culturally sensitive more accurate than existing instruments in assessing substance abuse behaviors among border town residents?	Administer each instrument to a sample of residents in treatment for substance abuse and a sample of residents not in treatment for substance abuse, and see which instrument depicts greater average differences in the extent of substance abuse between the two groups. Ensure that an adequate proportion of each sample is composed of residents for whom English is not their main language.

4.2f Multiple Purposes

Although it is useful to distinguish the purposes of social work research, we emphasize again that most social work studies have elements of several of these purposes. Because studies can have more than one purpose, sometimes it is difficult to judge how best to characterize a particular study's purpose. This is complicated further by the sometimes fuzzy distinction between exploratory and explanatory purposes. For example, what if you set out to explore why so many homeless people refuse to sleep in a shelter for the homeless? Your ultimate aim is to explain this phenomenon, but we call it an exploratory study if your methods aim merely to gain familiarity with the phenomenon and generate tentative possible explanations or insights that can be tested out more carefully later in an explanatory study. If your study is seeking to develop a beginning understanding of a

phenomenon, it is more likely to be exploratory than explanatory, even though it might include questions asking respondents to explain why they did something. On the other hand, your study is more likely to be explanatory to the extent that it seeks to rigorously test out predictions (hypotheses) implied by tentative explanations derived from previous work on the topic.

The distinction between descriptive and exploratory studies can be confusing, too. For example, suppose you don't know where to locate many homeless people in your community, and you decide to use very flexible methods to get a sense of where they may be. On the one hand, you seek to describe their whereabouts. But unless you are using a carefully structured survey with a representative sample, your study is more likely to be considered exploratory than descriptive.

4.2g Explaining and Predicting

EP 2.1.3b
EP 2.1.6b

Although quantitative explanatory studies commonly test out predictions, we should recognize the difference between being able to predict something and being able to explain or understand it. Often we are able to predict without understanding—you may be able to predict rain when your trick knee aches. And often, even if we don't understand why, we are willing to act on the basis of a demonstrated predictive ability. Our ancient ancestors could predict sunrises and sunsets every day and plan their activities accordingly, without understanding why the sun rose and set. And even if they thought they understood, using an explanation involving a flat, stationary earth, they could predict accurately although their explanation was incorrect.

In the same vein, when the findings of social work research studies support a particular hypothesis, the findings might not explain why the hypothesis (prediction) was correct. Suppose a researcher hypothesizes that Caucasians are more likely to engage in and continue to use outpatient mental health services than are African Americans or Mexican Americans. Finding that to be true would not, by itself, explain *why* it is true. Are mental health services less likely to be valued in some cultures? Is there perhaps a greater sense of stigma associated with mental illness in those cultures? To what extent can the finding be attributed to economic factors, such as the greater likelihood that Caucasians can get away from work during service provision hours or can afford agency fees or transportation costs? To what extent can the finding be attributed to the nature of the services offered or the characteristics of the practitioners providing those services? Perhaps the difference in treatment engagement and retention rates would disappear if the services were more culturally sensitive and were being provided by a greater proportion of African American and Hispanic practitioners.

To sort all of this out, more studies testing more hypotheses would be needed. For example, suppose the findings of a new study supported the prediction that the differences in engagement and retention

rates would disappear in agencies that emphasized a culturally competent approach to service provision. Findings supporting that prediction would help explain—at least partially—the findings supporting the earlier prediction of a difference in engagement and retention rates. Thus, although an accurate prediction about a phenomenon does not necessarily imply an accurate explanation of it, it is possible to improve our understanding of phenomena through a cumulative research process in which subsequent studies test hypotheses that build on and attempt to explain the findings supporting the hypotheses of earlier studies.

4.3 THE TIME DIMENSION

EP 2.1.3a
EP 2.1.3b
EP 2.1.6b

Another factor influencing the research process—one that is related to the purpose of the research—is the time period during which the research observations will be conducted. Research observations may be made more or less at one time, or they may be deliberately stretched over a long period. If, for example, the purpose of your study is to describe the living arrangements of mentally ill patients immediately after their hospital discharge, then you might decide to observe each patient's living arrangements at a predetermined point after their discharge. If, on the other hand, the purpose of your study is to describe how these living arrangements change over time, then you would need to conduct repeated observations of these individuals and their living arrangements over an extended period.

4.3a Cross-Sectional Studies

A research study that examines a phenomenon by taking a cross section of it at one time and analyzing that cross section carefully is called a **cross-sectional study**. Such a study may have an exploratory, descriptive, or explanatory purpose. A single U.S. census, for example, exemplifies a cross-sectional study for descriptive purposes. If you conducted one open-ended, unstructured interview with each client who prematurely terminated treatment in your agency during a specified period in order to generate insights about why your agency's treatment termination rate is so high, you would be conducting a

cross-sectional studies   Studies based on observations that represent a single point in time.

cross-sectional study for exploratory purposes. If you conducted one structured interview both with these clients and with those who completed their planned treatment to test the hypothesis that practitioner–client disagreement about treatment goals is related to whether treatment is completed, then you would be conducting a cross-sectional study for explanatory purposes.

Explanatory cross-sectional studies have an inherent problem. They typically aim to understand causal processes that occur over time, yet their conclusions are based on observations made at only one time. For example, if your cross-sectional study of patients recently discharged from a psychiatric hospital found that those who were living with their families were functioning better and had less symptomatology than those who were not living with their families, then you would not know whether the differences in functioning or symptomatology between the two groups commenced before or after they entered their current living arrangements. In other words, you wouldn't know whether different living arrangements helped cause differences in functioning and symptoms, or whether the latter differences helped to explain placement in particular living arrangements. Although merely finding in a cross-sectional study that such a relationship existed might have significant value, a better understanding of the causal processes involved in that relationship could be obtained using methods we will discuss later on, in the chapters on research designs and statistical analysis.

4.3b Longitudinal Studies

Studies that are intended to describe processes occurring over time and thus conduct their observations over an extended period are called **longitudinal studies**. For example, researchers carry out a longitudinal study if they participate in or observe the activities of a support group for battered women, or an advocacy group for families of the mentally ill, from its beginnings to the present. Other examples of longitudinal studies would be analyses of newspaper editorials or of U.S. Supreme Court decisions over time on a subject such as abortion or psychiatric commitment. In the latter instances, the researcher may conduct the analyses at one point in time, but because the study's data correspond to events that occur at different chronological points, the study is considered longitudinal.

Longitudinal studies can be of great value in assessing whether a particular attribute increases one's risk of developing a later problem. To do this, longitudinal studies might follow over time individuals possessing or not possessing such an attribute. At a later time, the incidence of the problem between the two groups can then be compared. For example, children who do have a parent diagnosed with schizophrenia and those who do not might be followed and compared over many years to see if they become afflicted with schizophrenia. If the incidence of schizophrenia among the children of parents with schizophrenia is significantly higher than it is among the other children, then having a parent with schizophrenia would be deemed a risk factor for developing schizophrenia. Similar longitudinal studies could be conducted to assess the relative risk of contracting HIV or AIDS between groups with particular risk factors and those without. By comparing the incidence rates of a problem between two groups, longitudinal studies can calculate the likelihood that individuals with a particular risk factor will develop the problem.

Three special types of longitudinal studies should be noted here. *Trend studies* are those that study changes within some population over time. One could, for example, assess whether the types of clients or problems that make up an agency's caseload are changing over time, and perhaps use that analysis to make projections as to what these trends imply for future staffing patterns or in-service training needs.

Cohort studies examine more specific subpopulations (cohorts) as they change over time. For example, we might be interested in what happens to the incidence of substance abuse among young adults with schizophrenia as they age, because such abuse is particularly dangerous for this group owing to the nature of their illness and the prescribed medications they take for the illness. In 2000 we might survey a sample of such persons 20 years of age (born in 1980) and ask them about their use of alcohol or drugs. In 2010 we might survey another sample of such persons 30 years of age, and another sample of those 40 years of age in 2020. Although the people being described

longitudinal studies Studies that conduct observations at different points in time.

in each of the three age groups are different, each set of them represents the same cohort: those who were born in 1980.

Panel studies examine the same set of people each time. Suppose you wanted to learn how teenagers from different ethnic groups adapt to their child-rearing responsibilities. You could conduct interviews with those who became mothers in 2010 and then conduct follow-up interviews with the same mothers at different points over time. You might see what they learned from other family members, the roles played by their children's fathers, and so on. By getting to know a specific set of such mothers in depth, you would be able to understand a wide range of changes occurring in their lives.

Longitudinal studies have an obvious advantage over cross-sectional ones in providing information describing processes over time. But this advantage often comes at a heavy cost in both time and money, especially in a large-scale survey. Observations may have to be made at the time events are occurring, and the method of observation may require many research workers.

Panel studies, which offer the most comprehensive data on changes over time, face a special problem: panel attrition. Some of the respondents studied in the first wave of the study might not participate in later waves. The danger is that those who drop out of the study may be atypical, thereby distorting the results of the study. Over the years, researchers have developed many techniques for tracking down the missing people. Rhodes and Marks (2011) used Facebook as a vehicle for tracking down members of a longitudinal study who had been unreachable by telephone or mail. They were successful in locating a third of the subjects. Figure 4.2 compares these three types of longitudinal designs as well as cross-sectional designs.

---

paradigm A set of philosophical assumptions about the nature of reality—a fundamental model or scheme that organizes our view of some things.

contemporary positivism A paradigm that emphasizes the pursuit of objectivity in our quest to observe and understand reality.

social constructivism A paradigm that emphasizes multiple subjective realities and the difficulty of being objective.

FIGURE 4.2 Comparing Types of Study Design

	Cross-Sectional	Longitudinal		
		Trend	Cohort	Panel
Snapshot in time	X			
Measurements across time		X	X	X
Follow age group across time			X	
Study same people over time X				X

4.4 THE INFLUENCE OF PARADIGMS

Whether and how researchers use or emphasize qualitative or quantitative methods will be influenced by the paradigm they favor. A **paradigm** is a set of philosophical assumptions about the nature of reality—a fundamental

EP 2.1.3a

model or scheme that organizes our view of some things. Two contrasting paradigms that influence social work research are **contemporary positivism** and **social constructivism**. The contemporary positivist paradigm emphasizes the pursuit of objectivity in our quest to observe and understand reality. In contrast, the **social constructivist** paradigm emphasizes multiple subjective realities and the difficulty of being objective. Contemporary positivist researchers often use quantitative methods and formulate all or most of their research procedures for a specific study in advance, and then attempt to adhere precisely to those procedures with maximum objectivity as they collect data. In contrast, social constructivist researchers are more likely to use qualitative methods and begin with a more flexible plan, one that values subjective processes and the need for the research processes to evolve as more observations are gathered, rather than being determined completely in advance. Although social constructivist researchers typically use qualitative methods, and positivist researchers typically use quantitative methods, there are exceptions. Contemporary positivist researchers, for example, occasionally conduct qualitative studies when they think the problem they are investigating calls for such. When they do, however, they will typically be more concerned with assessing the objectivity of their qualitative observations than social constructivist researchers are when they conduct qualitative investigations.

Another paradigm associated with qualitative research is called **interpretivism**. Like social constructivism, interpretivism values subjectivity. Interpretive researchers attempt to develop an in-depth subjective understanding of people's lives. They are likely to hang out with people and observe them in their natural settings, where they attempt to gain an empathic understanding of how people feel inside, seeking to interpret individuals' everyday experiences, deeper meanings and feelings, and idiosyncratic reasons for their behaviors. Rather than convey statistical probabilities for particular causal processes within a large number of people, interpretive researchers attempt to help readers of their reports sense what it is like to walk in the shoes of the small number of people they study.

Interpretive researchers believe that you cannot adequately learn about people by relying solely on objective measurement instruments that are used in a standardized manner from person to person. Instead, interpretive researchers believe that the best way to learn about people is to be flexible and subjective in one's approach so that the subject's world can be "seen" through the subject's own eyes. It is not enough to simply measure the subject's external behaviors or questionnaire answers. The subjective meanings and social contexts of an individual's words or deeds must be examined more deeply.

A fourth paradigm that can influence the research process is called **critical social science**. This paradigm has been labeled in various ways; some have called it a **feminist paradigm**. Labeling it an *empowerment* or *advocacy* paradigm might also make sense. Regardless of its name, its chief distinguishing feature is its focus on oppression and its commitment to using research procedures to empower oppressed groups. Toward that end, investigators committed to this paradigm might use quantitative or qualitative research procedures or selected elements of other paradigms.

When researchers who adhere to a critical social science paradigm use qualitative methods, they are distinguished by their stance toward their findings. Whereas positivist researchers attempt to minimize the influence of political or ideological values in interpreting their findings, critical social science researchers set out to interpret findings through the filter of their empowerment and advocacy aims. Likewise, they are likely to use a research process that fits those empowerment and advocacy aims.

When critical social scientists use interpretivist research methods, they are distinguished from interpretivists by going beyond the subjective meanings of the people they study, and by attempting to connect their observations to their a priori notion of an unjust, broader objective reality they are seeking to change. Thus, a feminist researcher guided by the critical social science paradigm and taking an interpretive approach to the study of battered women would not stop at seeing reality through the eyes of the battered women, but would also address aspects of the feminist vision of reality that might not be shared by the women being studied. For example, if the battered women deny or minimize the severity of the battering, find excuses for the batterer, or think they cannot leave the batterer, a feminist researcher might note the discrepancy between the women's subjective views and the objective reality as seen by the researcher. A feminist researcher also might raise questions about the reasons for these undesirable discrepancies, and attempt to derive from them recommendations for

---

interpretivism A research paradigm that focuses on gaining an empathic understanding of how people feel inside, seeking to interpret individuals' everyday experiences, their deeper meanings and feelings, and the idiosyncratic reasons for their behaviors.

critical social science A research paradigm distinguished by its focus on oppression and its commitment to using research procedures to empower oppressed groups.

feminist paradigm A research paradigm, like the critical social science paradigm, distinguished by its commitment to using research procedures to address issues of concern to women and to empower women.

FIGURE 4.3 How Might a New Welfare Reform Policy Be Researched Differently from the Perspective of Different Paradigms?

Paradigm	Research Question	Research Design
Positivism	Is the new policy effective in reducing poverty?	Conduct an experiment, comparing the proportion of people who move out of poverty in areas that do and do not have the new policy.
Interpretivism	How do welfare recipients experience their lives changing under the new policy?	Conduct in-depth, qualitative interviews, reporting the impact of the new policy on their lives from the perspectives of the welfare recipients.
Critical social science	Does the new policy really help the poor, or does it keep them oppressed?	Organize poor people to design and carry out their own study about the question as a way to mobilize them and help them gather evidence that they can use to lobby legislators for policy changes that are less oppressive.
Feminist	What impact does the new policy have on poor women?	Conduct in-depth, qualitative interviews, reporting the impact of the new policy on their lives from the perspectives of female welfare recipients. or Organize poor women to design and carry out their own study about the question as a way to empower them and help them gather evidence that they can use to lobby legislators for policy changes that are less oppressive to women.

raising the women's feminist consciousness and empowering them.

The foregoing are just a few examples of how paradigms can influence social work research. We could probably fill a whole book with additional examples, but that probably wouldn't be a lot of fun for us or for you; so instead, we'll provide Figure 4.3, which shows how different paradigms might influence research into a new welfare reform policy.

4.5 THE INFLUENCE OF THEORIES

EP 2.1.3a

Just as paradigms can influence how an investigation proceeds, so can theories. In fact, the distinction between the terms *theory* and *paradigm* is fuzzy, because some people can become so enamored of and entrenched in one particular theory that they tend to interpret a wide range of phenomena in terms of that theory only;

theory   A systematic set of interrelated statements intended to explain some aspect of social life or enrich our sense of how people conduct and find meaning in their daily lives.

they miss (or dogmatically dismiss) the alternative insights and perspectives that other theories might offer. Thus, certain theories—psychoanalytic theory, role theory, behavioral theory, and so on—can be construed as paradigms.

Although they sometimes are used interchangeably, there are important differences between the terms *paradigm* and *theory*. As noted in Chapter 1, paradigms are general frameworks for looking at life. A **theory** is a systematic set of interrelated statements intended to explain some aspect of social life or enrich our sense of how people conduct and find meaning in their daily lives. Different people who share the same paradigm may or may not share the same theoretical orientations. For example, some positivist social work researchers might seek to verify the effectiveness of interventions that are rooted in cognitive or behavioral theory, while other positivist social work researchers might want to verify the effectiveness of interventions arising from psychoanalytic theory.

Theory plays an important role in social work research, as it does in social work practice. In both practice and research, theory helps us make sense of and see patterns in diverse observations. It helps direct our inquiry into those areas that seem more likely to show useful patterns and explanations. It also helps us distinguish between chance occurrences and observations that have value in anticipating future occurrences.

Imagine a colleague telling you that she allowed a young boy to play with small toys in a sand tray, and commented to him on the themes of his play in a nondirective manner. In this way, she tried to help the boy better cope with the tragic death of his mother and move on with his life. If you had not studied child development theory and learned about the importance of play, then you might respond with bewilderment, wondering how letting a boy just play and talking to him about it could be a powerful professional intervention. In fact, if you asked your colleague to explain why her intervention worked and she could not explain it, then you might be more skeptical about its likelihood of working with your clients than you would be if she could explain it theoretically. Without considering theory, you might flounder around in your practice, trying anything and everything anyone told you in the hopes of stumbling on something that seemed to work. Then, if something did work with one client, you might continue to apply it indiscriminately with other clients for whom it might be inapplicable.

Suppose you decide to test your colleague's sand-play idea with one of your clients, a 6-year-old girl who has been depressed and withdrawn after surviving a traffic accident that killed her mother. After several sessions of sand play, the girl's father reports to you that the girl has begun to have angry outbursts and spells of intense sobbing in which she cries out for her mother. Without theory, you might be inclined to stop the sand play, fearing that it was having harmful effects. If, on the other hand, you were aware of theory on child development and grieving, then you might interpret the change in the girl's behavior as a necessary and therefore positive early step in the grieving process, and you would not stop the intervention.

Imagine you were conducting research on the effectiveness of the sand-play intervention in helping children of victims of Hurricane Katrina in New Orleans and nearby areas along the Gulf coast. If you were operating without theory, you would likely encounter analogous problems. You might, for example, measure the impact of the intervention prematurely or look for the wrong indicators of success. Without theory, you might be clueless in designing your study. How long should the intervention last? What are the minimum and maximum ages for subjects?

Theories also help researchers develop useful implications from their findings for practice and policy. Suppose a researcher finds that single-parent homes produce more delinquency than two-parent homes. Our understanding of why this is so and what we might do about it would be rather limited without the use of theory. Suppose, however, that we have a theoretical understanding of why single-parent homes produce more delinquency, and that a lack of supervision and the absence of positive role models are two important reasons. This would improve our position to develop effective social programs, such as after-school mentoring programs.

Some valuable social work research studies, however, do not involve theory. For example, some studies focus exclusively on methodological issues, rather than attempt to explain something. Thus, they might survey published studies, perhaps seeking to identify the types of research methods used most and least frequently, how often researchers use inappropriate research methods, or the frequency of particular types of findings. Other atheoretical studies might seek to describe something without attempting to explain it. For example, they might assess the average salaries of social workers in various areas, the needs for various services expressed by prospective or current service consumers, and so on.

Some atheoretical studies are conducted when agencies must provide evidence to funding sources that clients received the types of services the funders intended them to receive, that the clients felt highly satisfied with those services, and that treatment dropout rates were low. The social workers could get that evidence by surveying clients and agency records. They would conduct that study not to test or develop theory, but merely to meet the pragmatic purpose of program maintenance. This type of atheoretical study, despite lacking linkages to theory, would have some immediate practical value. Depending on its results, for example, the study could determine whether funding was continued (and perhaps even expanded) or discontinued (or perhaps just reduced).

Although social work research studies can have value without any linkages to theory, their value may be enhanced by such linkages. The above study, for example, might contribute more to the profession's knowledge base if it aimed to go beyond the agency's immediate funding concerns and attempted to build social work practice theory about factors that influence client satisfaction and treatment completion, and the consequent implications for what social workers in other agencies can do to improve service delivery.

4.5a Inductive and Deductive Uses of Theory

EP 2.1.3a

Theory can influence the research process using either inductive or deductive methods. Using the **inductive method**, we would begin with a set of observations. Suppose we want to study the problem of adolescent runaways. We might conduct unstructured, open-ended interviews with many runaways. We might also interview their families as well as social workers and other practitioners who work with runaways and their families. The patterns in our interview data might generate tentative conclusions about family dysfunction being the cause of running away, and family therapy as a way to reunite adolescents with their families. The conclusions are tentative—they are hypotheses that we have not yet tested.

In the **deductive method** we would start with hypotheses and then test them. The hypotheses might come from a theory or from tentative conclusions that were generated from research using the inductive method. Next, we would define the variables in each hypothesis and the operations to be used to measure them in specific, observable terms.

---

inductive method   A research process based on inductive logic, in which the researcher begins with observations, seeks patterns in those observations, and generates tentative conclusions from those patterns.

deductive method   A research process based on deductive logic, in which the researcher begins with a theory, then derives hypotheses, and ultimately collects observations to test the hypotheses.

In the final step, we would implement the specified measurements, thus observing the way things really are, and seeing if those observations confirm or fail to confirm the hypotheses. Sometimes this final step involves conducting experiments, interviewing people, or visiting and watching the subject of interest.

Research can begin by using either method. Using the inductive method in our study of adolescent runaways, we can begin by immersing ourselves in observations of runaways until we are struck by certain consistent patterns that seem to point us in a particular theoretical direction that in turn will lead to hypotheses and observations. Using the deductive method, we might begin with family systems theory and see dysfunctional families as the reason that adolescents run away. From this theoretical understanding, we derive one or more specific hypotheses—for example, that providing family systems therapy will reduce the likelihood of future runaway episodes. Next, we define in observable terms exactly what constitutes a runaway episode, and the substance and processes that constitute the type of family systems therapy being tested. Finally, observations are made to test our hypotheses.

In actual practice, then, theory and research interact through a never-ending alternation of deduction, induction, deduction, and so forth. Walter Wallace (1971) has represented this process nicely as a circle, which is presented in modified form in Figure 4.4. In the Wallace model, theories generate hypotheses, hypotheses suggest observations, observations produce generalizations, and those generalizations result in modifications of the theory. The modified theory then suggests somewhat modified hypotheses and a new set of observations that produce somewhat revised generalizations, further modifying the theory. In this model there is clearly no beginning or ending point. You can begin anywhere in examining what interests you. Thus, if we seek to understand and do something about the problem of adolescent

FIGURE 4.4 The Wheel of Science

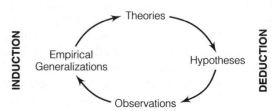

runaways, we can begin by deriving hypotheses from family systems theory (or some other theory) and then making observations to test those hypotheses; or we can begin by immersing ourselves in observations of runaways until we are struck by certain consistent patterns that seem to point us in a particular theoretical direction that in turn will lead to hypotheses and observations.

In summary, the scientific norm of logical reasoning provides a bridge between theory and research—a two-way bridge. Scientific inquiry in practice typically involves an alternation between deduction and induction. During the deductive phase, we reason toward observations; during the inductive phase, we reason from observations. Both logic and observation are essential. In practice, both deduction and induction are routes to the construction of theories.

4.6 SOCIAL WORK PRACTICE MODELS

EP2.1.3a,b

In social work, we may apply existing social science theories in an effort to alleviate problems in social welfare. But texts on social work practice are less likely to cite social science theories as guides to social work practice than they are to cite something called *practice models*. These models help us organize our views about social work practice, and may or may not reflect a synthesis of existing theories.

The social work literature contains a diverse array of practice models. Chapter 2, for example, discussed the evidence-based practice model. If you have taken other social work courses, then you may have encountered the following terms for other practice models: *psychosocial, functionalist, problem-solving, cognitive-behavioral, task-centered, case management, crisis intervention, ecological perspective, life model, generalist, empirically based practice,* and *eclectic* among many others. Social work practice models tend not to be mutually exclusive. Many of them, for example, stress the importance of the worker–client relationship and the need to forge a therapeutic alliance.

We won't delve here into the characteristics of all the various models of social work practice or

into the subtleties of how they are similar and different. You can study that in courses on practice or in courses that introduce you to the profession of social work. Instead, we'll simply illustrate how certain models can influence the way we choose to research social work problems.

Let's consider how a researcher's orientation to the psychosocial model or the cognitive-behavioral model might influence the research process in a study of the effectiveness of the treatment of parents at risk of child abuse. The cognitive-behavioral model looks at problems such as child abuse in terms of dysfunctional emotions connected to irrational beliefs, and the need to restructure cognitions and learn better coping skills and parenting skills. Rather than focusing on long-term personality change and dealing with unresolved issues stemming from the parents' own childhoods, this model deals in the present with specific skills, cognitions, and behaviors that can be changed in the short term through behavior modification and cognitive therapy techniques.

When researching the outcome of the treatment of at-risk parents, individuals influenced by this model might administer paper-and-pencil tests that attempt to gauge whether parents have become less angry, have changed their attitudes about normal childhood behaviors that they first perceived as provocative, and have learned new child-rearing techniques (such as using time-outs and so forth). These researchers might also directly observe the parents with their children in situations that require parenting skills and count the number of times the parents exhibit desirable (praise, encouragement, and so forth) and undesirable (slapping, threatening, and so forth) parenting behaviors.

Those who are influenced by the psychosocial model might be somewhat skeptical of the adequacy of the preceding approach to researching treatment outcome. In particular, they might doubt whether any observed improvements would last long after treatment ended, and whether the parents' ability to give desired test answers or act in an acceptable manner while being observed would really reflect the normal home environment when observers aren't present. They might suggest that a better indicator of outcome would be whether parents were actually court-reported for abusive behavior over the longer haul.

Although the foregoing illustration is essentially hypothetical, note that the bulk of actual research with favorable outcomes has evaluated interventions that are associated with the cognitive or behavioral models of practice. Most other models have received less research, and their outcomes have not been as consistently favorable. Proponents of some other models often attribute the apparent relative success of the cognitive and behavioral models to the "superficiality" of outcome indicators used in cognitive-behavioral evaluations, and the difficulty of assessing the more complex, longer-range goals of their models. We won't resolve this debate here, and we expect it to continue for quite a while.

4.7 THE INFLUENCE OF ETHICAL CONSIDERATIONS

EP 2.1.2b,c

Before they can implement their studies, social workers and other professionals who conduct research involving human participants must ensure that their research procedures are ethical. As you will see in Chapter 5, which is devoted to ethical issues in social work research, in some studies the ethical concerns are subtle and arguable, and it is not always easy to judge whether the expected benefits of a research study outweigh those concerns. In other studies, that judgment is easier, and Chapter 5 will describe some medical and psychological experiments done long ago in which the ethical violations were egregious.

In response to such notoriously unethical studies, federal law now governs research ethics in studies involving humans. Any organization wishing to receive federal research support must establish an Institutional Review Board (IRB) that reviews all of the organization's research proposals involving human participants and rules on their ethics. Chapter 16 will delve in depth into IRB regulations and procedures with which researchers must comply. It will also discuss how it is sometimes difficult for IRB panelists to decide whether to approve a proposed study in light of the study's expected benefits and the extent to which it might violate the following ethical questions:

- **Voluntary Participation and Informed Consent.** Will the research participants be fully informed about the features of the study that might affect their decision to participate, particularly regarding the risks of harm resulting from the study procedures? Will they understand that their participation is entirely voluntary and that they can refuse to participate in the study or can stop their participation at any time without experiencing any negative consequences (such as losing benefits or being denied treatment)?

- **No Harm to Participants.** Does the research risk harming participants in any way? This includes not only physical harm or serious forms of psychological harm, but also harm associated with revealing information that may embarrass them, make them feel uncomfortable, or endanger their jobs or interpersonal relationships.

- **Anonymity and Confidentiality.** Will it be impossible for the researchers or anyone else to identify what participants are connected to what research data? If the answer to that question is yes, then *anonymity* is ensured. If the research procedures require that someone on the research team be able to identify what data came from what participant (such as when the researchers interview participants or need to connect their pre-intervention scores to their post-intervention scores), will the research procedures include safeguards that prevent anyone else from learning the identity of the participants providing the data? If the answer to that question is yes, then *confidentiality* is ensured.

- **Deceiving Participants.** Will research participants be deceived in any way, and if so, will the deception be relatively harmless and justifiable? (For example, if a study seeking to assess whether entitlement eligibility intake workers respond differently to applicants of different ethnicities, is it justified not to inform those workers that the study is being conducted and which particular applicants are part of the study?)

The need to obtain IRB approval regarding the above ethical guidelines can influence social work researchers to rethink or revise their originally planned research procedures. For example, suppose they want to conduct an experiment to test the comparative effectiveness of two promising new interventions for treating military combat veterans suffering from posttraumatic stress disorder (PTSD). Suppose—to ensure the comparability of three groups—that they plan to use coin tosses to determine which veterans seeking treatment in their center will receive which of the two promising new treatments and which ones will receive the ongoing treatment as usual. Their IRB would require them to inform the prospective recipients of the research design (including a description of the treatment procedures). It might also require that they give participants choices as to which treatment they will receive. Moreover, the researchers might be required to inform prospective recipients that the new treatments have the potential to be more effective (and perhaps less effective) than treatment as usual. The informed consent and voluntary participation guidelines therefore could lead the researchers to change their planned protocol for assigning veterans to the three different treatments. It might even result in their not having enough participants in one or more of the treatment groups. Many veterans, for example, might refuse treatment as usual and insist on receiving one of the promising new treatments. Conversely, if either of the new treatments involved procedures that could be emotionally painful—such as using virtual reality technology depicting traumatic combat scenarios (which, by the way, is currently being done in the treatment of some veterans of the wars in Iraq and Afghanistan)—some veterans might prefer treatment as usual.

Here is another hypothetical example of how IRB approval and ethical considerations could influence the research process. Suppose the researchers planned to pose as homeless people and to stay in shelters for the homeless for a period of time so that they could observe what goes on there and experience what it is like to stay there. Their IRB might insist that they first inform the shelter staff of their true identities and gain their consent, which (assuming the consent were granted) could bias how the shelter staff members behaved during their observations. Moreover, the IRB might refuse to approve the study even with such informed consent, with the rationale that the researchers would be harming homeless participants by taking away shelter beds that the researchers would be using. Consequently, these ethical considerations might influence the researchers to replace their planned observational research design with one in which they just interview homeless people about their attitudes about or experiences staying in shelters.

4.8 THE INFLUENCE OF MULTICULTURAL FACTORS

Perhaps more than any other profession, social work is practiced with minority and oppressed populations. Consequently, social work research needs to be culturally sensitive, and social workers conducting research **EP 2.1.4a** with minority and oppressed populations have to be culturally competent with respect to those populations. In research, as we will discuss in Chapter 6, being culturally competent means being aware of and appropriately responding to the ways in which multicultural factors should influence what we investigate, how we investigate it, and how we interpret our findings. Chapter 6 also will discuss in depth the ways in which efforts to be culturally competent can influence the research process. We'll just touch upon a few examples here.

Researchers who want to conduct studies in areas heavily populated by Alaskan Natives or American Indians may need to obtain permission for their studies from the tribal leaders of their prospective Native Americans. To obtain that permission, they might have to tweak their plans to conform to the demands of tribal leaders regarding the research questions they'll ask, how their studies will be designed and implemented, and how their results will be portrayed and disseminated. For example, they may need to change their original plans to alleviate tribal leader fears that their studies might (unintentionally) exacerbate stereotypes about their people regarding such things as their work ethic, their alcohol consumption, and so on.

Researchers whose studies involve interviewing or administering self-report scales to people who recently immigrated from other countries, or for whom English is not their primary language, might need to employ bilingual interviewers and modify the questions they intended to ask in order to ensure that even when translated into the respondent's language, the questions have the intended conceptual meaning to the respondent. For example, suppose they translate a question to recently immigrated adolescents about whether their parents get on their nerves. Even if their literal translation of the idiom "get on their nerves" is accurate, the respondents are apt to think they are being asked about some form of undesirable physical pressure. Many additional examples will be discussed in Chapter 6.

4.9 THE INFLUENCE OF ORGANIZATIONAL AND POLITICAL CONCERNS

Social work researchers also may have to modify their plans in light of organizational or political concerns. Agency administrators or practitioners, for example, might not allow researchers to assign clients to different treatment conditions. Instead, they might agree to allow the study only if the treatment assignment is done according to existing agency procedures. As will be discussed later in this book, such procedures might make the groups very different in terms of client attributes, and those differences, rather than differences in the treatments, might be the reason that the one group's treatment outcome is better than another's. Consequently, the researchers might need to add some procedures to their design that can alleviate this potential bias, or they might need to find a different agency in which to conduct their research.

However, the influence of organizational concerns need not be negative. Organizational concerns might be the reason the research was conceived in the first place. For example, agency administrators might ask researchers to evaluate the effectiveness of their services, survey a target community regarding unmet service needs, assess whether practitioners are providing agency services in the intended manner, measure the extent to which clients are satisfied or dissatisfied with the services they received, and so on. Chapter 14, on program evaluation, will delve in more detail into the various ways that organizational concerns can stimulate research studies or influence them to be modified.

The final influence that we'll introduce here involves political concerns. Actually, some multicultural and organizational concerns can be political in nature, as well. For example, tribal leaders' concerns about the potential results of a research study might be connected to their fears about how those findings might impact their efforts to seek funding for local municipal projects. Administrators

concerned with obtaining future funding for their agency might insist that their programs be evaluated in biased ways that increase the chances that the findings will portray their services favorably.

Some political concerns may emanate from the researchers themselves. For example, researchers might have conceived of their study in the first place because they wanted to use its findings as ammunition to support a noble cause, such as improving the ways our society cares for certain needy populations, reforming a social policy, exposing certain forms of prejudice or other forms of social injustice, and so on. On the flip side, researchers might shy away from certain politically sensitive research questions, or they might tone down the way they interpret their findings to make them more politically correct and to protect their own reputations and careers.

All of the factors that we've discussed in this chapter will re-emerge again and again throughout this book. Now that you see how they can influence the questions that researchers study, the research methods and designs that they employ, and the way they interpret and disseminate their research findings, we can examine the specific elements and methods of the research process in more depth. We'll begin to do that in the next chapter.

4.10 MAIN POINTS

- A social work research study can have one or more of the following research purposes: exploration, description, explanation, evaluation, and construction of measurement instruments.
- Exploratory studies can employ qualitative or quantitative methods in an attempt to develop an initial understanding of a topic.
- Descriptive and explanatory studies can follow a quantitative or qualitative research process, or combine both processes.
- Evaluation studies can be conducted with exploratory, descriptive, and explanatory purposes.
- In quantitative studies, *description* typically refers to surface attributes that can be easily quantified; objectivity, precision, and generalizability are paramount concerns.
- In qualitative studies, *description* is more likely to involve a thicker examination of phenomena

and their deeper meanings, rather than generalizing with precision to a larger population.

- A qualitative explanatory study might conduct in-depth, probing, and relatively unstructured interviews.
- A quantitative explanatory study might start out with a hypothesis about some factor (or factors) that helps explain a phenomenon and then test that hypothesis.
- Cross-sectional studies examine phenomena at one point in time.
- Longitudinal studies describe processes occurring over time and conduct their observations over an extended period.
- Trend studies study changes within some population over time. Cohort studies examine more specific subpopulations (cohorts) as they change over time. Panel studies examine the same set of people each time.
- A variety of paradigms influence the ways in which research can be done.
- A paradigm is a fundamental model or scheme that organizes our view of something.
- The positivist paradigm emphasizes the pursuit of objectivity in our quest to observe and understand reality. On the other side is the social constructivist paradigm, which emphasizes multiple subjective realities and the difficulty of being objective.
- The interpretivist paradigm emphasizes describing how people feel inside, describing how they interpret their everyday experiences, and describing whatever idiosyncratic reasons they may have for their behaviors.
- The critical social science paradigm focuses on oppression and uses research procedures to empower oppressed groups.
- A theory is a systematic set of interrelated statements intended to explain some aspect of social life or to enrich our sense of how people conduct and find meaning in their daily lives.
- In attempting to explain things, theories inescapably get involved in predicting them. Although prediction is implicit in explanation, it is important to distinguish between the two. Often we are able to predict without understanding.
- In the deductive method, the researcher begins with a theory and then derives one or more hypotheses from it for testing. In induction, the researcher starts from observed data and develops a hypothesis to explain the specific observations.
- Social work practice models, like theories, can influence the way we choose to research social work problems.
- Other factors influencing the research process include ethical considerations, multicultural factors, and organizational and political concerns.

4.11 PRACTICE-RELATED EXERCISES

1. Find an article that reports a research study that illustrates exploration, description, or explanation. Identify which of these three purposes the study illustrates, and briefly justify your judgment in that regard.
2. Locate the following longitudinal study from the July 2002 issue of the journal *Social Work*: "Welfare Use as a Life Course Event: Toward a New Understanding of the U.S. Safety Net" by M. R. Rank and T. A. Hirschl. Describe the nature of the study design, its primary findings, and the implications of those findings for social work practice and social welfare policy.
3. Find information on the Internet for at least two of the following paradigms: positivism, interpretivism, social constructivism, critical social science, feminism, and postmodernism. Give the Internet locations and report on the main themes you find in the discussions.

4.12 ADDITIONAL READING

Sokal, A. D., & Bricmont, J. (1998). *Fashionable nonsense: Postmodern intellectual's abuse of science*. New York: Picador USA. This book criticizes postmodern paradigms, including the critical social science paradigm.

4.12a Competency Notes

EP 2.1.2b: Make ethical decisions by applying standards of the National Association of Social Workers Code of Ethics (p. 72): Social workers apply the NASW code of ethics as part of conducting ethical research and appraising whether the research completed or proposed by others is ethical.

EP 2.1.2c: Tolerate ambiguity in resolving ethical conflicts (p. 72): Social workers understand that in some studies the ethical concerns are subtle and arguable, and it is not always easy to judge whether the expected benefits of a research study outweigh those concerns.

EP 2.1.3a: Distinguish, appraise, and integrate multiple sources of knowledge, including research-based knowledge (pp. 62, 64, 66, 68, 70): Social workers distinguish qualitative, quantitative, and mixed methods sources of knowledge.

EP 2.1.3b: Analyze models of assessment, prevention, intervention, and evaluation (pp. 62, 64): Social workers understand qualitative, quantitative, and mixed methods of assessment and evaluation.

EP 2.1.4a: Recognize the extent to which a culture's structures and values may oppress, marginalize, alienate, or create or enhance privilege and power (p. 73): Social work researchers need to be culturally sensitive and culturally competent when conducting research with minority and oppressed populations.

EP 2.1.6b: Use research evidence to inform practice (pp. 62, 64): Understanding qualitative, quantitative, and mixed methods of assessment evaluation—and understanding the research process—enhances social workers' ability to use research evidence to inform their practice.

Ethical and Cultural Issues in Social Work Research

part 3

Qualitative or quantitative methodological priorities are not the only things that influence decisions made in planning how best to structure and conduct social work research. Other important influences involve ethical and cultural considerations, as we discussed in Chapter 3. In Chapter 5, we'll delve more thoroughly into the special ethical considerations that arise in social work research. We'll also address the fine line that can exist between ethical issues and the influence of politics and values. Chapter 6 will explore how social work researchers can use qualitative and quantitative methods to improve the cultural competence of all phases of the research process. We'll see how cultural competence can help researchers obtain and provide information that is relevant and valid for minority and oppressed populations, and thus improve practice and policy with those populations.

Ethical Issues in Social Work Research

5.1   INTRODUCTION

Before researchers can implement studies that involve people, they confront questions about the ethics of their proposed investigations. Concern about the ethics of research that involves human subjects has not always been as intense as it is today. Many decades ago, studies on human subjects could be conducted with little scrutiny of the ethics involved, and some research became notorious for its inhumane violations of basic ethical standards. The most flagrant examples are the Nazi atrocities in medical experimentation that were conducted during the Holocaust.

Although the depraved Nazi experiments stand apart as by far the most atrocious examples of inhumane "research," they were not the only studies being done around that time that involved inhumane ethical violations. The most notorious example in the United States was the Tuskegee syphilis study, which started in 1932 in Alabama. In that study, medical researchers diagnosed several hundred poor African American male sharecroppers as suffering from syphilis, but did not tell them they had syphilis. Instead, they told the men that they were being treated for "bad blood." The researchers merely studied the disease's progress and had no intentions of treating it. Even after penicillin had been discovered as a cure for syphilis, the study continued without providing penicillin or telling the subjects about it. Thirteen journal articles reported the study during this time, but it continued uninterrupted. As reported by James Jones in his book on the Tuskegee experiment, *Bad Blood* (1981), "None of the health officers connected with the Tuskegee Study expressed any ethical concern until critics started asking questions" (p. 190).

In December 1965, Peter Buxtun, who was trained as a social worker while in the U.S. Army, was hired by the Public Health Service as a venereal disease interviewer. Buxtun learned of the Tuskegee study from coworkers, and after studying published articles on it, he became relentless in his efforts to intervene. A series of letters to, and difficult meetings with, high-ranking officials ultimately prompted them to convene a committee to review the experiment, but that committee decided against treating the study's subjects.

Buxtun then went to the press, which exposed the study to the public in 1972. This exposure prompted U.S. Senate hearings on the study. Subsequently, in the mid-1970s, the men were treated with antibiotics, as were their wives, who had contracted the disease, and their children, who had it congenitally (Royse, 1991). According to Jones (1981, p. 203), it is the social worker Peter Buxtun, aided by the press, who deserves the ultimate responsibility for stopping the Tuskegee study.

5.2   ETHICAL GUIDELINES IN SOCIAL WORK RESEARCH

When we consider research such as the Tuskegee study, it is not hard to find the ethical violations and to agree that the research was blatantly unethical. However, some ethical violations in social work research can be subtle, ambiguous, and arguable. Sometimes there is no "correct" answer to the situation, and people of good will can disagree.

In most dictionaries and in common usage, ethics is typically associated with morality, and both deal with matters of right and wrong. But what *is* right, and what wrong? What is the source of the distinction? For individuals, the sources vary. They may be religious beliefs, political ideologies, or the pragmatic observation of what seems to work and what doesn't.

Webster's New World Dictionary is typical among dictionaries in defining ethical as "conforming to the standards of conduct of a given profession or group." Although the idea may frustrate readers in search of moral absolutes, what we regard as morality and ethics in day-to-day life is a matter of agreement among members of a group. And it is no surprise that different groups have agreed on different codes of conduct. If you are going to live in a particular society, then it is extremely useful for you to know what that society considers ethical and unethical. The same holds true for the social work research "community." The sections that follow discuss some of the more important ethical agreements that prevail in social work research, as well as in research in allied fields. (As you may recall, we touched briefly on these ethical issues in Chapter 4.) Let's begin by examining relevant sections of the National Association of Social Workers (NASW) Code of Ethics.

5.2a   NASW Code of Ethics

If decisions about the ethics of research involve subjective value judgments in which we must weigh the potential

EP 2.1.2b

Photo from the Tuskegee Syphilis Study.
SOURCE: The National Archives and Records Administration

benefits of the research against its potential costs to research participants, and if we must make those decisions in light of various idiosyncratic factors, then those decisions pose dilemmas for which there may be no right or wrong answers. But researchers can do some things to be as ethical as possible. They can obtain collegial feedback as to the ethics of their proposed research. They can (and perhaps must) obtain approval from an institutional review board (IRB), which we'll discuss later in this chapter. They should carefully consider whether there are ethically superior alternatives, and strive to ensure that their research proposal is the most ethical one that they can conceive.

To guide them in this endeavor, various professional associations have created and published formal codes of conduct to cover research ethics. Figure 5.1 shows the codes from the "5.02 Evaluation and Research" section of the National Association of Social Workers Code of Ethics. Although this section provides ethical guidelines for conducting research, another section—on social workers' ethical responsibilities as professionals—reminds us that we can

violate our ethical responsibilities as professionals not only when we conduct research, but also when we refrain from using research to guide our practice. The latter section is worded as follows:

> *Social workers should critically examine and keep current with emerging knowledge relevant to social work. Social workers should routinely review the professional literature.... Social workers should base practice on recognized knowledge, including empirically based knowledge, relevant to social work and social work ethics.*
> *(NASW, 1999, Section 4.01)*

5.2b Voluntary Participation and Informed Consent

Social work research often represents an intrusion into people's lives. The interviewer's knock on the door or the arrival of a questionnaire in the mail signals the beginning of an activity that the respondent has not

EP 2.1.2c

FIGURE 5.1 NASW Code of Ethics

NASW Code of Ethics:
Section 5.02 Evaluation and Research

(a) Social workers should monitor and evaluate policies, the implementation of programs, and practice interventions.

(b) Social workers should promote and facilitate evaluation and research to contribute to the development of knowledge.

(c) Social workers should critically examine and keep current with emerging knowledge relevant to social work and fully use evaluation and research evidence in their professional practice.

(d) Social workers engaged in evaluation or research should carefully consider possible consequences and should follow guidelines developed for the protection of evaluation and research participants. Appropriate institutional review boards should be consulted.

(e) Social workers engaged in evaluation or research should obtain voluntary and written informed consent from participants, when appropriate, without any implied or actual deprivation or penalty for refusal to participate; without undue inducement to participate; and with due regard for participants' well-being, privacy, and dignity. Informed consent should include information about the nature, extent, and duration of the participation requested and disclosure of the risks and benefits of participation in the research.

(f) When evaluation or research participants are incapable of giving informed consent, social workers should provide an appropriate explanation to the participants, obtain the participants' assent to the extent they are able, and obtain written consent from an appropriate proxy.

(g) Social workers should never design or conduct evaluation or research that does not use consent procedures, such as certain forms of naturalistic observation and archival research, unless rigorous and responsible review of the research has found it to be justified because of its prospective scientific, educational, or applied value and unless equally effective alternative procedures that do not involve waiver of consent are not feasible.

(h) Social workers should inform participants of their right to withdraw from evaluation and research at any time without penalty.

(i) Social workers should take appropriate steps to ensure that participants in evaluation and research have access to appropriate supportive services.

(j) Social workers engaged in evaluation or research should protect participants from unwarranted physical or mental distress, harm, danger, or deprivation.

(k) Social workers engaged in the evaluation of services should discuss collected information only for professional purposes and only with people professionally concerned with this information.

(l) Social workers engaged in evaluation or research should ensure the anonymity or confidentiality of participants and of the data obtained from them. Social workers should inform participants of any limits of confidentiality, the measures that will be taken to ensure confidentiality, and when any records containing research data will be destroyed.

(m) Social workers who report evaluation and research results should protect participants' confidentiality by omitting identifying information unless proper consent has been obtained authorizing disclosure.

(n) Social workers should report evaluation and research findings accurately. They should not fabricate or falsify results and should take steps to correct any errors later found in published data using standard publication methods.

(o) Social workers engaged in evaluation or research should be alert to and avoid conflicts of interest and dual relationships with participants, should inform participants when a real or potential conflict of interest arises, and should take steps to resolve the issue in a manner that makes participants' interests primary.

(p) Social workers should educate themselves, their students, and their colleagues about responsible research practices.

---

requested and that may require a significant portion of his or her time and energy. Participation in research disrupts the subject's regular activities.

Social work research, moreover, often requires that people reveal personal information about themselves—information that may be unknown to their friends and associates. And social work research often requires that such information be revealed to strangers. Social work practitioners also require such information, but their requests may be justified on the grounds that the information is required for them to serve the respondent's personal interests. Social work researchers cannot necessarily make this claim, perhaps only being able to argue that their efforts will ultimately help the entire target population of people in need.

A major tenet of research ethics is that participation must be *voluntary*. No one should be forced to participate. All participants must be aware that they are participating in a study, be *informed* of all the consequences of the study, and *consent* to participate in it. This norm might not apply to certain studies. For example, if a community organization measures the amount and speed of automobile traffic at a busy intersection near a school as part of an effort to convince the city to erect a traffic light, it would not need to obtain informed consent from the drivers of every automobile it observes passing through the intersection.

The norm of voluntary participation is far easier to accept in theory than to apply in practice. When the instructor in a social work class asks students to fill out a questionnaire that he or she hopes to analyze and publish, students should always be told that their participation in the survey is completely voluntary. Even so, most students will fear that nonparticipation will somehow affect their grade. The instructor should be especially sensitive to such beliefs in implied sanctions and make special provisions to obviate them. For example, the instructor could leave the room while the questionnaires are being completed. Or students could be asked to return the questionnaires by mail or drop them in a box near the door just before the next course meeting.

You should be clear that this norm of voluntary participation goes directly against several scientific concerns that we have discussed earlier in this text. One such concern involves the scientific goal of *generalizability,* which is threatened to the extent that the kinds of people who would willingly participate in a particular research study are unlike the people for whom the study seeks generalizations. Suppose the questionnaire assesses student attitudes about the feminization of poverty, and only a minority of students voluntarily participate—those who care the most deeply about feminism and the poor. With such a small group of respondents, the instructor would have no basis for describing student attitudes in general, and if he or she did generalize the findings to the entire student population, then the generalizations might be seriously misleading.

The need, in some studies, to conceal the nature of the study from those being observed is another scientific concern that is compromised by the norm of voluntary participation and informed consent. This need stems from the fear that participants' knowledge about the study might significantly affect the social processes being studied among those participants. Often the researcher cannot reveal that a study is even being done. Rosenhan (1973), for example, reported a study in which the research investigators posed as patients in psychiatric hospitals to assess whether hospital clinical staff members, who were unaware of the study, could recognize "normal" individuals (presumably the investigators) who (presumably) did not require

continued hospitalization. (The results suggested that they could not.) Had the subjects of that study—that is, the clinical staff members—been given the opportunity to volunteer or refuse to participate, then the study would have been so severely compromised that it would probably not have been worth doing. What point would there be to such a study if the clinical staff were aware that the investigators were posing as patients?

But the fact that the norm of voluntary participation and informed consent may be impossible to follow does not alone justify conducting a study that violates it. Was the study reported by Rosenhan justified? Would it have been more ethical not to conduct the study at all? That depends on whether the long-term good derived from that study—that is, observations and data on the identification, understanding, and possible amelioration of problems in psychiatric diagnosis and care—outweighs the harm done in denying clinical staff the opportunity to volunteer or refuse to participate in the study. The need to judge whether a study's long-term benefits will outweigh its harm from ethically questionable practices also applies to ethical norms beyond voluntary participation, and thus we will return to this topic later. The norm of voluntary participation and informed consent is important. In cases where you feel ultimately justified in violating it, it is all the more important that you observe the other ethical norms of scientific research, such as bringing no harm to the people under study.

Regardless of how you may feel about the norm of voluntary participation and informed consent, if your study involves human subjects, you will probably have to obtain the approval of its ethics from an independent panel of professionals called an *institutional review board* (IRB). Use of IRBs became widespread during the 1970s as a result of federal legislation and increased public concern about the ethics of biomedical and behavioral research. Today, all organizations that engage in research and receive federal money are required to have an IRB that reviews the ethics of proposed studies that involve human subjects. Investigators in organizations that wish to conduct such studies must get the advance approval of their organization's IRB. This applies to *all* studies that use human subjects, not just those that receive government funding. The boards may continue to oversee studies after they have been implemented, and they may decide to suspend or terminate their approval of a study.

A later section of this chapter will focus on IRBs. For now—in regard to informed consent—we want to point out that your IRB will probably require that before participating in your study, participants sign a *consent form*. The consent form should provide full information about the features of the study that might affect their decision about whether they want to participate in it, particularly regarding the procedures of the study, potential harm, anonymity, and confidentiality. The IRB consent forms can be quite detailed. Separate forms are required if research participants include children. If you conduct a study involving parents and children, for example, you probably will have to use one consent form for parents that might be several pages long, another form for parents to consent to their child's participation, and a third form for the child to sign. The last form usually is called an *assent form*, which will be briefer and use simpler language that a child can understand. Likewise, to obtain truly informed consent you should consider the reading level of prospective research participants and have a translated version of it if they are not English speakers.

5.2c No Harm to the Participants

EP 2.1.2c

Social work research should never injure the participants in a study, regardless of whether they volunteered for it. Perhaps the clearest instance of this norm in practice concerns the revealing of information that would embarrass them or endanger their home lives, friendships, jobs, and so forth.

Research participants can be harmed psychologically in the course of a study, and the researcher must be aware of the often subtle dangers and guard against them. Research participants are often asked to reveal deviant behavior, attitudes they feel are unpopular, or personal characteristics they may feel are demeaning, such as low income, the receipt of welfare payments, and the like. Revealing such information is likely to make them feel, at the very least, uncomfortable.

Social work research projects also may force participants to face aspects of themselves that normally they are not fully aware of. This can happen even when the information is not revealed directly to the researcher. In retrospect, for example, a certain past behavior may appear unjust or immoral to the participant, for whom, then, the project can be the source of a continuing, personal agony. Or, if the study concerns codes of ethical conduct, the participant may begin questioning his or her own morality, and that personal concern may last long after the research has been completed and reported.

By now, you should have realized that just about any research you might conduct runs the risk of injuring other people somehow. There is no way for the researcher to guard against all possible injuries, yet some study designs make them more likely than others. If a particular research procedure seems likely to produce unpleasant effects for participants—asking survey respondents to report deviant behavior, for example—the researcher should have the firmest of scientific grounds for doing the procedure. If the research design is essential and also likely to be unpleasant for participants, then you will find yourself in an ethical netherworld and may find yourself forced to do some personal agonizing. Although agonizing has little value in itself, it may be a healthy sign that you have become sensitive to the problem.

Although the fact often goes unrecognized, participants can be harmed by data analysis and reporting. Every now and then, research participants read the books published about the studies in which they have participated. Reasonably sophisticated participants will be able to locate themselves in the various indexes and tables. Having done so, they may find themselves characterized—though not identified by name—as bigoted, abusive, and so forth. At the very least, such characterizations are likely to trouble them and threaten their self-images. Yet the whole purpose of the research project may be to explain why some people are prejudiced and others are not.

Like voluntary participation, not harming people is an easy norm to accept in theory but often difficult to ensure in practice. Sensitivity to the issue and experience with its applications, however, should improve the researcher's tact in delicate areas of research.

Increasingly, in recent years, social researchers have been getting support for abiding by this norm. Federal and other funding agencies typically require an independent evaluation of the treatment of human subjects for research proposals, and most universities now have human subject committees to serve that evaluative function. Although sometimes troublesome and inappropriately applied, such requirements not only guard against unethical research but also can reveal ethical issues that have been overlooked by even the most scrupulous of researchers.

5.2d Anonymity and Confidentiality

The protection of participants' identities is the clearest concern in the protection of their interests and well-being in survey research. If revealing their survey responses would injure them in any way, adherence to this norm becomes all the more important. Two techniques—anonymity and confidentiality—will assist you in this regard, although the two are often confused.

Anonymity

A respondent may be considered anonymous when the researcher cannot identify a given response with a given respondent. This means that an interview survey respondent can never be considered anonymous, because an interviewer collects the information from an identifiable respondent. An example of anonymity would be a mail survey in which no identification numbers are put on the questionnaires before their return to the research office.

Ensuring anonymity makes it difficult to keep track of who has or has not returned the questionnaires. Despite this problem, you may be advised to pay the necessary price in some situations. If you study drug abuse, for example, assuring anonymity may increase the likelihood and accuracy of responses. Also, you can avoid the position of being asked by authorities for the names of drug offenders. When respondents volunteer their names, such information can be immediately obliterated on the questionnaires.

Confidentiality

In a confidential survey, the researcher is able to identify a given person's responses but essentially promises not to do so publicly. In an interview survey, for instance, the researcher would be in a position to make public the income reported by a given respondent, but the respondent is assured that this will not be done.

You can use several techniques to ensure better performance on this guarantee. To begin, interviewers and others with access to respondent identifications should be trained in their ethical responsibilities. As soon as possible, all names and addresses should be removed from questionnaires and replaced with identification numbers. A master identification file should be created that links numbers to names to permit the later correction of missing or contradictory information, but this file should not be available to anyone else except for legitimate purposes. Whenever a survey is confidential rather than anonymous, it is the researcher's responsibility to make that fact clear to respondents. Never use the term *anonymous* to mean "confidential."

As in social work practice, situations can arise in social work research when ethical considerations dictate that confidentiality not be maintained. Suppose in the course of conducting your interviews that you learn children are being abused, or respondents are at imminent risk of seriously harming themselves or others. It would be your professional (and perhaps legal) obligation to report this to the proper agency. Participants need to be informed as part of the informed consent process before they agree to participate in a study.

There may be other situations when government agents take legal action to acquire research data that you believe should remain confidential. For example, they may subpoena data on participants' drug use, and thus legally force you to report this information. To protect research participants from such efforts, the United States National Institutes of Health began issuing certificates of confidentiality in 1989. Researchers can submit proposals to apply for these certificates. By obtaining a *certificate of confidentiality*, researchers eliminate the risk of having their data subpoenaed.

5.2e Deceiving Participants

We've seen that handling the identities of the participants in a study is an important ethical consideration. Handling your own identity as a researcher can be tricky also. Sometimes it's useful and even necessary to identify yourself as a researcher to those you want to study. You'd have to be a master con artist to get people

EP 2.1.2c

to complete a lengthy questionnaire without revealing that you were conducting research.

Even when it's possible and important to conceal your research identity, there is an important ethical dimension to consider. Deceiving people is unethical, and within social research, deception needs to be justified by compelling scientific or administrative concerns. Even then, the justification will be arguable.

Sometimes, researchers admit they are doing research but fudge about why they are doing it or for whom. Suppose you've been asked by a public welfare agency to conduct a study of living standards among aid recipients. Even if the agency is looking for ways of improving conditions, the recipient participants are likely to fear a witch hunt for "cheaters." They might be tempted, therefore, to give answers that make themselves seem more destitute than they really are. Unless they provide truthful answers, however, the study will not produce accurate data that will contribute to an effective improvement of living conditions. What do you do? One solution would be to tell participants that you are conducting the study as part of a university research program—concealing your affiliation with the welfare agency. Doing that improves the scientific quality of the study but raises a serious ethical issue in the process.

5.2f Analysis and Reporting

As a social work researcher, then, you have several ethical obligations to the participants in your study. At the same time, you have ethical obligations to your professional colleagues. A few comments on the latter obligations are in order.

In any rigorous study, the researcher should be more familiar than anyone else with the study's technical shortcomings and failures. You have an obligation to make them known to your readers. Even though you may feel foolish admitting mistakes, you should do it anyway.

Negative findings should be reported if they are at all related to your analysis. There is an unfortunate myth in scientific reporting that only positive discoveries are worth reporting (and journal editors are sometimes guilty of believing this as well). In science, however, it is often just as important to know that two variables are not related as to

know that they are. If, for example, an experiment finds no difference in outcome between clients treated and those not treated with a tested intervention, then it is important for practitioners to know that they may need to consider alternative interventions—particularly if the same null finding is replicated in other studies. And replication would not be possible if the original experiment were not reported.

The ethical importance of reporting negative findings in studies evaluating the effectiveness of interventions, programs, or policies is particularly apparent in the evidence-based practice process (as discussed in Chapter 2). Suppose you are conducting an evidence-based practice search looking for interventions with the best evidence supporting their effectiveness with the problem presented by your client, and you find a well-designed study supporting the effectiveness of a relevant intervention (that we'll call Intervention A). If you find no other studies with contradictory findings, you might be tempted to deem Intervention A the one with the best evidence base for your client's problem. But suppose several other studies found Intervention A to be ineffective for that problem but were not reported because the investigators believed that no one is interested in hearing about interventions that don't work. In reality, then, interventions other than Intervention A might have better, more consistent evidence supporting their effectiveness, and if you knew of the studies with negative findings about Intervention A, you might propose one of those other interventions to your client. Moreover, suppose your client is African American or Hispanic, and that the one study supporting Intervention A involved only Caucasian clients, while the other studies—the ones with negative results—involved African American or Hispanic clients. The ethical implications of not reporting those other studies should be apparent to you; not reporting them would mislead you into proposing the wrong, unhelpful intervention to your client.

Researchers also should avoid the temptation to save face by describing their findings as the product of a carefully preplanned analytic strategy when that is not the case. Many findings arrive unexpectedly, even though they may seem obvious in retrospect. So they uncovered an interesting relationship by accident—so what? Embroidering such situations with descriptions of fictitious hypotheses is dishonest and tends to mislead inexperienced researchers into thinking that all scientific inquiry is rigorously preplanned and organized.

In general, science progresses through honesty and openness, and it is retarded by ego defenses and deception. Researchers can serve their fellow researchers—and scientific discovery as a whole—by telling the truth about all the pitfalls and problems they have experienced in a particular line of inquiry. Perhaps that candor will save their colleagues from the same problems.

5.3 WEIGHING BENEFITS AND COSTS

EP 2.1.2c

We have noted that ethical considerations in the conduct of social work research often pose a dilemma. The most ethical course of action for researchers to take is not always clear-cut. Sometimes it is difficult to judge whether the long-term good to be derived from a study will outweigh the harm done by the ethically questionable practices that may be required for adequate scientific validity. Consider, for example, the study in which a team of researchers deceptively posed as hospitalized mental patients, concealing their identity from direct care staff members to study whether the staff could recognize their normalcy. Earlier we asked whether the potential benefits of the study—regarding psychiatric diagnosis and care—justified violating the norm of voluntary participation by direct staff. What if the purpose of that study had been to verify whether suspected physical abuse of patients by staff was taking place? Suppose an appalling amount of staff neglect and abuse of patients really was occurring and that the researchers uncovered it. Would the potential benefits to current and future patients to be derived from exposing and perhaps reforming the quality of care outweigh using deception in the research?

If alternative ways to conduct the research are available—that is, ways that can provide equally valid and useful answers to the research question without engaging in ethically questionable research practices—then the dilemma will be resolved and an alternative methodology can be chosen. But sometimes no such alternatives appear. If not, then how researchers resolve this dilemma will depend on the values they attach to the various costs and benefits of the research, and whether they believe that some ends ever justify some means. No objective formula can be applied to this decision; it is inherently subjective. Some individuals would argue that the end never justifies the means. Others might disagree about which particular ends justify which particular means.

5.3a An Illustration: Living with the Dying—Use of Participant Observation

In Chapter 3 we briefly discussed a study by Robert Buckingham and his colleagues (1976) that sought to compare the value of routine hospital care with that of hospice care for the terminally ill. As we mentioned, the emphasis in hospice care is on minimizing discomfort and maximizing quality of life, and this might entail eschewing medical procedures that prolong life but hinder its quality. Routine hospital care, in contrast, is more likely to emphasize prolonging life at all costs, even if that requires a lower quality of life for the dying patient. The routine approach is less attentive to the psychosocial and other nonmedical needs of the patient and family.

Our discussion of the Buckingham study in Chapter 3 focused on how it illustrated the difference between qualitative and quantitative methods of inquiry. Here we reexamine the study in light of ethical considerations because it provides one example of how the long-term good to be derived from a study may be argued to have justified violating ethical guidelines. This study, which involved deceiving participants and not obtaining their informed consent to participate, might be of special interest to students who are interested in practicing social work in a medical or hospice setting.

Buckingham and his colleagues wanted to observe and experience the treatment of a terminally ill patient in two wards of a hospital: the surgical-care (nonhospice) ward and the palliative-care (hospice) ward. For his observations to be useful, it was necessary that staff members and other patients on his ward not know what he was doing. The steps that he took to carry out his deception are quite remarkable. Before entering the hospital, he lost 22 pounds on a six-month diet. (He was naturally thin before starting it.) He submitted himself to ultraviolet radiation so he would look as if he had undergone radiation therapy. He had puncture marks from intravenous needles put on his hands and arms so he would look as if he had undergone chemotherapy. He underwent minor surgery for the sole purpose of producing biopsy scars. He learned how to imitate the behavior of patients dying with pancreatic cancer by reviewing their medical charts and maintaining close contact with them. Finally, for several days before entering the hospital, he grew a patchy beard and abstained from washing.

Buckingham stayed in the hospital 10 days, including 2 days in a holding unit, 4 days in the surgical-care unit, and 4 days in the hospice unit. His findings there supported the advantages of hospice care for the terminally ill. For example, on the surgical-care ward he observed staff communication practices that were insufficient, impersonal, and insensitive. Physicians did not communicate with patients. Staff members in general avoided greeting patients, made little eye contact with them, and often referred to them by the names of their diseases rather than by their personal names. Complacent patients did not receive attention. The negative aspects of the patients' conditions were emphasized.

Buckingham's observations on the hospice ward, however, were quite different. Staff maintained eye contact with patients. They asked questions about what the patients liked to eat and about other preferences. They asked patients how they could be more helpful. They listened to patients accurately, unhurriedly, and empathically. Physicians spent more time communicating with patients and their families. Staff encouraged family involvement in the care process. It is not difficult to see the value of Buckingham's findings in regard to enhancing the care of the terminally ill and their families. In considering whether the benefits of those findings justify Buckingham's particular use of deception, several other aspects of the study might interest you.

Before entering the hospital, Buckingham engaged the hospital's top medical, administrative, and legal staff members in planning and approving the study. The heads of both the surgery ward and the hospice ward also participated in the planning and approved the study. In addition, the personnel of the hospice ward were informed in advance that their unit was going to be evaluated, although the nature of the evaluation was not revealed. Finally, an ad hoc committee was formed to consider the ethics of the study, and the committee approved the study. In light of these procedures and this study's benefits, it may not surprise you to learn that no ethical controversy emerged in response to this study.

5.3b Right to Receive Services versus Responsibility to Evaluate Service Effectiveness

EP 2.1.2c

Perhaps the most critical ethical dilemma in social work research pertains to the right of clients in need to receive services, and whether the benefit of improving the welfare of clients in the long run ever justifies delaying the provision of services to some clients in the short run. This debate has to do with experiments and quasi-experiments (as discussed in Chapter 12) that evaluate the effectiveness of social work interventions by comparing the fates of clients who receive the interventions being evaluated and those from whom we withhold the interventions. The debate also is relevant to evidence-based practice in that practitioners engaged in the evidence-based practice process will search for the best available evidence about the effectiveness of services, and rigorous experiments are the strongest designs for making inferences about whether the service provided or something else most plausibly explains variations in client outcome. Two values are in conflict here: doing something to try to provide immediate help to people in need, and ensuring that the services clients receive have had their effects—whether beneficial or harmful—scientifically tested.

Some researchers argue that individuals in need should never be denied service for any period or for any research purpose. Others counter that the service being delayed is one whose effects, if any, have not yet been scientifically verified—otherwise, there would be no need to test it. How ethical, they ask, is it to provide the same services perennially without ever scientifically verifying whether those services are really helping anyone, or are perhaps harmful? And if they are potentially harmful, are those who receive them actually taking a greater risk than those who are temporarily denied them until their effects are gauged? Using another medical parallel, would you think your physician was ethical if he or she treated you with a drug while knowing that the beneficial or harmful effects of that drug were as yet untested? If you were being paid to participate in a medical experiment to test the effectiveness of a drug whose benefits and negative side effects were as yet unknown, which group would you feel safer in: the group receiving the drug or the group not receiving it?

The seriousness of the client's problem is one factor that bears on this dilemma. It would be much harder to justify the delay of service to individuals who are experiencing a dangerous crisis or who are at risk of seriously harming themselves (suicidal clients, for example) than to those in less critical need. Another factor is the availability of alternative interventions to which the tested intervention can be compared. Perhaps those who are denied the tested service can receive another one that might prove to be no less beneficial.

If alternative interventions are available, then the conflict between the right to service and the responsibility to evaluate can be alleviated. Instead of comparing clients who receive a new service being tested to those who receive no service, we can compare them to those who receive a routine set of services that was in place before the new one was developed. This is a particularly ethical way to proceed when insufficient resources are available to provide the new service to all or most clients who seek service. This way, no one is denied service, and the maximum number that resources permit receive the new service.

Another way to reduce the ethical dilemma when resources don't permit every client to receive the new service is to assign some clients to a waiting list for the new service. As they await their turn, they can be compared to the clients currently receiving the new service. Ultimately, everyone is served, and the waiting-list clients should be free to refuse participation in the study without risk of being denied service eventually.

5.4 THREE ETHICAL CONTROVERSIES

As you may already have guessed, the adoption and publication of professional codes of conduct has not

totally resolved the issue of research ethics. Social scientists still disagree on some general principles, and those who seem to agree in principle still debate specifics. In this section we will briefly describe three research projects that have provoked ethical controversy and discussion. These are not the only controversial projects that have been done, but they illustrate ethical issues in play in the real world and we thought you'd find them interesting and perhaps provocative.

5.4a Observing Human Obedience

One of the more unsettling rationalizations to come out of World War II was the German soldier's common excuse for atrocities: "I was only following orders." From the point of view that gave rise to this comment, any behavior—no matter how reprehensible—could be justified if someone else could be assigned responsibility for it. If a superior officer ordered a soldier to kill a baby, then the fact of the order was said to exempt the soldier from personal responsibility for the action.

Although the military tribunals that tried the war crimes cases did not accept the excuse, social scientists and others have recognized the extent to which this point of view pervades social life. Often people seem willing to do things they know would be considered wrong by others—if they can cite some higher authority as ordering them to do it. Such was the pattern of justification after the My Lai tragedy in Vietnam, in which U.S. soldiers killed more than 300 unarmed civilians—some of them young children—simply because their village, My Lai, was believed to be a Viet Cong stronghold. This sort of justification appears less dramatically in day-to-day civilian life. Few would disagree that this reliance on authority exists, yet Stanley Milgram's (1963, 1965) study of the topic provoked considerable controversy.

To observe people's willingness to harm others when following orders, Milgram brought 40 adult men—from many different walks of life—into a laboratory setting that he designed to create the phenomenon under study. If you had been a subject in the experiment, you would have had something like the following experience.

First you would have been informed that you and another subject were about to participate in a learning experiment. As the result of drawing lots, you would have been assigned the job of "teacher," and your fellow subject the job of "pupil." Your pupil then would have been led into another room, been strapped into a chair, and had an electrode attached to his wrist. As the teacher, you would have been seated in front of an impressive electrical control panel covered with dials, gauges, and switches. You would have noticed that each switch had a label giving a different number of volts, ranging from 15 to 315. The switches would have had other labels, too, some with the ominous phrases "Extreme-Intensity Shock," "Danger—Severe Shock," and "XXX."

The experiment would run like this: You would read a list of word pairs to the learner and then test his ability to match them. You couldn't see him, but a light on your control panel would indicate his answer. Whenever the learner made a mistake, you would be instructed by the experimenter to throw one of the switches—beginning with the mildest—and administer a shock to your pupil. Through an open door between the two rooms, you'd hear your pupil's response to the shock. Then you'd read another list of word pairs and test him again.

As the experiment progressed, you'd be administering ever more intense shocks until your pupil was screaming for mercy and begging for the experiment to end. You'd be instructed to administer the next shock anyway. After a while, your pupil would begin kicking the wall between the two rooms and screaming. You'd be told to give the next shock. Finally, you'd read a list and ask for the pupil's answer—and there would only be silence from the other room. The experimenter would inform you that no answer was considered an error and instruct you to administer the next higher shock. This process would continue up to the " XXX " shock at the end of the series.

What do you suppose you really would have done when the pupil first began screaming? When he began kicking on the wall? Or when he became totally silent and gave no indication of life? You'd refuse to continue giving shocks, right? And surely the same would be true of most people.

So we might think—but Milgram found otherwise. Of the first 40 adult men Milgram tested, nobody refused to continue administering the shocks until they heard the pupil begin kicking the wall between the two rooms. Of the 40, five did so

then. Two-thirds of the subjects, 26 of the 40, continued doing as they were told through the entire series—up to and including the administration of the highest shock.

As you've probably guessed, the shocks were phony, and the "pupil" was another experimenter. Only the "teacher" was a real subject in the experiment. You wouldn't have been hurting another person, even though you would have been led to think you were. The experiment was designed to test your willingness to follow orders—presumably to the point of killing someone.

Milgram's experiments have been criticized both methodologically and ethically. On the ethical side, critics particularly cited the effects of the experiment on the subjects. Many seem to have personally experienced about as much pain as they thought they were administering to someone else. They pleaded with the experimenter to let them stop giving the shocks. They became extremely upset and nervous. Some had uncontrollable seizures.

How do you feel about this research? Do you think the topic was important enough to justify such measures? Can you think of other ways in which the researcher might have examined obedience? There is a wealth of discussion regarding the Milgram experiments on the web. Search for "Milgram experiments," "human obedience experiments," or "Stanley Milgram."

5.4b Trouble in the Tearoom

The second illustration was conducted by a graduate student and published in a 1970 book called *Tearoom Trade: Impersonal Sex in Public Places.* Researcher Laud Humphreys wanted to study homosexual acts between strangers meeting in public restrooms in parks; the restrooms are called "tearooms" by those who used them for this purpose. Typically, the tearoom encounter involved three people: the two men actually engaged in the homosexual act and a lookout.

To gather observations for his study, Humphreys began showing up at public restrooms and offering to serve as a lookout whenever it seemed appropriate. Humphreys wanted to go beyond his observations as lookout and learn more about the people he was observing. Many of the participants were married men who wanted to keep their homosexuality secret and thus avoid being stigmatized and losing their status in their communities. They probably would not have consented to being interviewed. Instead of asking them for an interview, Humphreys tried to note the license plate numbers of their vehicles and then track down their names and addresses through the police. Then disguising himself enough to avoid recognition, he visited the men at their homes and announced that he was conducting a survey. In that fashion, he collected the personal information he was unable to get in the restrooms.

Humphreys's research provoked considerable controversy both within and outside the social scientific community. Some critics charged Humphreys with a gross invasion of privacy in the name of science. What men did in public restrooms was their own business and not his. Others were mostly concerned about the deceit involved: Humphreys had lied to the participants by leading them to believe he was only participating as a voyeur. Some were more concerned with Humphreys's follow-up survey than with what he did in public facilities. They felt it was unethical for him to trace the participants to their houses and interview them under false pretenses. Still others justified Humphreys's research. The topic, they said, was worthy of study and could not be studied any other way. They considered the deceit to be essentially harmless, noting that Humphreys was careful not to harm his subjects by disclosing their tearoom activities.

The tearoom trade controversy, as you might imagine, has never been resolved. It is still debated, and probably will be for a long time, because it stirs emotions and contains ethical issues about which people disagree. What do you think? Was Humphreys ethical in doing what he did? Are there parts of the research you feel were acceptable and other parts that were not? Whatever you feel in the matter, you are sure to find others who disagree with you.

5.4c Social Worker Submits Bogus Article to Test Journal Bias

EP 2.1.2c

Our third illustration is the first well-publicized ethical controversy to involve a social worker's research. The social worker, William Epstein, started with the hypothesis that journal editors were biased in favor of publishing research articles whose findings confirmed the effectiveness of evaluated social work interventions and biased against publishing research articles whose findings failed to support the effectiveness of tested interventions. To test his hypothesis, Epstein fabricated a fictitious study that pretended to evaluate the effectiveness of a social work intervention. Epstein concocted two versions of the bogus study. In one version, he fabricated findings that supported the effectiveness of the intervention; in the other version, he fabricated data that found the intervention to be ineffective.

Epstein submitted the fictitious article to 146 journals. Half of the journals received the version that supported the effectiveness of the intervention, and half received the other version. Epstein did not enter his own name as author of his fabricated article, instead using a pair of fictitious names.

In his real study, Epstein interpreted his findings as providing some support for his hypothesis: Journal editors were biased in favor of publishing the version of the bogus article with positive findings and against publishing the version with negative findings.

After being notified of the acceptance or rejection of his fictitious article, Epstein informed each journal of the real nature of his study. Later, he submitted a true article under his own name that reported his real study to the *Social Service Review*. That journal rejected publication of his real study, and its editor, John Schuerman, led a small group of editors who filed a formal complaint against Epstein with the National Association of Social Workers. The complaint charged Epstein with unethical conduct on two counts: (1) deceiving the journal editors who reviewed the bogus article, and (2) failing to obtain their informed consent to participate voluntarily in the study.

Schuerman recognized that sometimes the benefits of a study may warrant deceiving participants and not obtaining their informed consent to participate. But he argued that in Epstein's (real) study, the benefits did not outweigh the time and money costs associated with many editors and reviewers who had to read and critique the bogus article and staff members who had to process it. In addition to the time and money costs, Schuerman argued that Epstein's experiment had exacted an emotional cost: "The chagrin and embarrassment of those editors who accepted the [bogus] article" (*New York Times*, September 27, 1988, p. 25).

Epstein countered that journal editors are not the ones to judge whether the benefits of his (real) study justified its costs. In his view, the editors are predisposed to value their own costs very dearly. Thus, they are unlikely to judge any study that would deceive them as being worth those costs. Epstein argued that the journals are public entities with public responsibilities. Testing whether they are biased in deciding what to publish warranted his deception and the lack of informed consent to participate, actions that were necessary to test for their bias.

One might argue that if journal editors and reviewers are biased against publishing studies that fail to confirm the effectiveness of tested interventions, then the field may not learn that certain worthless interventions in vogue are not helping clients. Moreover, if several studies disagree about the effectiveness of an intervention, and only those that confirm its effectiveness get published, then an imbalanced and selective set of replications conceivably might be disseminated to the field. This would mislead the field into believing that an intervention is yielding consistently favorable outcomes when in fact it is not. This could hinder the efforts of social workers to provide the most effective services to their clients—and therefore ultimately reduce the degree to which we enhance clients' well-being.

One could argue that Epstein's study could have been done ethically if he had forewarned editors that they might be receiving a bogus paper within a year and obtained their consent to participate in the study without knowing the specifics of the paper. An opposing viewpoint is that such a warning might affect the phenomenon being studied, tipping off the reviewers in a manner that predisposes them to be on guard not to reveal a real bias that actually does influence their publication decisions.

Some scholars who have expressed views that are somewhat sympathetic to Epstein's thesis have argued that journal editors and reviewers exert great influence on our scientific and professional knowledge base and therefore need to have their policies and procedures investigated. Schuerman, who filed the charges against Epstein, agreed with this view, but he argued that Epstein's study was not an ethical way to conduct such an investigation.

The initial ruling of the ethics board of the National Association of Social Workers was that Epstein had indeed violated research rules associated with deception and failure to get informed consent. Epstein appealed the decision before any disciplinary action was taken. His appeal was upheld by the executive committee of the association, which concluded that his research did not violate its ethical rules. It did not publicize additional details of its rationale for upholding Epstein's appeal and reversing the initial ruling.

5.5 INSTITUTIONAL REVIEW BOARDS

The foregoing examples illustrate that reasonable people might disagree about the ethics of some research projects. Determining whether a particular study is ethical can be difficult, and should not be based solely on the judgment of the individuals proposing the research. As we saw earlier, researchers can try to ensure that their studies are ethical by obtaining the consent of an independent panel of professionals, called an *institutional review board* (IRB).

In Chapter 4 we discussed how the need to obtain IRB approval might influence social work researchers to rethink or revise their originally planned research procedures. As mentioned in our earlier discussion, IRB reviews are mandatory for research in agencies receiving federal money. Board panelists review research proposals involving human subjects and rule on their ethics. Although there is no guarantee that every IRB decision will be the "correct" or best decision about the ethics of a proposed project, at least that decision is being made by an independent panel of professionals who—unlike the investigator proposing the study—have no vested interests or ego involvement in the proposed study.

Suppose Epstein had obtained the advance approval of an IRB at his university for his study using a bogus article to test for journal bias. (Epstein recently told us that his university had no IRB at that time but that he did obtain informal feedback from some of his colleagues, who agreed that his study was ethical.) Had Epstein been able to obtain IRB approval, even those who later depicted his study as unethical would have had no basis for charging *him* with unethical conduct. Instead, their complaint would have been with the IRB, if the board had approved his study. By not making the decision himself—and thus avoiding the chances that his own vested interests or ego involvement, if any, could have influenced his decision—Epstein would have been operating responsibly, regardless of how some might later judge the ethics of the research method. Even if we deem Epstein's study to have been ethical, we can say that obtaining IRB approval (had it been possible for him to do so) would have protected Epstein from any ensuing ethical controversy. As an epilogue to this account, Epstein (2004) published a replication of his earlier study in which the only change was to obtain advance permission from his university's IRB to waive informed consent.

Institutional review boards vary in the amount and format of materials they require to describe the proposed research. In the process of deciding whether to approve a research proposal, an IRB may require that certain modifications be made to make the research acceptable, such as providing additional information to participants before their consent to participate is obtained. For example, some social work research studies might involve situations in which ethical considerations dictate that confidentiality not be maintained, such as when child abuse is unexpectedly encountered or when respondents are at imminent risk of seriously harming themselves or others. You may need to add this contingency to your own consent form and IRB application form. You also may need to assure your participants and your IRB that you will arrange for services to be offered to any subject you encounter who needs them. Because they vary so much, we suggest that you examine your university's IRB forms and procedures, which may be accessible online. Alternatively, you can examine Figure 5.2, which presents condensed and partial excerpts from the template used by the University of Texas at Austin to guide investigators as to what materials to submit in their applications for IRB approval. It will give you an idea of the kinds of things that are commonly required by other IRBs.

If your research instructor requires that you design and carry out a research project, then you may find that you have to get your study approved by your university's IRB before you can begin

collecting data. Moreover, if your research project is to be carried out in an agency that receives federal money, you may have to obtain approval from both your school's IRB and the agency's IRB. Just what you needed, right? Don't panic. Perhaps your study will qualify for an exemption from a full review and you'll be able to obtain approval within a few days. Federal regulations allow IRBs to grant exemptions to certain kinds of studies, although institutions vary considerably in interpreting the federal regulations. The actual wording of the exemptions ought to be available from your IRB. Most student research (with the exception of doctoral dissertations) qualifies for at least one exemption.

5.6 BIAS AND INSENSITIVITY REGARDING GENDER AND CULTURE

EP 2.1.4a

Gender and cultural bias and insensitivity can impair the methodological quality of a study and therefore the validity of its findings. Some critics have suggested that when researchers conduct studies in a sexist or a culturally insensitive manner, they are not just committing methodological errors but also going awry ethically.

The question of ethics arises because some studies are perceived to perpetuate harm to women and minorities. Feminist and minority scholars have suggested a number of ways that such harm can be done. Interviewers who are culturally insensitive can offend minority respondents. If they conduct their studies in culturally insensitive ways, then their findings may yield implications for action that ignore the needs and realities of minorities, may incorrectly (and perhaps stereotypically) portray minorities, or may inappropriately generalize in an unhelpful way. By the same token, studies with gender bias or insensitivity may be seen as perpetuating a male-dominated world, or failing to consider the potentially different implications for men and women in the research.

Various authors have recommended ways to avoid cultural bias and insensitivity in one's research. We will cover these recommendations in greater depth in Chapter 6 on culturally competent research. For now, let's examine some recommendations for avoiding gender bias. In her book

FIGURE 5.2 Partial Excerpts from the University of Texas at Austin's Institutional Review Board's Template to Guide Research Proposals

---

   I. **Title**
  II. **Investigators (co-investigators)**
  III. **Hypothesis, Research Questions, or Goals of the Project**
  IV. **Background and Significance**
  V. **Research Method, Design, and Proposed Statistical Analysis**
  VI. **Human Subject Interactions**

        A. Identify the **sources of potential participants**, derived materials, or data. Describe the characteristics of the subject population such as their anticipated number, age, sex, ethnic background, and state of health. Identify the criteria for inclusion and/or exclusion. Explain the rationale for the use of special classes of participants whose ability to give voluntary informed consent may be in question. Such participants include students in one's class, people currently undergoing treatment for an illness or problem that is the topic of the research study, people who are mentally retarded, people with a mental illness, people who are institutionalized, prisoners, etc. When do you expect human subject involvement in this project to begin and when do you expect it to end?

        If the participants are prisoners or residents of correction facilities, the composition of the IRB must be augmented by a prisoner's advocate. Please inform the IRB if this applies to your project.

If some of the potential participants or the parents of child participants are likely to be more fluent in a language other than English, the consent forms should be translated into that language. Both English and the other language versions of the form should be provided, with one language on one side of a page and the other on the other side of the page. This translation may be completed after IRB approval of the study and consent forms. Specify here your intentions with respect to the languages of the consent forms. (If you plan to conduct your study with students from the Austin Independent School District, you will be required to provide a Spanish language version of your parental consent form.)

        B. Describe the **procedures for the recruitment of the participants**. Append copies of fliers and the content of newspaper or radio advertisements. If potential participants will be screened by an interview (either telephone or face-to-face) provide a script of the screening interview.

If the potential participants are members of a group that may be construed as stigmatized (e.g., spousal abusers, members of support groups, people with AIDS, etc.) your initial contact with the potential participants should be through advertisements or fliers or through people who interact with the potential participants because of their job duties. These people may describe your study to the potential participants and ask them to contact you if they are interested in talking to you about the study.

        C. Describe the **procedure for obtaining informed consent**.

        D. Research Protocol: What will you ask your participants to do? When and where will they do it? How long will it take them to do it? Describe the type of research information that you will be gathering from your subjects, i.e., the data that you will collect. *Append copies of all surveys, testing materials, questionnaires, and assessment devices. Append copies of topics and sample questions for non-structured interviews and focus group discussions.*

  VII. Describe any **potential risks** (physical, psychological, social, legal, or other) and assess their likelihood and seriousness.

        Describe the procedures for protecting against (or minimizing) any potential risks and include an assessment of their effectiveness. Discuss the procedures that will be used to maintain the confidentiality of the research data.

        If your study involves deception, describe the procedures for debriefing the participants.

 VIII. Describe and assess the **potential benefits** to be gained by participants (if any) and the benefits that may accrue to society in general as a result of the planned work. Discuss the risks in relation to the anticipated benefits to the participants and to society.

  IX. Indicate the specific **sites or agencies involved in the research project** besides The University of Texas at Austin. These agencies may include school districts, day care centers, nursing homes, etc. Include, as an attachment, approval letters from these institutions or agencies on their letterhead. The letter should grant you permission to use the agency's facilities or resources; it should indicate knowledge of the study that will be conducted at the site. If these letters are not available at the time of IRB review, approval will be contingent upon their receipt.

Source: Reprinted with permission of the University of Texas at Austin Institutional Review Board.

Nonsexist Research Methods (1988), Margrit Eichler recommends the following feminist guidelines to avoid gender bias and insensitivity in one's research:

- If a study is done on only one gender, make that clear in the title and the narrative, and don't generalize the findings to the other gender.
- Don't use sexist language or concepts (for example, don't refer to males as "heads of household," and to females as "spouses").
- Don't use a double standard in framing the research question (such as looking at the work-parenthood conflict for mothers but not for fathers).
- Don't overemphasize male-dominated activities in research instruments (such as by assessing social functioning primarily in terms of career activities and neglecting activities in homemaking and child rearing).
- In analyzing your data, look for ways in which the findings might differ for men and women.
- Don't assume that measurement instruments used successfully with males are automatically valid for women.
- Be sure to report the proportion of males and females in your study sample.

5.7 POLITICS AND VALUES

The line between ethical issues and politics and values in social work research is extremely fine. People disagree on political aspects of research just as they disagree on ethical ones. Although ethics and politics are often intertwined, the ethics of social work research deals more with the methods employed, whereas political issues are more concerned with the practical costs and use of research. Thus, for example, some social workers raise ethical objections to experiments that evaluate the effectiveness of social work services by providing those services to one group of clients while delaying their provision to another group of clients. Those who voice these objections say that the harm done to clients in delaying service provision outweighs the benefits to be derived from evaluating the effectiveness of those services. A political objection, on the other hand, might be that if the results of the evaluation were to suggest that the services were not

effective, then those negative results might hurt agency funding. Another political objection might be that withholding services would reduce the amount of fees for service or third-party payments received, not to mention the bad publicity that would be risked regarding agency "neglect" of people in need.

Another distinction between ethical and political aspects of social work research is the absence of formal codes of accepted political conduct that are comparable to the codes of ethical conduct we discussed earlier. The only partial exception to the lack of political norms is in the generally accepted view that a researcher's personal political orientation should not interfere with or unduly influence his or her scientific research. It would be considered improper for you to use shoddy techniques or lie about your research as a way to further your political views. However, studies are often enough attacked for allegedly violating this norm.

Many scholars do not believe that social work research is ever entirely value-free. For example, researchers of homelessness may be influenced by their values in the way they define homelessness, which in turn influences whom they include in their sample of homeless individuals. Do the homeless include only people living in the streets? Or do they also include people "doubling up" with friends or relatives or living in squalid, temporary quarters who cannot find a decent place they can afford? It is difficult to make such decisions independently of our values. Researchers who have been active in social action efforts to alleviate homelessness may be predisposed to choose the broader definition, which will indicate a greater number of the homeless; researchers who believe social welfare spending is wasteful and incurs too much dependency among the poor may be predisposed to choose the narrower definition.

Scholars who believe that social research is never really value-free typically recommend that we should be aware of our values and describe them in an upfront manner rather than kidding ourselves or others that we are completely objective. Indeed, not all social scientists agree that researchers should try to separate their values from their research activities. Some have argued that social science and social action cannot and should not be separated. Social work has a long tradition of using research as a tool to try to make society more humane. For example, our profession embraced the social survey movement at the turn of the 20th century as a way to convince society to enact environmental reform to alleviate a host of urban problems. More recently, surveys on homelessness have been conducted in the hope that their findings would influence legislators and their tax-averse constituents to spend more public funds to alleviate homelessness.

When we conduct research to alleviate human suffering and promote social welfare, we should not let our humanitarian aims spur us to hide from or distort the truth by biasing the way we conduct our research or interpret its findings. Attempting to be completely objective and value-free in the way we conduct research is an impossible ideal, and it is risky to kid ourselves into thinking that we are completely neutral. This does not mean, however, that we shouldn't *try* to keep our beliefs from distorting our pursuit of truth. Being aware of our biases throughout all phases of our research helps us minimize their impact on our work. And being upfront in describing our predilections to readers better prepares them to evaluate the validity of our findings.

Some social science research studies have stimulated considerable controversy about whether their findings were merely intrusions of a researcher's own political values. Typically, researchers have denied the intrusion, and the denial has been challenged. Let's look at examples of the controversies that have raged and continue to rage over this issue.

5.7a Social Research and Race

Nowhere have social research and politics been more controversially intertwined than in the area of race relations. Social scientists have studied the topic for a long time, and often the products of the research have found their way into practical politics. For the most part, social scientists during the 20th century supported the cause of African American equality in the United States. Many were actively involved in the civil rights movement, some more radically than others. Thus, social scientists were able to draw research conclusions that support the cause of equality without fear of criticism from colleagues. To recognize the solidity of the general social science position in the matter of equality, we need to examine only a few research projects that have produced conclusions that disagreed with the predominant ideological position.

Most social scientists—overtly, at least—supported the end of (even de facto) school segregation. Thus, an immediate and heated controversy was provoked in 1966 when James Coleman, a respected sociologist, published the results of a major national study of race and education. Contrary to general agreement, Coleman found little difference in academic performance between African American students attending integrated schools and those attending segregated ones. Indeed, such obvious things as libraries, laboratory facilities, and high expenditures per student made little difference. Instead, Coleman reported that family and neighborhood factors had the most influence on academic achievement. Coleman's findings were not well received by many of the social scientists who had been active in the civil rights movement. Some scholars criticized Coleman's work on methodological grounds, but many others objected hotly on the grounds that the findings would have segregationist political consequences.

Another example of political controversy surrounding social research in connection with race concerns the issue of IQ scores. In 1969 Arthur Jensen, a Harvard psychologist, was asked to prepare an article for the *Harvard Educational Review* that would examine the data on racial differences in IQ test results (Jensen, 1969). In the article, Jensen concluded that genetic differences between African Americans and Whites accounted for the lower average IQ scores of African Americans. He became so identified with that position that he appeared on college campuses across the country to discuss it.

Jensen's position was attacked on numerous methodological bases. It was charged that many of the data on which Jensen's conclusion was based were inadequate and sloppy, given that there are many IQ tests, some worse than others. Similarly, critics argued that Jensen had not sufficiently accounted for social–environmental factors. Other social scientists raised other appropriate methodological objections.

Beyond the scientific critique, however, Jensen was condemned by many as a racist. He was booed, and his public presentations were drowned out by hostile crowds. Jensen's reception by several university audiences was not significantly different from the reception received by abolitionists a century before, when the prevailing opinion had favored leaving the institution of slavery intact.

A similar reaction erupted in response to a book titled *The Bell Curve*, published in 1994 and coauthored by Charles Murray, a sociologist, and the late Richard J. Herrnstein, a psychologist. A small portion of their lengthy book argued that ethnic differences in intelligence can be attributed in part (but not exclusively) to genetic factors.

In their book, Murray and Herrnstein saw intelligence as a crucial factor that influences whether Americans will prosper or wind up in an underclass culture of poverty and other social ills. Based on the thesis that intelligence is so hard to change, the book recommended against spending money on a variety of social programs, including those aimed at improving the intellectual performance of disadvantaged youths.

Critics pointed to serious methodological shortcomings in the procedures and conclusions in the Murray and Herrnstein study. But as with the earlier controversy involving Jensen, what is most germane to this chapter is not the methodological critique of *The Bell Curve*, but its political condemnation. When the book first appeared, its early critics gave more attention to political objections than to the study's serious methodological shortcomings. It was attacked in a *Boston Globe* editorial before it was even published. The *Washington Post* reported that former education secretary William Bennett, a politically conservative supporter and friend of Murray, strongly praised the book but was made nervous by the section on race and intelligence. Because of that section, Bennett reportedly characterized Murray as a "marked man."

New Republic magazine devoted its October 31, 1994, issue to the book. The issue contains a 10-page article by Murray and Herrnstein, based on the section of their book that dealt with intelligence and genetics. Preceding that article are 17 pages of editorials by 20 different authors about both *The Bell Curve* and Murray and Herrnstein's *New Republic* article. Some of the editorials debate whether the magazine was ethical to even consider publishing the article, and most sharply attack the article or criticize the magazine's decision to publish it. One editorial depicts Murray and Herrnstein as dishonest. Another portrays them as seeking to justify oppression. Others liken them to racists trying to justify their racism or to bigots practicing pseudoscientific racism. One harsher editorial, titled "Neo-Nazis," implies that the relevant chapter from Murray and Herrnstein's book is "a chilly synthesis" of the findings of previous works published by neo-Nazis.

In an editorial that justified the decision to publish the Murray and Herrnstein article on grounds of free inquiry, the magazine's editor argued that the burden of proof for suppressing debate on the topic rests with those who seek to suppress the debate. The editorial argues for judging the issue on scientific and logical grounds, not tarring and feathering the authors by impugning their motives or associating them with Nazis. The editorial also responds to critics who claim that *The Bell Curve* hurts the feelings of African Americans, especially African American children, who don't want to be called genetically inferior. The editor argues that the view that African Americans are vulnerable people who must be shielded from free and open intellectual exchange is itself inherently racist.

Many social scientists limited their objections to the notorious Coleman, Jensen, and Murray and Herrnstein research on scientific, methodological grounds. The purpose of our account, however, is to point out that political ideology often gets involved in matters of social research. Although the abstract model of science is divorced from ideology, the practice of science is not.

Although the role of politics and values is not unique to social work research (the natural sciences have experienced similar situations), it is frequently discussed. We study things that matter to people—things about which they have firm, personal feelings, and things that affect their lives. Social work researchers, like all scientists, are human beings, and their human feelings often show through in their professional lives. To think otherwise would be naive. But science does proceed even under political controversy and hostility. Even when researchers get angry and call each other names, or when the research community comes under attack from the outside, the job of science gets done anyway. Scientific inquiry persists, studies are done, reports are published, and new things are learned. In short, political disputes do not bring science to a halt; they can simply make it more exciting.

5.8 MAIN POINTS

- In addition to technical, scientific considerations, social work research projects are likely to be shaped by administrative, ethical, and political considerations.
- What's ethically "right" and "wrong" in research is ultimately a matter of what people agree is right and wrong.
- Scientists agree that participation in research should, as a general norm, be voluntary. This norm, however, can conflict with the scientific need for generalizability.
- Probably all scientists agree that research should not harm those who participate in it, unless the participants willingly and knowingly accept the risks of potential harm.
- Anonymity refers to the situation in which even the researcher cannot identify an individual by the specific information that has been supplied.
- Confidentiality refers to the situation in which the researcher, although knowing which data describe which subjects, agrees to keep that information confidential.
- In some instances, the long-term benefits of a study are thought to outweigh the violation of certain ethical norms. But determining whether a study's ends justify its means is a difficult and often highly subjective process. Nowadays, institutional review boards (IRBs) make such determinations in approving studies.
- Bias and insensitivity about gender and culture have become ethical issues for many social scientists.
- Guidelines have been proposed to avoid bias and insensitivity about gender and culture.
- Although science is neutral on political matters, scientists are not.
- Ideological priorities can restrict inquiry out of a fear that certain truths can be misperceived or misused in a manner that will harm certain vulnerable groups; this restriction can lead to incomplete or distorted knowledge-building that risks harming the people it seeks to protect.

5.9 PRACTICE-RELATED EXERCISES

1. Suppose a social worker conducts a study in which she interviews children who were placed for adoption in infancy by their biological parents. She will focus on their feelings about someday meeting their biological parents. Discuss the ethical problems she would face, and how those might be avoided.

2. Suppose a social worker who has strong religious or personal beliefs against abortion wants to conduct an interview survey to explore the emotional impact of abortion on young women who have had an abortion. Discuss the personal involvement problems the social worker would face, and how those might be avoided.

3. Consider the following real and hypothetical research situations. Identify the ethical component in each. How do you feel about it? Do you feel the procedures described are ultimately acceptable or unacceptable? It might be useful to discuss some of these with classmates.

   a. A social work professor asks students in a social work practice class to complete questionnaires assessing their knowledge and attitudes about culturally competent practice that the instructor will analyze and use in preparing a journal article for publication.

   b. A community organizer conducts qualitative interviews at an impromptu peaceful demonstration in a low-income neighborhood where residents are protesting plans to build an expressway through the neighborhood. Unexpectedly, some of the residents who were interviewed start rioting and destroying property after being inter viewed. Police demand that the community organizer identify those people who were observed breaking the law. Rather than risk arrest as an accomplice after the fact, the community organizer complies.

   c. After a clinical program director completes the final draft of a research report supporting the effectiveness of her agency's services, the director discovers that 20 of the 200 agency cases were accidentally excluded from the data analysis. The excluded cases all involved clients whose data reflected poorly on the agency's effectiveness. The director chooses to ignore that fact and publish the report as is, unrevised.

   d. Social work students with field placements in a child welfare agency obtain a list of abusive parents they wish to study for a paper for their field seminar class. They contact the parents with the explanation that each has been selected "at random" from among the general population to take a sampling of "public opinion."

e. A social worker employed in a child guidance center decides to study the disciplinary styles of abusive parents with toddlers who are served in her agency. Each parent and his or her child enter a room with toys scattered around it, and the parent is asked to have the child straighten up the toys before playing with them. The parent is told that the researcher will observe the parent–child interactions from behind a one way mirror.

f. A school social worker conducts a survey in which she finds that 85 percent of the students in her high school smoke marijuana regularly. Dissemination of this finding will probably create a furor in the community. She decides to ignore the finding and keep it quiet.

g. To test the extent to which social work practitioners may try to save face by expressing clinical views on matters about which they are wholly uninformed, a social worker in charge of in-service training in his agency asks the practitioners for their clinical opinion of a fictitious practice model.

h. A research questionnaire is circulated among clients as part of their agency's intake forms. Although clients are not told they must complete the questionnaire, the hope is that they will believe they must—thus ensuring a higher completion rate.

i. A participant–observer pretends to join a group that opposes family planning services so she can study it, and she is successfully accepted as a member of the inner planning circle. What should the researcher do if the group makes plans for (1) a peaceful, though illegal, demonstration against family planning services, or (2) the bombing of an abortion clinic during a time when it is sure to be unoccupied?

5.10 INTERNET EXERCISES

1. Find an article that discusses ethical issues in social research. (You might enter one of the following search terms: *research ethics*, *informed consent*, or *institutional review boards*.) Read an article that piques your interest. Write down the bibliographic information for the article and summarize the article in a few sentences.

2. Repeat Internet Exercise 1, this time entering the search term *research politics*.

3. Skim some research articles that come up when you use the search term *informed consent*. Write down the groups of people for whom informed consent may be problematic—people who may not be able to give it. Suggest some ways in which the problem might be overcome.

4. Visit the website, Protecting Human Research Participants (https://phrp.nihtraining.com). If you take the online tutorial at this site, you will receive a certificate of completion that some IRBs now require of principal investigators and their research assistants working on studies involving human subjects. This certificate might therefore come in handy later on if you become a research assistant or need IRB approval for your research. You might also ask your instructor if extra credit could be granted for obtaining this certificate.

5. For more information on the Tuskegee syphilis study and additional web links on that topic, you can go to http://www.google.com and search using the key word *Tuskegee*.

5.11 ADDITIONAL READINGS

Jones, J. H. (1981). *Bad blood: The Tuskegee syphilis experiment*. New York, NY: Free Press. This remarkable book provides a fascinating account of the Tuskegee study we discussed in this chapter. Its account of the history of that study may astound you, and you may be inspired by the tale of a social worker who, after waging relentless battles with public health authorities for several years and ultimately deciding to engage the press in the service of his cause, managed to put a halt to the study.

Potocky, M., & Rodgers-Farmer, A. Y. (Eds.). (1998). *Social work research with minority and oppressed populations*. New York, NY: Haworth Press. This collection of articles contains innovative ideas for avoiding cultural bias and insensitivity in research with minority and oppressed populations; these groups include people living with HIV or AIDS, low-income urban adolescents, women of color, non-White ethnic elders, and African American children.

5.11a Competency Notes

EP 2.1.2b: Make ethical decisions by applying standards of the National Association of Social Workers Code of Ethics (p. 80): Social workers apply the NASW code of ethics as part of conducting ethical research as well as appraising whether the research completed or proposed by others is ethical.

EP 2.1.2c: Tolerate ambiguity in resolving ethical conflicts (pp. 81, 84, 85, 87, 88, 91): Social workers understand that in some studies the ethical concerns are subtle and arguable, and it is not always easy to judge whether the expected benefits of a research study outweigh those concerns.

EP 2.1.4a: Recognize the extent to which a culture's structures and values may oppress, marginalize, alienate, or create or enhance privilege and power (p. 93): When social workers conduct research in a culturally biased or culturally insensitive manner, they can alienate oppressed populations and further contribute to their oppression.

chapter

6

Culturally Competent Research

6.1 INTRODUCTION

EP 2.1.4b

Much of social work practice—at the macro as well as micro levels—involves minority and oppressed populations. Consequently, a heavy emphasis in social work education is placed on helping students learn more about cultural diversity and become more culturally competent practitioners. Cultural competence is also important in research. In Chapter 5 we noted that cultural bias and insensitivity are ethical issues. Avoiding them requires cultural competence. In this chapter we will go beyond ethics and examine how cultural competence can influence all phases of the research process. We'll see how cultural competence can help researchers obtain and provide information that is relevant and valid for minority and oppressed populations and thus can improve practice and policy with those populations.

In research, the term *cultural competence* means being aware of and appropriately responding to the ways in which cultural factors and cultural differences should influence what we investigate, how we investigate, and how we interpret our findings. When designing **culturally competent research** studies, for example, we will not overlook the need to include a sufficient and representative sample of participants from minority and oppressed populations. However, just seeking representation of minorities in our sample does not guarantee that we will get it. As we will discuss in this chapter, successfully recruiting and retaining minority participants in research requires special, culturally sensitive knowledge and efforts.

You may be surprised to learn that emphasis on cultural competence in research in social work and allied fields is a relatively recent development. Acknowledging that minority participants historically have not been adequately represented in clinical research, the National Institutes of Health (NIH) in 1994 issued a new policy mandating that all

---

culturally competent research   Research that is sensitive and responsive to the ways in which cultural factors and cultural differences influence what we investigate, how we investigate, and how we interpret our findings.

NIH-funded research projects involving human subjects must include adequate representation of women and members of ethnic minority groups in their samples. Moreover, the new policy stipulated that research proposals must include detailed plans for how women and minority participants would be recruited and retained in the study. Investigators are now required to describe their prior experience in recruiting and retaining such participants, report collaborations with other researchers who have this experience, and provide letters of support for their study from relevant community groups (Hohmann & Parron, 1996).

6.2 RECRUITING AND RETAINING THE PARTICIPATION OF MINORITY AND OPPRESSED POPULATIONS IN RESEARCH STUDIES

Recruiting a sufficient and representative sample of research participants from minority and oppressed populations can be a daunting challenge. So can retaining their participation throughout the study after they have been recruited. Many reasons have been postulated to explain difficulties in the recruitment and retention of participants from minority and oppressed populations. One is the poisoned climate for research created by previous studies that were conducted in a culturally insensitive manner. A related reason is the perception that the research question may have value for the larger society but little value to a particular minority group. Perhaps members of a particular minority group are likely to distrust research in general or members of the majority culture in general.

Some prospective participants can get turned off by *culturally insensitive informed consent procedures.* (We discussed informed consent procedures in Chapter 5.) For example, Norton and Manson (1996) observe, "The sophisticated language required by IRB protocols may be intimidating to American Indians and Alaska Natives, particularly those for whom English is a second language" (p. 858).

Another barrier pertains to *not knowing where to look for participants.* Suppose you want to study the impact of parental depression on the child-rearing practices of parents who recently immigrated to the United States from South Korea or from Latin America. Because such immigrants have extremely low rates of utilization of traditional mental health services, you may have meager success if you try to recruit participants only through referral sources or advertisements at traditional mental health service providers, where you think they may be in treatment for depression.

Locating or identifying prospective participants can be a special challenge when dealing with populations who lack a known residence—such as homeless individuals, migrant workers, or undocumented immigrants. Another hard-to-locate population is made up of people with known residences who have some characteristic that is stigmatized by society and therefore risky for them to disclose. People in need of intervention for HIV or AIDS, for example, comprise one such "hidden" population (Roffman, Picciano, Wickizer, Bolan, & Ryan, 1998).

In light of the many barriers to the recruitment and retention of participants from minority and oppressed populations, what can be done to alleviate or overcome those barriers? The literature on this issue is still emerging. It recommends a number of potentially useful approaches, as described below.

6.2a Obtain Endorsement from Community Leaders

If prospective participants in your study see that it has been endorsed by community leaders whom they respect, their distrust of the researchers or their skepticism about the value of the research to their community may be alleviated. Norton and Manson (1996), for example, discuss the need for investigators who seek to recruit American Indian or Alaskan Natives to obtain permission first from the prospective participant's tribe. They note that the Navajo nation now has a board staffed by tribal representatives who review, approve, and monitor all health-related research proposed for their community. Tribal governments aggressively evaluate the value of proposed research projects to the tribe. One tribal council even asserted that it had the authority to grant collective consent to participate on behalf of its members.

Seeking consent from community leaders can be a major undertaking. When done in a thorough and

careful manner, it involves obtaining their input into how the research questions are formulated, how the study is to be designed and implemented, and how its results are to be presented and disseminated. However, the effort can pay off not only by enhancing recruitment and retention of participants, but also by improving the design of your study or the interpretation of its results. Norton and Manson (1996) cite an example of how dialoguing with a tribal government alerted them to the greater reluctance of study participants in one of their research sites to disclose alcohol consumption to local staff than to clinicians from external communities. This development led them to change their plans to use local interviewers, enabling them to obtain responses that were less biased.

6.2b Use Culturally Sensitive Approaches Regarding Confidentiality

For those minority groups that value collective identity, it may not be enough to assure individual confidentiality. They might also require community confidentiality. Norton and Manson (1996) advise that, when publishing research in American Indian and Alaska Native communities, investigators should not identify specific communities. Press releases should not come from the investigators; instead, they should be initiated by the tribal government. Research findings should be in the form of generalizations; readers should not be able to ascertain the identity of the local communities associated with those findings.

6.2c Employ Local Community Members as Research Staff

If you have adequate funding, you can hire local community members to help locate and recruit prospective participants and obtain their informed consent. If the folks you hire also happen to be community leaders, all the better, because they can enhance your efforts to publicize your research and express their enthusiastic support for it. Employing community members to obtain informed consent also might help overcome any problems in understanding the consent forms or in being intimidated by them, since the members can explain the study verbally and answer questions about it in ways that prospective participants may be more likely to understand. Another benefit of employing local community members in your research is that your study thereby benefits the community just by providing more jobs. One drawback of employing local community members as research staff is its implications regarding confidentiality. Prospective participants may not want members of their own community interviewing them or knowing of their participation.

6.2d Provide Adequate Compensation

It is often advisable to reimburse participants for their time and effort in providing data and for any other ways in which they participate in your research. The payment should be large enough to provide an incentive, yet not so large that it becomes coercive. Compensation for participating in research is particularly applicable to studies of minority and oppressed populations. In light of the high poverty rates in some minority communities, compensation might provide a strong inducement for members to participate. Those same high poverty rates, however, may lead some to view high levels of compensation as coercive and thus unethical. Although you do not want to pay too much, an appropriate level of compensation can be another way your study benefits the local community. Norton and Manson (1996) add that compensation need not be limited to individual participants. They cite a request by a Pueblo community that compensation be provided to the tribe as a whole, in keeping with the tribe's emphasis on collective identity.

Money is not the only form of compensation you can use. If you are studying the homeless, for example, responding quickly to their need for some food or clothing can build trust and reward their participation. A sandwich, some cigarettes, or a cup of coffee can be significant to them. Perhaps you can accompany them to an agency that will give them some shelter, financial assistance, or health care. Food vouchers are a commonly used noncash way researchers can reward homeless or other low-income individuals for their research participation. Perhaps a fast-food chain will be willing to donate vouchers worth about five dollars each to your study.

6.2e Alleviate Transportation and Child Care Barriers

Because of the high poverty rates in some minority communities, some barriers to recruitment and retention pertain not to cultural issues per se, but to economic difficulties. For example, suppose you work in a child guidance center and want to evaluate a new, culturally sensitive intervention for an economically disadvantaged minority group in which the parent and child are treated together. Many of the parents you seek to recruit might experience transportation or childcare barriers to coming to your child guidance center for the treatment sessions. A culturally competent approach to your research, therefore, might include the provision of free transportation and child care (for their other young children). An alternative to providing free transportation would be to conduct the treatment and data collection sessions at their homes, although many families might still need child care during those sessions.

6.2f Choose a Sensitive and Accessible Setting

If your treatment or data collection sessions are not conducted in the participants' homes, you should make sure that the choice of setting in which they are conducted is sensitive to participant needs, resources, and concerns. Areán and Gallagher-Thompson (1996) have provided some useful insights concerning the culturally sensitive choice of a setting. For example, even if minority group members have transportation and are not dissuaded from participating because of economic barriers, some might be reluctant to travel to a particular setting in a different neighborhood out of fear of a racially motivated crime. Or perhaps the setting is in a dangerous section of their neighborhood. These fears might be particularly salient to elderly minority individuals. The site you choose, therefore, should be located somewhere that participants will perceive as convenient as well as safe. You should also consider whether some participants might be uncomfortable with the nature of the building you choose. If you choose a community church, for example, some prospective participants who don't belong to that church might be uncomfortable entering it. Others might not want their neighbors to see them receiving services or participating in a research study. Perhaps a nearby university site, where friends won't know of their participation, would be preferable. If you can implement some of the recommendations we've already mentioned—such as conducting focus groups, involving community leaders in planning your study, and employing local community members as research staff—you should try to ascertain which settings would or would not be accessible to your prospective participants and sensitive to their concerns.

6.2g Use and Train Culturally Competent Interviewers

It may seem obvious to you that one of the most important ways to enhance the recruitment and retention of minority group participants in your research is to make sure that the research staff who will come into contact with prospective participants are culturally competent. One way to do this, of course, is to employ members of the local community as your research staff, as we mentioned earlier. We also mentioned that in some cases employing local community members might conflict with confidentiality concerns. What other steps can you take to maximize cultural competence when employing local community members is deemed undesirable or infeasible? One recommendation commonly found in the literature on culturally competent research is to use interviewers who are of the same ethnicity as the members of the minority population whom you seek to recruit. Thus, if you seek to recruit and retain African American participants in a particular community, you might employ African American interviewers from a different community.

Matching interviewer and participant ethnicity probably won't impede your recruitment efforts; however, several studies have suggested that successful interviewing depends more on interviewer competence than on racial matching (Jackson & Ivanoff, 1999). In a study by Thompson, Neighbors, Munday, and Jackson (1996), for example, racial matching had no effect on the likelihood of African American psychiatric inpatients agreeing to be interviewed. According to Thompson and her associates, more important than racial matching

is whether the interviewer has adequate previous experience or training in working with members of the target population. Their interviewer training consisted of practicing how to approach participants, practicing how to give them an overview of the study, practicing how best to discuss confidentiality and voluntary participation, and thoroughly learning the intricacies of the survey instruments they were to use. The interviewers had to review every line on every page of the instructions for introducing the study and of the interviewing protocols. Using a script prepared by the research staff, they had to rehearse introducing and explaining the study. They also had to role-play practice interviews with each other and complete two practice interviews with real patients. These practice interviews were reviewed and critiqued.

Although the Thompson et al. study illustrates that with ample interviewer training, interviewer–participant matching may not be necessary, we should not overgeneralize their results. They may have had different findings had their subjects not been psychiatric inpatients. What if they had been unable to find interviewers who had ample previous experience working with members of the target population? What if they lacked the resources to train their interviewers so extensively? Under those conditions, matching the ethnicity of interviewers and participants might have made a huge difference.

6.2h Use Bilingual Staff

If you are trying to recruit participants from communities where many members have difficulty speaking English, your recruitment staff should be able to communicate in the language with which prospective participants are most comfortable. For example, if your study is to take place in a heavily Latino community, your interviewers should be able to converse in Spanish. If they cannot, your recruitment efforts are unlikely to succeed. Likewise, after recruiting participants, your data collection efforts will also need to be conducted in Spanish. And if you are evaluating a treatment, that treatment should be conducted in Spanish. Otherwise, even successful recruitment efforts are likely to have been wasted because you will have been able to retain so few non-English-speaking participants in the study.

6.2i Understand Cultural Factors Influencing Participation

Earlier in this chapter we discussed the important role played by tribes in the lives of Native Americans. We noted that researchers might need to interact with tribal leaders before individuals are permitted or willing to participate in a study. Researching related phenomena among Latino families, Miranda and her associates (Alvidrez, Azocar, & Miranda, 1996; Miranda, 1996) identified other cultural factors bearing upon recruitment and retention of low-income traditional Latinos in research on mental health services. *Familismo* refers to strong, traditional family values among traditional Latinos. *Machismo* refers to the power of the father in decision making, economic and emotional stability, and protecting the family from danger. *Marianismo* refers to the mother's spiritual superiority in her capacity for suffering and self-sacrifice to help her husband and children. *Personalismo* refers to the preferences of many traditional Latinos for a dignified approach when you associate with them, such as by using formal language and formal greetings that convey respect. At the same time, however, recruitment efforts should not be too formal. *Simpatía* refers to the expectation of traditional Latinos that the person treating them with respect will also interact in a warm and friendly manner. To illustrate how sensitivity to these cultural factors can enhance recruitment and retention, Miranda and her associates cite studies whose research staff experienced success in recruiting and retaining Latinos by being warm and personable while using such touches as formal titles (such as *señor* or *señora*), the polite forms of words (such as *usted* for "you"), and remembering the names of participants' children and asking about the children during each interview.

6.2j Use Anonymous Enrollment with Stigmatized Populations

Locating and recruiting prospective participants can be a special challenge if your study concerns people who have some characteristic that is stigmatized by society and therefore risky for them to disclose. People in need of intervention for HIV and AIDS constitute one such population. Roffman and his associates (1997, 1998) evaluated the effectiveness of a telephone group approach to AIDS prevention counseling with gay and bisexual men who had recently engaged in unprotected anal or oral sex with men. It was not easy for the researchers to find prospective participants for their study. Their recruitment period lasted almost two years and included "advertising in the gay press, news coverage in the mainstream press, distributing materials to HIV testing centers and gay/lesbian/bisexual health and social service agencies, and mailing posters to gay bars and baths" (Roffman, 1998, p. 9). By implementing both the study and the intervention by telephone, Roffman and his associates were able to assure prospective participants anonymity if they desired it. Publicizing *anonymous enrollment* in their recruitment materials enabled prospective participants to feel safer in responding to the recruitment effort and thus helped the research team obtain a pool of prospective participants, many of whom normally would have remained hidden because of the societal risk involved in being identified. In addition to helping obtain a pool of prospective participants, anonymous enrollment further helped secure their willingness to engage in the study.

Roffman and his associates were creative in their efforts to ensure anonymity and make the prospective applicants feel safe participating in the study. Anonymously enrolled clients were reimbursed (with no name entered on the payee line of the mailed check) for the cost of renting postal boxes in nearby post offices. They used pseudonyms to receive mailed materials from the research staff. The research team succeeded in engaging 548 participants in the study and therefore concluded that anonymous enrollment is an effective way to facilitate participation in research by hidden groups who might otherwise remain unreached. The team also acknowledged, however, that its approach applied only to prospective participants who had telephones and to interventions that can be delivered by telephone. The researchers also acknowledged that although anonymous enrollment appeared to be an important component of contacting and engaging prospective participants in the study, maintaining their participation was facilitated by having a staff that was culturally competent for this population.

6.2k Use Special Sampling Techniques

Anonymous enrollment is just one way to identify, engage, and maintain hidden groups in your sample. The literature on researching hard-to-reach populations is in its infancy, and future inquiries are likely to identify alternative innovative approaches. Some approaches involve specialized sampling techniques that will be discussed in Chapter 11. One technique is *purposive (judgmental) sampling*. In studying the homeless, for example, you may need to use your judgment, or the judgment of people who work with the homeless, to identify certain areas of town where the homeless may be found. Another technique is *snowball sampling*. Once you found homeless individuals, you would attempt to expand your snowball sample by asking them for information to help you locate other homeless people whom they know.

A technique particularly appropriate for sampling minority and oppressed populations is *disproportionate stratified sampling*, which can be used to ensure that enough cases of certain minority groups are selected to allow for subgroup comparisons within each of those minority groups. Thus, if you wanted to compare the attributes of members of a small minority group who live in urban areas with those who live in rural areas, and if only a tiny proportion of that small minority group lives in rural areas, then you probably would select a larger proportion of those who live in rural areas.

6.2l Learn Where to Look

Culturally competent researchers have learned not to rely exclusively on traditional agencies as referral sources in seeking to recruit certain minority group participants or members of hidden and stigmatized populations. But what are the alternatives? The answer to this question will vary depending on your target population. In their study of people in need of intervention for HIV and AIDS, for example, Roffman and his associates advertised in the gay press, distributed materials at HIV testing centers and gay/lesbian/bisexual health and social service agencies, and mailed posters to gay bars and baths. A study of the homeless that will be examined in Chapter 14 recruited homeless participants in such places as steam tunnels, loading docks, park benches, bus terminals, missions and flophouses, and abandoned buildings.

Culturally competent researchers studying African Americans who have emotional problems have learned that many such individuals do not seek help from traditional mental health services. These researchers therefore request help in recruiting participants for their studies from ministers, primary care physicians, and informal support networks in addition to traditional service agencies (Thompson et al., 1996). We do not mean to imply that traditional agencies should be ignored, however—just that they should not be relied on *exclusively*.

6.2m Connect with and Nurture Referral Sources

Whether you are relying on traditional or nontraditional organizations for referrals to your study, your success in securing sufficient referrals from those sources will be enhanced if you have established rapport with the individuals working in them. For example, you might attend their meetings and see whether you can volunteer your assistance to them. The more extensive your earlier interactions with key individuals upon whom you will rely for referrals, and the better your established relationship with them, the more helpful they are likely to be when you seek their assistance in recruiting participants for your research.

After establishing rapport with referral sources, you should inform them of the benefits your study can provide to the field as well as to individual participants. For example, perhaps the participants will receive a promising new service as well as compensation and other rewards for participating. Perhaps the field will learn whether the promising new service is really effective. Discuss their questions about your study and attempt to assuage their fears about it. You should also nurture your relationships with your referral sources throughout your study. Continue to attend their meetings and assist them. Keep them apprised of how your study is going. Let them know incrementally of any preliminary findings as they emerge.

6.2n Use Frequent and Individualized Contacts and Personal Touches

Although many of the techniques we've discussed so far bear on retention as well as recruitment, much of our discussion has emphasized recruitment more than retention. But as we've noted, in studies that involve multiple sessions with participants, successful recruitment efforts will be in vain if they are not followed by successful retention efforts. Studies assessing treatment outcome, for example, will need to undertake special efforts to retain clients in treatment. Clients also will need to be reminded and motivated to participate in pretesting, posttesting, and perhaps several administrations of follow-up testing. Miranda and her associates (Alvidrez et al., 1996; Miranda, 1996) recommended some approaches to enhance retention that have been successful in several treatment outcome studies involving low-income Latino participants. We believe that their recommendations might apply to some other low-income minority groups, as well. For example, Miranda and her associates advocate the telephoning of participants regularly, perhaps monthly, by research assistants who are warm and friendly and who ask about the well-being of the participants and their families. The same research assistant should call each time and should remember and discuss the details of the participant's situation and his or her family's situation. This builds rapport and continuity between phone calls. As we mentioned earlier, transportation to and from each assessment session along with modest cash or food voucher reimbursements to participants after each assessment session will also help. Providing coffee, cold drinks, and perhaps some sandwiches or snacks is also a nice touch.

In addition to the regular contacts and personal touches that we've just mentioned, it is crucial that you be sure to make reminder calls to participants before their scheduled treatment or assessment sessions. In fact, in addition to calling them a day or two in advance, you should try calling them a week or two in advance. If they are poor, they may not own an answering machine. Perhaps they've moved, and you will need time to track them down.

6.2o Use Anchor Points

Making reminder calls and other contacts is not easy if your participants are homeless or residentially

---

anchor points   Pieces of information about the various places you may be able to find a particular research participant.

transient. Based on their review of the research on the homeless mentally ill, Hough and his associates (1996) recommend using **anchor points**, which are pieces of information about the various places you may be able to find a particular participant. The more anchor points you identify when you first engage individuals in your study, the more likely you will be to find them later. If your participant is a homeless woman, for example, some anchor points might include where she usually sleeps, eats, or hangs out. You might also ask if she has any nearby family or friends and how you can contact them. Are there any social service workers, landlords, or other individuals in the community who might know how to locate her? Is there an address where she goes to pick up her mail, her messages, or Supplemental Security Income checks? What, if any, nicknames or aliases does she use? All this information should be recorded systematically on a tracking form. In your subsequent contacts with the participant or others who know of her whereabouts, you should continually update your anchor point information.

6.2p Use Tracking Methods

Hough and his associates recommend additional techniques for tracking and contacting your participants. If your anchor points include a telephone number, you can use *phone tracking*. As we mentioned above, you should start calling a week or two in advance of an interview. With a homeless individual, expect to make quite a few calls to the anchor points just to arrange a single interview. You should also give homeless participants a toll-free number where they can leave messages about appointment changes, changes in how to locate them, or other relevant information. You might even offer incentives, such as food vouchers, for leaving such messages. To help participants remember appointments and how to contact the research project, you should give them a card that lists useful information (such as key community resources) on one side; on the other side, the card should show appointment times and the research project's address and telephone number.

In addition to phone tracking, you can use *mail tracking*, in which you mail reminder notices about impending interviews or ask participants to call in to update any changes in how to contact them. Mail tracking also might include sending birthday cards, holiday greetings, and certificates of appreciation for participation. All correspondence should be signed by the research staff member the participant knows.

You can also use *agency tracking*, in which you ask service providers or other community agencies whether they have been in recent contact with participants whom you are unable to locate. Some of these agencies may have been identified in your anchor points. If they are unable to tell you where to locate the participant, you can contact additional agencies, such as social service agencies, hospitals, police, probation and parole officers, substance abuse programs, shelters, public housing staff, social security offices, or even the coroner's office. The cooperation you get from these agencies will be enhanced if you follow some of the other recommendations we've mentioned earlier in this chapter, such as obtaining endorsement for your study from community leaders and connecting with and nurturing your relationships with community agencies relevant to your study.

If your efforts at phone tracking and agency tracking fail to locate a participant, you can resort to *field tracking*. Field tracking, which is particularly relevant to research on the homeless, involves talking with people on the streets about where to find the participant. You might go to where other homeless people who know the participant hang out and ask them. Offering them small gifts, such as coffee or cigarettes, might help. You can also use your anchor points to identify neighbors, friends, family, or previous hangout spots that might help you find the participant.

Regardless of which tracking methods you use, Hough and his associates argue that your persistence is probably the most important factor in obtaining satisfactory retention rates. With some homeless mentally ill participants, for example, you may need to seek out 10 anchor points several times each, make 15 attempts to contact the participant, or show up for a fifth scheduled interview with a participant who has not shown up for the previous four.

These tracking techniques can conflict with the ethical guideline of protecting anonymity and privacy, as discussed in Chapter 5. Consequently, before you can use them, you will be required to

account for them in your informed consent procedures. Participants will need to give you advance permission to seek their whereabouts from the various sources we've been discussing. In addition, you will need to make sure that you do not inadvertently reveal sensitive information about your participant to these sources. The sources should not, for example, be informed that your study is on mental illness or AIDS. If these sources are given an address or phone number for the research study, neither should contain anything that would hint at the sensitive nature of the research topic.

6.3 CULTURALLY COMPETENT PROBLEM FORMULATION

If you want to conduct research on an ethnic minority population, it would behoove you to know quite a bit about that population's culture. Thus, before you begin any investigation, it is crucial that you are well read in the literature on the culture of minority or oppressed populations relevant to your study. This should include readings that describe the culture and its values as well as research studies dealing with issues bearing on the participation of its members in your study.

In other words, you should develop *cultural competence* regarding the population you want to include in your study. As discussed by Vonk (2001), cultural competence involves knowledge, attitudes, and skills. You should understand the minority culture's historical experiences—including the effects of prejudice and oppression—and how those experiences influence the ways in which its members live and view members of the dominant culture. You also should understand the minority culture's traditions, values, family systems, socioeconomic issues, and attitudes about social services and social policies. You should be aware of how your own attitudes are connected to your cultural background and how they may differ from the worldview of members of the minority culture. You should develop skills in communicating effectively both verbally and nonverbally with members of the minority culture and establishing rapport with them.

Miranda and her associates (Alvidrez et al., 1996; Miranda, 1996) discuss how misconceptions about Latino attitudes and Latino utilization of mental health services can impede the efforts of psychotherapy researchers to recruit and retain Latinos in their studies. If you plan to conduct a study evaluating mental health services in an area where many Latinos reside, it is important that you have accurate knowledge about what will influence utilization of such services among Latinos. Otherwise, you might not undertake appropriate efforts to recruit and retain the participation of Latinos in your study, and you might too readily attribute their lack of participation to negative attitudes rather than to your inadequate efforts to recruit and retain them. For example, Miranda and associates discuss how the individual is valued less among many traditional Latinos than is the family, including extended as well as nuclear family members. Consequently, researchers may need to interact with family members before individuals are permitted or willing to participate in treatment outcome studies.

Even if you already have accumulated considerable knowledge and sensitivity regarding the culture of interest, you should review recent literature, especially the research literature, before commencing your research. Doing so will enhance your assessment of your own cultural competence and will check to see whether your conceptions are accurate and consistent with the latest findings. Moreover, cultures are not monolithic. They contain diverse subcultures that might be related to differences in factors such as geographic origin, socioeconomic status, and acculturation. In assessing your own cultural competence, therefore, be sure not to overlook the diversity within the culture in which you already have expertise.

In addition to reviewing the literature, another helpful early step in seeking to improve the cultural competence of your research involves using various qualitative methods. Using qualitative sampling methods, for example, you might seek the advice of *key informants* who are members of the culture or who have a great deal of experience in working with its members. These colleagues should include practitioners as well as scholars whose works have dealt with the culture of interest. Other key informants are community members and their leaders. In fact, it is essential that representatives of the minority cultures be included in the formulation of the research questions and in all subsequent stages of the research. This will not only help you formulate research questions that are responsive to minority group needs and concerns, it also can help you prevent or deal with culturally related problems that might arise in later stages of the research design and implementation—problems that you might not otherwise have anticipated. Likewise, it can foster a sense of community commitment to the research and more receptivity to future studies.

By using qualitative methods, you also can immerse yourself directly in the culture of interest and enhance your assessment of your own cultural competence. Alvidrez and associates (1996), for example, mention how conducting a focus group consisting of young African American women before initiating investigations about parenting interventions can help researchers to better understand attitudes about child rearing among this population. The researchers can be better prepared to develop culturally specific hypotheses about how young African American women might respond to the parenting interventions of concern. Focus groups can also help you to anticipate barriers to recruiting and retaining participants in your study and to identify steps you can take that might enhance recruitment and retention. Let's turn now to issues in data analysis and reporting.

6.4 CULTURALLY COMPETENT DATA ANALYSIS AND REPORTING

Cultural competence can affect how data are analyzed and reported. Culturally competent researchers will not just be interested in whether minority groups differ from the majority group. If they have a sufficiently diverse sample, rather than combine all minority groups together as one category to compare to the majority group in the data analysis, they will compare the various minority groups to each other. There are two reasons for this. First, it would be culturally insensitive to be concerned only with how minority groups as a whole compare to the majority group and not with each other. Second, different minority groups differ from the majority group in different ways. For example, Asian Americans on average currently have higher levels of academic achievement than American Caucasians, whereas some other minority groups in the

United States on average currently have lower levels of academic achievement than Caucasians. Thus, if the Asian Americans' achievement levels were combined with the levels of one or more of the minority groups with lower levels, their combined (average) level might be close to that of Caucasians. This would mask the real differences as compared to Caucasians and would overlook important differences between the minority groups.

Cultural insensitivity in the data analysis and reporting phases of research also can result in interpreting ethnic differences in a prejudicial manner, focusing too much on the deficits of minorities and too little on their strengths. Miranda (1996), for example, cites studies that interpreted as an innate deficit the lower likelihood of delaying gratification among inner-city minority children, as compared to middle-class White children. Miranda depicts this interpretation as racist because it overlooks the possibility that the inner-city minority children were merely responding in an adaptive manner to their disadvantaged environment.

Norton and Manson (1996) discuss the harmful impact of news headlines resulting from press releases put out by investigators in a 1979 study of alcohol use among the Inupiat tribe in Alaska. One headline read, "Alcohol Plagues Eskimos." Another read, "Sudden Wealth Sparks Epidemic of Alcoholism." Overnight, Standard & Poor's dramatically reduced the bond rating of the Inupiat community, which halted funding to some major municipal projects. Consequently, some Alaska Native tribes are no longer receptive to research on alcoholism, despite the importance of that problem in their communities.

Cultural insensitivity in interpreting data can also occur when ethnic minorities are not even included in a study and yet its findings are generalized to them as if they had been included. Likewise, studies whose samples include only one gender should clarify that their results do not generalize to the other gender.

6.5 ACCULTURATION

Culturally competent researchers will also consider the *immigration experience* and *acculturation* as factors to include in their research as they study differences between minority and majority populations. Sensitivity to these factors will also alert researchers to study differences within a particular minority group. For example, Latinos or Asians who have recently immigrated to the United States are likely to have different needs and problems, have different attitudes about child rearing or marital roles, and respond to social services differently than Latinos or Asians whose parents or grandparents have lived in the United States for several decades or longer. The longer a member of a minority culture has lived among a majority culture, the more likely they are to be acculturated to the majority culture. **Acculturation** is the process in which a group or individual changes after coming into contact with a majority culture, taking on the language, values, attitudes, and lifestyle preferences of the majority culture. If you want to study factors influencing service utilization patterns or child-rearing attitudes among Korean Americans, for example, degree of acculturation is one of the factors you should examine.

6.6 CULTURALLY COMPETENT MEASUREMENT

Earlier in this chapter we mentioned some problems that cultural insensitivity can create, such as offending participants and dissuading them from participating in your study. At this point, we'll look at how culturally competent measurement procedures attempt to avoid the problem of producing unreliable or invalid information.

6.6a Language Problems

Regardless of whether we interview people or ask them to complete questionnaires, we need to modify our procedures when some of our research participants are not fluent in the majority language. Three rather obvious steps to be taken under these circumstances are using bilingual interviewers, translating the measures into the language of the respondents, and pretesting the measures in dry runs to see if they

acculturation The process by which a group or individual changes after coming into contact with a majority culture, taking on the language, values, attitudes, and lifestyle preferences of the majority culture.

are understood as intended. But even these steps will not guarantee success in attaining reliable and valid measurement, or what can be called *translation validity*. The translation process, for example, is by no means simple.

One problem pertains to the fluency of the bilingual interviewers or translators. Perhaps they are not as fluent in the minority language as we think they are. Or there may be language differences regarding a particular foreign language between those who can speak only in that language and those who are bilingual. United States residents who are bilingual in English and Spanish, for example, might use some English words with a Spanish sound when speaking Spanish—words that might be unintelligible to recent immigrants from Latin America who speak only in Spanish (Grinnell, 1997).

But even if words are accurately translated, that does not guarantee that you have accurately translated the concept being conveyed by those words. Consider North American terms such as "feeling blue" or "downhearted," which are commonly used in instruments that measure depression. It is difficult to translate these terms into other languages. For example, if you ask Latino or Asian respondents in their own language if they are "feeling blue," they may think you are asking them if they literally have blue skin.

One procedure that deals with complexities in translating instruments from one language into another is called **back-translation**. This method begins with a bilingual person translating the instrument and its instructions to a target language. Then another bilingual person translates from the target language back to the original language (without seeing the original version of the instrument). Then the original instrument is compared to the back-translated version, and items with discrepancies are

---

back-translation A method aimed at attaining translation validity that begins with a bilingual person translating an instrument to a target language, followed by another bilingual person translating it from the target language back to the original language (without seeing the original version of the instrument). Then the original instrument is compared to the back-translated version, and items with discrepancies are modified further.

modified further. But back-translation is by no means foolproof. It does not guarantee translation validity or the avoidance of *cultural bias*.

6.6b Cultural Bias

A measurement procedure has a cultural bias when it is administered to a minority culture without adjusting for the ways in which the minority culture's unique values, attitudes, lifestyles, or limited opportunities alter the accuracy or meaning of what is really being measured. Avoiding cultural bias goes beyond resolving language difficulties. For example, asking about sexual issues is extremely taboo in some cultures. As another example, the reluctance among Chinese respondents to acknowledge pride is not a translation problem, but one of understanding unique cultural values and their implications for social desirability. Likewise, consider a true-false item on a scale measuring different types of psychopathology worded as follows: "When I leave home, I worry about whether the door is locked and the windows closed." African American youths may be more likely than Whites to answer "true," even when they have no more psychopathology than Whites. This is because the African American youths are more likely than Whites to live in high-crime neighborhoods where an unlocked door is an invitation to burglars (Nichols, Padilla, & Gomez-Maqueo, 2000).

Cultural bias also can mar data collected using direct observation. Cauce, Coronado, and Watson (1998), for example, cite research showing that when viewing videotaped interactions of African American mothers and daughters, African American observers rated the interactions as having less conflict than did the other observers. The African American raters also rated the mothers as less controlling. Thus, if your study uses observers or raters, it is critical that they be culturally competent.

6.6c Measurement Equivalence

All of the steps that we've been recommending for developing culturally competent measurement won't guarantee that a measurement instrument that appeared to be valid when tested with one culture will be valid when used with another. Allen and Walsh (2000) point out that most of the validated personality tests currently used in the United States were validated with samples consisting mainly of Euro-Americans. When we modify such instruments, we should assess whether the modified instrument used with the minority culture is really equivalent to the version validated with the dominant culture. We need to do the same when a measure is validated in one country but then applied in another country.

The term **measurement equivalence** means that a measurement procedure developed in one culture will have the same value and meaning when administered to people in another culture (Burnette, 1998; Moreland, 1996). Three types of measurement equivalence that tend to be of greatest concern are *linguistic equivalence, conceptual equivalence,* and *metric equivalence.*

Linguistic equivalence, also known as **translation equivalence,** is attained when an instrument has been translated and back-translated successfully. **Conceptual equivalence** means that instruments and observed behaviors have the same meanings across cultures. For example, Moreland (1996) notes that some cultures consider a belch to be a compliment, whereas others consider it to be an insult. If you are monitoring antisocial behaviors among children, you will not have conceptual equivalence if you count belching as an antisocial behavior among subjects in a culture that considers it to be a compliment. Metric equivalence means that scores on a measure are comparable across cultures.

To illustrate the difference between conceptual equivalence and metric equivalence, suppose that you devise an instrument that intends to measure the degree of burden experienced by caregivers of frail, elderly parents. Some items on the instrument might refer to "objective" burden, such as how much time is spent on caregiving. Other items might refer to "subjective" burden, such as how depressed the caregiver feels about caregiving. At the level of *conceptual equivalence,* you might be concerned that items about depression, such as "I feel blue," might not have the same meaning across two or more different cultures. At the level of **metric equivalence,** you might wonder whether in some cultures the amount of time spent in caregiving is really an indicator of burden, because some cultures may so esteem their elderly and the care-giving role that the act of caregiving is not seen or experienced as a burden.

An instrument cannot have metric equivalence unless it has linguistic and conceptual equivalence.

However, as we have illustrated above, linguistic and conceptual equivalences do not guarantee metric equivalence. Accurately understanding the intended meaning of a question about how much time one spends in caregiving does not guarantee that a higher score on time spent indicates more of the concept of "burden." Eight hours a day may be perceived in one culture as spending a moderate amount of time on caregiving, whereas in another it may seem huge and burdensome.

6.6d Assessing Measurement Equivalence

Various procedures can be used to assess the measurement equivalence of an instrument. For example, we can see whether the more acculturated members of a particular minority culture on average score differently on the instrument than the less acculturated members (such as recent immigrants) on average do. If the average scores do not differ according to level of acculturation, that would support the notion that the scale might be equivalent. Conversely, if the average scores differ according to level of acculturation, that would suggest problems in measurement equivalence.

You should be cautious in making this inference, however. Suppose you are measuring something like emotional stress or caregiver burden. Perhaps the immigration experience and being new and less acculturated in a foreign land actually do create more emotional stress or make the caregiving role more burdensome. If so, then the differences in average scores by level of acculturation would not mean the scale lacked measurement equivalence. To get a better handle on this issue, you might want to use some of

measurement equivalence An attribute of a measurement procedure developed in one culture when it has the same value and meaning when administered to people in another culture.

linguistic equivalence (also known as **translation equivalence**) An attribute of a measurement instrument attained by translating it and back-translating it successfully.

conceptual equivalence An attribute of a measurement procedure that has the same meanings across cultures.

metric equivalence An attribute of a measure whose scores are comparable across cultures.

the methods that will be discussed in Chapter 8, such as exploring whether several individual items on the instrument statistically correlate with the culture-related factors and whether deleting or modifying those items would improve the measurement equivalence of the instrument.

6.7 MAIN POINTS

- Cultural competence means being aware of and appropriately responding to the ways in which cultural factors and cultural differences should influence what we investigate, how we investigate, and how we interpret our findings.
- Studies that do not include adequate representation from specific minority and oppressed populations in their samples are not generalizable to those populations.
- Cultural insensitivity can result in interpreting research findings on ethnic differences in a prejudicial manner, focusing too much on the deficits of minorities and too little on their strengths.
- Culturally competent researchers will include socioeconomic factors in their analyses when they are studying other ways in which minority and majority populations differ.
- Culturally competent researchers will also consider the immigration experience and acculturation as factors to include in their research as they study differences between minority and majority populations.
- Acculturation is the process by which a group or individual changes after coming into contact with a majority culture, taking on the language, values, attitudes, and lifestyle preferences of the majority culture.
- Before you begin any investigation with minority or oppressed populations, it is crucial that you develop cultural competence regarding those populations, including being well read in the literature on their cultures.
- Representatives of the minority cultures being studied should be included in the formulation of the research questions and in all subsequent stages of the research.
- To alleviate barriers to the recruitment and retention of research participants from minority and oppressed populations, you should obtain

endorsement from community leaders; use culturally sensitive approaches regarding confidentiality; employ local community members as research staff; provide adequate compensation; alleviate transportation and child care barriers; choose a sensitive and accessible setting; use and train culturally competent interviewers; employ bilingual staff; understand cultural factors influencing participation; use anonymous enrollment with stigmatized populations; use special sampling techniques; learn where to look; connect with and nurture referral sources; use frequent and individualized contacts and personal touches; and use anchor points and tracking methods.

- Three main threats to culturally competent measurement are (1) the use of interviewers whose personal characteristics or interviewing styles offend or intimidate minority respondents or in other ways make them reluctant to divulge relevant and valid information; (2) the use of language that minority respondents do not understand; and (3) cultural bias.
- When some of your research participants are not fluent in the majority language, you should employ bilingual interviewers, translate measures into the language of the respondents, and pretest the measures to see if they are understood as intended.
- Back-translation is one means of attempting to attain translation validity. It begins with a bilingual person translating the instrument and its instructions to a target language. Then another bilingual person translates from the target language back to the original language. Then the original instrument is compared to the back-translated version, and items with discrepancies are modified further.
- Measurement equivalence means that a measurement procedure developed in one culture will have the same value and meaning when administered to people in another culture.
- Linguistic equivalence is attained when an instrument has been translated and back-translated successfully.
- Conceptual equivalence means that instruments and observed behaviors have the same meanings across cultures.
- Metric equivalence means that scores on a measure are comparable across cultures.

6.8 PRACTICE-RELATED EXERCISES

1. Suppose you are employed as a community organizer working with migrant farm workers who recently emigrated from Mexico to the United States. You want to conduct a survey whose findings might help improve services or policies affecting the farm workers.

   a. Contrast how taking a culturally competent approach would differ from a culturally insensitive approach in each of the following phases of the research process: (1) formulating the research question, (2) measurement, and (3) interpreting findings.
   b. Discuss the steps you would take to recruit and retain the participation of the migrant farm workers in your study.

2. Examine the tables of contents and abstracts of recent issues of the journal *Research on Social Work Practice* until you find an article reporting on a study asses sing the measurement equivalence of an instrument related to social work practice. Briefly summarize how that study attempted to improve and assess the instrument's measurement equivalence.

6.9 INTERNET EXERCISES

1. Find an article titled "Translation of the Rosenberg Self-Esteem Scale into American Sign Language: A Principal Components Analysis," by Teresa V. Crowe, which appeared in the March 2002 issue of *Social Work Research*. Briefly describe and critically appraise the steps taken in the reported study to achieve and assess measurement equivalence.
2. Find an article titled "Korean Social Work Students' Attitudes toward Homosexuals," by Sung Lim Hyun and Miriam McNown Johnson, which appeared in the Fall 2001 issue of the *Journal of Social Work Education*. Briefly describe how the study reported in this article illustrates the concept of *metric equivalence*.
3. Find an article titled "Ethnic Pride, Biculturalism, and Drug Use Norms of Urban American Indian Adolescents," by Stephen Kulis, Maria Napoli, and Flavio Francisco Marsiglia, which appeared in the June 2002 issue of *Social Work Research*.

Briefly describe and critically appraise how that study illustrates research that is culturally sensitive.

4. Go to a website developed and operated by Dr. Marianne Yoshioka, a social work professor at Columbia University, called "Psychosocial Measures for Asian American Populations" and located at www.colum-bia.edu/cu/ssw/projects/pmap/. Download some of the abstracts of measures you find at the site and briefly describe how they illustrate at least two main points about culturally sensitive measurement discussed in this chapter.

6.10 ADDITIONAL READINGS

Cuéllar, I., & Paniagua, F. A. (Eds.). (2000). *Handbook of multicultural mental health: Assessment and treatment of diverse populations*. San Diego, CA: Academic Press. This edited volume contains chapters covering material that can enhance your cultural competence in practice as well as research. Among the research concepts covered are cultural bias in sampling and interpreting psychological test scores and how to assess measurement equivalence. Several chapters also focus on specific minority groups in discussing culturally competent practice and research with each group.

Fong, R., & Furuto, S. (Eds.). (2001). *Culturally competent practice: Skills, interventions, and evaluations*. Boston, MA: Allyn & Bacon. As its title implies, most of the chapters in this book focus on culturally competent social work practice. Developing cultural competence is important in its own right, and it will also help you become more culturally competent in your research. In addition, Part 4 of this five-part book focuses on applying culturally competent practice concepts and skills in the evaluation of programs and practice. Key concepts addressed include applying culturally competent evaluation skills, the strengths perspective, and the empowerment process in designing evaluations and in interacting with African American, Mexican American and Latino, Native American, Asian American, and Hawaiian and Pacific Islander individuals, families, organizations, and communities.

Hernandez, M., & Isaacs, M. R. (Eds.). (1998). *Promoting cultural competence in children's mental health services*. Baltimore, MD: Paul H. Brookes. In addition to offering a useful perspective on various dimensions of cultural competence in children's mental health services, this book provides three chapters focusing specifically on cultural competence in evaluation and research.

Potocky, M., & Rodgers-Farmer, A. Y. (Eds.). (1998). *Social work research with minority and oppressed populations*. New York, NY: Haworth Press. This handy collection of articles contains innovative ideas for avoiding cultural bias and insensitivity in research with minority and oppressed populations. Most pertinent to this chapter are two articles that describe issues in the construction of instruments to measure depression among women of color and gerontological social work concerns among non-White ethnic elders.

6.10a Competency Note

EP 2.1.4b: Gain sufficient self-awareness to eliminate the influence of personal biases and values in working with diverse groups (p. 102): All of the concepts in this chapter aim to help social workers become more culturally competent in their research, which entails eliminating the influence of personal biases and values when engaged in research efforts with diverse groups.

Problem Formulation and Measurement

Now that you have an overview of the research process and the factors affecting it, we can examine various research phases and methods more closely. Chapter 7 presents the problem formulation phase in which research topics are selected and research questions formulated, hypotheses are developed, and their variables are defined and observed.

Knowing how we plan to observe variables sets the stage for deciding how to measure them. Chapter 8 will discuss measurement reliability and validity and sources of error in alternative forms of measurement. Finally, Chapter 9 will examine guidelines for asking questions, interviewing, and critically appraising measurement instruments.

chapter
7

Problem Formulation

7.1 INTRODUCTION

EP 2.1.3a

Social work research, like social work practice, follows a problem-solving process in seeking to resolve social welfare problems. Both research and practice begin with formulating a problem, which includes recognizing a difficulty, defining it, and specifying it. This chapter will examine the problem formulation phase of social work research. We'll begin by discussing the process of selecting a topic.

7.2 SELECTING A TOPIC

In social work research, as distinguished from social scientific research in other disciplines, the impetus for selecting a topic should come from decisions that confront social service agencies, or from a need for information to solve practical problems in social welfare. The researcher's intellectual curiosity and personal interests certainly come into play (as they do in all research), but a study is more likely to have value to the social work field (and to be considered social work research) if the topic is selected because it addresses information needed to guide policy, planning, or practice decisions in social welfare. One way to gauge the practical value of a research topic is to discuss it with key people who work in the area to which your research question pertains. Another is to conduct a thorough review of the literature relevant to your research question. The *literature review* is perhaps the most important step in formulating a research question. It not only will help you assess the general utility of your question, but it will also provide you with an excellent basis for selecting a research question to begin with.

7.3 LITERATURE REVIEW

Novice researchers commonly make the mistake of putting off their literature reviews until they have sharpened their research question and come up with a design to investigate it. Research can be done that way, but it is not the most efficient use of time. Doing it that way may be reinventing the wheel or failing to benefit from the mistakes and experiences of others. Until we review the literature,

we have no way of knowing whether the research question has already been adequately answered, of identifying the conceptual and practical obstacles that others have already encountered in this line of research, of learning how those obstacles have been overcome, or of deciding what lines of research can best build on the work that has already been done in a particular problem area.

Another reason to review the literature early is that it is a prime source for selecting a research question. What better way to reduce the chances of selecting an irrelevant or outdated research question than by knowing what has already been done in a particular problem area and the implications of that work for future research? What better way to ensure that your study will be valued as part of a cumulative knowledge-building effort, as opposed to being seen as an obscure study that does not seem to address anything that anyone else is addressing or cares about?

Building on prior research does not necessarily imply that your study should never depart radically from previous work or that it should never duplicate a previous study. There may be sound reasons for both. The point is that you make that decision not in ignorance of the prior research, but in light of it and of what your judgment tells you to do. You may wish to repeat a previous study if you think replication is warranted and would be the best contribution you can make. Perhaps your research question has already been answered, but the limitations of the methodologies used to investigate it make you skeptical of the validity of the currently accepted answer. So you might decide to study the same question with a better methodology. On the other hand, you may be inspired to look at the problem in a way no one else ever has. You would do this not just to satisfy your own curiosity, but also because careful consideration of what's been done before has convinced you that this radical departure is precisely what the field now needs. There are countless examples of how an early search of the literature can enrich your study and save you from later headaches. Identifying valid measurement instruments, for example, lets you adapt existing measures instead of spending endless hours constructing and testing your own instruments. Another benefit of the literature search is that you can identify alternative conceptions of the problem or variables that had not occurred to you.

Some qualitative researchers who seek to construct theory in an inductive fashion might opt to delay the literature review until near the end of the research process in order to avoid being influenced by other people's theories in what they observe or how they interpret what they observe. Other qualitative researchers do a thorough literature review before beginning their research. Although they want to conduct their observations with minds as open as possible, they want to start out with an understanding of the current knowledge base and its gaps. This is an issue about which reasonable people can disagree.

Regardless of the timing of your literature review, you should be familiar with how to go about conducting one. Some tips for conducting literature reviews were provided in Chapter 2, in the section on searching for evidence in Step 2 of the evidence-based practice process. That section emphasized electronic searches. Appendix A, on Using the Library, provides more detail about conducting a literature review, in connection to manual as well as online approaches. It also provides an extensive list of professional journals related to social work and some time saving tips for examining them.

7.4 SELECTING A RESEARCH QUESTION

EP 2.1.6a
EP 2.1.10m

If you have conducted your literature review for the purpose of formulating a research study, your next step will be to narrow your broad topic into a research question. For example, the treatment of sexually abused girls is a topic, not a research question. In contrast, a good research question might be, "Is play therapy effective in alleviating trauma symptoms among sexually abused girls aged six to eight?" Just wording a broad topic in question form does not guarantee that you will have a *good* research question. The question needs to be *narrow* and *specific*. Thus, "Is childhood sexual abuse an important issue in the treatment of depression among women?" would be a better research question if it were worded as follows: "What proportion of women currently in treatment for major depression report having been sexually abused as a child?"

Research questions need to be *posed in a way that can be answered by observable evidence*. Asking whether criminal sentences for perpetrators of sexual abuse should be stiffer is not a research question. Its answer will depend not on observable evidence, but on arguments based largely on value judgments. Of course, it is conceivable that people could marshal known evidence to support their argument in this debate. Perhaps they could mention the high recidivism rate among perpetrators or studies documenting the failure of rehabilitation programs, but that would not make the question being debated a research question. The studies being cited in the debate, however, might have investigated good research questions, such as, "What are the recidivism rates for certain kinds of juvenile sex offenders who have and have not received certain kinds of treatment?"

We noted above that the most important criterion that should guide you in narrowing your research topic into a research question is that its answer should have significant potential *relevance for guiding social welfare policy or social work practice*. By the same token, a crucial attribute of a good research question is whether it addresses the decision-making needs of agencies or practical problems in social welfare. This does not mean that researchers must ask planners, practitioners, administrators, or other significant social welfare figures to select research questions for them (although getting feedback from those individuals about their needs and priorities is a valuable step in the process). Inspiration for useful research questions can come from many sources—sometimes it's something you read, something you observe in an agency, or something a colleague says to you. Sometimes a neat idea pops into your head from out of the blue.

7.4a Feasibility

Another attribute of a good research question is whether it will be feasible to answer it. If you lack the means or cooperation to conduct the sort of study needed to answer the research question you have posed, then that question won't work for you. You'll need to change it to a question that you have the resources to investigate adequately. Experienced and inexperienced researchers alike find it much easier to conceive rigorous, valuable studies than to figure out how they can actually implement them. One of the most difficult problems that confront researchers is how to make a study feasible without making the research question so narrow that it is no longer worth investigating, or without sacrificing too much methodological rigor or inferential capacity. Inexperienced researchers commonly formulate idealistic, far-reaching studies and then become immobilized when they find out how much they must scale down their plans if their study is to be feasible. With seasoning, we learn how to strike a happy medium—that is, we learn to formulate and appreciate those research questions that are not so narrow that they are no longer worth doing, yet not so grandiose that they are not feasible to investigate.

Common issues in determining the feasibility of a study are its scope, the time it will require, its fiscal costs, ethical considerations, and the cooperation it will require from others. The fiscal costs of a study are easily underestimated. Common expenses are personnel costs, computer costs for data processing and analysis, travel to collect data, printing and copying expenses, data collection instruments, and postage. Postage costs are easily underestimated— bulky questionnaires may require more stamps than expected, and nonresponse problems may necessitate multiple mailings. In each mailing, we also may need to enclose a stamped return envelope. Personnel costs commonly involve the hiring of interviewers, coders, and data entry personnel for computer processing.

Time constraints also may turn out to be much worse than anticipated. Inexperienced researchers in particular may underestimate the time required to recruit participants for the study, or to make multiple follow-up contacts to urge survey nonrespondents to complete and mail in their questionnaires. Scheduled interviews are often missed or canceled, requiring the scheduling of additional ones. Time may be needed to develop and test data collection instruments, perhaps through several dry runs, before actual data collection takes place. A great deal of unanticipated time may be needed to reformulate the problem and revise the study based on unexpected obstacles encountered in trying to implement the research. And, of course, time is needed for each additional phase of the research process: data processing and analysis, writing the report, and so forth.

One time constraint that can be extremely frustrating is obtaining advance authorization for the study. Approval may need to be secured from a variety of sources, such as agency administrators and practitioners, the agency board, and a human subjects review committee that assesses the ethics of the research. Political squabbles within an agency can impede obtaining approval for a study simply because the battling forces will be suspicious of almost anything that its adversaries support. Administrative turnover also can cause frustrating delays. You may have to delay implementing a study when, for example, an executive director moves on to another agency after you have spent considerable time involving him or her in the formulation of your research.

Sometimes, lack of cooperation in one setting forces the researcher to seek a different setting in which to implement a study. Agency members in the original setting may be skeptical about research and refuse to authorize it at all. Perhaps they fear that the research findings will embarrass the agency or certain units or staff. Perhaps in the past they have had bad experiences with other researchers who were insensitive to agency needs and procedures. A common complaint is that researchers exploit agencies so they can get the data they need for their own intellectual interests and career needs (doctoral dissertations, for example) and then give nothing back to the agency in useful findings that can help solve agency problems. Some of these agency resistances to research are quite rational, and it is a mistake to treat them lightly or to assume that they result from the insecurity or ignorance of agency members.

7.4b Involving Others in Formulating Research Questions

Several activities can enhance our chances of identifying a useful research question that is feasible for us to investigate. By engaging in these activities, we progressively sharpen the original research question and its conceptual elements in line with the above criteria. Or we may reject the original question and formulate a new one that better meets these criteria.

Obtaining critical feedback from colleagues and others is an important step in this process, one that helps us more rigorously appraise the study's utility, the clarity of our ideas, alternative ways of looking at the problem, and pragmatic or ethical considerations that pose potential obstacles to the study's feasibility. You must stress to these individuals that you are *not* looking for their approval and that you want them to be critical or skeptical. Otherwise, it may be expedient for them to think they are currying favor with you by patting you on the back, complimenting you for your initiative and fine mind, and then letting you fall on your face at no cost to themselves.

In Chapter 14, on program evaluation, we will discuss some of the steps researchers can take to try to overcome or prevent agency resistances to research. One important step is to involve all relevant agency figures as early as possible in all phases of problem formulation and research design planning. Interact with them and ask for their ideas about what needs to be done. Don't pretend to involve them solely to get their support. Be responsive to what they say, not only in the interaction but also in how you actually formulate the study. If you are responsive to their needs, and if they feel they have made a meaningful contribution to the study's design, then chances are better that they will find the study useful and will support it. The dialogue may also build a better, more trusting relationship that can dispel some anxieties about a researcher investigating something in their agency. Moreover, it may help them better understand the purpose and necessity for some of the inconveniences your methodology creates.

One last note before we leave this topic: Lack of cooperation can come not only from agency staff and board members, but also from clients or other individuals we hope will be the subjects of our research. Perhaps they will refuse to be observed or interviewed or to respond to a mailed questionnaire (particularly when the data collection procedure is cumbersome or threatening). Even if they are willing to participate, will we be able to find them? Suppose you were trying to carry out a longitudinal study of the homeless mentally ill over a period of years. Imagine how difficult it would be to keep track of them and find them for follow-up interviews (not to mention locating them in the first place for initial interviews). To ensure that your study is sensitive to the needs, lifestyles, and concerns of service consumers, do not overlook representatives of service consumers' groups when involving relevant agency figures in the research planning.

7.5 CONCEPTUALIZATION

After the research question has been formulated, the next step in the research process is conceptualization, which involves identifying the things you want to study and providing a theoretical or conceptual rationale as to how they are interrelated and why you have chosen them for study.

Suppose, for example, you want to evaluate the effectiveness of a program that aims to prevent recidivism among prison inmates by involving them in a series of small group meetings in which crime victims tell their stories of the devastating effects that the crimes had on their lives. You should provide a theoretical basis explaining why that intervention might be effective and is worth studying. You should also identify the processes by which it is expected to reduce recidivism. Thus, you might hypothesize that by hearing the victims' stories, the inmates develop more empathy for crime victims and that this new or increased empathy might be the reason they become less likely to commit crimes after release from prison. If so, then you would also identify empathy as something you will want to measure in your study, along with recidivism. That is, does the intervention increase empathy, and is the increased empathy associated with less recidivism? Also, you will need to define what you mean by empathy and how it will be observed. This will in turn set the stage for planning the measurement phase of your study, which we will discuss in the next chapter.

The nature of your conceptualization and measurement will vary depending on whether your study is using quantitative or qualitative research methods (or both). As we discussed in Chapter 3, studies following a quantitative process typically attempt to define in advance and in precise, observable terms all the things that the study will observe. Studies following a qualitative process might have an elaborate theoretical framework but are less likely to attempt to anticipate all the important things that might be observed, and less likely to attempt to define them in advance in precise and observable terms. Essentially, qualitative studies tend to use a more flexible, open-ended approach that allows research procedures and lines of inquiry to evolve as more observations are gathered and new insights are generated. Because quantitative and qualitative methods of inquiry differ with respect to the conceptualization and measurement phases, we'll look at each type separately. Let's begin with the essential features of quantitative approaches to conceptualization.

7.6 CONCEPTUALIZATION IN QUANTITATIVE INQUIRY

EP 2.1.6b

The concepts that researchers plan to investigate are called *variables*. A **concept** is a mental image that symbolizes an idea, an object, an event, a behavior, a person, and so on. We can also think of concepts as words that people agree upon to symbolize something. The words can represent something relatively easy to observe, like gender, height, residence, ethnicity, or age. Or they can represent something more difficult to observe, like level of self-esteem, morale, level of social functioning, racism, sexism, ageism, homophobia, and so on.

Instead of just sticking to the term *concepts*, we call the concepts investigated by researchers **variables** because they must be expected to vary in order to be worth studying. For example, the term *empathy* is a concept, but we are not likely to research it unless we think that the level of empathy varies among different individuals who have different characteristics or experiences.

When concepts vary, we call the different variations or categories of the concept **attributes**. Gender, for example, is a variable that consists of the

---

concept A mental image that symbolizes an idea, an object, an event, a behavior, or a person.

variable A concept being investigated that is characterized by different attributes.

attributes Characteristics of persons or things.

relationship Variables changing together in a consistent, predictable fashion.

hypothesis A tentative and testable statement about how changes in one variable are expected to explain changes in another variable.

---

attributes "male" and "female." Likewise, social class is a variable composed of a set of attributes such as "upper class," "middle class," "lower class," or some similar set of divisions. Thus, a variable is a concept being investigated that is characterized by different attributes.

Suppose we want to investigate whether the effectiveness of the program to build victim empathy among prison inmates is different for male and female inmates. In this case, one variable might be "program attendance," and it would be characterized by the attributes "attended" and "did not attend" (referring to each individual inmate and whether or not each attended the program). Another variable would be "inmate gender," and it would be characterized by the attributes male and female. Another variable would be "level of empathy," and it would be characterized by attributes at higher or lower levels of empathy. A third variable might pertain to "postrelease outcome," and it might be characterized by the attributes "rearrested" and "not rearrested." Perhaps we would find that participation in the program led to higher levels of empathy and fewer rearrests only among women.

Not all researchers use the term *attributes*, however, when referring to the categories of their variables. Some might instead use the term *categories*. You should realize that the terms *attributes* and *categories* mean the same thing when researchers are mentioning them in reference to their variables. Other researchers might use the term *values* to mean the same thing as the attributes or categories of their variables. Although that term can be synonymous with the terms *attributes* and *categories*, it is more likely to be used than the other two terms when the categories of the variable in question are numeric, such as with variables such as age, score on a test, and so on.

In many quantitative studies, the researchers predict in advance the relationships they expect to find between or among variables. By **relationship**, we simply mean that a change in one variable is likely to be associated with a change in the other variable. In the above example, for instance, they might have predicted in advance that participation in the program would lead to increased empathy or fewer rearrests (or both). That prediction would be called a hypothesis. A **hypothesis** is a tentative and testable statement about how changes in one variable are expected to explain changes in another variable. In other words, hypotheses are tentative statements that predict what we expect to find about the way our variables covary (vary together). Thus, the hypothesis that participation in the program would lead to fewer rearrests consists of two variables: (1) whether inmates participate in the program and (2) whether (or how often) they are rearrested.

Most hypotheses predict which variable influences the other—in other words, which is the cause and which the effect. A variable that explains or causes something is called the **independent variable**. It is called independent because it is doing the explaining or causing, and is not dependent on the other variable. Conversely, the variable being explained or caused—that is, the variable that is the effect—is called the **dependent variable**. In the foregoing hypothesis, for example, whether inmates participate in the program constitutes the independent variable, and whether (or how often) they are rearrested constitutes the dependent variable.

7.6a Developing a Proper Hypothesis

EP 2.1.10m

A good hypothesis has some of the attributes of a good research question. It should be clear and specific and have more than one possible outcome. It should also be value-free and testable.

For example, the statement, "Welfare reform legislation should be repealed," is not a hypothesis. It is a judgmental recommendation, not a predicted relationship between two variables that is stated in terms that can be verified or refuted. If we modify the statement to read, "Welfare reform is harmful to the children of welfare recipients," we have made it sound more like a hypothesis. But it would still not qualify as a proper hypothesis statement. Although it is predicting that a concept, welfare reform, is harming children, it is not clear and specific regarding the nature of the harm—that is, the specific nature of the concept that is meant to be the dependent variable. Moreover, the concept intended as the independent variable, welfare reform, is also vague. What specific aspect of welfare reform are we referring to? We could change the statement into a good hypothesis by being more

clear and specific about both variables. One way to do so would be to postulate, "Welfare reform policies that move parents off welfare by increasing recipient work requirements will increase the number of children who lack health insurance coverage." The latter statement predicts a relationship between two clearly stated variables that can be verified or refuted by examining whether increases in the number of children who lack health insurance coverage occur after such policies are implemented or by examining whether states that implement such policies have greater increases in the number of children who lack health insurance coverage than do states not implementing them.

7.6b Mediating and Moderating Variables

Additional variables can affect the relationship between the independent and dependent variables. **Mediating variables**, for example, can be the mechanisms by which independent variables affect dependent variables. If we think our intervention reduces recidivism by first increasing prisoner empathy for crime victims, then "level of empathy for crime victims" would be our mediating variable. It would come between our independent variable (whether prisoners receive the intervention) and our dependent variable (whether they get rearrested for another crime). In other words, we would be conceptualizing a causal chain in which the independent variable affects the mediating variable, which in turn affects the dependent variable, as illustrated in Figure 7.1. Because mediating variables come between independent and dependent variables, they also can be called *intervening variables*.

Moderating variables are those that are not influenced by the independent variable, but that

---

independent variable A variable that explains or causes a dependent variable.

dependent variable A variable that is being explained or caused by an independent variable.

mediating variable (intervening variable) The mechanism by which an independent variable affects a dependent variable.

moderating variable A variable that influences the strength or direction of a relationship between independent and dependent variables.

FIGURE 7.1 Illustration of a Mediating (or Intervening) Variable

can affect the strength or direction of the relationship between the independent and dependent variables. Thus, if we predict that our intervention will be effective only among female inmates and not among male inmates, "gender" would be a moderating variable. Likewise, if we predict that our intervention will be effective only among offenders who committed nonviolent crimes, then "type of crime" would be a moderating variable.

Sometimes moderating variables represent alternative explanations for relationships that are observed between independent and dependent variables. Suppose, for example, that the economy improves at the same time that a new welfare policy is implemented. If the living standards of poor people improve after the policy has been implemented, then "change in the economy" (the moderating variable) might be the real reason for the change in the dependent variable (living standards). Perhaps our independent variable (change in welfare policy) has nothing to do with the dependent variable, or perhaps its effect on the dependent variable is weakened when we take changes in the economy into account.

As noted above, sometimes the direction of a relationship between an independent and dependent variable can be reversed when a moderating variable is taken into account. Suppose that a study finds that the more social services that are received by hospital patients, the shorter their life span. That relationship would probably be explained away by the fact that the cases involving the most serious illnesses—particularly terminal

illnesses—need to receive more social services. Thus, severity of illness might be conceptualized as a moderating variable. If we examine the impact of social services separately for patients with the most severe illnesses, we might find that among those patients, receiving more social services actually lengthens life span.

7.6c Controlling for the Effects of Variables

Authors of studies that examine the impact of moderating variables sometimes refer to moderating variables as **control variables**. That's because those variables are controlled for in the study design. For example, a study might separate all cases into subgroups according to seriousness of illness. For the sake of simplicity, assume it would divide them into only two groups: (1) those with life-threatening illnesses, and (2) those whose illnesses are not life-threatening. Next, it would assess the relationship between life span and amount of social services received just for those cases with life-threatening illnesses. Then it would do the same just for those cases whose illnesses are not life-threatening. Thus, it would be controlling for seriousness of illness by examining whether the original relationship between the independent and dependent variables changes or stays the same for each level of serious illness. The term *control* in this context does not mean that the researcher has control over the nature of the illness. It simply means that the researcher examines the hypothesized relationship separately for each category of the control variable. If the original relationship disappears when a third variable is controlled for, it means that the original relationship was *spurious*. Thus, a **spurious relationship** is one that no longer exists when a third variable is controlled. Figure 7.2 provides a pictorial illustration of the type of spurious relationship we have been discussing.

---

control variable   A moderating variable that we seek to control by holding it constant in our research design.

spurious relationship   A relationship between two variables that are no longer related when a third variable is controlled.

FIGURE 7.2 Illustrations of a Spurious Causal Relationship That Disappears When Controlling for a Third Variable

Spurious Causal Relationship:
Social services in health care increase risk of death
(Arrows indicate incorrect causal interpretation.)

Amount of social
services provided
to patient and family   Patient death rate

More   ⟹   Higher

Less   ⟹   Lower

Actual Causal Relationship:
Severity of illness affects both the amount of social
services and the risk of death
(Receiving more social services is associated with a higher
death rate only because terminally ill patients receive more social services.)
(Arrows indicate correct causal interpretation.)

Terminal   Severity of   Not Terminal
                  Patient's
                  Illness

More Social   Higher Death   Less Social   Lower Death
Services   Rate   Services   Rate

7.6d Constants

Another way to control for the effects of a variable is to study only cases sharing one particular attribute of that variable. For example, by studying only women, you rule out any effect that gender might have on the variables under study. Likewise, in the above health care spurious relationship researchers might include only those cases with terminal illnesses in the study and then assess the impact of social services with those cases and no others. Although such a study would *control* for any potentially misleading findings that would result from also including cases with less severe illnesses (such as the spurious finding that recipients of social services are more likely to have shorter life spans), severity of illness would *not* be a control (moderating) variable. It would not be a variable because it would not *vary* in the study since only one of its categories had been included. Nevertheless, the researchers could correctly say that they controlled for the effects of that variable by including only one of its attributes and thus not letting its variation confound the study results. The correct terminology in such an instance would be to refer to terminal illness as a **constant.**

Although it is incorrect to call a *constant* a *variable*, it is not uncommon to hear researchers

correctly say that they *controlled* for the effects of a particular variable by holding it constant. It is therefore an understandable technical mistake when some refer to a constant as a control variable. For example, a common mistake is to call gender a control variable in studies that include only males or only females in their samples. Nevertheless, it would be correct to say that such studies control for the effects of gender by including men, only, or females, only (e.g., treating it as a constant). Likewise, if an evaluation of the effectiveness of an intervention for PTSD excludes from its sample clients who are at risk for suicide, it would be correct to depict the study as controlling for the potential impact of suicidality by holding it constant, but technically incorrect to call suicidality a control variable.

7.6e The Same Concept Can Be a Different Type of Variable in Different Studies

Most concepts can be an independent, dependent, mediating, or moderating variable, depending on how they are being conceptualized in a particular study. For example, although type of intervention is more commonly conceptualized as an independent variable, some studies can conceptualize it as a dependent variable. To illustrate, a study could hypothesize that the type of intervention received by clients of practitioners with social work degrees will be different than the type received by practitioners with degrees in other fields. Thus, "type of degree" would be the independent variable, and "type of intervention" would be the dependent variable (because the latter is being influenced by the kind of degree held by the practitioner).

EP 2.1.6b

You should also realize that whether a variable is independent or dependent does not depend on the sequence in which it is specified in the hypothesis. For example, if we postulate that case management intervention is more likely to be provided by practitioners with social work degrees, then "type of intervention" can be the dependent variable even though it is specified first in the hypothesis. This

constant   One attribute that is included in a study without including other attributes of the same variable.

can be confusing, because even though the cause must happen before the effect, putting the effect first in the hypothesis does not mean you are saying that it will happen first.

Another thing to remember is that the same concept can be a variable in one study and a constant in another. For example, if we include both men and women in our study, then gender could be an independent variable or a moderating variable. But if we include only men, or only women, then the concept of gender is being held constant.

7.6f Types of Relationships between Variables

EP 2.1.6b

Some hypotheses predict a positive, negative (inverse), or curvilinear relationship between variables. In a **positive relationship**, the dependent variable increases as the independent variable increases (or decreases as the independent variable decreases)—that is, *both variables move in the same direction.* Thus, we might postulate a positive relationship between the amount of symbolic rewards citizens receive for participating in community organizations and the extent to which they participate.

We might also postulate a positive relationship between client satisfaction with social services and the extent to which the delivered service focused on the problem or goal for which the client originally sought help (as opposed to a problem or goal that the practitioner chose to work on without involving the client in the decision). The top graph in Figure 7.3 pictorially represents this hypothesized positive relationship.

---

positive relationship A relationship in which the dependent variable increases as the independent variable increases (or decreases as the independent variable decreases)—that is, both variables move in the same direction.

negative, or inverse, relationship A relationship between two variables that move in opposite directions—that is, as one increases, the other decreases.

curvilinear relationship A relationship in which the nature of the relationship changes at certain levels of the variables.

FIGURE 7.3 Graphic Display of Types of Hypothetical Relationships between Variables

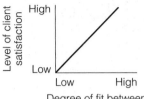

1. POSITIVE RELATIONSHIP

The better the fit between the client's reason for seeking help and the service goal formulated by the practitioner, the higher the client satisfaction.

2. NEGATIVE RELATIONSHIP

The lower the family income, the higher the level of family stress.

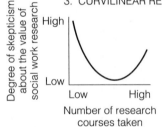

3. CURVILINEAR RELATIONSHIP

Skepticism decreases as students take more research courses up to a point, but after that skepticism increases as more research courses are taken.

A **negative, or inverse, relationship** means that the two variables move in opposite directions— that is, *as one increases, the other decreases.* We might postulate a negative relationship between the caseload size of direct-service practitioners and their degree of effectiveness, because those whose caseloads are too large might be expected to have less time to provide quality services. A negative relationship might also be postulated between family income and level of family stress. The middle graph in Figure 7.3 pictorially represents this hypothesized negative relationship.

A **curvilinear relationship** is one in which the nature of the relationship changes at certain levels of the variables. For example, some social work educators believe that the students who are most skeptical about the value of published social work research are those who have either taken many research courses or none at all. Those who have never had a research course may not yet have learned to appreciate research's potential utility. Those with a great deal of knowledge about research might be disillusioned by the many serious methodological flaws they detect in much of the published research. Consequently, those with the least skepticism may be the ones in the middle—those who have enough knowledge to appreciate the value of good research but have not yet critically scrutinized enough of the literature to realize how many published studies are seriously flawed. Educators who believe this notion might hypothesize a U-curve that begins with a negative relationship between the number of courses taken and the degree of skepticism about research, and ends with a positive relationship between them. In other words, skepticism decreases as more courses are taken up to a certain number of courses, then it increases as more courses are taken beyond that. The bottom graph in Figure 7.3 pictorially represents this hypothesized curvilinear relationship.

7.6g Operational Definitions

EP 2.1.10m

As we noted, a concept is a variable if (1) it is characterized by more than one attribute, or value, and thus is capable of varying; and (2) it is chosen for investigation in a research study. In quantitative research studies, a third condition must be met before a concept can be called a variable: It must be translated into observable terms. The term **operational definition** refers to that translation—that is, to the operations (or indicators) we will use to determine the attribute we observe about a particular concept. Thus, a family's "risk of child abuse" could be operationally defined as a score on the Family Risk Scale (a scale completed by child welfare workers based on their observations of the family).

Operational definitions differ from nominal definitions. **Nominal definitions** can be like dictionary definitions: conceptual or theoretical definitions. They use a set of words to help us understand what a term means, but do not tell us what indicators to use in observing the term in a research study. For example, a nominal definition of social

adjustment might be "appropriate performance of one's major roles in life"—as parent, student, employee, spouse, and so on. This definition may give us clues about how we might develop an operational definition, but it does not specify precisely what indicators we will observe and the exact categories of social adjustment we will note in our research on social adjustment.

We can operationally define abstract variables in many ways. One operational definition of social adjustment might be a score on a scale that measures level of social adjustment. Another operational definition might be whether an individual is receiving social services aimed at restoring social functioning. Those who receive such services might be categorized as having lower levels of social adjustment than others who do not receive them. Here's a contrasting example: In an institutional facility for the severely developmentally disabled, our operational definition might identify individuals with higher levels of social adjustment as those whose case records indicate that they are deemed by staff to be ready to be placed in a sheltered workshop. Operational definitions point the way to how a variable will be measured.

To summarize, an operational definition and a nominal definition are two different ways to define the same concept. One way (nominal) helps us understand the conceptual or theoretical meaning of the concept. The other way (operational) tells us how it will be observed.

7.6h The Influence of Operational Definitions

How we choose to operationally define a variable can greatly influence our research findings. Suppose a community organizer wants to study factors that influence citizen participation in a barrio in Los Angeles. Her results may vary depending on

operational definition A definition of a variable that identifies the observable indicators that will be used to determine that variable's attributes.

nominal definition A dictionary-like definition that uses a set of words to help us understand what a term means, but does not tell us what indicators to use in observing the term in a research study.

whether she operationally defines citizen participation as attendance by barrio residents at meetings of a social action organization, their attendance at city government meetings where issues of concern to the barrio are being discussed, contacts they make with governmental officials, or participation in protest demonstrations. The factors that motivate people to attend a protest demonstration might be different than those that motivate them to attend a meeting or to write their city council member.

Suppose we want to evaluate a child welfare program aimed at preventing child abuse and preserving families. If we operationally define child abuse rates in terms of the number of children placed in foster care, and the program reduces that number, the program would be deemed successful. However, what if the rate of abuse actually increases because so few children at great risk for abuse were not placed in foster care? Had the operational definition of "child abuse rates" included other indicators of abuse, the same program, with the same results, might have been considered a failure.

7.6i Alternative Sources of Data for Operational Definitions in Social Work

EP 2.1.10m

Typically, we use three broad categories of choices for operationally defining variables in social work: self-reports, direct observation, and the examination of available records. These options are also called *sources of data*. In Chapters 8 and 13 we will discuss each of these sources in more depth, including the strengths and weaknesses of each. At this point, however, we will limit our focus to how they come into play as different ways to operationally define variables.

In a study on marital problems, you might simply ask the couples involved if they have recently sought help for marital problems. In this case you would be using **self-reports** as the source of data.

---

self-reports A source of data that can be used when operationally defining variables according to what people say about their own thoughts, views, or behaviors.

direct observation A source of data that can be used when operationally defining variables based on observing actual behavior.

You might consider those who answer "Yes" to have less marital satisfaction than those who say "No." Similarly, you might just ask the couples whether they consider themselves to have high, medium, or low degrees of marital satisfaction. You might understandably have some qualms about whether the answers you get are sufficiently accurate and objective indicators of marital satisfaction, and we are not necessarily recommending either approach. However, you should understand that either one would be an operational definition.

There can be very different ways to operationally define the same variable using self-reports. For example, a more thorough self-report option would be an existing scale previously devised to measure marital satisfaction. You would ask each person in your study to complete the scale. The higher the score on the scale, the more marital satisfaction. (If both spouses respond, perhaps you would add both scores to get a combined score per couple.) Existing scales that have been formulated to measure certain constructs build the indicators of the construct into the scale. Thus, a scale to measure marital satisfaction might ask either spouse how often he or she is annoyed with the spouse, has fun with the spouse, feels he or she can rely on the spouse, wants to be with the spouse, is proud of the spouse, feels controlled by the spouse, resents the spouse, and so on. Each item on the scale gets a score, and the scores are summed for a total score of marital satisfaction. For instance, an individual might get a score of 5 for each positive item (such as "feeling proud of spouse") to which he or she responds "Always" and for each negative item (such as "resenting the spouse") to which the response is "Never." If there are 20 items on the scale and the individual responds "Always" to every positive item and "Never" to every negative item, then the total score would be 100. This total would indicate that this person had more marital satisfaction than another person who responded "Sometimes" to every item, receiving a score of, say, 3 for every item and therefore a total score of 60.

Alternatively, you might interview each couple about their marriage and count the number of times either partner makes a derogatory statement about the marriage or the spouse. This option would be using **direct observation** as the source of data. If you go this route, you'll have to grapple with the ground rules for considering a statement

Operationally Defining Positive Parenting: Illustration of Three Sources of Data for Operationalization Choices

Suppose you work in a state child welfare agency that is evaluating an innovative intervention program to improve positive parenting among parents referred for child abuse or neglect. The agency's assumption is that by improving positive parenting skills it will reduce the incidence of child neglect and abuse. Several similar counties have been selected for the evaluation. Some counties will implement the new program, and some comparable counties will receive the traditional program. The hypothesis for the evaluation is that parents referred for child abuse or neglect in the counties receiving the innovative

program will improve their parenting more than their counterparts in the counties receiving the traditional program. An important task in designing the evaluation is developing an operational definition of the dependent variable "positive parenting." You have been given that task. Three sources of data that can be used for the operational definition are illustrated in Figure 7.4, along with how each could be used in testing the hypothesis. The illustrations are just some of the ways you could operationally define positive parenting. You may be able to come up with some superior alternatives.

derogatory. Perhaps you'll just have to leave that to the judgment of the interviewer and see whether an independent observer (perhaps viewing a videotape of the interview) tends to agree with the interviewer's counts. We'll say more about this when we discuss sources of data and the concept of *reliability* in the next chapter.

Another way to use direct observation might be to ask the spouses to conduct a typical 15-minute conversation while you observe and count the number of times they interrupt one another, raise their voices, or make various physical gestures that seem to indicate frustration or dissatisfaction with the other. This can be tricky. If the couple is disagreeing about an intellectual or political issue (such as foreign policy, for example), perhaps the partners actually enjoy having heated, animated debates. Although you have an observable definition, you might wonder whether it is really measuring marital satisfaction. We'll get into that issue as well in the next chapter when we discuss self-reports and the concept of *validity*.

Of course, we might attempt to operationally define marital satisfaction in many other ways. For example, if we are doing cross-cultural research, we might compare divorce rates in different geographic areas as one operational indicator of marital satisfaction. This illustrates the use of **available records** as the source of data. Again, this does not mean that such rates would be a true indicator of the construct, just that they would be operational. Perhaps the culture with the lower divorce rates has no more marital satisfaction, just stricter taboos against divorce. Probably the most commonly used source

of available data in social work research is agency case records. We will say more about that source in the next chapter.

The box titled "Operationally Defining Positive Parenting: Illustration of Three Sources of Data for Operationalization Choices" and the accompanying Figure 7.4 further illustrate alternative ways to operationally define variables and some of the advantages and disadvantages of each alternative.

7.6j Existing Scales

Although responses to existing scales do not necessarily accurately reflect actual behavior, existing scales are a popular way to operationally define variables. They spare researchers the costs in time and money of devising **EP 2.1.10d** their own measures, and provide an option that has been used successfully to measure the concept in previous studies. Therefore, let's examine how you find relevant scales and salient information about them.

The most thorough procedure would be to conduct a literature review on the construct you seek to measure. For example, you might review the literature on marital satisfaction to locate materials that report measures of marital satisfaction. Of course, this would be a relatively quick literature review,

---

available records   A source of data for a study, in which the information of concern has already been collected by others.

FIGURE 7.4 Sources of Data for Choices for Operationally Defining Level of Positive Parenting

Category	Operational Definition	Testing the Hypothesis	Some Advantages and Disadvantages
Direct Observation	You might begin by making a list of positive parenting behaviors—praising, encouraging, modeling, consistency, use of time-outs, and so on. Another list might specify undesirable parenting behaviors—threatening, slapping, screaming, criticizing, bribing, belittling, and so on. Then you might *directly observe* the parents or foster parents in a challenging parenting situation (such as getting children to put away their toys) and count the number of times the parents show positive and negative behaviors. Perhaps you will give them +1 for every positive behavior and −1 for every negative behavior; tally up the points to get a parenting skill score.	See if the average scores of parents in the counties receiving the innovative program are higher (better) than the average scores of parents in the counties receiving the traditional program.	Advantages: 1. Behaviors are observed first-hand. Disadvantages: 1. Time-consuming. 2. Parents will know they are being observed and may not behave the same as when they are not being observed. 3. Possibility of observer bias.
Self-Report	Ask the parents to complete an *existing self-report scale* that purports to measure knowledge or attitudes about parenting. Such a scale might ask parents questions about what they would do in various child-rearing situations or how they perceive various normal childhood behaviors that some parents misperceive as provocative.	See if the average scale scores of parents in the counties receiving the innovative program are better than the average scale scores of parents in the counties receiving the traditional program.	Advantages: 1. Less costly and less time-consuming than direct observation. 2. If scales are completed anonymously, parents might be more likely to reveal undesirable attitudes. Disadvantages: 1. Parents might distort their true attitudes to convey a more socially desirable impression. 2. The scale may not be valid. 3. Knowledge and attitudes may not always reflect actual behaviors.
Examination of Available Records	Examine county records of the number of documented incidents of child abuse and neglect.	See if the number of documented incidents of child abuse and neglect in the counties receiving the innovative program is lower than the number in the counties receiving the traditional program.	Advantages: 1. Less costly and time-consuming than either direct observation or self-report. 2. You don't have to assume that positive parenting knowledge and skills translate into less abuse; you measure abuse per se. Disadvantages: 1. Reliance on adequacy of county records. 2. Won't show whether the parents who received your intervention improved their parenting. 3. Possibility of biased reporting.

FIGURE 7.5 Reference Volumes for Existing Scales That Can Operationally Define Variables in Social Work

American Psychiatric Association. 2000. *Handbook of Psychiatric Measures.* Washington, DC: American Psychiatric Association.

Beere, C. A. 1990. *Sex and Gender Issues: A Handbook of Tests and Measures.* New York: Greenwood Press.

Corcoran, K. J., and J. Fischer. 2000a. *Measures for Clinical Practice, Vol. 1, Couples, Families, Children* (3rd ed.). New York: Free Press.

Corcoran, K. J., and J. Fischer. 2000b. *Measures for Clinical Practice, Vol. 2, Adults* (3rd ed.). New York: Free Press.

Hudson, W. W. 1982. *The Clinical Measurement Package: A Field Manual.* Homewood, IL: Dorsey Press.

LaGreca, A. M. 1990. *Through the Eyes of the Child:Obtaining Self-Reports from Children and Adolescents.* Boston: Allyn & Bacon.

Magura, S., and B. S. Moses. 1987. *Outcome Measures for Child Welfare Services.* Washington, DC: Child Welfare League of America.

Martin, R. P. 1988. *Assessment of Personality and Behavior Problems: Infancy through Adolescence.* New York: Guilford Press.

Maruish, M. E. 2000. *Handbook of Psychological Assessment in Primary Care Settings.* Mahwah, NJ: Erlbaum.

Maruish, M. E. (ed.). 2002. *Psychological Testing in the Age of Managed Behavioral Health Care.* Mahwah, NJ: Erlbaum.

McCubbin, H. I., and A. I. Thompson (eds.). 1987. *Family Assessment Inventions for Research and Practice.* Madison: University of Wisconsin–Madison.

Mullen, E. J., and J. L. Magnabosco (eds.). 1997. *Outcomes Measurement in the Human Services.* Washington, DC: NASW Press.

Ogles, B. M., and K. S. Masters. 1996. *Assessing Outcome in Clinical Practice.* Boston: Allyn & Bacon.

Ollendick, T. H., and M. Hersen. 1992. *Handbook of Child and Adolescent Assessment.* Des Moines, IA: Allyn & Bacon.

Sawin, K. J., M. P. Harrigan, and P. Woog (eds.). 1995. *Measures of Family Functioning for Research and Practice.* New York: Springer.

Suzuki, L., P. J. Meller, and J. G. Ponterotto (eds.). 1996. *Handbook of Multicultural Assessment.* San Francisco, CA: Jossey-Bass.

because the purpose is to locate measures of a construct, not to review all the research on the construct.

One way to expedite the search for measures is to consult reference volumes that list and describe many existing measures. Figure 7.5 lists a number of volumes that might be useful. Some of them reprint the actual measurement instrument; others describe it and provide additional references. Usually, they will discuss the quality of the instrument (such as its reliability and validity) and tell you how to obtain it and more information about it. You will also be told whether it's copyrighted, which will indicate whether you must purchase it or use it with the author's permission.

Let's now examine criteria we would use in selecting an existing scale as an operational definition. Beginning on a practical note, we might ask: How lengthy is the scale? Will it take too long for the participants in your study to complete? Suppose, for example, a lengthy scale that takes more than an hour to complete was tested on people who were paid $20 to complete the scale. Its success under those circumstances would not be relevant to a study of busy people who were mailed the scale and asked to volunteer that much time—without pay—to complete and mail back the scale.

Another practical question is whether the scale will be too difficult for your participants to complete. For example, will it be too cumbersome or too complexly worded for them? Suppose you want to study depression among undocumented immigrants from Mexico. Chances are you would not be able to use a scale that was developed to assess depression among American college students, no matter how successful it proved to be with the latter population.

If your study seeks to measure change over time (perhaps before and after receiving a social work intervention), you will need a scale that is sensitive to small changes over relatively short periods. Some clients, after being treated for low self-esteem, for example, might still have lower self-esteem compared to the rest of the population but higher self-esteem than they did before the intervention. Some self-esteem scales might be able to detect this movement, while others might not, simply indicating that these people have much lower self-esteem than the rest of the population.

Two critical issues to consider in choosing a scale are its reliability and validity. In the next chapter we'll discuss in depth these two terms, which deal with consistency of instruments and whether they really measure what they intend to measure. For now, we'll just note that the reference literature on existing scales will usually report whatever reliability and validity figures have been established for a particular scale. But you should interpret those figures with caution. If they are based on studies that tested the instrument on a population dissimilar to yours or under study conditions unlike those of your study, they may have no bearing on the instrument's suitability for your particular study. No matter how reliable and valid the reference literature says a scale may be, you may find that you have to modify it for your particular study, or that you cannot use it at all. You should also realize that existing scales are often used in more than one source of data. For example, children could complete a scale themselves to *self-report* how often they engage in certain behaviors. Alternatively, or in addition to the child's self-report, an adult (such as the child's parent, teacher, or cottage parent) could complete a scale to report how often the child engaged in those behaviors based on their *direct observation* of the child.

7.6k Levels of Measurement

Variables can be operationally defined at one or more of four levels of measurement: nominal, ordinal, interval, and ratio. At the **nominal level of measurement**, variables are defined in terms of

---

nominal level of measurement   A level of measurement that describes variables (such as gender or ethnicity) whose different attributes are categorical only, and can be described in terms of how many cases are in each category of the variable, but not degree of the variable.

ordinal level of measurement   A level of measurement describing variables whose attributes may be rank-ordered according to degree. An example would be socioeconomic status as composed of the attributes high, medium, and low.

interval level of measurement   A level of measurement that describes variables (such as IQ or Fahrenheit temperature) whose attributes are rank-ordered and have equal distances between adjacent attributes, but which do not have a true zero point.

ratio level of measurement   A level of measurement that describes variables (such as age or number of children) whose attributes have all the qualities of interval measures and are also based on a true zero point.

qualitative attributes that are categorical only. For example, defining social adjustment in terms of whether a person is receiving social services (yes or no) is at the nominal level of measurement. So is defining it in terms of whether a person is deemed ready for a sheltered workshop (again, yes or no). Other examples of variables at the nominal level of measurement are gender, ethnicity, and birthplace. It makes no sense to assess how much a person is male or born in Mexico. They either are or they aren't.

Variables at the **ordinal level of measurement** can be rank-ordered in that different attributes represent relatively more or less of the variable. But the differences between the attributes are not precise. At the ordinal level, we know only whether one case has more or less of something than another case, but we don't know how much more. For example, we have an ordinal measure if we know that the horse Seabiscuit won the race and the talking TV horse Mr. Ed came in second, but we don't know by how much. Likewise, if clients say they are very satisfied with Service A, but only slightly satisfied with Service B, then we have an ordinal measure because we don't know the precise difference in degree of satisfaction.

In contrast, with variables at the **interval level of measurement**, differences between different levels have the same meanings. Thus, the difference between IQ scores of 95 and 100 is considered to be of the same magnitude as the difference between 100 and 105. If social adjustment is defined in terms of a practitioner's rating of low, medium, and high, it is no longer at the nominal level because the different categories represent higher or lower degrees of adjustment. However, it would not be at the interval level because the differences between low, medium and high are quite imprecise. It would be at the ordinal level because we cannot assume that the difference between low and medium is the same as the difference between medium and high.

Variables at the **ratio level of measurement** have the same attributes as interval measures, but in addition have a true zero point. Thus, a person can have no arrests, one arrest, two arrests, and so on. Because there is a true zero point, we know that the person with four arrests has been arrested exactly twice as many times as the person with

FIGURE 7.6 Levels of Measurement

Nominal Measure Example: Sex

Male   Female

Ordinal Measure Example: Religiosity
"How important is religion to you?"

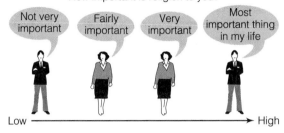

Not very important   Fairly important   Very important   Most important thing in my life

Low ⟶ High

Interval Measure Example: IQ

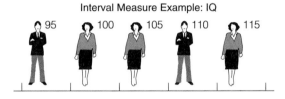

95   100   105   110   115

Ratio Measure Example: Income

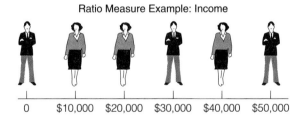

0    $10,000 $20,000 $30,000 $40,000 $50,000

two arrests. Figure 7.6 presents a graphic illustration of the four levels of measurement.

Above, we mentioned nominal definitions and contrasted them with operational definitions. Using the term *nominal* in connection to definitions is different than using it in connection to levels of measurement. For example, a nominal definition of income such as the amount of money earned implies a ratio level of measurement (exact amount earned), or at least an ordinal level of measurement (poverty level, middle class, affluent, and so on).

7.7 CONCEPTUALIZATION IN QUALITATIVE INQUIRY

EP 2.1.3a

Very often, the specification of reliable operational definitions seems to rob such concepts of their richness of meaning. For example, level of marital satisfaction involves much more than whether a couple is receiving marital counseling. Recognizing this, qualitatively oriented researchers do not restrict their observations to predetermined operational indicators. Instead, they emphasize methodological freedom and flexibility so that the most salient variables, and their deeper meanings, will emerge as they immerse themselves in the phenomena they are studying. In fact, the term *operationalization* is virtually absent from most texts that deal exclusively with qualitative research methods.

Here are three reasons for not operationally defining variables in advance in qualitative studies. First, we may not know in advance what all the most salient variables are. Second, limitations in our understanding of the variables we think are important may keep us from anticipating the best way to operationally define those variables. Third, even the best operational definitions are necessarily superficial, because they are specified only in terms of observable indicators. Although operational definitions are necessary in quantitative studies, they do not pertain to probing into the deeper meanings of what is observed. These deeper meanings are the purview of qualitative studies.

In a purely quantitative study, we assume that we know enough in advance about a phenomenon to pose a narrow research question about a limited set of variables, and to develop precise, objective, and observable indicators of those variables that can be counted to answer the research question. In a purely qualitative study, we assume that we need to develop a deeper understanding of a phenomenon and its subjective meanings as it occurs in its natural environment. We take it for granted that we will not be able to develop that richer understanding if we limit ourselves to observable indicators that can be anticipated in advance and counted. In qualitative research, we immerse ourselves in a more subjective fashion in open-ended, flexible observations of phenomena as they occur naturally,

Illustrations of the Qualitative Perspective on Operationalization and Its Complementarity with a Quantitative Perspective

Here are two research questions that help illustrate the qualitative perspective on operationalization, as well as its complementarity with the quantitative perspective:

Research Question 1. *Is burnout among social workers more likely to occur when they work in public welfare agencies or in private family service agencies?*

A qualitative study would not pose this research question. Instead of defining burnout operationally in terms of one or two observable indicators and then looking at it in relationship to a predetermined independent variable (or set of such variables), it might examine the experiences of a small group of social workers in depth, and attempt to portray in a richer and deeper sense what it feels like to be burned out and what it means to the social worker. The study might, for example, be in the form of a biography of the career of one or more social workers who are burned out, perhaps contrasted with a biography of one or more who are not burned out. Conceivably, the qualitative study could be done in conjunction with a quantitative study—that is, the quantitative component could look at which of the two types of agencies had more burnout, whereas the qualitative component could try to discover the underlying reasons for the quantitative differences.

Research Question 2. *Who are the most popular social work instructors: those who teach practice, research, or policy?*

A qualitative study would not pose this research question, either. Instead of using an operational definition of popularity and then seeing if it's related to the type of

course taught, it might involve observations of all aspects of instructor interactions with students in and out of the classroom, analysis of course materials, and in-depth, open-ended interviews with instructors and students to try to identify what makes instructors popular and what it means to be popular (perhaps popularity doesn't necessarily imply the most effective instruction). Identifying instructors who appear to be the most popular could be part of a qualitative study, but the point of the study would be to probe more deeply into the meaning and experience of their popularity, not to see if a particular operational indicator of popularity is quantitatively related to another predetermined variable. Rather than report numbers on how popular one group of instructors is compared to another group, a qualitative study might begin by identifying instructors who students generally agree are the most and least popular. It might then provide a wealth of information about each of those instructors, attempting to discern themes and patterns that appear to distinguish popular from unpopular instructors, or to provide the field with ideal or undesirable case study types of instructional patterns to emulate or avoid emulating. As with the previous question, the qualitative component of a study could be done in conjunction with a quantitative component. There is no reason why the hypothesis that popularity will be related to curriculum area taught could not be tested as part of a larger study that looks qualitatively at the deeper meaning of other aspects of popularity.

then try to discern patterns and themes from an immense and relatively unstructured set of observations. Also, in qualitative research, the social context of our observations is emphasized.

To illustrate the importance of social context, as well as the qualitative perspective, imagine a quantitative study that tests the hypothesis that increasing the number of home visits by child welfare practitioners will improve parental functioning and therefore preserve families. Studies like this have been done, and the dependent variable is often operationally defined in quantifiable terms of whether or not (or for how long) children are placed in foster care. A problem with many of these studies is that the increased home visitation might also increase the practitioner's awareness of neglectful or abusive

acts by parents. If so, then it is conceivable that any reductions in foster care placement because of improved parental functioning are canceled out by the increases in foster care placement because of increased practitioner monitoring. Thus, the hypothesis might not be supported even though the increased home visits are improving service outcomes.

A qualitative inquiry, in contrast, might probe into the deeper meaning and social context of the processes and outcomes in each case. Instead of merely counting the number of placements, it might learn that a foster care placement in one case, and the avoidance of a placement in another case, could both mean that the practitioner has achieved a valuable outcome. Moreover, a qualitative study might observe in detail what practitioners and clients did, probe into the deeper meanings of what was observed, and attempt to discern patterns that indicated the conditions under which practitioners appear to be more or less effective.

In describing this qualitative perspective on operational definitions, we are not implying that it is a superior one. It's neither superior nor inferior. Nor are we implying that the qualitative and quantitative perspectives are mutually exclusive. In the foregoing family preservation illustration, for example, a qualitative inquiry could be conducted simultaneously with the quantitative inquiry, and both could be part of the same study. The qualitative component could shed light on why the quantitative hypothesis was not supported. The box "Illustrations of the Qualitative Perspective on Operationalization and Its Complementarity with a Quantitative Perspective" provides two additional examples of this issue.

7.8 MAIN POINTS

- Conducting the literature review is an important early phase when planning a research study. Usually, a thorough grounding in the literature should precede, and provide a foundation for, the selection of an important topic and the formulation of a research question.
- A good research question should be narrow and specific, feasible to study, posed in a way that can be answered by observable evidence, and have significant potential relevance for guiding social welfare policy or social work practice.
- Time constraints, fiscal costs, lack of cooperation, and ethical dilemmas are essential things to consider when assessing the feasibility of a study.
- Concepts are mental images that symbolize ideas, objects, events, or people. We use concepts as summary devices for bringing together observations and experiences that seem to have something in common.
- A variable is a concept that is being investigated and that contains a logical grouping of attributes.
- A variable that explains or causes something is called the independent variable. The variable

being explained or caused is called the dependent variable.
- Hypotheses predict relationships among variables—that a change in one variable is likely to be associated with a change in the other variable.
- Hypotheses consist of independent variables (the postulated explanatory variable) and dependent variables (the variable being explained).
- Mediating variables (also called intervening variables) are the mechanisms by which independent variables affect dependent variables.
- Moderating variables influence the strength or direction of relationships between independent and dependent variables.
- Control variables are moderating variables that we seek to control by holding them constant in our research design.
- A relationship between two *variables* that are no longer related when a third variable is controlled is called a spurious relationship.
- Hypotheses should be clear and specific, value-free, testable, and have more than one possible outcome.
- Relationships between variables can be positive, negative, or curvilinear.
- Operational definitions, unlike nominal definitions, translate variables into observable terms.
- We can operationally define abstract variables in many ways.
- How we choose to operationally define a variable can greatly influence our research findings.
- Three broad categories of choices for operationally defining variables in social work include self-reports, direct observation, and the examination of available records.
- Existing self-report scales are a popular way to operationally define many social work variables, largely because they have been used successfully by others and provide cost advantages in terms of time and money, but scales need to be selected carefully and are not always the best way to operationally define a variable.
- Rather than predetermine specific, precise, objective variables and indicators to measure, qualitative studies begin with an initial set of anticipated meanings that can be refined during data collection and interpretation.

7.9 PRACTICE-RELATED EXERCISES

1. Consider a problem in social welfare in which you have a special interest (such as child abuse, mental illness, the frail elderly, and so on). Formulate a research question about the problem that it would be important for the field to answer.

2. Pick a social work concept (such as child neglect or abuse, quality of life, or level of informal social support) and operationally define that concept so that it could be studied in a research project. Be sure to specify the indicators and dimensions you wish to include (and exclude) in your operational definition.

3. Specify two hypotheses in which a particular concept is the independent variable in one hypothesis and the dependent variable in the other. Try to hypothesize one positive relationship and one negative (or inverse) relationship.

4. Describe how a qualitative researcher and a quantitative researcher might take different approaches regarding operationally defining the level of staff sensitivity to the needs of residents in nursing homes.

5. Another researcher is not sure whether to use self-reports, direct observation, or available records to operationally define the degree of staff sensitivity to the needs of residents in nursing homes. Describe the advantages and disadvantages of each approach, and the advice you would give the researcher in light of them.

6. Suppose a study found that students in research courses requiring this textbook are more likely to have productive research careers than students in research courses not using this textbook. In discussing the findings, the authors of the fictitious study noted several plausible explanations. Perhaps it is this book's use of humor that made research more interesting to students. Maybe it has to do with the many practice examples in the book. Perhaps it is not the book alone that makes the difference, but the fact that it inspires students to take additional research courses as electives. On the other hand, perhaps it is not the book per se that impacts the students' future careers. Instead, perhaps it is the case that the more effective teachers of research are more likely to require this text. Which of the above plausible explanations would you classify as a mediating variable, and which

would you classify as a moderating variable? Explain your reasoning. Don't feel you have to hold back on your praise for the book.

7.10 INTERNET EXERCISES

1. Find two quantitative research articles in the journal *Health and Social Work*. For each study, write down how the main variables in the study were operationally defined. Critically appraise the advantages and disadvantages of the operational definition used in each study. Describe how a qualitative investigation may have used a different approach to assess the same phenomena.

2. Find the article titled "Social Justice and the Research Curriculum" by John F. Longres and Edward Scanlon in the Fall 2001 issue of the journal *Health and Social Work*. Also, examine the reactions to that article (in that same issue). Based on what you read, discuss the difficulties in operationally defining the term *social justice*.

3. Go to a website developed and operated by Dr. Marianne Yoshioka, a social work professor at Columbia University. The site is called "Psychosocial Measures for Asian-American Populations" and is located at http://www.columbia.edu/cu/ssw/projects/pmap/. Download three of the abstracts of existing scales you find at the site that operationally define three different concepts. Identify the concepts that are operationally defined by the scales.

7.11 ADDITIONAL READING

Denzin, N. K., & Lincoln, Y. S. (2000). *Handbook of qualitative research* (2nd ed.). Thousand Oaks, CA: Sage. This edited volume includes informative and provocative papers, many of which illustrate how conceptualization in qualitative inquiry differs from conceptualization in quantitative inquiry.

7.11a Competency Notes

EP 2.1.3a: Distinguish, appraise, and integrate multiple sources of knowledge, including research-based knowledge (pp. 120, 135): Social workers distinguish qualitative, quantitative, and mixed methods sources of knowledge.

EP 2.1.6b: Use research evidence to inform practice (pp. 124, 127, 128): Understanding conceptualization in research enhances social workers' ability to use research evidence to inform their practice.

EP 2.1.10d: Collect, organize, and interpret client data (p. 131): Existing scales are often used to collect client data.

EP 2.1.10m: Critically analyze, monitor, and evaluate interventions (pp. 121, 125, 129, 130): Understanding conceptualization in research enhances social workers' ability to use research methods to evaluate interventions.

Measurement in Quantitative and Qualitative Inquiry

8.1 INTRODUCTION

In quantitative inquiry, operational definitions provide the bridge from conceptualization to measurement. In the previous chapter, we saw that researchers have a wide variety of options available when they want to operationally define a concept. Some options might make more sense than others. For example, we can operationally define a child's risk of abuse by simply asking a parent whether the child is at risk (yes or no). That would tell us how we choose to measure risk, but the fact that it is an operational definition would not ensure our obtaining accurate, unbiased answers.

EP 2.1.6b
EP 2.1.10d
EP 2.1.10m

No matter how we operationally define abstract concepts, we need to be mindful of the extreme vulnerability of the measurement process to sources of measurement error. We must carefully plan to minimize the likelihood that those errors will occur and then take certain steps to check on the adequacy of our measures. This chapter examines how to do that in both quantitative and qualitative research.

8.2 SOURCES OF MEASUREMENT ERROR

Measurement error occurs when we obtain data that do not accurately portray the concept we are attempting to measure. Some inaccuracies may be minor, such as when parents forget about one of the 11 temper tantrums their son had the previous week, and report that he had 10. Other inaccuracies

---

systematic error   A measurement error that occurs when the information we collect consistently reflects a false picture of the concept we seek to measure.

bias   A distortion in measurement based on personal preferences or beliefs.

acquiescent response set   The tendency to agree or disagree with all statements regardless of their content.

social desirability bias   The tendency of people to say or do things that will make them or their reference group look good.

---

may be serious, such as when a measure portrays an abusive parent as nonabusive.

Two sources of measurement error emphasized in quantitative inquiry are systematic error and random error. **Systematic error** occurs when the information we collect consistently reflects a false picture of the concept we seek to measure, because of either the way we collect the data or the dynamics of those who are providing the data. Sometimes our measures really don't measure what we think they do. For example, words don't always match deeds. Measuring what parents say they think about child abuse will not necessarily reflect whether they themselves actually ever abuse their children.

Perhaps the most common way our measures systematically measure something other than what we think they do is when **biases** are involved in the data collection. Biases can come in various forms. We may ask questions in a way that predisposes individuals to answer the way we want them to, or we may smile excessively or nod our heads in agreement when we get the answers that support our hypotheses. Or individuals may be biased to answer our questions in ways that distort their true views or behaviors. For instance, they may be biased to agree with whatever we say, or they may do or say things that will convey a favorable impression of themselves. The former bias, agreeing or disagreeing with most or all statements regardless of their content, is called the **acquiescent response set**. The latter bias, the tendency of people to say or do things that will make them or their reference group look good, is called the **social desirability bias**.

Simply identifying an attitude or position with a prestigious person or agency can bias responses. For example, it would be hard for social work students to disagree with the question, "Do you agree or disagree with the call by the NASW for a new welfare policy that ...?" Some students might disagree, but stating that the policy is endorsed by our professional association would probably increase the likelihood that students will agree with the new policy. Questionnaire items also can be biased negatively as well as positively. Consider the following question: "Do you agree or disagree with the position of Adolf Hitler when he stated that ...?" How would you be tempted to respond?

In quantitative inquiry, we should be especially wary of the social desirability bias. Whenever you ask people for information, they answer through a filter of concern about what will make them look good. This is especially true if they are being interviewed in a face-to-face situation. Thus, for example, a particular man may feel that things would be a lot better if women were kept in the kitchen, not allowed to vote, forced to be quiet in public, and so forth. Asked whether he supports equal rights for women, however, he may want to avoid looking like a staunch male chauvinist. Recognizing that his views might have been progressive in the 15th century but are out of step with current thinking, he may choose to say "Yes."

Unlike systematic errors, **random errors** have no consistent pattern of effects. Random errors do not bias our measures; they make them inconsistent from one measurement to the next. This feature does not mean that whenever data change over time we have random error; sometimes things really do change, and when they do, our measures should detect that change. What this feature does mean is that if the things we are measuring do not change over time but our measures keep coming up with different results, then we have inconsistencies in measurement, or random error.

Random errors can take various forms. Perhaps our measurement procedures are so cumbersome, complex, boring, or fatiguing that our subjects say or do things at random just to get the measurement over with as quickly as possible. For example, halfway through a lengthy questionnaire full of complicated questions, respondents may stop giving much thought to what the questions really mean or how they truly feel about them.

Another example might be when two raters are recording the number of times a social worker gives an empathic response in a videotaped interview with a client. If the raters are not really sure how to recognize an empathic response when they see one, they may disagree substantially about how many empathic responses they observed in the same videotape. Note the difference between this sort of error and systematic error. If one rater was the videotaped social worker's mentor or fiancée and the other rater was the social worker's rival for a promotion, then the differences in the ratings would probably result from systematic error.

8.2a Errors in Alternate Sources of Data

In Chapter 7 we examined three alternative sources of data that can be used when operationally defining variables in social work research: self-reports, direct observation, and examination of available records. We also noted that each of these sources is vulnerable to measurement error. Let's now look at each of the three sources separately, and see some of the similarities and differences in the ways each is vulnerable to measurement errors.

Self-Reports

As we noted above, people's *words* don't necessarily match their *deeds*. For example, parents referred for abuse or neglect who have completed a mandatory parent education program can learn and check off the desired answers to a written test of their knowledge, attitudes, and skills about child rearing without becoming any less likely to neglect or abuse their children. Their written responses about their behavior may be grossly inaccurate, because they may want to portray themselves in a socially desirable light. Having them complete the instruments anonymously might alleviate some of this bias, but it does not guarantee the avoidance of gross inaccuracies, since people tend to see themselves in a socially desirable manner.

Direct Observation

Rather than rely on what people say, we can observe their behavior directly. For example, if we want to assess the effects of an intervention program on the parenting behaviors of parents who were referred for abuse or neglect, we could make home visits and observe how they interact with their children. Or we could have their children play with a bunch of toys in a playroom and then observe through a one-way mirror how the parents handle the challenging task of getting the children to put away their toys.

Although direct observation can be more time-consuming and costly than using self-report measures, it has the advantage of seeing behavior for ourselves and not having to wonder whether the way people answer questions really reflects how

random error A measurement error that has no consistent pattern of effects.

they actually behave. Yet direct observation, too, can be highly vulnerable to systematic error, such as social desirability biases. As we noted earlier, people who know they are being observed may act in a much more socially desirable manner than when they are not being observed or when they do not know they are being observed. In addition, the observers themselves might be biased to perceive behaviors that support their study's hypothesis. Random errors can result from inconsistencies in the way different observers observe and record things, perhaps stemming from differences in how well they understand the phenomena they are looking for and recording.

Examining Available Records

Perhaps the least costly and time-consuming measurement option is the examination of available records. In assessing practitioner orientations about their practice, for example, we might want to examine process notes in their case records, looking to see how often they employ different techniques or provide different services. But some practitioners might exaggerate their records regarding the amount of time they spend on certain activities in the belief that someone might use those records to evaluate their performance. Maybe they resent all the record keeping that is expected of them and thus aren't careful in documenting their tasks. That would create random errors.

8.3 RELIABILITY

In light of the vulnerability of the measurement process to error, quantitative researchers ideally should assess whether the measurement procedures they plan to use sufficiently avoid systematic and random sources of error before they implement their study. This typically involves assessing whether their measurement procedures have acceptable levels of reliability and validity.

Reliability has to do with the amount of random error in a measurement. The more reliable the measure, the less random error in it. Reliability is a matter of whether a particular technique, applied

---

reliability The degree of consistency in measurement (impeded by random error).

repeatedly to the same object, would yield the same result each time. Suppose a large classmate—a tackle on your school's football team—asks you and another classmate to guesstimate how much he weighs. You look him over carefully and guess that he weighs 260 pounds. Your classmate guesstimates 375 pounds. This would suggest that the technique of having people estimate how much other people weigh is not very reliable. Suppose, however, that each of you had used his bathroom scale to measure his weight. The scale would have indicated virtually the same weight each time, indicating that the scale provided a more reliable measure of weight than did your guesstimates.

Reliability, however, does not ensure accuracy. Suppose he set his bathroom scale to shave 10 pounds off his weight just to make him feel better. Although the scale would (reliably) report the same weight for him each time, you and your classmate would both be wrong because of systematic error (that is, a biased scale).

Reliability problems crop up in many forms in social work research. For example, sometimes we ask questions for which people don't know the answers. Just imagine, for example, how you'd respond if a researcher asked you how many times you've disagreed with your parents. Sometimes people don't understand what our questions mean, such as when we use words that children have not yet learned or terms that have different meanings in different cultures. And sometimes we ask questions that are so complicated that a person who had a clear opinion on the matter might arrive at a different interpretation on being asked the question a second time.

8.3a Types of Reliability

The type of measurement reliability that is most relevant to a particular study varies according to the study's purpose and design. If the study involves judgments made by observers or raters, for example, then we need to assess the extent of agreement, or consistency, between or among observers or raters. If the study involves using a written self-report scale that respondents complete to measure certain constructs such as self-esteem, depression, job satisfaction, and so on, then reliability is usually measured in one of two ways. If the self-report scale is being used to measure changes in people over time, then we need to assess the *stability* of the scale in providing consistent measurements from one administration to the next. A particularly expedient alternative way to assess a scale's reliability, without concern as to stability over time, is to measure its *internal consistency*.

The term for the degree of agreement or consistency between or among observers or raters is **inter-observer reliability** or **inter-rater reliability**. Suppose you are studying whether an in-service training program for paraprofessionals or volunteers increases the level of empathy they express in videotaped role-play situations. To assess inter-rater reliability, you would train two raters and then have them view the same videotapes and independently rate the level of empathy they observed in each. If they agree approximately 80 percent or more of the time in their ratings, then you can assume that the amount of random error in measurement is not excessive. Some researchers would argue that even 70 percent agreement would be acceptable.

In studies that seek to assess changes in scale scores over time, it is important to use a stable measure—that is, a scale that provides consistency in measurement over time. If the measurement is not stable over time, then changes that you observe in your study may have less to do with real changes in the phenomenon being observed than with changes in the measurement process. The term for assessing a measure's stability over time is **test–retest reliability**.

To assess test–retest reliability, simply administer the same measurement instrument to the same individuals on two separate occasions. If their scores on the two sets of responses to the instrument are similar, then the instrument may be deemed to have acceptable stability. But assessing test–retest reliability can be tricky. What if the individual actually changes between testing and retesting? What if the conditions (time of day and so forth) of the test are different from those of the retest? In assessing test-retest reliability, you must be certain that both tests occur under identical conditions, and that the time lapse between test and retest is long enough—so the individuals do not recall their answers from the first testing—yet short enough to minimize the likelihood that individuals will change significantly between the two testings. Approximately 2 weeks is a common interval between the test and the retest.

Whether or not we plan to assess changes on a measure over time, it is important to assess whether the various items that make up the measure are *internally consistent*. This method, called **internal consistency reliability**, assumes that the instrument contains multiple items, each of which is scored and combined with the scores of the other items to produce an overall score. Using this method, we simply assess the correlation of the scores on each item with the scores on the rest of the items. Or we might compute the total scores of different subsets of items and then assess the correlations of those subset totals. Using the *split-halves method* for example, we would assess the correlations of subscores among different subsets of half of the items. Because this method only requires administering the measure one time to a group of respondents, it is the most practical and most commonly used method for assessing reliability.

Before the advent of computers made it easy to calculate internal consistency correlations, research texts commonly mentioned a more time-consuming, more difficult, and impractical method for measuring a scale's reliability that is akin to internal consistency reliability. It is called *parallel-forms reliability*. This method requires constructing a second measuring instrument that is thought to be equivalent to the first. It might be a shorter series of questions, and it will always attempt to measure the same thing as the other instrument. Both forms are administered to the same set of individuals, and then the two sets of responses are analyzed to assess whether they are adequately correlated. This reliability assessment method is extremely rare in social work research because constructing a second instrument and ensuring its equivalence to the first are both cumbersome and risky. Inconsistent results on the two "parallel" forms might not indicate that the main measure is unreliable; instead, it may merely result from shortcomings in the effort to make the second instrument truly equivalent to the first.

---

interobserver reliability or **inter-rater reliability** The degree of agreement or consistency between or among observers or raters.

test–retest reliability A method for assessing a measure's consistency or stability.

internal consistency reliability The degree to which scores among scale items, or scores among subsets of items, correlate with each other.

The most common and powerful method used today for calculating internal consistency reliability is **coefficient alpha**. The calculation of coefficient alpha is easily done using available computer software. The formula for calculating coefficient alpha is a bit complicated, but it in simple terms it involves subdividing all of the items of an instrument into all possible split halves (subsets of half of the items), calculating the total subscore of each possible split half for each subject, and then calculating the correlations of all possible pairs of split half subscores. Coefficient alpha equals the average of all of these correlations (or is somewhat less than the average after statistically correcting for differences in item standard deviations). When coefficient alpha is at about .90 or above, internal consistency reliability is considered to be excellent. Alphas at around .80 to .89 are considered good, and somewhat lower alphas can be considered acceptable for relatively short instruments. The types of reliability that we've been discussing are illustrated in Figure 8.1.

8.4 VALIDITY

We'll return to the issue of reliability more than once in the chapters ahead. For now, however, let's note that even perfect reliability doesn't ensure

---

coefficient alpha The average of the correlations between the scores of all possible subsets of half the items on a scale.

face validity Whether a measure merely seems to be a reasonable way to measure some variable, based only on subjective judgment.

content validity The degree to which a measure seems to cover the entire range of meanings within a concept.

criterion-related validity The degree to which an instrument relates to an external criterion that is believed to be another indicator or measure of the same variable that the instrument intends to measure.

predictive validity The degree to which an instrument accurately predicts a criterion that will occur in the future.

---

that our measure measures what we think it does—that is, it does not ensure that our measure is *valid*. In conventional usage, the term *validity* refers to the extent to which an empirical measure adequately reflects the *real meaning* of the concept under consideration.

8.4a Types of Validity

There are several types of validity. At the crudest and least persuasive level, there's a feature called **face validity**, which is merely a subjective assessment of validity made by the researcher, or perhaps by other experts. Having face validity does not mean that a measure really measures what the researcher intends to measure, only that in the judgment of one or more people it *appears* to do so.

A technically more legitimate type of validity, one that includes elements of face validity, is known as **content validity**. The term refers to the degree to which a measure covers the range of meanings included within the concept. For example, a test of mathematical ability, Carmines & Zeller (1979) point out, cannot be limited to addition alone but would also need to cover subtraction, multiplication, division, and so forth. Like face validity, however, content validity is established on the basis of judgments; that is, researchers or other experts make judgments about whether the measure covers the universe of facets that make up the concept. Although we must make judgments about face and content validity when we construct a particular measure, it is important to test out the adequacy of those judgments. No matter how much confidence we may have in those judgments, we need evidence to ascertain whether the measure really measures what it is intended to measure. The two most common ways of testing whether a measure really measures what it's intended to measure are called *criterion-related validity* and *construct validity*.

Criterion-related validity is based on some external criterion. When we assess the criterion-related validity of an instrument, we select an *external* criterion that we believe is another indicator or measure of the same variable that our instrument intends to measure. Two subtypes of criterion-related validity are **predictive validity** and

FIGURE 8.1 Illustration of Types of Reliability for a Scale Measuring Interviewing Skill

Test–Retest Reliability: Does the same individual score similarly at Time 1 and Time 2 on a self-report scale?

Example of Strong Reliability:

	Time 1	Time 2
Ann	47	48
Bob	63	65
Eve	93	91
Hal	84	83

Example of Weak Reliability:

	Time 1	Time 2
Ann	47	94
Bob	63	96
Eve	93	58
Hal	84	27

Internal Consistency Reliability: Does the same individual score similarly on different scale items?

Example of Strong Reliability:

	Item 1	Item 2	Item 3
Ann	4	4	5
Bob	7	6	7
Eve	1	2	2
Hal	3	3	3

Example of Weak Reliability:

	Item 1	Item 2	Item 3
Ann	4	1	7
Bob	7	2	5
Eve	1	7	4
Hal	3	1	6

Inter-rater Reliability: Do raters give similar ratings for the same interview they observe?

Example of Strong Reliability:

	Rater 1	Rater 2
Ann	10	9
Bob	2	3
Eve	5	6
Hal	8	8

Example of Weak Reliability:

	Rater 1	Rater 2
Ann	10	5
Bob	2	6
Eve	5	9
Hal	8	1

concurrent validity. The difference between them has to do with whether the measure is being tested according to (1) its ability to predict a criterion that will occur in the future (such as later success in college), or (2) its correspondence to a criterion that is known concurrently. Suppose your introductory practice course instructor devises a multiple-choice test to measure your interviewing skills before you enter your field placement. To assess the concurrent validity of the test, she may see if scores on it correspond to ratings students received on their interviewing skills in videotapes they made in which they role-played interviewing situations. To assess the predictive validity of the test, she may see if scores on it correspond to field instructor evaluations of their interviewing skills after the students complete their fieldwork. The predictive validity might also be assessed by comparing the test scores to client satisfaction ratings of the students' interviews after they graduate.

If you read studies that assess the criterion validity of various instruments, you will find many that ascertain whether an instrument accurately differentiates between groups that differ in respect to the variable being measured. For example, the validity of an instrument designed to measure depression might be tested by seeing if it accurately differentiates between people who are and are not in treatment for depression. When the criterion validity of a measure is assessed this way—that is, according to its ability to differentiate between "known groups," the type of validity being assessed may be called **known groups validity**, which is simply a subtype of criterion-related validity. For example, to test the known groups validity of a scale designed to measure racial prejudice, you might see whether the

scores of social work students differ markedly from the scores of Ku Klux Klan members.

Assuming you are comfortable with the issue of criterion-related validity, let's turn to a more complex form of validity, **construct validity**. This form is based on the way a measure relates to other variables within a system of theoretical relationships. Let's suppose, for example, that you are interested in studying "marital satisfaction"—its sources and consequences. As part of your research, you develop a measure of marital satisfaction, and you want to assess its validity. In addition to developing your measure, you also will have developed certain theoretical expectations about the way marital satisfaction "behaves" in relation to other variables. For example, you may have concluded that family violence is more likely to occur at lower levels of marital satisfaction. If your measure of marital satisfaction relates to family violence in the expected fashion, then that constitutes evidence of your measure's construct validity. If "satisfied" and "dissatisfied" couples were equally likely to engage in family violence, however, that would challenge the validity of your measure.

In addition to testing whether a measure fits theoretical expectations, construct validation can involve assessing whether the measure has *both* convergent validity and discriminant validity. A measure has *convergent validity* when its results correspond to the results of other methods of measuring the same construct. Thus, if the clients whom clinicians identify as having low levels of marital satisfaction tend to score lower on your scale of marital satisfaction than clients who clinicians say have higher levels of marital satisfaction, then your scale would have convergent validity.

A measure has *discriminant validity* when its results do not correspond as highly with measures of other constructs as they do with other measures of the same construct. Suppose, for example, that the results of a measure of depression or self-esteem correspond more closely to clinician assessments of maritally satisfied and dissatisfied clients than do the results of your marital satisfaction scale. Then your scale would not have construct validity, even if it had established convergent validity. The idea here is that if your scale were really measuring the construct of marital satisfaction, it should correspond more highly to other measures

---

concurrent validity The degree to which an instrument corresponds to an external criterion that is known concurrently.

known groups validity Whether an instrument accurately differentiates between groups known to differ in respect to the variable being measured.

construct validity The degree to which a measure relates to other variables as expected within a system of theoretical relationships and as reflected by the degree of its convergent and discriminant validity.

of marital satisfaction than to measures of conceptually distinct concepts. Likewise, if your scale is really measuring marital satisfaction, it should not correspond more highly with measures of self-esteem or depression than it does with measures of marital satisfaction.

It is possible that a scale that intends to measure marital satisfaction will correspond to another measure of marital satisfaction and yet not really be a very good measure of the construct of marital satisfaction. If we assume, for example, that people who have low self-esteem or who are depressed are less likely to be maritally satisfied than other people, then a scale that really has more to do with depression or self-esteem than with marital satisfaction will still probably correspond to a measure of marital satisfaction. The process of assessing discriminant validity checks for that possibility and thus enables us to determine whether a measure really measures the construct it intends to measure, and not some other construct that happens to be related to the construct in question. The types of validity that we've been discussing are illustrated in Figure 8.2.

FIGURE 8.2 Illustration of Types of Validity for a Scale Measuring Interviewing Skill

Face Validity: Do the scale items seem to be reasonable for measuring interviewing skill?

Example of Strong Face Validity:

Item 1. Interviewers should maintain eye contact with interviewees.	True	False
Item 2. Interviewers should use neutral probes.	True	False

Example of Weak Face Validity:

Item 1. Interviewers should be good in math.	True	False
Item 2. Interviewers should be artistic.	True	False

Content Validity: Do the scale items cover the complete range of interviewing skills?

Example of Strong Content Validity:

Scale contains items on all aspects of interviewing skills, such as empathy, warmth, attentiveness, posture, neutrality, and so on.

Example of Weak Content Validity:

Scale lacks items on some important aspects of interviewing skills.

Criterion-Related Validity: Do scale scores correlate with another independent indicator of interviewing skill?

Predictive Validity: Do current scale scores accurately predict future client satisfaction ratings?

Example of Strong Predictive Validity:

	Current Scale Score	Future Evaluation Rating
Ann	10	9
Bob	2	3
Eve	5	6
Hal	8	8

Example of Weak Predictive Validity:

	Current Scale Score	Future Evaluation Rating
Ann	10	5
Bob	2	6
Eve	5	9
Hal	8	1

(Continued)

FIGURE 8.2 (*continued*)

Concurrent Validity: Do current scale scores accurately correlate with current observer ratings?

Example of Strong Concurrent Validity:

	Current Scale Score	Current Evaluation Rating
Ann	10	9
Bob	2	3
Eve	5	6
Hal	8	8

Example of Weak Concurrent Validity:

	Current Scale Score	Current Evaluation Rating
Ann	10	5
Bob	2	6
Eve	5	9
Hal	8	1

Known Groups Validity: Do scale scores accurately differentiate between groups known to differ in interviewing skills?

Example of Strong Known Groups Validity:

	Average Scale Score
Experienced clinical social workers	97
First-year MSW students	78
Undergraduate engineering majors	43

Example of Weak Known Groups Validity:

	Average Scale Score
Experienced clinical social workers	73
First-year MSW students	74
Undergraduate engineering majors	71

Construct Validity: Does the scale have **both** convergent and discriminant validity?

Example of Strong Construct Validity:

Good convergent validity:
High correlation between scale scores and field instructor rating of interviewing skill

PLUS

Good discriminant validity:
Low or no correlation between scale scores and field instructor gender or ethnicity

Two Examples of Weak or No Construct Validity:

1. *Poor convergent validity*
2. *Good convergent validity:*

    High correlation between scale scores and field instructor rating of interviewing skill

    BUT

    Poor discriminant validity:
    Similarly high correlation between scale scores and field instructor gender or ethnicity

The Difference Between Reliability and Validity

Question: "Have you smoked a cigarette since receiving the smoking cessation intervention?"

Participant 1 (Reliable and valid)

October 7

October 21

Participant 2 (Neither reliable nor valid)

October 7

October 21

Participant 3 (Reliable but not valid)

October 7

October 21

8.5 RELATIONSHIP BETWEEN RELIABILITY AND VALIDITY

As we noted earlier, although it is desirable that a measure be reliable, its reliability does not ensure that it is valid. Suppose an abusive mother and father were referred by the courts to family therapy as a precondition for keeping their child. As involuntary clients, they might be reluctant to admit abusive behaviors to the therapist, believing that such admissions would imperil maintaining custody of their child. Even if they continued to abuse their child, they might deny it every time the therapist asked them about it. Thus, the therapist would be getting highly reliable (that is, consistent) data. No matter how many times and ways the therapist asked about abusive behaviors, the answer would always be the same.

Nonetheless, the data would not be valid: The answer would not really measure the construct in question—the amount of child abuse that was occurring. Instead, what was really being measured was the reluctance of the parents to convey a socially undesirable image to the therapist.

Figure 8.3 graphically portrays the difference between validity and reliability. If you can think of measurement as analogous to hitting the bull's-eye on a target, you'll see that reliability looks like a "tight pattern," regardless of where it hits, because reliability is a function of consistency. Validity, on the other hand, is a function of shots being arranged around the bull's-eye. The failure of reliability in the figure can be seen as random error, whereas the failure of validity is a systematic error. Notice that neither an unreliable nor an invalid measure is likely to be useful. Notice also that you can't have validity without also having reliability.

The box on the difference between reliability and validity further clarifies these two concepts, this time in relation to follow-up telephone calls to assess whether recipients of a smoking cessation intervention have ever smoked a cigarette again after receiving the intervention. To assess the reliability of the measure, three participants are called twice, with 2 weeks elapsing between the calls (thus illustrating test–retest reliability). Alas, all three participants have continued smoking despite having received the intervention. Participant 1 admits to having smoked in both phone calls, thus reporting reliable and valid data. Participant 2 denies the smoking at time 1, but admits it at time 2, thus reporting information that is neither reliable (i.e., consistent) nor valid. Participant 3 denies the smoking in both calls, thus reporting information that is reliable but not valid.

8.6 RELIABILITY AND VALIDITY IN QUALITATIVE RESEARCH

Although much of the basic logic about reliability and validity is the same in qualitative and quantitative research, qualitative researchers may approach the issues somewhat differently than quantitative researchers. In a quantitative study of adolescent depression, the researcher would conceivably administer a standardized depression scale to a sizable sample of adolescents, perhaps to assess the extent of depression among adolescents or perhaps to see if the extent of depression was related to other variables. In planning the study, or in reading

FIGURE 8.3 An Analogy to Validity and Reliability

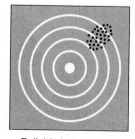

Reliable but not valid

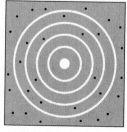

Neither reliable nor valid

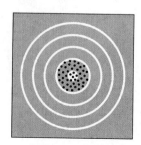

Valid *and* reliable

about it, a critical issue would be the depression scale's reliability and validity. But we know that even the best depression scale is not 100 percent reliable and valid. Even using the best scale, the study would be dealing with probabilistic knowledge—that is, specific scores would indicate a higher or lower probability that the adolescent is depressed. A good clinical scale would be correct about 90 percent of the time in depicting an adolescent as depressed or not depressed, and it would be important to know how often the scale is accurate and how often it's mistaken. But if all we have on each adolescent is quantitative data from a scale score, we will not know which adolescents are being accurately depicted and which are among the 10 percent or so who are not.

In a qualitative study of adolescent depression, the researcher would not rely on a standardized instrument. The researcher would be more likely to study a much smaller sample of adolescents and conduct extensive and varied direct observations and in-depth interviews with each one of them and their significant others. Perhaps the scope would be limited to a biographical case study of the impact of adolescent depression on one family, or perhaps the sample would include several families. In either case, the sample would be small enough to permit the researcher to describe the everyday lives of the subjects in such rich detail that the reader would not question the existence of depression or simply would not care what construct was used to label the observed phenomenon.

Suppose the qualitative report described an adolescent girl whose academic and social functioning began to deteriorate after the onset of puberty. After achieving high grades throughout her previous schooling, she began staying awake all night, sleeping all day, and refusing to go to school. On the days when she did attend school, she was unable to concentrate. Her grades fell precipitously. She began to isolate herself from family and friends and refused to leave her room. She began to express feelings of hopelessness about the future and negative thoughts about her looks, intelligence, likeability, and worthiness. She no longer had the energy to do things she once did well, and started to neglect basic daily tasks associated with cleanliness and grooming. She began to wear the same black clothes every day, refusing to wear any other color. When family or friends reached out to her, she became unresponsive or irritable. She displayed no signs of substance abuse but began to wonder if that might make her feel better. She began to have thoughts of suicide and started to cut herself. She showed no signs of schizophrenia such as delusions or hallucinations.

A good qualitative report would depict the above clinical deterioration in a format replete with detailed observations and quotations that would be many pages long and would leave the reader with a sense of having walked in the shoes of the girl and her family, sensing the girl's depression and agony as well as the burden placed on the family. The detail of the study and its report would be so rich that if the girl did not score in the depressed range of a standardized scale, the reader would be likely to conclude that this was one of the 10 percent or so of cases in which the scale got it wrong. The reader might not even care whether the phenomenon described fit best under the rubric of "Depression" or under some other label. Rather than verifying a label for it that could be generalized to others, the study would be geared more to giving the reader a deeper sense of the situation that the girl and her family were struggling with, the ways in which the various family members experienced the situation and the subjective meanings it had for them, and what they felt they needed.

The point of qualitative studies, in other words, is to study and describe things in such depth and detail, and from such multiple perspectives and meanings, that there is less need to worry about whether one particular measure is really measuring what it's intended to measure. In quantitative studies, on the other hand, we are more likely to rely heavily on one indicator, or a few indicators, administered perhaps in a matter of minutes, to determine the degree to which a hypothetical construct applies to a large number of people, and with an eye toward generalizing what we find to an even larger number of people. In such studies, it is critical to assess the reliability and validity of the indicators we use. It is thus possible to recognize the critical role of reliability and validity in quantitative studies while at the same time appreciating the need to take a different perspective on the role of reliability and validity in qualitative studies. In fact, without even attempting to quantitatively assess the validity of in-depth qualitative measurement, one could argue that the directness, depth, and detail of its observations often give it better validity than quantitative measurement.

We are not, however, saying that the concepts of reliability and validity have no role in qualitative studies. Qualitative researchers disagree on the nature and extent of the role of reliability and validity in their work, and their disagreement is connected to the assumptions they make about the feasibility of objectivity in measurement. At one extreme are the researchers who believe we can improve or assess our objectivity. These researchers use varied criteria to judge whether the evidence reported in qualitative studies is to be trusted as accurate and unbiased. One way they may do this is by using the concept of **triangulation,** which involves using several measurement alternatives and seeing if they tend to produce the same findings. For example, they might see if different interviewers or observers generate the same findings. They might even compare the qualitative interpretations with data from quantitative measures. To the degree that the quantitative data support the qualitative interpretations, the qualitative material may be seen as more credible (or reliable).

Some researchers judge the reliability of qualitative interpretations according to criteria that are not really quantitative but that resemble the underlying logic of quantitative approaches to reliability. As in determining interobserver reliability in quantitative studies, for example, one might assess whether two independent raters arrive at the same interpretation from the same mass of qualitative field notes. What distinguishes this from a quantitative approach is that the consistency between the two raters would not be calculated through quantitative indicators such as percentages of agreement or correlations. Instead, one would merely ask whether the two arrived at the same particular overarching interpretation. (Some researchers might argue that this is still a quantitative indicator—that is, agreement is either 100 percent or 0 percent.) Akin to internal consistency reliability, one might examine whether different sources of data fit consistently with the researcher's observations and interpretations. Rather than calculate quantitative reliability coefficients, however, one would attempt to illustrate how, on an overall basis, the different sources were in qualitative agreement.

triangulation   The use of more than one imperfect data collection alternative in which each option is vulnerable to different potential sources of error.

Some researchers use indicators of reliability of a more distinctly qualitative nature. They might, for example, ask research participants to confirm the accuracy of the researcher's observations. Or the participants might be asked whether the researcher's interpretations ring true and are meaningful to them. Some researchers judge reliability according to whether the report indicates ways in which the researcher searched thoroughly for disconfirming evidence, such as by looking for other cases or informants whose data might not fit the researcher's interpretation. They might also ask whether the researcher sufficiently varied the time, place, and context of the observations, and whether the interpretation fit consistently across the observations taken at different times, places, and contexts.

Jane Kronick (1989) proposed four criteria for evaluating the validity of qualitative interpretations of written texts. The first is analogous to internal consistency reliability in quantitative research—that is, the interpretation of parts of the text should be consistent with other parts or with the whole text. Likewise, the "developing argument" should be "internally consistent." Second, Kronick proposed that the interpretation should be complete, taking all of the evidence into account. Her third criterion involves "conviction," which means that the interpretation should be the most compelling one in light of the evidence within the text. Fourth, the interpretation should be meaningful. It should make sense of the text and extend our understanding of it.

As in quantitative research, limitations inhere in some of the qualitative approaches to reliability and validity. For instance, the subjects of the research may not confirm the accuracy of a researcher's observations or interpretations because they do not like the way they are portrayed, may not understand the researcher's theoretical perspective, or may not be aware of patterns that are true but that only emerge from the mass of data. A second rater may not confirm the interpretations of the principal investigator because certain insights might require having conducted the observations or interviews and might not emerge from the written notes alone.

Although some qualitative researchers disagree about which of the above types of approaches to reliability and validity to use and how to use them, others reject the whole idea of reliability and validity in keeping with their view that it is impossible to be objective. Or they define reliability and validity in terms that are worlds apart from what other researchers mean by those two words. Sometimes they define reliability and validity in terms that researchers who do not share their assumptions would perceive as nonscientific, or even antiscientific. For instance, some would deem a study valid if a particular group deemed as oppressed or powerless experienced it as liberating or empowering. Thus, rather than define validity in terms of objectivity and accuracy, some define it according to whether findings can be applied toward some political or ideological purpose (Altheide & Johnson, 1994). Others point to writing style as a validity criterion, deeming a study valid if the report is written in a gripping manner that draws the reader into the subjects' worlds so closely that readers feel as though they are walking in the subjects' shoes, recognize what they read to correspond to their own prior experiences, and perceive the report to be internally coherent and plausible (Adler & Adler, 1994). One qualitative study, for example, used fictional novels and plays as sources of data for developing insights about the experience of family caregiving of relatives with Alzheimer's disease (England, 1994).

As you encounter the terms *reliability* and *validity* throughout the remainder of this book, they will be used primarily in reference to their quantitative meanings, because these terms are more commonly used in quantitative research. But we also will be discussing qualitative research in the remaining chapters, and we hope you'll keep in mind the distinctive ways in which reliability and validity are considered in qualitative research as you read that material.

8.7 MAIN POINTS

- Measurement error can be systematic or random. Common systematic errors pertain to social desirability biases and cultural biases. Random errors have no consistent pattern of effects, make measurement inconsistent, and are likely to result from difficulties in understanding or administering measures.
- Alternative forms of measurement include written self-reports, interviews, direct behavioral observation, and examining available records.

Each of these options is vulnerable to measurement error.

- Because no form of measurement is foolproof, applying the principle of triangulation—using several different research methods to collect the same information—we can use several imperfect measurement alternatives and see if they tend to produce the same findings.
- Reliability concerns the amount of random error in a measure and measurement consistency. It refers to the likelihood that a given measurement procedure will yield the same description of a given phenomenon if that measurement is repeated. For instance, estimating a person's age by asking his or her friends would be less reliable than asking the person or checking the birth certificate.
- Different types of reliability include interobserver reliability or inter-rater reliability, test-retest reliability, parallel-forms reliability, and internal consistency reliability.
- Validity refers to the extent of systematic error in measurement—the extent to which a specific measurement provides data that relate to commonly accepted meanings of a particular concept.
- Content validity refers to the degree to which a measure covers the range of meanings included within the concept.
- Two subtypes of criterion-related validity are predictive validity and concurrent validity. The difference between these subtypes has to do with whether the measure is being tested according to the ability to predict a criterion that will occur in the future or according to its correspondence to a criterion that is known concurrently.
- Known groups validity is another subtype of criterion-related validity. It assesses whether an instrument accurately differentiates between groups known to differ in respect to the variable being measured.
- Construct validation involves testing whether a measure relates to other variables according to theoretical expectations. It also involves testing the measure's convergent validity and discriminant validity.
- A measure has convergent validity when its results correspond to the results of other methods of measuring the same construct.
- A measure has discriminant validity when its results do not correspond as highly with

measures of other constructs as they do with other measures of the same construct and when its results correspond more highly with the other measures of the same construct than do measures of alternative constructs.

- Reliability and validity are defined and handled differently in qualitative research than they are in quantitative research. Qualitative researchers disagree about definitions and criteria for reliability and validity, and some argue that they are not applicable to qualitative research at all. These disagreements tend to be connected to differing assumptions about objectivity.
- Rigorous qualitative studies describe things in such depth and detail, and from such multiple perspectives and meanings, that there is less need to worry about whether one particular measure is really measuring what it's intended to measure.

8.8 PRACTICE-RELATED EXERCISES

1. Suppose a geriatric social worker assesses whether a life history review intervention improves the level of depression among frail nursing-home residents by administering a depression measure to them before and after the intervention. Suppose the measure had its validity assessed by comparing scores of frail nursing-home residents on it to the scores of healthy elderly folks living independently.

   a. What type (and subtype) of validity was assessed?
   b. What more would be needed to establish the measure's construct validity?
   c. If the measure is valid, can we assume it is also reliable? Why?

2. A geriatric social worker develops a very lengthy scale to assess the degree of staff sensitivity to the needs of residents in nursing homes. The scale is designed to be completed by both staff and residents.

   a. Identify reasons why the scale might be vulnerable to both systematic and random error.
   b. Describe two ways to test the reliability of the scale.

8.9 INTERNET EXERCISES

1. Go to a website developed and operated by Dr. Marianne Yoshioka, a social work professor at Columbia University. The site is called "Psychosocial Measures for Asian-American Populations" and is located at www.columbia.edu/cu/ssw/projects/pmap/. Find two abstracts at the site that assessed different forms of reliability and validity. Briefly describe and contrast how each assessed reliability and validity and their results.

2. Find several research articles in the journal *Health & Social Work* that employed existing scales to measure variables. How adequately do the articles report the reliability and validity of the scales they used? What type of reliability and validity do they report? What types of reliability and validity tend to get reported more and less often than others?

3. Access one of your college's literature databases and enter the key words *qualitative research* to find two articles that report studies using qualitative approaches to measurement. Describe and critically appraise the advantages and disadvantages of the measurement approaches used in each.

8.9a Competency Notes

EP 2.1.6b: Use research evidence to inform practice (p. 142): Social workers must understand all the measurement concepts in this chapter so they can recognize flawed measurement when using research evidence to inform their practice.

EP 2.1.10d: Collect, organize, and interpret client data (p. 142): Social workers must understand all the measurement concepts in this chapter in order to collect and interpret client data in a reliable and valid way.

EP 2.1.10m: Critically analyze, monitor, and evaluate interventions (p. 142): Social workers must understand all the measurement concepts in this chapter to design a competent evaluation and to minimize measurement error when monitoring client progress.

Quantitative and Qualitative Measurement Instruments

9.1   INTRODUCTION

In Chapter 8 we discussed various sources of measurement error. It is virtually impossible to avoid all possible types of measurement error. Even if all we do is examine an agency's caseload to describe the proportions of male and female clients of different ages and ethnic groups, chances are we will have some measurement error. For instance, there may be clerical oversights in recording data, coding them, or typing them for computer input.

No one should be dissuaded from pursuing research simply because of the inevitability of measurement errors. No one expects a social work research study to have perfect measurement. What matters is that you try to minimize any major measurement errors that would destroy the credibility and utility of your findings, and that you assess how well your measures appear to have kept those errors from exceeding a reasonable level.

In this chapter, we examine how to minimize measurement error when constructing measurement instruments that are widely used in social work research: questionnaires, interview schedules, and scales. We'll also discuss how to critically appraise such instruments. As we examine the construction and appraisal of these types of instruments, bear in mind that the principles guiding their design will vary depending on whether the research is primarily qualitative or quantitative. We'll begin by examining some broad guidelines for asking people questions that apply to both quantitative and qualitative inquiry.

9.2   GENERIC GUIDELINES FOR ASKING QUESTIONS

EP 2.1.10d

One of the most common ways that social work researchers get data for analysis and interpretation is by asking people questions. As we'll see, several general guidelines should guide framing and asking questions. There are also pitfalls that can result in useless and even

---

questionnaire   A document that contains questions and other types of items that are designed to solicit information appropriate for analysis.

misleading information. This section should assist you in differentiating the two. Let's begin with some of the options for creating questionnaires.

9.2a Questions and Statements

The term **questionnaire** suggests a collection of questions. In quantitative studies, questionnaires might also contain as many statements as questions. For example, if researchers are interested in determining the extent to which respondents hold a particular attitude or perspective, they might summarize the attitude in a fairly brief statement and ask respondents whether they agree or disagree with it.

9.2b Open-Ended and Closed-Ended Questions

In asking questions, researchers have two options. They may ask *open-ended questions*, in which the respondent is asked to provide his or her own answer to the question. Open-ended questions can be used in interview schedules as well as in self-administered questionnaires. For example, the respondent may be asked, "What do you feel is the most important problem facing your community today?" and be provided with a space to write in the answer or be asked to report it orally to an interviewer. Although open-ended questions can be used in both quantitative and qualitative studies, they are much more prominent in qualitative research. The interviewer may be instructed to probe for more information as needed. For instance, if the respondent replies that the most important problem facing the community is "urban decay," the interviewer may probe for more clarification by saying, "Could you tell me some more about that problem?"

With *closed-ended questions*, the respondent is asked to select an answer from among a list provided by the researcher. Closed-ended questions can be used in self-administered questionnaires as well as interview schedules, and are popular in quantitative research because they provide a greater uniformity of responses and are more easily processed. The chief shortcoming of closed-ended questions lies in the researcher's structuring of responses. When the relevant answers to a given question are relatively clear, there should be no problem. In other cases, however, the researcher's structuring of responses may overlook some important responses. In asking about "the most important problem facing your community," for example, your checklist of problems might omit certain ones that respondents would have said were important.

In the construction of closed-ended questions, you should be guided by two structural requirements. The response categories provided should be *exhaustive*: They should include all of the possible responses that might be expected. Often, researchers ensure this by adding a category labeled something like "Other."

Second, the answer categories must be *mutually exclusive*: The respondent should not feel compelled to select more than one. For example, the following response categories regarding ethnicity would *not* be mutually exclusive: White, Black, Hispanic. That's because Hispanic individuals can be both Hispanic and White as well as Hispanic and Black. (In some cases, researchers may wish to solicit multiple answers, but these may create difficulties in data processing and analysis later on.) To ensure that categories are mutually exclusive, researchers should carefully consider each combination of categories, asking themselves whether a person could reasonably choose more than one answer. In addition, it is useful to add an instruction to the question that asks the respondent to select the *one best answer*, but this technique is not a satisfactory substitute for a carefully constructed set of responses.

9.2c Make Items Clear

Questionnaire items should be *clear* and *unambiguous*. Often researchers can become so deeply involved in the topic under examination that opinions and perspectives are clear to them but will not be clear to their respondents—many of whom have given little or no attention to the topic. Or if they have only a superficial understanding of the topic, researchers may fail to specify the intent of their question sufficiently. The question, "What do you think about the proposed residential facility for the developmentally disabled in the community?" may evoke in the respondent a counter question: "*Which* residential facility?" or "What's a residential facility?" In quantitative studies, questionnaire

items should be precise so that the respondent knows exactly what question the researcher wants answered. It helps to be precise in qualitative studies, too; however, in qualitative studies the investigator typically can clarify any questions that respondents aren't sure they understand.

9.2d Avoid Double-Barreled Questions

Frequently, researchers ask respondents for a single answer to a combination of questions. For example, they might ask respondents to agree or disagree with the statement, "The state should abandon its community-based services and spend the money on improving institutional care." Although many people would unequivocally agree with the statement and others would unequivocally disagree, still others would be unable to answer. Some would want to abandon community-based services and give the money back to the taxpayers. Others would want to continue community-based services but also put more money into institutions. These latter respondents could neither agree nor disagree without misleading researchers.

As a general rule, whenever the word *and* appears in a question or questionnaire statement, researchers should check whether they are asking a *double-barreled question*. However, some questions can be implicitly double-barreled without using the word *and*. For example, suppose we ask an adolescent the following question: "Do you get along well with your parents?" What if they get along well with their mom but not their dad (or vice versa)? What if they come from a single-parent family? If so, they might be unable to answer. Of course, if you are taking a qualitative approach to measurement, you'll probably be able to resolve the problem by modifying the question. However, if the question is contained in a questionnaire administered by mail in a quantitative study, you won't have that opportunity.

9.2e Respondents Must Be Competent to Answer

In asking respondents to provide information, researchers should continually ask themselves whether respondents are able to do so accurately. In a study of child rearing, researchers might ask respondents to report the age at which they first talked back to their parents. Aside from the problem of defining "talking back to parents," it is doubtful whether most respondents would remember with any degree of accuracy. The same difficulty would pertain if researchers asked people entering treatment for alcohol addiction how many alcoholic drinks they consumed during the past 30 days.

Inability to remember accurately is not the only way in which respondents may not be able to answer questions. Another way is that they might not know about the relevant information in the first place. For example, if a survey asks practitioners about their attitudes regarding a treatment that is so new that most respondents have never heard of it, few respondents will be able to provide meaningful answers. Some respondents may be unable to answer certain questions due to psychological or biological impairments. Rather than ask a person with Alzheimer's disease how often they get lost wandering off, for example, it would be better to ask their caregiver.

9.2f Respondents Must Be Willing to Answer

Often, researchers would like to learn things from people that they are unwilling to share. For example, it might be difficult to get candid answers from people in totalitarian countries to questions about their political views. Fear is not the only reason why a respondent may be reluctant to answer a question. Another might be shame or embarrassment, such as when asked questions about sensitive topics like masturbation, marital infidelity, abusive behaviors, and so on.

9.2g Questions Should Be Relevant

Similarly, questions asked in a questionnaire should be relevant to most respondents. When attitudes are requested on a topic that few respondents have thought about or really care about, the results are not likely to be useful. For example, if you ask clients about their attitudes regarding a community issue they have never heard of, they might express attitudes even though they have never given any thought to that issue. You may have no way of telling which responses genuinely reflect attitudes and which reflect meaningless answers to an irrelevant question.

9.2h Short Items Are Best

In the interest of being unambiguous and precise and pointing to the relevance of an issue, the researcher is often led into long and complicated items. That should be avoided. Respondents are often unwilling to study an item to understand it. The respondent should be able to read an item quickly, understand its intent, and select or provide an answer without difficulty. In general, researchers should assume that respondents will read items quickly and give quick answers; therefore, researchers should provide clear, short items that will not be misinterpreted under those conditions.

9.2i Avoid Negative Items

The appearance of a negation in a questionnaire item paves the way for easy misinterpretation. Asked to agree or disagree with the statement, "The community should not have a residential facility for the develop-mentally disabled," a sizable portion of the respondents will read over the word *not* and answer on that basis. Thus, some will agree with the statement when they are in favor of the facility, and others will agree when they oppose it. And you may never know which is which.

9.2j Avoid Biased Items and Terms

The meaning of someone's response to a question depends in large part on the wording of the question that was asked. Some questions seem to encourage particular responses more than other questions. Questions that encourage respondents to answer in a particular way are said to be *biased*.

In our discussion of the social desirability bias in Chapter 8, we noted the need to be especially wary of this bias whenever we ask people for information. This applies to the way questionnaire items are worded, as well. Thus, for example, in assessing the attitudes of community residents about a halfway house proposed for their neighborhood, we would not ask if residents agreed with prominent clergy in supporting the facility. Likewise, we would not ask whether they endorsed "humanitarian" proposals to care for the needy in the community.

Although the avoidance of bias is more likely to be emphasized in quantitative studies than in qualitative ones, and although many qualitative studies are more interested in developing an in-depth understanding of subjective views than in preventing biased responses, both methods of inquiry typically prefer using neutral items and terms when asking people questions and avoiding biased ones. After all, what is to be gained in qualitatively probing for in-depth information about the attitudes of community residents about a halfway house proposed for their neighborhood by framing the question in such a (biased) way that they are reluctant to reveal their true attitude?

There are exceptions to this rule in some qualitative studies, however—especially those following a critical social science or feminist paradigm. (This paradigm was discussed in Chapter 4.) For example, a researcher employing a feminist research paradigm might think that the prior research on the burden people experience when caring for disabled loved ones focused too much on the negative aspects of caregiving and too little (or not at all) on the positive aspects that women experience when caring for their loved ones. Consequently, the researcher might intentionally ask respondents to talk about the things they like about caring for their disabled parent or disabled partner and not about the undesirable burdens of such care-giving. Of course, even here we can note the preference for avoiding bias in the way questions are posed. That is, even if the researcher biases the questions toward the positive aspects of caregiving, she probably will want to ask about those positive aspects in a neutral manner. Thus, rather than asking, "Do you agree with most women that caregiving gratifies their nurturing instincts?" she might ask, "Could you comment whether you find fulfillment in caring for your loved one, and if so, how?"

9.2k Questions Should Be Culturally Sensitive

EP 2.1.3c

Some of the illustrations above about problems in asking questions pertain to issues of cultural bias and insensitivity. For example, items that are clear in one culture may not be clear in another.

Respondents living in totalitarian societies might be unwilling to answer some questions that respondents in freer societies are willing to answer. Consequently, even if we find that our measurement instruments are reliable and valid when tested with one culture, we cannot assume that they will be reliable and valid when used with other cultures. Chapter 6, on culturally competent research, discussed the issue of cultural competence in measurement in more depth.

Before moving on to the topic of formatting questionnaires, we'd like to call your attention to the box "Learning from Bad Examples," which illustrates problems in asking questions that we've just discussed.

9.3 CRITICALLY APPRAISING QUANTITATIVE INSTRUMENTS

Now that we've examined some generic guidelines for asking people questions in both quantitative and qualitative studies, let's look separately at things to consider when critically appraising measurement instruments using each approach to inquiry. We'll begin with questionnaires in quantitative inquiry.

9.3a Questionnaires

When critically appraising a questionnaire, we would examine whether any of the generic guidelines discussed above have been violated. Even experienced researchers, for example, might inadvertently construct some questions that are unclear, too long, or subtly double-barreled. But the first thing we might notice is the questionnaire's overall format. The *format* of a questionnaire is just as important as the nature and wording of the questions asked. An improperly laid-out questionnaire can lead respondents to miss questions, confuse them about the nature of the data desired, and, in the worst case, lead them to throw the questionnaire away. Both general and specific guidelines are suggested here.

As a general rule, the questionnaire should be spread out and uncluttered. Inexperienced researchers tend to fear that their questionnaire will look too long and thus squeeze several questions onto a single line, abbreviate questions, and use as few pages

Learning from Bad Examples

by Charles Bonney, Department of Sociology, Eastern Michigan University

Here's a questionnaire I've used to train my students in some of the problems of question construction. These are questions that might be asked in order to test the hypothesis "College students from high-status family backgrounds are more tolerant toward persons suffering mental or emotional stress" (where *status* has been operationally defined as the combined relative ranking on family income, parents' educational level, and father's occupational prestige—or mother's, if father not present or not employed). Each question has one or more flaws in it. See if you can identify these problems. (A critique of the questionnaire appears at the end of the box.)

Questionnaire

1. What is your reaction to crazy people? _____

2. What is your father's income? _____

3. As you were growing up, with whom were you living?

   _____ both parents

   _____ mother only

   _____ father only

   _____ other (please specify)

4. What is your father's occupation? _____
   (If father is deceased, not living at home, or unemployed or retired, is your mother employed?

   _____ yes _____ no)

5. Did your parents attend college?

   _____ yes _____ no

6. Wouldn't you agree that people with problems should be sympathized with?

   _____ yes _____ no

7. The primary etiology of heterophilic blockage is unmet dependency gratification.

   _____ agree

   _____ undecided

   _____ disagree

8. If a friend of yours began to exhibit strange and erratic behavior, what do you think your response would be? _____

9. Has anyone in your immediate family ever been institutionalized?

   _____ yes _____ no

Critique

The most fundamental critique of any questionnaire is simply, "Does it get the information necessary to test the hypothesis?" Although questions can be bad in and of themselves, they can be good only when seen in terms of the needs of the researcher. Good questionnaire construction is probably about as much an art as a science, and even "good" questions may contain hidden pitfalls or be made even better when the overall context is considered, but the following flaws definitely exist:

1. Derogatory and vague use of a slang term. Because it's the first question it's even worse: it may contaminate your results either by turning off some people enough to affect your response rate or it may have a "funneling effect" on later responses.

2. The operational definition of *status* calls for family income, not just the father's. Also, it's been found that people are more likely to answer a question as personal as income if categories are provided for check-off, rather than this open-ended format.

3. "As you were growing up" is a vague time period. Also, the question is of dubious relevance or utility in the current format, although it could have been used to organize questions 2, 4, and 5.

4. The format (asking about mother's employment only if there's no employed father) may well be sexist. Although it follows the operational definition, the operational definition itself may well be sexist. There are two additional problems. First, a checklist nearly always works better for occupation-open-ended questions often get answers that are too vague to be categorized. Also, in cases where status will be measured by mother's occupation, the question only elicits whether or not she's employed at all.

5. Limited measure of educational levels. Also, it's double-barreled: what if one parent attended college and the other didn't?

6. "Wouldn't you agree" is leading the respondent. Also, "sympathized" and "problems" are vague.

7. Technical jargon. No one will know what it means. (In fact, I'm not even sure what it means, and I wrote it! As close as I can translate it, it says, "The main reason you can't get a date is because your folks ignored you.")

8. Asks for speculation regarding a vague, hypothetical situation—which is not always bad, but there's usually a better way. Note, however, that the question is not double-barreled as many have said: it asks only about behavior that is both "strange" and "erratic."

9. "Institutionalized" is a vague term. Many types of institutionalization would clearly be irrelevant.

as possible. All these efforts are ill-advised and even dangerous. Putting more than one question on a line will lead some respondents to miss the second question altogether. Some respondents will misinterpret abbreviated questions. And more generally, respondents who find they have spent considerable time on the first page of what seemed a short questionnaire will be more demoralized than respondents who quickly completed the first several pages of what initially seemed a long form. Moreover, the latter will have made fewer errors and will not have been forced to reread confusing, abbreviated questions. Nor will they have been forced to write a long answer in a tiny space.

Formats for Respondents

In one of the most common types of questionnaire items, the respondent is expected to check one response from a series. For this purpose, our experience has been that boxes adequately spaced apart are the best format. Modern word processing makes the use of boxes a practical technique these days; setting boxes in type can also be accomplished easily and neatly. Here are some easy examples:

Rather than providing boxes to be checked, a code number might be placed beside each response and the respondent asked to circle the appropriate number (see Figure 9.1). If numbers are to be circled, however, clear and prominent instructions must be provided because many respondents will be tempted to cross out the appropriate number, which makes data processing even more difficult. (Note that the technique can be used more safely when interviewers administer the questionnaires, since the interviewers themselves *record* the responses.)

Contingency Questions

Quite often in questionnaires, certain questions will be clearly relevant only to some respondents and irrelevant to others. This situation often arises when the researcher wishes to ask a series of questions about a certain topic. Researchers may want to ask whether respondents belong to a particular organization and, if so, how often they attend meetings, whether they have held office in the organization, and so forth. Or they might want to ask whether respondents have heard anything about a certain community issue and then learn the attitudes of those who have heard of it.

The subsequent questions in series such as these are called **contingency questions**. Whether they are to be asked and answered is contingent on responses to the first question in the series. The proper use of contingency questions can facilitate the respondents' task in completing the questionnaire because they are not faced with trying to answer questions that are irrelevant to them.

There are several formats for contingency questions. The one shown in Figure 9.2 is probably the clearest and most effective. Note two key elements in this format: (1) the contingency question is set off to the side and enclosed in a box and thus isolated from the other questions; (2) an arrow connects the contingency question to the answer on which it is contingent. In the illustration, only respondents who answer "yes" are expected to answer the contingency question. The rest of the respondents should simply skip it.

The foregoing discussion should show how seemingly theoretical issues of *validity* and *reliability* are involved in so mundane a matter as putting questions on a piece of paper. Used properly, even rather complex sets of contingency questions can be constructed without confusing the respondent. Figure 9.3 illustrates a more complicated example.

Sometimes a set of contingency questions is long enough to extend over several pages. Suppose you are studying the voting behaviors of poor people, and you wish to ask a large number of questions of individuals who have voted in a national, state, or local election. You could separate out the relevant respondents with an initial question such as, "Have you ever voted in a national, state, or local election?" but it would be confusing to place the

FIGURE 9.1 Circling the Answer

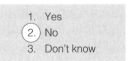

---

contingency question A question asked only of *some* respondents, depending on their response to some other question.

FIGURE 9.2 Contingency Question Format

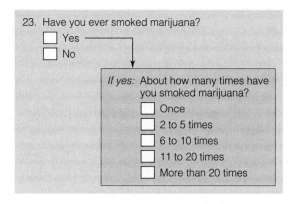

FIGURE 9.3 Contingency Table

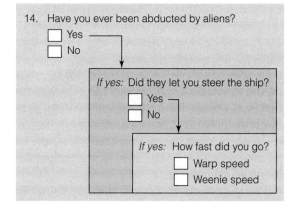

FIGURE 9.4 Instructions to Skip

> 13. Have you ever voted in a national, state, or local election?
>   ☐ Yes (Please answer questions 14–25.)
>   ☐ No   (Please skip questions 14–25. Go
>   directly to question 26 on page 8.)

Ordering Items

The *order* in which questions are asked also can affect the answers given. First, the appearance of one question can affect the answers given to later ones. For example, if respondents are asked to assess their overall religiosity ("How important is your religion to you in general?"), their responses to later questions about specific aspects of religiosity will be aimed at consistency with the prior assessment.

Some researchers attempt to overcome this effect by *randomizing* the order of questions. This is usually a futile effort. To begin, a randomized set of questions will probably strike respondents as chaotic and worthless. It will be difficult to answer, moreover, because they must continually switch their attention from one topic to another. And, finally, even in a randomized ordering of questions the appearance of one question can affect the answers given to later ones—except that you will have no control over this effect.

The safest solution is sensitivity to the problem. Although the effect of question order cannot be avoided, researchers should attempt to estimate the resulting effect and thus be able to interpret results in a meaningful fashion. If the question order seems especially important in a given study, then researchers might construct more than one version of the questionnaire with different possible orderings of questions. They would then be able to determine the effects. At the very least, the different forms of the questionnaire should be pretested.

The desired ordering of questions differs somewhat between self-administered questionnaires and interviews. In the former, it might be best to begin the questionnaire with the most interesting set of questions. The potential respondents who glance casually over the first few questions should want

contingency questions in a box that stretched over several pages. It would make more sense to enter instructions in parentheses after each answer, telling respondents to answer or skip the contingency questions. Figure 9.4 illustrates this method.

In addition to these instructions, it would be worthwhile to place an instruction at the top of each page that contains only the contingency questions. For example, you might say, "This page is only for respondents who have voted in a national, state, or local election." Clear instructions such as these spare respondents the frustration of reading and puzzling over questions that are irrelevant to them, as well as decreasing the chance of getting responses from those for whom the questions are not relevant.

to answer them. Perhaps the questions will ask for attitudes that they are aching to express. At the same time, however, the initial questions should not be threatening. (Beginning with questions about sexual behavior or drug use is probably a bad idea.) Requests for duller demographic data (age, gender, and the like) might be placed at the end of a self-administered questionnaire.

Just the opposite is generally true for interview surveys. When the potential respondent's door first opens, the interviewer must begin to establish rapport quickly. After a short introduction to the study, the interviewer can best begin by enumerating the members of the household, getting demographic data about each. Such questions are easily answered and are generally nonthreatening. Once the initial rapport has been established, the interviewer can move into the area of attitudes and more sensitive matters. An interview that began with the question "Do you believe in God?" would probably end rather quickly.

Questionnaire Instructions

Every questionnaire, whether it is to be completed by respondents or administered by interviewers, should contain clear instructions and introductory comments where appropriate.

It is useful to begin every self-administered questionnaire with basic instructions to be followed in completing it. Although many people these days are pretty familiar with forms and questionnaires, you should begin by telling them exactly what you want: that they are to indicate their answers to certain questions by placing a check mark or an "X" in the box beside the appropriate answer, or by writing in their answer when asked to do so. If many open-ended questions are used, respondents should be given some guidance about whether brief or lengthy answers are expected. If researchers wish to encourage their respondents to elaborate on their responses to closed-ended questions, that should be noted.

If a questionnaire is arranged into content subsections—political attitudes, religious attitudes, background data—each section should be introduced with a short statement about its content and purpose. For example, "In this section, we would like to know what people around here consider to be the most important community problems."

Demographic items at the end of a self-administered questionnaire might be introduced thus: "Finally, we would like to know just a little about you so we can see how different types of people feel about the issues we have been examining."

Short introductions such as these help make sense out of the questionnaire for the respondent. They make the questionnaire seem less chaotic, especially when it taps a variety of data. And they help put the respondent in the proper frame of mind for answering the questions.

Some questions may require special instructions to facilitate proper answering, especially if their format varies from the general instructions that pertain to the whole questionnaire. Specific examples will illustrate this situation. Despite the desirability of mutually exclusive answer categories in closed-ended questions, more than one answer may often apply for respondents. If you want a single answer, then make this clear in the question. An example would be, "From the list below, please check the *primary reason* for your decision to attend college." Often the main question can be followed by a parenthetical note: "Please check the one best answer." If, on the other hand, you want the respondent to check as many answers as apply, that should be made clear as well.

Pretesting the Questionnaire

No matter how carefully researchers design a data-collection instrument such as a questionnaire, there is always the possibility—indeed the certainty—of error. They will always make a mistake: an ambiguous question, a question respondents cannot answer, or a question that violates the rules just discussed in some other way.

To guard against such errors, researchers should pretest the questionnaire in a dry run. The pretest sample can be small—perhaps 10 people or less. They should be like the people researchers intend to include in their study. The ones who participate in the pretest, however, should *not* later participate in the actual study.

When pretesting the instrument, by and large, it's better to ask people to complete the questionnaire than to read through it looking for errors. All too often, a question seems to make sense on a first reading, but proves to be impossible to answer.

9.3b Scales

Some variables are too complex or multifaceted to be measured with just one item on a questionnaire. Examples of complex variables that social work researchers may find difficult to tap adequately with a single questionnaire item are marital satisfaction, level of social functioning, level of client satisfaction with services, attitudes about women or minorities, and level of caregiver burden—to mention just a few.

The composite or cumulative measures of complex variables are called **scales**. Scales allow us to represent complex variables with scores that provide greater potential for variance than would a single item. Suppose, for example, we are providing play therapy for children who have been abused and have a posttraumatic stress disorder (PTSD) as a result of that abuse. Suppose we want to assess whether their PTSD improves as a result of the play therapy. It is hard to imagine how we could assess that improvement in a reasonable way by just asking one question. Instead, we might want to develop a list of PTSD symptoms, such as having nightmares, difficulties concentrating, worrying about bad things happening, self-blame, hypervigilance (we wouldn't use that term with kids), bad memories, and so on. Beside each symptom, the children (or their parent) might check whether in the past week they've had that symptom.

Excerpts from such a scale appear in Figure 9.5. By adding up the numbers that a parent circles for the items in the scale, we can get a total PTSD score. The higher the score, the worse the PTSD symptoms appear to be. We can assess whether the PTSD symptoms got better (or perhaps worse) after our play therapy by having parents complete the scale before the play therapy treatment commences and at points after the entire play therapy treatment regimen has been completed. We could also administer the scale at weekly intervals during the play therapy treatment period to monitor whether the symptoms are improving, worsening, or staying the same. We would not need to analyze separately the responses to the individual items; instead, we would need only to examine the summated score to represent the multifaceted PTSD variable.

As you can tell from the lengthy list of reference volumes for existing scales appearing in Appendix A, scales can come in a seemingly endless variety of formats. Some scaling procedures are highly complex and require a tremendous expenditure of labor to develop. Less complex scales can be as simple as one-item scales that may have minimal wording and can be administered in a conversational format. For example, if you want to assess the moods of very young children (perhaps before and after receiving some form of treatment such as play therapy), you might present them with a handful of simple cartoonish faces, with a smiley face at one end of the continuum and a frowning, sad face at the other end. You would then ask them to select the face that best fits how they were feeling. Or you might assess how well your adult clients were responding to your intervention for anxiety by asking them to rate their anxiety on a scale from 1 to 10, with 1 representing no anxiety and 10 representing the worst anxiety imaginable.

One commonly used scaling format is called Likert scaling. **Likert scales** present respondents with statements followed by response choices for respondents to indicate whether they "strongly agree," "agree," "disagree," "strongly disagree," or are "undecided." Modifications of the wording of the response categories (e.g., "approve") may be used, of course. Sometimes there are additional categories, like "strongly agree," "moderately agree," "slightly agree," "slightly disagree," "moderately disagree," "strongly disagree," and so on. Sometimes the respondents are not given the "undecided" choice to avoid having too many respondents duck taking a position. Whether or not to include choices such as "undecided," "uncertain," or "neutral" is usually a judgment call by the researcher; there is no formula or hard-and-fast guideline determining whether to provide the undecided choice. Likewise, whether to include the "moderately" and "slightly" choices also is a judgment call. If the "undecided," "uncertain," or "neutral" choice is included, it

---

Likert scale A type of measure that presents respondents with statements followed by response choices so that respondents can indicate their degree of agreement or disagreement with each statement.

FIGURE 9.5 Condensed Excerpts from Parent Report of Posttraumatic Symptoms Scale*

Please circle a number that best indicates how well each item describes your child **in the past week.** Please do **NOT** skip any item, even if you are not sure.

Not True or Rarely True	Somewhat or Sometimes True	Very True or Often True	
0	1	2	Difficulty concentrating
0	1	2	Mood swings
0	1	2	Thinks of bad memories
0	1	2	Sad or depressed
0	1	2	Hyper-alert
0	1	2	Worries
0	1	2	Fearful
0	1	2	Withdrawn
0	1	2	Nervous
0	1	2	Startles easily
0	1	2	Irritable
0	1	2	Difficulty sleeping
0	1	2	Nightmares or bad dreams

*Copies of the full scale can be obtained from Dr. Ricky Greenwald, rg@childtrauma.com, who has the copyright for it. Reproduced by permission.

would be placed in the middle of the continuum of choices; that is, between the agree choices and the disagree choices.

With five response categories, scores of 1 to 5 might be assigned, taking the direction of the items into account (for instance, assign a score of 5 to "strongly agree" for positive items and to "strongly disagree" for negative items). Each respondent would then be assigned an overall score that represents the summation of the scores he or she received for responses to the individual items. For example, if there are 20 items on the scale, with the respondent getting a score from 1 to 5 for each item, then the respondent's total score can range from 20 (a score of 1 per item) to 100 (a score of 5 per item). With more than five response categories, the maximum total score will be higher. For example, if seven response categories are used (i.e., "strongly agree," "moderately agree," "slightly agree," "undecided," "slightly disagree," "moderately disagree," "strongly disagree") with 20 items, then respondents could get a score of 1 to 7 for each item and a possible total score ranging from 20 to 140 (7 times 20 items).

9.4 CRITICALLY APPRAISING QUALITATIVE MEASURES

Although scales like those we've been discussing can be used in studies that combine quantitative and qualitative methods, they are typically associated with quantitative inquiry. Let's now examine some of the ways that instrument construction is different in qualitative measurement than in quantitative measurement. But first let's remember that earlier in this chapter we discussed guidelines for asking questions that are just as applicable to gathering information from respondents in qualitative studies as they are in quantitative studies. In either type of study, for instance, one should avoid wording that is biased, too complex, or irrelevant to respondents. Likewise, both methods of inquiry might involve gathering data by directly observing people in addition to asking them questions. In this chapter, we are limiting the discussion to measures for asking people questions, not instruments used for recording direct observations. The latter types of instruments will be discussed in later chapters.

The chief difference between quantitative and qualitative measures for asking people questions is that quantitative measures are always highly structured, tend to use closed-ended questions primarily, and may be administered in either an interview or questionnaire format, whereas qualitative measures rely primarily on interviews that are usually unstructured and that mainly contain open-ended questions with in-depth probes.

9.5 QUALITATIVE INTERVIEWING

Qualitative interviews can range from completely unstructured, informal conversational interviews that use no measurement instruments to highly structured, standardized interviews in which interviewers must ask questions in the exact order and with the exact wording in which they are written in advance. Between these two extremes are semistructured interviews that use interview guides that list in outline form the topics and issues the interview should ask about, but that allow the interviewer to be flexible, informal, and conversational and to adapt the style of the interview and the sequencing and wording of questions to each particular interviewee.

A relatively *unstructured qualitative* interview is an interaction between an interviewer and a respondent in which the interviewer has a general plan of inquiry but not a specific set of questions that must be asked in particular words and in a particular order. It is essentially a conversation in which the interviewer establishes a general direction for the conversation and pursues specific topics raised by the respondent. Ideally, the respondent does most of the talking. If the interviewer is talking more than 5 percent of the time, that's probably too much.

Patton (1990, p. 280) identifies three forms of qualitative, open-ended interviewing:

1. the informal conversational interview,
2. the general interview guide approach, and
3. the standardized open-ended interview.

9.5a Informal Conversational Interviews

An *informal conversational interview* is an unplanned and unanticipated interaction between an interviewer and a respondent that occurs naturally during the course of observation. It is the most open-ended form of interviewing. When this type of interviewing occurs, the person with whom you are talking may not even think of the interaction as an interview. Consequently, you'll probably not want to develop or use a measurement instrument when your research involves conducting informal conversational interviews.

When you conduct an informal conversational interview, you should be extremely flexible so that you can pursue relevant information in whatever direction seems appropriate. Your questions should be generated naturally and spontaneously from what you happen to observe at a particular point in a particular setting or from what individuals in that setting happen to say to you. In other words, this is the type of interviewing that will occur spontaneously when you are conducting observations and want to maximize your understanding of what you are observing and what the people whom you are observing think about what is happening.

Because you cannot anticipate the situation beforehand, you conduct informal conversational interviews with no predetermined set of questions. Nonetheless, it is important for you to use your skills in asking questions and listening—skills that you probably learned as part of your social work practice training.

Asking questions and noting answers is a natural process for all of us, and it seems simple enough to add it to a researcher's bag of tricks as a researcher. However, as we've discussed earlier in this chapter, question wording is a tricky business. All too often, the way researchers ask questions subtly biases the answers they get. Sometimes, researchers put the respondent under pressure to look good. Sometimes researchers put the question in a particular context that completely precludes the most relevant answers.

Suppose you want to find out why a group of youths in a residential facility for emotionally distressed children is running amok. You might be tempted to focus your questioning on how the youths feel about the disciplinary style of their cottage parents. Although you may collect a great deal of information about their attitudes toward their cottage parents, they may be rioting for some other reason. Or perhaps most are simply joining in for the excitement. Properly done, informal conversational interviewing would enable you to find out.

One of the special strengths of this type of interviewing is its *flexibility*. It allows you to respond to things you see or hear that you could not anticipate. The answers evoked by your initial questions should shape your subsequent ones. In this situation, merely asking preestablished questions and recording answers doesn't work. You need to ask a question, hear the answer, interpret its meaning for your general inquiry, and frame another question either to dig into the earlier answer in more depth or to redirect the person's attention to an area more relevant to your inquiry. In short, you need to be able to listen, think, and talk almost at the same time.

The use of neutral **probes** provides a useful guide to getting answers in more depth without biasing later answers. For instance, in response to a question about agency services, a service recipient might simply reply, "Pretty bad." The interviewer could obtain an elaboration on this response through a variety of probes. Sometimes the best probe is silence; if the interviewer sits quietly with pencil poised, the respondent will probably fill the pause with additional comments. (This technique is used effectively by journalists.) Appropriate verbal probes might be, "How is that?" or, "In what ways?" Perhaps the most generally useful probe is, "Anything else?"

Frequently, it is necessary to probe for answers that will be sufficiently informative for analytic purposes. In every case, however, such probes *must* be completely neutral. The probe cannot affect the nature of the subsequent response in any way.

If you have already studied interviewing in your social work practice courses, you might recognize the similarities between interviewing in social work *practice* and conducting informal conversational interviews in social work *research*. In both, you should learn the skills of being a good listener. Be more interested than interesting. Learn to ask such questions as, "How is that?" "In what ways?" "How do you mean that?" "What would be an example of that?" Learn to look and listen expectantly, and let the person you are interviewing fill the silence.

At the same time, you can't afford to be a totally passive receiver in the interaction. You'll probably have some general (or specific) questions in mind based on what you are observing, and you will have to learn the skills of subtly directing the flow of conversation.

Because informal conversational interviewing is so much like normal conversations, it is essential that researchers keep reminding themselves that they are not having a normal conversation. In normal conversations, we want to come across as interesting, worthwhile people. If you watch yourself the next time you are chatting with someone you don't know well, you may find that much of your attention is directed toward thinking up interesting things to say—contributions to the conversation that will make a good impression. Often, we don't really hear each other because we're too busy thinking of what we'll say next. For an interviewer, the desire to appear interesting is counterproductive to the job. You need to make the other person seem interesting—by being interested. (Do this in ordinary conversations, by the way, and people will actually regard you as a great conversationalist.)

9.5b Interview Guide Approach

Besides including the unplanned interviews that emerge spontaneously in the conduct of observations (interviews that probably won't involve using a measurement instrument), qualitative inquiry can include the use of interviews that are planned in advance. These interviews are therefore more structured than informal conversational interviews and will involve using a measurement instrument. Although all qualitative interviewing is open-ended and allows respondents to express their own perspectives in their own words, qualitative interviewing measurement instruments can vary in the extent to which the sequencing and wording of the open-ended questions are predetermined.

Highly structured measurement instruments attempt to ensure that all respondents are asked the same questions in the same sequence to maximize the comparability of responses and to ensure that complete data are gathered from each person on all relevant questions. Greater structure can also reduce interviewer biases and inconsistencies in the way different interviewers conduct their interviews. More structure also eases the researcher's task of organizing and analyzing interview data, and helps readers of the research report judge the quality of the interviewing methods and instruments used.

---

probe A technique for soliciting in a nondirective and unbiased manner a more complete answer to a question.

The downside to the highly structured approach, however, is that it reduces the natural, conversational nature of the interview and the interviewer's flexibility to follow up on important unanticipated circumstances or responses. Patton (1990) suggests that one way to provide more structure than in the completely unstructured informal conversational interview, while maintaining a relatively high degree of flexibility, is to use the interview guide strategy.

An *interview guide* is a qualitative measurement instrument that lists in outline form the topics and issues that the interviewer should cover in the interview, but it allows the interviewer to adapt the sequencing and wording of questions to each particular interview. Thus, the interview guide ensures that different interviewers will cover the same material and keep focused on the same predetermined topics and issues, while at the same time remaining conversational and free to probe into unanticipated circumstances and responses. Interview guides will vary in the extent of detail they provide. How much detail you provide in your guide will depend on the extent to which you are able to anticipate the important topics and issues in advance, and how much detail you think your interviewers need to ensure that they will all cover the same material in a thorough fashion (Patton, 1990).

Suppose, for example, that you want to use intensive interviews of social workers in a qualitative evaluation of an in-service training program aimed at improving their own interviewing skills in conducting clinical assessments. A relatively brief interview guide might list a handful or so of broad question areas to ask about, such as:

1. What interviewing training activities and assignments did the trainee do in the program?
2. In what areas of interviewing, if any, does the trainee feel more or less skillful as a result of the program?
3. What service functions, if any, does the trainee feel better (or worse) prepared to provide as a result of the training?
4. Has the program influenced the trainee's career plans, and if so, how?
5. What did the trainee like and dislike most about the program? What are its strengths and weaknesses, and what changes, if any, does the trainee suggest?

A more detailed interview guide for the same type of evaluation might look something like the following rough example:

I. Overall impression of program
   A. Likes? Dislikes?
   B. Strengths? Weaknesses?
   C. Suggested changes?
   D. Perceived influence of program on trainee?
     1. Service functions prepared to provide
     2. Career plans
     3. Interviewing skills, in general

II. Activities in program
   A. Readings?
   B. Written experiential assignments?
   C. Role plays?
   D. Peer or instructor feedback?
   E. Instructor modeling of interview skills?

III. Progress made or not made in specific areas of interviewing
   A. Beginning the interview
     1. Meeting and greeting client
     2. Introductions
     3. Putting client at ease
     4. Explaining purpose of interview
     5. Obtaining client's reason for coming
   B. Physical attending
     1. Eye contact
     2. Posture
     3. Intermittent positive gestures
     4. Appropriately relaxed and professionally comfortable?
   C. Verbal attending
     1. Nonjudgmental prompts
     2. Brief pauses before responding
     3. Appropriate paraphrasing
     4. Encouraging client to talk
     5. Sensitivity to differences in culture or ethnicity
     6. Conveying empathy and warmth
     7. Speaking in a natural, spontaneous, genuine manner
   D. Exploring the problem
     1. Taking social histories
     2. Examining problem from different perspectives
     3. Assessing situational and systemic factors
   E. Questioning and probing
     1. Asking clear and succinct questions
     2. Asking questions in an unbiased manner
     3. Asking exploratory questions in an open-ended manner
     4. Interspersing closed- and open-ended questions
     5. Pursuing important details with neutral probes

6. Knowing not to bombard with too many questions

7. Logical sequencing of questions

8. Sensitivity to privacy concerns

Regardless of how much detail is in the interview guide, researchers should make sure that their interviewers are completely familiar with its contents and purposes before they begin any interviews. If they are not, the interview will not flow smoothly, and the researcher's efforts to ensure that all of the material is covered in the context of a natural, conversational interview will be imperiled.

Interviewers also have to be prepared to decide when and when not to follow up in a neutral probing manner on unanticipated topics that emerge during the interview, depending on their importance to the respondent and to the purpose of the research. Thus, interviewers should be trained carefully before embarking on any interviews.

9.5c Standardized Open-Ended Interviews

As we just mentioned, sometimes researchers will want to ensure that all interviews are conducted in a consistent, thorough manner—with a minimum of interviewer effects and biases. When this is the aim, the most appropriate strategy is to conduct standardized open-ended interviews. This strategy also may be needed when resource limitations leave insufficient time to pursue less structured strategies in a comprehensive way with large numbers of respondents, or when researchers are tracking individuals over time and therefore want to reduce the chances that changes observed over time are being caused by changes in the way interviews are being conducted.

In light of these concerns, the standardized open-ended interview measurement instrument consists of questions that are "written out in advance exactly the way they are to be asked in the interview" (Patton, 1990, p. 285). Great care goes into the wording of the questions and their sequencing. Probes are to be limited to where they are indicated on the measurement instrument, which, as we noted at the beginning of this chapter, is called an *interview schedule*. However, some studies that use highly skilled interviewers may permit more flexibility in probing than other studies that use this standardized open-ended interviewing.

9.5d Illustration of a Standardized Open-Ended Interview Schedule

Figure 9.6 presents excerpts from an exemplary, highly structured, standardized open-ended interview schedule that has been used in a qualitative study of openness in adoption by Ruth McRoy and Harold Grotevant. The entire schedule consists of 179 items. We think that the 22 items we have excerpted for Figure 9.6 sufficiently illustrate a superbly crafted standardized interview schedule and some of the points we made about constructing measurement instruments that apply to both quantitative and qualitative research. Notice, for example, the open-endedness, neutrality, and logical arrangement and sequencing of the questions. Notice also where and how the schedule systematically instructs interviewers to probe for detail and clarification and how it provides parenthetical details to help interviewers clarify the point of the question for respondents who may initially have difficulty in answering. Finally, be sure to notice its use of contingency questions.

9.6 A COMPARISON OF QUANTITATIVE AND QUALITATIVE APPROACHES TO ASKING PEOPLE QUESTIONS

As we end this chapter, we remind you that, despite the differences between quantitative and qualitative measures for asking people questions, the two approaches share a number of commonalities. We'd also like to reiterate that the same study can use both approaches; they need not be seen as mutually exclusive or in conflict. We summarize these points in the box entitled "A Comparison of Quantitative and Qualitative Approaches to Asking People Questions."

9.7 MAIN POINTS

- Questionnaires provide a method of collecting data by (1) asking people questions, or (2) asking them to agree or disagree with statements that represent different points of view.

- Questions may be open-ended (respondents supply their own answers) or closed-ended (they select from a list of answers provided them).

FIGURE 9.6 Excerpts from a Standardized Open-Ended Interview Schedule on Openness in Adoptions

ADOPTIVE PARENT INTERVIEW

Begin the interview process by reviewing with the parent the number of adopted children s/he has, their names and ages.

BACKGROUND REGARDING ADOPTION

1. Could you begin by telling me a little bit about why you decided to adopt?

2. Whom did you talk to about adoption before you reached your decision? What advice did you receive?

3. What did you expect the adoption process to be like?

   .

   .

   .

34. How old were you when _____ (child) was adopted?

35. How did your relatives react to your decision to adopt?

36. In what ways is _____ (child) like you (temperament, appearance)?

37. In what ways is _____ (child) dissimilar to you (temperament, appearance)?

38. Did you anticipate that the arrival of_____ (child) would mean making changes in your life style? If so, what changes did you anticipate?

   .

   .

   .

41. Please describe the time around the arrival of_____in your family. How would you describe _____'s early behavior (Probe: pleasant, easy, fussy, difficult, etc.)? What were some of the satisfactions and problems you encountered in the first 3 years? What was your relationship like with_____during those early years? (Probe for specific events and behaviors rather than global evaluations.)

KNOWLEDGE ABOUT DEGREES OF OPENNESS IN ADOPTION

42. What options did your adoption agency offer regarding open or closed adoptions (non-identifying information, photos of birthparents, continued sharing of information, meeting parents, ongoing contact, etc.)?

43. Had you heard of open adoptions before you came to_____(agency)?

44. If so, what did you think the term meant?

45. What does the term "semi-open adoption" mean to you?

46. What does the term "traditional or closed adoption" mean to you?

47. Describe the process you went through before deciding what form of openness you would choose.

48. What option did you choose?

49. Why did you choose this option?

50. What do you see as the advantages and the disadvantages of:
    a. traditional "closed" adoption

    b. semi-open adoption

    c. open adoption

(Continued)

FIGURE 9.6 (*Continued*)

IF FAMILY CHOSE A TRADITIONAL (CLOSED) ADOPTION, CONTINUE DIRECTLY ON TO THE PINK SECTION, PAGES 6-7.

IF FAMILY CHOSE TO SHARE INFORMATION ONLY, NOW GO TO THE GREEN SECTION, PAGES 8-9.

IF FAMILY CHOSE TO MEET THE BIRTHPARENTS, NOW GO TO THE YELLOW SECTION, PAGES 10-11.

IF FAMILY RESPONDENT CHOSE TO HAVE ONGOING FACE TO FACE CONTACT, NOW GO TO THE BLUE SECTION, PAGES 12-14.

IF FAMILY INITIALLY CHOSE SEMI-OPEN AND LATER CHANGED TO FULLY DISCLOSED, NOW GO TO THE ORANGE SECTION, PAGES 15-18.

IF FAMILY CHOSE CONFIDENTIAL (CLOSED) ADOPTION [This section appears on pink paper]

  ·

  ·

  ·

58. If there are other siblings in the household, do they ever try to use (child's) adoption against him/her? If so, please describe.

    ·

    ·

    ·

IF FAMILY CHOSE TO SHARE INFORMATION ONLY.... [This section appears on green paper]

  ·

  ·

  ·

75. What impact do you think sharing information will have on:
    a. your child?

    b. you and your spouse?

    c. birthparents?

    d. other children in the family (if applicable)?...

      ·

      ·

      ·

IF FAMILY CHOSE TO HAVE ONGOING CONTACT.... [This section appears on blue paper]

  ·

  ·

  ·

111. How would you describe your relationship with the birthparent(s)? (Probe: as a relative, friend, etc.)...

    ·

    ·

    ·

179. We've talked about quite a few things, but I wonder if there might be something that we have skipped which you might feel to be important to understanding you and your family. Is there anything that you would like to add to what we have discussed?

SOURCE: Used by permission of Ruth McRoy.

A Comparison of Quantitative and Qualitative Approaches to Asking People Questions

	Quantitative Approaches	Qualitative Approaches
Similarities in Measurement Principles		
Try to use language that respondents will understand	Always	Always
Ask one question at a time; avoid double-barreled questions	Always	Always
Only ask questions that respondents are capable of answering and that are relevant to them	Always	Always
Avoid biased items and terms	Always	Always
Stylistic Differences		
Questionnaires or scales	Often	Rarely
Interviews	Sometimes	Usually
Same wording and sequence of questions for all respondents	Always	Rarely
Interviewer flexibility regarding wording, sequencing, and conversational style	Never	Very often
Open-ended questions	Rarely	Usually
Probes	Rare and brief	Frequent and in-depth
Closed-ended questions	Usually	Sometimes
Formality of interview	Relaxed, friendly demeanor, but professional tone and not overly casual	More likely to resemble a spontaneous, informal, friendly conversation
Complementary Functions		
Objectivity and consistency versus flexibility and subjective meanings	Develop measures to be administered to many respondents in ways that attempt to minimize random and systematic measurement error, but that may be at a superficial level, requiring an investigation of their validity	Develop measures that allow for researcher flexibility and subjectivity in order to pursue deeper, more valid levels of understanding of subjective meanings among fewer respondents
Generalizability versus in-depth, theoretical understanding	Verify, in a precise, statistical fashion, whether understandings emerging from qualitative measurement are generalizable	Develop a deeper theoretical understanding of the meanings of statistical findings emerging from quantitative measurement
Test hypotheses versus generating hypotheses and deeper understandings	Test hypotheses, perhaps generated from qualitative studies, generating new findings that might require further qualitative study to be sufficiently understood	Study phenomena whose meanings are not sufficiently understood, perhaps generating hypotheses for quantitative study

- Usually, short items in a questionnaire are better than long ones.
- Negative items and terms should be avoided in questionnaires because they may confuse respondents.
- In questionnaire items, bias is the quality that encourages respondents to answer in a particular way to avoid or support a particular point of view. Avoid it.
- Contingency questions are questions that should be answered only by people giving a particular response to some preceding question. The contingency question format is highly useful because it doesn't ask people questions that have no meaning for them. For example, a question about the number of times a person has been pregnant should be asked only of women.
- Scales include several indicators of a variable in one summary measure.
- Likert scaling is a measurement technique that is based on the use of standardized response categories (for instance, "strongly agree," "agree," "disagree," "strongly disagree") for several questionnaire items. The Likert format for questionnaire items is popular and extremely useful.
- Although qualitative and quantitative measurement approaches share certain principles, quantitative measures are always highly structured, tend to use closed-ended questions primarily, and may be administered in either an interview or questionnaire format, whereas qualitative measures rely on interviews that are usually unstructured and mainly contain open-ended questions and in-depth probes.
- Three forms of qualitative, open-ended interviewing are (1) the informal conversational interview, (2) the interview guide approach, and (3) the standardized open-ended interview.

9.8 PRACTICE-RELATED EXERCISES

1. Find a questionnaire in a magazine or newspaper (a reader survey, for example). Bring it to class and critique it.
2. For each of the open-ended questions listed below, construct a closed-ended question that could be used in a questionnaire.

   a. What was your family's total income last year?
   b. How do you feel about increasing public spending on social welfare?
   c. How important is learning theory in your approach to social work practice?
   d. What was your main reason for studying to be a social worker?
   e. What do you feel is the biggest problem that faces this community?

3. Construct a set of contingency questions for use in a self-administered questionnaire that would solicit the following information:

   a. Is the respondent employed?
   b. If unemployed, is the respondent looking for work?
   c. If the unemployed respondent is not looking for work, is he or she retired, a student, or a homemaker?
   d. If the respondent is looking for work, how long has he or she been looking?

4. Using the Likert format, construct a brief scale to measure client satisfaction with service delivery.
5. Develop two versions of a brief questionnaire asking your classmates about their satisfaction with the chapters of this text that they have read so far. Make one version entirely open-ended and the other entirely closed-ended. Administer each version to several classmates. Compare the answers you get to the two versions. What advantages and disadvantages of each approach are illustrated by the different sets of answers?

9.9 INTERNET EXERCISES

1. Find an article that discusses scale development. Write down the bibliographic reference information for the article and summarize the article in a few sentences. If the article reports the development of a particular scale, critique the scale, its development, or both—either positively or negatively.
2. Find a questionnaire on the Internet. (Hint: Search for "questionnaire.") Critique at least five of the questions contained in it—either

positively or negatively. Be sure to give the Web address (URL) for the questionnaire and the exact wording of the questions you critique.

9.9a Competency Notes

EP 2.1.3c: Demonstrate effective oral and written communication in working with individuals, families, groups, organizations, communities, and colleagues (p. 162): Social workers will communicate more effectively by following this chapter's guidelines for asking questions.

EP 2.1.10d: Collect, organize, and interpret client data (p. 158): Social workers understand how to ask questions in collecting client data so that the answers can be interpreted properly.

Sampling and Surveys

part

5

The next two chapters will describe procedures geared toward obtaining findings from study participants that can be generalized with accuracy to a larger population. Chapter 10 will describe survey research, which involves collecting data by asking people questions. It will emphasize quantitative methods that attempt to maximize the objectivity, accuracy, and generalizability of the information provided by respondents in self-administered questionnaires or through interviews. Chapter 11, on sampling, also deals with generalizability. As we'll see, it is possible for us to select a few people or things for observation and then apply what we observe to a much larger group of people or things. Chapter 11 will also discuss qualitative methods for obtaining study participants, which tend to be more flexible than quantitative sampling methods and which put less emphasis on generalizability and more emphasis on in-depth understanding and generating tentative new ideas and insights.

Sampling and Surveys

Part

5

Surveys

10.1　INTRODUCTION

EP 2.1.6b
EP 2.1.10d
EP 2.1.10m

Much of what we discussed in Chapter 9—such as asking questions, constructing questionnaires, and conducting interviews—applies to survey research. You probably have been a **respondent** in a survey more than once. In a typical survey, the researcher selects a sample of respondents and administers a questionnaire to them. Surveys may be used for descriptive, explanatory, and exploratory purposes. They can be limited to one point in time in cross-sectional surveys or repeated at different points in time in longitudinal surveys. Although surveys tend to be associated with quantitative research, they can be improved through combination with qualitative methods.

Survey research is probably the best method available to describe a population that is too large to observe directly. If appropriate methods are used to select a group of respondents whose characteristics reflect those of the larger population, survey researchers can accurately describe the attributes of large populations based on data from a small fraction of the population. The methods for selecting small groups that accurately represent a larger population are called *sampling*. Sampling methods, however, apply to other types of research, too—not just surveys—and thus will be the focus of our next chapter. We'll see how the outcomes of presidential elections with millions of voters can be accurately predicted when proper sampling methods are used to select less than 2,000 respondents, and how they can be inaccurately predicted when flawed sampling procedures are used with a much larger group of respondents. In this chapter, however, we just need to bear in mind that the value of a survey may depend on whether the people who respond to it do or do not accurately represent the larger population that the survey may be attempting to portray.

Sometimes people use the pretense of survey research for nonscientific purposes. For example, you may receive a telephone call indicating you've been selected for a survey, only to find the first question is, "How would you like to make thousands of dollars a week right there in your own home?" Or you may be told you can win a prize if you can name the president whose picture is on the penny. (Tell them it's Elvis.) Unfortunately, a few unscrupulous telemarketers will try to prey on the general cooperation people have given to survey researchers.

Done properly, however, survey research can be a useful tool of social inquiry. The key task for you is separating the wheat from the chaff. We trust this chapter will help you in that task.

There are four main methods of administering survey questionnaires to a sample of respondents: (1) by mail, (2) online, (3) through face-to-face interviews, and (4) by telephone. This chapter will examine each of those four methods in that order.

10.2　MAIL SURVEYS

Both mail surveys and online surveys ask respondents to complete self-administered questionnaires themselves. Some studies, however, ask respondents to complete *self-administered questionnaires* in other contexts. For example, they might administer the questionnaire to a group of respondents who have gathered at the same place at the same time. A survey of students taking an introductory social work course, for example, might be conducted in this manner during class. High school students might be surveyed during homeroom period. Or a research worker might deliver the questionnaire to the home of sample respondents and explain the study. The questionnaire is left for the respondent to complete and the researcher to pick up later.

Home delivery and mailings can be used in combination as well. Questionnaires can be mailed to families, and then research workers visit homes to pick up the questionnaires and check them for completeness. In just the opposite method, questionnaires have been hand-delivered by research workers with a request that the respondents mail the completed questionnaires to the research office.

On the whole, when a research worker delivers the questionnaire or picks it up (or does both), the completion rate seems higher than for straightforward mail surveys. Additional experimentation with this method is likely to point to other techniques for improving completion while reducing costs.

---

respondent　A person who provides data for analysis by responding to a survey questionnaire.

10.2a Mail Distribution and Return

The basic method for collecting data through the mail has been to send a questionnaire accompanied by a letter of explanation and a self-addressed, stamped envelope for returning the questionnaire. The respondent is expected to complete the questionnaire, put it in the envelope, and return it by mail. If, by any chance, you've received such a questionnaire and failed to return it, it would be valuable to recall the reasons you had for not returning it and keep them in mind any time you plan to send questionnaires to others.

A common reason for not returning questionnaires is that it's too much trouble. To overcome this problem, researchers have developed several ways to make returning them easier. For instance, a *self-mailing questionnaire* requires no return envelope: When the questionnaire is folded a particular way, the return address appears on the outside. The respondent therefore doesn't have to worry about losing the envelope.

More elaborate designs are available also. For example, the questionnaire can be bound in a booklet with foldout panels on the front and back cover: one for sending the questionnaire out and the other for getting it back—thus avoiding the use of envelopes. The point here is that anything you can do to make the job of completing and returning the questionnaire easier will improve your study. Imagine receiving a questionnaire that made no provisions for its return to the researcher. Suppose you had to (1) find an envelope, (2) write the address on it, (3) figure out how much postage it required, and (4) put the stamps on it. How likely is it that you would return the questionnaire?

You may be wondering at this point why it's so important to make it easier for people to return their questionnaires? Didn't we say just a while ago that a survey of a smaller grouping of people can accurately portray the characteristics of a larger population? Yes, we said that. But we also said that the accuracy depends on whether the characteristics of the smaller grouping really represent the characteristics of the population. To the extent that those who choose not to respond to a survey differ from respondents in important ways relevant to the research question, the representativeness of the survey suffers from **non-response bias**.

Imagine a survey of low-income social service recipients to assess their satisfaction with the services they received. Imagine further that a questionnaire is mailed to them with no return envelope, or perhaps with an unstamped return envelope. The respondents in all likelihood would be an atypical and tiny proportion of the population whose extreme feelings (perhaps extremely favorable or extremely unfavorable) about the services are so strong that they are willing to go to the trouble and expense of completing and returning the questionnaire. They might also have more money than those who refuse to purchase a stamp. Consequently, the survey results would probably misrepresent the larger population, because the folks with less money or less extreme feelings about the services would be much less likely to respond. One of the most important criteria, therefore, in distinguishing useful mailed surveys from misleading ones is whether sufficient steps are taken to maximize the number of people who respond.

10.2b Cover Letters

An important factor influencing response rates to mailed surveys is the quality of the cover letter that accompanies the questionnaire. The cover letter is usually what prospective respondents read first, so it should be constructed in a way that will motivate them to respond and alleviate any resistance they may have about participating in the survey.

To motivate individuals to respond, explain the purpose and importance of the survey in terms that the prospective respondent can understand. Obtain an endorsement of or sponsorship for the study from organizations or people who are esteemed by prospective respondents and then identify those organizations or people in the cover letter. Explain why each individual's response is important to the success of the study and to solving a problem that respondents care about.

To alleviate resistance to participating, assure potential participants of the anonymity of their

---

non-response bias A threat to the representativeness of survey findings, the seriousness of which depends upon the extent to which survey respondents differ from non-respondents in important ways relevant to the research question.

responses, explain how the sample was selected, and indicate how long it takes to complete the questionnaire (the quicker, the better).

Figure 10.1 is a cover letter that accompanied a 2008 survey of social workers. It illustrates the elements just discussed for motivating participation and reducing resistance.

10.2c Follow-Up Mailings

If respondents have been identified for purposes of follow-up mailing, then such mailings should be prepared for as the questionnaires are returned. Follow-up mailings may be administered in several ways. The simplest is to send non-respondents a letter of additional encouragement to participate. A better method, however, is to send a new copy of the survey questionnaire with the follow-up letter. If potential respondents have not returned their questionnaires after two or three weeks, the questionnaires probably have been lost or misplaced. Receiving a follow-up letter might encourage them to look for the original questionnaire, but if they can't find it easily, the letter may go for naught.

The methodological literature on follow-up mailings strongly suggests that it is an effective method for increasing return rates in mail surveys. Three mailings (an original and two follow-ups) are the norm. In general, the longer a potential respondent delays replying, the less likely he or she is to do so at all. Properly timed follow-up mailings thus stimulate more responses. Roughly two or three weeks is a reasonable interval between mailings.

If the individuals in the survey sample are not identified on the questionnaires, it may not be possible to re-mail only to non-respondents. In such a case, you should send your follow-up mailing to all members of the sample, thanking those who may have already participated and encouraging the participation of those who have not.

A less costly alternative is to include a stamped, self-addressed postcard with the original mailing and perhaps with each subsequent mailing. The postcard can identify who has responded to the survey and who chooses not to participate in it.

The person completing the postcard simply enters their name on it and then mails it back to you separately from the survey questionnaire. That way the anonymity of the questionnaire is protected, and you will know not to send a follow-up mailing to those whose names are on the postcards. The box "Postcard Contents" shows what you can say on the postcard so that you will know not to send that person another mailing and yet not know whether they chose to participate in your survey or not.

10.2d Response Rates

A question that new survey researchers frequently ask concerns the response rate that should be achieved in a mail survey. The **response rate** is the number of people participating in a survey divided by the number of people who were asked to respond, in the form of a percentage. The overall response rate is one guide to the representativeness of the sample respondents. If a high response rate is achieved, then there is less chance of significant non-response bias than if a low rate is achieved. In the past, response rates of at least 50 percent were usually considered adequate, and response rates as high as 60 or 70 percent were considered good or very good.

Today, however, there is less agreement as to what constitutes an acceptable response rate. Some surveys with lower response rates can have value. For example, suppose an agency mails a questionnaire to all of its clients, and on it clients are asked to indicate their level of satisfaction with agency services. Suppose further that the response rate is only 40 percent and that most respondents indicate that they are very dissatisfied, and only a small minority of respondents say they are satisfied. Although agency staff members would not know the exact proportion of very dissatisfied clients, they would know that it is more than 20 percent (which is half of 40 percent). They therefore would be able to conclude that even if the non-respondents are much more satisfied than the respondents (which may or may not be the case), the proportion of dissatisfied clients appears to be an important problem for the agency.

The above hypothetical example, however, does not mean that the potential for non-response bias should be taken lightly. It is always an important

---

response rate   The number of people participating in a survey divided by the number of people who were asked to respond, in the form of a percentage.

FIGURE 10.1 A Sample Cover Letter

SCHOOL OF SOCIAL WORK

THE UNIVERSITY OF TEXAS AT AUSTIN

1925 San Jacinto Blvd. · Austin, Texas 78712-1203 · MC D3500 · Fax (512) 471-9600 · email utssw@utxvms.cc.utexas.edu

Dear Colleague,

A critical issue being debated in social work these days involves whether and how the evidence-based practice (EBP) model should be guiding our practice decisions. However, our profession lacks adequate information about the way practitioners view and use EBP and the factors associated with those views. If you would take about 15 to 20 minutes to complete the enclosed questionnaire and return it in the enclosed stamped self-addressed envelope, you will make an important contribution to a survey that seeks to enhance our profession's gathering of such information from practitioners.

The Department of Field Education at the Columbia University School of Social Work (CUSSW) is collaborating with us on the project, and for this reason, you are among 800 licensed clinical social workers selected randomly in four areas (New York, St. Louis, Texas, and Toronto) to be asked to participate in this survey. Your participation is voluntary and your responses are anonymous. Neither I nor anyone else will be able to identify from whom any completed questionnaire came. However, if you would complete and return the enclosed stamped self-addressed postcard, you will help us know whom to contact in follow-up mailings to colleagues who intend to participate but who need to be reminded. By mailing the postcard back separately from the questionnaire, the anonymity of your questionnaire responses will be maintained.

Please return your completed questionnaire and postcard as soon as possible. If you wish to discuss the information above or any concern you may have with this survey, please do not hesitate to contact me, Allen Rubin, Ph.D., at (512) 471-9218. If you have any questions about your rights as a research participant, complaints, concerns, or questions about the research, please contact the Institutional Review Board at Columbia University, 475 Riverside Drive, New York, NY 10115; Phone: (212) 870-3481; E-mail: askirb@columbia.edu.

Your current or future relationship with CUSSW will not be affected whether you choose to participate or not.

Your response is very important to this survey. The value of its results will depend on how many practitioners choose to respond.

Thank you for your attention and time.

Respectfully,

Allen Rubin, Ph.D.

Admissions and Academic Programs (512) 471-5457 · Dean's Office (512) 471-1937 · General Information (512) 471-5456

Postcard Contents

Please complete this postcard and return it separately from the questionnaire. Doing so will let us know that you have either responded to the survey or choose not to participate in it. In turn, that information will let us know not to send you a subsequent follow-up mailing.

By mailing this postcard back separately, the anonymity of your questionnaire responses will be maintained.

I, _____ have either responded to the survey or choose not to participate in it.

Thank you!

consideration, even when response rates are relatively high. Thus, if the response rate to the above survey were 50 percent, and most respondents indicated high levels of satisfaction, it would be quite risky to conclude that most clients overall were highly satisfied. Maybe the vast majority of the non-respondents were dissatisfied and because of their dissatisfaction opted not to bother with responding to the survey.

When appraising the implications of a survey's response rate, you should bear in mind that a demonstrated lack of non-response bias is far more important than a high response rate. Suppose that in the example with the 40-percent response rate, the researchers had conducted a special follow-up effort with 10 percent of the non-respondents and found that most of them were also very dissatisfied with the agency's services. Moreover, suppose that they found that the personal characteristics (age, ethnicity, presenting problem, and so on) of the non-respondents were similar to those of the respondents. That follow-up effort and its findings would therefore suggest that although the survey's response rate was not high, its results do not appear to be highly vulnerable to a serious non-response bias.

10.2e Increasing Response Rates

As you might imagine, one of the more persistent discussions among survey researchers concerns ways of increasing response rates, and thus reducing the likelihood of non-response bias. Survey researchers have developed many techniques for addressing this problem. We've already discussed some of them, such as preparing a cover letter that will motivate people to respond and let them know that it won't take much time (10 to 15 minutes *at most* is recommended), making it easy for them to respond, and using follow-up mailings. Offering to share the survey results with those who respond might also help. In addition, some have tried paying people to respond. One problem with paying, of course, is that it can be expensive, but some imaginative alternatives have been used. Some researchers have said, "We want to get your two-cents' worth on some issues, and we're willing to pay"—enclosing two pennies. Another enclosed a quarter, suggesting that the respondent make some little child happy. Still others have enclosed paper money. More commonly, a raffle has been used as an incentive to respond, and the lucky respondent whose name is drawn wins a prize.

From an ethical standpoint, another concern about compensating survey respondents is that such incentives may be somewhat coercive and reduce the voluntary nature of participation. And if some respondents are inspired to participate while others are not, a bias may be introduced in the sample responding. This is not a settled issue for social researchers as a whole, and experimentation with incentives has proceeded. In a 1999 review of studies of this topic, Singer, Groves, and Corning found that with very few exceptions, response rates are increased by the use of incentives in mail surveys, face-to-face interviews, and telephone polls. Also, the authors found no evidence of negative effects on the quality of responses collected. A decade later, Petrolia and Bhattacharjee (2009) reviewed past experience with incentives and conducted their own study. They confirmed that incentives increase response rates, and they found that prepaid incentives had a greater effect than those introduced later in the process.

10.3 ONLINE SURVEYS

An increasingly popular method of survey research involves the use of the Internet. Some online surveys are conducted completely via e-mail; others are conducted via websites. Commonly, potential respondents will receive an e-mail asking them to go to a web link where the survey resides. Web design software can be used to design your questionnaire on a website for online use by respondents who would be directed to go to that site.

10.3a Advantages and Disadvantages of Online Surveys

The main advantage of online surveys is that they can quickly and inexpensively be sent to very large numbers of prospective respondents anywhere in the world. For example, you can quickly disseminate your request for participation by using an up-to-date e-mail address list and asking recipients to click on the link to your survey website. (The link would be provided within your e-mail message.) Moreover, survey response data are automatically entered for computer processing, eliminating the need for manual data entry and facilitating a quick online tabulation of results. Online survey tools, such as SurveyMonkey™, can check whether respondents are skipping an item or in other ways responding inappropriately while taking the survey, and then prompt them to correct any omission or other mistake before proceeding to the next item.

The main disadvantage of online surveys concerns the representativeness of the respondents. This disadvantage is particularly relevant to social work surveys of people who are poor or elderly. People who use the Internet and who are most apt to respond to online surveys are likely to be younger, more affluent, and more highly educated than the rest of your target population. However, this problem may be waning as more and more people gain access to the Internet. In fact, some believe that online surveys soon will replace other, more traditional survey methods. Depending on the type of respondents being targeted, evidence is emerging to suggest that online survey response rates may be comparable to mail surveys (Kaplowitz et al., 2004), especially when the online survey is accompanied by a postcard reminder encouraging respondents to participate. This "mixed method" of combining online surveys and postal surveys has largely been developed by Don Dillman (2000). Nevertheless, the poor and the elderly remain likely to be underrepresented in online social work surveys in the foreseeable future.

10.3b Using SurveyMonkey™

If you are interested in testing the water of online surveys, SurveyMonkey™ may provide you an opportunity to try your hand at this emerging technique. At this writing, you can experiment with a limited version of the online survey program at no charge. Visit http:// www.surveymonkey.com/ and select "Create Survey" to get started. The program is very user-friendly with regard to designing questionnaire items. You will have to enter the e-mail addresses of your intended respondents, and they will receive an e-mail invitation to visit the survey webpage and participate. The free beginner package will also provide you with a basic analysis of the survey results.

10.3c Tips for Conducting Online Surveys

If the underrepresentation of the poor and elderly is not a reason to eschew conducting your survey online (e.g., maybe you are surveying social work students or practitioners), here are some do's and don'ts:

- Use plain, simple language in your e-mail message inviting respondents to participate.
- Address your message to each respondent by his or her name. If respondents see the names of many other recipients, they might be less likely to respond. Do not list more than one address in the "TO" or "CC" field.
- Keep the e-mail message brief and clear. You want to motivate respondents to click on the survey's website link, where you can place more details. The e-mail invitational message should be limited to the survey's aim, why respondents have been selected, how much time it takes to complete the survey, the deadline for responding, the link to the survey website, and a password that is unique for each respondent.
- The password that respondents will use to gain access to the survey will prevent them from skewing the results with multiple submissions ("ballot stuffing"). Keep the password terminology consistent; for example, don't confuse respondents by referring to it as a "unique

number" in your e-mail message and then as a "password" when they access the survey online.

- Present the password and link to the survey website early in the e-mail message (no more than one third of the way down); don't force respondents to scroll down the screen to find them.
- Consider using a reward—such as a prize drawing—as an incentive to participate. As an additional incentive, offer to share selected results with everyone who completes the survey.
- Mention that the respondents have been specially selected for participation.
- Limit the time required for survey completion to 15 minutes or less.
- Set a deadline for participation.
- Send the e-mail message at a time when respondents are most likely to be reading their e-mail and apt to respond to the survey. The best time to send your message will depend on the type of respondents to your survey. For example, if you are surveying faculty or students, don't send it during spring break or some other time when they are likely to be on vacation. If you have completed your work on the e-mail message late at night, wait until the next day to send it (unless you are surveying insomniacs or night watch guards). If a parent-child questionnaire is planned, send the invitation around late afternoon when children are home, not early in the day when respondents can't complete the study because children are at school.
- Send frequent follow-up e-mail reminders to participate.
- Your survey website tool should enable respondents to take a break and then reenter the survey if they need to.
- Limit the number of questions per screen to just a few, to avoid excessive scrolling and to make completion seem less burdensome.
- The website should introduce the survey in a manner that motivates participation—for example, by providing simple instructions as to how to respond and an illustration of the ease of responding.

One of the trickier problems regarding non-response to online surveys is the growth of spam-blocking e-mail systems. In e-mail jargon, "spam" refers to unsolicited and typically unwanted e-mail messages that have been sent as mass mailings to a large number of recipients. If you send your invitational e-mail message out in a way that increases its likelihood of being flagged as spam, many intended recipients may never receive it, and you will have no way of knowing what proportion of them do and do not receive it. If many do not receive it, that will of course substantially reduce your response rate and perhaps make your survey look more biased than it actually is. In other words, many non-respondents might have responded had they seen your e-mail message in the first place, and their non-response will have had nothing to do with them having different characteristics or views than respondents.

To reduce the chances that your invitational e-mail message will be perceived as "spam," you should word your subject field in a way that does not sound like a mass solicitation. Likewise, do not include many recipients, because some e-mail systems automatically block messages as spam when they detect that. Instead, you should use a broadcast/e-mail merge option that sends an individual message to each recipient. Your message is more likely to be flagged as bulk mail and blocked as spam if it includes many addresses in the "TO," "CC," or "BCC" (blind copy) field. You can test whether your message will be perceived as spam by sending it to some friends or colleagues who you know have spam filters and ask them to respond letting you know they received the message.

The box "Online Survey of Views about Evidence-Based Practice" presents an illustration of an online survey in social work. It illustrates some of the advantages of online surveys and also might help you avoid some of the pitfalls encountered by investigators using this technique.

10.3d Emerging Developments in Online Surveys

Technological advances are developing so quickly that new innovations will surely have arisen by the time this book reaches your hands. For example, tablets and smartphones have been rapidly gaining in computing power, and increasingly they have been used as vehicles for online surveys. Respondents probably led researchers in this innovation.

Online Survey of Views about Evidence-Based Practice

In 2005 the *Journal of Social Work Education* disseminated a call for papers, encouraging prospective authors to submit manuscripts that would be reviewed for possible publication in a special issue on the topic of evidence-based practice (EBP) in social work education. Upon seeing this call for papers, Allen Rubin asked his doctoral student research assistant, Danielle Parrish, if she'd like to collaborate with him in writing a conceptual article on that topic to be submitted for the special issue. She agreed, and they began reviewing the literature and developing ideas. As things progressed, they realized that the value of their work might be enhanced if they could augment their conceptual ideas with evidence from a national survey about how social work faculty members were viewing EBP.

At first, the idea of such a survey seemed impractical for two reasons: (1) The deadline for submitting their manuscript for the special issue was in about six months; and (2) they had no special funding for such an ambitious survey. Upon further reflection, however, Rubin thought it just might be doable if done online, and Parrish agreed. They estimated that it would take only about 30–40 hours for a team of MSW student assistants to go to the website of every graduate school of social work and download the e-mail addresses listed there for each program's faculty members. They estimated that the labor costs for this would be about $500. Rubin knew that he could cover those costs with the small amount of funds left over in his annual professorship endowment, but nevertheless was successful in procuring with a quick turnaround the funds in a special research grant from his university. Six MSW students were hired, and they were able to download the e-mail addresses of all faculty ($N= 3,061$) from 170 of the 181 accredited graduate schools of social work with accessible websites as listed on the website of the Council on Social Work Education.

While their assistants were downloading the e-mail addresses, Rubin and Parrish developed an online survey instrument consisting of 10 items that they estimated would take faculty member respondents only about five minutes to complete. The survey items were posted on a university website, and a link to the website was created and inserted into the e-mails sent to potential respondents. Whereas an e-mail reply to the survey would have shown the respondent's e-mail address, the website survey ensured the anonymity of each participant's response, and the link made it convenient to use. In addition, the e-mail that went out to faculty members detailed the purpose of the research, the importance of each recipient's participation, the anonymous and voluntary nature of the study, and Rubin's contact information. (It was not terribly time-consuming to send out 3,061 e-mail messages because, by cutting and pasting the addresses into 10 groups with a different e-mail nickname for each group,

only 10 messages had to be sent, with each automatically going to about 300 recipients.)

Immediately after sending the e-mail, technological problems emerged. First, Rubin's e-mail system was deluged with 135 undeliverable e-mails, due primarily to obsolete addresses. Some folks sent e-mails to Rubin indicating that his e-mail message had been delivered to their school's "spam jam," decreasing the likelihood that their colleagues received it. Others informed Rubin by e-mail that the survey website link somehow was deleted from his e-mail message by their university's e-mail system. Still others responded by e-mail to say that they could not access the survey website.

To address these technical difficulties, the researchers corresponded by e-mail with those who had reported difficulties to improve access to the survey. In addition, the researchers consulted with university technology support, and created a new university-hosted website address that was sent out in subsequent follow-up mailings. However, it is likely that technical problems precluded the response of many potential participants who did not take the time to obtain assistance in accessing the website or to respond to later e-mails.

In all, there were three follow-up e-mails to the potential respondents. The final mailing asked respondents to either complete the survey by accessing the website link or respond to Rubin by e-mail with the reason why they did not complete the survey (for example, perhaps they could not access the website). This was done to assess how representative or biased the respondent sample might be.

All of these efforts yielded a final sample of 973 respondents, which was 32 percent of the original list of 3,061 e-mail addresses. Because of the various technical problems there was no way to know the exact response rate among those who actually received the e-mail messages and were able to access the survey website. With various adjustments for the technical problems, Rubin and Parrish estimated that the response rate was at least 47 percent among those who actually received their e-mails and were able to access the survey website. Moreover, the e-mailed responses to the final follow-up message suggested that decisions about responding to the survey generally were not influenced by views about EBP.

Despite the tech-related non-response problems encountered, the findings of the survey proved to be quite valuable. A surprisingly large proportion of respondents reported teaching students that certain interventions deserved special recognition as being "evidence-based" even if the types of "evidence" supporting those interventions are generally considered weak sources of evidence-sources that reside at or near the bottom of the EBP research hierarchy. The proportion was so large that even if every non-respondent did not teach about EBP in the problematic way, the adjusted proportion of faculty members saying that they teach about EBP this way would still be troubling. For example, even if the proportion fell from 50 percent (in the sample) to 20 percent (in the population), the prospects of one out of five faculty members teaching about EBP this way would be unsettling.

Based on feedback received after e-mailing the survey findings to all potential respondents, the findings appeared to have created quite a stir among many faculty members and spurred some schools to hold faculty meetings to discuss how faculty members were viewing and teaching about evidence-based practice. The reactions to the survey findings spurred the convening of a national symposium on improving the teaching of evidence-based practice.

The Rubin and Parrish survey illustrates how an online survey can be conducted with a limited amount of time and money, and how it might have value even with non-response problems. Yet it also illustrates some of the potential technical difficulties you should anticipate if you plan to conduct an online survey-difficulties that can make such surveys a lot more time-consuming than some might imagine them to be. Finally, it illustrates that despite these technical difficulties, when done well, online surveys can produce useful information that otherwise could only have been obtained with survey methods beyond the means of investigators with limited time and funds.

As respondents attempted, sometimes unsuccessfully, to use smart phones to complete questionnaires designed for desktop computers, survey researchers realized the need and potential for adapting their questionnaires to a variety of devices that may be used by respondents. Screen size, of course, is a major concern, but so are the different navigation systems used by different devices.

Researchers are also learning we must accommodate respondents' device preferences. For example, Morgan M. Millar and Don A. Dillman (2012) conducted an experiment in which they attempted to encourage respondents use participate via smartphones while allowing the use of other platforms, but they experienced only a slight increase in smartphone usage over those who were given no encouragement.

This line of methodological research will continue, but consider this: we will surely see the development of new devices, some we can't currently imagine, that will have to be accommodated in the future.

To stay abreast of these developments, your best single source is the American Association for Public Opinion Research (AAPOR) and two key publications: *Public Opinion Quarterly* (POQ) and the online journal *Survey Practice* (www.surveyprac tice.org). Although neither of these is dedicated to online research solely, an increasing percentage of their articles address that topic. University survey research offices such as those at the University of Michigan, NORC at the University of Chicago, and many other universities around the globe are very active in developing this new technique. Similarly, commercial research firms such as Pew, Harris, and others are equally involved.

10.4 INTERVIEW SURVEYS

The **interview** is an alternative method of collecting survey data. Rather than asking respondents to read questionnaires and enter their own answers, researchers send interviewers to ask the questions orally and record respondents' answers. Interviewing is typically done in a face-to-face encounter, but telephone interviewing, as we'll see, follows most of the same guidelines. Also, most interview surveys require more than one interviewer, although you might undertake a small-scale interview survey yourself.

10.4a The Role of the Survey Interviewer

Having a questionnaire administered by an interviewer rather than the respondent has several advantages. To begin, interview surveys typically attain higher response rates than mail surveys. A properly designed and executed interview survey ought to achieve a completion rate of at least 80 to 85 percent. Respondents seem more reluctant to turn down an interviewer who is standing on their doorsteps than they are to throw away mail questionnaires.

Within the context of the questionnaire, the presence of an interviewer generally decreases the

---

interview A data collection encounter in which one person (the interviewer) asks questions of another (the respondent).

number of "Don't knows" and "No answers." If minimizing such responses is important to the study, then the interviewer can be instructed to probe for answers—for example, "If you had to pick one of the answers, which do you think would come closest to your feelings?"

Interviewers also can provide a guard against confusing questionnaire items. If the respondent clearly misunderstands the intent of a question or indicates that he or she does not understand it, then the interviewer can clarify matters, thereby obtaining relevant responses.

Finally, the interviewer can observe as well as ask questions. For example, the interviewer can note the quality of the dwelling, the presence of various possessions, the respondent's ability to speak English, the respondent's general reactions to the study, and so forth.

Unlike some of the less structured qualitative interviewing methods discussed in Chapter 9, survey interviews typically involve the use of either closed-ended questions or highly structured, standardized interview schedules (like the one displayed in Figure 9.6 in the previous chapter). The intent is to have questionnaire items that will mean the same thing to every respondent. That way, the same responses have the same meaning when given by different respondents. Although this is an impossible goal, survey questions are drafted to approximate the ideal as closely as possible.

The interviewer also must fit into this ideal situation. The interviewer's presence should not affect a respondent's perception of a question or the answer given. The interviewer, then, should be a neutral medium through which questions and answers are transmitted.

If this goal is successfully accomplished, then different interviewers will obtain exactly the same responses from a given respondent. (Recall earlier discussions of reliability.) Let's suppose that a survey is being done to determine attitudes toward low-cost housing to help in the selection of a site for a new government-sponsored development. An interviewer who is assigned to a given neighborhood might—through word or gesture—communicate his or her own distaste for low-cost housing developments. Respondents might therefore tend to give responses that generally agree with the interviewer's own position. The survey results would indicate that the neighborhood in question strongly resisted construction of the development in its area, although the apparent resistance might only reflect the interviewer's attitudes.

10.4b General Guidelines for Survey Interviewing

The manner in which interviews ought to be conducted will vary somewhat by survey population and by the nature of the survey content. Nevertheless, we can provide general guidelines that apply to most, if not all, interviewing situations.

Appearance and Demeanor

As a general rule, the interviewer should dress in a fashion that is similar to that of the people who will be interviewed. A richly dressed interviewer will probably have difficulty getting good cooperation and responses from poorer respondents. And a poorly dressed interviewer will have similar difficulties with richer respondents.

To the extent that the interviewer's dress and grooming differ from those of the respondents, it should be in the direction of cleanliness and neatness in modest apparel. Although middle-class neatness and cleanliness may not be accepted by all sectors of American society, they remain the primary norm and are more likely to be acceptable to the largest number of respondents.

Dress and grooming are typically regarded as signals of a person's attitudes and orientations. At the time this is being written, wearing torn jeans, green hair, and a razor-blade earring may communicate—correctly or incorrectly—that you are politically radical, sexually permissive, favorable to drug use, and so forth. Any of these impressions could bias responses or affect the willingness of people to be interviewed.

In demeanor, interviewers should be pleasant if nothing else. Because they will be prying into the respondents' personal lives and attitudes, they must communicate a genuine interest in getting to know each respondent without appearing to spy. They must be relaxed and friendly without being too casual or clinging. Good interviewers also are able to determine quickly the kind of person the respondent will feel most comfortable with and the kind of person with whom the respondent would most enjoy talking. This ability serves a double purpose. Clearly, the interview will be more successful if the interviewer can become that kind of person. Further, because respondents are asked to volunteer a portion of their time and to divulge personal information about themselves, they deserve the most enjoyable experience the researcher and interviewer can provide.

Familiarity with Questionnaire

If an interviewer is unfamiliar with the questionnaire, then the study suffers and an unfair burden is placed on the respondent. The interview is likely to take more time than necessary and be generally unpleasant. Moreover, the interviewer cannot acquire familiarity by skimming through the questionnaire two or three times. It must be studied carefully, question by question, and the interviewer must practice reading it aloud.

Ultimately, the interviewer must be able to read the questionnaire items to respondents without error, without stumbling over words and phrases. A good model for interviewers is the actor who is reading lines in a play or motion picture. The lines must be read as naturally as though they constituted a natural conversation, but that conversation must follow exactly the language set down in the questionnaire.

By the same token, the interviewer must be familiar with the specifications prepared in conjunction with the questionnaire. Inevitably, some questions will not exactly fit a given respondent's situation, and the interviewer must determine how the question should be interpreted in that situation. The specifications provided to the interviewer should give adequate guidance in such cases, but the interviewer must know the organization and contents of the specifications well enough to refer to them efficiently. It would be better for the interviewer to leave a given question unanswered than spend five minutes searching through the specifications for clarification or trying to interpret the relevant instructions.

Following Question Wording Exactly

Earlier we discussed the significance of question wording for the responses obtained. A slight change in the wording of a given question may lead a respondent to answer "Yes" rather than "No."

Even though you have very carefully phrased your questionnaire items to obtain the information you need and to ensure that respondents will interpret items precisely as you intend, all this effort will be wasted if interviewers rephrase questions in their own words.

Recording Responses Exactly

Whenever the questionnaire contains open-ended questions—that is, those that solicit the respondent's answer—it is critical that the interviewer record that answer exactly as given. No attempt should be made to summarize, paraphrase, or correct bad grammar.

Sometimes the respondent may be so inarticulate that the verbal response is too ambiguous to permit interpretation. However, the interviewer may be able to understand the respondent's intention through his or her gestures or tone. In such a situation, the exact verbal response should still be recorded, but the interviewer should add marginal comments that give both the interpretation and the reasons for arriving at it.

More generally, researchers can use marginal comments to explain aspects of the response that are not conveyed in the verbal recording, such as the respondent's apparent uncertainty in answering, anger, embarrassment, and so forth. In each case, however, the exact verbal response also should be recorded.

Probing for Responses

Sometimes, respondents will answer a question inappropriately. For example, the question may present an attitudinal statement and ask the respondent to strongly agree, agree somewhat, disagree somewhat, or strongly disagree. The respondent, however, may reply: "I think that's true." The interviewer should follow this reply with: "Would you say you strongly agree or agree somewhat?" If necessary, interviewers can explain that they must check one or the other of the categories provided. If the respondent adamantly refuses to choose, the interviewer should write in the exact response given by the respondent.

Probes are more frequently required in eliciting responses to open-ended questions. In every case, however, such probes *must* be completely neutral (as we discussed in Chapter 8 in the context of qualitative interviewing). The probe cannot affect the nature of the subsequent response in any way. Suppose a community resident responds to a question about community needs for new services by saying, "We need all *sorts* of things!" An appropriate neutral probe might be to say, "Could you identify some of the things you have in mind?" Or maybe, "All *sorts* of things, eh?" An inappropriate probe, one that is *not* neutral, might be, "How about more day care services?" or "What about the unsafe streets?"

Whenever you anticipate that a given question may require probing for appropriate responses, you should present one or more useful probes next to the question in the questionnaire. This practice has two important advantages. First, you will have more time to devise the best, most neutral probes. Second, all interviewers will use the same probes whenever they are needed. Thus, even if the probe is not perfectly neutral, all respondents will be presented with the same probe. This is the same logical guideline discussed for wording questions. Although questions should not be loaded or biased, it is essential that every respondent be presented with the same questions, even biased ones.

10.4c Coordination and Control

Most interview surveys require the assistance of several interviewers. In the large-scale surveys, of course, such interviewers are hired and paid for their work. As a student researcher, you might find yourself recruiting friends to assist you. Whenever more than one interviewer is involved in a survey, their efforts must be carefully controlled. There are two aspects of this control: training interviewers and supervising them after they begin work.

The interviewer training session should begin with a description of the study and a discussion of general guidelines and procedures, such as those discussed earlier in this chapter. Then you should turn to the questionnaire itself. The whole group should go through the questionnaire together—question by question. You should also prepare *specifications* to accompany an interview questionnaire. Specifications are explanatory and clarifying comments about how to handle difficult or confusing situations that may occur with specific questions in the questionnaire. When you are drafting the

questionnaire, try to think of all the problem cases that might arise—the bizarre circumstances that might make a question difficult to answer. The survey specifications should provide detailed guidelines on how to handle such situations. Go over your specifications with the interviewers when you review the individual questions in the questionnaire. Make sure your interviewers fully understand the specifications as well as the questions themselves and the reasons for them. Once you have gone through the whole questionnaire, conduct one or two demonstration interviews in front of everyone.

After the demonstration interviews, pair off your interviewers and have them practice on each other. When they have completed the questionnaire, have them reverse roles and do it over again. The final stage of the training for interviewers should involve "real" interviews. Have your interviewers conduct questioning under actual final survey conditions. Do not have them practice on people you have selected in your sample, however. After each interviewer has completed three to five interviews, have him or her check back with you. Look over the completed questionnaires to see if there is any evidence of misunderstanding. Again, answer any questions that individual interviewers may have. Once you are convinced that a given interviewer knows what to do, assign actual interviews—using the sample you have selected for the study. You should continue to supervise the work of interviewers over the course of the study.

If you are the only interviewer in your study, then these comments may not seem relevant to you—but that's not wholly the case. You would be advised, for example, to prepare specifications for potentially troublesome questions in your questionnaire. Otherwise, you run the risk of making ad hoc decisions during the course of the study that you will later regret or forget. Also, the emphasis that has been placed on practice applies just as much to the one-person project as to the complex, funded survey with a large interviewing staff.

10.5 TELEPHONE SURVEYS

For years, telephone surveys had a bad reputation among professional researchers. These surveys are limited by definition to people who have telephones. Years ago, then, this method produced a substantial social class bias by excluding poor people from the surveys. Over time, however, the telephone has become a standard fixture in almost all American homes. By 2003, the U.S. Bureau of the Census (2006, p. 737, Table 1117) estimated that 95.5 percent of all housing units had telephones, so the earlier form of class bias has substantially diminished.

A related sampling problem involves unlisted numbers. If the survey sample is selected from the pages of a local telephone directory, then it would omit all of those people who have unlisted numbers—typically richer people who request that their numbers not be published. This potential bias has been alleviated through a technique called *random-digit dialing*, in which phone numbers are generated using random numbers (see Appendix C) rather than using a telephone directory.

Imagine that you were to select a set of seven-digit telephone numbers at random. Even those whose numbers were unlisted would have the same chance of selection as those who were in the directory. However, if you were to start dialing randomly selected numbers, a high proportion of those would turn out to be "not in service," government offices, commercial enterprises, et cetera. Fortunately, it is possible to obtain ranges of numbers that are (mostly) active residential numbers. Selecting a set of those numbers at random will provide a representative sample of residential households. As a consequence, random-digit dialing has been a standard procedure in telephone surveys.

Telephone surveys have many advantages that underlie the method's growing popularity. Probably the greatest advantages are money and time, in that order. To conduct a face-to-face, household interview, you may have to drive several miles to a respondent's home only to find no one there, return to the research office, and drive back the next day—possibly finding no one there again. It's cheaper and quicker to let your fingers make the trips.

When interviewing by telephone, you can dress any way you please without affecting the answers respondents give. And sometimes respondents will be more honest in giving socially disapproved answers if they don't have to look you in the eye. Similarly, it may be possible to probe into more sensitive areas, though that is not necessarily the case. (People are, to some extent, more suspicious when they can't see the person asking them questions—perhaps a

consequence of "surveys" aimed at selling magazine subscriptions and time-share condominiums.) Realize, however, that people can communicate a lot about themselves over the phone, even though they can't be seen. For example, researchers worry about the impact of an interviewer's name (particularly if ethnicity is relevant to the study) and debate the ethics of having all interviewers use plain-vanilla "stage names" such as Smith or Jones. (Female interviewers sometimes ask permission to do this to avoid subsequent harassment from men they interview.)

Telephone surveys can give you greater control over data collection if several interviewers are engaged in the project. If all of the interviewers are calling from the research office, then they can get clarification from the person in charge whenever the inevitable problems occur. Alone in the boondocks, an interviewer may have to wing it between weekly visits with the interviewing supervisor.

Another important factor involved in the growing use of telephone surveys has to do with personal safety and concerns for the same. Don Dillman (1978, p. 4) describes the situation this way:

Interviewers must be able to operate comfortably in climate in which strangers are viewed with distrust and must successfully counter respondents' objections to being interviewed. Increasingly, interviewers must be willing to work at night to contact residents in many households. In some cases, this necessitates providing protection for interviewers working in areas of a city in which a definite threat to the safety of individuals exists.

Concerns for safety thus work to hamper face-to-face interviews in two ways. First, potential respondents may refuse to be interviewed, fearing the stranger interviewer. Second, the interviewers themselves may be in danger. All this is made even worse by the possibility of the researchers being sued for huge sums if anything goes wrong.

Telephone interviewing still has problems. As we've already mentioned, the method is hampered by the proliferation of bogus "surveys," which are actually sales campaigns disguised as research. If you have any questions about any such call you receive, by the way, ask the interviewer directly whether you've been selected for a survey only, or if a sales "opportunity" is involved. It's also a good idea, if you have any doubts, to get the interviewer's name, phone number, and company. Hang up if they refuse to provide that information.

Another potential problem for telephone interviewing is the prevalence of answering machines and caller identification features that enable prospective respondents to screen out calls they don't want to answer. And if they do answer, the ease with which they can hang up is another problem. Once you've been let inside someone's home for an interview, that person is unlikely to order you out of the house in mid-interview. It's much easier to terminate a telephone interview abruptly, saying something like, "Whoops! Someone's at the door. I gotta go," or "OMIGOD! The pigs are eating my Volvo!" (That sort of thing is much harder to fake when you're sitting in their living room.)

The growth in popularity of cell phones has become a new source of concern for survey researchers. The Telephone Consumer Protection Act of 1991 put limitations on telephone solicitations and, because calls to a cell phone may incur an expense to the target of the call (depending on their service plan), the Act made it illegal for automatic dialing systems (e.g., the robocalls alerting you to a special sale on widgets) to call cell phones (FCC 2012). But where does this leave survey researchers, who aren't selling anything? Although efforts are underway to officially exempt research projects from that ruling, the American Association for Public Opinion Research (AAPOR, 2010) advised members that:

> To ensure compliance with this federal law, in the absence of express prior consent from a sampled cell phone respondent, telephone research call centers should have their interviewers manually dial cell phone numbers (i.e., where a human being physically touches the numerals on the telephone to dial the number).

Those who use cell phones exclusively, moreover, tend to be younger, and in 2004 they were more likely to vote for John Kerry than older voters were. In 2008, they were more likely than the average to support Barack Obama. Scott Keeter (2006) found, however, that researchers who weighted their results in terms of age avoided bias in this respect.

In a study of this matter, Keeter, Dimock, Christian, and Kennedy (2008) found a distinct bias by age and the variables closely related to it (e.g., marital status), distinguishing those who were reachable only by cell phone and those reachable by landline. One of the most striking differences between cell-only respondents and people reached on a landline telephone is their age. Nearly half of the cell-only respondents (46%) are under age 30 compared to only 12 percent in the landline sample. Related to their younger age, only 26 percent of cell-only respondents are married, compared with 57 percent of those in the landline sample. Similarly, about half of cell-only respondents have never been married (51%), compared with only 16 percent in the land-line sample (Keeter et al., 2008).

At the 2008 meetings of the American Association for Public Opinion Research, several research papers examined the implications of cell phone popularity. Overall, most of the researchers found that for most purposes, ignoring those with cell phones only (because of their relatively small portion of all telephone customers) does not seriously bias survey results. However, virtually all of the researchers concluded by saying that this situation was likely to change in the years ahead. The role of cell phones is clearly a development that social researchers will continue to examine and deal with.

10.5a Computer-Assisted Telephone Interviewing

Computers are changing the nature of telephone interviewing. One innovation is *computer-assisted telephone interviewing (CATI)*. This method is often used by academic, government, and commercial survey researchers. Though there are variations in practice, here's what CATI can look like.

Imagine an interviewer wearing a telephone operator headset, sitting in front of a computer screen. The central computer randomly selects a telephone number and dials it. (This feature avoids the problem of unlisted telephone numbers.) The video screen shows an introduction ("Hello, my name is ...") and the first question to be asked ("Could you tell me how many people live at this address?").

When the respondent answers the phone, the interviewer says hello, introduces the study, and asks the first question displayed on the screen. When the respondent answers, the interviewer types it into the computer terminal—either the verbatim response to an open-ended question or the code category for the appropriate answer to a closed-ended question. The answer is immediately stored in the central computer. The second question appears on the video screen, is asked, and the answer is entered into the computer. Thus, the interview continues. In addition to the obvious advantages in terms of data collection, CATI automatically prepares the data for analysis; in fact, the researcher can begin analyzing the data before the interviewing is complete, thereby gaining an advanced view of how the analysis will turn out.

10.6 COMPARISON OF THE DIFFERENT SURVEY METHODS

Now that we've seen several ways to collect survey data, let's take a moment to compare them directly.

Self-administered questionnaires are generally cheaper and quicker than face-to-face interview surveys. These considerations are likely to be important for an unfunded student wishing to undertake a survey for a term paper or thesis. Moreover, if you use the self-administered mail format, it costs no more to conduct a national survey than a local one of the same sample size. In contrast, a national interview survey would cost far more than a local one. Also, mail surveys typically require a small staff: One person can conduct a reasonable mail survey alone, although you shouldn't underestimate the work involved. Further, respondents are sometimes reluctant to report controversial or deviant attitudes or behaviors in interviews but are willing to respond to an anonymous self-administered questionnaire.

Interview surveys also have many advantages. For instance, they generally produce fewer incomplete questionnaires. Although respondents may skip questions in a self-administered questionnaire, interviewers are trained not to do so. Computers offer a further check on this in CATI surveys. Interview surveys, moreover, have typically achieved higher completion rates than self-administered ones.

Although self-administered questionnaires may deal with sensitive issues more effectively, interview surveys are definitely more effective in dealing with complicated ones. Prime examples would be the enumeration of household members and the determination of whether a given household address contains more than one housing unit. Although the concept of housing unit has been refined and standardized by the Bureau of the Census and interviewers can be trained to deal with the concept, it's extremely difficult to communicate in a self-administered questionnaire. This advantage of interview surveys pertains more generally to all complicated contingency questions.

With interviewers, it is possible to conduct a survey based on a sample of addresses or phone numbers rather than on names. An interviewer can arrive at an assigned address or call the assigned number, introduce the survey, and even—following instructions—choose the appropriate person at that address to respond to the survey. By contrast, self-administered questionnaires addressed to "Occupant" receive a notoriously low response.

Finally, interviewers who question respondents face-to-face are able to make important observations aside from responses to questions asked in the interview. In a household interview, they may note the characteristics of the neighborhood, the dwelling unit, and so forth. They may also note characteristics of the respondents or the quality of their interaction with the respondents—whether the respondent had difficulty communicating, was hostile, seemed to be lying, and so forth.

The chief advantages of telephone surveys over those conducted face-to-face are primarily a matter of time and money. Telephone interviews are much cheaper and can be mounted and executed quickly. Also, interviewers are safer when interviewing residents in high-crime areas. Moreover, we've seen that the impact of the interviewers on responses is somewhat lessened when they can't be seen by the respondents.

Online surveys have many of the strengths and weaknesses of mail surveys. However, the costs of online surveys are substantially less than the costs of conventional mail surveys. In mail surveys, for example, the cost of paper, printing, and postage alone can constitute a large expense. An important weakness, however, lies in the difficulty of assuring that respondents to an online survey will be representative of some more general population of concern to social workers, especially the poor and elderly.

Table 10.1 summarizes the advantages and disadvantages that we've been discussing regarding the different survey methods. Clearly, each survey method has its place in social research. Ultimately, you must balance the advantages and disadvantages of the different methods in relation to your research needs and your resources.

10.7 STRENGTHS AND WEAKNESSES OF SURVEY RESEARCH

Like other modes of observation in social scientific research, surveys have special strengths and weaknesses. It is important to know these in determining whether the survey format is appropriate to your research goals.

Surveys are particularly useful when we describe the characteristics of a large population. A well-selected representative sample in combination with a standardized questionnaire offers the possibility of making refined descriptive assertions about a student body, a city, a nation, or another large population. Surveys determine unemployment rates, voting intentions, and the like, with uncanny accuracy. Although examining official documents such as marriage, birth, and death records can provide equal accuracy for a few topics, no other method of observation can provide this general capability.

Surveys—especially the self-administered variety—make very large samples feasible. Surveys of 2,000 people are not unusual. A large number of cases is important for both descriptive and explanatory analyses. Whenever several variables are to be analyzed simultaneously, it is essential to have a large number of cases.

Because surveys make large samples feasible, their findings may be more generalizable than the findings of experiments. As we will see in Chapter 11, experiments in social work typically are unable to obtain large samples that are representative of the population. This advantage in generalizability, however, is offset by the limited ability of surveys to show causality. For example, a survey of the moods of thousands of elderly people can tell us in general whether elderly people with pets have better moods than elderly people without pets. It wouldn't, however, be able to sort out whether having pets caused their moods to improve, or whether being less depressed in the first place is what leads to getting a pet. (In Chapter 11 we'll examine designs for sorting out what causes what.)

The survey would also enable us to analyze multiple variables simultaneously; thus, we could see whether the relationship between mood and pets applied to elderly people of different ethnicities, different income levels, different living arrangements, different levels of dependency, and so on. But we'd still be uncertain as to causality. By conducting a longitudinal survey—for example, assessing over an extended period the same elderly folks' moods and whether they own pets or not—we'd be in a better position to speculate about causality. In other words, we could ascertain whether the moods were changing before or after the pets were obtained, although we'd still have less confidence regarding causal inferences than in an experiment. Despite the uncertainty about causality, the high level of generalizability of the findings to the population as a whole, as well as to various subgroups of the population in their natural settings, is an advantage of surveys that few experiments can offer.

In one sense, surveys are flexible. Many questions may be asked on a given topic, giving you considerable flexibility in your analyses. Although experimental design may require you to commit yourself in advance to a particular operational definition of a concept, surveys let you develop operational definitions from actual observations.

Finally, standardized questionnaires have an important strength in regard to measurement generally. Earlier chapters have discussed the ambiguous nature of many concepts. One person's spirituality might be quite different from another's. Although you must be able to define concepts in ways that are most relevant to your research goals, you may not find it easy to apply the same definitions uniformly to all research participants. The survey researcher is bound to this requirement by having to ask exactly the same questions of all respondents and having to impute the same intent to all respondents giving a particular response.

Survey research has weaknesses, though. First, the requirement for standardization just mentioned often seems to result in the fitting of round pegs into

Table 10.1 Advantages and Disadvantages of Different Survey Methods

SURVEY TYPE	ADVANTAGES	DISADVANTAGES
Mail Surveys	• Cheaper and quicker than interviews • Large samples • Anonymity facilitates responses regarding sensitive areas	• More expensive and time-consuming than online surveys • Lower response rates than face-to-face interviews
Online Surveys	• Less expensive • Less time-consuming • Largest samples • Automatic data entry • Tools to check and correct inappropriate responses • Growth in public use of Internet • Anonymity facilitates responses regarding sensitive areas	• Representativeness (especially the poor and elderly) • Lower response rates than face to-face interviews
Face-to-Face Interview Surveys	• High response rates • Fewer "don't knows" • Fewer missing answers • Opportunity to clarify confusing items • Opportunity to observe • Opportunity to probe	• More expensive and time-consuming • Lack of anonymity can impede responses regarding sensitive areas • Interviewer safety
Telephone Surveys	• Less expensive and less time-consuming than face-to-face interviews • Interviewer's physical appearance won't bias respondents • Fewer "don't knows" • Fewer missing answers • Opportunity to clarify confusing items • Opportunity to probe • Interviewer safety • Opportunity to get supervision during interview • Can be computer-assisted	• Unlisted numbers* • Cell phones* • Ease of hanging up • Caller ID

*Random-digit dialing can alleviate these two problems.

square holes. Standardized questionnaire items often represent the least common denominator in assessing people's attitudes, orientations, circumstances, and experiences. By designing questions that will be at least minimally appropriate to all respondents, you may miss what is most appropriate to many respondents. In this sense, surveys often appear superficial in their coverage of complex topics. Although this problem can be partly offset through sophisticated analyses, it is inherent in survey research.

Similarly, survey research can seldom deal with the *context* of social life. Although questionnaires can provide information in this area, the survey researcher can seldom develop the feel for the total life situation in which respondents are thinking and

acting that, say, the participant–observer can (see Chapter 14).

Although surveys are flexible in the sense mentioned earlier, they are inflexible in other ways. Studies that use direct observation can be modified as field conditions warrant, but surveys typically require that an initial study design remain unchanged throughout. In qualitative research, for example, you can become aware of an important new variable operating in the phenomenon you are studying and begin to observe it carefully. The survey researcher would likely be unaware of the new variable's importance and could do nothing about it in any event.

Finally, surveys are subject to artificiality. Finding out that a person gives conservative answers to a questionnaire does not necessarily mean the person is conservative; finding out that a person gives prejudiced answers to a questionnaire does not necessarily mean the person is prejudiced. This shortcoming is especially salient in the realm of action. Surveys cannot measure social action; they can only collect self-reports of recalled past action or of prospective or hypothetical action. This problem has two aspects. First, the topic of study may not be amenable to measurement through questionnaires. Second, the act of studying that topic—an attitude, for instance—may affect it. A survey respondent may have given no thought to whether the governor should be impeached until asked for his or her opinion by an interviewer. At that point, he or she may form an opinion on the matter.

Survey research is generally strong on reliability. By presenting all subjects with standardized wording, survey research goes a long way toward eliminating unreliability in observations made by the researcher. Moreover, careful wording of the questions can also reduce significantly the subject's own unreliability.

10.8 COMBINING SURVEY RESEARCH METHODS AND QUALITATIVE RESEARCH METHODS

As with all methods of observation, a full awareness of the inherent or probable weaknesses of survey research can partially resolve them in some cases. Ultimately, though, you are on the safest ground when you can use a number of different research methods in studying a given topic.

By combining qualitative research methods with survey research methods, we can benefit from the strengths of survey research while offseting its weaknesses regarding superficiality, missing social context, inflexibility, artificiality, and questionable validity. Mark Rank (1992) conducted a study that illustrates the blending of qualitative and quantitative methods, and shows the benefits of it in a study of childbearing among welfare recipients.

Rank was interested in the debate over whether welfare programs encouraged women to have more children by increasing the payments when additional children are born. He began his study with qualitative interviews at various agencies serving welfare recipients and in neighborhoods where many recipients lived. The people he observed and talked to in these settings did not agree with the stereotype of women choosing to bear more children so their public assistance payments would increase. Instead, they believed that most women receiving welfare wanted to get off welfare and did not want any more children.

Were their beliefs accurate? To find out, Rank conducted a secondary analysis of survey data from the databases of the Wisconsin (Rank's state) Department of Health and Social Services and the U.S. Bureau of the Census. (We'll discuss secondary analysis in Chapter 16.) His quantitative analysis supported his preliminary qualitative findings. Women on welfare had a "substantially lower fertility rate than women in the general population" (1992, p. 289).

Rank then wondered what accounted for his dramatic findings. To find out, he and his assistant conducted in-depth qualitative interviews with 50 families on welfare. None of the nonpregnant women they interviewed wanted to have another child in the near future. They consistently cited financial and social forces that are not conducive to having more children. Virtually all of them expressed wanting to get off of welfare, and they appeared to recognize that the meager increase in payments for having more children was far outweighed by the increase in economic, social, and psychological costs that would come with having more children. Rank concluded that his quantitative and qualitative data reinforced each other and enhanced the validity of his findings, findings that challenged the assumption of conservative policy analysts that welfare payments encourage women to have more children.

10.9 USE OF SURVEYS IN NEEDS ASSESSMENT

Early in your career as a professional social worker, you may be assigned to assess the needs of your program's target population in order to inform your agency of potential ideas for providing new services. For example, you might assess the extent and location of the problems the program seeks to ameliorate, as well as the target population's characteristics, problems, expressed needs, and desires. This information could then be used to guide program planning and development concerning such issues as what services to offer, how to maximize service utilization by targeted subgroups, where to locate services, and so on.

The process of researching needs is called **needs assessment**. The term *needs assessment* applies to a variety of research techniques for collecting data for program planning purposes. The specific techniques for conducting a needs assessment are usually classified in five categories: (1) the key informants approach, (2) the community forum approach, (3) the rates under treatment approach, (4) the social indicators approach, and (5) the community survey approach. Let's look at each one.

10.9a Key Informants

The key informants approach utilizes questionnaires or interviews to obtain expert opinions from individuals who are presumed to have special knowledge about a target population's problems and needs, as well as about current gaps in service delivery to that population. The **key informants** selected to be surveyed might include leaders of groups or organizations that are in close contact with the target population and that have special knowledge of its problems. They might also include practitioners who work closely with the target population.

In assessing the needs of the homeless, for instance, key informants might include professionals who work in public shelters or soup kitchens; researchers or other personnel who address homelessness as part of their work for local

---

needs assessment   Systematic research on diagnostic questions about the needs of a target population—for program planning purposes.

key informants   An approach to needs assessment that is based on obtaining expert opinions from individuals who are presumed to have special knowledge about the target population's problems and needs, as well as about current gaps in service delivery to that population.

community forum   An approach to needs assessment that involves holding a meeting where concerned members of the community can express their views and interact freely about their needs.

---

planning agencies; neighborhood leaders who live in communities where the homeless tend to congregate; administrators and case managers who work in community mental health programs; public officials who advocate legislation to help deal with the problem of homelessness; leaders of citizen advocacy groups who work on behalf of the poor, homeless, or mentally ill; and law enforcement officials who have been dealing with the problem.

The prime advantage of the key informants approach is that a sample can be obtained and surveyed quickly, easily, and inexpensively. Also, conducting the survey can provide the fringe benefits of building connections with key community resources that are concerned about the problem and of giving some visibility to the agency conducting the needs assessment. The chief disadvantage of this method, however, is that the information is not coming directly from the target population; that information's quality depends on the objectivity and depth of knowledge underlying the expressed opinions.

To illustrate this disadvantage, consider the following possible pitfalls in an assessment of homelessness. Perhaps key informants who are affiliated with public shelters are unaware of those individuals who refuse to use the shelters, their reasons for doing so, and the unique problems they have. Perhaps advocates for poverty legislation will be likely to downplay needs associated with the mentally ill homeless because they see homelessness primarily as an economic problem and do not want to foster the notion that people are homeless because of either defects in character or voluntary preferences. Perhaps mental health officials will be biased toward exaggerating mental illness as the cause of homelessness, or perhaps their bias will be to downplay the problem of homelessness among the mentally ill because that problem may reflect negatively on the mental health policies they have implemented. Perhaps neighborhood leaders where the homeless tend to congregate may be biased toward perceiving the need for services that get the homeless out of their neighborhood.

10.9b Community Forum

The **community forum** approach involves holding a meeting in which concerned members of the community can express their views and interact freely about their needs. This approach offers several non-scientific advantages, including its feasibility, its ability to build support and visibility for the sponsoring agency, and its ability to provide an atmosphere in which individuals can consider the problem in depth, and be stimulated by what others have said to consider things they might otherwise have overlooked. Still, from a scientific standpoint this approach is risky.

Those who attend such meetings might not be representative of the people in the best position to know about the needs of the target population and of those whose views are relatively unbiased. Instead, those who have vested interests or particular axes to grind are likely to be overrepresented. The views expressed at such meetings are expressed publicly, and therefore strong social pressures might inhibit certain individuals from speaking at all or from expressing minority viewpoints. In light of these problems, rather than hold an open meeting for anyone to attend, it may be advisable to hold a series of closed meetings, each for a different, pre-selected homogeneous group.

10.9c Rates under Treatment

The **rates under treatment** approach involves estimating the need for a service and the characteristics of its potential clients, based on the number and characteristics of clients who already use that service. This method makes the most sense when the rates under treatment are examined in a community other than, but similar to, a target community that does not yet provide the service in question. The assumption is that if the two communities really are comparable, then the size and characteristics of the target population in the community without the service will parallel the size and characteristics of those already being treated in the comparison community.

The prime advantages of the rates under treatment approach are that it is relatively quick, easy to administer, inexpensive, and unobtrusive. Its prime disadvantage is that it assesses only that portion of the target population that is already using services and thus may underestimate need by failing to account for people who need services but don't utilize them. Another disadvantage is the potential for unreliability or bias in the existing data. For example, accurate recordkeeping may be a low priority in many agencies in the comparison community, particularly if service delivery demands leave little time for it. Also, agencies may exaggerate the number of clients served or their needs for services so that they will look good to funding sources or others to whom they are accountable.

10.9d Social Indicators

Another type of needs assessment that makes use of existing statistics is the **social indicators** approach. This approach does not look just at treatment statistics; it examines aggregated statistics that reflect conditions of an entire population. For example, infant mortality rates (the number of infants who die during their first year of life) can be an indicator of the need for prenatal services in a particular community. Such rates also could be examined to identify communities that have the greatest need for these services. Likewise, rates of reported child abuse in a community can be used as an indicator of that community's need for a newly developed abuse prevention program. School dropout rates can indicate the need for a school district to hire school social workers. Using social indicators can be done quickly and inexpensively. But those advantages need to be weighed against potential problems in the reliability of a particular existing database. Also, this approach's utility depends on the degree to which the existing indicators can be assumed to reflect future service use patterns accurately.

10.9e Surveys of Communities or Target Groups

The most direct way to assess the characteristics and perceived problems and needs of the target group is

---

rates under treatment An approach to needs assessment that involves the secondary analysis of existing statistics to estimate the need for a service and the characteristics of its potential clients, based on the number and characteristics of clients who already use that service.

social indicators A type of needs assessment that makes use of existing statistics that reflect conditions of an entire population.

to survey its members. This usually involves surveying a sample drawn from the population. As with most surveys, a key issue is whether the sample is representative of the population. Techniques for maximizing the likelihood that the sample will be representative will be discussed in the next chapter.

Data collection methods might use highly structured, quantitative questionnaires or less structured qualitative interviews, depending on the nature of the target group and what is already known or not known about its possible needs. The advantages and disadvantages of the direct survey approach parallel those of surveys in general. Evaluators ought to be particularly mindful of the potential biases associated with low response rates, social desirability, and acquiescent response sets. Suppose, for example, that the survey is conducted by mail. Those who bother to respond cannot be assumed to represent those who do not respond. In all likelihood, the respondents will feel a greater need for the program than the non-respondents, and they are likely to differ in other ways as well. Suppose the questions are phrased only in general terms concerning whether a particular service ought to be available. Respondents might be predisposed to agree. Why not agree with the provision of a new service if no mention is made of its costs or whether the respondent would actually use it? But if respondents who agree that a service sounds nice are asked if they think it's worth specific costs or whether they intend to use it, they might respond negatively.

Thus, the advantages of this method—its directness and its potential for ascertaining how prospective service consumers perceive their need for and likely use of programs—need to be weighed against potential biases in measurement or in response rates. Of course, what you have learned and will learn in this book about sampling, measurement, and surveys might enable you to design a needs assessment survey that adequately minimizes those biases. But doing so would be time-consuming and expensive, and feasibility constraints might instead require that you use one or more of the foregoing four approaches to needs assessment.

Like research methods in general, each of the five approaches to needs assessment has its own advantages and disadvantages. Ideally, then, we should combine two or more approaches to needs assessment to get a more complete picture of needs and the likely utilization of prospective services.

10.10 MAIN POINTS

- Survey research, a popular social research method, is the administration of questionnaires to a sample of respondents selected from a population.
- Survey research is especially appropriate for making descriptive studies of large populations; survey data also may be used for explanatory purposes.
- Questionnaires may be administered in three different ways: (1) self-administered questionnaires can be completed by the respondents themselves; interviewers can administer questionnaires in face-to-face encounters, reading the items to respondents and recording the answers; and interviewers can conduct telephone surveys.
- Plan to send follow-up mailings for self-administered questionnaires to respondents who fail to respond to the initial appeal.
- Online surveys have many of the strengths and weaknesses of mail surveys. The costs of online surveys are substantially less than the costs of conventional mail surveys. In mail surveys, for example, the cost of paper, printing, and postage alone can constitute a large expense. An important weakness, however, lies in the difficulty of assuring that respondents to an online survey will be representative of some more general population of concern to social workers, especially the poor and elderly.
- One of the trickier problems regarding non-response to online surveys is the growth of spam-blocking e-mail systems. When you conduct an online survey, it is important to structure your invitational e-mail message in a way to reduce the chances that it will be flagged as spam.
- The essential characteristic of interviewers is that they be neutral; their presence in the data collection process must not have any effect on the responses given to questionnaire items.
- Interviewers must be carefully trained to be familiar with the questionnaire, to follow the question wording and question order exactly,

and to record responses exactly as they are given.

- A probe is a neutral, nondirective question designed to elicit an elaboration on an incomplete or ambiguous response that is given in an interview in response to an open-ended question. Examples include: "Anything else?" "How is that?" "In what ways?"

- The advantages of a self-administered questionnaire over an interview survey are economy, speed, lack of interviewer bias, and the possibility of anonymity and privacy to encourage more candid responses on sensitive issues.

- Surveys conducted over the telephone have become more common and more effective in recent years, and computer-assisted telephone interviewing (CATI) techniques are especially promising.

- The advantages of an interview survey over a self-administered questionnaire are fewer incomplete questionnaires and fewer misunderstood questions, generally higher return rates, and greater flexibility in terms of sampling and special observations.

- Survey research in general has advantages in terms of economy and the amount of data that can be collected. The standardization of the data collected represents another special strength of survey research.

- Survey research has the weaknesses of being somewhat artificial and potentially superficial. It is not good at fully revealing social processes in their natural settings.

- Five approaches to needs assessment are: (1) surveying key informants, (2) holding a community forum, (3) examining rates under treatment, (4) analyzing social indicators, and (5) conducting a direct survey of the community or target group. Each approach is imperfect but offers its own unique advantages and disadvantages. Ideally, a needs assessment will combine more than one approach.

10.11 PRACTICE-RELATED EXERCISES

1. For each of the following scenarios, which survey method (mailed, online, face-to-face interview, or telephone interview) would you choose to administer a structured questionnaire? State the reasons for your choice and identify any additional information that would make it easier to choose among these four options.

   a. National survey of parents of children in treatment for psychotic disorders. The parents are members of the National Association for the Mentally Ill. The purpose of the survey is to assess the way mental health professionals have related to the parents, and the parents' satisfaction with the services provided to their children.

   b. National survey of licensed mental health professionals who treat children with psychotic disorders. The purpose of the survey is to assess the perspectives of mental health professionals on the causes of childhood psychoses and on working with parents.

   c. Survey of the students in your school of social work to assess how they view the causes of child hood psychoses and working with parents of children in treatment for psychosis.

2. If you were to conduct a mail survey for each of the above scenarios, what would you do to maximize the response rate? What else would you do to maximize the response rate if you were to conduct the survey online?

3. Locate an online survey being conducted on the Internet. Briefly describe the survey and discuss its strengths and weaknesses.

4. Look at your appearance right now. Identify aspects of your appearance that might create a problem if you were interviewing a general cross-section of the public.

5. Consider a social problem that is currently receiving a lot of media attention in your community. Design a needs assessment study regarding that problem or a specific service you have in mind for alleviating it. Assume a data collection budget of $5,000 and a six-month deadline for designing and completing the assessment.

6. Prepare a cover letter for a mailed survey to social work majors in your college or university, asking about their attitudes about an issue or issues of your choosing. Try to construct the letter so that it motivates students to respond to the survey.

7. Prepare several open-ended questions about the attitudes of interest in the survey outlined in

Exercise 6. Form a group of three or four students and take turns interviewing each other with the questions you've each prepared. Use neutral probes in the interviews. When it's not your turn to interview or be interviewed, observe and critique the interviews of the other students in your group. Follow that with a discussion of each interview. Focus on how well you use neutral probes in this exercise.

10.12 INTERNET EXERCISES

1. Find a study in a social work journal (such as *Social Work* or *Health and Social Work*) that used a survey design. Identify the strengths and weaknesses of the survey methods used in the study.
2. Go to the following website that deals with online survey methodology: http://www.websm.org/. Briefly describe something you find there that makes you more optimistic or more skeptical about the likelihood of obtaining representative samples of respondents when using online surveys in social work research.
3. Go to the following Gallup, Inc., website: www.gallup.com/poll/faqs.aspx. As of this writing, the information needed can be found under "How

does Gallup polling work?" which links to a six-page document, "How Polls Are Conducted." Briefly summarize what you learn there and why you think the Gallup survey methodology is or is not likely to yield accurate, representative findings.

10.12a Competency Notes

EP 2.1.6b: Use research evidence to inform practice (p. 180): Understanding all of the concepts in this chapter will help social workers distinguish between surveys that supply research evidence that can inform their practice and surveys that are too flawed to merit guiding their practice.

EP 2.1.10d: Collect, organize, and interpret client data (p. 180): Understanding all of the concepts in this chapter will help social workers collect client data (such as in client needs assessment surveys or client satisfaction surveys) in ways that will maximize the quality and utility of those data.

EP 2.1.10m: Critically analyze, monitor, and evaluate interventions (p. 180): Social workers must understand all of the concepts in this chapter in order to use surveys in a competent manner for the purpose of monitoring or evaluating programs or interventions.

chapter 11

Sampling: Quantitative and Qualitative Approaches

11.1 INTRODUCTION

EP 2.1.6b
EP 2.1.10d
EP 2.1.10m

In Chapter 10 we saw that one of the most important criteria influencing the value of a survey is the representativeness of the survey respondents. Do their attributes accurately reflect those of the larger population? We alluded to sampling methods that can be used to maximize the likelihood that people selected for a survey will be representative of the population. Those sampling methods will be the focus of this chapter.

In quantitative studies, sampling deals with generalizability. As we'll see, it is possible for us to select a few people or things for observation and then apply what we observe to a much larger group of people or things. The first part of the chapter will focus on quantitative sampling methods. Later, we'll examine more flexible, qualitative sampling methods.

11.2 QUANTITATIVE SAMPLING METHODS

The key ingredient that enables researchers to *generalize* accurately from a segment of the population to the whole population is the use of **probability sampling** techniques, which involve random sampling. **Random Sampling** is an unbiased, precise, scientific procedure for selecting research respondents. There is nothing haphazard about it. Sampling techniques can allow us to determine or control the likelihood of specific individuals being selected for study. In the simplest example, flipping a coin to choose between two individuals gives each person exactly the same probability of selection:

---

probability sampling The use of random procedures to select a sample that can allow us to estimate the expected degree of sampling error in a study and determine or control the likelihood of specific units in a population being selected for the study.

random sampling A precise, scientific procedure for selecting research population elements for a sample that guarantees an equal probability of selection of each element when substantial samples are selected from large populations.

---

50 percent. More complex techniques guarantee an equal probability of selection when substantial samples are selected from large populations.

The history of political polling illustrates how researchers using unbiased sampling procedures can generalize accurately to a large population based on data collected from a tiny fraction of that population. For example, Table 11.1 reports polls conducted during the few days preceding the election. Despite some variations, the overall picture they present is amazingly consistent and pretty well matched the election results.

Now, how many interviews do you suppose it took each of these pollsters to come within a couple of percentage points in estimating the behavior of more than 131 million voters? Often fewer than 2,000!

Although probability sampling is precise, it is not always feasible to use probability sampling techniques. Consequently, social work research studies often use *nonprobability* sampling. Therefore, after we examine probability sampling methods, we'll look at a variety of nonprobability methods as well, including those used in qualitative research.

Table 11.1 Election Eve Polls Reporting Presidential Voting Plans, 2008

POLL	DATE ENDED	OBAMA	MCCAIN
FOX	Nov 2	54	46
NBC/WSJ	Nov 2	54	46
Marist College	Nov 2	55	45
Harris Interactive	Nov 3	54	46
Reuters/ C-SPAN/Zogby	Nov 3	56	44
ARG	Nov 3	54	46
Rasmussen	Nov 3	53	47
IBD/TIPP	Nov 3	54	46
DailyKos.com/ Research 2000	Nov 3	53	47
GWU	Nov 3	53	47
Marist College	Nov 3	55	45
Actual vote	**Nov 4**	**54**	**46**

Source: Poll data are adapted from data presented at Pollster.com (http://www.pollster.com/polls/us/08-us-pres-ge-mvo.php) on January 29, 2009. The official election results are from the Federal Election Commission (http://www.fec.gov/pubrec/fe2008/2008presgeresults.pdf) on the same date. For simplicity's sake, as there were no undecideds in the official results and each of the third-party candidates received less than one percentage of the vote, we've apportioned the undecided and other votes according to the percentages saying they were voting for Obama or McCain.

Although not based on random selection, these methods have their own logic and can provide useful samples for social work research. We'll examine both the advantages and the shortcomings of such methods, and we'll see where they fit within the social work research enterprise. Let's begin by examining a few political polls that illustrate some of the risks of using nonprobability sampling.

11.2a President Alf Landon

In 1936 the *Literary Digest*, a popular newsmagazine published in the United States between 1890 and 1938, conducted a poll that attempted to predict the outcome of the presidential election. Ten million ballots were sent to people listed in telephone directories and to automobile registration lists. More than 2 million responded, and the poll results gave Republican contender Alf Landon a stunning 57 to 43 percent landslide over the incumbent, President Franklin Roosevelt. Two weeks later, in the actual election, voters gave Roosevelt a second term in office by the largest landslide in history, with 61 percent of the vote.

Why was the *Digest*'s prediction so wrong? A part of the problem lay in the poll's 22 percent return rate. Another was in its sampling frame: telephone subscribers and automobile owners. Such a sampling design selected a disproportionately wealthy sample, especially coming during the worst economic depression in the nation's history. The sample effectively excluded poor people—who predominantly voted for Roosevelt's New Deal recovery program.

11.2b President Thomas E. Dewey

The 1936 election also saw the emergence of a young pollster whose name was to become synonymous with public opinion. In contrast to the *Literary Digest*, George Gallup correctly predicted that Roosevelt would beat Landon. Gallup's success in 1936 hinged on his use of quota sampling, about which we'll have more to say later in the chapter. For now, you need only know that **quota sampling** is based on a knowledge of the characteristics of the population being sampled: what proportions are men and women, and what proportions are of various incomes, ages, and so on. People are selected to match the population characteristics: the right number of poor, White,

rural men; the right number of rich, Black, urban women; and so on. The quotas are based on those variables that are most relevant to the study. By knowing the numbers of people with various incomes in the nation, Gallup selected his sample to ensure the right proportion of respondents at each income level.

Gallup and his American Institute of Public Opinion used quota sampling to good effect in 1936, 1940, and 1944—correctly picking presidential winners in each year. Then, in 1948, Gallup and most political pollsters suffered the embarrassment of picking New York Governor Thomas Dewey over incumbent President Harry Truman. The pollsters' embarrassing miscue continued right up to election night. A famous photograph shows a jubilant Truman—whose followers' battle cry was "Give 'em hell, Harry!"—holding aloft a newspaper with the banner headline "Dewey Defeats Truman."

Several factors accounted for the pollsters' 1948 failure. First, most of the pollsters stopped polling in early October, despite a steady trend toward Truman during the campaign. In addition, many voters were undecided throughout the campaign but went disproportionately for Truman when they stepped into the voting booth. More important for our present purposes, however, Gallup's failure rested on the unrepresentativeness of his samples.

Quota sampling—which had been effective in earlier years—was Gallup's undoing in 1948. This technique requires that the researcher know something about the total population (of voters in this instance). For national political polls, such information came primarily from census data. By 1948, however, a world war had produced a massive movement from country to city and radically changed the character of the U.S. population from the one described by the 1940 census—whose data Gallup used. City dwellers, moreover, were more likely to vote Democratic; hence, the overrepresentation of rural voters also underestimated the number of Democratic votes.

---

quota sampling A type of nonprobability sampling in which units are selected into the sample on the basis of prespecified characteristics so that the total sample will have the same distribution of characteristics as are assumed to exist in the population being studied.

11.2c President John Kerry

Improvements made in political polling enabled election eve polls to accurately predict the outcomes of presidential elections in the decades that followed. Today, probability sampling is the primary method for selecting large, representative samples for social science research. Basically, this technique selects a "random sample" from a list that contains the names of everyone in the population of study interest. By and large, current probability sampling methods are far more accurate than earlier sampling techniques, such as those used in predicting that Alf Landon would beat Franklin Roosevelt in a landslide.

The value of probability sampling techniques was underscored in the presidential election of 2004. Most election eve polls conducted with probability samples accurately predicted that George Bush would be reelected, beating John Kerry by a small margin. But on election day various news media and political groups attempted to get an early scoop on the outcome by conducting exit polls, asking voters who they voted for as the voters left the voting sites. The exit polls did not use rigorous probability sampling. Instead, they were most likely to interview those voters who happened to be near and willing (and perhaps eager) to reveal whom they voted for. As it turned out, Kerry voters were more likely to participate in the exit polls than were Bush voters. Knowing the results of the exit polls, various conservative TV pundits looked gloomy throughout the day before the actual results came in, as they anticipated a Kerry presidency and speculated about what went wrong in the Bush campaign. Likewise, various Kerry supporters looked exuberant. Their moods reversed as the actual vote counts came in showing Bush leading in key states predicted to go for Kerry in the exit polls.

11.3 PROBABILITY SAMPLING

If all members of a population were identical in all respects—demographic characteristics, attitudes, experiences, behaviors, and so on—we wouldn't need careful sampling procedures. Any sample would be sufficient. In this extreme case of

Based on early political polls that showed Dewey leading Truman, the *Chicago Tribune* sought to scoop the competition with this unfortunate headline.

homogeneity, in fact, one case would be enough as a sample to study the whole population's characteristics.

Of course, the human beings who make up any real population are quite heterogeneous, varying in many ways from one another. Figure 11.1 shows a simplified heterogeneous population: the 100 members of this small population differ by sex and race. We'll use this hypothetical micropopulation to illustrate various aspects of sampling throughout the chapter.

If a sample of individuals from a population is to provide useful descriptions of the total population, then it must contain essentially the same variations that exist in the population as a whole. This is not as simple as it might seem, however.

Let's look at some of the ways in which researchers might go astray. This will help us see how probability sampling provides an efficient method for selecting a sample that should adequately reflect variations in the population.

11.3a Conscious and Unconscious Sampling Bias

At first glance, it may look as though sampling is a pretty straightforward matter. To select a sample of 100 university students, you might simply go to campus and interview the first 100 students you find walking around campus. This kind of sampling method is often used by untrained researchers, but it has serious problems.

Figure 11.1 shows what can happen when you simply select people who are convenient for study. Although women are only 50 percent of our micropopulation, those closest to the researcher (in the upper-right corner) happen to be 70 percent women; and although the population is 12 percent African American, not one African American individual was selected into the sample.

Beyond the risks inherent in simply studying people who are convenient, we find other potential problems. To begin, a sample selected in this manner may be affected by our own personal leanings or biases; the sample therefore would not truly represent the student population. Suppose you're intimidated by students who look particularly "cool," feeling they might ridicule your research effort. You might consciously or unconsciously avoid interviewing such people. Or you might feel that the attitudes of "super-straight-looking" students would be irrelevant to your research purposes, and avoid interviewing them.

FIGURE 11.1 A Sample of Convenience: Easy, but Not Representative

Even if you sought to interview a "balanced" group of students, you wouldn't know the exact proportions of different types of students who make up such a balance, and you wouldn't always be able to identify the different types just by watching them walk by.

Even if you made a conscientious effort to interview every 10th student who entered the university library, you could not be sure of getting a representative sample, because different types of students visit the library with different frequencies. Your sample would overrepresent students who visit the library often.

When we speak of "bias" in connection with sampling, this simply means those selected are not "typical" or "representative" of the larger populations from which they have been chosen. This kind of bias is virtually inevitable when people are picked via a seat-of-the-pants approach.

Similarly, public opinion call-in polls—in which radio or TV stations or newspapers ask people to call specified telephone numbers or use the Internet to register their opinions—cannot be trusted to represent general populations. At the very least, not everyone in the population will be aware of the poll or have Internet access. This problem also invalidates polls by magazines and newspapers that publish coupons for readers to complete and return. Even among readers or viewers who are aware of such polls, not all of them will express opinions, especially if it will cost a stamp, an envelope, or a telephone charge. The possibilities for inadvertent sampling bias are endless and not always obvious. Fortunately, probability sampling techniques let us avoid bias.

11.3b Representativeness and Probability of Selection

Although the term *representativeness* has no precise, scientific meaning, its commonsense meaning makes

---

element   The unit selected in a sample about which information is collected.

population   The theoretically specified aggregation of study elements.

study population   The aggregation of elements from which the sample is actually selected.

it a useful concept in our discussion of sampling. As we'll use the term here, a sample will be representative of its population if the sample's aggregate characteristics closely approximate those same aggregate characteristics in the population. If the population, for example, contains 50 percent women, then a representative sample would also contain "close to" 50 percent women.

A basic principle of probability sampling is that a sample will be representative of its population if all members of that population have an equal chance of being selected in the sample. Moving beyond this basic principle, we must realize that probability samples seldom, if ever, perfectly represent the populations from which they are drawn. Nevertheless, probability sampling offers two special advantages.

First, probability samples, even if never perfectly representative, are typically more representative than other types of samples because selection biases are avoided. Second, probability theory permits us to estimate the sample's accuracy or representativeness. Conceivably, an uninformed researcher might, through wholly haphazard means, select a sample that nearly perfectly represents the larger population. The odds are against that happening, however, and we would be unable to estimate the likelihood that he or she has achieved representativeness. The probability sampler, on the other hand, can provide an accurate estimate of success or failure.

We've said that probability sampling ensures that samples are representative of the population we wish to study. As we'll see in a moment, probability sampling rests on the use of a random selection procedure. To develop this idea, though, we need to give more precise meaning to two important terms: *element* and *population*.

An **element** is that unit about which information is collected. Typically, in survey research, elements are people or certain types of people. However, other kinds of units can constitute the elements for social work research—for example, families, social clubs, or corporations might be the elements of a study.

Up to now we've used the term *population* to mean the group or collection that we're interested in generalizing about. More formally, a **population** is the theoretically specified aggregation of study elements. A **study population** is that aggregation of elements from which the sample is actually selected. As a practical matter, you are seldom in a position to guarantee that every element that meets established theoretical definitions actually has a chance of being selected in the sample. Even where lists of elements exist for sampling purposes, the lists are usually somewhat incomplete. Some students are always omitted, inadvertently, from student rosters. Some telephone subscribers request that their names and numbers be unlisted. The study population, then, is the aggregation of elements from which the sample is selected.

Researchers often decide to limit their study populations more severely than indicated in the preceding examples. National polling firms may limit their national samples to the 48 contiguous states, omitting Alaska and Hawaii for practical reasons. A researcher who wishes to sample social work practitioners may limit the study population to those whose names appear on the membership list of the National Association of Social Workers or on a list of those licensed by a particular state. (In a sense, we might say that these researchers have redefined their universes and populations, in which case they must make the revisions clear to their readers.)

11.3c Random Selection

With these definitions in hand, we can define the ultimate purpose of probability sampling: to select a set of elements from a population in such a way that descriptions of those elements accurately portray the total population from which the elements are selected. Probability sampling enhances the likelihood of accomplishing this aim and also provides methods for estimating the degree of probable success.

Random selection is the key to this process. In **random selection**, each element has an equal chance of selection independent of any other event in the selection process. Flipping a coin is the most frequently cited example: Provided that the coin is perfect (i.e., not biased in terms of coming up heads or tails), the "selection" of a head or a tail is independent of previous selections of heads or tails. No matter how many heads turn up in a row, the chance that the next flip will produce "heads" is exactly 50/50.

Such images of random selection, although useful, seldom apply directly to sampling methods in social work research. More typically, social work researchers use tables of random numbers or computer programs that provide a random selection of sampling units. A **sampling unit** is that element or set of elements considered for selection in some stage of sampling.

The reasons for using random selection methods are twofold. First, this procedure serves as a check on conscious or unconscious bias on the part of the researcher. The researcher who selects cases on an intuitive basis might very well select cases that would support his or her research expectations or hypotheses. Random selection erases this danger. More important, random selection offers access to the body of probability theory, which provides the basis for estimating the characteristics of the population as well as estimates of the accuracy of samples. Let's now examine the logic of probability sampling in greater detail.

11.3d The Logic of Probability Sampling

Probability theory is a branch of mathematics that provides researchers with tools to devise sampling techniques that produce representative samples and to analyze the results of their sampling statistically. More formally, probability theory provides the basis for estimating the parameters of a population. A **parameter** is the summary description of a given variable in a population. The mean income of all families in a city is a parameter; so is the age distribution of the city's population. When researchers generalize from a sample, they're using sample observations to estimate population parameters. Probability theory enables them both to make these estimates and to arrive at a judgment of how likely it is that the estimates will accurately represent the actual parameters in the population. So,

---

random selection A sampling method in which each element has an equal chance of selection independent of any other event in the selection process.

sampling unit An element or set of elements considered for selection in some stage of sampling.

parameter The summary description of a given variable in a population.

for example, probability theory allows pollsters to infer from a sample of 2,000 voters how a population of 100 million voters is likely to vote—and to specify exactly what the probable margin of error in the estimates is.

Although some complex statistical concepts and formulas are required to specify the exact probable margin of error in probability sampling, we can understand the logic involved without getting into the heavy math. Let's start by imagining that we are tossing a coin to see if it is more likely to come up heads or tails. Suppose we flip it twice and it comes up heads both times. We would not conclude that the coin always comes up heads or even that it is predisposed to come up heads. We don't need math to recognize that a coin that comes up heads half the time and tails half the time easily can come up heads twice in a row or tails twice in a row. If, based on our two coin flips, we concluded that the coin comes up heads 100 percent of the time, our estimate of the population of flips of that coin would be off by 50 percent. That is, our estimate of 100 percent heads and zero percent tails would be 50 percent away from the true population parameter of 50 percent heads and 50 percent tails. The difference between the true population parameter (50%) and our estimate (100%) is called **sampling error**. Thus, our sampling error would be 50 percent.

Now imagine that instead of tossing the coin twice we tossed it 20 times. The likelihood that we would get 100 percent heads (or 100 percent tails) would be quite tiny. Thus, because we increased our sample size, we reduced the likelihood that we would have 50 percent sampling error. And the larger the number of coin tosses, the lower that likelihood becomes. Thus, as sample size increases, the likelihood of random error in sampling decreases. Conversely, the larger the sample size, the greater the likelihood that our estimate will be close to the true population parameter.

To further illustrate this logic, suppose we had the name of every person in the United States written on a tiny piece of paper, had all the pieces crumpled up so that the names were not visible, and put

---

sampling error The difference between the true population parameter and the estimated population parameter.

them all in an enormous container. Suppose we shook the container vigorously and then with eyes closed drew names out of the container at random. Suppose the first two names we drew were female, and we therefore concluded that the percentage of females in the population is 100 percent. Just like with the coins, our sampling error would be about 50 percent (assuming that the population is evenly split between males and females). Next, suppose we randomly drew 1,000 slips of paper. The odds are quite high that we would get very close to having 500 (50%) males and 500 (50%) females. It probably wouldn't be exactly 50/50. We might, for example, get 510 (51%) males and 490 (49%) females. If so, our sampling error would be 1 percent.

When political polls based on random samples (not exit polls!) predict the outcomes of presidential elections, the same logic is involved, and that's why their predictions quite often are so accurate. If you've noticed the results of such polls in the newspaper or on television, you may recall that they come with an estimate of the margin of sampling error. For example, a poll predicting that the vote will be 51 percent for candidate X and 49 percent for candidate Y might say that the margin of error is plus or minus 3 percent. That means that there is a very high probability that the true population parameters are between 48 percent and 54 percent for candidate X and 46 percent and 52 percent for candidate Y. (That is, 3 percent is added to and subtracted from the estimates for each candidate to identify the range of likely outcomes in the larger population.) That is why sometimes news reporters will characterize such poll results as a "statistical dead heat." In other words, if the margin of sampling error is 3 percent, but the poll results show only a 2 percent difference between the two candidates, then it is quite conceivable that the candidate with 49 percent in the poll might really be favored by 50 percent or more of the larger population, and the candidate with 51 percent in the poll might really be favored by 50 percent or less of the population.

The same logic applies when we are trying to generalize from a sample to a population about other attributes, such as age, income, ethnicity, educational level, and so on. If a sufficiently large sample is selected randomly, we can estimate those parameters with a small margin of sampling error as well. When we say "sufficiently large" we do not mean large in the sense of percentage of the population. Accurate presidential polls are conducted with less than 2,000 people—much less than 1 percent of the population of voters.

Probability theory gives us a formula for estimating how closely sample statistics are clustered around a true population value. To put it another way, probability theory enables us to estimate the degree of sampling error to be expected for a given sample design. This statistical formula is too advanced for this text; however, if you are interested in examining it, you can find it in our more advanced text (Rubin & Babbie, 2011). The formula enables us to be confident (at some level) of being within a certain range of a population parameter, and to estimate the expected degree of error on the basis of one sample drawn from a population. Using this formula, for example, a presidential pollster might report that she is 95 percent confident that between 48 and 54 percent of the population of voters will vote for candidate X.

The formula also provides a basis for determining the appropriate sample size for a study. Once you have decided on the degree of sampling error you can tolerate, you'll be able to calculate the number of cases needed in your sample. Thus, for example, if a pollster assumes that the election will be close, and wants to be 95 percent confident of predicting the election results within plus or minus 5 percentage points of the actual votes, then she'll need to select a sample of at least 400 people. Although you may not use the formula in any of your own research, Table 11.2 is a convenient guide for estimating the sample size you will need for the degree of sampling error you can tolerate. It also illustrates how, as sample sizes reach a certain point, further increases in sample size yield diminishing returns in reducing sampling error and may not be worth the additional data collection costs.

To use Table 11.2, find the intersection between the sample size and the approximate percentage distribution that you anticipate in the population. For example, suppose we assume that roughly 50 percent of the population intends to vote for candidate X, and 50 percent intend to vote for candidate Y. It shows that increasing the sample size from 100 to 1,100 will reduce the estimated

Table 11.2 Estimated Sampling Error

SAMPLE SIZE	ESTIMATED PERCENTAGE DISTRIBUTION				
	50/50	60/40	70/30	80/20	90/10
100	10	9.8	9.2	8	6
200	7.1	6.9	6.5	5.7	4.2
300	5.8	5.7	5.3	4.6	3.5
400	5	4.9	4.6	4	3
500	4.5	4.4	4.1	3.6	2.7
600	4.1	4	3.7	3.3	2.4
700	3.8	3.7	3.5	3	2.3
800	3.5	3.5	3.2	2.8	2.1
900	3.3	3.3	3.1	2.7	2
1000	3.2	3.1	2.9	2.5	1.9
1100	3	3	2.8	2.4	1.8
1200	2.9	2.8	2.6	2.3	1.7
1300	2.8	2.7	2.5	2.2	1.7
1400	2.7	2.6	2.4	2.1	1.6
1500	2.6	2.5	2.4	2.1	1.5
1600	2.5	2.4	2.3	2	1.5
1700	2.4	2.4	2.2	1.9	1.5
1800	2.4	2.3	2.2	1.9	1.4
1900	2.3	2.2	2.1	1.8	1.4
2000	2.2	2.2	2	1.8	1.3

sampling error by 7 percentage points. But increasing it from 1,100 to 2,000 will reduce it by only another eight-tenths of 1 percent.

This, then, is the basic logic of probability sampling. Random selection permits the researcher to link findings from a sample to the body of probability theory so as to estimate the accuracy of those findings. The researcher may report that he or she is x percent confident that the population parameter is between two specific values.

11.3e Populations and Sampling Frames

Although it is necessary for the research consumer, student, and researcher to understand the logic of probability sampling, it is no less important that they appreciate the less-than-perfect conditions that exist in the field. The present section is devoted to a discussion of one aspect of field conditions that requires a compromise with regard to theoretical conditions and assumptions. Here we'll consider the congruence of or disparity between populations and sampling frames.

Simply put, a **sampling frame** is the list or quasi-list of elements from which a sample is selected. If a sample of students is selected from a student roster, the roster is the sampling frame. If the primary sampling unit for a complex population sample is the census block, the list of census blocks is the sampling frame—in the form of a printed booklet or a computer file. Here are some reports of sampling frames appearing in research journals:

The data for this research were obtained from a random sample of *parents of children in the third grade in public and parochial schools in Yakima County, Washington.*

(Petersen & Maynard, 1981, p. 92)

The sample at Time 1 consisted of 160 names drawn randomly from the *telephone directory of Lubbock, Texas.*

(Tan, 1980, p. 242)

The data reported in this paper … were gathered from a probability sample of *adults aged 18 and over residing in households in the 48 contiguous United States.* Personal interviews with 1,914 respondents were conducted by the Survey Research Center of the University of Michigan during the fall of 1975.

(Jackman & Senter, 1980, p. 345)

In each of these examples, we've highlighted and italicized the actual sampling frames.

Properly drawn samples provide information appropriate for describing the population of elements making up the sampling frame—nothing more. It is necessary to make this point in view of the all-too-common tendency for researchers to select samples from a given sampling frame and then make assertions about a population similar to, but not identical to, the study population defined by the sampling frame.

For an example of an overgeneralized sampling frame, take a look at this report, which is discussing the drugs most frequently prescribed by American physicians:

Information on prescription drug sales is not easy to obtain. But Rinaldo V. DeNuzzo, a professor of pharmacy at the Albany College of Pharmacy, Union University, Albany, NY, has been tracking prescription drug sales for 25 years by polling nearby drugstore. He publishes the results in an industry trade magazine, MM&M. DeNuzzo's latest survey, covering 1980, is based on reports from 66 pharmacies in 48 communities in New York and New Jersey. Unless there is something peculiar about that part of the country, his findings can be taken as representative of what happens across the country.

(Moskowitz, 1981, p. 33)

The main thing that should strike you is the casual comment about whether there is anything peculiar about New York and New Jersey. There is. The lifestyle in these two states is hardly typical of the other 48. We cannot assume that residents in these large, urbanized, Eastern-seaboard states necessarily have the same drug-use patterns as residents of Mississippi, Utah, New Mexico, and Vermont.

Does the survey even represent prescription patterns in New York and New Jersey? To determine that, we would have to know something about the manner in which the 48 communities and the 66 pharmacies were selected. We should be wary in this regard, given the reference to "polling nearby drugstores." As we'll see, there are several methods for selecting samples that ensure representativeness, and unless they are used, we should not generalize from the study findings.

A sampling frame, then, must be consonant with the population we wish to study. In the simplest sample design, the sampling frame is a list of the elements making up the study population. In practice, though, existing sampling frames often define the study population rather than the other way around. That is, we often begin with a population in mind for our study, then search for possible sampling frames. Having examined and evaluated the frames available for our use, we decide which frame presents a study population most appropriate to our needs.

Studies of organizations are often the simplest from a sampling standpoint because organizations typically have membership lists. In such cases, the list of members constitutes an excellent sampling frame. If a random sample is selected from a membership list, the data collected from that sample may

---

sampling frame The list or quasi-list of elements from which a sample is selected.

be taken as representative of all members—if all members are included in the list.

Populations that can be sampled from good organizational lists include elementary school, high school, and university students and faculty; church members; factory workers; fraternity and sorority members; members of social, service, and political clubs; and members of professional associations.

The preceding comments apply primarily to local organizations. Often, statewide or national organizations do not have a single, easily available membership list. There is, for example, no single list of Episcopalian church members. However, a slightly more complex sample design could take advantage of local church membership lists by first sampling churches and then subsampling the membership lists of those churches selected. (More about that later.)

Other lists of individuals may be especially relevant to the research needs of a particular study. Government agencies maintain lists of registered voters, for example, that might be used if you wanted to conduct a preelection poll or an in-depth examination of voting behavior—but you must ensure that the list is up-to-date. Similar lists contain the names of automobile owners, welfare recipients, taxpayers, business permit holders, licensed professionals, and so forth. Although it may be difficult to gain access to some of these lists, they provide excellent sampling frames for specialized research purposes.

Realizing that the sampling elements in a study need not be individual persons, we may note that the lists of other types of elements also exist: universities, businesses of various types, cities, academic journals, newspapers, unions, political clubs, professional associations, and so forth.

Street directories and tax maps are often used for easily obtained samples, but they may also suffer from incompleteness and possible bias. For example, in strictly zoned urban regions, illegal housing units are unlikely to appear on official records. As a result, such units would have no chance for selection, and sample findings could not be representative of those units, which are often poorer and more overcrowded than the average.

Most of the above comments apply to the United States; the situation is quite different in some other countries. In Japan, for example, the government maintains quite accurate population registration lists. Moreover, citizens are required by law to keep their information up-to-date, as it may change by a residential move or births and deaths in the household. As a consequence, it is possible to select *simple random samples* of the Japanese population by the process described later in this chapter. Such a registration list in the United States would conflict directly with American norms regarding individual privacy.

11.3f Non-Response Bias

We have just discussed errors in overgeneralization that can occur when sampling frames are not consonant with the population to which we seek to generalize. Another common error occurs when a substantial proportion of people in the randomly selected sample choose not to participate in the study.

Suppose, for example, you want to survey the social workers in your state regarding their views of evidence-based practice and how often they engage in it. You plan to conduct the survey by mailing each social worker a paper questionnaire to complete and return in the stamped, self-addressed envelope enclosed with the questionnaire. Your first step would be to obtain a list of all the social workers and their addresses. Let's assume that the only list available to you is the membership roster of your state's chapter of National Association of Social Workers. Let's further suppose that there are 10,000 social worker names on that list and that your limited research budget has only $1,000 for postage. Obviously, you cannot afford to survey all 10,000 members. Let's say you can afford the postage for a sample of 500 social workers, which you randomly select from the list of 10,000.

Your sampling frame is the list of 10,000 names, and you *hope* your sample will be the 500 social workers whose names you randomly selected from that list. We emphasize the word *hope* because many of the 500 randomly selected social workers may choose not to respond to your survey. Suppose only 200 respond. That would not be a probability sample. Why not? Because the reasons for inclusion ultimately were not random. Perhaps most of the 200 who responded are familiar with evidence-based practice and engage in it frequently. Perhaps most of the 300 who did not respond chose not to because they had never heard of evidence-based practice, don't care about it, or dislike it. Perhaps many of them don't engage in it and feel embarrassed about admitting that. Clearly then, despite choosing the 500 names randomly, your 200 respondents would comprise a nonprobability sample—moreover, a quite biased and unrepresentative one!

Although you used random procedures to generate what you hoped would be your sample, what you really wound up with was a nonprobability sample of 200 available subjects—those who for whatever reasons took the trouble to participate. It also bears noting that even if you had 100 percent participation from all 500 social workers, you might have had some bias in your sample. That's because many social workers in your state might not be current members of NASW. This refers back to our discussion above, regarding the distinction between sampling frames and populations. (We used the term *sampling frame* in this illustration, and not study *population*, because your aim is to generalize to all social workers in your state, not just NASW members.)

In light of the refusal to participate by some randomly selected individuals, many samples that are considered to be random may, from a technically pure standpoint, not be random at all. That is, when one or more randomly selected individuals opt not to participate in a study, the randomly selected sample only represents those elements in the population who agree to participate. There might be important differences between those who so choose and those who refuse regarding the variables being assessed. However, when the proportion of the selected elements who refuse to participate is trivial, it is usually reasonable—from a practical standpoint—to call the participants a probability sample. Suppose, for example, that 490 (98%) of the 500 social workers respond to your survey, and that 343 (70%) of them express favorable views about evidence-based practice. Even if all 10 of the nonrespondents dislike evidence-based practice, your estimate of the proportion favoring evidence-based practice would be off by less than 2 percentage points. That is, the true percentage favoring evidence-based practice out of the 500 would be 343 divided by 500, or 68.6 percent—only 1.4 percentage points less than your finding of 70 percent. But this raises the question of where

the cutoff point is for deeming the refusal rate to be too high to still interpret your findings as if they were based on probability sampling. There is no scientific or mathematical answer to this question. Our best guidance on this is to examine whether the proportion of refusals is large enough that their numbers could have changed your findings to a meaningful extent had they participated and been unlike the actual participants in regard to the variables of your study.

11.3g Review of Populations and Sampling Frames

Surprisingly little attention has been given to the issues of populations and sampling frames in social research literature. With this in mind, we've devoted special attention to them here. To further emphasize the point, here is a summary of the main guidelines to remember:

1. Findings based on a sample can be taken as representative only of the aggregation of elements that make up the sampling frame.
2. Often, sampling frames do not truly include all the elements that their names might imply. Omissions are almost inevitable. Thus, a first concern of the researcher must be to assess the extent of the omissions and to correct them if possible. (Realize, of course, that the researcher may feel he or she can safely ignore a small number of omissions that cannot easily be corrected.)
3. Even to generalize to the population comprising the sampling frame, it is necessary for all elements to have equal representation in the frame. Typically, each element should appear only once. Elements that appear more than once will have a greater probability of selection, and the sample will, overall, overrepresent those elements.

11.3h Other Considerations in Determining Sample Size

The importance of the foregoing material notwithstanding, decisions about sample size in social work research rarely involve estimating sampling error. Often, this is due to practical limitations. It may not be possible to obtain an adequate sampling frame for some populations of concern to social workers, such as the homeless, undocumented recent immigrants, and so on. Meager budgets for conducting research or time constraints may preclude conducting preliminary surveys to estimate population parameters. Inadequate resources also may force researchers simply to select the largest sample the budget will permit, knowing in advance that that maximum sample size will fall short of the number needed for a desired estimated sampling error.

In studies that have meager resources but seek to conduct complex statistical analyses, the selected sample size often will be determined by multiplying the number of variables to be simultaneously analyzed by the minimum number of cases per variable required by the appropriate statistical procedure.

11.4 TYPES OF PROBABILITY SAMPLING DESIGNS

Four commonly used types of probability sampling designs are: (1) simple random sampling, (2) systematic sampling, (3) stratified random sampling, and (4) multistage cluster sampling. So far, the illustrations we have been using pertain primarily to simple random sampling, and we'll examine that type more closely now. Then we'll discuss the other three options for obtaining a probability sample.

11.4a Simple Random Sampling

Once a sampling frame has been established in accord with the preceding discussion, the researcher can use **simple random sampling** by assigning a single number to each element in the sampling frame list without skipping any number in the process. A table of random numbers (Appendix D) is then used to select elements for the sample. The box entitled "Using a Table of Random Numbers" explains its use.

Figure 11.2 illustrates simple random sampling. Note that the members of our hypothetical micropopulation have been numbered from 1 to 100. Moving to Appendix D, we decide to use the last two digits of the first column and to begin with the third number from the top. This yields person number 30 as the first one selected into the sample. Number 67 is next, and so forth. (Person 100 would have been selected if "00" had come up in the list.)

11.4b Systematic Sampling

Simple random sampling is less efficient than systematic sampling, and it can be rather laborious if done manually. Consequently, when manually selecting a sample from a list of sampling elements, researchers often prefer to employ a less laborious alternative: **systematic sampling**.

In systematic sampling, every kth element in the total list is chosen (systematically) for inclusion in the sample. If the list contains 10,000 elements and you want a sample of 1,000, you select every 10th element for your sample. To guard against any possible human bias in using this method, you should select the first element at random. Thus, in the preceding example, you would begin by selecting a random number between 1 and 10. The element having that number is included in the sample, plus every 10th element following it. This method is technically referred to as a systematic sample with a random start. Two terms are frequently used in connection with systematic sampling. The **sampling interval** is the standard distance between elements selected in the sample: in the preceding sample, 10. The **sampling ratio** is the proportion of elements in the population that are selected: 1/10 in the example.

In practice, systematic sampling is virtually identical to simple random sampling. If the list of elements is indeed randomized before sampling, one might argue that a systematic sample drawn from that list is, in fact, a simple random sample. By now, debates over the relative merits of simple random sampling and systematic sampling have been resolved largely in favor of the simpler method: systematic sampling. Empirically, the results are virtually identical.

---

simple random sampling Using a table of random numbers to select sampling units after assigning a single number to each element in the sampling frame list.

systematic sampling An efficient alternative to random sampling, in which every kth element in the sampling frame list—after a random start—is chosen for inclusion in the sample.

sampling interval The standard distance between elements selected in systematic sampling.

sampling ratio The proportion of elements in the population that are selected in a systematic sample.

FIGURE 11.2 A Simple Random Sample

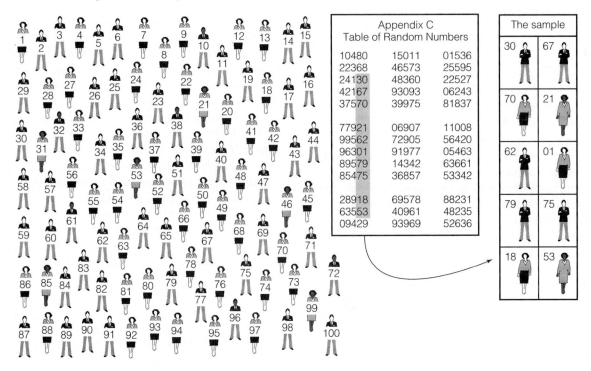

There is one danger involved in systematic sampling. The arrangement of elements in the list can make systematic sampling unwise. Such an arrangement is usually called *periodicity*. If the list of elements is arranged in a cyclical pattern that coincides with the sampling interval, then a grossly biased sample may be drawn. Two examples will illustrate.

In one study of soldiers during World War II, researchers selected a systematic sample from unit rosters. Every 10th soldier on the roster was selected for the study. The rosters, however, were arranged in a table of organizations: sergeants first, then corporals and privates, squad by squad. Each squad had 10 members. As a result, every 10th person on the roster was a squad sergeant. The systematic sample selected contained only sergeants. It could, of course, have been the case that no sergeants were selected for the same reason.

As another example, suppose we select a sample of apartments in an apartment building. If the sample is drawn from a list of apartments arranged in numerical order (e.g., 101, 102, 103, 104, 201, 202, and so on), there is a danger of the sampling interval coinciding with the number of apartments on a floor or some multiple thereof. Then the samples might include only northwest-corner apartments or only apartments near the elevator. The sample of these types of apartments will be biased if they have some other particular characteristic in common (e.g., higher rent). The same danger would appear in a systematic sample of houses in a subdivision arranged with the same number of houses on a block.

In considering a systematic sample from a list, then, you should carefully examine the nature of that list. If the elements are arranged in any particular order, you should figure out whether that order will bias the sample to be selected and take steps to counteract any possible bias (e.g., take a simple random sample from cyclical portions).

11.4c Stratified Sampling

In the two preceding sections, we discussed two methods of sample selection from a list: random and systematic. **Stratification** is not an alternative to these methods, but it represents a possible modification in their use.

Simple random sampling and systematic sampling both ensure a degree of representativeness and permit an estimate of the error present. Stratified sampling is a method for obtaining a greater degree of representativeness—for decreasing the probable sampling error. The reason for this is that a homogeneous population produces samples with smaller sampling errors than does a heterogeneous population. If 99 percent of the population agrees with a certain statement, then it is extremely unlikely that any probability sample will greatly misrepresent the extent of agreement. If the population is split 50/50 on the statement, then the sampling error will probably be much greater. With stratified sampling, rather than selecting a sample from the total population at large, we ensure that appropriate numbers of elements are drawn randomly from homogeneous subsets of that population.

Suppose you seek to obtain a stratified sample of clients in a large social service agency in order to assess client satisfaction with the services they received. You suspect that ethnic minority clients might be relatively dissatisfied with services, and you want to ensure that they are adequately represented in the sample. Consequently, you might first organize your list of cases so that clients of the same ethnicity are grouped together. That's what's meant by the term *stratifying*. Then you would randomly draw appropriate numbers from each ethnic group (each *stratum*). You could use either a simple or systematic approach to the random selection, but whichever approach you use should be the same for each group. In a nonstratified sample, representation by ethnicity would be subjected to the same sampling error as other variables. In a sample stratified by ethnicity, the sampling error on this variable is reduced to zero.

Even more complex stratification methods are possible. In addition to stratifying by ethnicity, you might also stratify by age group, type of presenting problem, and so forth. In this fashion, you might be able to ensure that your sample would contain the proper numbers of Hispanic children with behavior disorders, African American families experiencing marital discord, elderly Asian American clients, and so forth.

The ultimate function of stratification, then, is to organize the population into homogeneous subsets (with heterogeneity between subsets) and to randomly select the appropriate number of elements from each. To the extent that the subsets are homogeneous on the stratification variables, they may be homogeneous on other variables as well. If the age group is related to type of presenting problem, then a sample stratified by age group will be more representative in terms of presenting problem as well. If socioeconomic status is related to ethnicity, then a sample stratified by ethnicity will be more representative in terms of socioeconomic status.

Figure 11.3 offers a graphic illustration of stratified, systematic sampling. As you can see, we lined up our micropopulation according to sex and race. Then, beginning with a random start of "3," we've taken every 10th person thereafter: 3, 13, 23, ..., 93.

Stratified sampling ensures the proper representation of the stratification variables to enhance the representation of other variables related to them. Taken as a whole, then, a stratified sample is likely to be more representative on several variables than a simple random sample. Although the simple random sample is still regarded as somewhat sacred, we often can do better.

Proportionate and Disproportionate Stratified Samples

So far, we have been illustrating stratified random sampling with a uniform proportion of cases drawn from each homogeneous grouping. This is called *proportionate stratified sampling*. For example, if our overall sample is to be 10 percent of the population, then we would draw 10 percent of each homogeneous group. In some studies, however, it may be advisable to select a larger proportion of cases from some groups than from others. Suppose, for example, that the preceding client satisfaction survey is being conducted in an agency whose 1,000 clients include 600 White clients, 300 African American clients, 40 Hispanic clients, 30 Asian American clients, 20 Native American clients, and 10 clients whose ethnicity falls in a catchall "other" category. We could select 10 percent of the White and African American clients and have 60 and 30 cases in each group. But if we selected

---

stratification The grouping of the units making up a population into homogeneous groups (or strata) before sampling.

Using a Table of Random Numbers

In social research, it is often appropriate to select a set of random numbers from a table such as the one in Appendix D. Here's how to do that.

Suppose you want to select a simple random sample of 100 people (or other units) out of a population totaling 980.

1. To begin, number the members of the population—in this case, from 1 to 980. Now the problem is to select 100 random numbers. Once you've done that, your sample will consist of the people having the numbers you've selected. (Note: It's not essential to actually number them, as long as you're sure of the total. If you have them in a list, for example, you can always count through the list after you've selected the numbers.)

2. The next step is to determine the number of digits you will need in the random numbers you select. In our example, there are 980 members of the population, so you will need three-digit numbers to give everyone a chance of selection. (If there were 11,825 members of the population, you'd need to select five-digit numbers.) Thus, we want to select 100 random numbers in the range from 001 to 980.

3. Now turn to the first page of Appendix D. Notice that there are many rows and columns of five-digit numbers over three pages. The table represents a series of random numbers in the range from 00001 to 99999. To use the table for your hypothetical sample, you have to answer these questions:

   a. How will you create three-digit numbers out of five-digit numbers?

   b. What pattern will you follow in moving through the table to select your numbers?

   c. Where will you start?

   Each of these questions has several satisfactory answers. The key is to create a plan and follow it. Here's an example.

4. To create three-digit numbers from five-digit numbers, let's agree to select five-digit numbers from the table but consider only the leftmost three digits in each case. If we picked the first number on the first page—10480—we would consider only the three digits 104. (We could also agree to take the digits furthest to the right, 480, or the middle three digits, 048; any of these plans would work.) The key is to make a plan and stick with it. For convenience, let's use the leftmost three digits.

5. We can also choose to progress through the table any way we want: down the columns, up them, across to the right or to the left, or diagonally. Again, any of these plans will work just fine so long as we stick to it. For convenience, let's agree to move down the columns. When we get to the bottom of one column, we'll go to the top of the next; when we exhaust the first page, we'll start at the top of the first column of the next page.

6. Now, where do we start? You can close your eyes and stick a pencil into the table and start wherever the pencil point lands. (We know it doesn't sound scientific, but it works.) Or, if you're afraid you'll hurt the book or miss it altogether, close your eyes and make up a column number and a row number. ("We'll pick the number in the fifth row of column 2.") Start with that number. If you prefer more methodological purity, you might use the first two numbers on a dollar bill, which are randomly distributed, to determine the row and column on which to start.

7. Let's suppose we decide to start with the fifth number in column 2. If you look on the first page of Appendix D, you'll see that the starting number is 39975. We have selected 399 as our first random number, and we have 99 more to go. Above (in step 5) we decided to move down the columns. Therefore, the next number that we would select is 069, which is immediately below the first number we selected. Continuing to move down the second column, we select 729, 919, 143, 368, 695, 409, 939, and so forth. At the bottom of column 2, we select number 104 and continue to the top of column 3: 015, 255, and so on.

8. See how easy it is? But trouble lies ahead. When we reach column 5, we are speeding along, selecting 816, 309, 763, 078, 061, 277, 988.... Wait a minute! There are only 980 students in the senior class. How can we pick number 988? The solution is simple: Ignore it. Any time you come across a number that lies outside your range, skip it and continue on your way: 188, 174, and so forth. The same solution applies if the same number comes up more than once. If 399 reappears, for example, just ignore it the second time.

9. That's it. You keep up the procedure until you've selected 100 random numbers. Returning to your list, your sample consists of person number 399, person number 69, person number 729, and so forth.

FIGURE 11.3 A Stratified, Systematic Sample with a Random Start

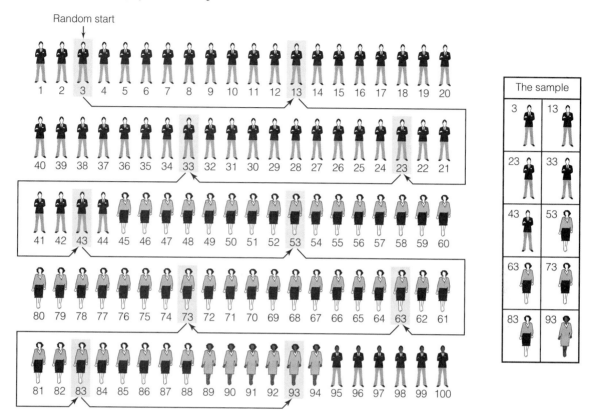

10 percent of the clients in the other groups, we would have only four Hispanics, three Asian Americans, two Native Americans, and one "other." There would be nothing wrong with this if all we sought to do was to come up with an overall satisfaction rating for the entire agency.

But what if we sought a detailed analysis about each ethnic group, or sought to generalize about which ethnic groups were more satisfied or dissatisfied than others? Such an analysis would not be possible for groups represented by only a handful of cases. Therefore, we would have to take a larger proportion of the very small homogeneous groupings than of the larger ones. This is called *disproportionate stratified sampling*. This sampling procedure gives cases from specified small subgroups a disproportionately better chance of being selected than cases from larger subgroups.

For example, we might select 10 percent of the White and African American clients and 50 percent

from each of the remaining groups. That would give us 20 Hispanics, 15 Asian Americans, 10 Native Americans, and 5 "other." This would permit us to undertake our detailed analyses. But if we also wanted to portray an overall agency composite of client satisfaction, then we would have to weight the average satisfaction level of each ethnic group in accordance with its overall proportion in the agency population. (If you'd like to see the math involved in this weighting, you can examine the sampling chapter in our more advanced text [Rubin & Babbie, 2011].)

11.4d Multistage Cluster Sampling

The preceding sections have dealt with reasonably simple procedures for sampling from lists of elements. Such a situation is ideal. Unfortunately, however, much research requires the selection of samples from populations that cannot easily be listed for sampling purposes. Examples would be the population of a city, state, or nation; all university students in the United States; and so forth. In such cases, the sample design must be much more complex and typically involves the initial sampling of groups of elements—clusters—followed by the selection of elements within each selected cluster.

Cluster sampling may be used when it's either impossible or impractical to compile an exhaustive list of the elements that make up the target population. All church members in the United States would be an example of such a population. It is often the case, however, that the population elements are already grouped into subpopulations, and a list of those subpopulations either exists or can be created practically. Thus, church members in the United States belong to discrete churches, and it would be possible to discover or create a list of those churches. Following a *cluster sample* format, then, the list of churches would be sampled in some manner as discussed previously (e.g., a stratified, systematic sample). Next, you would obtain lists of members from each selected church. Each list would then be sampled to provide samples of church members for study.

11.4e Probability Sampling in Review

The preceding discussions have been devoted to the key sampling method used in controlled survey research: probability sampling. In each examined variation, we have seen that elements are chosen for study from a population on a basis of random selection. Depending on the field situation,

---

cluster sampling A multistage sampling procedure that starts by sampling groups (clusters) of elements in the population and then subsampling individual members of each selected group afterward.

nonprobability sampling The use of procedures to select a sample that does not involve random selection.

availability sampling A sampling method that selects elements simply because of their ready availability and convenience. Frequently used in social work because it is usually less expensive than other methods and because other methods may not be feasible for a particular type of study or population.

---

probability sampling can be extremely simple or extremely difficult, time-consuming, and expensive. Whatever the situation, however, it remains the most effective method for selecting a representative sample of study elements in quantitative research. There are two reasons for this.

First, probability sampling avoids conscious or unconscious biases in element selection on the part of the researcher. If all elements in the population have an equal (or unequal and subsequently weighted) chance of selection, then there is an excellent chance that the selected sample will closely represent the population of all elements.

Second, probability sampling permits estimates of sampling error. Although no probability sample will be perfectly representative in all respects, controlled selection methods permit the researcher to estimate the degree of expected error.

11.5 NONPROBABILITY SAMPLING IN QUANTITATIVE AND QUALITATIVE RESEARCH

Social work research is often conducted in situations in which it is not feasible to select a probability sample. Suppose you wanted to study homelessness: No list of all homeless individuals is available, and you're not likely to create such a list yourself. Neither are you likely to have a list of clusters from which to sample. Moreover, as we'll see, there are times when probability sampling wouldn't be appropriate even if it were possible. In many such situations, **nonprobability sampling** procedures are called for, and we'll examine four types in this section: (1) reliance on available subjects, (2) purposive or judgmental sampling, (3) quota sampling, and (4) snowball sampling. These procedures are applicable in qualitative research as well as quantitative research. After we examine them, we'll move on to procedures that are unique to qualitative research.

11.5a Reliance on Available Subjects

Relying on *available* subjects—sometimes called **availability sampling**, *accidental sampling*, or *convenience sampling*—is a frequently used sampling method in social work because it is usually less expensive than other methods and because other methods may not be feasible for a particular type of study or population. As one indicator of the popularity of this sampling method in social work, some form of availability sampling was reported in the majority of research articles published from 1994 through 1999 in the journal *Social Work Research* (Monette, Sullivan, & DeJong, 2002).

As we noted earlier in our discussion of conscious and unconscious sampling bias in selecting people who are convenient to study, availability sampling can be an extremely risky sampling method. For example, stopping students who happen to be walking near your school of social work would be a risky way to assess student attitudes about social issues like welfare policies, affirmative action, reproductive rights, and so on. Social work students tend to have liberal attitudes about those issues and would be more likely to be near the school than students with more conservative attitudes about them.

Despite their risk of bias, however, some forms of availability sampling can seem more useful than others. Not all samples of convenience are equally biased. Even if bias is evident, some convenience samples can provide useful tentative findings, especially when care is taken not to overgeneralize their findings. Suppose, for example, that a local foundation is concerned about a dangerous new drug that recently caused several deaths among teens in the United States. It wants to find out how widespread the use of that drug is among high school students in your Midwestern city. It gives you a small grant to survey high-school students in your city about whether and how much they've experimented with the new drug. There are 10 high schools in your city, but you manage to obtain permission to conduct your survey in only two of them. One of the high schools is in a poor neighborhood, and has a relatively large proportion of African American students. The other high school is in a middle-class neighborhood, and has relatively few ethnic minority students.

You conduct your survey by having teachers disseminate your questionnaire about drug use to all the students in each of the two schools. A cover letter asks each student to voluntarily participate in the study by completing the questionnaire and returning it anonymously in a sealed envelope into a large drop box located at the school. Suppose that 50 percent of the students at each school

participate, and the other 50 percent do not. Suppose further that your findings indicate that exactly 30 percent of the survey respondents in each school report having experimented with the new drug, and that exactly 20 percent of them say they will continue using it on occasion.

What would be the value of your findings? In considering the answer to this question, we should note that yours is a risky convenience sample containing likely biases because it does not include the 50 percent of those students who were either unwilling to answer questions about drug use or not motivated to take the time and effort to respond to your survey. Perhaps the students experimenting with drugs were more interested in a drug survey than those not into drugs, and thus were much more motivated to respond than the other students. Another possibility is that the students experimenting with drugs were more likely to be threatened by your survey and therefore less likely to respond. Moreover, not only did your survey not include the nonrespondents in the two schools, it did not include the other eight high schools that refused to participate in your survey. Perhaps drug experimentation in those eight schools is more (or less) prevalent than it is in the two schools that agreed to participate.

Should the community therefore disregard your findings because they were based on an availability sample that likely is biased? In answering this question, you might note that even if all of the students in the two participating schools who had experimented with the new drug were included among your respondents, your findings would nevertheless mean that 15 percent of all the students in the two schools say they have experimented with the drug. (Thirty percent of *half* of the students is 15 percent of *all* the students.) Likewise, the findings would mean that 10 percent of all the students (half of the 20 percent) in those two schools say they will continue using it on occasion. Moreover, your findings would mean that these figures are minimum estimates, because it is conceivable that students experimenting with the new drug were less likely than others to respond to your survey.

Assuming that the students were not lying about experimenting with the dangerous new drug, we think your findings would have significant value. We think your findings would spur the community to implement a program to educate students about the dangers of the new drug and to try in other ways to prevent its usage. Moreover, we think that the community would be concerned about the students in not only the two schools that participated in your survey, but the remaining schools as well. In fact, we think your findings would spur the remaining schools to replicate your survey among their students. Although your findings should not be generalized to other schools, they certainly would provide a tentative—but still valuable—basis for concern about the scope of the problem elsewhere, even including other cities.

The foregoing example is hypothetical and does not mean that you should disregard our earlier comments about the risks of conscious and unconscious biases in selecting convenience samples. We are merely illustrating how some studies using convenience samples might be more useful than others, depending on the research question and the way findings are interpreted. Although this form of sampling is always risky, not all convenience samples are equally risky. Not all produce worthless and misleading results.

Suppose you conduct a mailed survey of all the clients in your agency to assess their satisfaction with your agency's services. Unless they all respond to your survey, you will have a sample of available subjects that includes only those who took the time to respond. Perhaps they are more likely to be extremely satisfied or extremely dissatisfied than the nonresponders. But if about 80 percent of them respond and almost all say they are extremely dissatisfied, you would have good reason to try to improve your services. If, on the other hand, only 10 percent respond and all say they are extremely satisfied, you would *not* have grounds for concluding that things are hunky-dory. The room for bias in the latter sample is huge, and the 90 percent who did not take the time to respond might be much less satisfied than those who did respond.

11.5b Purposive or Judgmental Sampling

Sometimes you may appropriately select your sample on the basis of your own knowledge of the population, its elements, and the nature of your research aims—in short, based on your judgment and the

---

purposive sampling   Selecting a sample based on your own judgment about which units are most representative or useful.

purpose of the study. Especially in the initial design of a questionnaire, you might wish to select the widest variety of respondents to test the broad applicability of questions. Although the study findings would not represent any meaningful population, the test run might effectively uncover any peculiar defects in your questionnaire. This situation would be considered a pretest, however, rather than a final study.

In some instances, you may wish to study a small subset of a larger population in which many members of the subset are easily identified, but enumerating all of them would be nearly impossible. For example, you might want to study the homeless. Many homeless people might be visible in certain areas of town, such as near shelters, a Salvation Army facility, or other social welfare facilities. But it would not be feasible to define and sample all of them. In studying all or a sample of the most visible homeless individuals, you might collect data sufficient for your purposes, particularly if your study is exploratory. Thus, you might ask personnel in those facilities to use their judgment in handpicking cases that they think represent those segments of the homeless population with which they are familiar.

Suppose you are writing a grant proposal to secure funding for new social services to be targeted to the homeless, and the funding source requires that your proposal include an assessment of the social service needs of the homeless in your community. Suppose, given your agency's meager resources and the nearness of the proposal submission deadline, you have neither the time nor money to conduct a communitywide survey of the homeless using probability sampling. One option would be to select a **purposive sampling** of community leaders, experts, and professionals known for their work with and expertise on the problem of homelessness in your locality. You could use your knowledge of the community to handpick key people who, in your judgment, best represented the range of those persons who would best know the needs of the homeless in your community and then survey them as to their estimates of those needs. (For an example of this sampling procedure, recall our discussion in Chapter 10 of the key informants approach to needs assessment.)

Sometimes purposive sampling is used to select not typical cases, but atypical ones. This approach is commonly used in qualitative studies that seek to compare opposite extremes of a phenomenon in order to generate hypotheses about it. For example, in seeking to gain insights into the attributes of effective practice, we might handpick for intensive study those cases with whom practitioners felt extremely successful and those cases with whom they felt extremely ineffectual.

Researchers conducting qualitative studies are often particularly interested in studying deviant cases—cases that don't fit into fairly regular patterns of attitudes and behaviors—to improve their understanding of the more regular pattern. This approach is called **deviant case sampling**, and it is another form of purposive sampling. For example, you might gain important tentative insights into the processes of a support group for battered women by interviewing women who remain relatively quiet during support group meetings or by interviewing group members who only rarely attend the meetings. We will return to deviant case sampling later in this chapter, in connection with qualitative sampling methods.

11.5c Quota Sampling

Quota sampling begins with a matrix that describes the target population's characteristics: what proportion of the population is male and female, for example; and, for each sex, what proportions fall into various age categories, educational levels, ethnic groups, and so forth. In establishing a national quota sample, we would need to know what proportion of the national population is urban, Eastern, male, under 25, white, working class, and the like, and all the other permutations of such a matrix.

Once we have created such a matrix and assigned a relative proportion to each cell in the matrix, we would collect data from people who had all of the characteristics of a given cell. All the people in a given cell would then be assigned a weight proportionate to their presence in the total population (a process called *weighting*). When all of the sample elements are so weighted, the overall data should provide a reasonable representation of the total population.

Quota sampling has several inherent problems. First, the quota frame (the proportions that different cells represent) must be accurate, and getting up-to-date information for this purpose is often difficult. Second, biases may exist in the selection of sample elements within a given cell—even if its proportion of the population is accurately estimated. An interviewer instructed to interview five persons

meeting a given, complex set of characteristics may still avoid people living at the top of seven-story walkups, occupying particularly run-down homes, or owning vicious dogs. Researchers using quota sampling should be aware of potential problems like this and work to prevent them. For example, they should do all they can to obtain an accurate count of the number and characteristics of individuals who make up a particular cell. They should make sure that interviewers are properly trained and supervised to minimize the chances that the interviewers will violate the sampling protocol to skip certain undesirable interviews. But there is no guarantee that all potential problems like these will be anticipated or prevented. Therefore, you would be advised to treat quota sampling warily if your purpose is statistical description.

11.5d Snowball Sampling

Another nonprobability sampling technique, one that some researchers consider a form of accidental sampling, is called **snowball sampling**. Snowball sampling is appropriate when the members of a special population are difficult to locate. It might be appropriate, for example, to find a sample of homeless individuals, migrant workers, undocumented immigrants, and so on. This procedure is implemented by collecting data on the few members of the target population whom one is able to locate, and then asking those individuals to provide the information needed to locate other members of that population they happen to know. The term *snowball* refers to the process of accumulation as each located subject suggests other subjects. This sampling procedure also results in samples that have questionable representativeness, so it is used primarily for

---

deviant case sampling A form of purposive sampling in which cases that don't fit into regular patterns are selected to improve understanding of regular patterns.

snowball sampling A nonprobability sampling method used when the members of a special population are difficult to locate. Each selected member of the target population whom one is able to locate is asked to provide the information needed to locate other members of that population that they happen to know.

exploratory purposes. Nevertheless, snowball sampling is an important and commonly used technique in qualitative research, and in research on minority and oppressed populations it is often necessary.

Let's now turn to sampling methods that are commonly used in qualitative research. We'll look further at some of the nonprobability sampling methods we've been discussing, as well as some others that are uniquely associated with qualitative inquiry.

11.6 ADDITIONAL QUALITATIVE SAMPLING METHODS

In qualitative research, sampling can be more complicated than in quantitative research. Qualitative researchers often attempt to observe everything within their field of study; thus, in a sense they do not sample at all. In reality, of course, it is impossible to observe everything. To the extent that qualitative researchers observe only a portion of what happens, then, what they do observe is a de facto sample of all the possible observations that might have been made. If several people are shouting support for the speaker in a community meeting, those shouts the researcher hears and understands represent a sample of all such shouts. Or if a qualitative researcher observes acts of violence during a riot, the observed acts are a sample of all such acts of violence. Qualitative researchers may seldom be able to select a controlled sample of such observations, but they should bear in mind the general principles of representativeness and interpret their observations accordingly.

Although qualitative researchers often must rely on availability sampling, sometimes they can do better. If they are studying the development of a grassroots community organization over time, for instance, they may choose to interview different members of that organization by listing all of the members and then selecting a probability sample. When they must use nonprobability sampling methods, they might try to improve on availability sampling by using quota sampling, studying persons

---

intensity sampling A qualitative sampling technique similar to deviant case sampling in which cases are selected that are more or less intense than usual, but not so unusual that they would be called deviant.

---

representing all different participation categories. In the study of a community organization, for instance, they might interview leaders and non leaders, radical and more moderate members, both men and women, young people and old people, and the like.

11.6a Deviant Case Sampling

Qualitative researchers also often use snowball sampling, which we just discussed. Or they might use deviant case sampling. As you may recall, when we discussed deviant case sampling earlier, we promised to elaborate on it in this section on qualitative sampling. Examining cases that deviate from regular patterns might improve our understanding of the regular patterns of attitudes and behaviors that we observe. For example, we might gain important insights into the nature of group morale as exhibited at a meeting by interviewing people who did not appear to be caught up in the emotions of the crowd, or by interviewing people who did not attend the meeting at all.

Deviant cases are unusual in some respect. Suppose, for example, you are interested in conducting a case study of several case management programs to describe the diversity of case management practice and generate hypotheses about factors that influence the case management process. If you suspect that the nature of case management may vary considerably depending on the size of the case manager's caseload, you might want to select a couple of programs known for their extremely high caseloads and a couple known for their extremely low caseloads.

For another example, suppose you seek to generate hypotheses about the extent of family involvement in nursing home care. You might want to study intensively several families that are known among nursing home staff as being the most highly involved in the care of their relatives, and several that are known to be the least involved.

11.6b Intensity Sampling

Perhaps, however, you might suspect that extreme or deviant cases are so unusual that they provide a distorted portrayal of the phenomenon you want to study. If so, Patton (1990) suggests that you consider using **intensity sampling**: Select cases that are more or less intense than usual, but not so unusual that they would be called *deviant*. Thus, rather than selecting families that are most and least involved in nursing home care, you might select families known to be more or less involved than most families, but that are not so involved or uninvolved that they represent aberrations whose information might be misleading or not particularly useful.

11.6c Maximum Variation and Homogeneous Sampling

Maximum variation sampling is another qualitative sampling option identified by Patton. This strategy aims to capture the diversity of a phenomenon within a small sample to be studied intensively. By observing a phenomenon under heterogeneous conditions, we are likely to generate more useful insights about it. Thus, if you want to study case management processes, you might select programs with high, medium, and low caseload sizes; some in urban, suburban, and rural areas; some that are old, some that are new; and so on.

On the other hand, you might opt for a *homogeneous sample*. Suppose you are interested in studying how case managers attempt to handle role overload. You probably would restrict your sample to programs in which the case managers' caseload sizes were unusually large.

11.6d Theoretical Sampling

Another qualitative sampling approach is called **theoretical sampling**. This method is associated with the grounded theory paradigm of qualitative research, which we'll discuss in Chapter 15. Theoretical sampling begins by selecting new cases that seem to be similar to those that generated previously detected concepts and hypotheses, but once the researcher perceives that no new insights are being generated from observing similar cases, a different type of case is selected, and the same process is repeated until the observation of different types of cases seems to be generating no new insights. Theoretical sampling thus combines elements of homogeneous sampling and deviant case sampling.

The types of nonprobability sampling strategies and samples that we've been discussing can all be called *purposive sampling* and *purposive samples*, which we discussed earlier. In qualitative research, purposive sampling involves selecting a sample of observations that you believe will yield the most comprehensive understanding of your subject of

study, based on the intuitive feel for the subject that comes from extended observation and reflection. You can use purposive sampling procedures to select deviant cases or critical cases, but you can also use them to try to obtain a fairly representative portrayal of the phenomenon you are studying.

11.7 MAIN POINTS

- A sample is a special subset of a population that is observed for purposes of making inferences about the nature of the total population itself.
- The chief criterion of the quality of a probability sample is the degree to which it is representative—the extent to which the characteristics of the sample are the same as those of the population from which it was selected.
- Probability sampling methods provide one excellent way to select samples that will be quite representative.
- The chief principle of probability sampling is that every member of the total population must have some known nonzero probability of being selected into the sample.
- The most carefully selected sample will almost never perfectly represent the population from which it was selected. There will always be some degree of sampling error.
- Probability sampling methods allow us to estimate the amount of sampling error that should be expected in a given sample.
- A sampling frame is a list or quasi-list of the members of a population. It is the resource used in the selection of a sample. A sample's representativeness depends directly on the extent to which a sampling frame contains all the members of the total population that the sample is intended to represent.

---

theoretical sampling A sampling method associated with the grounded theory paradigm of qualitative research, in which new cases are selected that seem to be similar to those that generated previously detected concepts and hypotheses, but once the researcher perceives that no new insights are being generated from observing similar cases, a different type of case is selected, and the same process is repeated until the observation of different types of cases seems to be generating no new insights.

- Simple random sampling is the most fundamental technique in probability sampling.
- Systematic sampling involves the selection of every kth member from a sampling frame. This method is functionally equivalent to simple random sampling, with a few exceptions.
- Stratification is the process of grouping the members of a population into relatively homogeneous strata before sampling. This practice improves the representativeness of a sample by reducing the degree of sampling error.
- Multistage cluster sampling is a more complex sampling technique that is frequently used in those cases in which a list of all the members of a population does not exist. An initial sample of groups of members (clusters) is selected first, and then all members of the selected cluster are listed, often through direct observation in the field. Finally, the members listed in each selected cluster are subsampled, thereby providing the final sample of members.
- Nonprobability sampling involves the use of procedures to select a sample that does not involve random selection.
- Reliance on available subjects (availability sampling) is a very risky form of nonprobability sampling, but it can be useful in some instances.
- Purposive sampling is a type of nonprobability sampling method in which the researcher uses his or her own judgment in selecting sample members. It is sometimes called a judgmental sample.
- Snowball sampling is used when the members of a special population are difficult to locate. Researchers ask each selected member of the target population they are able to locate to provide the information needed to locate other members of that population whom the selected members happen to know.
- Sampling strategies used in qualitative inquiry typically differ from those used in quantitative inquiry and are less likely to employ probability sampling procedures.

11.8 PRACTICE-RELATED EXERCISES

1. Using Appendix D of this book, select a simple random sample of 10 numbers in the range from 1 to 9,876. Describe each step in the process.

2. In a paragraph or two, describe the steps involved in selecting a multistage cluster sample of nursing home residents throughout the nation.

3. Suppose you wanted to interview migrant farm workers who recently immigrated to the United States from Latin America. Discuss the problems inherent in relying exclusively on probability techniques to select your sample. Identify nonprobability sampling techniques that would be needed to obtain an adequate sample, and discuss why and how you would use them.

4. Suppose you want to learn how to increase the voluntary participation of parents in your treatment program for their substance-abusing youths. To begin, you want to understand why some treatment staff members seem to be more effective in motivating parents to participate than others. You also want to identify whether certain parent or youth characteristics help explain the participation or nonparticipation of the parents. Discuss the conditions under which you would use a quantitative or a qualitative sampling strategy in interview surveys of the parents or staff members, the specific sampling technique or techniques you would employ, and your rationale for each.

5. Suppose you are a social worker in a nursing home and want to survey relatives of nursing home residents to identify factors associated with the extent of their involvement in the care of the resident. For your sampling frame, obtain a list of the main contact person for each resident in your nursing home. You then select a random sample from that list.

   a. Critically appraise this sampling strategy from the standpoint of representativeness in quantitative inquiry. Would it be problematic even if you only wanted to generalize to the nursing home where you work? Why? Is there a better quantitative sampling approach that would be feasible for you to use? If so, identify it and your rationale for preferring it.

   b. Critically appraise this sampling strategy from the standpoint of qualitative inquiry. Is there a better qualitative sampling approach that would be feasible for you to use? If so, identify it and your rationale for preferring it.

11.9 INTERNET EXERCISES

1. Find two research articles in the journal *Health & Social Work*—one that used probability sampling and one that used nonprobability sampling. Critique the sampling procedures used in each—either positively or negatively.
2. Find and briefly examine four additional research articles in the journal *Health & Social Work*. How many used probability sampling methods? How many relied exclusively on nonprobability methods?
3. Surf some of your favorite websites on the Internet until you find one conducting a survey of visitors to that site. For example, certain news media sites conduct daily polls about political issues. Discuss the sampling problems connected to the survey you find, addressing issues such as the sampling frame, the representativeness of the sample, and so on.
4. Go to the website for the Crime Victimization Survey of the Bureau of Justice Statistics at http://bjs.ojp.usdoj.gov/index.cfm?ty=dcdetail&iid=245. Download and then examine the "Methodology" file: "Survey Methodology of Criminal Victimization in the United States." Summarize and critique the multistage sampling procedures used in the survey and described in the downloaded file.
5. Find the following article in the July 2002 issue of the journal *Social Work*: "Living on the Edge: Examination of People Attending Food Pantries and Soup Kitchens" by M. A. Biggerstaff, P. M. Morris, and A. Nichols-Casebolt. Critically appraise the multistage cluster sampling procedure used in that study.
6. Find two research articles that used qualitative sampling methods. Describe the sampling methods used and their rationale. Discuss why probability sampling methods would have been less appropriate for those studies.

11.9a Competency Notes

EP 2.1.6b: Use research evidence to inform practice (p. 204): Social workers must understand all of the concepts in this chapter so they can critically appraise the sampling methods of studies that might inform their practice.

EP 2.1.10d: Collect, organize, and interpret client data (p. 204): Social workers must understand all of the concepts in this chapter so they can use appropriate sampling methods when they collect and interpret client data.

EP 2.1.10m: Critically analyze, monitor, and evaluate interventions (p. 204): Social workers must understand all the measurement concepts in this chapter in order to use appropriate sampling methods when they monitor and evaluate interventions.

Designs for Evaluating Programs and Practice

part

6

Whereas the previous two chapters focused on methods and issues related to our ability to generalize from a sample to a population, we now turn to logical arrangements that permit us to make inferences about causality in the sample we observe. In Chapter 1, we discussed the need to assess the effectiveness of social work practice and programs. Chapter 12 will discuss how logical arrangements in experiments and quasi-experiments bear on our ability to infer whether our interventions—and not some alternative explanations—are responsible for client outcomes. Chapter 13 will examine logical arrangements for evaluating practice effectiveness in the context of single-case evaluation designs. It will show how practitioners can implement these designs to evaluate their own practice effectiveness, and how these designs can yield causal inferences about the effects of a particular intervention on a particular case. Chapter 14 will depart from focusing on logic and methods for making inferences about effectiveness and instead will focus on issues and practical guidelines for conducting program evaluations. It will show how vested interests can influence the ways in which evaluations are conducted and utilized, and how evaluators can deal with those political forces.

Experiments and Quasi-Experiments

12.1 INTRODUCTION

EP 2.1.6b
EP 2.1.10m

The logic of probability sampling, which we discussed in Chapter 11, bears on our ability to make inferences about whether one variable is causing another. For example, suppose we want to know what really causes lower rearrest rates after release from prison among those inmates who volunteer to participate in a faith-based intervention. Was it the intervention that made the difference? Or were the inmates who volunteered for the intervention different from the other inmates to begin with? Was their participation in the intervention therefore merely an indication of preexisting remorse and a reflection that they were already strongly motivated to turn their lives around—rather than a cause of their lower rearrest rates?

To answer these questions, suppose that instead of comparing prisoners who volunteered for the intervention to those who refused it, we used probability sampling techniques to divide those volunteering into two groups—with one group receiving the intervention and one group not receiving it (or receiving an alternative intervention approach). With a large enough sample (say, about 100 inmates or so) *randomly* split in half into two groups, we could assume that the two groups were both representative of the total sample and thus representative of each other. Then, if one group had lower rearrest rates after release than the other, we would be able to infer that the type of intervention they received caused the difference, and not some preexisting difference in the motivation or other characteristics between the two groups.

When our research design has features (like the one we've just described) that permit us to ascertain whether it really was our independent variable (such as intervention type) that caused change in our dependent variable (such as rearrest rates)—and not some alternative explanation (such as preexisting differences in the characteristics of people receiving and not receiving an intervention), then our research study is said to have *internal validity*. The alternative explanations for the change are called *threats to internal validity*. After we examine some prominent threats to internal validity, we'll see why and how *experimental designs* are thought to

have the most internal validity, and why they are thus thought to be the best way to determine whether one thing is really the cause of another. Let's begin by examining the three criteria for inferring causality.

12.2 CRITERIA FOR INFERRING CAUSALITY

Before we can infer that our independent variable is really causing change in our dependent variable, we have to check which change came first. Was it change in the independent variable? Or change in the dependent variable? That's because it makes no sense to imagine something being caused by something else that happened later on. Thus, the *first criterion* for inferring causality is that *the cause must precede the effect in time.*

As simple and obvious as this criterion may seem, we will discover endless problems in this regard in the analysis of social work research findings. Often, the time order that connects two variables is simply unclear. Suppose, for example, that a study finds that children with antisocial behavioral problems have worse relationships with their parents than well-behaved children. Did the poor relationship cause the behavioral problems? Or did the child's problems cause them to have poorer relationships with their parents? Which came first? Perhaps the behavior problems are caused by biological factors or other pathological factors in their environment beyond their parents' control.

The *second requirement in* a causal relationship is that *the two variables must covary with one another.* It would make no sense to say that an intervention caused lower rearrest rates if there was no difference in rearrest rates between people who received the intervention and people who did not receive it. That is, there would be no covariation between the intervention variable and the rearrest variable.

The *third requirement* for a causal relationship is that *the covariation between two variables cannot be explained away as the result of the influence of some third variable that causes the two under consideration.* For instance, as we just noted, a difference in rearrest rates might be explained away by the greater preexisting motivation to "go straight" among inmates who volunteered for an intervention.

12.3 INTERNAL VALIDITY

When we consider the extent to which a research study permits causal inferences to be made about relationships between variables, we again encounter the term *validity*. You may recall that when we were discussing measurement validity in Chapter 8, we referred to validity as the extent to which a measure really measures what it intends to measure. When discussing causal inference, however, we use the term differently. Two forms of validity are important when considering causality: *internal validity* and *external validity*.

As we just noted, **internal validity** refers to the confidence we have that the results of a study accurately depict whether one variable is or is not a cause of another. To the extent that the preceding three criteria for inferring causality are met, a study has internal validity. Conversely, to the extent that we have not met these criteria, we are limited in our grounds for concluding that the independent variable does or does not play a causal role in explaining the dependent variable. **External validity** refers to the extent to which the causal relationship depicted in a study can be *generalized* beyond the study conditions. We will examine internal validity in depth at this point and return to the concept of external validity later in this chapter. To clarify how we assess the extent to which a study has internal validity, let's examine specific threats to internal validity.

12.3a Threats to Internal Validity

Threats to internal validity refer to things other than the independent variable that can affect the dependent variable. When evaluating the effectiveness of programs or practice, for example, investigators might erroneously conclude that differences in outcome were caused by the evaluated intervention, when in fact something else really caused the differences. Here are seven prominent threats to internal validity:

1. **History** During the course of the research, extraneous events may occur that will confound the results. The term *history* is tricky. The extraneous events need not be major news events that one would read about in a history book, but simply extraneous events that coincide in time with the manipulation of the independent variable. For example, suppose a study evaluates the effectiveness of social services in improving resident morale in a nursing home merely by measuring the morale of a group of residents before and after they receive social services. Perhaps some extraneous improvement in the nursing home environment—an improvement independent of the social services—was introduced between the before and after measures. That possibility threatens the internal validity of the research because it, rather than the independent variable (social services), might cause the hypothesized improvement in the dependent variable (morale).

2. **Maturation or the passage of time** People continuously grow and change, whether they are a part of a research study or not, and those changes affect the results of the research. In the earlier nursing home illustration, for example, it would be silly to infer that because residents were physically frailer several years after receiving social services, the social services caused the physical deterioration. Maturation, through the aging process, would represent a severe threat to the internal validity of such a conclusion. But this threat to internal validity does not require that basic developmental changes occur; it also can refer simply to the effects of the passage of time. Consider bereavement counseling, for example. It would be silly also to conclude that, just because the functioning level or mood of clients whose loved one died immediately before counseling was somewhat better after counseling, the bereavement counseling must have caused the improvement.

3. **Testing** Often the process of testing will itself enhance performance on a test without any

---

internal validity The degree to which an effect observed in a dependent variable was actually caused by the independent variable and not other factors.

external validity The extent to which a causal relationship depicted in a study can be generalized beyond the study conditions.

corresponding improvement in the real construct that the test attempts to measure. Suppose we want to see if a workshop helps social workers perform better on their state licensure exam. We might construct a test that we think will measure the same sorts of things as are measured on the licensure exam and then administer that test to social workers before and after they take our workshop. If their scores on the exam improve, then we might wish to attribute the improvement to the effects of our workshop. But suppose the social workers, after taking the first test, looked up answers to test items before our workshop began and remembered those answers the next time they took the same test? They would then score higher on the posttest without even attending our workshop, and we therefore could not claim that taking our workshop caused their scores to improve.

4. **Instrumentation changes** If we use different measures of the dependent variable at posttest than we did at pretest, how can we be sure that they are comparable to each other? Suppose in evaluating the workshop to help social workers perform better on their state licensure exam we do not want workshop participants to take the same test twice (to avoid testing effects). We might therefore construct two versions of the outcome test—one for the pretest and one for the posttest—that we think are equivalent. Although we would like to conclude that our workshop caused any improvement in scores, it is conceivable that the real reason may have been that, despite our best efforts, the posttest version was an easier exam than the pretest version. And if their scores worsened, rather than indicating that our workshop made them less well prepared for the exam, perhaps the posttest version was more difficult.

5. **Statistical regression** Sometimes it's appropriate to evaluate the effectiveness of services for clients who were referred because of their extreme scores on the dependent variable. Suppose, for example, that a new social work intervention to alleviate depression among the elderly is being pilot-tested in a nursing home for residents whose scores on a depression inventory indicate the most severe levels of depression. From a clinical standpoint, it would be quite appropriate to provide the service to the residents who appear most in need of the service. But consider from a methodological standpoint what is likely to happen to the depression scores of the referred residents even without intervention. In considering this, we should consider that, with repeated testing on almost any assessment inventory, an individual's scores on the inventory are likely to fluctuate somewhat from one administration to the next—not because the individual really changed, but because of the random testing factors that prevent instruments from having perfect reliability. For example, some residents who were referred because they had the poorest pretest scores may have been having atypically bad days at pretest and may typically score better on the inventory on an average day. Perhaps they didn't sleep well the night before the pretest, perhaps a chronic illness flared up that day, or perhaps a close friend or relative passed away that week.

When we provide services to only those people with the most extremely problematic pretest scores, the odds are that the proportion of service recipients with atypically bad pretest scores will be higher than the proportion of nonrecipients with atypically bad pretest scores. Conversely, those who were not referred because their pretest scores were better probably include some whose pretest scores were atypically high (i.e., people who were having an unusually good day at pretest). Consequently, even without any intervention, the group of service recipients is more likely to show some improvement in its average depression score over time than is the group that was not referred. There is a danger, then, that changes occurring because subjects started out in extreme positions will be attributed erroneously to the effects of the independent variable.

6. **Selection biases** Comparisons don't have any meaning unless the groups being compared are really *comparable*. Suppose we sought to evaluate the effectiveness of an intervention to promote positive parenting skills by comparing the level of improvement in parenting skills of parents who voluntarily agreed to participate in the intervention program with the level of improvement of parents who refused to participate.

We would not be able to attribute the greater improvement among program participants to the effects of the intervention—at least not with a great deal of confidence about the internal validity of our conclusion—because other differences between the two groups might explain away the difference in improvement. For example, the participants may have been more motivated than program refusers to improve and thus may have been trying harder, reading more, and doing any number of things unrelated to the intervention that may really explain why they showed greater improvement. Selection biases are a common threat to the internal validity of social service evaluations because groups of service recipients and nonrecipients are often compared on outcome variables in the absence of prior efforts to verify that the groups being compared were initially truly equivalent. Perhaps this most typically occurs when individuals who choose to use services are compared with individuals who were not referred to those services or who chose not to utilize them (as is the case when inmates who volunteer to participate in an intervention are compared in rearrest rates to those who refuse the intervention).

7. **Ambiguity about the direction of causal influence** As we discussed earlier in this chapter, there is a possibility of ambiguity concerning the time order of the independent and dependent variables. Whenever this occurs, the research conclusion that the independent variable caused the changes in the dependent variable can be challenged with the explanation that the "dependent" variable may have actually caused changes in the independent variable.

Suppose, for example, a study finds that clients who completed a substance abuse treatment program are less likely to be abusing substances than those who dropped out of the program. There would be ambiguity as to whether the program influenced participants not to abuse substances or whether the abstinence from substance abuse helped people complete the program.

We can illustrate further the foregoing threats to internal validity by examining how they bear on some research designs that are commonly used for evaluating social work practice and programs.

Although research consumers may disagree over approximately how well specific studies have controlled for particular threats to internal validity, it is usually possible to differentiate those studies whose internal validity is very low, those with very high internal validity, and those that merit a "mixed review." A large part of this assessment depends on which of the following types of designs a study employs. We'll begin with some designs that have a low degree of internal validity, called *preexperimental designs*.

12.4 PREEXPERIMENTAL DESIGNS

As we noted earlier, to the extent that studies look only at the covariation between two variables without controlling for threats to internal validity, they have low internal validity. But some studies don't even establish covariation. Consider the **one-shot case study**, for example. The shorthand notation for this design is:

$$X \quad O$$

The X in this notation represents the introduction of a stimulus, such as an intervention. The O represents observation, which yields the measurement of the dependent variable. In this design, a single group of subjects is measured on a dependent variable after the introduction of a stimulus (i.e., an intervention) without comparing the obtained results to anything else.

For instance, a service might be delivered and then the service recipients' social functioning measured. This design offers no way for us to ascertain whether the observed level of social functioning is any higher (or lower!) than it was to begin with, or any higher (or lower!) than it is among comparable individuals who received no service. Thus, this design—in addition to failing to assess covariation—fails to control for any of the threats to internal validity.

Even if time order is established and the hypothesized change is observed, we still have

---

one-shot case study A preexperimental research design, with low internal validity, that simply measures a single group of participants on a dependent variable at one point in time after they have been exposed to an intervention or another type of stimulus.

met only two of the three criteria for inferring causality. Meeting only these two criteria means that we cannot rule out the possibility that *extraneous variables* or *extraneous events* caused the observed change. Consider, for example, the **one-group pretest–posttest design**. The shorthand notation for this design is:

$$O_1 \quad X \quad O_2$$

The subscripts 1 and 2 in this notation refer to the sequential order of the observations; thus, O_1 is the pretest before the intervention, and O_2 is the posttest after the intervention. This design assesses the dependent variable before and after the stimulus (intervention) is introduced. Thus, in the evaluation of the effectiveness of social services, the design would assess the outcome variable before and after services are delivered.

Although this design assesses covariation and controls for causal time order, it does not account for factors other than the independent variable that might have caused the change between pretest and posttest results—factors usually associated with the following threats to internal validity: history, maturation, testing, and statistical regression.

Suppose, for example, that we assess the attitudes of social work students about social action strategies of community organization—strategies that emphasize tactics of confrontation and conflict (protests, boycotts, and so on)—before and at the end of their social work education. Suppose we find that over this time they became less committed to confrontational social action strategies and more in favor of consensual community development approaches.

---

one-group pretest–posttest design A preexperimental design, with low internal validity, that assesses a dependent variable before and after an intervention or another type of stimulus is introduced, but does not attempt to control for alternative explanations of any changes in scores that are observed.

posttest-only design with nonequivalent groups A preexperimental design that involves two groups that may not be comparable, in which the dependent variable is assessed after the independent variable is introduced for one of the groups.

Would such a finding permit us to infer that the change in their attitude was *caused* by their social work education? No, it would not. Other factors could have been operating during the same period and caused the change. For instance, perhaps the students matured and became more tolerant of slower, more incremental strategies for change (the threat to internal validity posed by *maturation or the passage of time*). Or perhaps certain events extraneous to their social work education transpired during that period and accounted for their change (the threat of *history*). For example, perhaps a series of protest demonstrations seemed to backfire and contribute to the election of a presidential candidate they abhorred, and their perception of the negative effects of these demonstrations made them more skeptical of social action strategies.

A third preexperimental design is the **posttest-only design with nonequivalent groups**. The shorthand notation for this design, which has also been termed the *static-group comparison design*, is:

$$X \quad O$$
$$O$$

This design assesses the dependent variable after the intervention is introduced for one group, while also assessing the dependent variable for a second group that may not be comparable to the first group and that was not exposed to the intervention. In the evaluation of the effectiveness of social services, this design would entail assessing clients on an outcome variable only after (not before) they receive the service being evaluated, and comparing their performance with a group of clients who did not receive the service and who plausibly may be unlike the treated clients in some meaningful way.

Let's return, for example, to the preceding hypothetical illustration about evaluating the effectiveness of a cognitive-behavioral intervention with abusive parents. Using the posttest-only design with nonequivalent groups rather than comparing the pretest and posttest scores of parents who received the intervention, we might compare their posttest scores to the scores of abusive parents who were not referred or who declined the intervention. We would hope to show that the treated parents scored better than the untreated parents, because this would indicate a desired covariation between the independent variable (treatment status) and the dependent variable (test score). But this covariation would not permit us to infer that the difference between the two groups was caused by the intervention. The most important reason for this is the design's failure to control for the threat of *selection biases*. Without pretests, we have no way of knowing whether the scores of the two groups would have differed as much to begin with—that is, before the treated parents began treatment.

Moreover, these two groups may not really have been equivalent in certain important respects. The parents who were referred or who chose to participate may have been more motivated to improve or may have had more supportive resources than those who were not referred or who refused treatment.

12.4a Pilot Studies

As we prepare to move on to designs with higher levels of internal validity, a parting qualification is in order. When we say that a particular design has low internal validity, we are not saying that you should never use that design, or that studies that do so never have value. Remember, not all research studies strive to produce conclusive, causal inferences. Many studies have an exploratory or descriptive purpose. Suppose, for example, that your agency has initiated a new, innovative intervention for a small target group about which little is known. It might be quite useful to find out whether clients' posttest scores are better (or perhaps worse!) than their pretest scores in a one-group pretest-posttest design. You might implement that design on a *pilot study* basis, purely for the purpose of generating tentative exploratory or descriptive information. Pilot studies such as this are commonly produced in practice settings where stronger designs are not feasible and are often reported in practice-oriented journals. If the posttest scores are much better than at pretest, then you might be encouraged to view the hypothesis that the intervention is effective as more plausible, even if it does not allow you to claim that you verified conclusively that the intervention caused the desired effects. With such results, you would have established covariation and time order, and may have provided a reasonable basis for continued testing of the intervention, including perhaps finding resources for conducting a larger

study with more internal validity. Two types of designs with higher levels of internal validity than preexperimental studies are *experimental* and *quasi-experimental* designs. First we'll look at experimental designs.

12.5 EXPERIMENTAL DESIGNS

Experimental designs attempt to provide maximum control for threats to internal validity. They do so by giving the researchers greater ability to manipulate and isolate the independent variable. In social work, the most common use of experimental designs is to evaluate the effectiveness of our services or practice methods. The essential components of experiments involve (1) randomly assigning individuals to an **experimental group** and a **control group**, (2) introducing one category of the independent variable to the experimental group and the other category to the control group (for example, the experimental group might receive an innovative intervention, whereas the control group receives routine services), and (3) comparing the amount of experimental and control group change on the dependent variable.

For example, suppose we wanted to assess the effectiveness of an intervention used by social workers in nursing home facilities, an intervention that engages clients in a review of their life history to alleviate depression and improve morale. Rather than just compare residents who previously had requested and received the intervention with those who did not—which would constitute a preexperimental approach because we could not assume the two groups were equivalent to begin with—our experimental approach would use a table of random numbers, or flip a coin, or use systematic sampling procedures to assign randomly each resident who agrees to participate in our study and for whom the intervention is deemed appropriate to an experimental group

---

experimental group The group of individuals in an experiment who receive the intervention or program being evaluated.

control group The group of individuals in an experiment who do not receive the intervention or program being evaluated.

(which would receive the intervention) or a control group (which would not receive it). Observations on one or more indicators of depression and morale (the dependent variables) would be taken before and after the intervention is delivered, and to the extent that the experimental group's mood improves more than that of the control group, the findings would support the hypothesis that the intervention causes the improvement.

The preceding example illustrates the classic experimental design, also called the **pretest–posttest control group design**. This design is diagrammed in Figure 12.1. The shorthand notation for this design is:

$$R \quad O_1 \quad X \quad O_2$$
$$R \quad O_1 \qquad O_2$$

The R in this design stands for random assignment of research participants to either the experimental group or the control group. The O_1s represent pretests, and the O_2s represent posttests. The X represents the tested intervention.

Notice how this design controls for many threats to internal validity. If the improvement in mood were caused by history or maturation, then there would be no reason the experimental group should improve any more than the control group. Likewise, because the residents were assigned on a randomized basis, there is no reason to suppose that the experimental group was any more likely to statistically regress to less extreme scores than was the control group. Random assignment also removes

---

pretest–posttest control group design   The classic experimental design in which participants are assigned randomly to an experimental group that receives an intervention being evaluated and to a control group that does not receive it. Each group is tested on the dependent variable before and after the experimental group receives the intervention.

posttest-only control group design   A variation of the classic experimental design that avoids the possible testing effects associated with pretesting by testing only after the experimental group receives the intervention, based on the assumption that the process of random assignment provides for equivalence between the experimental and control groups on the dependent variable before the exposure to the intervention.

FIGURE 12.1 Diagram of Basic Experimental Design

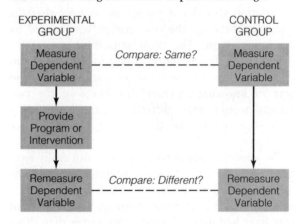

any reason for supposing that the two groups were different initially with respect to the dependent variable or to other relevant factors such as motivation or psychosocial functioning. The box "A Social Work Experiment Evaluating the Effectiveness of a Program to Treat Children at Risk of Serious Conduct Problems" summarizes a published report of a social work study that used a pretest–posttest control group design.

Notice also, however, that the pretest–posttest control group design does not control for the possible effects of testing and retesting. If we think that taking a pretest might have an impact on treatment effects, or if we think that it might bias a group's posttest responses, then we might opt for an experimental design called the **posttest-only control group design**. Another, more common, reason for choosing the posttest-only control group design is that pretesting may not be possible or practical, such as in the evaluation of the effectiveness of programs to prevent incidents of child abuse. The shorthand notation for this design is:

$$R \quad X \quad O$$
$$R \qquad O$$

This design assumes that the process of random assignment removes any significant initial differences between experimental and control groups. This assumption of initial group equivalence permits the inference that any differences between the two groups at posttest reflect the causal impact of the independent variable. The box "A Social Work Experiment Evaluating Motivational Interviewing"

A Social Work Experiment Evaluating the Effectiveness of a Program to Treat Children at Risk of Serious Conduct Problems

Mark Fraser and his associates evaluated the effectiveness of a multicomponent intervention to treat children referred by teachers for aggressive antisocial behavior and rejection by their prosocial peers. The children were assigned randomly to an experimental group or a wait-list control group. The experimental group children participated in a social skills training program in after-school or school settings, and their parents or caretakers participated in an in-home family intervention program designed to increase parenting skills. The control group children "continued to participate in any routine services they may have [already] been receiving." At the conclusion of the study, the children and parents in the control condition were offered the same intervention package as the experimental group participants received. Outcome was measured by having teachers complete a form at pretest and posttest on which they rated each child's behaviors in classroom and play environments. The results showed the experimental group children had significantly more improvement than control group children on ratings of prosocial behavior, ability to regulate emotions, and increased social contact with peers.

Source: Fraser, M., Day, S. H., Galinsky, M. J., Hodges, V. G., and Smokowski, P. R. 2004. "Conduct Problems and Peer Rejection in Childhood: A Randomized Trial of the Making Choices and Strong Families Programs," *Research on Social Work Practice*, 14, 5, 313–324.

A Social Work Experiment Evaluating Motivational Interviewing

Robert Schilling and his colleagues evaluated a motivational interviewing intervention designed to encourage detoxified alcohol users to participate in self-help groups after alcohol detoxification. Ninety-six clients were randomly assigned to either a three-session motivational interviewing condition or a standard care condition. Motivational interviewing is directive but uses client-centered relationship skills (such as being empathic, warm, and genuine) in providing information and feedback to increase client awareness of the problem and consideration of change by helping clients see the discrepancy between their problematic behavior and their broader goals. Outcome was assessed two months after discharge from inpatient care via self-reported attendance at self-help meetings and drinking behavior. Although motivational interviewing currently is widely accepted as an evidence-based intervention, this study's results were portrayed by its authors as somewhat disappointing. No differences in drinking behavior were found between the experimental and control groups; however, motivational interviewing recipients averaged twice as many days participating in 12-step self-help groups.

Source: Schilling, R. F., El-bassel, N., Finch, J. B., Roman, R. J., and Hanson, M. 2002. "Motivational Interviewing to Encourage Self-Help Participation Following Alcohol Detoxification," *Research on Social Work Practice*, 12, 6, 711–730.

summarizes a published report of a social work study that used a posttest-only control group experimental design.

If we would like to know the amount of pretest-posttest change but are worried about testing effects, then we could use a fancy design called the **Solomon four-group design**. The shorthand notation for this design is:

$$
\begin{array}{cccc}
R & O_1 & X & O_2 \\
R & O_1 & & O_2 \\
R & & X & O_2 \\
R & & & O_2 \\
\end{array}
$$

This design, which is highly regarded by research methodologists but rarely used in social work studies, combines the classic experimental design with the posttest-only control group design. It does this simply by randomly assigning research participants to four groups instead of two. Two of the groups are control groups and two are experimental groups. One control group and one experimental

---

Solomon four-group design An experimental design that assesses testing effects by randomly assigning participants to four groups, introducing the intervention being evaluated to two of them, conducting both pretesting and posttesting on one group that receives the intervention and one group that does not, and conducting posttesting only on the other two groups.

group are pretested and posttested. The other experimental and control groups are posttested only. If special effects are caused by pretesting, then they can be discerned by comparing the two experimental groups' results with each other and the two control groups' results with each other.

Sometimes experiments are used to compare the effectiveness of two alternative treatments. Pretests are recommended in such experiments, so that the comparative amounts of change produced by each treatment can be assessed. This design is called the **alternative treatment design with pretest** (Shadish, Cook, & Leviton, 2001). The shorthand notation for this design is:

$$
\begin{array}{llll}
R & O_1 & X_A & O_2 \\
R & O_1 & X_B & O_2 \\
R & O_1 &   & O_2
\end{array}
$$

The first row above represents the participants randomly assigned to treatment A. The second row represents the participants randomly assigned to treatment B. The third row represents the participants randomly assigned to a control group. To show that treatment A is more effective than treatment B, the first row would need to show more improvement from O_1 to O_2 than both of the other rows. If the first two rows both show approximately the same amounts of improvement, and both amounts are more than in the third row,

---

alternative treatment design with pretest An experiment that compares the effectiveness of two alternative treatments. Participants are assigned randomly to two experimental groups, each of which receives a different intervention being evaluated, and to a control group that does not receive any intervention. Each group is tested on the dependent variable before and after the experimental groups receive the intervention.

dismantling studies Experiments designed to test not only whether an intervention is effective but also which components of the intervention may or may not be necessary to achieve its effects. Participants are assigned randomly to groups that receive either the entire intervention package, separate components of it, or a control condition, and then tested on a dependent variable before and after the intervention components are provided.

that would indicate that both treatments are approximately equally effective. But if the third row shows the same degree of improvement as the first two rows, then neither treatment would appear to be effective. Instead, we would attribute the improvement in all three rows to an alternative explanation, such as history or the passage of time.

Some experiments use the first two rows of this design, but not the third. That is, they compare the two treatments to each other, but not to a control group. Such experiments can have conclusive, valid findings if one group improves significantly more than the other. But suppose they both have roughly the same amount of improvement? The temptation would be to call them equally effective. However, with no control group, we cannot rule out threats to internal validity, like history or the passage of time, as alternative explanations of the improvement in both groups. An illustrative study is summarized in the box, "A Social Work Experiment Comparing the Effectiveness of Two Court Mandated Approaches to Spouse Abuse Treatment."

A similar type of design can be used to see not only whether an intervention is effective, but also which components of the intervention may or may not be necessary to achieve its effects. Experiments using this design are called **dismantling studies**. The shorthand notation for this design is:

$$
\begin{array}{llll}
R & O_1 & X_{AB} & O_2 \\
R & O_1 & X_A & O_2 \\
R & O_1 & X_B & O_2 \\
R & O_1 &   & O_2
\end{array}
$$

The first row above represents the participants randomly assigned to a treatment that contains components A and B.

The second row represents the participants randomly assigned to receive the A component only. The third row represents the participants randomly assigned to receive the B component only. The fourth row represents the participants randomly assigned to a control group. If the first row shows more improvement from O_1 to O_2 than all of the other rows, that would indicate that the treatment is effective and that both components (A and B) are needed. If either of the next two rows shows as much improvement as the first row does, that would indicate that the component

A Social Work Experiment Comparing the Effectiveness of Two Approaches to Court Mandated Spouse Abuse Treatment

For his dissertation, Stephen Brannen conducted an experiment with intact couples desiring to stay in their current relationship who were referred by a court in San Antonio for spouse abuse treatment. The couples were assigned to one of two approaches to group cognitive-behavioral therapy. In one approach the couples participated together in the group; in the other approach they participated apart in separate groups for each gender. Outcome was measured using standardized self-report scales that measured the couples' conflict resolution ability, the level of violence in the relationship, the level of communication and marital satisfaction within the relationship, and recidivism. Data were collected both from the victims and perpetrators of the abuse. Significant pretest to posttest gains were found for both groups; however, there was no difference between the groups. Consequently, although the findings were consistent with the notion that both interventions are about equally effective, without a no-treatment or routine treatment control group Brannen could not rule out threats like history or the passage of time as possible causes of the improvement.

Source: Brannen, S. J. and Rubin, A. 1996. "Comparing the Effectiveness of Gender-Specific and Couples Groups in a Court Mandated Spouse Abuse Treatment Program," *Research on Social Work Practice*, 6, 4, 405–424.

A Social Work Experiment Evaluating Cognitive-Behavioral Interventions with Parents at Risk of Child Abuse

Whiteman, Fanshel, and Grundy (1987) tested the effectiveness of different aspects of a cognitive-behavioral intervention aimed at reducing parental anger in the face of perceived provocation by children in families in which child abuse had been committed or in families at risk for child abuse. Fifty-five clients were randomly assigned to four intervention groups and a control group that received no experimental intervention but instead continued to receive services from the referral agency. The first intervention group received cognitive restructuring interventions that dealt with the parents' perceptions, expectations, appraisals, and stresses. The second intervention group was trained in relaxation procedures. The third intervention group worked on problem-solving skills. The fourth intervention group received a treatment package comprising the three interventional modalities delivered separately to the first three intervention groups. The results revealed no significant differences among the experimental and control groups at pretest. At posttest, however, the treated (experimental group) participants had significantly greater reductions in anger than the untreated (control group) participants. The intervention group with the greatest reduction in anger was the one that received the composite package of interventions delivered separately to the other three intervention groups.

In light of their findings, Whiteman and associates recommended that social workers use the composite intervention package to attempt to reduce anger and promote positive child-rearing attitudes among abusive or potentially abusive parents. Their results also indicated the importance of the problem-solving skills component in reducing anger, the importance of the cognitive restructuring component in improving childrearing attitudes, and the relative unimportance of including the relaxation component in the intervention package.

Source: Whiteman, Martin, David Fanshel, and John F. Grundy. 1987. "Cognitive-Behavioral Interventions Aimed at Anger of Parents at Risk of Child Abuse," *Social Work*, 32, 6, 469–474.

signified in that row is all that is needed to achieve the effects shown in the first row, and that the other component may not be needed. The box "A Social Work Experiment Evaluating Cognitive-Behavioral Interventions with Parents at Risk of Child Abuse" illustrates the use of a dismantling study in social work.

12.5a Randomization

It should be clear at this point that the cardinal rule of experimental design is that the experimental and control groups must be comparable. Ideally, the control group represents what the experimental group would have been like had it not been exposed to the intervention or other experimental stimulus

Random Assignment versus Random Sampling
RANDOM ASSIGNMENT FOR AN EXPERIMENT

Participant's Name	Result of Coin Toss	Group Assigned to (heads-experimental; tails-control)
Ann	Heads	Experimental
Dan	Tails	Control
Jan	Tails	Control
Jack	Heads	Experimental
Jill	Tails	Control
Bill	Heads	Experimental
Lil	Heads	Experimental
Phil	Tails	Control

RANDOM SAMPLING FOR A SURVEY

Numbered Names in Sampling Frame	Numbers encountered in Table of Random Numbers	Names Chosen for Survey Participation
1. Ann	1	Ann
2. Dan		
3. Jan		
4. Jack	4	Jack
5. Jill	5	Jill
6. Bill		
7. Lil		
8. Phil	8	Phil

being evaluated. There is no way to guarantee that the experimental and control groups will be equivalent in all relevant respects. There is no way to guarantee that they will share exactly the same history and maturation processes, or that they will not have relevant differences before the evaluated intervention is introduced. But there is a way to avoid biases in the assignment of clients to groups and to guarantee a high mathematical likelihood that their initial, pretreatment group differences will be insignificant: through random assignment to experimental and control groups, a process also known as *randomization.*

Randomization, or random assignment, is not the same as random sampling, although it is based

on the same logic and techniques. The research participants to be randomly assigned are rarely randomly selected from a population. Instead, they are individuals who voluntarily agreed to participate in the experiment, a fact that *limits* the *generalizability* of the experiment. Unlike random sampling, which pertains to generalizability, randomization is a device for increasing internal validity. It does not seek to ensure that the research participants are representative of a larger population; instead, it seeks to maximize the likelihood that the experimental group and the control group are representative of each other. The difference between random assignment and random sampling is illustrated in the box *Random Assignment versus Random Sampling.*

The principal technique of randomization simply entails using procedures based on probability theory to assign research participants to experimental and

---

randomization A technique that uses procedures based on probability theory to assign research participants to experimental and control groups.

control groups. Having recruited, by whatever means, the group of all participants, the researchers might flip a coin to determine to which group each participant is assigned; or researchers may number all of the participants serially and assign them by selecting numbers from a random number table; or researchers may put the odd-numbered participants in one group and put the even-numbered ones in the other.

Put within the framework of our earlier discussions of sampling, in randomization the research participants are a population from which we select two probability samples, each consisting of one-half of the population. Because each sample reflects the characteristics of the total population, the two samples mirror each other. And, as we saw in Chapter 11, the number of research participants involved is important. Like random selection, random assignment works best with large numbers. It would be very risky to predict the outcome of an election by randomly sampling only a few voters, owing to sampling error. In the same vein, if we recruited only two participants and assigned, by the flip of a coin, one as the experimental participant and the other as the control, there would be no reason to assume that the two participants were similar to each other. With larger numbers of research participants, however, randomization makes good sense.

12.5b Providing Services to Control Groups

As we discussed in Chapter 5, the withholding of services from people in need raises ethical concerns. Withholding services also may be unacceptable to agency administrators, who fear bad publicity or the loss of revenues based on service delivery hours. We must therefore point out that when we discuss withholding the intervention being tested from the control group, we do not mean that people in the control group should be denied services. We simply mean that they should not receive the *experimental* intervention that is being tested during the period of the test.

When experiments are feasible to carry out in social work settings, control group participants are likely to receive the usual, routine services provided by an agency. Experimental group participants will receive the new, experimental intervention being tested, perhaps in addition to the usual, routine

services. Thus, the experiment may determine whether services that include the new intervention are more effective than routine services, rather than attempt to ascertain whether the new intervention is better than no service. Moreover, control group participants may be put at the top of a waiting list to receive the new intervention once the experiment is over. If the results of the experiment show that the tested intervention is effective, or at least not harmful, it can then be offered to control group participants. The researcher may also want to measure whether control group participants change in the desired direction after they receive the intervention. The findings of this measurement can buttress the main findings of the experiment.

12.6 QUASI-EXPERIMENTAL DESIGNS

In many social work agencies, we cannot use randomization to determine which participants are assigned to which treatment condition. If practitioners have a client who they think needs a particular type of intervention, they may not want to see that client be assigned to a different type of intervention, or perhaps to a control group with no intervention, based on something random like a coin toss. Administrators may not want to alienate resistant practitioners or have to deal with complaints from board members, consumers, or the community about having randomly withheld new services from certain clients.

Rather than forgo doing any evaluation in such instances, alternative research designs sometimes can be created and executed that have less internal validity than randomized experiments, but still provide more support for causal inferences than do preexperimental designs. These designs are called **quasi-experimental designs** and are distinguished from "true" experiments primarily because they do not use random procedures to assign research participants to alternative

---

quasi-experimental designs Designs that attempt to control for threats to internal validity and thus permit causal inferences, but that are distinguished from true experiments primarily by the lack of random assignment of participants.

treatment conditions. Let's examine two commonly used quasi-experimental designs that, when designed and conducted properly, can attain a reasonable degree of internal validity.

12.6a Nonequivalent Comparison Groups Design

The **nonequivalent comparison groups design** can be used when we find an existing group that appears similar to the experimental group and thus can be compared to it. Suppose, for example, that we want to evaluate the effects on depression of an intervention that gives pets to nursing home residents. It's unlikely that any nursing home will permit you to randomly select the residents who will and will not receive pets. You can probably imagine the administrative hassles that might erupt because some residents or their relatives feel they are being deprived. As an alternative to a true experimental design, then, you may be able to find two nursing homes that agree to participate in your research and that appear very similar in all of the respects that are relevant to internal validity: for example, the same numbers and types of residents and staff, the same level of care, and so on. In particular, you would want to make sure that the resident populations of the two homes were quite similar in terms of age, socioeconomic status, mental and physical disabilities, psychosocial functioning, ethnicity, and so on. You could then introduce the intervention in one home, and use the other as a comparison group. (The term *comparison group* is used instead of *control group* when participants are not assigned randomly.)

The two homes could be compared in a pretest to make sure that they really are equivalent on the dependent variable before introducing the intervention. If their average depression scores are about the same, then it would be reasonable to suppose that differences at posttest represent the effects of the

---

nonequivalent comparison groups design   A quasi-experimental design in which the researcher finds two existing groups that appear to be similar, and measures change on a dependent variable before and after an intervention is introduced to one of the groups.

intervention. Of course, such a causal inference would be even more credible had the participants been randomly assigned. But to the extent that you could provide convincing data as to the comparability of the two homes on plausible extraneous variables, and if the differences on their average pretest scores are trivial, then your causal inference would be credible and your study would have value. The shorthand notation for this design is:

$$O_1 \quad X \quad O_2$$
$$O_1 \qquad \quad O_2$$

You may note that the preceding notation is the same as the pretest–posttest control group design except that it lacks the R for random assignment.

When you read a report of a study that used a nonequivalent comparison groups design, it is important to remember that if selection biases seem highly plausible in that study, then the notion that the groups are really comparable is severely undermined. Unless the researcher can present compelling evidence documenting the comparability of the groups on relevant extraneous variables and on pretest scores, any differences in outcome between the two groups are highly suspect. In other words, depending on how well the researcher documents the comparability of the groups, studies using this design can be strong enough to guide practice or can be very weak.

But even when much evidence is supplied supporting the notion that the groups are comparable, nagging doubts often remain. Rarely can researchers obtain evidence about every possible extraneous variable that might really account for differences in outcome between the groups. For example, the fact that two groups are comparable in their pretest scores and in various background characteristics does not ensure that they are equally motivated to change. Suppose an evaluation is being conducted to see whether a prison bible studies program reduces rearrest rates after prisoners are released. Suppose further that the prisoners who attend the bible studies program do so voluntarily, and that the study compares the rearrest rates of those prisoners to a matched group of prisoners who share the same background characteristics as the bible studies group but who chose not to attend the bible studies program. No matter how much data are provided documenting the background similarities of the two groups, we might remain quite skeptical about their comparability regarding the prisoners' notions of morality, sense of remorse, and motivation to go straight—extraneous variables that might have a greater influence on rearrest rates than many of the background variables on which the groups have been shown to be comparable.

Our advanced text (Rubin & Babbie, 2011) describes some more complex procedures that can be used to help offset some of the doubts about the comparability of nonequivalent comparison groups. One such procedure adds a *switching replications* component to this design by providing the tested intervention to the comparison group after both groups complete the posttest. After the comparison group completes the intervention, they receive a second posttest. If their second posttest shows a level of improvement that is similar to the amount of improvement made by the experimental group after it received the intervention, then the effectiveness of the intervention is supported, and the notion that the difference at the first posttest was because of the lack of comparability of the two groups (i.e., a selection bias) is ruled out.

12.6b Time Series Designs

Another commonly used set of quasi-experimental designs is called **time series designs**. These designs use multiple pretests and multiple posttests. A particularly feasible time series design—feasible because it does not require a comparison group—is called the *simple interrupted time series design.* The shorthand notation for this design is:

$$O_1 \; O_2 \; O_3 \; O_4 \; O_5 \; X \; O_6 \; O_7 \; O_8 \; O_9 \; O_{10}$$

Each O in the notation represents a different observation point for measuring the dependent variable over time. No particular number of measurements is required, although the more the better. The preceding notation indicates that the dependent variable was measured at five points in time before the intervention (X) was introduced, and another five times after that.

To illustrate the time series design, we will begin by asking you to assess the meaning of some hypothetical data. Suppose your colleague—a child therapist working in a child guidance center—tells you that she has come up with an effective new

technique for reducing hostile antisocial behaviors by children with behavioral disorders during their group play therapy sessions. To prove her assertion, she tells you about a play therapy group that has had four sessions. During the first two sessions she noticed that there seemed to be an unusually high number of time-outs required in response to hostile antisocial behaviors, but she did not count them. After the second session, she developed her new technique and decided to test it out. To test it, she counted the number of time-outs in each of the next two sessions, not employing her new technique in the third session, and then employing it in the fourth session.

She tells you that during the third session, when she did not employ her technique, there were 10 time-outs, whereas the number of time-outs fell to 4 during the fourth session. In other words, she contends, her new technique cut the number of time-outs by 60 percent. This simple set of data is presented graphically in Figure 12.2.

FIGURE 12.2 Two Observations of Time-Outs: Before and After Using New Technique

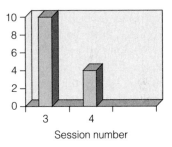

Session number

---

switching replications A procedure to assess whether posttest differences in a nonequivalent comparison groups design were due to selection bias. This procedure involves providing the tested intervention to the comparison group after both groups complete the posttest. If the comparison group then improves like the experimental group did, then the notion that the difference at the first posttest was because of a selection bias can be ruled out.

time series designs A set of quasi-experimental designs in which multiple observations of a dependent variable are conducted before and after an intervention is introduced.

Are you persuaded that the new technique employed during session 4 was the cause of the drop in time-outs? You'd probably object that her data don't prove the case. Two observations aren't really enough to prove anything. The improvement in time-outs could have been because of history, maturation, or statistical regression. Ideally, she should have had two separate play therapy groups with children assigned randomly to each, employed the new technique in only one group after one or more pretest sessions, and then compared the two groups in later sessions. But she doesn't have two groups of randomly assigned children. Neither does she have a nonequivalent comparison group. All she has is the one group.

Suppose, however, that instead of counting the time-outs only in sessions 3 and 4, she had been counting them in every session throughout a 10-session treatment period and recording each number in a running log. Suppose further that instead of introducing her new technique during session 4, she introduced it during session 6, and then continued employing it through session 10. Her log would allow you to conduct a time series evaluation.

Figure 12.3 presents three possible patterns of time-outs over time. In each pattern, the new technique is introduced after the fifth session (i.e., during the sixth session). In each pattern, the vertical line between the fifth and sixth sessions separates the five sessions before the new technique was used and the five sessions during which it was used. Which of these patterns would give you confidence that the new technique had the impact she contends it did?

If the time series results looked like Pattern 1 in Figure 12.3, you'd probably conclude that a trend of fewer time-outs with each session had begun well before the new technique was introduced and had continued unaffected after the new technique was introduced. The long-term data suggest that the trend would have occurred even without the new technique. Pattern 1, then, contradicts the assertion that the new technique decreased the number of time-outs.

Pattern 2 contradicts her assertion also. It indicates that the number of time-outs had been bouncing up and down in a regular pattern throughout the 10 sessions. Sometimes it increases from one session to the next, and sometimes it decreases; the new technique simply was introduced at a point

FIGURE 12.3 Three Patterns of Number of Time-outs in a Longer Time Series Perspective

Pattern 1

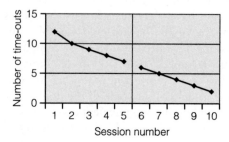

Pattern 2

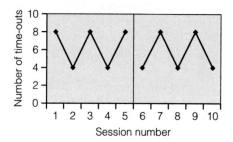

Pattern 3

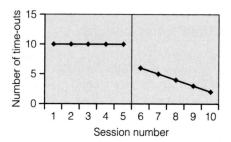

where there would have been a decrease in time-outs anyway. More to the point, we note that the number of time-outs kept fluctuating cyclically between increases and decreases during the 5 sessions when the new technique was used in the same way it fluctuated during session 1 through 5, before the new technique was introduced.

Only Pattern 3 in Figure 12.3 supports her contention that the new technique mattered. As we see, the number of time-outs before the new technique was introduced had been steady at 10 time-outs per session. Then, beginning immediately with session 6, when the new technique was introduced, the number of time-outs fell to 6 and continued dropping with each successive session. The data in Pattern 3 therefore exclude the possibility that the decrease in time-outs results from a process of maturation (indicated in Pattern 1) or from regular fluctuations (indicated in Pattern 2). As well, they rule out the possibility of statistical regression, because the improvement was not based on movement from one extreme, atypical pretest score.

The Pattern 3 data do not, however, rule out history as a possible explanation. That is, it is conceivable that some extraneous event may have caused the change. Perhaps the child guidance center's new psychiatrist started prescribing a new medication for attention deficit hyperactivity disorder at the same time the new play therapy technique was introduced. Or perhaps a family therapy service for the same children commenced at that time. Nevertheless, the data in Pattern 3 do reduce somewhat the *plausibility* of the explanation that history caused the change, because the extraneous event would have had to occur at the same time that the new technique was introduced—in a way that could be portrayed as an unlikely coincidence.

12.7 ADDITIONAL THREATS TO THE VALIDITY OF EXPERIMENTAL AND QUASI-EXPERIMENTAL FINDINGS

So far, we have seen how the logic of experimental designs and quasi-experimental designs can control for most threats to internal validity. Additional threats to the validity of the conclusions we draw from experiments and quasi-experiments require methodological efforts that go beyond their design logic. Let's now look at each of these additional threats and the steps that can be taken to alleviate them.

12.7a Measurement Bias

No matter how well an experiment or quasi-experiment controls for other threats to internal validity, the credibility of its conclusions can be damaged severely if its measurement procedures appear to have been biased. Suppose, for example,

that a clinician develops a new therapy for depression that promises to make her rich and famous and then evaluates her invention in an experiment by using her own subjective clinical judgment to rate improvement among the experimental and control group participants, knowing which group each participant is in. Her own ego involvement and vested interest in wanting the experimental group participants to show more improvement would make her study so vulnerable to *measurement bias* that her "findings" would have virtually no credibility. Although this example may seem extreme, serious measurement bias is not as rare in experimental evaluations as you might imagine. It is not difficult to find reports of otherwise well-designed experiments in which outcome measures were administered or completed by research assistants who knew the study hypothesis, were aware of the hopes that it would be confirmed, and knew which group each participant was in.

Whenever measurement of the dependent variable in experimental or quasi-experimental studies involves using research staff to supply ratings (through either direct observation or interviews), the individuals who supply the ratings should not know the experimental status of the subjects they are rating. The same principle applies when the people supplying the ratings are practitioners who are not part of the research staff, but who still might be biased toward a particular outcome. In other words, they should be "blind" as to whether any given rating refers to someone who has received the experimental stimulus (or service) or someone who has not. The term *blind ratings* or *blind raters* means that the study has controlled for the potential—and perhaps unconscious—bias of raters toward perceiving results that would confirm the hypothesis. Likewise, whenever researchers fail to inform you that such ratings were blind, you should be skeptical about the study's validity. No matter how elegant the rest of a study's design might be, its conclusions are suspect if results favoring the experimental group were provided by raters who might have been biased.

The use of blind raters, unfortunately, is often not feasible in social work research studies. When we are unable to use them, we should look for alternative ways to avoid rater bias. For example, we might use validated self-report scales to measure the dependent variable, rather than rely on raters who may be biased. But even when such scales are used, those administering them can bias the outcome by the comments they make. The term *research reactivity refers* to changes in outcome data that are caused by researchers or research procedures rather than the independent variable. Let's now look at the various ways in which research reactivity can threaten the validity of experimental or quasi-experimental findings.

12.7b Research Reactivity

Two similar forms of **research reactivity** are called *experimental demand characteristics and experimenter expectancies.* Research participants learn what experimenters want them to say or do, and then they cooperate with those "demands" or expectations. For example, some therapists will repeatedly ask clients at different points during therapy sessions to rate on a scale from 0 to 10 how much distress they are feeling during therapy when they think of a traumatic event in their life. Through the therapist's verbal communication as well as nonverbal communication (smiles or looks of concern, for example), clients can learn that the therapist hopes the rating number will diminish over the course of therapy. Some studies evaluating trauma therapy administer the same 0 to 10 rating scale at pretest and posttest that the therapist administers throughout treatment. Even if the pretests and posttests are administered by research assistants who are unaware of clients' experimental group status, clients will have learned from the therapist that they are expected to report lower distress scores at posttest than at pretest. Worse yet, in some studies it is the therapist herself who administers the same

---

research reactivity   A process that refers to changes in outcome data that are caused by researchers or research procedures rather than the independent variable.

obtrusive observation   Observation in which the participant is keenly aware of being observed and thus may be predisposed to behave in socially desirable ways.

unobtrusive observation   Observation in which the participant does not notice the observation.

0–10 scale at posttest that she has been using repeatedly as part of the therapy.

One way to alleviate the influence of experimenter expectancies and demand characteristics is to separate the measurement procedures from the treatment procedures. Another way is to use measurement procedures that are hard for practitioners or researchers to influence. Instead of using the above 0–10 scale at pretest and posttest, for example, a research assistant could administer physiological measures of distress (such as pulse rate and so on) while the client thinks of the traumatic event. It would also help if the assistants administering pretest scales were blind as to the study's hypothesis or the experimental status of the participants—to avoid giving cues about expected outcomes (Shadish, Cook, & Campbell, 2001).

Sometimes we can use raters or scale administrators who are not blind but do not seem likely to be biased. We may, for instance, ask teachers to rate the classroom conduct of children who receive two different forms of social work intervention. The teachers may know which intervention each student is receiving but not have much technical understanding of the interventions or any reason to favor one intervention over another.

A related option is to directly observe and quantify the actual behavior of participants in their natural setting, rather than rely on their answers to self-report scales or on someone's ratings. It matters a great deal, however, whether that observation is conducted in an *obtrusive* or *unobtrusive* manner. **Obtrusive observation** occurs when the participant is keenly aware of being observed and thus may be predisposed to behave in ways that meet experimenter expectancies. In contrast, **unobtrusive observation** means that the participant does not notice the observation. Suppose an experiment is evaluating the effectiveness of a new form of therapy in reducing the frequency of antisocial behaviors among children in a residential treatment center. If the child's therapist or the researcher starts showing up with a pad and pencil to observe the goings on in the child's classroom or cottage, he or she might stick out like a sore thumb and make the child keenly aware of being observed. That form of observation would be obtrusive, and the child might exhibit atypically good behavior during that observation. A more unobtrusive option would be to have teachers or cottage parents tabulate the number of antisocial behaviors of the child each day. Their observation would be less noticeable to the child because they are part of the natural setting and because being observed by a teacher or cottage parent is part of the daily routine and not obviously connected to the expectations of a research study.

Whenever we are conducting experimental research (or any other type of research) and are unable to use blind raters, blind scale administrators, unobtrusive observation, or some other measurement alternative that we think is relatively free of bias, we should try to use more than one measurement alternative. This involves the principle of *triangulation*, which, as we saw in Chapter 8, means using two or more measurement strategies, each vulnerable to different biases. If both produce the same results, then we can have more confidence in the validity of those results.

Another form of research reactivity can occur when the research procedures don't just influence participants to respond to our measures in misleading ways to tell us what they think we want to hear, but when those procedures really truly do produce desired changes. For instance, suppose as part of the research data collection procedures to measure outcome, participants in a parent education intervention self-monitor how much time they spend playing with or holding a friendly conversation with their children. That means that they will keep a running log, recording the duration of every instance that they play with or hold a conversation with their child. Keeping such a log might make some parents realize that they are spending much less quality time with their children than they previously had thought. This realization might influence them to spend more quality time with their children; in fact, it might influence them to do so more than the parent education intervention did.

It is conceivable that desired changes might occur among experimental group participants simply because of their sense of getting special attention or special treatment. To illustrate this form of reactivity, suppose a residential treatment center for children conducts an experiment to see if a new recreational program will reduce the frequency of antisocial behaviors among the children. Being assigned to the experimental group might make some children feel better about themselves and about the

center. If this feeling—and not the recreational program per se—causes the desired change in their behavior, then a form of research reactivity will have occurred. This form of reactivity has been termed *novelty and disruption effects*, because introducing an innovation in a setting where little innovation has previously occurred can stimulate excitement, energy, and enthusiasm among recipients of the intervention (Shadish et al., 2001).

A similar form of reactivity is termed *placebo effects*. **Placebo effects** can be induced by experimenter expectancies. If experimental group participants get the sense that they are about to receive a special new treatment that researchers or practitioners expect to be very effective, then the mere power of suggestion—and not the treatment itself—can bring about the desired improvement.

If we are concerned about potential placebo effects or novelty and disruption effects and wish to control for them, we could employ an experimental design called the **placebo control group design**. The shorthand notation for this design is:

$$
\begin{array}{cccc}
R & O_1 & X & O_2 \\
R & O_1 & & O_2 \\
R & O_1 & P & O_2
\end{array}
$$

This design randomly assigns clients to three groups: an experimental group and two different control groups. One control group receives no experimental stimulus, but the other receives a placebo (represented by the P in the preceding notation). Placebo group subjects would receive special attention of some sort other than the tested stimulus or intervention. Perhaps practitioners would meet regularly to show special interest in them and listen to them, but without applying any of the tested intervention procedures.

---

placebo effects Changes in the dependent variable that are caused by the power of suggestion connected to receiving a special intervention, and not by the intervention itself.

placebo control group design An experimental design that controls for placebo effects by randomly assigning subjects to an experimental group and two control groups and exposing one of the control groups to a stimulus that is designed to resemble the special attention received by subjects in the experimental group.

Placebo control group designs pose complexities from both a planning and interpretation standpoint, particularly when experimental interventions contain elements that resemble placebo effects. For example, in some interventions that emphasize constructs such as "empathy" and "unconditional positive regard," intervention effects are difficult to sort from placebo effects. But when they are feasible to use, placebo control group designs provide greater control for threats to the validity of experimental findings than do designs that use only one control group.

Before leaving this topic, we should clarify that we do not want to convey the impression that an experiment's findings lack credibility unless it can guarantee the complete absence of any possible research reactivity or measurement bias. It is virtually impossible for experiments in social work or allied fields to meet that unrealistic standard. Instead, the key issue should be whether reasonable efforts were taken to avoid or minimize those problems and whether or not the potential degree of bias or reactivity seems to be at an egregious level. That said, let's move on to a different type of threat to the validity of experimental or quasi-experimental findings.

12.7c Diffusion or Imitation of Treatments

Sometimes, service providers or service recipients are influenced unexpectedly in ways that tend to diminish the planned differences in the way a tested intervention is implemented among the groups being compared. For instance, consider research that evaluates the effectiveness of case management services. Many social workers who are not called case managers nevertheless conceptualize and routinely provide case management functions—such as outreach, brokerage, linkage, and advocacy—as an integral part of what they learned to be good and comprehensive direct social work practice. Consequently, when outcomes for clients referred to case managers are compared to the outcomes of clients who receive "traditional" social services, the true effects of case management as a treatment approach may be blurred by the *diffusion* of that approach among practitioners who are not called case managers. In other words, despite their different labels, the two treatment groups may not be as different in the independent variable as we think they are.

Preventing the *diffusion or imitation of treatments* can be difficult. Shadish et al. (2001) suggest separating the two treatment conditions as much as possible, either geographically or by using different practitioners in each. Another possibility is to provide ongoing reminders to practitioners about the need not to imitate the experimental group intervention when seeing control group clients. To monitor the extent to which the imitation of treatment is occurring or has occurred, researchers can use qualitative methods to observe staff meetings, conduct informal conversational interviews with practitioners and clients, and ask practitioners to keep logs summarizing what happened in each treatment session. If these efforts detect imitation while the experiment is still underway, further communication with practitioners may help alleviate the problem and prevent it from reaching a level that seriously undermines the validity of the experiment.

12.7d Compensatory Equalization, Compensatory Rivalry, or Resentful Demoralization

Suppose you conduct an experiment or quasi-experiment to see if increasing the involvement of families in the treatment of substance abusers improves treatment effectiveness. Suppose the therapists in one unit receive special training in working with families and are instructed to increase the treatment involvement of families of clients in their unit, whereas the therapists in another unit receive no such training or instructions. Assuming that the staff in the latter unit—and perhaps even their clients and the families of their clients—are aware of the treatment differences, they may seek to offset what they perceive as an inequity in service provision. The staff in the latter unit therefore might decide to compensate for the inequity by providing enhanced services that go beyond the routine treatment regimen for their clients. This eventuality is termed *compensatory equalization*. If compensatory equalization happens, as was the case above with diffusion or imitation of treatments, the true effects of increasing family involvement could be blurred.

What if the therapists not receiving family therapy training in the above example decide to compete with the therapists in the other unit who do receive the training? Perhaps they feel their job security or prestige is threatened by not receiving the special training and try to show that they can be just as effective without the special training. They may start reading more, attending more continuing education workshops, and increasing their therapeutic contact with clients. This eventuality is called *compensatory rivalry*. The control group therapists' extra efforts might increase their effectiveness as much as the increased family involvement might have increased the effectiveness of the experimental group therapists. If so, this could lead to the erroneous impression that the lack of difference in treatment outcome between the two groups means that increasing family involvement did not improve treatment effectiveness. The same problem could occur if the clients in one group become more motivated to improve because of the rivalry engendered by their awareness that they are not receiving the same treatment benefits as another group.

The converse of compensatory rivalry is *resentful demoralization*. This occurs when staff or clients become resentful and demoralized because they did not receive the special training or the special treatment. Consequently, their confidence or motivation may decline and may explain their inferior performance on outcome measures. To detect whether compensatory equalization, compensatory rivalry, or resentful demoralization is occurring—and perhaps intervene to try to minimize these problems—you can use qualitative methods, such as participant observation of staff meetings and informal conversational interviews with clients and practitioners.

12.7e Attrition

Let's now look at one more threat to the validity of experimental or quasi-experimental findings: **attrition**. Often, participants will drop out of an experiment or quasi-experiment before it is completed, and the statistical comparisons and conclusions that are drawn can be affected by that. In a pretest–posttest control group design evaluating the effectiveness of an intervention to alleviate a distressing problem, for example, suppose that experimental group participants who perceive no improvement in their target problem prematurely drop out of treatment and refuse to be posttested. At the posttest, the only experimental group participants left would be those

who felt they were improving. Suppose the overall group rate of perceived improvement among control group participants is exactly the same as the overall rate among those assigned to the experimental group (including the dropouts), but all of the nonrecipients agree to be posttested because none had been disappointed. The experimental group's average posttest score is likely to be higher than the control group's—even if the intervention was ineffective—merely because of the attrition (experimental mortality) of experimental group participants who perceived no improvement.

When the rate of attrition among experimental group participants is disconcerting, researchers can use a technique called *intent-to-treat analysis*. Using **intent-to-treat analysis**, all participants who originally enrolled in the study—including those who dropped out of treatment—have their outcomes assessed, and those outcomes are included in the data analysis. Including the dropouts in the data analysis is based in part on the notion that an intervention that fails to retain a client in treatment is not being effective with that client. Including the dropouts in the data analysis is also done to avoid the bias that would result from the notion that the participants who are the least motivated or most dysfunctional are the ones most likely to drop out of treatment. For example, if the control condition places few demands on its participants but the intervention being provided to experimental group participants places heavier demands, then the least motivated and most dysfunctional participants are more likely to drop out from the experimental group. If they are not included in the analysis, then despite random assignment, the groups are no longer equivalent. Instead, the deck is stacked in favor of the experimental group because the control group would have a greater proportion of participants who are the least motivated and the most dysfunctional.

A converse attrition problem can occur when participating in the control group protocol is more

---

attrition A threat to the validity of an evaluation that occurs when participants drop out of the study before it is completed.

intent-to-treat analysis An analysis of outcome data on intervention effectiveness in which everyone who originally enrolled in the study–even the treatment dropouts–are included in the data analysis.

boring or arduous than participating in the experimental treatment. If so, then the least motivated and most dysfunctional clients might be more likely to drop out of the control group. For example, consider an evaluation that compares the effectiveness of family therapy and discussion groups in the treatment of drug addiction. Shadish et al. (2001) point out that addicts with the worst prognoses are more likely to drop out of discussion groups than they are to drop out of family therapy. Consequently, the family therapy intervention may have poorer results at posttest not because it is less effective than discussion groups but because the different attrition rates left more difficult cases in the family therapy group at posttest.

Researchers conducting experimental or quasi-experimental evaluations of the effectiveness of practice or programs should strive to minimize attrition. One way to do that is by *reimbursing participants for their participation* in research. Reimbursement might not only alleviate attrition, it might enhance your ability to recruit people to participate in your study at the outset. The level of reimbursement should be sensitive to the time and efforts of participants in pretesting and posttesting. The payment should be large enough to work as an incentive without being so great that it becomes coercive. (Discount department store gift certificates sometimes are used instead of cash payments.) The amount should fit the difficulties that clients experience in participating, as well as fit their income levels and emotional states. With low-income participants, for example, you should anticipate difficulties in child care and in transportation to and from pretesting and posttesting (and perhaps follow-up testing). If feasible, an alternative to extra payments for transportation and child care costs might be to provide the transportation to the testing site, as well as a small child care service there. Alternatively, it might make sense to conduct the testing at the participant's residence (if doing so did not introduce serious measurement biases).

Another way to try to minimize attrition is by using the *tracking methods* that were discussed in Chapter 6. Many recipients of social work interventions are transient or secretive about where they live. Many are unemployed. Some lack telephones. The poor, the homeless, substance abusers, and battered women are prominent examples. Researchers can obtain as much location information as possible at the outset of their participation, not only from the participants themselves, but also from their friends, relatives, and other agencies with which they are involved. As was discussed in Chapter 6, there are various ways by which researchers can use this information to track research participants and attempt to retain their participation.

12.8 EXTERNAL VALIDITY

The threats to validity that we have been discussing so far in this chapter pertain primarily to internal validity. When a study has a high degree of internal validity, it allows causal inferences to be made about the sample and setting that were studied. But what about other settings and larger populations? Can we generalize the same causal inferences to them?

We defined *external validity* earlier as the extent to which we can *generalize* the findings of a study to settings and populations beyond the study conditions. A major factor that influences external validity is the representativeness of the study sample, setting, and procedures. Suppose a well-funded mental health case management program is implemented in an urban community where there is a comprehensive range of noninstitutional community support resources accessible to the case-managed clients residing in the community. Suppose, in turn, that the well-funded program can afford to hire high-caliber staff members, give them small caseloads, and reward them amply for good work. Finally, suppose that an evaluation with high internal validity finds that the program improves the clients' quality of life.

Would those findings imply that legislators or mental health planners in other localities could logically conclude that a similar case management program would improve the quality of life of mentally disabled individuals in their settings? Not necessarily. It would depend on the degree to which their settings, populations, and procedures matched those of the studied program.

Suppose their community is rural, has fewer or more geographically dispersed community-based resources for the mentally disabled, or has more neighborhood opposition to residences being located in the community. Suppose legislators view deinstitutionalization primarily as a cost-saving device and therefore do not allocate enough funds to enable the program to hire or keep high-caliber staff members, or give them caseload sizes that are small enough to manage adequately. And what about differences in the characteristics of the mentally disabled target population? Notice that we have said nothing about the attributes of the clients in the tested program. Perhaps they were different in age, diagnosis, ethnicity, average length of previous institutionalization, and degree of social impairment than the intended target population in the communities generalizing from the study findings. To the extent that such differences apply, similar programs implemented in other settings might not have the same effects as did the program in the tested setting.

Would such differences mean that this study had low external validity? Not necessarily. On the one hand, we could say that a study has low external validity if its conditions are far removed from conditions that could reasonably be expected to be replicated in the "real" world. On the other hand, a study's external validity could be adequate even if it cannot be generalized to many other settings. A study must be generalizable to some real-world settings, and it must represent that which it intends to represent. It does not have to represent every conceivable population or setting.

For example, a study that evaluates a case management program for the profoundly and chronically disabled in rural settings does not need to be generalizable to the mildly or acutely disabled or to the disabled residing in urban settings in order to have external validity. It just has to be representative of those attributes that it intends to represent, no matter how narrowly it defines them.

Problems in external validity abound in the literature that evaluates social work practice and programs. One common problem that limits external validity is ambiguity or brevity in reportage. Many studies do not adequately articulate the specific attributes of the clients who participated in the evaluated service. Many are vague about the practitioners' attributes. Some studies generalize about the effectiveness of *professional* social work practitioners based on findings about the effectiveness of *student* practitioners. Some studies leave out

important details about the evaluated clinical setting, such as caseload size and the like. Consequently, while it may be clear that the evaluated intervention did or did not cause the desired change among the studied clients—that is, that the study had high *internal validity*—it is often not clear to whom those findings can be *generalized*. Thus, some studies find services to be effective but do not permit the generalization that those services would be effective beyond the study conditions. Likewise, other studies find no support for the effectiveness of services, but do not permit the generalization that those services would be ineffective when implemented under other conditions.

12.9 CROSS-SECTIONAL STUDIES

Because most experimental and quasi-experimental research designs focus on controlling for threats to *internal* validity, they are highly desirable designs to use when we seek to derive causal inferences from our research. We have noted, however, that these designs are not flawless, and their *external* validity, in particular, often can be limited. Researchers who lack the means to conduct experimental or quasi-experimental designs, or who may be interested in studying larger, more representative samples, might opt to conduct cross-sectional studies. Cross-sectional studies often involve using survey and sampling methods discussed in Chapters 10 and 11.

Cross-sectional studies examine a phenomenon by taking a cross section of it at *one point in time*. For example, they might examine the plausibility of parent–child discord as a cause of childhood behavioral disorders by administering two measures to children at the same point: One assesses the degree of parent–child discord and the other assesses whether the child has a behavioral disorder. If the two measures are highly and positively correlated—that is, if the probability of behavioral disorder is higher when the amount of parent–child discord is greater—then the results support the *plausibility* of the supposition that the discord contributes to the causation of behavioral disorders.

Although the results are consistent with the notion that discord helps cause the disorder, however, they do not themselves demonstrate that the nature of the relationship is indeed causal. For instance, time order is not taken into account. Perhaps the causal order of the relationship is the other way around—that is, perhaps parent–child discord, rather than causing the behavioral disorder, increases as a result of the disorder. Also, the preceding correlation by itself does not rule out alternative variables that might cause both the discord and the behavioral disorder. For example, perhaps stressful life events produce both problems simultaneously.

Recognizing that simple correlations at one point do not permit causal inferences, researchers using cross-sectional designs may attempt to rule out the plausibility of rival hypotheses by controlling for alternative variables through multivariate statistical procedures. They do this by collecting data on as many plausible alternative explanatory variables as they can and then analyzing all of the variables simultaneously, using multivariate techniques. These statistical techniques go beyond the scope of this introductory text. To learn more about them you can examine our more advanced text (Rubin & Babbie, 2011). For now, it is sufficient to alert you to the fact that these multivariate procedures markedly enhance the internal validity of cross-sectional studies by enabling much greater control over alternative hypotheses, thereby increasing the plausibility of causal inferences drawn from cross-sectional data.

As we have seen, social work settings often do not permit the kinds of sophisticated methodological arrangements needed to manipulate variables and meet all of the criteria for inferring causality in an ideal manner. Because of their feasibility, cross-sectional designs have always been popular in social work research, and with recent advances in multivariate statistical analysis, the internal validity of these designs is improving. Cross-sectional designs are also commonly used in descriptive and exploratory research.

---

case-control design Instead of dividing cases up into treatment and control groups and then *prospectively* measuring outcomes, this design compares groups of cases that have had contrasting outcomes and then collects *retrospective* data about past differences that might explain the difference in outcomes.

12.10 CASE-CONTROL DESIGN

Another design that relies on multivariate statistical procedures is called the case-control design. The case-control design is popular because of its feasibility. As in cross-sectional designs, data can be collected at just one point in time. Instead of dividing cases up into treatment and control groups, and then *prospectively* measuring outcomes, the **case-control design** compares groups of cases that have had contrasting outcomes and then collects *retrospective data* about past differences that might explain the difference in outcomes.

Suppose we want to learn what interventions may be effective in preventing children who are victims of child abuse from becoming perpetrators of abuse as adults. To maximize our internal validity, we might conduct an experiment that tested one or more particular interventions. But experiments in general are often not feasible, and in this case an additional obstacle to feasibility would be the need to follow and measure the participating children over many years, even after they reach parenthood. Using the case-control design as an alternative, we could find a sample of two groups of parents who had been victims of child abuse: one group that had been referred at least once as adults to public child welfare agencies as perpetrators of child abuse, and another group that had never been so referred. We could then collect retrospective data from the adults in each group, asking about their past experiences, seeking to find some intervention that the non-perpetrators were much more likely than the perpetrators to have received earlier in life. (Or perhaps we'll find something harmful that the perpetrators were more likely to have experienced.) Suppose we find that after controlling statistically for a variety of relevant personal attributes and experiences, the main past experience that distinguishes the two groups is whether a volunteer from a Big Brother/Big Sister agency or some similar program provided them with a long-term positive, caring relationship that commenced very soon after they had been abused as children. That finding would suggest that practitioners intervening with abused children might want to do all they can to secure such a relationship for the children.

But despite their popularity, case-control designs can be fraught with problems that limit what can be inferred or generalized from their findings. Cases may need to be selected using nonprobability sampling procedures that create doubt about how *representative* they are of the population of people with their outcomes or past experiences. For example, snowball sampling or advertisements may be needed to find adults who were abused as children and who did and did not become perpetrators. The people recruited in that fashion may be quite unlike those who cannot be found or who are unwilling to participate in such a study. Their *memories* of childhood experiences may be *faulty*. What about ambiguity *in the direction of causal influence*?

Also, perhaps the good relationships children had with caring volunteers is explained more by their preexisting childhood resilience than by the effect of the relationships on the children's resilience. That is, perhaps the children who were already more resilient were more motivated and better able to connect with the adult volunteers.

In addition, perhaps adult memories of childhood experiences may be faulty. Forgetting is only one way in which their memories could be faulty. Another way is termed **recall bias**. Maybe the perpetrators had relationships with adult volunteers that were just as good as the relationships that the nonperpetrators had, but their current recollections of the quality and value of those relationships are tainted by knowing that things didn't work out for them later in life. Likewise, perhaps the adults who are leading happier and more successful lives are more predisposed to attribute their well-being to happy childhood memories, while perhaps blocking out the negative ones.

Despite the preceding problems, case-control designs, like cross-sectional designs, can be used in an exploratory fashion to generate hypotheses about the possible effects of interventions. Consequently, they can provide a valuable basis for designing studies using more valid designs to test the effectiveness of those interventions. An example of a valuable case-control study is summarized in the box entitled "A Case-Control Study of Adverse Childhood Experiences as Risk Factors for Homelessness."

12.11 MAIN POINTS

- There are three basic criteria for the determination of causation in scientific research: (1) the independent (cause) and dependent (effect) variables must be empirically related to each other, (2) the independent variable must occur earlier in time than the dependent variable, and (3) the observed relationship between these two variables cannot be explained away as being due to the influence of some third variable that causes both of them.

- The classic experiment evaluates the effectiveness of an intervention by randomizing clients to experimental and control groups and then pretesting and posttesting clients in each group.

- The logic of experimental design aims to control for the various threats to internal validity, such as history, maturation or the passage of time, testing, instrumentation, regression, selection bias, and causal time order.

- Control group participants in experiments in social work settings need not be denied services. They can receive alternative, routine services, or be put on a waiting list to receive the experimental intervention.

- Although the classic experiment with random assignment of participants guards against most threats to internal validity, additional methodological efforts may be needed to prevent or alleviate problems such as measurement bias, research reactivity, diffusion or imitation of treatments, compensatory equalization, compensatory rivalry, resentful demoralization, and attrition.

- Experimental demand characteristics and experimenter expectancies can hinder the validity of experimental findings if they influence research participants to cooperate with what experimenters want them to say or do.

- Obtrusive observation occurs when the participant is keenly aware of being observed and thus may be predisposed to behave in ways that meet experimenter expectancies. In contrast, unobtrusive observation means that the participant does not notice the observation.

---

recall bias A common limitation in case-control designs that occurs when a person's current recollections of the quality and value of past experiences are influenced either positively or negatively by knowing whether things did or did not work out for them later in life.

A Case-Control Study of Adverse Childhood Experiences as Risk Factors for Homelessness

Along with three associates, Daniel Herman, a social work professor at Columbia University, conducted a case-control study to ascertain whether adult homelessness could be explained in part by certain adverse childhood experiences (Herman, Susser, Struening, & Link, 1997). They began by analyzing available data from an earlier survey of 1,507 adults that was conducted in 1990. They then reinterviewed respondents to that survey, including all 169 who reported having been homeless at some time in their adult lives, and a comparable group who had never been homeless but who had attributes typically associated with a higher risk of homelessness (being poor, mentally ill, and so on).

In their follow-up interviews they used a scale designed to assess respondents' recollections of the quality of parental care during childhood. The answers to various items on the scale enabled the researchers to determine whether the respondent recalled the following types of adverse childhood experiences: lack of parental care, physical abuse, sexual abuse, lack of care plus either type of abuse, and any childhood adversity.

Their initial results indicated that lack of care and physical abuse were each strongly correlated with a greater likelihood of homelessness. The combination of lack of care plus either physical or sexual abuse during childhood was even more strongly correlated with a greater likelihood of adult homelessness.

What made this study particularly valuable, however, was its use of multivariate statistical procedures to control for extraneous variables that might explain away the above findings. Using these procedures, the researchers were able to control for the respondent's gender, age, ethnicity, current residence (urban versus rural), parental socioeconomic status, whether the family was on welfare during childhood, and the extent of current depressive symptoms. It was important to control for these variables. For example, growing up in poverty might be the real explanation for an increased likelihood of homelessness as an adult, and also explain adverse childhood experiences. Parents living in poverty are less likely to be able to care well for their children. Thus, the relationship between adverse parental care and adult homelessness might be spurious—with both attributes being explained by poverty.

A noteworthy strength of this study was its control for the respondent's current emotional well-being. Herman and his colleagues astutely reasoned that a current depressed mood among some respondents might bias them toward recalling more adverse aspects of their childhood experiences. Likewise, respondents who were currently better off emotionally might be biased against recalling adverse childhood experiences.

After controlling for all these variables in their multivariate analyses, Herman and his colleagues found that their initial results changed somewhat. Lack of care and physical abuse continued to be strongly correlated with homelessness, and so did the combination of the two. But the combination of lack of care and sexual abuse was no longer a significant correlate of adult homelessness.

Another nice feature of this study was the way its authors discussed the strengths and limitations of their case-control design. It's easy for authors to point out their study's strengths, and indeed there were many in this study. Not so easy, yet more impressive, is when authors correctly discuss their study's limitations. Thus, Herman and his colleagues point out that people with particularly lengthy homelessness experiences were probably underrepresented in their sample and that although the study controlled for current level of depression, recall bias is still a potential threat to the validity of its findings because respondents who had been homeless might be predisposed toward recalling more adverse childhood experiences. But recall bias comes with the territory when conducting even the best case-control studies, and this one certainly deserves recognition as among the best in social work.

Source: Herman, D. B., Susser, E. S., Struening, E. L., and Link, B. L. 1997. "Adverse Childhood Experiences: Are they Risk Factors for Adult Homelessness?" *American Journal of Public Health*, 87, 249–255.

- Experiments also face problems of external validity: Experimental findings may not reflect real life or be generalizable to other settings or populations.
- Many experimental studies fail to include measurement procedures, such as blind raters, to control for researcher or practitioner bias toward perceiving results that would confirm the hypothesis.
- Techniques for minimizing attrition include reimbursing participants for their participation and using methods to track participants.

- When the rate of attrition among experimental group participants is disconcerting, researchers can use a technique called *intent-to-treat analysis*, in which all participants who originally enrolled in the study—including those who dropped out of treatment—have their outcomes assessed, and those outcomes are included in the data analysis.
- It is often impossible to assign participants randomly to experimental and control groups in real agency settings, and quasi-experimental designs can provide credible, although less ideal, alternatives when experimental designs are not feasible.
- Two types of quasi-experimental designs that can have a reasonable degree of internal validity are time series designs and nonequivalent comparison group designs.
- Cross-sectional studies with multivariate statistical controls can provide another credible alternative to experimental designs.
- The case-control design compares groups of cases that have had contrasting outcomes and then collects retrospective data about past differences that might explain the difference in outcomes.

12.12 PRACTICE-RELATED EXERCISES

1. Pick six of the threats to internal validity discussed in this chapter and make up examples (not discussed in the chapter) to illustrate each.
2. Briefly sketch an experimental design for testing a new intervention in a social work agency with which you are familiar. Then conduct a qualitative (open-ended, semi-structured) interview with one or two direct-service practitioners and an administrator in that agency, asking them how feasible it would be to carry out your study in their agency.
3. What potential threats to the validity of the findings can you detect in the following hypothetical design? In a residential treatment center containing four cottages, the clinical director develops a new intervention to alleviate behavior problems among the children residing in the four cottages. The center has four therapists, each assigned to a separate cottage. The clinical director selects two cottages to receive the new intervention. The other two will receive the routine treatment. To measure outcome, the clinical director assigns a social work student whose field placement is at the center to spend an equal amount of time at each cottage observing and recording the number of antisocial behaviors each child exhibits and the number of antisocial statements each makes.

4. Briefly sketch a nonequivalent comparison groups design for evaluating the effectiveness of a parent education program for parents at high risk for child abuse. What would you do to assure the readers of your study that the threat of a selectivity bias seems remote? Include in your sketch a description of the dependent variable, and when and how it would be measured.

5. Briefly sketch a case-control design to generate hypotheses about interventions that may be the most helpful in preventing teen runaways. What are the background variables that would be most important to control for? Identify and explain three uncontrolled threats to the validity of your study that would represent major reasons why the results would be exploratory only.

6. A study with an exceptionally high degree of internal validity conducted with Native Alaskan female adolescents who have recently been sexually abused concludes that an intervention is effective in preventing substance abuse among its participants. Explain how this study can have little external validity from one perspective, yet a good deal of external validity from another perspective—depending upon the target population of the practitioners who are utilizing the study as a potential guide to their evidence-based practice.

12.13 INTERNET EXERCISES

1. Find an experiment that evaluated the effectiveness of a social work intervention. How well did it control for the threats to validity discussed in this chapter? What efforts did it make to alleviate attrition? Were its measurement procedures obtrusive or unobtrusive? Do they appear to be free from serious bias? Also critique the study's external validity—either positively or negatively.

2. Find a study that used a preexperimental design to evaluate the outcome of a social work intervention. Critique the study's internal validity and discuss whether it had value despite its preexperimental nature.

3. Find a study in which placebo effects figured importantly. Briefly summarize the study, including the source of your information. (Hint: You might want to do a search using the term *placebo* as a keyword.)

4. Find a study that used a nonequivalent comparison groups design to evaluate the effectiveness of a social work intervention. How well did it control for selection biases?

5. Find a study that used a cross-sectional design or a case-control design to test or generate hypotheses about effective social work intervention with some problem. Critique the validity of the study, identifying its strengths as well as weaknesses.

6. Find a study that used a time series design to evaluate the effectiveness of a social work intervention.

How well did it control for history, maturation or passage of time, statistical regression, and selection biases?

7. The Federal Bureau of Prisons engages in evaluation research into various aspects of prison operations. Find and briefly critique one of their studies that used a quasi-experimental design. See http://www.bop.gov/news/index_research.jsp.

12.13a Competency Notes

EP 2.1.6b: Use research evidence to inform practice (p. 232): Understanding all of the concepts in this chapter will help social workers critically appraise outcome evaluations and judge which ones best merit guiding their practice.

EP 2.1.10m: Critically analyze, monitor, and evaluate interventions (p. 232): Social workers must understand all of the concepts in this chapter in order to evaluate interventions in a valid, competent manner.

chapter 13

Single-Case Evaluation Designs

13.1 INTRODUCTION

In Chapter 12, we saw that when people cannot be assigned to control or comparison groups, time series designs can help evaluate the impact of programs or interventions on groups of individuals. By taking repeated measures of the dependent variable (the service or policy goal, or target problem that one seeks to change), we can identify stable trends in the target problem. Marked deviations in these trends that coincide with the introduction or withdrawal of the service or intervention can support the plausibility of the hypothesis that changes in the dependent variable were caused by variation in the service or intervention (the independent variable).

Key concepts here are multiple measurement points and unlikely coincidences. The more measurement points one has and the more stable the trends identified in that measurement, the easier it is to infer whether any changes in the target problem can be attributed to the intervention or to alternative explanations like maturation, history, or statistical regression. In other words, identifying stable trends through many repeated measures enhances the internal validity of evaluations that cannot utilize control groups by enabling the researcher to pinpoint precisely where change in the dependent variable occurs and whether that change coincides with the onset of intervention.

Single-case designs apply the logic of time series designs to the evaluation of practice effectiveness with a single case. Such designs involve obtaining repeated measures of a client system with regard to particular outcome indicators of a target problem. Repeated measures of the trend in the target problem are obtained before a particular intervention is introduced, and these repeated measures are continued after intervention is introduced to see if a sustained pattern of improvement in the target problem commences shortly after the onset of intervention.

The phase of repeated measures that occurs before intervention is introduced is called the *baseline*. **A baseline** is a control phase—that is, it serves

---

baseline The phase of a single-case evaluation design that consists of repeated measures before a new intervention or policy is introduced.

the same function that a control group does in group experiments. The data patterns collected during the baseline (control) phases are compared to the data patterns collected during the *intervention* (experimental) phases. To infer that an intervention is effective—that is, that improvements in the dependent variable can be attributed to the intervention and not to some rival explanation such as history or maturation—we look for shifts in the trend or pattern of the data that coincide with shifts between baseline and intervention phases.

Consider the graph in Figure 13.1, for example. We see a shift from a stable pattern of no consistent change in the target problem during baseline to a sustained trend of improvement in the target problem at the start of and throughout the intervention phase. Something other than the intervention may have caused that change, but that would be a big coincidence given the large number of repeated measures and the absence of any marked shift in the data pattern at any time other than after intervention begins.

Now, for the sake of contrast, consider the graph in Figure 13.2. Here we see virtually the same intervention data as in Figure 13.1, but after a trend during baseline that shows that the target problem was already improving during baseline at the same rate at which it continued to improve during intervention. Here we would conclude that something other than the intervention, such as maturation or the mere passage of time, was probably

FIGURE 13.1 Graph of Hypothetical Single-Case Design Outcome Supporting Effectiveness of Intervention (Basic AB Design)

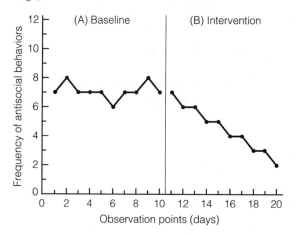

FIGURE 13.2 Graph of Hypothetical Single-Case Design Outcome Not Supporting Effectiveness of Intervention (Basic AB Design)

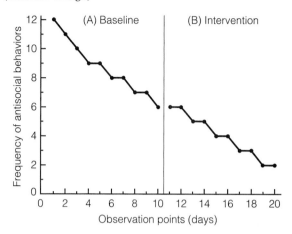

intervention phase. We will examine how that is done in depth later in this chapter. For now, let us consider the following illustration. Suppose a school social worker who seeks to enhance the self-esteem and social functioning of an acting-out adolescent at high risk of dropping out of school monitors the student's disciplinary referrals and administers a standardized self-esteem scale on a weekly basis. Suppose further that the social worker decided to interrupt the intervention phase for a few weeks, perhaps to take a well-deserved vacation or to see whether the student could maintain the improvement without being dependent on lengthy treatment. If a graph of the student's repeated measures resembled the data patterns displayed in Figure 13.3, then the social worker would have reasonable grounds for inferring that it was probably the intervention, and not history, that accounted for the student's improved functioning. Such an inference is reasonable because the shifts in the data patterns, or trends, occurred on three successive occasions that coincided with the introduction or interruption of intervention and at no other time. With this many successive trend shifts, the odds become extremely slim that other events are producing the desired change in the target problem and simply happen to coincide with variation in the independent variable. Thus, the history hypothesis becomes farfetched.

causing the improvement. This example illustrates how repeated measures during the baseline and intervention phases enable us to control for threats to internal validity that refer to processes that were underway before treatment begins. Without repeated measures in each phase—that is, with only one preintervention measure and one postintervention measure—we would have no way to detect such ongoing processes (for example, maturation) and thus would need experimental and control groups.

But what about history? Perhaps a big coincidence really did occur regarding the illustration depicted in Figure 13.1. Perhaps a dramatic and helpful change took place in the client's social environment precisely when intervention began. History cannot be ruled out with results like those in Figure 13.1, but note how history seems less plausible than in simple pretest–posttest group designs that contain only two data points (one before intervention and one after) and in which longer periods of time usually separate the two data points. In single-case designs, we can pinpoint the day or the week when the stable pattern of improvement begins, and we can discuss with the client what significant events or changes occurred at that point (other than the onset of intervention) to get a fairly good idea of whether history seems like a plausible explanation.

Single-case designs can increase their control for history by having more than one baseline and

FIGURE 13.3 Graph of Hypothetical Single-Case Design Outcome Supporting Effectiveness of Intervention (ABAB Design)

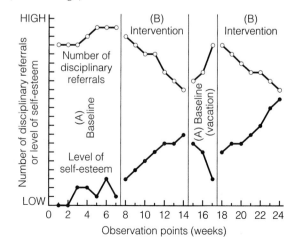

13.2 SINGLE-CASE DESIGNS IN SOCIAL WORK

When the preceding logic of time series analysis is applied to the evaluation of outcome with individual cases, the research designs can be termed *single-subject designs*, *single-case designs*, or *single-system designs*. The latter two terms are favored by those who seek to remind us that client systems need not be individual subjects, but can include a family unit, a community, and so on. The term *single-case designs* has become the more commonly used term in social work. Regardless of what we call them, a distinguishing feature of these designs is that the sample size is one. Whether our unit of analysis is one individual, one family, one community, or one organization, the number of sampling elements is one. Consequently, one of the chief limitations of these designs is their dubious external validity. In Chapter 11 we discussed the precariousness of generalizing from samples that lacked adequate size or selection procedures. What, then, are we to think of a sampling approach that contains only one element?

With a high degree of internal validity, single-case experiments can identify those interventions that seem to work in one, perhaps idiosyncratic, context, and can be tested for generalizability in subsequent studies. These later studies might include larger-scale experiments that use control groups, or they might be additional single-case experiments that attempt to replicate the original single-case experiment in other contexts. For example, suppose a gerontological social worker finds, based on his or her results in a single-case design, that reviewing life history with a particular client in a nursing home significantly improved the client's morale and diminished the client's depression. Gerontological social workers in other nursing homes with similar clients could attempt to replicate the intervention and study. To the extent that they also replicate the results, evidence would then accumulate that supported the generalizability of the findings. Ultimately, this evidence may be sufficient to secure the more extensive degree of support needed to make feasible a larger-scale experiment utilizing a control group. But even if a larger control group experiment is never conducted, the accumulation of single-case evidence will advance the scientific basis for continuing to deliver the tested intervention.

Accumulating findings of single-case experiments has value not only in advancing the scientific basis of particular interventions or of a particular practitioner's effectiveness, but also in evaluating an entire agency or program. Suppose, for example, that a funding source calls for a program evaluation to determine whether a family service agency is providing effective services and thus merits continued or perhaps increased levels of support. Suppose further that administrative and ethical considerations rule out the possibility of using a control group in the evaluation. One option might be to conduct a time series design. However, suppose target problems and service objectives vary substantially from case to case. The objective might be to reduce a child's antisocial behavior in one case, decrease marital conflict in another, prevent abusive parental behavior in a third, and so on. One option would be to conduct a separate single-case experiment on each case or on a representative subset of cases, and to use the idiosyncratic case objectives or target problems as the dependent variable in each experiment. The agency could then report not only the proportion of its cases that attain successful outcomes, but also (and more important) the proportion of those outcomes that the logic of time series analysis shows to have been caused specifically by receiving agency services.

A reverse process can also be cited to justify the value of single-case designs—that is, individual practitioners or agencies may wonder whether interventions supported initially by group experiments in other settings will work as well in their particular, and perhaps idiosyncratic, context. For instance, suppose a few gerontological social workers first learned about reviewing life histories from an experiment reported in a gerontological social work journal, and they wondered whether they were capable of implementing the reported intervention as effectively and whether their particular clients would be able to benefit from it as much as those in the reported study, whose characteristics may have been inadequately specified or may have differed slightly from those of their clients. They could conduct single-case experiments with one or more clients to answer these questions for themselves. Such experiments would reduce their doubt not only about the effectiveness of particular interventions with particular clients, but also about their own effectiveness as clinical practitioners.

13.2a Use of Single-Case Designs as Part of Social Work Practice

EP 2.1.6b
EP 2.1.10m

Single-case designs can be implemented by some social work practitioners as part of their own clinical practice with some clients. Because these designs require only one case, the practitioner need not worry about amassing large samples or assigning clients to control groups. Each experiment contains idiosyncratic objectives that are applicable to an individual case—objectives that the practitioner would be helping the client attain as a routine part of practice were no experiment to take place. Likewise, the practitioner would routinely want to monitor the client's progress in attaining those objectives. By taking repeated measures of changes in the target problem, the practitioner both monitors client progress (or lack thereof) and acquires a tool for a more systematic understanding of events or circumstances that may exacerbate or ameliorate the target problem. For example, suppose a child in a joint-custody arrangement is being treated for explosive and antisocial behaviors. Suppose further that the problematic behaviors tend to occur shortly before the child is about to go into the custody of one or the other parent. Repeated measures of the target behavior might help the practitioner chronologically identify this coincidence during the initial stages of service delivery, which in turn would help the practitioner better understand the causes of the target problem and develop an appropriate strategy to deal with it. Practitioners who spend considerable amounts of time unsystematically attempting to record and evaluate their practices might find conducting single-case designs to be one way to make that effort more systematic and valid.

There are, however, practical obstacles to integrating single-case designs as part of direct practice. These constraints make it unrealistic for many practitioners to utilize these designs, particularly when they are working in certain kinds of agency settings or with certain types of target problems. Client crises often do not allow practitioners enough time to take repeated measures to identify baseline trends before implementing an intervention. In some settings, heavy caseloads reduce the amount of time practitioners have to plan or conduct repeated measures during any phase. The practitioner's peers and supervisors in an agency may not recognize the value of researching one's own practice effectiveness and therefore may not support it. Clients may resent the extensive self-monitoring procedures that these designs may require.

Despite these obstacles, social work practitioners should strive to implement single-case designs whenever they can. Social work practice often entails providing interventions or services that have not yet received adequate scientific testing concerning their beneficial or harmful effects on clients. In light of this doubt about our effectiveness, the question may not be whether each of us can afford the time needed to use single-case methodology as part of our practices, but whether our profession can afford not to allocate the time. Given our commitment to the social welfare of our clients and our aspiration to call our work truly professional, we can conduct single-case experiments when implementing untested interventions to see whether they are helping clients, harming them, or merely wasting scarce resources that could be put to better use.

Wasting scarce resources in the social welfare arena is not just a question of efficiency or public accountability but also one of compassion and professional concern for clients. If we are wasting our own and the client's time on ineffectual services, then we are not ameliorating suffering. Neither are we able to use that time to implement alternative services that might really help that client. By conducting single-case designs as part of their practice, social work practitioners can obtain immediate feedback that will indicate whether they should modify the service program to better help (or perhaps stop hindering) specific clients.

13.2b Single-Case Design Methods in Evidence-Based Practice

Our point is not that practitioners would necessarily become researchers intent on publishing their findings, but that the use of scientific measurement procedures and single-case design logic is an important part of evidence-based practice, as we discussed in

Chapter 2. You may recall from that chapter that the final step in the evidence-based practice process involves assessing whether the selected intervention appears to be effective. When practitioners employ single-case design measurement procedures after having completed the earlier phases of the evidence-based practice process, the need for them to identify baseline trends before implementing the intervention becomes less important. That's because they already have determined—in the earlier steps of the evidence-based practice process—that the selected intervention has been shown in previous studies to have the best internally valid evidence supporting its probable effectiveness for the practice situation in question.

Earlier in this chapter we noted that a proper baseline with multiple measurement points serves the same function as a control group in controlling for threats to internal validity such as history and maturation. But if previous experiments or quasi-experiments have already controlled for those threats, then the practitioner has less need to rule out those threats as explanations for client progress. Because the earlier phases of the evidence-based practice process have already established causality regarding the intervention in question, the practitioner's concern is limited to assessing whether the desired outcome is achieved with his or her specific client.

You might ask, however, "If that's the case, why engage in the final step of the evidence-based practice process at all? That is, if we already know that the selected intervention has the best evidence regarding its probable effectiveness, why must we assess outcome?" The answer involves two key terms: *probable* and *external validity*.

In regard to the term *probable*, we know of no group experimental evaluation that found that any tested intervention was successful with *every* client. The most effective interventions are merely those that have the greatest *likelihood* of success. Suppose, for example, that a rigorous experiment finds that a new intervention for PTSD among Iraq war veterans reduces trauma symptoms significantly among 80 percent of the experimental group, compared to only 40 percent among control group recipients of routine treatment. That would be a very impressive finding indeed. Nevertheless, despite its superior effectiveness, the findings would indicate that 20 percent of the recipients of

the new intervention did not have a successful outcome. How would you know whether your client would be in that 20 percent? By monitoring whether his or her trauma symptoms are changing during treatment, you could find the answer. And if he or she appeared to be in that 20 percent, you would realize the need to try an alternative treatment approach.

In regard to *external validity*, you may recall from Chapter 12 that the findings of even the best, most internally valid experiments do not generalize to all clients and conditions outside of the experiment. In fact, the most tightly controlled experiments often exclude clients like those seen in real-world social work agencies. The clients in such experiments often are of the same ethnicity, are highly motivated, and do not suffer from multiple problems that impede treatment. Unlike those clients, social worker caseloads often are comprised of clients of minority ethnicity, involuntarily referred and less motivated clients, or clients whose target problems are combined with other problems (such as poverty or substance abuse) that complicate treatment efforts. Perhaps, for example, your Iraq war veteran client not only has PTSD, but also is addicted to drugs, homeless, and physically disabled.

In addition, the best, most internally valid experiments commonly are conducted under ideal practice conditions. The practitioners may have received extensive training and supervision in the evaluated intervention by the best trainers and supervisors possible, perhaps even being trained and supervised by the luminary who invented the tested intervention. Also, their caseload sizes are typically much smaller than those in real-world agency practice. Consequently, no matter how gifted you might be in your practice, you might not be nearly as effective in providing the new intervention to your client as the practitioners were in the published experiment in treating their clients. By using single-case design techniques you could monitor treatment progress. You might not know why the desired degree of progress was or was not being achieved, but at least you would know whether you should continue with the same treatment approach or modify it.

The main point of this section is that you could know these things without having to delay treatment to establish a baseline. If there were no obstacles to establish a pre-intervention baseline, all the better. But in the face of such obstacles, just monitoring progress during intervention would tell you whether to stick to the chosen intervention plan or change it. Later in this chapter we'll discuss alternative single-case designs. You'll see that the symbol for all but one of those designs begins with the letter A, which refers to the baseline phase. All of the designs also contain the letter B, which refers to the intervention phase. (Those symbols were also displayed in Figures 13.1, 13.2, and 13.3, discussed earlier.) You'll also see one design that contains the letter B only. That design pertains to situations in which practitioners have completed the previous steps of the evidence-based practice process, face obstacles in establishing a baseline (A) phase, and are limiting the purpose of the final step of the evidence-based practice process to monitoring client progress—not to ruling out threats to internal validity and thus inferring causality.

Before examining alternative designs, we'll discuss measurement issues. As we examine those issues, as well as alternative designs after that, we suggest that you bear the following in mind. Even if you think you will only use the B phase (and no A phase) in your practice—that is, even if you only anticipate monitoring client progress and not trying to rule out threats to internal validity when you employ single-case design techniques—the evidence you find in the earlier steps of the evidence-based practice process might come from studies employing single-case designs. If so, you'll need to understand the rest of the material in this chapter so that you will be better equipped to appraise the quality of that evidence and thus be better able to judge whether it should guide your decisions (in collaboration with your client) about what interventions to provide.

13.3 MEASUREMENT ISSUES

EP 2.1.10d

An early decision in using single-case design techniques involves identifying the target problem or goal that will serve as the dependent variable of the evaluation. Identifying target problems is chiefly a practice consideration and is treated in depth in various texts on practice and

assessment (such as Hepworth, Rooney, & Larsen, 2002). The next step is to develop an operational definition of that variable.

The operational definition might involve positive indicators that represent the target problem's absence or negative indicators that signify its presence. For instance, as discussed in Chapter 7, an operational definition might involve negative indicators such as slapping or threatening. The goal then would be a reduction in the observed indicators. The operational definition also might include positive indicators such as praising or using time-outs. If so, then the goal would be to increase those indicators. Practitioners might want to restrict their definition to positive indicators for clinical reasons, so that they and the client are not always thinking in negative terms about the problem. They might also choose to monitor several indicators of the problem or goal, perhaps including some that are positive as well as some that are negative.

13.3a What to Measure

Because of the need to obtain many repeated observations in single-case designs, the operational indicators should occur frequently enough to be measured on a regular basis. Thus, assessing indicators such as praising, encouraging, or using time-outs would be preferable to assessing an infrequent event such as how often the parent's abuse results in serious injury.

No strict rule determines how many operational indicators to measure. The fewer we measure, the greater the risk that we fail to detect client improvement on indicators other than those being measured. For example, a case manager might be effective in motivating a chronically mentally ill client to take medication as prescribed and in securing more community support services. But if the case manager only measured the client's degree of psychopathology or job-seeking behavior, then he or she might get negative results and erroneously conclude that the intervention was not working. On the other hand, it is unwise to try to measure so many indicators that the data-gathering process becomes unwieldy and overwhelms the client, practitioner, or both. Moreover, the greater the number of indicators that are monitored, the greater the risk that the data pattern of one or more of them will show improvement after intervention solely on the basis of chance fluctuations.

13.3b Triangulation

As a rule of thumb, two or three indicators are generally considered appropriate, enabling a feasible approach on the one hand, and meeting the criterion of triangulation on the other. As discussed in Chapter 8, *triangulation* is a principle that applies to all types of research designs, not just single-case experiments. It refers to situations in which researchers are confronted with a multiplicity of imperfect measurement options, each having advantages and disadvantages. To maximize the chances that the hypothesized variation in the dependent variable will be detected, more than one measurement option is used. Despite its connotation of a triangle, triangulation does not require using three options, only more than one.

In single-case designs, triangulation does not necessarily mean that more than one target problem is to be measured. It means that more than one indicator of the same target problem is to be measured. For instance, a school social worker whose client is underachieving might want to monitor the amount of time the client spends on homework each night, and teacher ratings of his or her class attentiveness and participation. Triangulation does not require that the social worker also monitor indicators of other problems, such as antisocial behaviors (fighting, disciplinary referrals, and so on). The practitioner may choose to monitor more than one problem, but the principle of triangulation does not require it. The principle of triangulation applies to all measurement options—not just what to measure—and we will consider it again in our discussion of data gathering.

13.4 DATA GATHERING

The options and decisions to be made in planning measurement and data collection in single-case experiments are not unlike those that confront researchers who are designing other types of studies. Researchers must decide whether the data sources should be available records, interviews, self-report scales, or direct observations of behavior. The advantages and disadvantages of these sources are largely the same in single-case experiments as those in other types of research.

13.4a Who Should Measure?

One issue involves who should do the measuring. When practitioners make measurements to evaluate their own practice, the risk of observer bias might be heightened, for it is only human to want to obtain findings that support our practice effectiveness and indicate that client suffering is being ameliorated. Perhaps even riskier is relying exclusively on clients to do the measuring themselves. Clients may be biased to perceive positive results not only to please themselves or to project a socially desirable image to the practitioner, but also to avoid disappointing the practitioner. Significant others (teachers, cottage parents, and so on) might be asked to monitor certain behaviors in the hope that they have less invested than the client or practitioner in seeing a positive outcome. However, neither their objectivity nor their commitment to the study can be guaranteed. This consideration is particularly important in light of the large amount of time and dedication that might be required to monitor the client's behavior carefully and systematically on a continuous basis. In light of the repeated measures required by single-case designs and the strong potential for bias, there is no easy answer about who should do the measuring. Here, then, we return to the principle of triangulation and perhaps use all three of the preceding options to gather the data. In this context, we see another advantage of triangulation—the opportunity it provides for assessing measurement reliability. To the extent that different data gatherers agree in their measures, we can have more confidence that the data are accurate.

13.4b Sources of Data

In considering alternative sources of data (available records, interviews, self-report scales, or direct behavioral observations), several issues are particularly salient in single-case designs. Available records, for example, might enable the researcher or practitioner to obtain a *retrospective baseline* of pretreatment trends (see later discussion) and therefore not have to delay treatment while collecting baseline data. This development, of course, can occur only when we are fortunate enough to have access to existing records that contain carefully gathered, reliable data that happen to correspond to the way the target problem has been operationally defined in the single-case experiment.

Self-report scales also merit special consideration in single-case designs. On the one hand, they can be quite convenient; repeated measures can be expedited by simply having clients complete a brief self-report scale each day where they reside or each time the practitioner sees them. Self-report scales also ensure that the repeated measures are administered and scored in a uniform fashion.

On the other hand, the use of these scales carries special risks in single-case experiments. For one thing, clients might lose interest in completing them carefully over and over again. Perhaps a more serious risk, however, is the potential for the client to be biased to complete these scales with responses that convey a socially desirable impression. This risk would be greatest when the single-case experiment is being conducted by practitioners to evaluate their own practice, because clients might be particularly predisposed to give inaccurate responses to please the clinicians about their helpfulness or favorably impress them.

13.4c Reliability and Validity

Readers might wonder at this point whether these risks could be avoided by using standardized self-report scales with established high levels of reliability and validity. All other things being equal (such as relevance to the problem or client, sensitivity to change, and instrument length and complexity), of course it is better to use scales whose reliability and validity have been empirically supported, if such scales are available for the particular variable one seeks to measure. However, the conditions under which the validity of standardized instruments is tested tend to contrast with single-case experimental conditions in critical ways. Standardized instruments tend to be validated in large-scale assessment studies in which (1) the respondent is part of a large group of individuals who have no special, ongoing relationship with the researcher and who are by and large anonymous; (2) the instrument will not be completed more than one or two times by each

respondent; and (3) a respondent's score on the instrument has no bearing on whether he or she is benefiting from some service.

In contrast, when clients complete these instruments as part of single-case experiments, they are not anonymous and have a special relationship with a service provider. They may therefore be sensitive about the impression they are conveying and be more intent on conveying a favorable impression than in a more anonymous situation. With each repeated completion of the instrument, their answers may become less valid, perhaps because of carelessness or because they remember their previous answers. Finally, and perhaps most important, they may be keenly aware of the difference between nontreatment (baseline) phases and treatment phases; they may know that if the service is being effective, then their scores should improve during the treatment phases. This awareness may predispose them to convey a more positive impression during the treatment phases. In light of these differences, we cannot assume that a particular self-report instrument will adequately avoid social desirability biases in a single-case experiment just because it has empirically been shown in other contexts not to have serious validity problems.

13.4d Direct Behavioral Observation

The large number of repeated measures desired in single-case experiments also complicates the decision to use direct behavioral observations as the data source. This feature is particularly problematic when the experiment is conducted as part of one's own practice, because busy practitioners may lack the time needed to conduct the observations themselves or the resources needed to induce someone else to observe the client. To the extent that observation of the target problem can be limited to office or home visits, the difficulty of practitioner observation is reduced.

Also, the direct observation of behavior does not always require continuous observation. *Spot-check recording* can be used to observe target behaviors that occur frequently, last a long time, or are expected to occur during specified periods. For instance, suppose a social worker in a residential treatment facility for distressed adolescents introduces a behavioral modification intervention that seeks to increase the amount of school homework that residents do during specified study periods each evening. The social worker or a cottage parent could briefly glance at the study area each evening, varying the precise time of the observation from day to day, and quickly record whether or not specified individuals were studying (yes or no) or simply count how many were studying at that particular moment.

But many target problems need to be observed on a more continuous basis. Barring the availability of a significant other (such as a teacher, relative, or cottage parent) who is willing to observe on a regular basis, we are commonly forced to rely on our clients to observe themselves. The term for client self-observation is *self-monitoring*. If the dependent variable is the number of a certain type of thoughts or feelings that a client has during a particular period—phenomena that only the client could observe—then self-monitoring would be the only direct-observation option.

The problem with self-monitoring is that, in addition to its vulnerability to measurement bias (as discussed earlier), it is highly vulnerable to the problem of *research reactivity*. (We discussed research reactivity in Chapter 12.) One way in which reactivity can occur is when the process of observing or recording the data—that is, the self-measurement process itself—brings about change in the target problem. For example, suppose a practitioner encourages a mother who has a conflictual relationship with her son to record each time she praises him and each time she scolds him. Regardless of what else the practitioner does, the mere act of recording may sensitize the mother to her tendency to scold her son too often and praise him too rarely. This sensitization in turn may bring her to praise him more and scold him less.

From a clinical standpoint, of course, reactivity might not be such a bad idea—that is, self-monitoring can be used as a clinical tool to help bring about the desired change. Indeed, it's often used that way, but when it's used as the only measurement procedure in research, it clouds the process of inferring whether the intervention alone brought about the change. This problem can be offset somewhat by the realization that if self-monitoring alone is bringing about the desired change, then the change might be detected by noticing an improving trend in a graph of the pretreatment (baseline) data.

13.4e Unobtrusive Versus Obtrusive Observation

As discussed in Chapter 12, *unobtrusive observation* means that the observer blends into the observation setting in such a way that the act of observing and recording is by and large not noticeable to those who are being observed. For example, a group worker who is attempting to reduce the amount of antisocial behavior by boys in a residential facility might ask a colleague who supervises their recreational activities to observe the number of fights, arguments, and so on the targeted boys get into, and record the numbers in the notebook that he or she always carries while supervising the boys.

The opposite of unobtrusive observation is *obtrusive observation*. Measurement is obtrusive to the extent that the subject is aware of the observation and therefore vulnerable to research reactivity or to acting in an atypical manner to convey a socially desirable impression. Self-monitoring is perhaps the most obtrusive form of observation because the client is both observee and observer, but many other forms of observation can be so obtrusive that the credibility of the entire study is imperiled. Some of these examples can be deceptive because researchers or practitioners may take steps that at first glance seem to provide some degree of unobtrusiveness.

For example, the researcher or practitioner may observe the client through a one-way mirror, thinking that because the client cannot see him or her, the client is less aware of the observation. To a certain extent this is true. But consider the following wrinkle. After taking pretreatment (baseline) measures through a one-way mirror of a conflictual mother–son dyad interacting, the practitioner introduces a task-centered intervention in which the practitioner and the mother agree that the mother's task will be to try to praise her son more when he acts appropriately. The practitioner continues to monitor the interactions through a one-way mirror to see if the intervention will be effective in increasing the number of statements of praise as compared to the pretreatment baseline.

Although it is commendable that the practitioner made observations while not visible by the clients, it is wrong to suppose that the observations were truly unobtrusive or that the baseline and intervention phases were really comparable in their degree of obtrusiveness. In both phases, the mother has some degree of awareness that the practitioner is watching from the other side of the mirror. And in the intervention phase, she knows precisely which behavior—praise—the practitioner is watching for, knowledge she did not have in the earlier, baseline phase.

Thus, the degree of obtrusiveness in both phases is compounded by the increased vulnerability to a social desirability bias during the intervention phase. And because the client is more inclined to provide the socially desirable response during the intervention phase, the problem of obtrusiveness becomes a bigger threat to the credibility of the findings. In other words, the desired increase in praise could easily have nothing to do with the efficacy of the intervention, but instead merely reflect the fact that after the intervention was introduced, the client became more predisposed to put on a socially desirable performance—one that might have no correlation whatsoever to the way the mother interacts with her child in a natural setting or when the practitioner is not watching.

13.4f Data Quantification Procedures

Data gathered through direct observation in single-case designs can be quantified in terms of their *frequency*, *duration*, or *magnitude*. For example, the target problem of temper tantrums could be recorded in terms of the number of temper tantrums observed in a specified period (frequency), how long each tantrum lasted (duration), or how loud or violent it was (magnitude). With the principle of triangulation, all three quantification procedures could be used simultaneously.

13.4g The Baseline Phase

The logic of single-case designs requires taking enough repeated measures to make it unlikely that extraneous factors (such as changes in the client's environment) would account for improvements that take place in the target problem with the onset of intervention. The logic also relies on comparing trends that are identified in the repeated measures to control for factors such as maturation or statistical regression. Based on this logic, the internal validity of single-case designs is enhanced when the baseline period has enough measurement points to show a stable trend in the target problem, and enough points to establish the unlikelihood that extraneous events that affect the target problem will coincide only with the onset of intervention. Although the ideal number of baseline measurement points needed will vary depending on how soon a stable trend appears, it is reasonable to plan for somewhere between 5 and 10 baseline measures. With some stable baselines, one can begin to see trends with as few as three to five data points. However, the more data points we have, the more confidence we can have in the stability of the observed trend and in the unlikelihood that extraneous events will coincide only with the onset of intervention.

The realities of practice do not always permit us to take an ideal number of baseline measures, however. For example, the client's problem might be too urgent to delay intervention any longer, even though the baseline trend appears unstable or is unclear. When an ideal baseline length is not feasible, we simply come as close to the ideal as the clinical and administrative realities permit.

A stable trend is one that shows the target problem to be occurring in a predictable and orderly fashion. The trend is identified by plotting the data points chronologically on a graph, drawing a line between each data point, and then observing whether the overall pattern is clearly increasing (Figure 13.4(A)), decreasing (Figure 13.4(B)), relatively flat (Figure 13.4(C)), or cyclical (Figure 13.4(D)). By contrast, Figure 13.4(E) illustrates an unstable baseline without an obvious clear trend.

The meaning of increasing or decreasing baselines depends on the operational definition of the target problem. If it involves undesirable phenomena such as temper tantrums, then an increasing baseline trend would mean the problem is worsening, and a decreasing baseline would indicate improvement. If the operational definition involves desirable indicators such as doing homework, then an increasing baseline would signify improvement and a decreasing baseline would signify deterioration.

FIGURE 13.4 Alternative Baseline Trends

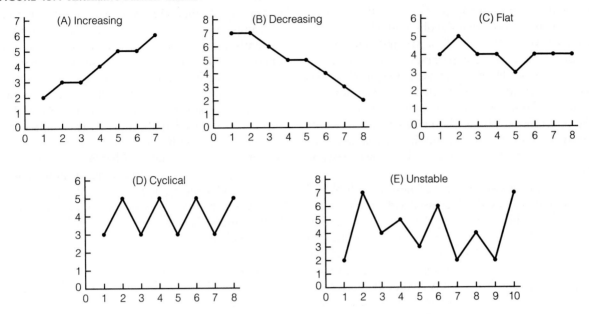

When the baseline trend signifies improvement, even if it is stable, it may be advisable to continue collecting baseline measures until the improving trend levels off, as illustrated in Figure 13.5. If intervention is introduced at the peak of an improving baseline trend (before it levels off), it will be difficult to achieve a dramatic improvement in the trend. In other words, the baseline trend would mean that the client was improving so steadily without any intervention that (1) even an effective intervention might not affect the rate of improvement, and (2) perhaps no intervention on that particular indicator was needed in the first place. Introducing an intervention

FIGURE 13.5 Graph of Hypothetical Outcome after Extending a Baseline with an Improving Trend (AB Design)

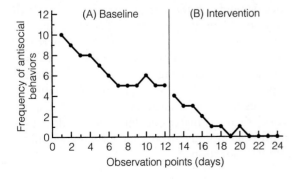

on the heels of a steadily improving baseline therefore makes it difficult to obtain results in the B phase that would depict even an effective intervention as being effective.

Suppose, for example, that the intervention being evaluated is effective in helping *most* clients quit smoking. Further suppose, however, that the data pattern like the one in Figure 13.5 pertains to that intervention being evaluated with a client who is so motivated and otherwise capable of quitting smoking that he is already engaged in a successful effort to quit smoking before the intervention commences and that his effort will soon result in a cessation of smoking with or without providing him with this intervention. The results in Figure 13.5 would not imply that the intervention was effective for this client, even though he succeeded in quitting smoking, because his rate of improvement during the baseline phase was not improved upon during the intervention phase. Although the results would not indicate that the intervention made a difference for *this* client, it would be wrong to conclude that the intervention is ineffective. We would not know whether it is effective or ineffective for most clients who are not already engaged in a successful effort to quit smoking.

We would also want to extend baseline measures beyond the point at which we initially planned to introduce the intervention if the baseline data collected up to that point were unstable (that is, if they failed to yield a predictable trend). As noted earlier, when we observe an unstable baseline, we ideally would extend the baseline measures until a stable pattern appears. However, it was also noted that the constraints of practice do not always permit us to extend the baseline until a desirable trend is obtained. Other priorities, such as client suffering or endangerment, may take precedence over the internal validity of the research design. If so, then we simply do the best we can with what we have. Perhaps the intervention is so effective that even an unstable or improving baseline pattern will prove to be clearly worse than the intervention data pattern. Figure 13.6 shows an unstable baseline juxtaposed with two alternative intervention data patterns. One pattern illustrates the difficulty of interpreting outcome with an unstable baseline; the other pattern shows that it is not necessarily impossible to do so. In a similar vein, Figure 13.7 illustrates that even with an improving baseline it may be possible to obtain results that support the efficacy of the intervention.

We also might want to deviate from the planned time of completion of the baseline phase when, after the design is implemented, we learn that extraneous environmental changes that may have a potentially important effect on the target problem will coincide with the beginning of the intervention period. For example, if the client has a severe hay fever problem and the target behavior is something like interpersonal irritability or school performance, then we would not want to introduce the intervention at

FIGURE 13.7 Graph of a Hypothetical Outcome Supporting Intervention Efficacy with an Improving Baseline (AB Design)

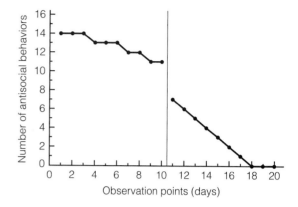

the beginning or end of the hay fever season. If we learn of such a situation after the baseline phase has begun, then we might extend the baseline longer than initially planned so that it includes enough data points to identify a stable trend after the relevant environmental conditions have changed. Another option would be to later withdraw the intervention for a short time and then reintroduce it, hoping that the hiatus from treatment would provide a second baseline whose beginning or end would not coincide with important environmental changes. (This latter option is called an ABAB design, and it will be examined in more depth shortly.)

When you cannot delay intervention to take baseline measures, you should consider whether it is possible to obtain a useful retrospective baseline. Also called a *reconstructed baseline*, a **retrospective baseline** is constructed again from past data. The two primary sources of data for a retrospective baseline are available records and the memory of the client (or significant others). An example of using available records would be obtaining school records on attendance, grades, detentions, and so on for a child who has behavioral problems in school. An example of using memory, provided in a study by Nugent (1991), would be asking clients with anger control problems to recall how many

retrospective baseline A type of pre-intervention single-case evaluation design phase that consists of chronologically ordered data points that are reconstructed from past data.

FIGURE 13.6 Graph of Two Hypothetical Outcomes with an Unstable Baseline (AB Design)

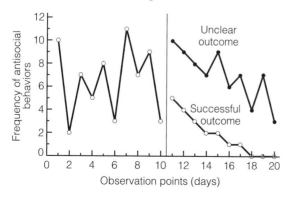

blowups they had during the previous week or two, and perhaps triangulating their data with spouse or parent recollections. Bloom, Fischer, and Orme (2009) offer the following two guidelines when relying on memory to reconstruct a baseline: (1) Use specific, identifiable events that are easy to recall (such as angry blowups, detention referrals, and so on) and therefore less vulnerable to distortion than things that are harder to recall (such as feelings of inadequacy, anxiety, and so on); and (2) for the same reason, use only the immediate past, such as the past week or two, and do not go back more than one month.

13.5 ALTERNATIVE SINGLE-CASE DESIGNS

13.5a AB: The Basic Single-Case Design

As illustrated in Figures 13.1, 13.2, 13.5, 13.6, and 13.7, the simplest single-case design includes one baseline phase (A) and one intervention phase (B). This is a popular design among practitioner/researchers because it involves only one baseline phase and therefore poses the least conflict with service delivery priorities. But this design is weaker than single-case designs with more baselines. With only one baseline, there is only one point at which the independent variable shifts from baseline to intervention. Consequently, only one unlikely coincidence can occur. Although taking many repeated measures reduces the plausibility that some extraneous event and not the intervention would explain a major shift in the data pattern of the dependent variable that occurs only after the onset of intervention, extraneous events are controlled much better when there are several shifts between baseline and intervention phases.

Despite its *relative* weakness, the AB design is still quite useful. More rigorous designs may not be feasible in many practice situations, and with enough repeated measures the AB design can provide some logical and empirical evidence about the effectiveness of interventions for which the impact on clients has not yet received enough scientific testing. Also, AB designs can be replicated, and if the results of various AB studies on the same intervention are consistent, then the evidence about the effectiveness of the intervention is strengthened.

For instance, suppose several AB studies at different times and with different clients all find that the same type of target problem begins to improve only shortly after the same intervention is introduced. How credible is the argument that with every client an extraneous event could have coincided only with the onset of intervention and caused the improvement? AB designs are also useful in that they provide practitioners with immediate feedback that enables them to monitor variations in the target problem, explore with the client alternative explanations of changes, and modify service delivery if the need for modification is indicated by this information.

13.5b ABAB: Withdrawal/Reversal Design

To better control for extraneous events, the ABAB design adds a second baseline phase (A) and a second intervention phase (B). This design was illustrated in Figure 13.3 and is also illustrated in Figures 13.8 and 13.9. The second baseline phase is established by withdrawing the intervention for a while. After a stable trend is identified in the second baseline, the intervention is reintroduced. This design assumes that if the intervention caused the improvement in the target problem during the first intervention period, then the target problem will reverse toward its original baseline level during the second baseline (after the intervention is withdrawn). When the intervention is reintroduced, the

FIGURE 13.8 Graph of Hypothetical Outcome of ABAB Design Supporting Intervention Efficacy Despite Failure to Obtain a Reversal during Second Baseline

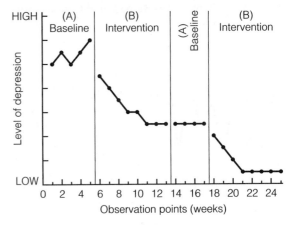

FIGURE 13.9 Graph of Hypothetical Outcome of ABAB Design with Unclear Results

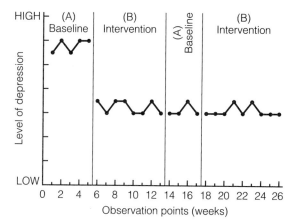

target problem should start improving again. The basic inferential principle here is that if shifts in the trend or level of the target problem occur successively each time the intervention is introduced or withdrawn, then it is not plausible that some extraneous event and not the intervention is causing the change. Because the independent variable is changed three times, there is more causal evidence than in the AB design. In other words, the number of unlikely successive coincidences that would have to occur in an ABAB design is three rather than one in the AB design.

The ABAB design has two major problems, although both often can be resolved. One is a practical or ethical problem. Practitioners may feel that withdrawing an intervention that appears to be working is indefensible in light of the suffering or other costs the client may bear if conditions revert to baseline. These concerns would be intensified with clients who had dangerous problems or who were particularly sensitive to setbacks. Practitioners may fear that withdrawal of the intervention would confuse or alienate the client and perhaps hurt the practitioner–client relationship or in other ways impede future efforts when the intervention is reintroduced. These are important and valid concerns, and researchers should not fault practitioners who resist implementing ABAB designs because of these concerns.

Practitioners, however, should not underestimate the opportunities they have for implementing ABAB designs without compromising intervention priorities. Occasionally, there are natural breaks in

the intervention phase when the practitioner attends a conference or takes a vacation, and these periods can be exploited to establish a second baseline (provided that the practitioner is not the only one observing and recording the extent of the target problem). Also, it is often consistent with good practice to withdraw an intervention temporarily at a point at which the target problem appears to have been overcome and then monitor whether the client can sustain his or her gains during the hiatus of treatment.

The second major, but potentially resolvable, problem with ABAB designs is that the assumption that the target problem can revert to baseline conditions may not be valid in many practice situations. Perhaps an intervention has had irreversible effects during the first intervention period. For instance, suppose the intervention involved social skills training, perhaps training individuals with mild developmental disabilities to interact at social gatherings or in the workplace. Once these skills are learned and the individuals are rewarded in the natural environment for using them, they may not need training to be reintroduced to be able to sustain the gains they have made. Or suppose the intervention was to help an elderly woman become less isolated, lonely, and depressed. Suppose further that the intervention was environmentally oriented and focused on securing a better residence for her, one where she would be among peers with whom she could easily interact and become friends. If this intervention succeeded during the first B period, is it reasonable to suppose that she would lose her new friends or become depressed again because the practitioner withdrew the intervention (that is, efforts to change her environment, not the new residence)?

To reduce the chances that effects will be irreversible, in some situations we might want to keep the first intervention period relatively short. Then, as soon as the second baseline shows a trend toward reversal, we could reintroduce the intervention and hope to reestablish the improving trend that was briefly interrupted during the second baseline. Irreversible effects also may be less problematic if, despite the failure to obtain a reversal during the second baseline, we observed a new, improving trend during the second intervention period. Suppose, for example, that in the case of the depressed and lonely elderly woman, we reintroduce the environmentally oriented intervention by getting her a pet and that this further alleviates her depression. This possibility is illustrated in Figure 13.8, in which we see a shift in the dependent variable each time the intervention is introduced, but gains made during the first intervention phase are maintained during the second baseline. Despite the absence of a reversal during the second baseline, the data's overall pattern would support the conclusion that it is the intervention and not some extraneous variable that accounts for the improvement and that the intervention's effects simply do not tend to reverse when the intervention is withdrawn.

So what do we conclude when the results of the ABAB design resemble those in Figure 13.9? Was the improvement that occurred only after the first introduction of the intervention caused by some extraneous event that happened to coincide with that introduction? In other words, should we refrain from attributing the improvement to the effects of the intervention because no other changes occurred in the target problem the next two times the intervention was introduced or withdrawn? Or can we speculate that perhaps the intervention was so effective, or the nature of the target problem made its improvement so irreversible, that only one shift in the trend or level of the target problem (that is, the shift at the onset of the first intervention phase) was possible? Depending on the nature of the target problem and what we learn from the client about extraneous events that coincide with changes in the design phases, it may be possible in some cases to decide which of these rival explanations seems to be the most plausible. But perhaps an even better way to resolve this dilemma is through **replication**. If results like those depicted in Figure 13.9 tend to be obtained consistently in future ABAB experiments on the same intervention, then the case for powerful or irreversible effects would be strengthened because there is no rational reason why extraneous events that cause shifts in the target problem

---

replication   The duplication of a study to expose or reduce error, or the reintroduction or withdrawal of an intervention to increase the internal validity of a quasi-experiment or single-case design evaluation.

multiple-baseline design   A type of single-case evaluation design that attempts to control for extraneous variables by having more than one baseline and intervention phase.

should occur with every client only at those points at which intervention is first introduced.

13.5c Multiple-Baseline Designs

Multiple-baseline designs also attempt to control for extraneous variables by having more than one baseline and intervention phase. But instead of withdrawing the intervention to establish more than one baseline, multiple-baseline designs initiate two or more baselines simultaneously, by measuring different target behaviors in each baseline or by measuring the same target behavior in two different settings or across two different individuals. Although each baseline starts simultaneously, the intervention is introduced at a different point for each one. Thus, as the intervention is introduced for the first behavior, setting, or individual, the others are still in their baseline phases. Likewise, when the intervention is introduced for the second behavior, setting, or individual, the third (if there are more than two) is still in its baseline phase.

The main logical principle here is that if some extraneous event, such as a significant improvement in the environment, coincides with the onset of intervention and causes the client's improved functioning, then that improvement will show up in the graph of each behavior, setting, or individual at the same time, even though some might still be in baseline. On the other hand, if the intervention is accountable for the improvement, then that improvement will occur on each graph at a different point that corresponds to the introduction of the intervention.

Figure 13.10 illustrates a hypothetical multiple-baseline design across three nursing home residents who feel an extreme sense of hopelessness. In this hypothetical illustration, the practitioner read a report of a group experiment by Mercer and Kane (1979), the findings of which supported the efficacy of reducing hopelessness in residents like these by having them care for a houseplant. The practitioner begins taking baseline measures of hopelessness via a self-report scale for each resident at the same time. Then he or she gives each resident a houseplant, along with instructions about caring for it, at three different times. Each resident's level of hopelessness, as reflected in the self-report scores, begins to decrease steadily only after the intervention is introduced. Therefore, it is not reasonable to suppose that some extraneous event, such as some other

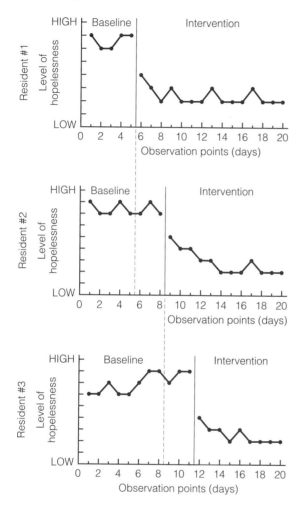

FIGURE 13.10 Graph of Hypothetical Outcome of Multiple-Baseline Design across Subjects Supporting Efficacy of Intervention

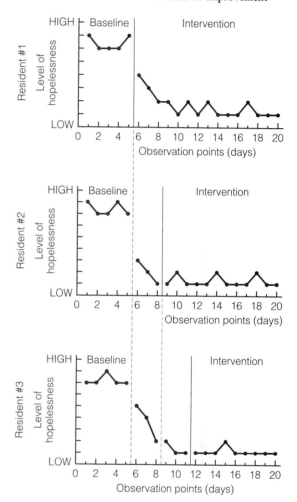

FIGURE 13.11 Graph of Hypothetical Outcome of Multiple-Baseline Design across Subjects Illustrating Extraneous Variable as Plausible Case of Improvement

improvement in the overall environment of the nursing home, really caused the change.

But suppose the results looked like those in Figure 13.11. There we see that the steady improvement in hopelessness commenced for each resident at the same time that the first intervention (houseplant) was introduced. It is not plausible to infer that the plant was causing the improvement because two of the residents had not yet received theirs. Instead, it is more plausible to suppose that some extraneous improvement in the broader nursing home environment coincided with the onset of the intervention with the first resident and caused the improvement in all three. This example illustrates how an AB

design (with the first resident) could yield misleading findings because of its weaker control for history than occurs in multiple-baseline designs.

Figures 13.12 and 13.13 illustrate the same logical principles with multiple-baseline designs across target behaviors or settings. Both figures refer to a hypothetical case that involves a boy referred to a residential treatment center because of his antisocial behaviors. There he participates in a cognitive-behavior modification intervention that includes teaching him how to say things to himself to help stop him from committing explosive, antisocial behaviors in situations in which he has been most vulnerable to losing control. In Figure 13.12, the first baseline ends and

FIGURE 13.12 Graph of Hypothetical Outcome of Multiple-Baseline Design across Target Behaviors, with Unclear Results

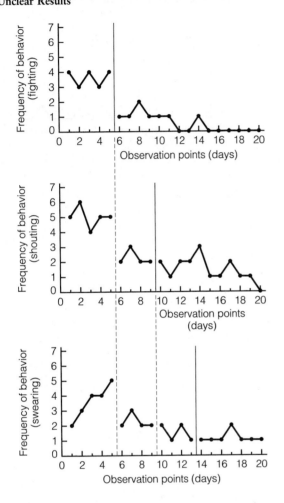

FIGURE 13.13 Graph of Hypothetical Outcome of Multiple-Baseline Design across Settings, with Unclear Results

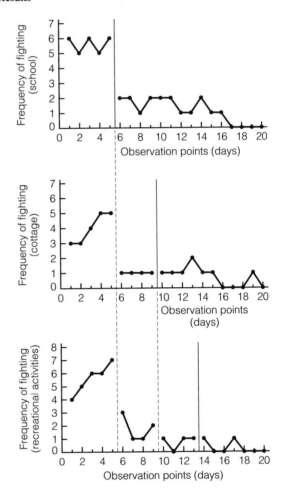

intervention begins as the client starts to rehearse the verbal self-instructions in connection to fighting. One week later, he begins to rehearse in connection to impulsive, inappropriate shouting. The following week he starts rehearsing in connection to swearing.

The graphs in Figure 13.12 show that once the client begins rehearsing for fighting, a dramatic shift in the data pattern occurs for all three target behaviors at the same time. What caused this reaction?

generalization of effects   A rival explanation in a multiple-baseline design that occurs when an intervention that is intended to apply to only one behavior or setting affects other behaviors or settings that are still in baseline.

Was it an extraneous event in the residential facility that happened to coincide with the end of the first baseline? Perhaps. But when multiple baselines are applied across different behaviors, a data pattern like this could also be caused by a rival explanation, one termed generalization of effects. **Generalization of effects** occurs when an intervention, although intended to apply to only one behavior or setting at a time, affects other target behaviors or settings that are still in the baseline phase as soon as it is applied to the first behavior or setting. In the current illustration, for instance, the rehearsals regarding fighting perhaps helped the boy simultaneously apply the verbal self-instructions to other behaviors that he knew got him into trouble.

Another way that generalization of effects could occur is when the intervention affects only one target behavior, but the change in that behavior changes the other behaviors in turn. In the preceding illustration, for example, the reduction in fighting conceivably gave the boy less to shout and swear about. The reduction in fighting also could have led to more positive feedback from peers and adults, and this improvement in his interpersonal relations (or the rewarding nature of the feedback) could have reduced his need to swear and shout or increased his desire to act appropriately.

The same sort of ambiguity in the data pattern appears in Figure 13.13. Here the three baselines end as the boy rehearses the verbal self-instructions across three different settings. At the end of the first baseline, he rehearses in connection to school. At the end of the second, he rehearses in connection to the cottage. At the end of the third, he rehearses in connection to recreational activities. As in Figure 13.12, we do not know whether the simultaneous improvement in all three settings at the end of the first baseline resulted from an extraneous event or from generalization of effects.

How do we decide which rival explanation—history or generalization of effects—is the more plausible? We may be unable to do so, but if it is feasible, we might try to replicate the experiment with other clients. If we continue to get results like those in Figures 13.12 and 13.13, then the generalization of effects hypothesis becomes more plausible, because it is not reasonable to suppose that some extraneous event would cause improvement in the target problem only at the point where the first baseline ends when clients were treated at different times.

With some interventions, however, it is difficult to conceive how they possibly could be applied to different behaviors or settings at different times. Suppose, for example, that the intervention involves family systems therapy in a case in which a child's poor functioning in various areas is theoretically thought to stem from problems in the parents' relationship with each other. If the practitioner seeks to resolve the target problem in the child by focusing intervention on the parental relationship, then it may not be realistic to try applying the intervention to different behaviors or settings regarding the child. Moreover, to do so might be deemed clinically inappropriate because it would continue to focus the intervention on the child.

13.5d Multiple-Component Designs

Several designs can be used to analyze the impact of changes in the intervention. These **multiple-component designs** are appropriate when we decide to modify an intervention that does not appear to be helping the client or when we seek to determine which parts of an intervention package really account for the change in the target problem. One such design is the ABCD design. As a hypothetical illustration of this design, suppose a chronically mentally disabled individual is unable to maintain steady employment. The intervention in the B phase might be social skills training to prepare him for job interviews and appropriate on-the-job behavior. If an inadequate degree of improvement is observed, then the social skills training might be replaced by a different intervention in the C phase. Perhaps during C a reward is offered for each real job interview the client undergoes or each week he keeps his job. So far, we would have an ABC design, in which B was the social skills training phase and C was the reinforcement phase. Suppose there still was no improvement, so a case advocacy phase is initiated in the D phase to investigate the possibility that we may need to convince prospective employers to consider hiring or be more tolerant of individuals whose illnesses impede their job-seeking skills or on-the-job behavior. The case advocacy phase, then, would add a fourth component to the design, and we would have an ABCD design.

The preceding design is flexible; it allows practitioners to change intervention plans as warranted by the data patterns that are observed in each successive phase. However, it must be used cautiously because of limitations associated with *carryover effects*, *order effects*, and *history*. In the ABCD illustration, suppose that a sustained pattern of improvement was obtained only during the D phase (case advocacy), as illustrated in Figure 13.14. It would be risky to conclude that for future clients like this one, all we needed to do

---

multiple-component design Single-case evaluation designs that attempt to determine which parts of an intervention package really account for the change in the target problem.

FIGURE 13.14 Graph of Hypothetical Outcome of Multiple-Component (ABCD) Design, with Unclear Results

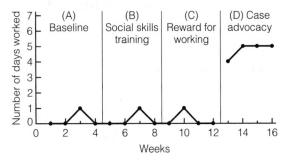

was to provide the case advocacy and not the other two interventions. It is plausible that had we changed the D phase to the B phase for this client, we may not have had the same positive results. Perhaps the client's social skills improved during the original B phase but those skills were insufficient in helping him stay employed, either because employers were unwilling to risk hiring someone with a history of mental illness or because they were unwilling to tolerate any deviance whatsoever from any employee. Conceivably, only with the addition of the case advocacy during the D phase did the improvement in social skills matter. Perhaps the case advocacy would have had no impact had it not been preceded by helping the client attain a level of social functioning that prospective employers could be convinced to tolerate. In other words, the case advocacy might not have worked without the order effects (that is, in coming after the social skills training, not before it) and the carryover effects of the social skills training on the case advocacy efforts. And with respect to the limitation of history, we must recognize that as we continue to substitute new interventions for those whose data patterns do not adequately differ from baseline, we increase the odds that one of those substitutions eventually will coincide with an extraneous improvement in the client's environment.

One way to sort out the preceding possibilities would be to replicate the interventions with future clients, introducing them in a different sequence while measuring outcome in the same way. Ultimately, we might find that the intervention that was originally in the D phase produced the desired results only when it was introduced after the interventions in the original B or C phase.

13.5e B or B+ Designs in Evidence-Based Practice

Earlier in this chapter we discussed how the earlier steps of the evidence-based practice process—in already having ascertained that the chosen intervention has the best internally valid evidence supporting its probable effectiveness for the practice situation in question—can lessen your need to identify baseline trends before implementing the selected intervention. If you have already judged through your appraisal of existing evidence that the chosen intervention has the best chance of success, and particularly if you face practical or ethical barriers to collecting repeated baseline measurement points, you can employ a practitioner friendly design that aims only to monitor client progress—not to help you infer the cause of that progress. Although a design lacking an adequate baseline will not permit causal inferences to be made, it will suffice in guiding decisions about whether to continue, modify, or replace the chosen intervention. That is, it will indicate whether the intervention with the best prior evidence appears to be generalizing to your practice situation.

Lacking a proper baseline, this design contains a B phase only. For example, consider the two graphs in Figure 13.15. Suppose the client's aim is to quit using cocaine. Although the data in the top graph won't tell you what caused him to quit, it will let you know that there is no reason to suppose that the chosen intervention is not applicable to this client or that it needs to be modified. In contrast, the longer data in the bottom graph continued unchanged, the more reason you would have to seek an alternative intervention for this client.

The graphs in Figure 13.15 contain no baseline measurement points whatsoever. However, it's often the case even in real-world agency practice that despite the barriers to collecting repeated baseline measurement points, there is no obstacle to collecting one baseline measurement point. For example, suppose you are trying to alleviate trauma symptoms with a woman who was very recently raped. Although you cannot delay treatment to collect repeated baseline measurement points, you might be able to measure the severity of her trauma symptoms during the assessment phase of your first contact with her. Although that would not be an adequate baseline, it would give you one data

FIGURE 13.15 Contrasting Results Using the B Design Regarding Cocaine Use

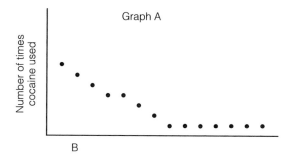

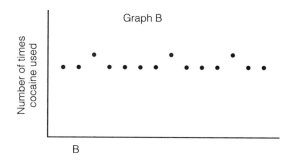

FIGURE 13.16 Contrasting Results Using the B+ Design Regarding Severity of Trauma Symptoms

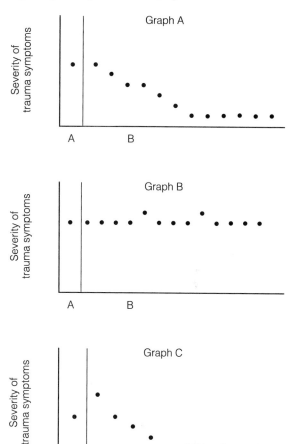

point before the intervention commences. Thus, it can be called a *B+ design* (Rubin, 2008).

The three graphs in Figure 13.16 display some alternative results you might obtain. The preintervention data point in each is signified by A, even though this is not really an AB design because the so-called A phase contains only one measurement point and thus does not establish a preintervention trend. The top graph (like the top one in Figure 13.15) would let you know that there is no reason to suppose that the chosen intervention is not applicable to this client or that it needs to be modified. In contrast, the middle graph, like the bottom one in Figure 13.15, would suggest considering an alternative intervention.

But what about the bottom graph? Things got worse at the start of intervention, but only very briefly. Notice that things soon started getting better. Moreover, it's not unreasonable to suppose that effective treatments for things like trauma (as well as some other problems) might generate some temporary distress as part of recounting in treatment the details of the traumatic experience. In that sense, a very temporary exacerbation can be viewed as consistent with treatment progress.

Finally, consider the graph in Figure 13.17. That graph started out with only a B phase, but with results like the bottom graph in Figure 13.15, which led to the introduction of an alternative intervention in the C phase. Because the B phase unexpectedly led to a new phase, this design, too, can be called a B+ design. Notice that this design is comparable to an AB design. That is, the lack of improvement during B, followed by the switch to a different intervention, made the B become a baseline for C. Thus, the results in Figure 13.17 would tell you three things: (1) the B intervention needed to be changed or abandoned, (2) the C intervention did not need to be changed or abandoned, and (3) the C intervention appears to be a very plausible cause of the improvement in trauma symptoms.

FIGURE 13.17 Illustration of B+ Results That Form an AB Design

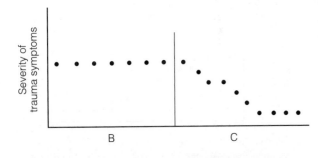

13.6 DATA ANALYSIS

In analyzing the results of single-case designs that attempt to rule out threats to internal validity (that is, designs that contain an ample baseline), we ask the following three questions:

1. Is there a *visual* pattern in the graph(s) that depicts a series of coincidences in which the level or trend of the target problem changes only after the intervention is introduced or withdrawn?
2. What is the *statistical* probability that the data observed during the intervention phase(s) merely are part of the normal, chance fluctuations in the target problem, fluctuations that we could have expected to occur had the baseline been extended and the intervention not introduced?
3. If change in the target problem is associated with the tested intervention, is the amount of change important from a *substantive*, or *clinical*, standpoint?

These three questions refer to the visual, statistical, and substantive significance of the findings.

When we analyzed the meaning of each graph in Figures 13.1 through 13.14, we dealt with **visual significance**. Visual significance is ascertained not through the use of fancy statistics, but merely by "eyeballing" the data pattern, as the term *visual* implies. To the extent that we can see that shifts in the target problem either do not occur when intervention is introduced or occur just as often at other times, there is less visual significance; that is, in those

---

visual significance   A pattern in single-case design graphs in which shifts in the level or trend of the target problem tend to coincide only with shifts in the independent variable.

---

instances there is less visual evidence for supposing that the intervention is affecting the target problem. To the extent that shifts in the level or trend of the target problem tend to coincide only with shifts in the independent variable—with movement from one phase to another—then there is more visual significance and thus more logical support for supposing that the intervention is affecting the target problem.

Sometimes our visual analysis of the data will remove the need for statistical analysis, particularly when the degree of visual significance (or lack thereof) is dramatic. Indeed, some single-case methodologists cite evidence that suggests that when experienced researchers judge whether an outcome is visually significant, their conclusions are usually supported by subsequent statistical analyses (Jayaratne, Tripodi, & Talsma, 1988). Practitioners who tend to be immobilized by their anxiety about statistics, therefore, can implement single-case designs in the hope that their visual analysis of the data will be sufficient.

Sometimes, however, the changes in the level or trend of the target problem from one phase to the next are subtle, or we are not sure whether our visual analysis of the data is being influenced by our desire to see a favorable outcome. At these times, it is helpful to augment our visual analysis with a statistical one.

Statistical and substantive significance mean the same thing in single-case designs as they do in other sorts of research, and they will be discussed in Chapter 17. However, analyzing the visual significance of the data pattern is usually sufficient when practitioners evaluate their own practice.

13.7 THE ROLE OF QUALITATIVE RESEARCH METHODS IN SINGLE-CASE EVALUATION

In Chapter 12 we saw that some techniques commonly used in qualitative studies can make valuable contributions when incorporated with quantitative methods in experimental and quasi-experimental designs. The same is true of single-case designs, which are generally considered quantitative. The utility of qualitative techniques as part of single-case designs is summarized in the box titled "Qualitative Techniques for Single-Case Evaluation."

Qualitative Techniques for Single-Case Evaluation

In this box we will list some prominent qualitative techniques and the important functions they can serve in single-case design evaluation studies. You can read more about these techniques in Chapter 15.

Qualitative Technique	Functions in Single-Case Evaluation
Informal conversational interviews with clients or others	• Identify extraneous events or forces connected with changes in the graphed data
	• Assess target problem and develop measurement and intervention plan
	• Assess what parts of the intervention client perceives to be most helpful and why
	• Corroborate the improvement (or lack thereof) self-reported or self-monitored by the client or by the significant other
Videotaping or audiotaping practitioner–client sessions	• Assess the fidelity of the intervention (Is it being implemented in a skillful manner, as intended?)
Event logs completed by client or significant others	• Assess where and when target problems occur and the circumstances that mediate them
	• Identify extraneous events occurring during baseline or intervention phases that might be helpful in interpreting whether changes that occur in the quantitative data are attributable to the intervention

13.8 MAIN POINTS

• Taking many repeated measures and identifying stable trends in the data enhances the internal validity of single-case designs by facilitating control for extraneous factors that affect the target problem.

• Baselines are control phases of repeated measures taken before an intervention is introduced. Baselines ideally should be extended until a stable trend in the data is evident.

• Including more than one baseline and intervention phase in a single-case experiment strengthens the control of history through the principle of unlikely successive coincidences. This is done in ABAB designs and multiple-baseline designs.

• AB designs have the weakest control for history, but they are the most feasible designs and can provide useful information.

• When we use designs with more phases than the AB design, we must exercise caution regarding possible carryover effects, order effects, generalization of effects, and the irreversibility of effects.

• The prime weakness of single-case designs is their limited external validity. With a sample of one, we are dealing with idiosyncratic conditions that cannot be generalized to other clients, practitioners, or settings. But this problem can be alleviated through replication.

• Single-case designs can be used by practitioners to monitor client progress or their own effectiveness more scientifically and systematically.

• Single-case designs have special measurement problems. Triangulating measures is therefore recommended—that is, simultaneously using more than one imperfect measurement option.

• Special caution must be exercised in single-case designs with regard to the measurement problems of reactivity, obtrusiveness, and social desirability bias.

When practitioners employ single-case design measurement procedures after having completed the earlier phases of the evidence-based practice process, the need for them to identify baseline trends before implementing the intervention becomes less important. That's because they already have determined—in the earlier steps of the evidence-based practice process—that the selected intervention has been shown in previous studies to have the best internally valid evidence supporting its probable effectiveness for the practice situation in question. Under these circumstances, although a design lacking an adequate baseline will not permit causal inferences to be made, it will suffice in guiding decisions about whether to continue, modify, or replace the chosen intervention.

- When practitioners have already judged through their appraisal of existing evidence that the chosen intervention has the best chance of success, and particularly if they face practical or ethical barriers to collecting repeated baseline measurement points, they can employ a practitioner friendly B or B+ design that aims only to monitor client progress—not to help them infer the cause of that progress.
- When the initial B phase of a design lacking an A phase shows no improvement, that B phase can become a baseline for evaluating the effects of a new intervention whose data points are graphed in a C phase, in which case the design morphs into an AB design.

13.9 PRACTICE-RELATED EXERCISES

1. Select some aspect of your own behavior that you would like to improve (for example, smoke less, eat less, exercise more, study more, and so on) and develop a plan to improve it. Conduct a single-case experiment and analyze the data to see if your plan is effective. Try to be aware of the degree to which you experience the measurement problems of reactivity and bias.
2. Think of a particular case or intervention that has piqued your curiosity about practice effectiveness. Design a single-case experiment that is relevant to that case or intervention. Try to design it in a way that would be feasible to implement.

13.10 INTERNET EXERCISES

1. Find a study that used a single-case evaluation AB design. Critique the study's design—either positively or negatively—and discuss whether you agree with the way its data were interpreted.

2. Find a study that used a single-case evaluation ABAB design or a multiple-baseline design. Critique the study's design—either positively or negatively—and discuss whether you agree with the way its data were interpreted.

13.11 ADDITIONAL READINGS

Bloom, M., Fischer, J., & Orme, J. G. (2009). *Evaluating practice: Guidelines for the accountable professional* (6th ed.). Boston, MA: Allyn & Bacon. This excellent, comprehensive text is an invaluable reference guide for social workers who plan to implement single-case designs as a regular part of their practice. All important aspects of single-case designs and ways to combine the roles of practitioner and researcher are covered in depth, and students often report that they learn a great deal about practice per se in this unique book.

Rubin, Allen. (2010). *Statistics for evidence-based practice and evaluation* (2nd ed.). Belmont, CA: Brooks/Cole. Chapter 19 of this practitioner friendly text discusses when and how to use various procedures for calculating the statistical significance and effect size of single-case design findings. One of the coauthors of the text you are reading recommends this book highly. Can you guess which one?

13.11a Competency Notes

EP 2.1.6b: Use research evidence to inform practice (p. 263): Social workers must understand all of the concepts in this chapter so they can critically appraise studies using single-case designs that might inform their practice.

EP 2.1.10d: Collect, organize, and interpret client data (p. 265): Social workers must understand how to collect, organize, and interpret client data as part of employing single-case designs to monitor and evaluate interventions.

EP 2.1.10m: Critically analyze, monitor, and evaluate interventions (p. 263): Social workers must understand all the measurement concepts in this chapter to employ single-case designs to monitor and evaluate interventions.

Program Evaluation

14.1 INTRODUCTION

EP 2.1.6b
EP 2.1.10m

The previous two chapters focused on the logic of methods of different designs for making causal inferences about the effectiveness of programs and interventions. Not all program evaluations, however, aim to generate causal inferences. Consequently, single-case or group experiments and quasi-experiments are not the only designs used in program and practice evaluation. Many other types of designs and methods can be used, such as surveys or various qualitative approaches. Even preexperimental designs can be used if the research question seeks only to describe whether change occurred without asking what caused it. *Program evaluation refers* to the *purpose* of research rather than to any specific research *methods*. Its purpose is to assess and improve the conceptualization, design, planning, administration, implementation, effectiveness, efficiency, and utility of social interventions and human service programs (Rossi & Freeman, 1993). In light of its purpose, program evaluation—when applied to social welfare settings and issues—is conceptually very similar to social work research, and many of the research studies conducted by social workers have a program evaluation purpose. Because the other chapters of this book are devoted to specific research designs and methods that can be employed in program evaluation (as well as in other research endeavors), this chapter will focus on issues and practical guidelines for conducting program evaluations. We'll start with an historical overview of program evaluation.

14.2 HISTORICAL OVERVIEW

Although the growth of program evaluation is a fairly recent phenomenon, planned social evaluation is really quite old. Some authors have traced it back to 2200 BC in China and connected it with personnel selection (Shadish et al., 1991). Whenever people have instituted a social reform for a specific purpose, they have paid attention to its actual consequences, even if they have not always done so in a conscious, deliberate, or systematic fashion, or called what they were doing program evaluation.

Modern approaches to program evaluation can be traced back to the beginning of the 20th century. In the 1940s, after the New Deal social welfare programs were implemented, studies examined the effects of work relief versus direct relief, the effects of public housing, and the impact of treatment programs on juvenile delinquency. After World War II, large public expenditures were committed to programs that attempted to improve housing, public health, attitudes toward minorities, and international problems in health, family planning, and community development. As expenditures grew, so did interest in data on the results of these programs.

14.2a Accountability

Program evaluation became widespread by the late 1950s as efforts increased to alleviate or prevent social problems such as juvenile delinquency and to test innovations in psychotherapy and new psychopharmacological discoveries. By the late 1960s and 1970s, interest in program evaluation accelerated as the public increasingly demanded evidence for a return on its investment in various programs to combat poverty, child abuse, substance abuse, crime and delinquency, mental illness, and so on. The increased demand that programs be accountable for their outcomes was prompted by more than just economic concerns. During the 1970s research studies emerged showing that some interventions and programs were not only ineffective, some were actually harmful. One notoriously harmful program was known as *Scared Straight*. It brought juvenile offenders and other at-risk youths into prisons where convicts would attempt to scare them away from criminal behavior by portraying the sordid nature of prison life. The program seemed to make sense and in 1979 was depicted in an Oscar-winning film shown to millions on national television. The film's narrator claimed that the program was 90 percent successful in scaring juveniles "straight." However, a rigorous program evaluation study that began in 1977 showed that juvenile offenders who participated in the program later engaged in much more crime than did a comparable group of offenders who did not participate. In trying to explain these surprising results the author of the study speculated that the "tough" juveniles who participated in the program may have been compelled to commit more crime to prove they were not scared (Finckenauer, 1979).

The "age of accountability" continued during the remainder of the 20th century, although the government provided less funding for program evaluation than it did prior to the 1980s. Liberals and conservatives alike demanded that programs be more accountable to the public and show whether they were really delivering what they promised to deliver. In fact, the need to evaluate may be greater when program funding is scarce than when it is abundant, because the scarcity of funds may intensify concerns that meager funding not be wasted on ineffectual programs. Individuals of all political persuasions have these concerns, including human service professionals who fiercely support increased social welfare spending but who are dedicated to finding better ways to help people and who do not want to see scarce welfare resources squandered on programs that don't really help their intended target populations. For example, the profession of social work was not immune from evaluations questioning effectiveness and harmfulness. During the 1970s several reviews concluded that social casework was ineffective (Fischer, 1973; Mullen & Dumpson, 1972; Wood, 1978), and one rigorous outcome study found that people suffering from schizophrenia who received social casework not combined with medications for schizophrenia actually relapsed faster than those who received the two interventions combined (Hogarty, 1979).

Thus, social workers should embrace accountability and evaluation out of a concern for our clients' well being even if we do not care about the public costs of our programs. Indeed, as was discussed in Chapter 1 and Chapter 5, our professional code of ethics requires that we promote, participate in, and keep abreast of program evaluation research.

14.2b Managed Care

The emphasis on program evaluation in health and human service agencies continued to grow because of the impact of "managed care." Defined in various ways, the term *managed care* refers to a variety of arrangements that try to control the costs of health and human services. These arrangements vary in the range of their components and proposed benefits, but the basic idea of managed care is to have a large organization contract with care providers who agree to provide services at reduced costs. Care providers are willing to reduce the costs because the organization pays for the cost of services for a very large number of people. The large organization paying for the care typically is the service recipient's employer or health insurance company. Providers are willing to meet the reduced cost demands of the large organizations so they will be eligible to have the cost of their services covered and thus get more referrals of clients covered under managed care plans. Some common types of managed care organizations are health maintenance organizations (HMOs), preferred provider organizations (PPOs), and employee assistance programs (EAPs). Public social service agencies also may employ managed care techniques to reduce the costs and inefficiencies of service provision.

One way in which managed care companies attempt to reduce costs is by reviewing requests for services by those they cover and approving— that is, agreeing to pay for—only those services they deem to be necessary and effective. This stipulation refers to both the type of service as well as the amount of service, putting pressure on service providers to come up with brief treatment plans as well as evidence as to how many sessions are needed to achieve certain effects. Suppose two alcohol abuse programs have two markedly different approaches to treating alcohol abuse. Suppose one program does not bother to evaluate the outcomes of treatment for its clients, whereas the other measures outcome from each client and shows that 90 percent of its clients never again evidence alcohol-related problems while at work after 10 treatment sessions. The latter program is more likely to be approved by a managed care company.

Most pertinent to this chapter is the effect that managed care is having on the way service providers use research methods to evaluate their services. This impact also should be pertinent to you, the reader of this text, because in your social work practice you are likely to experience pressures to use these methods to measure the outcomes of the services you provide.

14.2c Evidence-Based Practice

As discussed in Chapter 2, evidence-based practice has emerged as a prominent influence in the helping professions in recent decades. Although it differs from managed care concerns with cost saving, its emphasis on having practice decisions informed by research is consistent with concerns about accountability and effectiveness. Decisions about providing the type of program or intervention with the best chance for successful outcomes are often informed by **meta-analyses,** which are statistically oriented systematic reviews of research studies. Many meta-analyses aggregate effect-size statistics (to be discussed in Chapter 17) that convey the extent to which particular programs or interventions impact client outcomes. For example, using one type of effect-size statistic, a meta-analysis might show that a particular intervention reduces recidivism rates on average more than do alternative approaches. The implication of this finding for program evaluation would be twofold: (1) assuming the program staff chose to implement that intervention, the program evaluation might focus on assessing the extent to which the intervention is being implemented properly and identifying any implementation problems; and (2) assessing whether its recidivism rate outcome approximates the average outcome reported in the meta-analysis. Later in this chapter, as well as in Chapter 17 and Appendix E, we'll see how the results of meta-analyses can be used to enhance the value of a program evaluation findings when practical obstacles necessitate using scientifically limited research designs to assess program outcome.

As a result of the historical developments, program evaluation has become ubiquitous in the planning and administration of social welfare policies and programs. Let's turn now to the various types and purposes of program evaluation.

14.3 PURPOSES AND TYPES OF PROGRAM EVALUATION

A program evaluation might have one or more of the following three broad purposes: (1) to assess

---

meta-analyses statistically oriented systematic reviews of research studies

summative evaluations Evaluations that assess the ultimate success of programs and decisions about whether they should be continued or chosen in the first place from among alternative options.

formative evaluations Evaluations that focus on obtaining information for planning programs and improving their implementation and performance.

the ultimate *success* of programs, (2) to assess problems in how programs are being *implemented,* or (3) to obtain information needed in program *planning* and *development.* Program evaluations can be further classified as *summative* or *formative.*

14.3a Summative and Formative Evaluations

Summative evaluations are concerned with the first of the three purposes: involving the ultimate success of a program and decisions about whether it should be continued or chosen in the first place from among alternative options. The results of a summative evaluation convey a sense of finality. Depending on whether the results imply that the program succeeded, the program may or may not survive. Asking whether a program is achieving a successful outcome is perhaps the most significant evaluative question we might ask, and probably the question that immediately comes to mind when we think about program evaluation. It may also be the most politically charged question because it bears so directly on key vested interests, such as those that are associated with funding. But as we noted at the beginning of this chapter, program evaluation can have other purposes and other research questions that, although they may ultimately have some bearing on program outcome, focus on issues in the conceptualization, design, planning, administration, and implementation of interventions and programs.

Formative evaluations, for example, are not concerned with testing the success of a program. They focus instead on obtaining information that is helpful in planning the program and in improving its implementation and performance (Posavac & Carey, 1985). Whereas summative evaluations are usually quantitative in approach, formative evaluations may use quantitative methods, qualitative methods, or both. As you will see, these types or purposes of program evaluation are not mutually exclusive. Rather, they complement one another, and some evaluations can cover more than one of these purposes, such as when an evaluation finds that a program failed to attain its goals because it was never properly implemented in the first place. We'll continue our discussion of the various types of program evaluation by first examining in more depth the use of summative evaluations to evaluate program outcome and efficiency.

14.3b Evaluating Outcome and Efficiency

Evaluations of program outcome and efficiency may assess whether the program is effectively attaining its goals, whether it has any unintended harmful effects, whether its success (if any) is being achieved at a reasonable cost, and how the ratio of its benefits to its cost compares with the benefits and costs of other programs with similar objectives.

This approach to evaluation, sometimes called the *goal attainment model* of evaluation, refers to the formal goals and mission of the program—whether it's achieving what its funders or the general public want it to achieve. Typically, in designing goal attainment evaluations, the program's formal goals will be specified as dependent variables and operationally defined in terms of measurable indicators of program success. Ideally, but not necessarily, rigorous and internally valid experimental or quasi-experimental designs will be used to assess causal connections between program efforts and indicators of program outcome.

No matter how rigorous the assessment of outcome, the evaluation may be deemed incomplete unless it also assesses the costs of obtaining the outcome. In other words, how efficient is the program in achieving its outcome? Suppose, for example, that an evaluation of a case management program to prevent rehospitalization of people with psychotic disorders concludes that the program successfully reduces the number of days patients are hospitalized. Suppose further that the total number of days hospitalized for 50 case-managed patients during the course of the evaluation is 100, as compared to 500 for 50 controls. In other words, the case management program made a difference of 400 fewer hospitalized days. So far, so good. Suppose further that the extra cost of providing the case management services during the study period was $40,000. Thus, each day of hospitalization saved by providing case management had been costing $100 (which we get by dividing $40,000 by 400). If the cost of hospital care was more than $100 per day per patient, then in addition to being effective, the program was an efficient way to care for these people.

14.3c Monitoring Program Implementation

Some programs have unsuccessful outcomes simply because they are not being implemented properly.

Suppose a safe sex program develops a public education leaflet and decides to evaluate its effectiveness in a small pilot distribution in a particular high school. Suppose the program personnel deliver the leaflets to the school's vice principal, who agrees to disseminate them to all students. Suppose that for some reason—unanticipated opposition by the principal or the PTA, mere oversight, or whatever—the leaflets never get disseminated. Or perhaps they get disseminated in an undesirable way. Maybe instead of handing them out to every student in a school assembly, the vice principal merely deposits them in teachers' mailboxes with a vague message encouraging them to distribute the leaflets to their students. Maybe some teachers distribute the leaflets but most do not.

Suppose further that the program personnel never learn that the leaflets were not disseminated as intended. The implications of this turn of events would be quite serious. Because few or no students would have received the leaflet in the first place, the intervention was never implemented as planned and had no chance of succeeding. No matter what indicators of outcome were chosen, the leaflet dissemination effort would be doomed to fail. But it would fail not because it was a bad idea or an ineffectual leaflet but because it was never really tried. If the evaluators had merely conducted an outcome study without assessing whether and how the program got implemented, they would be in danger of abandoning a public education intervention that, if only implemented properly, might effectively prevent unsafe sex practices.

This example illustrates that no matter how well an outcome evaluation is designed, if it's not supplemented by an evaluation of program implementation, then it risks not identifying or misinterpreting the meaning of negative results. In turn, no matter how highly we value outcome studies, there is a clear need for the evaluation of program implementation.

An evaluation of program implementation can have value even without any evaluation of program outcome. Suppose, for example, an agency secures funding for a program to expand its services to poor people, but then uses the money merely to expand services to the type of clientele with whom agency staff are familiar and comfortable. If an evaluation of agency caseload attributes finds that the program was never implemented as planned—that poor people were not being served—those results would have great utility without an outcome evaluation.

Evaluations of program implementation are not necessarily concerned only with the question of whether a program is being implemented as planned. Many other possible questions might examine how best to implement and maintain the program. Here are just a few of the important questions that can be researched without getting into questions of outcome:

- What proportion of the target population is being served?
- What types of individuals are not being reached?
- Why are so many targeted individuals refusing services?
- How skillful are various types of practitioners in their clinical interventions?
- In what areas do practitioners seem least prepared and in need of continuing education?
- How are staff members reacting to new agency procedures? What difficulties are they experiencing with the procedures?
- Are clients satisfied with services? Why or why not?
- Why do so many clients drop out of treatment prematurely?

14.3d Process Evaluation

A term closely aligned with monitoring program implementation is called *process evaluation*. Process evaluations (which are an example of *formative evaluations*, mentioned earlier in this chapter) ask many of the same questions as indicated above in connection with monitoring program implementation, and they focus on identifying strengths and weaknesses in program processes and recommending needed improvements.

Often agency administrators will ask evaluators to conduct outcome evaluations of their programs while those programs are still in their infancy and have not yet had enough time to identify and resolve start-up bugs and other problematic processes in implementation. These administrators may be in a hurry for outcome data because they are under intense pressure from funding sources to prove their success at goal attainment. Seasoned evaluators, however, may try to persuade them to table

any outcome evaluation until a process evaluation has been completed so that outcome data are collected only after the program has been debugged. The administrators may or may not have the time or resources to conduct a process evaluation first and then an outcome evaluation. In contrast, other administrators, perhaps under less external pressure, may be content just to have the process evaluation, asking not whether their program works, but how to make it work better.

All of the methodologies covered in this book can be applied to evaluate program implementation. Choosing the most appropriate methodology to use depends on the nature of the research question. Surveys that use questionnaires or scales might assess staff, client, or community attitudes that affect program implementation decisions. Available records might be analyzed to assess whether the attributes of clients being served match program priorities regarding the intended target population. Experimental or quasi-experimental designs might be used to assess the effectiveness of alternative fund-raising strategies, to measure the impact of different organizational arrangements on staff attitudes, to determine which outreach strategies are most successful in engaging hard-to-reach prospective clients in treatment, and so on. Process evaluations, however, tend to rely heavily on qualitative methods, which we'll discuss at length in Chapter 15. Open-ended qualitative interviewing, for instance, might be the best way to learn how staff members are reacting to new agency procedures and the unanticipated difficulties they might be experiencing with them. Qualitative interviewing might also work best for discovering the reasons clients cite for service dissatisfaction or for refusing or prematurely terminating service delivery. Participant observation might be used to assess how staff members relate to clients or to one another. In some studies, evaluators have posed as clients and observed how staff members behaved and the ways in which their behavior affected clients.

14.3e Evaluation for Program Planning: Needs Assessment

Thus far, we have been discussing the evaluation of programs that have already been implemented. But the term *program evaluation* also connotes diagnostic evaluation. Just as clinical practitioners evaluate client problems and needs during a preintervention assessment period to develop the best treatment plan, program evaluators may assess a program's target population to enhance program planning. They might assess the extent and location of the problems the program seeks to ameliorate, as well as the target population's characteristics, problems, expressed needs, and desires. This information is then used to guide program planning and development concerning such issues as what services to offer, how to maximize service utilization by targeted subgroups, where to locate services, and so on.

For example, suppose you are planning a new statewide program to help the homeless. What would you need to know to guide your planning? You might want to find out the following: How many homeless people are there in the state? How many are there in specific locations in the state? What are the reasons for each individual's homelessness, and how many people are there for each reason? How many choose to be homeless? How many seem to be homeless because of mental illness or substance abuse? How many are homeless because they lost their jobs and cannot find work? How long have they been homeless? How many of the homeless are in different ethnic groups, and how many are recent immigrants or do not speak English? What proportion of the homeless consists of children and entire family units? What special problems do the children experience in such matters as education, health, nutrition, self-esteem, and so on? What special problems and needs are expressed by the adult homeless, those with emotional disorders, and others? These are just a few of the diagnostic questions you might ask; the answers will help you suggest what interventions to develop, where to locate them, how to staff them, and so on.

The process of systematically researching diagnostic questions like those just mentioned is called *needs assessment*. The term *needs assessment* is widely used to cover all sorts of techniques for collecting data for program planning purposes, and it has become essentially synonymous with evaluation for program planning.

We discussed the specific alternative techniques of needs assessment in Chapter 10 on surveys. We won't repeat that material here. Instead, let's consider a thorny conceptual issue that complicates the definition of needs: whether they're defined in normative terms or in terms of demand. If needs are defined normatively, then a needs assessment would focus on comparing the objective living conditions of the target population with what society, or at least that segment of society that is concerned with helping the target population, considers acceptable or desirable from a humanitarian standpoint. Normatively defining the needs of the homeless, for instance, might lead you to conclude that certain housing or shelter programs need to be developed for individuals who are living in deplorable conditions on the streets, even if those individuals don't express any dissatisfaction with their current homelessness.

If needs are defined in terms of demand, however, only those individuals who indicate that they feel or perceive the need themselves would be considered to be in need of a particular program or intervention. In this homelessness example, then, individuals who prefer to be homeless might not be counted as in need of the program. Defining needs in terms of demand can be tricky. Perhaps individuals express no need for a planned program because they don't understand how the planned program will help them or because they have come to expect that every time a social program is provided to them, it is stigmatizing or unacceptable to them in some other way. Thus, in an assessment of whether the homeless need a new shelter program, many homeless individuals might express no need for the program and might even disdain the idea because they have no reason to believe that the new program really will be more acceptable to them than the filthy, crowded, dangerous shelters they already refuse to use.

How we define *needs* affects the choice of specific techniques to assess them. For example, if we define needs normatively, we might be able to establish the need for a particular program by analyzing existing statistics. Thus, if census data showed a relatively high number of unmarried teenage mothers in a particular area, then we might be predisposed to conclude that more family planning or child-rearing education services are needed in that area. But if we take demand into account, then we might want to supplement the census information by conducting a survey of teenage mothers to determine under what conditions they would actually use the particular services we are contemplating.

14.4 PLANNING AN EVALUATION

Regardless of the ultimate purpose of an evaluation, program evaluators should collaborate with program *stakeholders* in planning the evaluation. In fact, the expressed needs and concerns of those stakeholders likely will determine the purpose of the evaluation. **Stakeholders** include everyone with an interest in the program, such as program administrators, service providers and staff, potential and current program funders, community members and their leaders (including politicians), clients (including previous and potential clients as well as current ones), and other community entities such as businesses and other programs and organizations that can affect or be affected by the program to be evaluated. As a first step in planning an evaluation, program evaluators should learn as much as possible about these stakeholders. For example, how do they perceive the need for an evaluation and its purposes? How might their beliefs, income, status or careers, or workload influence or be affected by the evaluation? To promote stakeholders' identification with the evaluation and their support of it during the data collection phase, it is essential that they be involved in a meaningful way in planning the evaluation.

14.4a Fostering Cooperation and Utilization

It is important at the outset to find out who wants the evaluation, why they want it, and who doesn't want it. For example, if program funders want the evaluation but program personnel either don't know about the evaluation or don't want it, then the evaluator should try to make the program personnel more comfortable with the evaluation to foster their cooperation in collecting and interpreting data. One way to do this, of course, is by involving them as stakeholders, and by sharing mutual incremental feedback throughout all phases of the evaluation. This involvement should begin early in the planning of the evaluation, not just after the research design is ready to be implemented. In addition to fostering cooperation with the evaluation, involving personnel in the planning is thought to improve the chances for identifying those daily organizational realities that might pose

Stakeholders everyone with an interest in a program

logistical obstacles to alternative research designs or data-collection methodologies.

Evaluators also can obtain staff feedback regarding a written proposal that reflects their input. The purpose of presenting them with the proposal is to make certain that they agree with evaluators about the components of the evaluation and the nature of the program being evaluated. In addition, by reconsidering everything in a final, written package, they might see logistical problems that were not apparent in earlier discussions. Planning an evaluation is a two-way street. The planning process should consider not only potential problems posed by stakeholders but also potential problems stemming from mistakes the evaluator might make in designing the evaluation. For example, involving decision makers who are likely to use the research helps ensure that evaluators will address questions that are relevant to their decision-making needs rather than questions that are trivial or of interest only to audiences who are not in a position to act on the research findings. Also, without adequate input from program personnel, evaluators might choose or develop the wrong data collection instruments, such as self-report scales that clients might not understand or be willing to complete. Evaluators also might not understand the unrealistic burden that their data collection procedures might place on practitioners who already strain to meet heavy paperwork requirements without sacrificing the quality of service they are providing to their many clients.

14.4b The Evaluation Report

The cooperation of program personnel might be fostered further by assuring them that they will get to see and respond to a confidential draft of the evaluation report before it is finalized and disseminated to other stakeholders. They should not be led to think that they will be able to censor the report, but they should be assured that their suggestions will be taken seriously. By meeting with key personnel to discuss the report, evaluators can point out and clarify implications of the findings that personnel might find particularly useful for improving the program. And this should be done in a timely fashion—not after it's too late for certain decisions to be made.

Finally, the evaluator can foster the evaluation report's utilization by tailoring its form and style to the needs and preferences of those who are in a position to use it. Clear, succinct, and cohesive composition always helps, as does careful typing and a neat, uncluttered layout. The briefer and neater the report, the more likely that busy administrators and practitioners will read it carefully. When adapting the report to an audience of program personnel, do not present every peripheral finding. And do not present negative findings bluntly and tactlessly. If program objectives are not being attained, couch the findings in language that recognizes the yeoman efforts and skills of program personnel and that does not portray them as inadequate. Try not to convey a message of success or failure; instead provide suggestions for developing new programs or improving existing ones. Alert program personnel in the planning stage that all reports bring both good and bad news and that the focus will be less on judging the program's value than on identifying feasible ways to improve it. And make sure that sufficient attention is given to realistic, practical implications of the findings.

A note of caution is in order here. We are not implying that if you follow all the steps we have proposed that you are certain to avoid problems in the way program personnel respond to a proposed evaluation or its findings. These steps are recommended as ways to reduce the likelihood of encountering those problems or the severity of those problems if they do arise. But even if you follow all of the proposed steps, under certain circumstances you may still encounter serious problems with program personnel. If, for example, they feel their funding is threatened by your findings, then they may still seek to discredit your evaluation, even if you went by the book in dealing with them.

14.4c Logic Models

In addition to involving stakeholders in planning an evaluation, it can be helpful to construct at the outset a **logic model**, which is a graphic portrayal that depicts the essential components of a program, shows how those components are linked to short-term process objectives, specifies measurable indicators of success in achieving short-term objectives, conveys how those short-term objectives lead to long-term program outcomes, and identifies measurable indicators of success in achieving long-term outcomes. Examining the components identified in

the logic model can facilitate decisions about the purpose of the evaluation as well as what aspects or indicators on which to focus within that purpose. For example, if the evaluation has a process or monitoring purpose, the illustration of a hypothetical logic model in Figure 14.1 might suggest assessing the adequacy of prisoner and victim volunteer recruitment, whether the group sessions were conducted as planned, the extent to which the prison leadership and staff cooperated with the program, participant views of the nature and value of the program, or whether the short-term objective of increasing prisoner empathy was actually achieved. If the evaluation's purpose is to evaluate longer-term outcome, the logic model identifies what outcome indicators to assess.

Program funding sources commonly require that the grant applications include a logic model because the model can help in considering the appropriateness of the proposed program as well as the program evaluation design. Logic models can be constructed in various ways. Some include a set of boxes identifying the underlying theories of the program components. Others might start with program inputs or resources. They might also vary regarding the extent to which they emphasize the details of the implementation process. Which approach to take in constructing a logic model will depend on program needs and the input of stakeholders. Regardless of which approach you might choose, you should try to find a happy medium between making your logic model so skimpy that it fails to adequately convey the various model components and their logical connections versus packing it with so much detail that the essence is hard to see. Figure 14.1 displays a basic, skeletal format of what a logic model might look like. The steps we have been discussing for planning an evaluation and fostering its utilization are summarized in the box "Steps to Enhance Compliance with and Utilization of Evaluations."

---

logic model A graphic portrayal that depicts the essential components of a program, shows how those components are linked to short-term process objectives, specifies measurable indicators of success in achieving short-term objectives, conveys how those short-term objectives lead to long-term program outcomes, and identifies measurable indicators of success in achieving long-term outcomes.

FIGURE 14.1 Template for Constructing an Outcomes Approach Logic Model for an In-Prison Prerelease Restorative Justice

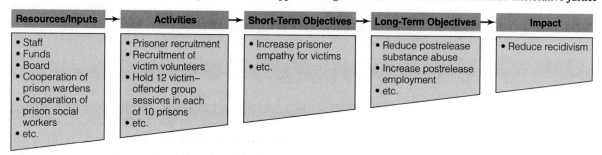

Steps to Enhance Compliance with and Utilization of Evaluations

- Learn about stakeholders
- Involve stakeholders early in planning the evaluation and in all of its phases
- Find out who wants the evaluation and why they want it
- Obtain stakeholder feedback to a draft of the evaluation proposal that reflects their input
- Include a logic model in the evaluation proposal
- Assure program personnel and other stakeholders that they will be able to respond to a draft of the report before it is finalized

- Tailor the form and style of the report to the needs of stakeholders
- Present negative findings, if any, tactfully, recognizing the yeoman efforts and skills of program personnel
- Instead of implying program failure, provide suggestions for developing new programs or improving existing ones
- Develop implications that are realistic and practical

14.5 THE POLITICS OF PROGRAM EVALUATION

Because the findings of program evaluation can influence program funding, intense political pressure is introduced into the program evaluation process. Especially when the purpose is to evaluate outcome, stakeholders' vested interests can impede the atmosphere for free scientific inquiry. Instead of pursuing truth as scientifically as possible to improve human well-being, program evaluation efforts may be implemented in ways that fit perceived program maintenance needs. Sometimes, as a result, there will be intense pressure to design the research or interpret its findings in ways that are likely to make the program look good. Other times, it may simply mean that the program evaluation is conducted in the cheapest, most convenient way possible, guided by the belief that funding

sources don't pay much attention to the quality of the research and just want to say that the programs they fund have been evaluated.

When you're in a position in your career to participate in, conduct, or use program evaluations, you should not be naive about the potential influence of vested interests on the integrity or quality of evaluations. Nevertheless, it would be misleading to imply that all program evaluation is corrupt. Agency administrators and others who have vested interests often have sufficient integrity and professional concern for learning the best ways to help clients that they are able to put their vested interests aside and act in a manner that fosters the most objective, scientific evaluation possible. Although it may be naive to assume that all (or even most) evaluations will be immune from the political pressures applied by those who have vested interests, it would be too cynical to assume that all evaluations are politically biased.

14.5a In-House Versus External Evaluators

When program evaluators work for the agency being evaluated, they are called *in-house* evaluators. Program evaluators also might work for external agencies such as government or regulating agencies and private research consultation firms (which often bid for government grants to evaluate programs that receive public funds). University faculty members also may secure research grants to evaluate programs, or they simply may wish to conduct applied research as part of their scholarly duties.

In-house evaluators may have certain advantages over *external* evaluators. They may have greater access to program information and personnel, more knowledge about program processes that might bear on the design of an evaluation or the meaning of findings, and more sensitivity to the program's research needs and the realistic obstacles to the feasibility of certain research designs or methods. They might also be more likely to be trusted by program personnel and consequently receive better cooperation and feedback from them. But the flip side of the coin is that their commitment to the program, their superiors, or the advancement of their own careers might make them less objective and independent than external evaluators.

But it would be naive to suppose that external evaluators are never subjected to the same kinds of political considerations as are in-house evaluators. External evaluators may have strong incentives to get and stay in the good graces of the personnel of the program being evaluated. If they alienate those personnel, then the quality of their evaluation may be imperiled by the lack of cooperation with the research agenda. In fact, one criterion for choosing the recipient of a program evaluation grant might be the quality of the relationship the evaluator has with the program and that relationship's potential for securing cooperation from program participants.

Also, it's incorrect to assume that external sponsors of the evaluation are always more objective than in-house personnel. Perhaps the sponsors of the evaluation want to stop funding the program and need negative evaluation results to justify the cessation of funding to their own constituents. On the other hand, the sponsors might fret that negative results would make them (the sponsors) look bad and in turn threaten their own fundraising efforts.

Fiscal concerns not only can affect the evaluation designs employed, but they also can lead to attempts to influence the way findings are interpreted, because administrators may believe that the prospects for future funding are enhanced by obtaining favorable evaluation outcomes. This influence can be exerted in various ways, some more subtle than others. External evaluators can be told, for example, that if the program has a successful outcome, then spin-off programs are likely to be funded, and the evaluator can receive the contract to be the "external" evaluator in those spin-off programs. Assuming additional program development further down the road, external evaluators may realize that staying in the good graces of the folks whose programs are being evaluated, and producing desired conclusions for those programs, can have significant long-term benefits for the evaluator's own job security, income, and career.

Another way to influence evaluators is by creating headaches for them when their evaluations are written in a manner that program administrators do not like. External evaluators quickly learn, for example, that if they produce reports that reflect favorably on the evaluated program, then program staff members are extremely unlikely to mobilize efforts to discredit the evaluation's credibility or the evaluator's competence. And they also learn that if their reports are not as positive as program staff members desire, especially if those members are worried about the impact of the evaluation findings on future funding, such mobilization efforts are likely to ensue, and the evaluator's standing with his or her employing agency might be seriously tarnished. A weak study with positive findings is unlikely to be attacked by program staff members who stand to benefit by those findings. However, a strong study with a few relatively minor flaws is likely to be vilified by staff members who see the findings as a threat to their funding prospects.

These things happen not just because there are good people and bad people. They happen because many program staff members work hard to secure scarce funding for programs that they believe are helping people. These program staff members may believe that even if we are unsure of the effectiveness of their programs, we should continue investing funds in and working to improve them. Negative findings, they may fear, will simply lead to funding cutbacks with no opportunity to improve on current efforts. Some might argue, from a more cynical perspective, that some staff members are also concerned with enhancing the fiscal well-being of their own agency and the status of their own jobs. There probably is a good deal of truth in both points of view, keeping individual differences in mind.

14.6 PRACTICAL PITFALLS IN CARRYING OUT EXPERIMENTS AND QUASI-EXPERIMENTS IN SOCIAL WORK AGENCIES

As the preceding discussion implies, various commitments and vested interests can influence whether and how program evaluation findings are used. The social context of program evaluation also affects the logistics involved in the implementation of program evaluation studies. *Logistics* refers to getting research participants to do what they're supposed to do, getting research instruments distributed and returned, and other seemingly unchallenging tasks. Sometimes practitioners or their supervisors are not exactly thrilled with the research requirements of the program evaluation. Not surprisingly, they may resist implementing them in a careful manner. At other times, logistical problems are unintentional, resulting from the uncontrollable context of daily life. For example, busy practitioners who are committed to the program evaluation, but whose main priority is service delivery, can simply forget to comply with research protocols. Let's now examine some of the most common logistical problems confronted by program evaluators who attempt to employ experimental or quasi-experimental designs to evaluate the effectiveness of programs.

14.6a Fidelity of the Intervention

The term *intervention fidelity* refers to the degree to which the intervention delivered to clients was delivered as intended. We often evaluate social work interventions that cannot be spelled out in step-by-step manuals. Instead, we rely on social work practitioners to implement general guidelines in skillful, creative, and idiosyncratic ways with each client. Some practitioners, however, might have better judgment than others. Some might misunderstand or misinterpret the intervention's intent. This means that the intervention we think we are evaluating may not be the one intended for experimental group participants, or that the services received by experimental and comparison group participants may be more similar than we intended. Related reasons why interventions may not be implemented as

intended include delays and startup problems in implementing new programs, the use of staff members who are inexperienced with or untrained in the new intervention, high initial staff turnover in new programs, organizational changes that affect the program, loss of staff enthusiasm over time, and ongoing supervision provided by agency supervisors who may not follow the research protocol.

A good way to assess intervention fidelity is to videotape several randomly selected treatment sessions from each of your practitioners. Have one or more experts in the intervention independently view each taped session and then complete a rating scale assessing their judgment of the degree to which the intervention in the session was implemented appropriately. For example, suppose the rating scale categories, with the corresponding score in parentheses, were (1) *unacceptable*, (2) *almost acceptable*, (3) *minimally acceptable*, (4) *acceptable*, and (5) *excellent*. If your study's intervention fidelity ratings are at or above a score of 4 (acceptable), but your main findings showed that the intervention was not effective, it would be difficult for critics to attribute your main findings to a lack of intervention fidelity.

But you do not have to wait until the end of your study to have the tapes rated and utilize the ratings. You could have that done incrementally throughout your study. If you find early in your study that the tapes are receiving low ratings, you can take steps to try to improve the way the practitioners in your study are implementing the intervention. Better yet, have some ratings done on a pilot basis before your study begins. If there are intervention fidelity problems, delay the onset of the study until you correct the problem and begin to consistently achieve acceptable ratings. This would not, however, remove the need to assess fidelity during your study, as well.

14.6b Contamination of the Control Condition

Even if the experimental group receives the intended intervention at an acceptable level of intervention fidelity, the comparison condition can be contaminated if comparison group and experimental group members interact. Suppose, for example, an experiment in a school social work intervention assigns students in the same school to either an experimental group that receives the new intervention being tested or a control group that receives the routine services.

The students in each group will interact in the school setting, and the improvements among the experimental group students may therefore have a beneficial spillover effect on the behavior of the control group students. If this happens, the two groups will not be as different on outcome measures (dependent variables) as was predicted, and we may therefore erroneously conclude that the new intervention did not make a difference. Solomon and Paulson (1995) suggest that contamination of the control condition can even occur if experimental and control group clients share the same agency waiting room.

14.6c Resistance to the Case Assignment Protocol

Practitioners may resent having to assign cases to treatment conditions on the basis of research requirements rather than on the basis of their own professional judgment about the best service match for each client. Practitioners tend to believe that the services they provide are effective, so they may not be committed to adhering to the research protocol in case assignment because they think they already "know" the answer to the research question. Believing they already know what services work best for what clients, they may feel compelled to violate—perhaps in a covert fashion—the research protocol to make sure that the client receives the service they think that client should receive. Even if they are unsure as to what service works best for what client, they may pressure to enroll clients with the greatest need into the experimental condition because it's new and innovative or offers more services than does the control condition.

Shadish et al. (2001) offer a number of recommendations to alleviate case assignment problems. Those most relevant to evaluations in social work agencies are as follows: (1) Carefully explain the purpose and nature of the case assignment protocol to agency staff; (2) provide incentives to them for implementing the protocol properly; (3) pilot test the case assignment procedure in the agency; (4) make sure that you develop clearly worded procedures—in operational terms—for implementing, controlling, and monitoring the case assignment protocol throughout the entire study; (5) have the case assignment protocol controlled by only one person who is part of the research team, and not an agency staff member; (6) keep the master list of case assignments in a secure place and a backup copy in a different secure place; (7) do not show the master assignment list to agency staff; (8) hold ongoing meetings with agency staff to discuss the case assignment process; (9) have a research staff member continually monitor the implementation of the case assignment protocol throughout the entire study; and (10) keep a log throughout the study of each case assignment and any violations of the case assignment protocol.

14.6d Client Recruitment and Retention

Recruiting a sufficient number of clients to participate in the study can be difficult when the research must rely on referrals of clients from outside agencies. This can be particularly problematic when the research design precludes joint involvement by referred clients in the services provided by the referring agencies. This can result in those agencies "dumping" cases they do not want to serve, perhaps because the dumped clients resist services or seem less likely to benefit from services. Alternatively, the agencies may be reluctant to refer any clients, because that might adversely affect the referring agency's reimbursement when it is based on the amount of services provided directly by the referring agency. Referring agencies also might not understand and even resent having their referrals assigned to a control condition, particularly if that assignment means referring control clients back to the referral agency.

Moreover, difficulties in client recruitment and retention can arise from the clients' own reactions to case assignment procedures and measurement requirements. Clients may resent the use of randomized procedures to determine which service they receive, and they may therefore not participate. Some clients might first agree to participate and then change their minds after learning that they have not been assigned to the new, innovative, experimental condition. Other clients might take longer to drop out of the control or comparison condition; perhaps after being inconvenienced by completing the pretesting, they will refuse to participate in the posttesting. (Problems in retention are the same as the problem of attrition, discussed in Chapter 12.)

Failing to recruit a sufficient number of clients can also result from overly optimistic estimates or promises by the staff in agencies where a study takes place. Relying on such estimates or promises can be particularly risky when that agency has never before served as a site for an experiment or quasi-experiment. If you plan to conduct an experiment or a quasi-experiment in an agency that has never before served as the main site for such a study, you should be skeptical about staff estimates regarding the number of participants it can provide in a specific time frame. Minimally, you should look for evidence that would assure you that the agency really can deliver the estimated number of participants who would meet your study's eligibility requirements and who would agree to participate. If you cannot obtain that evidence based on the agency's prior experiences or existing data, you probably should conduct a brief pilot test before starting your study in that agency—to see if the number of participants provided during that brief time span is consistent with the rate of participation projected for the entire study. For example, if an agency estimates that in one year it will provide 100 participants but provides only 3 during your 1-month pilot test, you'll probably want to revise your plans for obtaining a sufficient number of participants before implementing your study.

The above possibilities do not exhaust all of the pitfalls you are likely to encounter if you attempt to carry out experimental or quasi-experimental research. They're simply among the more common ones in a seemingly endless list. The point here is twofold: (1) be prepared to encounter pitfalls like these, and (2) build mechanisms into your design to prevent, detect, and deal with these pitfalls before they ruin your study.

14.7 MECHANISMS FOR AVOIDING OR ALLEVIATING PRACTICAL PITFALLS

One key way to try to avoid or alleviate the pitfalls discussed above, is, as discussed earlier in this chapter, to engage agency staff members in designing the research and to enlist their support and cooperation from its inception. Although this may help reduce the likelihood or degree of their resistance to the research, it will not guarantee that their resistance is eliminated. You should not assume that agency staff members' support for the research protocol will endure as they begin to encounter daily practice concerns. Instead, you should build into the study ongoing mechanisms in which some research staff members are onsite throughout the project to interact with program staff members and monitor whether they are complying with the research protocol and implementing the experimental and control conditions as intended.

You might also locate experimental and control conditions in separate buildings or agencies. This may help avoid contaminating the control condition. You might promote the fidelity of the intervention by developing a treatment manual that clearly and specifically defines the components and steps of both experimental and control interventions. You might anticipate and alleviate client recruitment and retention problems by planning to recruit clients assertively on an ongoing basis throughout your study, rather than assume that your initial cohort will be large enough and will remain intact. As we discussed in Chapter 12, client recruitment and retention might also be enhanced by reimbursing clients for their participation, particularly for their time and efforts in pretesting and posttesting.

14.7a Pilot Studies

Another good idea is to conduct a *pilot study* before implementing your main study. Previously, we mentioned conducting a brief pilot test just to see if the agency estimate about the projected number of study participants is accurate. A pilot study also can help you detect additional problems. Do you have intervention fidelity? Is imitation of treatments occurring in the control condition? Are there unanticipated problems in the way instruments are being administered or completed? Are there any other unanticipated data collection problems? Do staff who initially agreed to your protocol for assigning cases to experimental and comparison groups—perhaps because they really didn't understand the protocol and its implications, or perhaps because they just weren't paying that much attention and wanted to appear agreeable—start objecting to the protocol and perhaps try to undermine it when they realize that clients who they think should receive the new intervention are being assigned to the control group? Another good reason for conducting a pilot study is that if you submit a grant application to obtain funding for an experiment or quasi-experiment, showing that you completed a successful pilot study is likely to reassure the funding source that you have detected and resolved any of the above pitfalls likely to undermine your study. In light of all the foregoing reasons, some consider conducting a pilot study not just a good idea—but essential!

14.7b Qualitative Techniques

Detecting and alleviating practical pitfalls is one place in which techniques commonly employed in qualitative studies can come in handy as a valuable part of a quantitative research study. Qualitative methods offer a number of techniques that on-site research staff members can use in attempting to observe research implementation pitfalls. For example, they can interact formally or informally with agency staff members to identify compliance problems or learn how they are implementing the interventions. They can use videotapes or practitioner activity logs to assess intervention fidelity. They can also identify implementation problems by following along with (shadowing) practitioners in their daily activities. They can participate in in-service trainings or group supervision to identify discrepancies between the intended intervention and what agency trainers or supervisors are prescribing. The box titled "Qualitative Techniques for Experimental or Quasi-Experimental Research" summarizes the ways techniques commonly employed in qualitative studies can be used to help avoid or alleviate the many practical pitfalls that may be encountered in trying to carry out quantitative research studies employing experimental or quasi-experimental designs.

14.8 COMBINING QUANTITATIVE AND QUALITATIVE METHODS IN PROGRAM EVALUATION

Throughout this book we have emphasized that quantitative and qualitative methods complement each other and can be combined in many types of research studies. As you may have already surmised, program evaluation studies are no exception. To end this chapter, we'll reinforce this point by presenting the box titled "Combining Quantitative and Qualitative Methods in Program Evaluation."

14.9 MAIN POINTS

- Program evaluation applies different research methods and designs to assess and improve the conceptualization, design, planning, administration, implementation, effectiveness, efficiency, and utility of social interventions and human service programs.
- Summative evaluations are concerned with the ultimate success of a program and decisions about whether it should be continued or chosen in the first place from among alternative options.

- Formative evaluations focus on obtaining information that is helpful in planning the program and in improving its implementation and performance.
- Process evaluations are an example of formative evaluations and focus on identifying strengths and weaknesses in program processes and recommending needed improvements.
- Needs assessments use various data collection techniques to answer questions for program planning purposes.
- To alleviate potential problems in the logistics of their studies, as well as to alleviate resistance to them and their utilization, program evaluators should learn about the stakeholders and their vested interests in the evaluation, involve them in all phases of the evaluation, maintain ongoing mutual feedback with them, and tailor the evaluation and its reportage to their needs and preferences as much as possible without sacrificing scientific objectivity.
- Evaluations of program outcome and efficiency may assess whether the program is effectively attaining its goals, whether it has any unintended harmful effects, whether its success (if any) is being achieved at a reasonable cost, and how the ratio of its benefits to its cost compares with the benefits and costs of other programs with similar objectives.
- Although the evaluation of program outcome is one of the first things that comes to mind when people think of program evaluation, other important foci of evaluation research address research questions that are concerned with planning new programs and monitoring their implementation.
- Although evaluations of program outcome should strive to enhance causal inference by using the most internally valid experimental or quasi-experimental design possible, feasibility constraints often necessitate the use of preexperimental designs, and these designs can sometimes be of significant value for program evaluation purposes.
- Some programs have unsuccessful outcomes not because they are wrong in theory, but because they were never implemented as intended.
- Outcome evaluations ought to be supplemented by evaluations that monitor program implementation. Monitoring implementation can help resolve problems early on, keep agencies accountable, and identify the best ways to implement and maintain programs.

Qualitative Techniques for Experimental or Quasi-Experimental Research

It is not uncommon to hear researchers known primarily for their experimental or quasi-experimental quantitative findings say that almost all of their "quantitative" studies have included components that relied on qualitative methods. In this box we will list some prominent qualitative techniques and the important functions they can serve in experimental and quasi-experimental studies. You can read more about these techniques in Chapter 15.

Many of the ideas for this box were derived from a presentation by Phyllis Solomon and Robert I. Paulson at the first annual conference of the Society for Social Work and Research, in Washington, D.C., April 11, 1995. Their presentation was titled "Issues in Designing and Conducting Randomized Human Service Trials."

Qualitative Technique	Functions in Experimental and Quasi-Experimental Studies
Ethnographic shadowing (follow along and observe practitioners in their daily activities)	• Learn how practitioners actually implement the intervention • Learn if the interventions and other aspects of the research protocol are being implemented as intended
Participant observation during training or group supervision	• Identify discrepancies between the intended intervention and what agency trainers or supervisors are actually prescribing
Participant observation during agency staff meetings	• Determine whether agency staff are complying with the research protocol and identify difficulties they are having with compliance
Informal conversational interviews with agency staff	• Identify compliance problems with the research protocol • Learn how staff are actually implementing the interventions
Videotaping or audiotaping practitioner–client sessions	• Assess the fidelity of the intervention (Is it being implemented in a skillful manner, as intended?)
Practitioner activity logs	• Assess the fidelity of the intervention • Are the proper amounts and types of services being delivered to the clients for whom they were intended?
Event logs	• Identify major organizational and systems changes that may impede continued compliance with the research protocol
Focus groups	• Document the process of implementing the research design and interventions, and identify implementation problems • Develop possible explanations for unexpected, puzzling findings
Snowball sampling	• Recruit subjects from vulnerable or hard-to-find target populations
Semi-structured, open-ended interviews (using interview guides) with prospective clients who refuse services or clients who prematurely terminate services	• Learn why they are unwilling to participate or why they dropped out so as to figure out ways to improve client recruitment and retention
Content analysis of agency documents and service delivery manuals	• Identify potential practical pitfalls that need to be planned for in developing the research design • Develop specificity about the services being evaluated • Did the proper amounts and types of services get delivered to the clients for whom they were intended?
Semi-structured, open-ended interviews with practitioners or their clients following data analysis	• Develop possible explanations for unexpected, puzzling findings

Combining Quantitative and Qualitative Methods in Program Evaluation

Evaluative Function	Quantitative Methods	Qualitative Methods
Planning an evaluation		• Open-ended interviews with stakeholders • Content analysis of program documents • Participant observation of program activities
Needs assessment	• Survey of key informants, target group, or community • Rates under treatment • Social indicators	• Community forum • Focus groups
Process evaluation (monitoring program implementation and identifying needed improvements)	• Staff and client surveys • Analysis of agency records on amounts of various types of service delivery and to whom	• Case studies of model programs • Focus groups of program staff and service consumers • Open-ended interviews with staff about unofficial goals and implementation problems • Participant observation of service provision, staff training, and staff meetings • Open-ended interviews with service consumers • Content analysis of staff meeting documents or practitioner entries in client records • Videotaping or audiotaping service provision to assess practitioner skill or compliance with recommended procedures
Evaluating goal attainment	• Experimental and quasi-experimental designs combined with process evaluation to determine the nature of the program that did or did not attain its goals	• Supplement outcome evaluation with foregoing process evaluation methods to ascertain the nature of the successful program or to learn whether the unsuccessful program was really implemented as intended
Evaluating efficiency	• Cost-effectiveness analysis • Cost–benefit analysis	

- A good way to assess intervention fidelity is to videotape several randomly selected treatment sessions from each of your practitioners. Have experts in the intervention view each taped session and then complete a rating scale assessing their judgment of the degree to which the intervention in the session was implemented appropriately.
- A logic model graphically depicts the essential components of a program, shows how those components are linked to short-term process objectives, specifies measurable indicators of success in achieving short-term objectives, conveys how those short-term objectives lead to long-term program outcomes, and identifies measurable indicators of success in achieving long-term outcomes.
- The importance of program evaluation in funding decisions creates a highly political atmosphere in which stakeholders with vested interests can impede free scientific inquiry.
- Political considerations not only can affect in-house evaluators but also can bias external evaluators who seem to be more independent. Even funding sources and other external sponsors of an evaluation can have a stake in its outcome and may try to influence it for political reasons.

- Political and ideological forces can influence not only the methodology and interpretation of evaluative research, but also whether and how its findings are used. We cannot assume that the implications of evaluation research will necessarily be put into practice, especially if they conflict with official interests or points of view.
- Many practical pitfalls are likely to be encountered in attempting to implement experiments or quasi-experiments in service-oriented agencies. These pitfalls may compromise the fidelity of the interventions being evaluated, contaminate the control condition or the case assignment protocol, or hinder client recruitment and retention.
- The inclusion of various techniques commonly used in qualitative studies as part of an experiment or quasi-experiment can aid in avoiding or alleviating many of the practical pitfalls.

14.10 PRACTICE-RELATED EXERCISES

1. Interview an administrator and some practitioners at a social welfare agency. What evaluations, if any, have been conducted at the agency and with what outcomes? Were the findings used? Why or why not? Try to identify the stakeholders and their vested interests about those evaluations and findings. If no evaluation has ever been conducted, why not? Are politically or ideologically based resistances involved?
2. In the same or another agency, construct skeletal plans for evaluating program implementation and outcome. What resistances or logistical problems to the evaluation might be anticipated? How would the evaluation be useful to decision makers? What difficulties did you encounter in translating the agency's formal mission statement into observable indicators of outcome?
3. Find a research article in a social work journal that describes a study conducted for the purpose of evaluating program outcome. See if you can identify the stakeholders in the research, and critique the article from the standpoint of whether it showed how it controlled for potential biases associated with vested interests.
4. Identify six things you would do to avoid or alleviate practical pitfalls in carrying out an experiment to evaluate program outcome in an agency.

5. Read a program evaluation study that used quantitative methods only. A good place to look for one is the journal *Evaluation and Program Planning*. Summarize the study and discuss how adding qualitative methods might have improved its value.

14.11 INTERNET EXERCISE

1. Enter the search phrase "program evaluation" in Google Scholar to find two articles: one that reports a program evaluation study and one that discusses the politics of program evaluation. Write down the bibliographic reference information for each article. For the one reporting a study, briefly identify the strengths and weaknesses of that study. For the other article, summarize its main points about the politics of program evaluation.

14.12 ADDITIONAL READING

Alexander, L. B., & Solomon, P. (Eds.). (2006). *The research process in the human services: Behind the scenes*. Belmont, CA: Brooks/Cole. This book is a must-read for students who anticipate conducting program evaluation research in social work agencies. The chapters discuss efforts by esteemed researchers to implement different research methods and how those investigators grappled with the real-world agency challenges they encountered. The investigators discuss how they had to negotiate with agency stakeholders and modify their research designs in light of the obstacles they encountered. They also discuss the consequent strengths and weaknesses of the research methods they ultimately employed.

14.12a Competency Notes

EP 2.1.6b: Use research evidence to inform practice (p. 284): Understanding all of the concepts in this chapter will help social workers critically appraise outcome evaluations and judge which ones best merit guiding their practice.

EP 2.1.10m: Critically analyze, monitor, and evaluate interventions (p. 284): Social workers must understand all of the concepts in this chapter in order to evaluate interventions in a valid, competent manner.

Additional Qualitative and Quantitative Research Methods

Throughout this text we have discussed qualitative research methods and their value. The previous section, however, had to give more attention to quantitative methods, because those methods predominate in designs for making inferences about whether interventions cause certain outcomes. In Part 7 we will give more attention to qualitative methods. We'll begin by examining some qualitative methods in Chapter 15 that were not examined sufficiently in earlier chapters. In Chapter 16 we'll return to the topic of analyzing available records and examine the use of both quantitative and qualitative methods for conducting such analyses.

Additional Methods in Qualitative Inquiry

15.1 INTRODUCTION

EP 2.1.6b

Throughout this text we've been discussing ways in which research studies can combine quantitative and qualitative research methods. However, certain types of research—such as surveys and experiments—inescapably are more quantitative than qualitative in nature. In this chapter, then, we'll shift the emphasis of several recent chapters and focus on qualitative methods exclusively.

Unlike quantitative research methods, qualitative research methods typically are employed without precisely defined hypotheses to be tested. More typically, a purely qualitative study will attempt to make sense of an ongoing process that cannot be predicted in advance—making initial observations, developing tentative general conclusions that suggest particular types of further observations, making those observations and thereby revising conclusions, and so forth. The alternation of induction and deduction discussed in Chapter 4 of this book is perhaps nowhere more evident and essential than in good qualitative research.

One of the key strengths of qualitative research is the comprehensiveness of perspective it gives the researcher. By going directly to the social phenomenon under study and observing it as completely as possible, you can develop a deeper understanding of it. This mode of inquiry, then, is especially (though not exclusively) appropriate to research topics that appear to defy simple quantification. The qualitative researcher may recognize several nuances of attitude and behavior that might escape researchers using quantitative methods.

Qualitative research is especially appropriate to the study of phenomena that can best be understood within their natural setting. For example, if we want to learn what it feels like to be homeless, qualitative research methods might be more applicable than surveys or experiments.

---

ethnography A qualitative research approach that emphasizes observation in the natural environment and that focuses on detailed and accurate description of reality in terms of the people being observed.

15.2 PHENOMENOLOGY

Much qualitative research is associated with the term *phenomenology*, which refers to a philosophical paradigm for conducting qualitative research that emphasizes people's subjective experiences and interpretations of the world. One form of phenomenology is *heuristic inquiry*, in which researchers shed an effort to be detached observers and actually experience firsthand the phenomenon they are studying, using introspection to examine their own thoughts and feelings while experiencing that phenomenon. For example, they might stay in a shelter for the homeless for a while to better understand the meaning of that experience to the homeless, and perhaps to better understand why some homeless people refuse to use shelters.

An important phenomenological principle in qualitative research involves the German term *verstehen*, which means "understanding." Guided by this principle, qualitative researchers attempt to understand the people they observe from those people's own perspectives—to understand *their* feelings, *their* views of reality, and the special meanings to them of what the researchers observe. Thus, the term *verstehen* corresponds closely to the social work practice concept of empathy. Direct service social workers attempt to use empathy to understand their clients in much the same way that *verstehen* is used in qualitative research.

15.3 ETHNOGRAPHY

One form of phenomenological qualitative research is **ethnography**. Ethnography emphasizes observation in natural settings and focuses on providing detailed, accurate descriptions of the way people in a particular culture live and the way they interpret the meanings of things. By *culture*, we don't just mean societies in different countries. Ethnographic studies most relevant to social work will describe *subcultures* within our dominant culture, such as the homeless, street gangs, and so on.

Ethnographic research involves using qualitative interviewing and qualitative observation methods while immersing yourself in the culture you are attempting to understand and describe. Ethnographic researchers try to see the world through the eyes of the people they are studying and to understand their idiosyncratic belief systems and behavioral norms, as you can see in the following illustrations of ethnographic studies of homelessness.

15.3a Two Ethnographic Studies of Homelessness

Snow and Anderson (1987) sought to understand how the homeless construct and negotiate their identity while knowing that the society they live in attaches a stigma to homelessness. They found some key informants, whom they accompanied in their everyday journeys—following them to their day-labor pickup sites, for example, or to where they camped out under bridges. Snow and Anderson chose to memorize the conversations they participated in or the "talks" that homeless people had with each other. At the end of the day, the two researchers debriefed and wrote detailed field notes

about all the "talks" they encountered. They also taped in-depth interviews with their key informants.

Snow and Anderson reported "hanging out" with homeless people over the course of 12 months, for a total of 405 hours in 24 different settings. Out of these rich data, they identified three related patterns in homeless people's conversations. First, the homeless showed an attempt to "distance" themselves from other homeless people, from the low-status job they currently had, or from the Salvation Army they depended on. Second, they "embraced" their street-life identity, their group membership, or a certain belief about why they are homeless. Third, they told "fictive stories" that always contrasted with their everyday life. For example, they would often say that they were making much more money than they really were, or even that they were "going to be rich." The box titled "An Ethnographic Study of Homelessness in New York City" provides another illustration of this method.

An Ethnographic Study of Homelessness in New York City

Baxter and Hopper (1982) used ethnographic methods to show how the homeless in New York City "meet and resolve daily problems of survival in an often hostile environment" (p. 395). They conducted their observations wherever the homeless might sleep, stake out a domain, be fed, or receive services:

> ... park benches, street corners, doorways, subways, train stations, bus and ferry terminals, missions and flophouses, publicly and privately operated shelters, food programs, and emergency rooms. The terrain was initially mapped out through interviews with individuals and groups ... serving, researching, or advocating on behalf of the homeless. In the course of our own field work, additional sites were periodically discovered and investigated, including hallways and stairwells in occupied buildings, abandoned buildings, the piers along the East and Hudson rivers, alleyways, and heating vents—often with the homeless serving as guides. (p. 395)

They typically began their observations by initiating conversation with the offer of food, coffee, cigarettes, or change, and they introduced themselves as researchers on homelessness. But after encountering resistance, they began delaying this information awhile and describing their work in simpler terms, such as that of writers doing a story on homelessness.

In addition to their direct observations and interviews with the homeless, Baxter and Hopper interviewed others

who work with or who are connected in some way with homeless people. And on some occasions, they posed as homeless individuals themselves, such as when they entered public shelters to stay overnight. This enabled them to gain insights that would have been difficult to gain from the outside. For example, they were able to discover that from the standpoint of the homeless, refusal of service appears to have a more rational meaning than it does to professionals or to the public. The latter groups view service refusal as a reflection of defects in character or judgment, disinterest in being helped, or a preference to live on the street. Baxter and Hopper's observations indicated, however, that whenever services were offered, they were not adequate to accommodate the number of homeless individuals who sought to use them. Refusal of service seemed rational in light of the deplorable conditions they observed in the public shelters, conditions that sometimes made living in the streets and parks seem more attractive. In the public shelters, Baxter and Hopper observed overcrowding, lack of sanitation, and inadequate security—conditions that "would not meet federal regulations for prison cells" (1982, p. 398). Among other things, they noted the few toilets and showers that were often filthy or out of order, louse-infested mattresses and linens, the pilfering of clothing, the threat of violence, and fears of catching some dread disease.

But despite observing how service refusal can have an element of rationality, Baxter and Hopper also observed the harshness and toll of life on the streets, where the homeless are hungry, cold, socially isolated, and deprived of sleep. They observed how this strain can disorient individuals who were not mentally ill before they became homeless, and they noted that clinicians generally are not sensitive to the impact of this strain because they typically see the homeless only after their desperate straits have taken a toll on their mental health.

Through their immersion with the homeless, Baxter and Hopper also gained insights about the deeper meanings of other aspects of homelessness. For example, they observed the protective function of appearing bizarre and filthy and of having a noxious odor, which can protect homeless women by repelling men on the prowl. (Baxter and Hopper added, however, that foulness of appearance is virtually unavoidable, given the scarcity of toilets and bathing and laundry facilities.)

In light of these insights—insights that have escaped others—Baxter and Hopper concluded that practitioners' presumption of incompetence on the part of the homeless was a self-fulfilling prophecy because the homeless are eager to receive decent and humane care in those rare instances when such care is available. Despite the great hardships involved in living on the streets, the decision to refuse services can have the deeper meaning of salvaging a sense of defiant dignity and self-determination for the homeless in the face of the deplorable conditions of the shelters available to them. Baxter and Hopper ended their report with several proposals intended to make more and better services available to the homeless, to make it more rational for them to use those services, and to enhance the efforts of social workers to help the homeless.

15.4 CASE STUDIES

A **case study** is an examination of a single individual, family, group, organization, community, society, or phenomenon. Some case studies can be ethnographic. As with ethnography, the chief purpose of case studies is description, although attempts at explanation are also acceptable. Examples would include an in-depth description of a client system and an intervention with it, a depiction of the daily life and folkways of a street gang, an analysis of the organizational dynamics of a social welfare agency and how those dynamics influence the way social services are delivered, and a description of the emergence and experience of a grassroots community organization.

Although case studies are generally seen as a qualitative approach to research, the mode of observation used is not what distinguishes a case study. Instead, case studies are distinguished by their exclusive focus on a particular case (or several cases in a multiple-case study) and their use of a full variety of evidence regarding that case, including, perhaps, evidence gathered by quantitative research methods. Sources of evidence might include existing documents, observations, and interviews.

The rationale for using the case study method typically is the availability of a special case that seems to merit intensive investigation. For example, suppose a particular state decides to implement a massive program of deinstitutionalization by closing down many of its institutions for the mentally or developmentally disabled. A case study might be conducted to understand why and how it implemented that decision, what unanticipated problems occurred in the aftermath of the closings, and so on. Your case study of such an event and its impact might be useful in informing similar policy considerations in other states.

15.5 LIFE HISTORY

A method that emphasizes qualitative interviewing is called **life history**, or *life story*. Using this method, researchers ask open-ended questions to discover how the participants in a study understand the significant events and meanings in their own lives. Another term sometimes used in connection with this method is *oral history interviews*. (You may recall our discussion of qualitative interviews in Chapter 9.)

---

case study   An in-depth examination of a single individual, family, group, organization, community, society, or phenomenon.

life history   A qualitative interviewing method in which researchers ask open-ended questions to discover how the participants in a study understand the significant events and meanings in their own lives. (Other terms sometimes used in connection with this method are *life story* and *oral history interviews*.)

Researchers employing this method attempt to see how individuals subjectively remember and understand the significant events of their lives—even if the remembrances and interpretations lack objective accuracy. For example, Robinson (1994) sought to describe the significant events in the life stories of delinquent girls as told to her in oral history interviews. In particular, she was interested in life experiences that led to delinquent behaviors resulting in their referral for social services.

She interviewed 30 girls she randomly selected from purposively selected areas thought to be representative of Massachusetts. Robinson embarked on her study with the notion that a history of sexual abuse might be prevalent among this population of girls and that abuse might be a key factor in leading them to delinquent behaviors. Rather than operationally define "sexual abuse," however, she relied on the girls' own subjective experiences and perceptions. Robinson looked for cues suggestive of possible incidents of sexual abuse, and when she felt there was a cue she encouraged the girls to elaborate on the nature of the abuse and how they experienced it.

She began each interview with an open-ended question: "Tell me about your family" (1994, p. 81). In addition to observing their verbal responses during the interviews, Robinson took note of the girls' facial expressions, body language, and overall affect. The interviews were unstructured and conversational, although Robinson slowly and gently probed when the girls mentioned or hinted at sensitive events that were difficult for them to talk about. The girls discussed many painful and traumatic life events—including betrayal by parents, miscarriages and abortions, suicide attempts, and others—but Robinson focused on sexual abuse as the key event, noting that 23 of the 30 girls reported having been sexually abused. Ten of the girls reported being victimized by more than one person. Robinson's report cites various excerpts from her interviews, giving readers a sense of the girls' experiences of the abuse in their own voices. From this information, and guided by her theoretical framework and feminist perspective, Robinson concluded that correctional systems and social agencies should begin to view these girls not just as offenders, but as victims of horrendous experiences who need services specifically geared to sexual abuse.

15.6 FEMINIST METHODS

Robinson's study illustrates how the different types of qualitative studies we are discussing are not mutually exclusive. For example, her study combined life history interviews with a feminist perspective. We alluded to feminist studies back in Chapter 4, as an application of the critical social science paradigm. Many studies using feminist methods aim to generate findings that can be used to improve the well-being of women in a historically male-dominated society. Although feminist studies use both quantitative and qualitative methods, they are often associated with qualitative research. Qualitative feminist studies typically employ features of ethnography and oral history in that they attempt to let the voices of women be heard from their own point of view. In this connection, feminist studies typically rest on the assumption that women are different from men in the ways they acquire knowledge and view the world.

15.7 FOCUS GROUPS

Qualitative interviews can be conducted in **focus groups**. Focus group interviews can be structured, semistructured, or unstructured. They allow the researcher/interviewer to question several individuals systematically and simultaneously.

Focus groups are often used to assess whether a new social program or social service being considered is really needed in a community. In a focus group, a small group of people (some researchers recommend 12 to 15 people; others recommend no more than 8) are brought together in a room to engage in a guided discussion of a specified topic.

Participants in focus groups are likely to be selected using purposive sampling—based on their relevancy to the topic being discussed. For example, if the topic pertains to prospective consumer utilization of a new service that an agency is considering, then the participants may be community leaders, service providers from other agencies, referral

focus group A group of people interviewed together, prompting a discussion that might bring out aspects of the topic that researchers may not have anticipated and that may not have emerged in individual interviews.

sources, current service consumers, or perhaps a sample of community residents in targeted neighborhoods. If the topic concerns consumer satisfaction with agency services, then the participants may be drawn from current consumers. It's also common to convene more than one focus group; relying on only one group is generally considered too risky, because any one particular group may be atypical.

Despite the risks inherent in generalizing from focus groups, they offer several advantages. They are inexpensive, generate speedy results, and offer flexibility for probing. The group dynamics that occur in focus groups can bring out aspects of the topic that researchers may not have anticipated and that may not have emerged in individual interviews. Imagine, for example, that you, as a consumer in a social work education program, are being asked about your satisfaction with your social work curriculum and how it might be improved to offer better services. Suppose you are responding to a structured questionnaire or a structured interview with closed-ended questions about your degree of satisfaction with the classroom course offerings, field practicums, audiovisual or computer resources, the quality of the teaching, advising, instructor accessibility, and so forth.

Your responses would be limited to checking off things like "moderately satisfied," "slightly dissatisfied," and so on, to curriculum attributes anticipated by those who designed the survey. Suppose the survey questionnaire also contains open-ended items that ask you to think of anything else you particularly liked or disliked about the curriculum or recommendations you have for improvement. You may or may not give a great deal of thought to these open-ended items, and even if you give them considerable thought, you may not think of some things that others may think of, and with which you would agree.

Now suppose that you were being asked about these things not in a structured survey format but in a focus group. Instead of asking you to check off your degree of satisfaction with this or that, or to come up with new ideas for improvements by yourself, the focus group leader would ask you and some of your cohorts to engage in a sort of bull session discussion about your satisfaction or dissatisfaction with the curriculum and how it could be improved. Chances are, if one or more of your classmates began expressing dissatisfaction with something with which you also were dissatisfied, you might feel more comfortable in expressing the extent of your own dissatisfaction and its sources. As the members of the focus group interact about these issues, new ideas might be stimulated that would not have occurred to you in an individual interview or in completing a questionnaire.

For instance, someone might say, "Gee, I sure wish the curriculum offered an elective course on interventions connected to death and dying." This might spark someone else to say, "Yeah, and I would have loved to take a course on play therapy." Neither of these ideas may have occurred to you as an individual survey respondent, but on hearing them in a focus group you might respond, "Wow, I had assumed that the faculty knew best what courses were and were not appropriate to offer in a school of social work, but if those two courses had been offered I sure would have taken them both. They sound like they would have prepared me with specific practice intervention competencies more than a lot of the other electives offered."

These comments might spur other group participants who, like you, may not have thought of these courses in the context of an individual survey, and they might indicate that they also would love to take these two courses. And perhaps a few other possible elective courses would be identified that students would find highly relevant to their practice and that would, as a result of the courses' popularity, be fully enrolled. At the same time, the comments might prompt the group members to focus more on preparation for practice competency as their chief source of dissatisfaction with the curriculum, and a rich discussion might ensue identifying issues, potentially popular elective courses, and other ways to improve the curriculum that would not have been anticipated or identified by many respondents in a survey. Instead of only one or two prospective new elective courses being identified by one or two isolated individuals in a survey, the focus group might identify a larger number of new courses and show which would generate the most excitement and the largest potential enrollments.

That said, however, it's important to remember that focus groups also have disadvantages. As mentioned above, the representativeness of focus group members is questionable. Perhaps those who agree to participate or who are the most vocal are the ones with the biggest axes to grind about the program, the ones most satisfied with the program, or the ones most eager to curry favor with program providers. Although group dynamics can bring out information that would not have emerged in a survey, those dynamics also can create pressures for people to say things that may not accurately reflect their true feelings or prospective deeds. Whereas some individuals who feel dissatisfied with a program may feel more comfortable about expressing their dissatisfaction if others do so first, the same individuals may be less likely to express it if those who speak up first express great satisfaction with the program. If a couple of members show enthusiasm for a prospective service, then others may feel group pressure to say that they, too, would use the service even though, in reality, they would not.

In light of these potential pitfalls, special knowledge about group dynamics and special group work skills are needed to moderate focus groups. In a focus group interview—much more than in any other types of interviews—the interviewer has to develop the skills of a moderator. Controlling the dynamic within the group is a major challenge. Letting one interviewee dominate the focus group interview reduces the likelihood that the other participants will express themselves. This can generate the problem of group conformity, or groupthink, which is the tendency for people in a group to conform with opinions and decisions of the most outspoken members of the group. Interviewers need to be aware of this phenomenon and try to get everyone to participate fully on all the issues brought in the interview. Adding to the challenge, of course, is that you must resist overdirecting the interview and the interviewees, thus bringing your own views into play.

Another disadvantage of focus groups is that the data that emerge from focus groups are likely to be voluminous and less systematic than structured survey data. Analyzing focus group data, therefore, can be more difficult, tedious, and subject to the biases of the evaluator. And the analysis becomes more difficult to the extent that multiple focus groups yield inconsistent open-ended data. Thus, focus groups, like any other qualitative or quantitative research method, have certain advantages and disadvantages and are best used in combination with other research methods.

While focus group research differs from other forms of qualitative research, it further illustrates the possibilities for doing social research face-to-face with those we wish to understand. In addition, David Morgan (1993) suggests that focus groups are an excellent device for generating questionnaire items for a subsequent survey.

15.8 PARTICIPATORY ACTION RESEARCH

A qualitative research approach that is distinguished by its social action aims is called **participatory action research**. Using this approach, the researcher serves as a resource to those being studied—typically, disadvantaged groups—as an opportunity for them to act effectively in their own interest. The disadvantaged participants define their problems, define the remedies desired, and take the lead in designing the research that will help them realize their aims.

EP 2.1.5b

This approach rejects so-called elitist approaches to research that reduce the "subjects" of research to "objects" of research. According to many advocates of this perspective, the distinction between the researcher and the researched should disappear. They argue that the subjects who will be affected by research should also be responsible for its design. Implicit in this approach is the belief that research functions not only as a means of knowledge production, but also as a "tool for the education and development of consciousness as well as mobilization for action" (Gaventa, 1991, pp. 121–122). Advocates of participatory action research equate access to information with power, and argue that this power has been kept in the hands of the dominant class, sex, ethnicity, or nation. Once people see themselves as researchers, they automatically regain power over knowledge.

---

participatory action research An approach in which the researcher serves as a resource to those being studied and gives them control over the purpose and procedures of the research.

Examples of this approach include community power structure research, corporate research, and "right-to-know" movements (Whyte, Greenwood, & Lazes, 1991). Most germane to social work, participatory action research often involves poor people, as they are typically less able to influence the policies and actions that affect their lives. Bernita Quoss, Margaret Cooney, and Terri Longhurst (2000) reported on a research project involving welfare policy in Wyoming. University students, many of them welfare recipients, undertook research and lobbying efforts aimed at getting Wyoming to accept postsecondary education as "work" under the state's new welfare regulations.

> *This project began against the backdrop of the 1996 Personal Responsibility and Work Opportunity Act (PRWORA), which eliminated education waivers that had been available under the previous welfare law, the 1988 Family Support Act (FSA). These waivers had permitted eligible participants in the cash assistance AFDC program to attend college as an alternative to work training requirements. Empirical studies of welfare participants who received these waivers have provided evidence that education, in general, is the most effective way to stay out of poverty and achieve self-sufficiency. (Quoss et al., 2000, p. 47)*

The students began by establishing an organization, Empower, and making presentations on campus to enlist broad student and faculty support. They compiled existing research relevant to the issue and established relationships with members of the state legislature. By the time the 1997 legislative session opened, they were actively engaged in the process of modifying state welfare laws to take advantage of the shift in federal policy.

The students prepared and distributed fact sheets and other research reports that would be relevant to the legislators' deliberations. They attended committee meetings and lobbied legislators on a one-to-one basis. When erroneous or misleading data were introduced into the discussions, the student-researchers were on hand to point out the errors and offer corrections.

Ultimately, they were successful. Welfare recipients in Wyoming were allowed to pursue postsecondary education as an effective route out of poverty.

15.8a An Illustration of a Participatory Action Research Study Using Focus Groups and Feminist Methods: The Voices of Battered Women in Japan

Mieko Yoshihama was concerned about the dearth of research that examined the perspectives and experiences of battered women in Japan and the barriers to their seeking and using services. Consequently, she conducted "the first study in Japan to use face-to-face interviews with a community sample of battered women" (Yoshihama, 2002, p. 391). She used focus groups to conduct the interviews because she believed that hearing the experiences and perspectives of other battered women would help alleviate a sense of shame and isolation among study participants, would enhance their understanding of their own situation, and would make it easier for them to discuss how they perceived and coped with it.

EP 2.1.5c

She recruited battered women of various backgrounds to be study participants by sending flyers to organizations and professionals in Tokyo who come into contact with battered women, and by announcing the study in national and local newspapers. To facilitate the ability of women with diverse backgrounds and time constraints to participate in the study, she scheduled four focus groups during different times of the day, including one weekend group. On-site child care was provided. Participants received small cash reimbursements to partially cover their transportation and other costs of attending. They also received written materials about domestic violence and a list of assistance programs. Sessions were held at convenient and safe sites, and lasted two hours. To ensure anonymity, participants did not divulge their last names; some used pseudonyms or nicknames.

Each session was audiotaped, the tapes were transcribed, and the meanings or themes expressed by participants in the transcripts were coded. With the *grounded theory method* (see later discussion), repeated reviews of the transcripts yielded repeated revisions and improvements of the conceptual and thematic codes. Yoshihama's findings can be best summarized by the following excerpt from the abstract of her article:

> *Participants' narratives of their experience with their partners' violence suggest a web of entrapment, from which women saw little*

possibility of escape. The partners' physical violence, interference with the women's social participation, isolation from supportive networks, and degradation and debasement entrapped participants. The victim-blaming attitudes of family, friends, and professionals, as well as the lack of assistance programs and police protection often reinforced the web. When these women took the risk of exposing what was long considered private and shameful, isolation was broken. (p. 389)

In contrast with prevailing views, Yoshihama noted the similarities between the experiences of battered women in Japan and those in Western countries. Despite these similarities, Yoshihama pointed out that the victim-blaming reaction to this problem in Japanese society makes it harder for battered women there to obtain services and protection. Consequently, Yoshihama's study developed various implications for reforming social policy and social work practice in Japan to increase the amount of programs and services for battered women, and to make them more sensitive and responsive to the safety needs and rights of battered women instead of blaming them and emphasizing preservation of the marriage.

Her study also offered implications for social work practice with battered women immigrants from Japan in the United States, who may not be aware of their increased options in the United States and who may need several repeated explanations to understand the differences. Yoshihama also identified some limitations of her focus group study, specifically its limited generalizability in light of its small sample of self-selected women residing in one city. One of the strengths of the study pertained to its participatory action research function. By participating in the focus groups, the women were able to overcome their sense of shame and isolation, develop a shared understanding of their mutual problem, and obtain information about their legal rights and about available assistance programs. Consequently, the participants formed support groups for battered women.

15.9 GROUNDED THEORY

An overarching qualitative method that can be used in conjunction with most other forms of qualitative inquiry is called **grounded theory**. Grounded theory is an inductive qualitative method that begins with observations and looks for patterns, themes, or common categories. Although researchers using this method might have some preconceived ideas or expectations based on existing theory and research, the analysis is not set up to confirm or disconfirm specific hypotheses. By the same token, the openness of the grounded theory approach allows a greater latitude for the discovery of some unexpected regularity (or disparity) that probably would not have been anticipated by a pre-established theory or hypothesis.

Although grounded theory emphasizes an inductive process, it also can incorporate deductive processes. It does this through the use of **constant comparisons**. As researchers detect patterns in their inductive observations, they develop concepts and working hypotheses based on those patterns. Then they seek out more cases and conduct more observations, and compare those observations against the concepts and hypotheses developed from the earlier observations.

Their selection of new cases is guided by theoretical sampling concepts. As discussed in Chapter 11, theoretical sampling begins by selecting new cases that seem to be similar to those that generated previously detected concepts and hypotheses. Once the researcher perceives that no new insights are being generated from the observation of similar cases, a different type of case is selected, and the same process is repeated: Additional cases similar to this new type of case are selected until no new insights are being generated. This cycle of exhausting similar cases and then seeking a different category of cases can be repeated until the researcher believes that further seeking of new types of cases will not alter the findings.

---

grounded theory An inductive qualitative research approach that attempts to generate theory from the constant comparing of unfolding observations.

constant comparisons A grounded theory method in which as researchers detect patterns in their inductive observations, they develop concepts and working hypotheses based on those patterns, then seek out more cases and conduct more observations and compare those observations against the concepts and hypotheses developed from the earlier observations.

To understand the use of constant comparisons in the grounded theory process, imagine that you are seeking to discover the key components of effective community-based social work intervention aimed at forestalling relapse among young adults who have had schizophrenia. You might begin with open-ended interviews of several practitioners who have excellent reputations for their clinical effectiveness in this area. Perhaps you'd ask those practitioners to recall their most successful cases and discuss the interventions they used with them.

Let's suppose that you perceive a common pattern across every interview—a pattern in which each practitioner mentions the use of social skills training in the rehabilitation of the young adults, and communication skills training in helping their parents cope with them. You might therefore develop a working hypothesis that the use of such behavioral interventions distinguishes effective from ineffective practice in this area. To better ground your hypothesis in the empirical world, you might interview several additional practitioners with good clinical reputations to see if the same patterns are generated. If those interviews fail to generate new insights, you might reinterview the practitioners but use a different case-sampling approach. This time you might ask them to discuss the interventions they employed with their least successful cases. Suppose a few of them mention the same behavioral interventions that they mentioned with their most successful cases—the same behavioral interventions to which your working hypothesis refers. This would force you to modify your hypothesis. You might probe to uncover other aspects of their practice with their least successful cases—aspects that might help explain why the same interventions that seemed to work well with other cases did not work with these cases.

Let's suppose that these probes generate another common pattern—a pattern in which each of the least successful clients failed or refused to take their prescribed medications. Based on this observation, your modified working hypothesis might combine medication-monitoring interventions with behavioral interventions in distinguishing effective practice.

Continuing the grounded theory process, you would interview additional practitioners and ask about different types of cases. For example, you might learn of parents who did not benefit from the communications skills training because the practitioner did not adequately develop a therapeutic alliance with them before introducing that training. This knowledge might lead you to modify your working hypothesis further, perhaps by adding the prerequisite that family intervention be delivered in the context of a supportive relationship with the practitioner, one in which the parents understand that they are not being blamed for their children's illness.

At this point, you might realize that all of your cases have involved clients who live with their parents. Therefore, you might conduct interviews in reference to successful and unsuccessful cases in which the clients did not live with their parents. You might learn that with clients who do not live with their parents, effective practice also requires a lot of case management tasks such as attention to securing suitable living arrangements, and does not involve family communication skills training. Further sampling might identify many cases that involve dual diagnoses of schizophrenia and substance abuse. You might have to modify your hypothesis to include substance abuse interventions geared for this target population.

By the time you have completed the grounded theory process, you will have interviewed many different practitioners (perhaps including some with poor clinical reputations) and asked about many other types of cases. This additional empirical grounding will probably have led you to add many more modifications to your hypothesis. Some of them might deal with practitioner attributes such as empathy, warmth, and diagnostic skill. Some modifications might deal with client attributes, such as the need for different types of interventions depending on client degree of impairment, social support resources, and so on. Other modifications might deal with the full gamut of case management functions.

Gilgun (1991) sees several parallels between the grounded theory method and what social workers do in direct practice—particularly regarding clinical assessment. Both methods start where the case is and focus on the informant's perceptions. Both try to understand the case in a wider environmental context. Both combine induction and deduction and the constant comparison method in formulating working hypotheses based on observations, then modifying those hypotheses in light of further observations. Both try to avoid imposing preconceived ideas or theories on cases. Both rely heavily on open-ended interviewing and use largely the same interviewing skills (as will be evident later in this chapter when we discuss qualitative interviewing). The process of using notes and memos in grounded theory resembles the social worker's use of process recording and problem-oriented case record keeping. Both attempt "to keep a balance between being in tune with clients and maintaining an analytic stance" (1991, p. 17). Both like to conduct observations in natural settings, such as in the home or community.

15.10 SPECIAL CONSIDERATIONS IN QUALITATIVE OBSERVATION

Regardless of which of the foregoing approaches they use, qualitative investigators face decisions they must make about data collection. In Chapter 9, for example, we discussed decisions they will need to make about interviewing, and in Chapter 11 we discussed alternative sampling choices in qualitative inquiry. Other decisions involve the role they will play as an observer and their relations with the people they are observing. Let's examine some of the issues involved in these decisions.

15.10a The Various Roles of the Observer

In qualitative research, observers can play any of several roles, including participating in what they want to observe. In this chapter, we use the term *qualitative observation* rather than the frequently used term *participant observation* because qualitative researchers need not always participate in what they are studying, though they usually will study it directly at the scene of the action. Four roles that qualitative researchers may play include: *complete participant, participant-as-observer, observer-as-participant,* and *complete observer.* These roles can be viewed as forming a continuum, with the complete participant at one end and the complete observer at the other end.

The *complete participant,* in this sense, may either be a genuine participant in what he or she is studying (for example, a participant in a protest demonstration) or pretend to be a genuine participant. In any event, if you are acting as the complete participant, you let people see you only as a participant, not as a researcher.

Clearly, if you are not a genuine participant in what you are studying, you must learn to behave as

though you were. If you are studying a group of uneducated and inarticulate people, it would not be appropriate for you to talk and act like a university professor or student.

Here let us draw your attention to an ethical issue, one on which social researchers themselves are divided. Is it ethical to deceive the people you are studying in the hope that they will confide in you as they will not confide in an identified researcher? Do the interests of science—the scientific values of the research—offset such ethical considerations? Although many professional associations have addressed this issue, the norms to be followed remain somewhat ambiguous when applied to specific situations.

Related to this ethical consideration is a scientific one. No researcher deceives his or her participants solely for the purpose of deception. Rather, it is done in the belief that the data will be more valid and reliable, that the participants will be more natural and honest if they do not know the researcher is doing a research project. If the people being studied know they are being studied, they might modify their behavior in a variety of ways. First, they might expel the researcher. Second, they might modify their speech and behavior to appear more respectable than they would otherwise be. Third, the social process itself might be radically changed. Students making plans to burn down the university administration building, for example, might give up the plan altogether once they learn that a member of their group is a social scientist conducting a research project.

On the other side of the coin, if you are a complete participant, you may affect what you are studying. To play the role of participant, you must *participate.* Yet your participation may have important effects on the social process you are studying. Suppose, for example, that you are asked for your ideas about what the group should do next. No matter what you say, you will affect the process in some fashion. If the group follows your suggestion, your influence on the process is obvious. If the group decides not to follow your suggestion, the process by which the suggestion is rejected may affect what happens next. Finally, if you indicate that you just don't know what should be done next, you may be adding to a general feeling of uncertainty and indecisiveness in the group.

Ultimately, *anything* the participant observer does or does not do will have some effect on what is being observed; it is simply inevitable. More seriously, what you do or do not do may have an *important* effect on what happens. There is no complete protection against this effect, though sensitivity to the issue may provide partial protection.

Because of these several considerations, ethical and scientific, the qualitative researcher frequently chooses a different role from that of complete participant. For example, you might choose the role of *participant-as-observer*. In this role, you would participate fully with the group under study, but you would make it clear that you were also undertaking research. If you were a member of a community organization, for example, you might use your participation in the organization's activities to conduct a study of its social processes—letting other members know what you were doing. There are dangers in this role also, however. The people being studied may shift much of their attention to the research project rather than focus on the natural social process, and the process being observed may no longer be typical. Or conversely, you yourself may come to identify too much with the participants' interests and viewpoints. You may begin to "go native" and lose much of your scientific detachment.

The *observer-as-participant* is one who identifies himself or herself as a researcher and interacts with the participants in the social process but makes no pretense of actually being a participant. For example, you might study a social movement—such as the unionization of migrant farm workers. You might interview leaders and also visit workers where they live, watch strawberry picking, go with an injured worker to the hospital, and so on.

The *complete observer*, at the other extreme, observes a social process without becoming a part of it in any way. The participants in a study might not realize they are being studied because of the researcher's unobtrusiveness. Sitting at a bus stop to observe jaywalking behavior at a nearby intersection would be an example. Although the complete observer is less likely to affect what is being studied and less likely to "go native" than the complete participant, he or she is also less likely to develop a full appreciation of what is being studied. Observations may be more sketchy and transitory.

Ultimately, different situations require different roles for the researcher. Unfortunately, there are no clear guidelines for making this choice, and you must rely on your understanding of the situation and your own good judgment. In making your decision, however, you must be guided by both methodological and ethical considerations. Because these often conflict with one another, your decision will frequently be a difficult one, and you may find sometimes that your role limits your study.

15.10b Emic and Etic Perspectives

A paradoxical challenge in qualitative observation is the need to step outside of your own views and adopt those of the culture you are studying, while at the same time maintaining your objectivity and ability to question the views you are adopting. This requires a blending of two perspectives. The **emic perspective** involves trying to adopt the beliefs, attitudes, and other points of view shared by the members of the culture being studied. With this perspective, researchers try to gain an insider understanding in relating to research participants. In contrast, the **etic perspective** allows researchers to maintain their objectivity as an outsider, and to raise questions about the culture they are observing that would not occur to members of that culture.

15.11 CONDUCTING QUALITATIVE RESEARCH

Let's turn now to some generic ideas and techniques for conducting qualitative research, beginning with how researchers prepare for work in the field. Suppose that you want to study a grassroots community organization. Let's assume further that you are not a member of that group, that you do not know much about it, and that you will identify yourself to the participants as a researcher. You would be well-advised to begin with a search of the relevant

emic perspective   Trying to adopt the beliefs, attitudes, and other points of view shared by the members of the culture being studied.

etic perspective   Maintaining objectivity as an outsider and raising questions about the culture being observed that wouldn't occur to members of that culture.

literature, filling in your knowledge of the subject and learning what others have said about it.

In the next phase of your research, you may wish to discuss the community group with others who have already studied it or with anyone else who is likely to be familiar with it. In particular, you might find it useful to discuss the group with one of its members. Perhaps you already know a member or can meet one. This aspect of your preparation is likely to be more effective if your relationship with the informant extends beyond your research role. In dealing with members of the group as informants, you should take care that your initial discussions do not compromise or limit later aspects of your research. Realize that the impression you make on the member informant and the role you establish for yourself may carry over into your later effort. For example, creating the initial impression that you may be a spy for an opposing group is unlikely to facilitate later observations of the group.

You should also be wary about the information you get from informants. Although they may have more direct, personal knowledge of the subject under study than you, what they "know" is probably a mixture of fact and point of view. Members of the community group in our example are unlikely to give you completely unbiased information (neither would members of opposing groups).

Before making your first contact with the group, then, you should already be quite familiar with it, and you should understand the general, theoretical context within which it exists.

You can establish your initial contact with the people you plan to study in a variety of ways. How you do it will depend, in part, on the role you intend to play. Especially if you are to take on the role of complete participant, you must find a way to develop an identity with the people to be studied. If you wish to study dishwashers in a restaurant, the most direct method would be to get a job as a dishwasher. In the case of the community organization, you might simply join the group.

Whenever you wish to make a more formal contact with the people and identify yourself as a researcher, you must be able to establish a certain rapport with them. You might contact a participant with whom you feel comfortable and gain that person's assistance. If you are studying a formal group, you might approach the group leaders. Or you may

find that one of your informants who has studied the group can introduce you.

Although you will probably have many options in making your initial contact with the group, you should realize that your choice can influence your subsequent observations. Suppose, for example, that you are studying a community clinic and begin with high-level administrators. First, your initial impressions of the clinic are going to be shaped by the administrators' views, which will be quite different from those of patients or staff. This initial impression may influence the way you subsequently observe and interpret—even though you are unaware of the influence.

Second, if the administrators approve of your research project and encourage patients and staff to cooperate with you, then the latter groups will probably look on you as somehow aligned with the administration, which can affect what they say to you. Nurses might be reluctant to tell you about their plans to join a union, for example.

In making direct, formal contact with the people you want to study, you will be required to give them some explanation of the purpose of your study. Here again, you face an ethical dilemma. Telling them the complete purpose of your research might lose their cooperation altogether or have important effects on their behavior. On the other hand, giving only what you believe would be an acceptable explanation may involve outright deception. Realize in all this that your decisions—in practice—may be largely determined by the purpose of your study, the nature of what you are studying, observations you wish to use, and other such factors.

Previous qualitative research offers no fixed rule—methodological or ethical—to follow in this regard. Your appearance as a researcher, regardless of your stated purpose, may result in a warm welcome from people who are flattered that a scientist finds them important enough to study. Or you may end up being ostracized, or worse. (Do not, for example, burst into a meeting of an organized crime syndicate and announce that you are writing a term paper on organized crime.)

15.11a Recording Observations

Because of their in-depth, open-ended nature, qualitative interviews pose quite a challenge to the interviewer. The aims and philosophical roots of qualitative inquiry mandate that the respondent's answers should be recorded as fully as possible. Recording them verbatim is ideal. A tape recorder, therefore, is a powerful tool for the qualitative interviewer. It not only ensures verbatim recording but also frees interviewers to keep their full attention focused on respondents, to communicate that they are listening to what is being said, and to probe into important cues.

Noting these advantages of tape recording, Patton (1990) nevertheless urges interviewers who use tape recorders to take notes while they interview so they can refer back to something important said earlier in the interview, or to occasionally jot down summary points or key phrases to facilitate later analysis of the tape. He also suggests that note-taking (done in moderation) helps pace the interview and lets respondents know that you find what they are saying important.

Tape recorders, however, are not applicable for a great deal of the data gathering in field research, particularly data gathered as a result of observation outside the interview context. And even in interviews, tape recorders cannot capture all of the relevant aspects of social processes. Therefore, other basic tools of qualitative research include a notebook (or field journal) and a pencil. The greatest advantage of the qualitative field research method is the presence of an observing, thinking researcher on the scene. If possible, take notes on your observations as you make them. When that's not possible, write down your notes as soon as possible afterward.

Your notes should include both your empirical observations and your interpretations of them. You should record what you "know" has happened and what you "think" has happened. It is important, however, that these different kinds of notes be identified for what they are. For example, you might note that Person X spoke in opposition to a proposal made by a group leader, that you think this represents an attempt by Person X to take over leadership of the group, and that you think you heard the leader comment to that effect in response to the opposition.

Just as you cannot hope to observe everything, neither can you record everything you observe. Just as your observations represent a de facto sample of all possible observations, your notes represent a sample of your observations. Rather than record a random sample of your observations, you should, of course, record the most important ones.

Some of the most important observations can be anticipated before the study begins; others will become apparent as your observations progress. Sometimes your note-taking can be made easier if you prepare standardized recording forms in advance. In a study of the homeless, for instance, you might anticipate the characteristics of homeless individuals that are the most likely to be useful for analysis—age, gender, social class, ethnicity, psychiatric history, and so forth—and prepare a form in which actual observations can be recorded easily. Or you might develop a symbolic shorthand in advance to speed up recording. For studying citizen participation at a community meeting, you might want to construct a numbered grid to represent the different sections of the meeting room; then you would be able to record the location of participants easily, quickly, and accurately.

None of this advance preparation should limit your recording of unanticipated events and aspects of the situation. Quite the contrary, speedy handling of anticipated observations can give you more freedom to observe the unanticipated.

Every student is familiar with the process of taking notes. And as we said earlier, everybody is somewhat familiar with qualitative research in general. Like good qualitative research, however, good note-taking requires careful and deliberate attention and involves specific skills; some guidelines follow.

First, don't trust your memory any more than you have to; it's untrustworthy. Even if you pride yourself on having a photographic memory, it's a good idea to take notes either during the observation or as soon afterward as possible. If you are taking notes during observation, then do it unobtrusively, because people are likely to behave differently if they see you taking down everything they say or do.

Second, it's usually a good idea to take notes in stages. In the first stage, you may need to take sketchy notes (words and phrases) to keep abreast of what's happening. Then remove yourself and rewrite your notes in more detail. If you do this soon after the events you've observed, the sketchy notes should allow you to recall most of the details. The longer you delay, the less likely it is you will recall things accurately and fully.

We know this method sounds logical, and you've probably made a mental resolve to do it that way if you're ever involved in qualitative research. Let us warn you, however, that you will need self-discipline to keep your resolution in practice. Careful observation and note-taking can be tiring, especially if they involve excitement or tension and extend over a long period of time. If you've just spent eight continuous hours observing and making notes on how people have been coping with a disastrous flood, then your first thought afterward is likely to be directed toward getting some sleep, dry clothes, or a drink. You may need to take some inspiration from newspaper reporters who undergo the same sorts of hardships before writing their stories and meeting their deadlines.

Third, you will inevitably wonder how much you should record. Is it really worth the effort to write out all of the details you can recall right after the observation session? The general guideline here is, yes. Generally, in qualitative research you cannot be really sure of what is and is not important until you've had a chance to review and analyze a great volume of information, so you should even record things that don't seem important at the outset—they may turn out to be significant after all. Also, the act of recording the details of something "unimportant" may jog your memory on something that is important.

You should realize that most of your field notes will not be reflected in your final report on the project. Put more harshly, most of the notes you take will be "wasted." But take heart: Even the richest gold ore yields only about 30 grams of gold per metric ton, meaning that 99.997 percent of the ore is wasted. Yet that 30 grams of gold can be hammered out to cover an area 18 square feet—the equivalent of almost 700 book pages! So take a ton of notes, and plan to select and use only the gold.

Like other aspects of qualitative research (and all research, for that matter), proficiency comes with practice. The nice thing about qualitative research is you can begin practicing now and can continue practicing in almost any situation. You don't have to be engaged in an organized research project to practice observation and recording. You might start by volunteering to take the minutes at committee meetings, for example.

15.12 COMPARING THE STRENGTHS AND WEAKNESSES OF QUALITATIVE AND QUANTITATIVE RESEARCH

All research methods have their own distinctive strengths and weaknesses. Let's contrast some of the key strengths and weaknesses of qualitative and quantitative approaches to inquiry.

15.12a Depth of Understanding

Qualitative research is especially effective for studying subtle nuances in attitudes and behaviors, and for examining social processes over time. As such, the chief strength of this method lies in the depth of understanding it permits. Whereas some quantitative research methods may be challenged as "superficial," this charge is seldom lodged against qualitative research.

15.12b Flexibility

Flexibility is another advantage of qualitative research. In this method, you may modify your research design at any time, as discussed earlier. Moreover, you are always prepared to engage in qualitative research whenever the occasion arises; whereas you could not as easily initiate a survey or an experiment.

15.12c Subjectivity

Qualitative research measurements—although in-depth—are also often very personal. For example, if a researcher reports that the members of a club tend to be conservative, know that such a judgment may have been influenced by the researcher's own politics. However, researchers who use qualitative techniques can be conscious of this issue and take pains to address it. Not only are individual researchers often able to sort out their own biases and points of view, but also the communal nature of science means that their colleagues will help them in that regard. Depending on the purpose of a study—and on the researcher's paradigm regarding objectivity and subjectivity—the subjective nature of many qualitative studies might be seen as both an advantage and a disadvantage as compared to quantitative research.

15.12d Generalizability

One of the chief goals of science is generalization. Social scientists study particular situations and events to learn about social life in general. Usually, nobody would be interested in knowing about the specific participants observed by the researcher. Who cares, after all, how a sample of 1,500 voters is going to vote in a national election? We are interested only if the voters' intentions can be generalized to the total electorate.

Generalizability is a problem for qualitative research. It crops up in three forms. First, as we've already suggested, the personal nature of the observations and measurements made by the researcher can produce results that would not necessarily be replicated by another, independent researcher. If the observation depends in part on the particular observers, then it becomes more valuable as a source of insight than as proof or truth.

Second, because qualitative researchers get a full and in-depth view of their subject matter, they can reach an unusually comprehensive understanding. By its very comprehensiveness, however, this understanding is less generalizable than results based on rigorous sampling and standardized measurements. Let's say you set out to fully understand how your city council operates. You study each of the members in great depth, learning about their ideological positions, how they came to public life, how they got elected, who their friends and enemies are. You could learn about their family lives, seeing how personal feelings enter into their public acts. After such an in-depth study, you could probably understand the actions of the council really well. But would you be able to say much about city councils in general? Surely your study would have provided you with some general insights, but you wouldn't be able to carry over everything you learned from the specific to the general. Having mastered the operations of the Dayton City Council, you might not be able to say much about Cleveland's. You should, however, be in a position to organize a great study of the Cleveland City Council.

In reviewing reports of qualitative research projects, you should determine where and to what extent the researcher is generalizing beyond his or her specific observations to other settings. Such generalizations may be in order, but you need to judge that. Nothing in this research method guarantees it.

Finally, there is often a problem of generalizability even within the specific subject matter being observed. As an illustration, let's imagine you were interested in learning about Scientology. Suppose you were particularly interested in the church's recruitment practices: how it attracts new members, what kinds of people are attracted, and so on. One way to find the answers to such questions would be for you to express interest in the church yourself. Talk to members. Attend meetings and retreats. In this fashion, you'd be able to get a first hand experience of what you wanted to study. You could observe the way you were treated after expressing interest, and you could observe the treatment of other newcomers. By getting to know the other people who were considering joining the church, you would get an idea of the kinds of people who were joining.

Here's the problem of generalizability: Although you might talk to many church members, you couldn't be sure how "typical" they were. You might end up talking only to people assigned the job of talking to potential recruits. Or perhaps you make your contact through your English class and meet mostly members majoring in the humanities and none majoring in the sciences. The potentials for biased sampling are endless. The same would apply to the new recruits you got to know; they might not be typical of new recruits in general.

The problem of generalizability, however, is not unique to qualitative studies. Many quantitative studies also lack generalizability. Recall our discussion of potential limitations to external validity in Chapters 12 and 13 regarding group or single-case experimental and quasi-experimental designs. Recall also our discussion in Chapters 10 and 11 regarding how limitations of survey and sampling procedures can produce misleading results that are not representative of the population to which they are generalized.

15.13 STANDARDS FOR EVALUATING QUALITATIVE STUDIES

Because qualitative inquiry involves a variety of dissimilar research methods and paradigms, different perspectives can be found regarding how to critically appraise the rigor of qualitative research. Regardless of one's perspective, however, there is general agreement that one key issue in evaluating the rigor of qualitative research is *trustworthiness.* However, one's epistemological paradigm will influence the criteria used to assess trustworthiness as well as whether some other key issues are just as important as trustworthiness.

For those whose epistemological paradigm is mainly oriented toward contemporary positivism (as discussed in Chapter 4), trustworthiness will be the prime focus in evaluating the rigor of a qualitative study. They will be primarily concerned with the extent to which a study can take steps to maximize objectivity and minimize bias. Those who view research through the lens of the critical social science or participatory action research paradigm, however, will additionally ask whether people were empowered by the research. Those with a postmodern or social constructivist paradigm will also use trustworthiness as a key criterion, but they will approach that criterion somewhat differently than contemporary positivists in keeping with an emphasis on multiple subjective realities. The

different criteria each of these paradigms uses to assess trustworthiness are displayed in Table 15.1. In discussing these criteria, let's begin by examining the criteria used in the contemporary positivist perspective. Then we'll examine the similarities and differences between that approach and those that emphasize alternative paradigms.

15.13a Contemporary Positivist Standards

As we mentioned previously, for contemporary positivists the key issue in evaluating the rigor of qualitative research is trustworthiness. In her book, *Qualitative Methods in Social Work Research*, Deborah Padgett (1998b) identifies three key threats to trustworthiness: reactivity, researcher biases, and respondent biases. *Reactivity* occurs when the researcher's presence in the field distorts the naturalism of the setting and consequently the things being observed there. As we discussed earlier, *researcher biases* can distort what researchers perceive or how they selectively observe. *Respondent*

Table 15.1 Standards Used by Three Different Paradigms for Appraising the Trustworthiness of Qualitative Research

PARADIGM	STANDARDS
Contemporary Positivist	Maximize objectivity and minimize the distorting influences of reactivity, researcher biases, and respondent biases. Use one or more of the following six strategies: 1. Prolonged engagement 2. Triangulation 3. Peer debriefing and support 4. Negative case analysis 5. Member checking 6. Auditing a paper trail
Social Constructivist	Appraise whether multiple subjective realities are adequately depicted according to the following criteria: 1. Member checking 2. Fittingness or transferability (provision of thick background information with sufficient detail about the research context, setting and participants) 3. Triangulation not to check for reliability, but to improve chances of detecting the full range of subjective realities
Empowerment	Appraise whether the study empowered research participants. Did it: 1. Evoke action by participants to effect desired change and a redistribution of power? 2. Obtain and report participant testimonials suggesting a change in their views about the need for change and whether the research increased their optimism about the possibility for change?

bias is another concept you may recall from earlier sections; it refers most typically to the need to appear socially desirable.

To minimize the distorting influence of these threats, Padgett recommends six commonly used strategies to enhance the rigor of qualitative studies. Not every strategy is feasible or applicable to every qualitative investigation. You can evaluate the rigor of the qualitative studies you read by asking yourself which of these strategies are applicable to a given study and, if applicable, whether they were used.

Padgett terms the first strategy *prolonged engagement.* It is used to reduce the impact of reactivity and respondent bias. It assumes that a long and trusting relationship with the researcher gives respondents less opportunity to deceive and makes them less inclined to withhold information or to lie. Padgett adds that lengthy interviews or a series of follow-up interviews with the same respondent makes it easier for the researcher to detect distortion, or for the respondent ultimately to disclose socially undesirable truths.

Prolonged engagement can also have a drawback. A lengthy engagement can lead to bias if the researchers overidentify with their respondents and lose their objective, analytic stance, or their own sense of identity. Despite this risk, qualitative studies that lack prolonged engagement should be viewed with caution. Some authors, for example, seem to think that because qualitative inquiry emphasizes flexibility, the label "qualitative" means "anything goes." We have seen this in some manuscripts we've reviewed for publication in professional journals. The most common example occurs when an investigator thinks that one brief open-ended interview with each respondent is sufficient. (Conceivably, that may be sufficient in some unusual qualitative studies, but if so, the author should provide a compelling justification of that as opposed to ignoring the issue.)

The second strategy is *triangulation.* Triangulation occurs when researchers seek corroboration between two or more sources for their data and interpretations. Padgett describes five types of triangulation in qualitative inquiry. One approach is to have the data analyzed by colleagues who hold contrasting theoretical orientations. Another is to use more than one qualitative method (and perhaps some quantitative methods, too) to collect and analyze data. A third approach is to use multiple observers to collect the data and multiple coders to classify the collected observations. A fourth approach is to use more than one data source (such as direct observations, interviews, and existing records). A fifth type is called *interdisciplinary triangulation,* in which a team of researchers from different fields collaborate. Padgett cautions us, however, not to overreact to inconsistencies in triangulated data. Sometimes disagreement between different data sources simply reveals different perspectives about a phenomenon, such as when two conflicting family members express different versions of family problems.

A third strategy, one that overlaps somewhat with triangulation, is called *peer debriefing and support.* This occurs when teams of investigators meet regularly to give each other feedback, emotional support, and ideas. They might exchange alternative perspectives and new ideas about how they are collecting data, about problems, and about meanings in the data already collected. The idea here is that the peer debriefing process increases the likelihood of spotting and correcting for biases and other problems in data collection and interpretation.

The next two strategies are negative case analysis and member checking. *Negative case analysis* involves searching thoroughly for disconfirming evidence—looking for deviant cases that do not fit the researcher's interpretations. *Member checking* involves asking research participants to confirm or disconfirm the accuracy of the research observations and interpretations. Do the reported observations and interpretations ring true and have meaning to the participants?

The final strategy, *auditing,* occurs when the researcher leaves a paper trail of field notes, interview transcripts, journals and memos documenting decisions made along the way, and so on. This enables an impartial and qualitatively adept investigator who is not part of the study to scrutinize what was done to determine if efforts to control for biases and reactivity were thorough, if the procedures used were justifiable, and if the interpretations fit the data collected. Thus, auditing encompasses each of the preceding five strategies, because part of the purpose of the audit is to ascertain whether those strategies were appropriately implemented.

15.13b Social Constructivist Standards

Social constructivists also emphasize trustworthiness in appraising qualitative research, and they recommend the preceding strategies for enhancing the rigor of qualitative studies. However, they view trustworthiness and these strategies more in terms of capturing multiple subjective realities than ensuring the portrayal of an objective social reality, the objective of contemporary positivists. Thus, for example, minimizing respondent bias becomes less important than making sure that the research participants' multiple subjective realities are revealed as adequately as possible (Krefting, 1991). The point in member checking, then, becomes less concerned with whether the researcher's interpretations were objective and accurate, and more concerned with whether participants acknowledge that their subjective realities are being depicted as they see them.

Another criterion is whether the qualitative research report provides enough detail about the study contexts and participants to enable readers in other situations to judge whether the findings seem likely to apply to the context or population with which they are concerned. Guba (1981) referred to this criterion as *fittingness* or *transferability*. Lincoln and Guba (1985) added that this criterion is unlike the external validity or generalizability criteria that we have discussed in connection to quantitative studies. The onus is not on the qualitative researchers to demonstrate that their studies have external validity or to say to whom their findings generalize. Instead, the onus is on the research consumers to make the judgment as to whether the findings seem applicable to their situation or population of concern. To enable the consumer to make that judgment, however, the onus is on the researcher to provide "thick" background information about the research context, setting, and participants.

The constructivist approach also uses triangulation somewhat differently than does the contemporary positivist approach. The contemporary positivist approach would see inconsistencies revealed in triangulation as a reflection of unreliability in the data. It might also reflect researcher bias if two investigators derived contradictory interpretations of the data. In contrast, the constructivist approach would see inconsistencies as a possible reflection of multiple realities. They would want to

see the inconsistencies explained; perhaps the explanations of inconsistency in triangulated data would produce a better understanding of the range of subjective realities—especially those that are atypical.

15.13c Empowerment Standards

EP 2.1.5b
EP 2.1.5c

As we mentioned previously, those who take a critical social science or participatory action research approach to qualitative research would add empowerment standards to those mentioned. Rodwell (1998) discusses empowerment standards for evaluating qualitative research in terms of what she calls *catalytic authenticity* and *tactical authenticity*. According to her paradigm (which actually combines constructivism with empowerment), creating new knowledge is not sufficient in constructivist research. In addition, the research must evoke action by participants to effect desired change and a redistribution of power. She adds that although it will be impossible to prove that the research caused the change, a follow-up should obtain and report participant testimonials suggesting a change in their views about the need for change and whether the research increased their optimism about the possibility for change.

As we close this chapter, we should point out that we understand how some readers might get the impression that we give more attention to the limitations of qualitative research than to the limitations of quantitative research. Although that certainly is not our intention, readers might get that impression because this chapter focuses on qualitative methods in general and thus discusses the strengths and weaknesses of those methods in general. In contrast, we did not have a chapter on quantitative methods in general that contained a section on their strengths and weaknesses. However, we have been discussing flaws in quantitative research throughout most of the preceding chapters. For example, we discussed biases and other flaws in the wording of quantitative measurement instruments, quantitative scales that lack reliability and validity, unrepresentative surveys with inadequate response rates or biased sampling procedures, practice evaluations that lack internal validity or use biased measurement procedures, and so on. Moreover, even in this chapter we have discussed the strengths and limitations of qualitative research in the context of comparing them with the strengths and limitations of quantitative research. In that context, we noted that quantitative research can be superficial and sometimes not generalizable. It is our view that much of the quantitative research that gets published has significant additional methodological weaknesses.

To conclude, it is our hope that, in summarizing here our treatment of quantitative and qualitative research throughout the text, we will have managed to offset any unintended imbalance that readers may have perceived in the way we have covered the strengths and weaknesses of these two complementary approaches to inquiry.

15.14 MAIN POINTS

- Ethnography focuses on providing detailed, accurate descriptions of the way people in a particular culture live and the way they interpret the meanings of things.
- A case study is an examination of a single individual, family, group, organization, community, society, or phenomenon.
- Life histories involve asking open-ended questions to discover how the participants in a study understand the significant events and meanings in their own lives.
- Feminist studies aim to generate findings that can be used to improve the well-being of women in a historically male-dominated society.
- To create a focus group, researchers bring participants together and observe their interactions as they explore a specific topic.
- Using the participatory action research approach, the researcher serves as a resource to those being studied and gives them control over the purpose and procedures of the research.
- Grounded theory refers to the attempt to derive theories from an analysis of the patterns, themes, and common categories discovered among observational data.
- Using the constant comparisons method, researchers detect patterns in their inductive observations, develop concepts and working hypotheses based on those patterns, and then seek out more cases and conduct more observations and compare

those observations against the concepts and hypotheses developed from the earlier observations.
- You may or may not identify yourself as a researcher to the people you are observing. Identifying yourself as a researcher may have some effect on the nature of what you are observing, but concealing your identity may involve deceit.
- Because qualitative observation takes you into close contact with participants, you must negotiate your relationship with them; there are several options.
- You may or may not participate in what you are observing. Participating in the events may make it easier for you to conceal your identity as a researcher, but participation is likely to affect what is being observed.
- Participant observation is a form of qualitative observation in which the researcher participates as an actor in the events under study.
- Researchers using qualitative observation need to blend two paradoxical perspectives: (1) the emic perspective, in which they try to adopt the beliefs, attitudes, and other points of view shared by the members of the culture being studied; and (2) the etic perspective, which means maintaining objectivity as an outsider and raising questions about the culture being observed that would not occur to members of that culture.
- The field journal is the backbone of field research because that is where the researcher records his or her observations. Journal entries should be detailed, yet concise. If possible, observations should be recorded as they are made; otherwise, they should be recorded as soon afterward as possible.
- Compared with surveys and experiments, qualitative research measurements generally tap more depth of meaning but have less reliability, and qualitative research results cannot be generalized as safely as those based on rigorous sampling and standardized questionnaires.
- Although this chapter focused on the strengths of qualitative research methods in general, flaws in quantitative research have been discussed throughout most of the preceding chapters. Examples include biases and other flaws in the wording of quantitative measurement instruments, quantitative scales that lack reliability and validity,

unrepresentative surveys with inadequate response rates or biased sampling procedures, practice evaluations that lack internal validity or use biased measurement procedures, and so on.

- Diversity in epistemological paradigms is accompanied by different perspectives on how to critically appraise the rigor of qualitative research.
- The contemporary positivist paradigm emphasizes three key threats to the trustworthiness of qualitative research: reactivity, researcher biases, and respondent biases.
- Six contemporary positivist strategies for evaluating the rigor of qualitative studies are: (1) prolonged engagement, (2) triangulation, (3) peer debriefing and support, (4) negative case analysis, (5) member checking, and (6) auditing.
- The social constructivist paradigm views trustworthiness and strategies to enhance rigor more in terms of capturing multiple subjective realities than ensuring the portrayal of an objective social reality, the objective of contemporary positivists. Thus, minimizing respondent bias is less important than making sure the research participants' multiple subjective realities are revealed as adequately as possible.
- Those who take a critical social science or participatory action research approach to qualitative research include empowerment standards in critically appraising qualitative research studies.

15.15 PRACTICE-RELATED EXERCISES

1. Think of some group or activity that you know well or in which you participate. In two or three paragraphs, describe how an outsider might effectively go about studying that group or activity. Elaborate on details such as what he or she should read, what contacts should be made, and so on.
2. Formulate a separate applicable social work research question for each of the following qualitative research methods: ethnography, case study, life history, feminist studies, and focus groups. Discuss why you think each method is well suited to the particular question you formulate for it.
3. Write down the potential threats to the trustworthiness of the findings for each of the following hypothetical scenarios. Compare your

answers with those of your classmates and discuss any differences you encounter.

a. A researcher draws conclusions about the main reasons clients prematurely terminate treatment based on 15-minute interviews with each of the 20 clients who most recently dropped out of treatment (one interview per client).
b. A researcher who had been a victim of a violent crime interviews other such victims to generate a theory about the emotional impact of violent crimes on victims.
c. A young researcher uses participant observation seeking to understand why youths abuse drugs, begins to see the world through the eyes of the youths being observed, and draws conclusions based exclusively on their outlook.

4. What strategies could be used to alleviate the threats you identified regarding the scenarios in Exercise 3 above? Discuss your rationale for each strategy. Compare your answers with those of your classmates and discuss any differences you encounter.

15.16 INTERNET EXERCISES

1. Find five articles in the journal *Social Work* that debate how well clinical social work practice and qualitative research fit together. The article that sparked the debate, "Does the Glove Really Fit? Qualitative Research and Clinical Social Work Practice" by Deborah K. Padgett, appeared in the July 1998 issue. Three articles responding to Padgett's article, as well as her response to them, appeared in the May 1999 issue. Briefly describe the main points of each article and discuss your position on this debate.
2. Find two articles that discuss methodological issues in qualitative research. Write down the bibliographic reference information for each article and identify the methodological issues each discusses.
3. Find one to three articles illustrating the use of ethnography, grounded theory, and participatory action research. (One article might report a study using more than one of these paradigms.) Write down the bibliographic reference information for each article and identify its methodological strengths and weaknesses.

15.17 ADDITIONAL READINGS

Denzin, N. K., & Lincoln, Y. S. (2000). *Handbook of qualitative research* (2nd ed.). Thousand Oaks, CA: Sage. This compendium of readings provides a wide range of papers about doing qualitative research.

Gilgun, J., Daly, K., & Handel, G. (Eds.). (1992). *Qualitative methods in family research*. Thousand Oaks, CA: Sage. This useful compendium of qualitative studies on families with relevance to social work practice illustrates the use of qualitative interviewing, case studies, life history interviews, participant observation, and document analysis.

Padgett, D. K. (1998). *Qualitative methods in social work research*. Thousand Oaks, CA: Sage. This introductory text emphasizes the how-to of qualitative research methods for social workers.

Padgett, D. K. (Ed.). (2004). *The qualitative research experience*. Belmont, CA: Brooks/Cole. This text provides a valuable compendium of exemplary qualitative studies using many of the methods discussed in this chapter. The studies are followed by "behind the scenes" essays in which the authors describe their experiences while conducting the research.

Qualitative Social Work: Research and Practice. Thousand Oaks, CA: Sage. This journal provides articles about qualitative research and evaluation in social work and about qualitative approaches to social work practice.

Reissman, C. (Ed.). (1994). *Qualitative studies in social work research*. Thousand Oaks, CA: Sage. This is a useful compendium of qualitative research studies relevant to social welfare policy and social work practice.

15.17a Competency Notes

EP 2.1.5b: Advocate for human rights and social and economic justice (pp. 311, 323): Social workers conducting participatory action research or other types of research that are guided by empowerment standards will attempt to increase consciousness about social and economic injustice among research participants and attempt to empower them.

EP 2.1.5c: Engage in practices that advance social and economic justice (pp. 312, 323): Social workers conducting participatory action research or other types of research that are guided by empowerment standards have as the ultimate aim of their research the advancement of social and economic justice.

EP 2.1.6b: Use research evidence to inform practice (p. 306): All of the concepts in this chapter enhance social workers' ability to use research evidence to inform their practice.

chapter
16

Analyzing Available Records: Quantitative and Qualitative Methods

16.1   INTRODUCTION

EP 2.1.6b
EP 2.1.10m

Whether our inquiry uses qualitative or quantitative methods (or both), we have noted various disadvantages associated with using direct observation or self-reports to gather data. For example, social desirability biases can influence what people tell us. Likewise, obtrusive modes of direct observation can influence people to behave in a manner unlike how they behave when they are not being observed. In addition, gathering original data by any means can be costly and time-consuming.

An alternative that can avoid the foregoing problems is the analysis of available records. By *available records*, we do not mean just compilations of statistical data, although such compilations would be included as a prime example of available records. The term has a much broader meaning and includes an almost endless array of possible data sources, such as agency case records and practitioner process notes, reports or editorials in newspapers or on television, minutes of board meetings, agency memoranda and annual reports, books or professional journal articles, legal opinions or laws relevant to social welfare, and administrative rulings.

Three major advantages associated with the method of using available records are its unobtrusiveness, its expedience (it usually costs less and takes less time than do other methods of data collection), and the ability to study phenomena that have occurred in the past. In light of these advantages, this chapter will examine three methods of analyzing available records: secondary analysis, content analysis, and historical analysis.

16.2   SECONDARY ANALYSIS

Secondary analysis is a form of research in which the data collected and processed by one researcher are reanalyzed—often for a different purpose—by another. It is most typically associated with the

---

secondary analysis A form of research in which the data collected and processed by one researcher are reanalyzed—often for a different purpose—by another.

reanalysis of large-scale survey data. With the development of computer-based analyses, researchers can now easily *share* their data with one another. Data also may be obtained from various private and governmental agencies that regularly conduct large-scale surveys at the local, state, national, or international level. Suppose, for example, that you are concerned about and want to research a potential problem in social work education. Perhaps you have noticed that female faculty members tend to occupy the lower ranks in your school or that they are unlikely to have administrative positions. You might want to assess, on a national basis, whether women and men of equivalent backgrounds differ in regard to such variables as rank, academic responsibilities, salary, and scholarly productivity.

Conducting a nationwide survey of social work faculty members would be quite costly and time-consuming. Even if you could get the resources to conduct the survey, you would have to worry about the potential problem of nonresponse. As an alternative to conducting the survey yourself, you could purchase—for far less money than the cost of conducting a survey—a copy of all the data for a given year on the population of social work faculty members already collected by the Council on Social Work Education in its annual statistical canvass, which includes the information you seek to analyze and which uses faculty members as the unit of analysis.

Beginning in the 1960s, survey researchers became aware of the potential value that lay in archiving survey data for analysis by scholars who had nothing to do with the survey design and data collection. Even when one researcher had conducted a survey and analyzed the data, those same data could be further analyzed by others with slightly different interests. Thus, if you were interested in the relationship between political views and attitudes toward gender equality, you could examine that research question through the analysis of any data set that happened to contain questions relating to those two variables.

One type of data archive provides continuing time series surveys of different samples drawn from the same population. A well-known current example of this type is the General Social Survey (GSS). Every year or two, the federal government commissions the National Opinion Research Center

(NORC) at the University of Chicago to conduct a major national survey to collect data on a large number of social science variables. These surveys are conducted precisely for the purpose of making data available to scholars at little or no cost. You can learn more about the GSS at http://www.norc.org/projects/General+Social+Survey.htm. Another type of archive contains data collected in a national census of an entire population. Data collected in cross-sectional surveys and longitudinal surveys comprise two additional types of archives. Some archives contain more than one of the foregoing types of data sources.

Numerous resources are available for identifying and acquiring existing data for secondary analysis. Here are a few. The National Data Archive on Child Abuse and Neglect (http://www.ndacan.cornell.edu/) has data sets on child abuse and neglect. Another source with child welfare data is the Annie E. Casey Foundation (http://www.aecf.org/), which has a data set called "Kids Count" that contains variables relating to the well-being of children. The National Archive of Criminal Justice Data (http://www.icpsr.umich.edu/icpsrweb/NACJD/) has a data set from a domestic violence research project.

Esther Sales, Sara Lichtenwalter, and Antonio Fevola (2006) recommend several additional sources of data. The largest data repository they mention is at the Inter-University Consortium for Political and Social Research (ICPSR) at the University of Michigan. It is available to researchers working at member institutions worldwide. Its archives, which can be accessed at http://www.icpsr.umich.edu/, contain social work-related data on aging, substance abuse, mental health, criminal justice, health and medical care, and education. Another useful source mentioned by Sales and her associates is the Sociometrics Social Science Electronic Data Library (http://www.socio.com/ssedl.php). Its archive contains more than 200 studies on social work-related topics. For a website that provides links to a broad array of social science data, Sales and her associates recommend the University of California San Diego Social Science Data on the Net (http://3stages.org/idata/).

Data sets also can be derived from *existing statistics* in administrative and public records. This type of data is often in aggregate form in agency records. Suppose you wanted to assess the impact of a new statewide program to prevent child abuse. You could examine the existing statistics in the records compiled by the state's human services agency to see whether changes occurred in annual rates of removing children from their homes due to abuse after the program was implemented.

When the data are in aggregate form only, they can be analyzed only in the form of statistics that apply to the aggregate, such as the prevalence of child abuse in different geographic areas, the proportions of different types of services provided in different agencies, and so on. Aggregated data sets cannot be reanalyzed in terms of individual characteristics. Thus, suppose 1,000 children were removed from their homes in a given year. The data set would not provide the various individual characteristics of each of the 1,000 children. It might tell you how many were boys and how many girls and what the proportions were from various categories of ethnicity, but it would not list each child along with his or her ethnicity or other characteristics. In other words, it would give you one overall figure for each variable of interest, rather than 1,000 pieces of data per variable showing each child's attribute for that variable.

There are many sources of existing statistics provided at every level of government. To find out what's available, go to your library, find the government documents section, and spend a few hours browsing through the shelves. You can also visit the U.S. Government Printing Office website (http://www.access.gpo.gov/) and look around. Many additional sources are provided by nongovernment agencies, such as the Child Welfare League of America, the National Association for Welfare Research and Statistics, and others. World statistics are available through the United Nations. Its *Demographic Yearbook* presents annual vital statistics (births, deaths, and other data relevant to populations) for the individual nations of the world.

16.2a Advantages of Secondary Analysis

The advantages of secondary analysis are obvious and enormous—it is cheaper and faster than doing an original survey (or most other types of research). Moreover, the cost savings of this approach enable you to conduct research on very large samples—much larger samples than you would be able to study with typical levels of funding.

Another advantage is that, depending on who did the original study, you may benefit from the work of top flight professionals. In addition, the archived data may have been generated by studies that received well-funded federal research grants that made it feasible to implement rigorous sampling approaches and obtain high response rates.

Well-funded, large-scale studies also are likely to have assessed a much larger number of variables than most original social work research studies can assess. Secondary analysis thus provides the advantage of gathering information on a much larger number of variables. Moreover, in addition to examining information separately for many more variables, a very large sample size makes it possible to employ sophisticated multivariate statistical techniques for analyzing relationships among many variables simultaneously, thus ferreting out the relative explanatory power of each variable when the other variables are controlled.

Four Useful Sources of Existing Data in Child Welfare

Annie E. Casey's Kids Count

[http://datacenter.kidscount.org/]

The *Kids Count* database is provided by the Annie E. Casey Foundation. It compiles comparative data about the well-being of children state-by-state across the USA. The well-being indicators pertain to low birth rates, infant mortality, child deaths, teen deaths, teens who are neither attending school nor working, children living in families without a fully employed parent, children living in poverty, children in single-parent families, children in immigrant families, and children without health insurance. In addition to comparing states and cities, it enables analyses to be done within the bounds of a single state, territory, or community. It can create customized state profiles, maps, rankings, and graphs. For example, a bar graph that currently (as we write this book) appears near the top of the site shows the percentage of children who lived in poverty in each of the 50 states as of 2008. Mississippi had the highest percentage (30%), and most of the other states with relatively high rates (above 20%) were in the southern region.

National Data Archive on Child Abuse and Neglect

[http://www.ndacan.cornell.edu

This site makes available for secondary analysis high-quality data sets on child abuse and neglect that are acquired from researchers who have investigated this topic. The site also provides technical support for those seeking to conduct secondary analyses of its data sets. The following can give you a sense of the many data sets available at this site: National Family Violence Survey; Family Structure and Functioning in Neglectful Families; National Study of the Incidence of Child Abuse and Neglect; Runaway and Homeless Youth Management Information; Parenting Among Women Sexually Abused in Childhood; National Survey of Current and Former Foster Parents; Neighborhood and Household Factors in the Etiology of Child Maltreatment; Longitudinal Pathways to Resilience in Maltreated Children; and so on.

United States Children's Bureau Statistics & Research

[http://www.acf.hhs.gov/programs/cb/stats_research/index.htm]

This governmental site provides existing statistics (not databases) on adoption and foster care at the state and national levels. Its Adoption and Foster Care Reporting and Analysis System (AFCARS) reports case-level existing statistics on "all children in foster care for whom State child welfare agencies have responsibility for placement, care or supervision, and on children who are adopted under the auspices of the State's public child welfare agency." Among the many useful areas of existing statistics you can find at this site are yearly trends in foster care and adoption, the number of child fatalities, risk factors for child maltreatment, characteristics of perpetrators, child welfare outcomes, and so on.

Child Welfare Dynamic Report System

[http://cssr.berkeley.edu/ucb_childwelfare/]

This site is provided collaboratively by the California Department of Social Services and the University of California at Berkeley. It provides child welfare administrative data about children in California's child welfare system. Charts can be viewed on such topics as the numbers and rates of child abuse referrals, the recurrence of child maltreatment, and so on.

Another advantage of conducting a secondary analysis of a well-funded study is the likelihood that the original study was methodologically strong in general, not just in the size and representativeness of its sample. For example, to be successful in securing major funding for large-scale studies, research proposals had better reflect well-controlled designs and very strong measurement procedures. Chances are, no matter how well you understand the design and measurement concepts that we've discussed in this book, it will be difficult for you to obtain the level of funding needed to obtain the resources required to actually implement a study that is as rigorous as you'd like it to be.

Sales and her associates (2006) also identify some additional advantages of secondary analysis. If you are interested in studying a population that is hard to find, such as same-sex adoptive parents, accessing a data set from a well-funded study whose sample was large enough to include sufficient members from such populations may make more sense than trying to collect original data from those members yourself. If you want to study trends over time, you can save yourself years of work collecting original data by instead accessing a data set from a longitudinal study. Other advantages discussed by Sales and associates involve avoiding ethical concerns about your data collection procedures, being able to compare social problems across different nations, and the availability of technical support from government agencies to help researchers access and analyze their data. The box "Four Useful Sources of Existing Data in Child Welfare" provides further information on some of the above sources as well as some others that might be of particular interest to readers who might like to conduct research in the field of child welfare.

16.2b Limitations of Secondary Analysis

Secondary analysis does have its limitations. If you conduct a secondary analysis or analyze existing statistics in your research (or your practice), you should not assume that the data are free of problems just because they are "official" or because a prestigious agency published them. For example, the data may be outdated by the time they are released. Let's look now at some of the special problems this method presents in terms of missing data,

units of analysis, validity, and reliability. We'll conclude the discussion by mentioning some useful sources of existing statistics.

Missing Data

Whenever you base your research on an analysis of data that already exist, whether they were collected via a survey or by some other method, you are obviously limited to what exists. Before investing a great deal of time in planning a study that will use existing data, you should check the data source to see if the data you need are there at all. If they are there, you should check to see whether large chunks of the data on certain key variables are missing. If you conduct a national research study using existing data on ethnicity and poverty among retirees in the United States, for example, and states with relatively large numbers of relatively affluent White retirees (such as Florida and Arizona) are missing from the database—or are in the database but without reporting ethnicity—your results might be seriously inaccurate.

Sometimes a variable may have data entered on it, but the lack of variation in the data renders it missing in the sense of being a variable. You may recall from our earlier discussion of variables that to be a variable, a concept must *vary*. Suppose you want to evaluate the effectiveness of a play therapy intervention for traumatized 6-year-olds by examining its impact on their grades in first grade, using school grade records. You should first check the school records to see if sufficient variation exists in grades at that level. Suppose first grade teachers give virtually every student an A, to avoid discouraging the students or lowering their self-esteem. If that is the case, grades will be missing as a variable in the records, since they will not sufficiently vary.

Problems of Validity

You will encounter validity problems if the agency that collected the existing statistics you are analyzing defined your variables in ways that don't match your definitions of those variables. Suppose, for example, that a state welfare agency—perhaps seeking to show that its recent welfare reform policy succeeded in getting welfare recipients back to work—defines participation in a government job training program as being employed. Suppose you, however, are skeptical about how often such training leads to actual paid employment and therefore do not want to count such training in your definition of being employed. Maybe the government data do not distinguish between part-time and full-time employment, and in your definition success in getting welfare recipients back to work means full-time employment with wages that match or exceed welfare benefits. If you must rely on the government's existing statistics for your research, you would have a serious validity problem.

Another type of validity problem occurs when existing statistics deal with phenomena that often go unreported but include only reported incidents in the records. Thus, existing statistics may underestimate the number of individuals who have been physically abused by a spouse or a partner or the number of coeds who have been sexually abused on dates, because many such incidents go unreported. The actual incidence of these problems can be underestimated even further if the existing statistics include only incidents involving the filing of criminal charges, omitting incidents that were unreported as well as those that were reported but did not lead to criminal charges.

Improper data collection methods also can cause validity problems, such as when survey interviewers make up information so they can avoid dangerous areas. Likewise, direct service practitioners who resent having to spend so much time completing forms on their cases can become careless and sloppy in rushing to complete those forms.

Problems of Reliability

The analysis of existing statistics depends heavily on the quality of the statistics themselves: Are they accurate reports of what they claim to report? That can be a substantial problem sometimes because the weighty tables of government statistics are sometimes grossly inaccurate.

Because a great deal of the research into crime depends on official crime statistics, this body of data has come under critical evaluation. The results have not been encouraging. Suppose, for purposes of illustration, that you were interested in tracing the long-term trends in marijuana use in the United States. Official statistics on the numbers of people arrested for selling or possessing marijuana would seem to be a reasonable measure of use, right? Not necessarily.

To begin, you face a hefty problem of validity. Before the passage of the Marijuana Tax Act in 1937, marijuana was legal in the United States, so arrest records would not give you a valid measure of use. But even if you limited your inquiry to the post-1937 era, you would still have problems of reliability that stem from the nature of law enforcement and crime record keeping.

Law enforcement, for example, is subject to various pressures. Crime reports may rise or fall depending on increases or decreases in the budget for hiring police. A public outcry against marijuana, led perhaps by a vocal citizens' group, can result in a police "crackdown on drug trafficking"—especially during an election or budget year. A sensational story in the press can have a similar effect. In addition, the volume of other business that faces police affects marijuana arrests.

Similar problems of reliability can occur in existing statistics on many other variables of interest to social work researchers whose definitions or record-keeping methods change over time. Consider child abuse, for example. Some methods of corporal punishment that were deemed acceptable several decades ago are now considered to constitute child abuse.

Awareness is your first protection against the problems of validity and reliability in the analysis of existing statistics—knowing that the problems may exist. Investigating the nature of the data collection and tabulation may help you assess the nature and degree of these problems so that you can judge their potential impact on your research interest. Replication can also help alleviate the problem.

Despite the foregoing limitations, analyzing existing statistics is usually less costly and less time-consuming than collecting original data, and often can provide valuable findings for guiding policy and practice. A study that illustrates the applicability to social work practice of analyzing existing statistics—and that also illustrates some of the problems in using this method—is summarized in the box titled "An Illustration of the Analysis of Existing Statistics in Research on Social Welfare Policy." Now that you see the advantages and problems of secondary analysis, let's turn to another method for analyzing existing data, this time focusing on available data that are more qualitative in nature.

An Illustration of the Analysis of Existing Statistics in Research on Social Welfare Policy

Claudia Coulton, Shanta Pandey, and Julia Chow (1990) were concerned that economic forces in the United States during the 1980s were concentrating poor people in deteriorating central urban neighborhoods where they were becoming further isolated from economic opportunities and increasingly exposed to adverse social and physical conditions associated with extreme poverty. To study this phenomenon in depth, Coulton and her associates decided to limit their study to one urban area: Cleveland, Ohio. They recognized that this decision would limit the generalizability of their findings, but believed that others could replicate their study in other cities to see if the same patterns could be observed.

The researchers prefaced their study by noting that poverty rates rose sharply in the 1980s and that, to the extent that poverty was becoming more geographically concentrated, it was becoming more difficult for poor people to reach jobs located in the suburbs. Workers who could afford to move closer to suburban jobs were induced to do so, and this further concentrated the poverty of the inner-city neighborhood they left behind and reduced the opportunity of those who were left behind to find jobs close to home (to which they could travel). As the neighborhood deteriorated, the worsening social environment conceivably might have had harmful effects on the individuals left behind—particularly the youths—as they became increasingly exposed to such problems as teen pregnancy, delinquency, school dropouts, and so on.

The research team used a variety of sources of existing statistics for Cleveland, including data from the Center for Regional Economic Issues located at Case Western Reserve University, birth and death information reported by the Ohio Department of Health (which provided data on low birth weight, infant death rate, teen birth rate, and illegitimacy rates), crime rate data from the Federal Bureau of Investigation, juvenile delinquency data from the Cuyahoga County Juvenile Court, drug arrest rates from the Cleveland Police Department, and housing value data from the Housing Policy Research Program of Cleveland State University.

The existing statistics showed that by 1988 nearly 50 percent of Cleveland's poor people lived in neighborhoods of concentrated poverty, compared with 21 percent in 1970. Thus, poor people were becoming more spatially isolated from the rest of society and less likely to encounter nonpoor people in their neighborhoods. The statistics further indicated that as poor people were becoming more concentrated in high-poverty areas, the social and physical environments to which they were being exposed were deteriorating rapidly, particularly for people living in "emerging poverty areas" that lost many blue-collar workers in the early 1980s and consequently became poverty areas after 1980. Noting the importance of the person-in-environment framework for social work practice and the special vulnerability of poor children living in high-poverty neighborhoods, Coulton and her associates recommended that social workers consider interventions at the environmental level:

Social workers need practice models that combine their traditional approaches to service delivery with economic redevelopment of distressed parts of the city and mechanisms that reestablish connections between central city residents and distant, suburban job locations. Barriers to these connections are geographic but also involve social networks, information channels, and psychological distance. As poor neighborhoods become increasingly adverse environments due to economic and social decline, programs and interventions are needed that will disrupt their growing isolation from the mainstream. (1990, p. 15)

16.3 CONTENT ANALYSIS

Not all forms of available records are in the form of statistical data collected by others. Alternative forms, for example, might include books, journal or magazine articles, newspapers, television shows or commercials, agency reports, process notes recorded by direct service practitioners in their case records, and so on. The data available in these sources typically are qualitative in nature.

The method for analyzing such data is called *content analysis.*

Content analysis can be a quantitative or qualitative technique. As a qualitative technique, it is a way of discovering patterns and meanings from communications. As a quantitative technique, it involves transforming qualitative material into quantitative data. For example, it might involve attempting to see if certain types of social work faculty members or schools have more content on ethnic minorities than do others by counting the number of times words pertaining to ethnic minorities appear in their social work course syllabi. Or it might tabulate how often various types of issues are mentioned in the minutes of community organization meetings. Is the amount of citizen participation reflected in the minutes related to how frequently certain types of issues appear in the minutes?

Attempting to identify themes and meanings by counting the number of times certain terms or phrases appear in qualitative data can be misleading. Consider the following fictional research abstract, for example, which we've made up:

> We reviewed studies assessing the effectiveness of social service agencies that claimed to be providing programs of intervention emphasizing cultural competence with ethnic minority clients. Most of the programs were designed to be culturally competent with African Americans or Hispanic Americans. Others were designed for Asian Americans or Native Americans. None of the culturally competent programs, however, had outcomes that were better than programs that did not claim to be specially designed for particular ethnic minority clientele. In fact, some so-called culturally competent programs had worse outcomes. Consequently, we found no evidence to support the notion that culturally competent interventions are more effective than mainstream interventions, and some evidence that culturally competent programs may be less effective. We therefore recommend de-emphasizing cultural competence in the training of social workers.

Suppose we are doing a purely quantitative content analysis to assess whether certain types of author characteristics or certain types of journals are more likely to support cultural competence with ethnic minorities than others. Suppose we decide to count how many times they mention words like cultural competence, culturally competent, ethnic minority, African American, Hispanic American, Asian American, or Native American as a way of quantifying their commitment to cultural competence with ethnic minorities. In the above fictional abstract, these terms appear 13 times. Each of the terms contains 2 words; thus, the 13 terms are composed of 26 words. Because there are a total of

130 words in the above fictional abstract, the 26 words comprise one-fifth (20%) of the words in the abstract. That's a lot. But a qualitative interpretation of the overall meaning of the abstract would clearly conclude that it does *not* support the promotion of cultural competence in social work education or practice. In fact, it takes the opposite point of view.

Content analysis research can guide social work practice. For example, Marsden (1971) reviewed an extensive body of research studies that used content analysis to identify the core elements in the practitioner–client relationship—elements such as practitioner empathy, warmth, and genuineness. In these studies, written and taped excerpts from therapy sessions were rated according to the degree to which the core relationship conditions were observed. The findings tended to indicate that the more these three conditions were present, the better the clinical process and outcome.

Some topics are more appropriately addressed by content analysis than by any other method of inquiry. Suppose for a moment that you're interested in how mentally ill individuals are portrayed on television. Perhaps the National Alliance for the Mentally Ill plans to mount a campaign to educate the public about the nature of mental illness, alleviate fears about the mentally ill, and offset stereotypes about them. Suppose one facet of the campaign is aimed at the television medium and seeks to reduce the extent to which TV programs portray mentally ill individuals as violent or dangerous. Suppose further that you seek to evaluate the impact of that facet of the campaign on TV programming, and you will use a time series design to assess whether the campaign seems to be reducing the extent to which mentally ill individuals are portrayed as violent or dangerous. Content analysis would be the best mode of observation for your time series study.

Briefly, here's what you would do. First, you'd develop an operational definition of your dependent variable: the extent to which mentally ill individuals are portrayed as violent or dangerous. The section on coding later in this chapter will help you do that. Next, you'd have to decide what to watch. Probably you would decide (1) what stations to watch, (2) for what days or period, and (3) at what hours. Then you'd stock up on snacks and start watching, classifying, and recording. Once you had completed your observations, you would be able to analyze the data you collected and determine whether mentally ill individuals were being portrayed less violently after than before the campaign.

Content analysis, then, is particularly well suited to the study of communications and to answering the classic question of communications research: "Who says what, to whom, why, how, and with what effect?" As a mode of observation, content analysis requires a considered handling of the *what*, and the analysis of data collected in this mode, as in others, addresses the *why* and *with what effect*.

16.3a Sampling in Content Analysis

In the study of communications, as in the study of people, it is often impossible to observe directly everything in which you are interested. In your study of television portrayals of the mentally ill, for example, we'd advise against attempting to watch everything that's broadcast. It wouldn't be possible, and your brain would probably short-circuit before you got close to discovering that for yourself. Usually, then, it's appropriate to sample.

Sampling in content analysis involves some decisions. In the study of television portrayals of the mentally ill, for example, you would need to establish the universe to be sampled from. In this case, what TV stations will you observe? What will be the period of the study—which days and what hours of those days will you observe? Then, how many programs do you want to observe and code for analysis?

Now you're ready to design the sample selection. As a practical matter, you wouldn't have to sample among the different stations if you had assistants— each of you could watch a different channel during the same time period. But let's suppose you are working alone. Your final sampling frame, from which a sample will be selected and watched, might look something like this:

- Jan. 7, Channel 2, 7–9 P.M.
- Jan. 7, Channel 4, 7–9 P.M.
- Jan. 7, Channel 9, 7–9 P.M.
- Jan. 7, Channel 2, 9–11 P.M.
- Jan. 7, Channel 4, 9–11 P.M.
- Jan. 7, Channel 9, 9–11 P.M.
- Jan. 8, Channel 2, 7–9 P.M.
- Jan. 8, Channel 4, 7–9 P.M.

- Jan. 8, Channel 9, 7–9 P.M.
- Jan. 8, Channel 2, 9–11 P.M.
- Jan. 8, Channel 4, 9–11 P.M.
- Jan. 8, Channel 9, 9–11 P.M.
- Jan. 9, Channel 2, 7–9 P.M.
- Jan. 9, Channel 4, 7–9 P.M.
- and so on.

Notice that we've made several decisions for you in the illustration. First, we have assumed that channels 2, 4, and 9 are the ones appropriate to your study. We've assumed that you found the 7 to 11 P.M. prime-time hours to be the most relevant and that two-hour periods would do the job. We picked January 7 out of the hat for a starting date. In practice, of course, all of these decisions should be based on your careful consideration of what would be appropriate to your particular study.

In content analysis of written prose, sampling may occur at any or all of the following levels: words, phrases, sentences, paragraphs, sections, chapters, books, writers, or the contexts relevant to the works. Other forms of communication may also be sampled at any of the conceptual levels appropriate to them.

Any of the conventional sampling techniques discussed in Chapter 11 may be used in content analysis. We might select a *random or systematic* sample of agency memoranda, of state laws passed regarding the rights of mental patients, or of the minutes of community organization meetings. We might number all course syllabi in a school of social work and then select a random sample of 25.

Stratified sampling is also appropriate to content analysis. To analyze the editorial policies of American newspapers, for example, we might first group all newspapers by region of the country, size of the community in which they are published, frequency of publication, or average circulation. We might then select a stratified random or systematic sample of newspapers for analysis. Having done so, we might select a sample of editorials from each selected newspaper, perhaps stratified chronologically.

Cluster sampling is equally appropriate to content analysis. Indeed, if individual editorials were to be the unit of analysis in the previous example, then the selection of newspapers at the first stage of sampling would be a cluster sample. In an analysis of political speeches, we might begin by selecting a sample of politicians; each politician would represent a cluster of political speeches. The study of TV portrayals of the mentally ill described previously is another example of cluster sampling.

16.3b Coding in Content Analysis

Content analysis is essentially a coding operation. Communications—oral, written, or other—are coded or classified according to some conceptual framework. Newspaper editorials, for example, may be coded as liberal or conservative. Radio broadcasts might be coded as propagandistic or not. Novels might be coded as pro–social welfare or not. Political speeches might be coded as to whether or not they impugn the character of welfare recipients or the homeless. Recall that terms such as these are subject to many interpretations, and the researcher must specify definitions clearly.

16.3c Manifest and Latent Content

In the earlier discussions of qualitative research, we found that the researcher faces a fundamental choice between *depth* and *specificity* of understanding. Often, this represents a choice between *validity* and *reliability,* respectively. Typically, qualitative researchers opt for depth, preferring to base their judgments on a broad range of observations and information, even at the risk that another observer might reach a different judgment of the situation. But survey research—through the use of standardized questionnaires—represents the other extreme: total specificity, even though the specific measures of variables may not be fully satisfactory as valid reflections of those variables. The content analyst has more of a choice in this matter.

Coding the **manifest content**—the visible, surface content—of a communication more closely approximates the use of a standardized questionnaire. To determine, for example, how sexist certain books are, you might simply count the number of times male pronouns are used in conjunction with

manifest content   The directly visible, objectively identifiable characteristics of a communication, such as the specific words in a book, the specific colors used in a painting, and so forth.

latent content   The underlying meanings contained within communications.

generalized prestigious roles (such as referring to the role of some nonspecified physician as "his" role) or the average number of such uses per page. This strictly quantitative method of transforming qualitative data would have the advantage of ease and *reliability* in coding, and of letting the reader of the research report know precisely how the sexist language was measured. It would have a disadvantage, on the other hand, in terms of *validity*. Surely the term *sexist book* conveys a richer and deeper meaning than the number of times male pronouns are used.

Alternatively, you may take a more qualitative approach by coding the **latent content** of the communication: its underlying meaning. In the current example, you might read an entire book or a sample of paragraphs or pages and make an overall assessment of how sexist the book is. Although your total assessment might well be influenced by the inappropriate appearance of male pronouns, it would not depend fully on the frequency with which such words appeared.

Clearly, this qualitative method seems better designed for tapping the underlying meaning of communications, but its advantage comes at a cost of reliability and specificity. Somewhat different definitions or standards may be used, especially if more than one person is coding the novel. A passage—perhaps depicting boys as heroes and girls as being rescued—might be deemed sexist by one coder but not another. Even if you do all of the coding yourself, there is no guarantee that your definitions and standards will remain constant throughout the enterprise. Moreover, the reader of your research report would be generally uncertain about the definitions you have used.

Wherever possible, the best solution to this dilemma is to use *both* methods. A given unit of observation should receive the same characterization from both methods to the extent that your coding of manifest and latent content has been reasonably valid and reliable. If the agreement achieved by the two methods is fairly close, though imperfect, then the final score might reflect the scores assigned in the two independent methods. If, on the other hand, coding manifest and latent content produces gross disagreement, then you would be well advised to reconsider your theoretical conceptualization.

16.3d Qualitative Content Analysis

We've already mentioned that not all content analysis results in counting. Sometimes a qualitative assessment of the materials is most appropriate. Bruce Berg (1998, pp. 123–125) discusses "negative case testing" as a technique for qualitative hypothesis testing. First, in the grounded theory tradition, you begin with an examination of the data, which may yield a general hypothesis. Let's say that you're examining the leadership of a new community association by reviewing the minutes of meetings to see who made motions that were subsequently passed. Your initial examination of the data suggests that the wealthier members are the most likely to assume this leadership role.

The second stage in the analysis is to search your data to find all the cases that would contradict the initial hypothesis. In this instance, you would look for poorer members who made successful motions and wealthy members who never did. Third, you must review each of the disconfirming cases and either (1) give up the hypothesis or (2) see how it needs to be fine-tuned.

Let's say that in your analysis of the disconfirming cases, you notice that each of the nonwealthy leaders has a graduate degree, while each of the wealthy nonleaders has very little formal education. You may revise your hypothesis to consider both education and wealth as routes to leadership in the association. Perhaps you'll discover some threshold for leadership (a white-collar job, a level of income, and a college degree) beyond which those with the most money, education, or both are the most active leaders.

This process is an example of what Barney Glaser and Anselm Strauss (1967) called "analytic induction." It is inductive in that it primarily begins with observations, and it is analytic because it goes beyond description to find patterns and relationships among variables.

There are, of course, dangers in this form of analysis, as in all others. The chief risk is misclassifying observations so as to support an emerging hypothesis. For example, you may erroneously conclude that a nonleader didn't graduate from college or you may decide that the job of factory foreman is "close enough" to being white-collar.

Berg (1998, p. 124) offers the following techniques for avoiding these errors:

1. If there are sufficient cases, select some at random from each category to avoid merely picking those that best support the hypothesis.
2. Give at least three examples in support of every assertion you make about the data.
3. Have your analytic interpretations carefully reviewed by others uninvolved in the research project to see whether they agree.
4. Report whatever inconsistencies you do discover—any cases that simply do not fit your hypotheses. Realize that few social patterns are 100 percent consistent, so you may have discovered something important even if it doesn't apply to absolutely all of social life. However, you should be honest with your readers in that regard.

16.3e An Illustration of a Qualitative Content Analysis in Social Work Research

An example of a qualitative content analysis study in social work was reported by Ruth McRoy and her associates (1990) on adoption revelation. The researchers thought that the relatively high frequency of psychiatric treatment referrals of adopted children might indicate problems in the process of revealing to children that they were adopted. They decided to explore this issue by looking for patterns among case illustrations of problematic and nonproblematic revelations of adoption. Their nonprobability sample (an availability sample) consisted of 50 adoptive families whose adopted children were in residential treatment facilities and had been adopted before the age of 2.

Intensive, open-ended interviews were conducted with the parents, adopted child, and caseworker for each family. The interviews were tape-recorded and transcribed verbatim. A content analysis was then performed on the information on the tapes. Like many qualitative research reports, this one did not provide much detail as to methodological procedures—details that would enable the reader to assess the validity of its conclusions. As we discussed in Chapter 15, qualitative approaches eschew such structure in favor of more flexible approaches that permit deeper probing into subjective meanings—probes that usually seek to generate new insights more than they seek to test hypotheses.

McRoy and her associates presented the results of their content analysis of their interview data primarily in the form of lengthy quotes that they incorporated into composite case illustrations. In one case illustration, for example, a girl was not told by her parents that she was adopted until she was 10 years old. The quotation shows that she refused to believe them and was traumatized by the revelation. In two other case illustrations, boys who learned of being adopted when they were 5 years old reacted with anger or mistrust.

One theme that seemed to cut across the case illustrations was the need for social workers who worked with adoptive families to deal with issues concerning how, when, and by whom children are informed of their adoption. Social workers need to encourage adoptive parents to be the first to inform the child of the adoption.

Another recurrent theme was the need for ongoing communication between parents and their children about the adoption and the need to express empathy and understanding regarding the children's ongoing questions about their background and the reasons for being placed for adoption. The evidence for this conclusion is presented in several quotes that illustrate how learning of being adopted seemed to trigger problems in some families but not in others. In one, a daughter describes how she became rebellious against her parents when she found out at age 10 what adoption really means. The problem had been exacerbated, in her view, when her parents seemed to have difficulty discussing the adoption with her and were not always truthful with her about aspects of the adoption. Other quotes are provided from cases that involved better communication where the children reported less discomfort with the adoption issue.

This illustration of qualitative content analysis in action should give you a clearer picture of the procedures and potential that characterize this research method. Let's conclude the discussion of content analysis with an overview of its particular strengths and weaknesses.

16.3f Strengths and Weaknesses of Content Analysis

Probably the greatest advantage of content analysis is its economy in terms of both time and money. A single college student could undertake a content analysis, whereas undertaking a survey, for example, might not be feasible. There is no requirement for a large research staff; no special equipment is needed. As long as you have access to the material to be coded, you can undertake content analysis.

Ease of correcting mistakes is another advantage of content analysis. If you discover you have botched a survey, you may be forced to repeat the whole research project with all its attendant costs in time and money. If you botch your qualitative observational field research, it may be impossible to redo the project; the event under study may no longer exist. In content analysis, it's usually easier to repeat a portion of the study than it is for other research methods. You might be required, moreover, to recode only a portion of your data rather than repeat the entire enterprise.

Also important, content analysis permits you to study processes that occur over long periods of time. You might focus on the imagery of African Americans conveyed in American novels of 1850 to 1860, for example, or you might examine changing imagery from 1850 to the present.

Finally, content analysis has the advantage of being *unobtrusive*—that is, the content analyst seldom affects the subject being studied. Because the books have already been written, the case records already recorded, and the speeches already presented, content analyses can have no effect on them. Not all research methods have this advantage.

Content analysis has disadvantages as well. For one thing, it is limited to the examination of *recorded* communications. Such communications may be oral, written, or graphic, but they must be recorded in some fashion to permit analysis.

Content analysis, as we have seen, has both advantages and disadvantages in terms of validity and reliability. For validity, problems are likely unless you happen to be studying communication processes per se. For instance, does an increase in the mention of the term *case management* in the social work literature necessarily mean that social workers are now more likely to deliver case management services? Conceivably, the only thing that changed is the labels being used to describe the same forms of practice—perhaps *case management* has merely become the fashionable terminology for the same old practices.

Although validity is a common problem with content analysis, the concreteness of materials studied in quantitative approaches to content analysis strengthens the likelihood of reliability. You can always code and recode (and even recode again, if you want), making certain that the coding is consistent. In other forms of quantitative and qualitative research, by contrast, there's probably nothing you can do after the fact to ensure greater reliability in observation and categorization. Let's move from content analysis and turn to a related research method: historical analysis.

16.4 HISTORICAL ANALYSIS

Historical analysis is a method that overlaps somewhat with content analysis, as well as other forms of qualitative inquiry. Although it can involve some quantitative methods (such as time series analysis and other forms of longitudinal research), it is usually considered a qualitative method, one in which the researcher attempts to master many subtle details. The main resources for observation and analysis are historical records. Although historical research might include content analysis, it is not limited to communications.

Many historical writings can be found in the social work literature. Biographies of social work pioneers constitute a large segment of these writings. Another segment contains case studies that trace the development of social welfare policies and programs. Less common, but perhaps more useful for informing current practice, are studies that look for recurring patterns that help explain the past and imply possible lessons for the present.

In an excellent example of the latter type of study, Morrissey and Goldman (1984) examined recurrent cycles of reform in the care of the chronically mentally ill. They identified parallels between the deinstitutionalization movement of the late 20th century and Dorothea Dix's mid-19th-century crusade to build state hospitals to provide asylum and sanctuary to individuals too sick to fend for themselves in communities that did not want them. In Dix's era, the reform intended to make care more humane by shifting its locus from the community to the hospital. In the 20th-century era of deinstitutionalization, the reform intended to make care more humane by shifting its locus from the hospital

to the community. But today we hear of large numbers of mentally ill individuals who are homeless or in jails and who are living in squalor—many of the same conditions that prompted Dix's crusade back in the 1800s.

Morrissey and Goldman show how both reforms failed for the same reason: Each merely shifted the locus of care without garnering enough public fiscal support to ensure that the new locus of care would ultimately be any more humane than the old one. Without adequate financing, Dix's intended humane sanctuaries for the mentally ill too often became overcrowded, inhumane "snake-pits" where sick individuals who could not afford expensive private care could be warehoused and forgotten. Without adequate financing, the noble intentions of the 20th-century deinstitutionalization movement led for too many individuals to community-based conditions as bad as in the back wards of state hospitals.

One lesson for today from this research is that if we seek to ensure more humane care for the long-term mentally ill, we must go beyond conceptualizing idealized programs or notions about where to provide care; the real issue is convincing the public to allocate adequate fiscal support for that care. Without the latter, our reformist efforts may be doomed to repeat the unintended consequences of previous reforms.

16.4a Sources of Historical Data

As we saw in the case of existing statistics, there is no end of data available for analysis in historical research. To begin, historians may have already reported on whatever it is you want to examine, and their analyses can give you an initial grounding in the subject, a jumping-off point for more in-depth research. Ultimately, you will usually want to go beyond others' conclusions, and examine "raw data" and draw your own conclusions. These vary, of course, according to the topic under study. Raw data might, for example, include old letters or diaries, sermons or lectures, and so forth.

In discussing procedures for studying the history of family life, Ellen Rothman (1981) points to the following sources:

In addition to personal sources, there are public records which are also revealing of family history. Newspapers are especially rich in evidence on the educational, legal, and recreational aspects of family life in the past as seen from a local point of view. Magazines reflect more general patterns of family life; students often find them interesting to explore for data on perceptions and expectations of mainstream family values. Magazines offer several different kinds of sources at once: visual materials (illustrations and advertisements), commentary (editorial and advice columns), and fiction. Popular periodicals are particularly rich in the last two. Advice on many questions of concern to families—from the proper way to discipline children to the economics of wallpaper—fills magazine columns from the early nineteenth century to the present. Stories that suggest common experiences or perceptions of family life appear with the same continuity. (p. 53)

Organizations generally document themselves, so if you are studying the development of some organization, you should examine its official documents: charters, policy statements, speeches by leaders, and so on.

Often, official government documents provide the data needed for analysis. To better appreciate the history of race relations in the United States, A. Leon Higginbotham, Jr. (1978) examined 200 years of laws and court cases involving race. Himself the first African American appointed to a federal judgeship, Higginbotham found that the law, rather than protecting Blacks, was the embodiment of bigotry and oppression. In the earliest court cases, there was considerable ambiguity over whether Blacks were indentured servants or, in fact, slaves. Later court cases and laws clarified the matter—holding Blacks to be something less than human.

Many of the source materials for historical research can be found in academic libraries. Two broad types of source materials are *primary* sources and *secondary* sources. Primary sources provide firsthand accounts by someone who was present at an event—for example, diaries, letters, organizational bylaws, the minutes of a meeting, the orally reported memory of an eyewitness, and so on. Secondary sources describe past phenomena based on primary sources. Thus, if you cite a book on the history of Lyndon Johnson's Great Society social

welfare programs in his war on poverty, you are using a secondary source. But if you go to the LBJ Presidential Library in Austin, Texas, and cite letters, laws, and official documents from that period that you find there, then you are using primary sources.

A danger in working exclusively with secondary sources is that you may merely repeat the mistakes contained in those sources and fail to give yourself the opportunity to provide a new, independent perspective on past events. But primary sources can be flawed as well. For example, an eyewitness could have been biased or may experience faulty memory.

Stuart (1981) argues that people who produce or write primary sources based on events they witnessed probably had a vested interest in those events. He cites an example of bias in the statistical reports of the populations of Native Americans on reservations by Indian agents in the late 19th century. Some agents exaggerated the population size to obtain more supplies for their reservations from the federal government's Office of Indian Affairs.

In conducting historical research, then, keep these cautions in mind. As we saw in the case of existing statistics, you cannot trust the accuracy of records—official or unofficial, primary or secondary. You need always be wary of bias in your data sources. If all of your data on a pioneer social worker are taken from people who worked for that social worker, you are unlikely to get a well-rounded view of that person. If all of your data on the development of a social movement are taken from activists in the movement itself, then you are unlikely to gain a well-rounded view of the movement. The diaries of affluent, friendly visitors of the Charity Organization Societies from the late 19 century may not give you an accurate view of life among the immigrant poor they visited during those times.

Your protection against these dangers in historical research lies in *corroboration*. If several sources point to the same set of "facts," your confidence in them might reasonably increase. Thus, when conducting historical research, you should try not to rely on a single source or on one type of source. Try to obtain data from every relevant source you can find, and be sure to seek sources that represent different vested interests and different points of view. The box titled "Reading and Evaluating

Reading and Evaluating Documents

by Ron Aminzade and Barbara Laslett, University of Minnesota

The purpose of the following comments is to give you some sense of the kind of interpretive work that historians do and the critical approach they take toward their sources. It should help you to appreciate some of the skills that historians develop in their efforts to reconstruct the past from residues, to assess the evidentiary status of different types of documents, and to determine the range of permissible inferences and interpretations. Here are some of the questions historians ask about documents:

1. Who composed the documents? Why were they written? Why have they survived all these years? What methods were used to acquire the information contained in the documents?

2. What are some of the biases in the documents and how might you go about checking or correcting them? How inclusive or representative is the sample of individuals, events, etc. contained in the documents? What were the institutional constraints and the general organizational routines under which the documents were prepared? To what extent do the documents provide more of an index of institutional activity than of the phenomenon being studied?

What is the time lapse between the observation of the events documented and the witnesses' documentation of them? How confidential or public were the documents meant to be? What role did etiquette, convention, and custom play in the presentation of the material contained within the documents? If you relied solely upon the evidence contained in these documents, how might your vision of the past be distorted? What other kinds of documents might you look at for evidence on the same issues?

3. What are the key categories and concepts used by the writer of the documents to organize the information presented? What are the selectivities or silences that result from these categories of thought?

4. What sort of theoretical issues and debates do these documents cast light upon? What kinds of historical and/or sociological questions do they help answer? What sorts of valid inferences can one make from the information contained in these documents? What sorts of generalizations can one make on the basis of the information contained in these documents?

Documents" provides additional suggestions on how to use historical documents and what to make of them.

The critical review that Aminzade and Laslett urge for the reading of historical documents can serve you more generally in life, and not just in the pursuit of historical and comparative research. Consider applying some of the boxed questions with regard to presidential press conferences, advertising, or—gasp!—college textbooks. None of these offers a direct view of reality; all have human authors and human subjects.

16.4b Analytic Techniques

As a qualitative research method, historical research treats hypotheses differently from the way quantitative methods do when seeking to formulate explanations. Rather than sticking with a hypothesis throughout an entire study that has been rigidly designed in advance to test it, historical researchers are likely to revise and reformulate their hypotheses

continually throughout the process of examining, analyzing, and synthesizing the historical documents they encounter.

Because historical and comparative research is a fluid qualitative method, there are no easily listed steps to follow in the analysis of historical data. Max Weber used the German term *verstehen*—understanding—in reference to an essential quality of social research. Weber meant that the researcher must be able to mentally take on the circumstances, views, and feelings of those being studied to interpret their actions appropriately. More recently, social scientists have adopted the term *hermeneutics* for this aspect of social research. Originally a Christian theological term that referred to the interpretation of spiritual truth in the Bible, hermeneutics has been secularized to mean the art, science, or skill of interpretation.

Whereas the conclusions drawn from quantitative research methods can rest, in part, on numerical calculations—either x is greater than y or it isn't—hermeneutic conclusions are harder to pin down and more subject to debate. But hermeneutics involves more than mere opinions. Albert Einstein (1940) described the foundation of science this way:

> Science is the attempt to make the chaotic diversity of our sense-experience correspond to a logically uniform system of thought. In this system single experiences must be correlated with the theoretic structure in such a way that the resulting coordination is unique and convincing. (p. 487)

The historical researcher must find patterns among the voluminous details that describe the subject matter of study. Often, the "theoretic structure" Einstein mentioned takes the form of what Weber called *ideal types*: conceptual models composed of the essential characteristics of social phenomena. Thus, for example, Weber himself did considerable research on bureaucracy. Having observed numerous actual bureaucracies, Weber (1925) detailed those qualities essential to bureaucracies in general: jurisdictional areas, hierarchically structured authority, written files, and so on. Weber did not merely list characteristics common to all the actual bureaucracies he observed. Rather, he needed to understand fully the essentials of bureaucratic operation to create a theoretical model of the "perfect" (ideal type of) bureaucracy.

Often, historical research is informed by a particular theoretical paradigm. Thus, Marxist scholars may undertake historical analyses of particular situations (such as the history of Hispanic minorities in the United States) to determine whether they can be understood in terms of the Marxist version of conflict theory.

Although historical and comparative research is regarded as a qualitative rather than quantitative technique, historians often make use of quantitative methods. For example, historical analysts often use time series (see Chapter 12) data to monitor changing conditions over time, such as data on populations, crime rates, unemployment, and infant mortality rates. When historical researchers rely on quantitative data, their reports will rely on numbers, graphs, statistical trends, and the like to support their conclusions. When they rely on qualitative methods, their reports will contain less

quantitative data and instead cite narrative material in their sources to illustrate the recurring patterns that they think they have detected.

16.5 MAIN POINTS

- Secondary analysis is a form of research in which the data collected and processed by one researcher are reanalyzed—often for a different purpose—by another.
- A variety of government and nongovernment agencies provide aggregate data for secondary analysis.
- Two key advantages of secondary analysis are that it is cheaper and faster than doing an original survey.
- Two key disadvantages of secondary analysis are that the data may be outdated by the time they are released, and the data might not provide a valid measure of the variable you want to analyze.
- Before investing a great deal of time in planning a study that will use existing data, you should check the data source to see if the data you need are there at all. If they are there, you should check to see whether large chunks of the data on certain key variables are missing and whether the data contain sufficient variation on your intended variables.
- Existing statistics often have problems of validity and reliability, so use them with caution.
- Units of communication, such as words, paragraphs, and books, are the usual units of analysis in content analysis.
- Manifest content refers to the directly visible, objectively identifiable characteristics of a communication, such as the specific words in a book, the specific colors used in a painting, and so forth.
- Latent content refers to the meanings contained within communications. The determination of latent content requires judgments on the part of the researcher.
- The advantages of content analysis include economy, ease of correcting mistakes, and the ability to study processes occurring over a long time. Its disadvantages are that it is limited to recorded

communications and can raise issues of reliability and validity.

- Social work researchers use historical and comparative methods to discover common patterns that recur in different times and places.
- Two broad types of source materials for historical research are primary sources and secondary sources.
- Primary sources provide firsthand accounts by someone who was present at an event—for example, diaries, letters, organizational bylaws, the minutes of a meeting, the orally reported memory of an eyewitness, and so on. Secondary sources describe past phenomena based on primary sources.
- A danger in working exclusively with secondary sources is that you may merely repeat the mistakes contained in those sources and fail to give yourself the opportunity to provide a new, independent perspective on past events. But primary sources can be flawed as well. For example, an eyewitness could have been biased or may experience faulty memory recall.
- When conducting historical research, you should try not to rely on a single source or on one type of source. Your protection against dangers in using primary and secondary sources lies in corroboration. If several sources point to the same set of "facts," your confidence in them might reasonably increase.

16.6 PRACTICE-RELATED EXERCISES

1. In two or three paragraphs, outline a content analysis design to determine whether the Republican Party or the Democratic Party is more supportive of public spending on social welfare. Be sure to specify units of analysis, sampling methods, and the relevant measurements.

2. Suppose you assess the need for and likely utilization of a suicide prevention program on your campus by conducting a secondary analysis of existing data collected in a recent survey of students asking them about a wide range of issues, including whether they've ever contemplated suicide. Discuss the advantages and disadvantages of basing your needs assessment solely on this secondary analysis.

3. Suppose, in response to managed care pressures, 5 years ago your child and family services agency dramatically increased the amount of time practitioners had to spend filling out forms on each case, including the provision of details about diagnoses and other information bearing on whether and how long services for each case were eligible for reimbursement from managed care companies. Discuss the specific ways in which this development might create special problems in analyzing existing agency statistics regarding historical trends in the types of diagnoses of clients served by your agency, the nature and amount of services provided, and client background characteristics.

16.7 INTERNET EXERCISES

1. Find the following articles that utilized content analysis and were published in the October 2002 issue of the journal *Social Work*:
   - "Among the Missing: Content on Lesbian and Gay People in Social Work Journals," by R. V. Voorhis and M. Wagner.
   - "Client's View of a Successful Helping Relationship," by D. S. Ribner and C. Knei-Paz.
   Identify each study's methodological strengths and weaknesses, indicate whether it used manifest or latent coding (or both), and indicate whether its methods were quantitative or qualitative. Finally, briefly explain why, in your view, each study's findings did or did not provide important implications for social policy or social work practice.

2. Go to the Content Analysis Guidebook Online website (http://academic.csuohio.edu/kneuen dorf/content/). Once there, find the following:
   a. A list of software programs for conducting a qualitative content analysis.
   b. Lists of other websites and resources that might be helpful in conducting a content analysis.
   c. Lists of publications and bibliographies on content analysis.

16.8 ADDITIONAL READINGS

Elder, G. H., Jr., Pavalko, E. K., & Clipp, E. C. (1993). *Working with archival data: Studying lives*. Newbury Park, CA: Sage. This book discusses the possibilities and techniques for using existing data archives in the United States, especially those providing longitudinal data.

Weber, R. P. (1990). *Basic content analysis*. Newbury Park, CA: Sage. Here's an excellent beginner's book for the design and execution of content analysis. Both general issues and specific techniques are presented.

16.8a Competency Notes

EP 2.1.6b: Use research evidence to inform practice (p. 328): Understanding all of the concepts in this chapter will help social workers comprehend the evidence supplied by studies that analyze available records and thus use that evidence to inform their practice.

EP 2.1.10m: Critically analyze, monitor, and evaluate interventions (p. 328): Understanding all of the concepts in this chapter will help social workers use available records when appropriate to evaluate their interventions.

Data Analysis

part

8

This concluding section will provide an overview of the analysis and interpretation of data in quantitative and qualitative studies. Chapter 17 examines quantitative data analysis for both descriptive and inferential purposes. Its emphasis is on understanding statistics rather than on procedures for computing them. Chapter 18 examines qualitative data analysis.

Although processing qualitative data can be as much art as science—with no cut-and-dried steps that guarantee success—we'll discuss some of the theoretical grounding for this approach and some conceptual procedures useful in the search for meaning among qualitative data.

chapter 17

Quantitative Data Analysis

17.1 INTRODUCTION

EP 2.1.6b
EP 2.1.10m

This chapter will provide a brief overview of the main ideas involved in analyzing statistical data in quantitative research studies. Quantitative data analysis can be descriptive or inferential. When we analyze data for descriptive purposes, our focus is limited to the data we have collected on our study's sample. Descriptive analysis involving just one variable is called univariate analysis. Bivariate analysis pertains to relationships between two variables, and multivariate analysis pertains to examining the way three or more variables are interrelated.

We seldom conduct quantitative research just to describe our samples per se. In most instances, our purpose is to make assertions about the larger population from which our sample has been selected or about the causal processes in general that might explain why we have observed a particular relationship in our data. Descriptive analysis does not provide a basis for generalizing beyond our particular study or sample. Even when we describe relationships between different variables in our study, that alone does not provide sufficient grounds for inferring that those relationships exist in general or have any theoretical meaning. Therefore, after we examine descriptive statistics, we'll examine inferential statistics.

Statistics is a complicated topic, and we can merely scratch the surface here. But we hope this chapter helps you comprehend some of the main concepts you'll encounter when reading quantitative research reports.

17.2 CODING

Today, data analysis is usually done by computer programs. For those programs to work their magic, they must be able to read the data you've collected in your research. The first step in quantitative data analysis, therefore, is coding. (The same is true of qualitative data analysis, as we'll see in Chapter 18.) Coding involves assigning separate code numbers to each category of each variable in your study.

Some data are coded easily. If you've conducted a survey, for example, some of your data are inherently numerical: age or income, for example. If a respondent reports her age as "sixty-five" you can just enter "65" into the computer. Likewise, transforming "male" and "female" into "1" and "2" is hardly rocket science. Researchers can also easily assign numerical representations to such variables as "religious affiliation," "ethnicity," and "region of the country."

Other data are more challenging to code. Surveys with open-ended questions about community problems, for example, might yield many diverse and lengthy responses. The responses will need to be collapsed into a smaller list of code categories, assigning the same code to responses that seem to belong together.

After the data are transformed into quantitative codes, researchers need to enter the data into a computer. The next step is the elimination of coding and data entry errors: "cleaning" the data. Next, researchers can begin quantitative analysis. Let's look now at some basic descriptive statistics for analyzing and presenting data about a single variable.

17.3 DESCRIPTIVE UNIVARIATE ANALYSIS

Univariate analysis is the examination of the distribution of cases on only one variable at a time. For example, if "gender" was measured, we would look at how many of the participants were men and how many were women. We'll begin by examining a basic form of univariate analysis: frequency distributions.

17.3a Frequency Distributions

A cumbersome way to present univariate data would be to list the attributes of all individual cases for each variable. Suppose you are interested in the ages of clients served by your agency, and suppose hundreds of clients have been served. (Your data might have come from agency records.) Imagine how difficult it would be for readers of your report if you just listed the ages of hundreds of clients: 57, 49, 62, 80, 72, 55, and so forth. Alternatively, you could arrange your data in a somewhat more manageable form without losing any of the detail by reporting that 5 clients were 38 years old, 7 were 39, 18 were 40, and so forth. Such a format would avoid duplicating data on this variable.

For an even more manageable format—with a certain loss of detail—you could report clients' ages in **frequency distributions** of *grouped data*: 246 clients less than 45 years of age, 517 between 45 and 50 years of age, and so forth. In addition, your distribution could display percentages. Thus, for example, you could report that x percent of the clients were under 45, y percent were between 45 and 50, and so forth.

17.3b Central Tendency

You might also present your data in the form of summary averages or measures of *central tendency*. Your options in this regard are the **mode** (the most frequent attribute, either grouped or ungrouped), the arithmetic **mean**, and the **median** (the *middle* attribute in the ranked distribution of observed attributes). Here's how the three averages would be calculated from a set of data.

Suppose that you're analyzing the case records of an adolescent residential facility whose 40 clients range in age from 12 to 18, as indicated in the accompanying table.

AGE	NUMBER OF CLIENTS
12	4
13	4
14	7
15	10
16	9
17	5
18	1

Now that you've seen the actual ages of the 40 clients, how old would you say they are in general, or on the average? Let's look at three different ways to answer that question.

The easiest **average** to calculate is the mode, or the most frequent value. As you can see, there were more 15-year-olds (10 of them) than any other age, so the modal age is 15. A more commonly used average is the mean. To calculate the mean, we would first add up the ages of all 40 clients. Thus we would add four 12s, four 13s, and so on. Adding

all 40 ages we would get a sum of 595. Then we would divide that sum by the total number of clients (40). That would give us a mean age of 14.9.

The *median* represents the "middle" value: half are above it, half below. Our median for the 40 clients would be 15, because there are 15 clients older than 15 and 15 clients younger than 15.

In the research literature, you'll find both means and medians presented. Whenever means are presented, you should be aware that they are susceptible to extreme values: a few very large or very small numbers. As one example, the (mean) average person in Redmond, Washington, has a net worth in excess of a million dollars. If you were to visit Redmond, however, you would not find that the "average" resident lives up to your idea of a millionaire. The very high mean reflects the influence of one extreme case among Redmond's 40,000 residents—Bill Gates of Microsoft, who has a net worth (at the time this is being written) of tens of billions of dollars. Clearly, the median wealth would give you a more accurate picture of the residents of Redmond as a whole. Let's now turn to another basic statistical concept related to this example, the concept of *dispersion*.

17.3c Dispersion

Averages reduce raw data to the most manageable form: a single number (or attribute) that represents all of the detailed data collected for the variable. This advantage comes at a cost, of course, because the reader cannot reconstruct the original data from an average. This disadvantage of averages can be

---

frequency distributions   A description of the number or percentage of times the various attributes of a variable are observed in a sample.

mode   The most frequently observed value or attribute.

mean   The sum of the values of several observations divided by the number of observations.

median   The value of the "middle" case in a rank-ordered set of observations.

average   An ambiguous term that generally suggests "typical" or "normal." Mean, median, and mode are specific examples of mathematical averages.

FIGURE 17.1 Three Fictitious Distributions of Eight Family Incomes Differing in Dispersion but Not Central Tendency

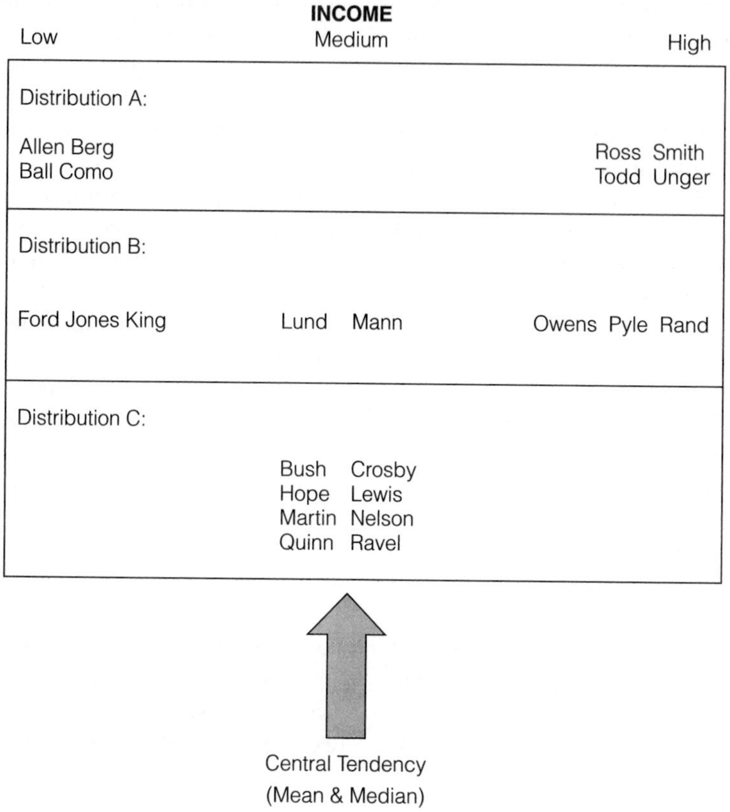

INCOME

Low	Medium	High

Distribution A:

Allen Berg   Ross Smith
Ball Como   Todd Unger

Distribution B:

Ford Jones King   Lund   Mann   Owens Pyle Rand

Distribution C:

                       Bush   Crosby
                       Hope   Lewis
                       Martin Nelson
                       Quinn Ravel

Central Tendency
(Mean & Median)

somewhat alleviated by reporting summaries of the **dispersion** of responses. The simplest measure of dispersion is the *range*: the distance separating the highest from the lowest value. Thus, besides reporting that our clients have a mean age of 14.9, we might also indicate that their ages ranged from 12 to 18.

There are many other measures of dispersion. The one you'll encounter most often is the **standard deviation**. Instead of examining its mathematical formula, we'll just consider what it means. In simple terms, the standard deviation reflects dispersion in a distribution by indicating how far away from the mean individual scores on average are located. For

example, if the mean age of clients is 14.9, and the standard deviation is 1.0, then we would know that a substantial portion of the ages are falling between 13.9 (one below the mean) and 15.9 (one above the mean). If, on the other hand, the standard deviation is, say, 5, then we would know that although the mean is 14.9, quite a few clients are up to 5 years older and 5 years younger than 14.9.

Figure 17.1 illustrates how distributions with different degrees of dispersion can have the same central tendency. Likewise, it illustrates how reports of descriptive findings that rely exclusively on central tendency can be incomplete and possibly misleading. For example, notice how in Distribution A none of the fictitious families is near the mean and median, whereas in Distribution C all of the families are near the very same mean and median. Thus, for Distribution A if you only knew the mean and median and not the dispersion and therefore concluded that the mean and median were good ways

---

dispersion   The distribution of values around some central value, such as an average.

standard deviation   A descriptive statistic that portrays how far away from the mean individual scores on average are located.

to portray the incomes of that group of families, you would be making a big mistake. A similar mistake, albeit not quite as misleading, would be made just knowing the central tendency of Distribution B. In that distribution, although two of the eight families are close to the central tendency, six of them are far from it. In Distribution C the mean and median would give you an accurate portrayal of the incomes of that group of families, but if you did not have any dispersion statistic (such as the standard deviation), you could not be sure of that.

17.3d Levels of Measurement

The calculations just described are not appropriate for all variables. The type of calculations that can be performed on a variable depends on that variable's *level of measurement*. There are four levels of measurement. Variables at the **nominal level of measurement** have qualitative attributes that are categorical only. Examples of nominal variables are gender, ethnicity, and birthplace. It makes no sense to assess *how much* a person is male or born in Mexico. Either they are or they aren't. We can only measure nominal variables in terms of **frequencies**—such as head counts. For example, we can ask what percentage of our clients are female or born in another country. We cannot calculate the mean gender or the mean country of origin.

Variables at the **ordinal level of measurement** can be rank-ordered in that different attributes represent relatively more or less of the variable. But the differences between the attributes are not precise. At the ordinal level, we know only whether one case has more or less of something than another case, but we don't know *how much* more. For example, we have an ordinal measure if we know that the horse Seabiscuit won the race and the talking TV horse Mr. Ed came in second, but we don't know by how much. Likewise, if clients say they are very satisfied with Service A, but only slightly satisfied with Service B, then we have an ordinal measure because we don't know the precise difference in degree of satisfaction.

In contrast, with variables at the **interval level of measurement**, differences between different levels have the same meanings. Thus, the difference between an IQ score of 95 and 100 is considered to be of the same magnitude as the difference between 100 and 105. Summated scores on various scales used in social work research are often treated as interval-level variables even though purists might deem them to be at the ordinal level. For example, suppose we administer a 10-item Likert scale assessing one's degree of agreement or disagreement with statements about legalizing gay marriage. Let's say that each item has a five-point response scale and that total scores thus can range from 10 to 50. We can't be sure that the difference between scores of 40 and 45 represents the same degree of difference in attitude as does the difference between scores of 20 and 25.

Variables at the **ratio level of measurement** have the same attribute as interval measures, but in addition have a true zero point. Thus, a person can have no arrests, one arrest, two arrests, and so on. Because there is a true zero point, we know that the person with four arrests has been arrested exactly twice as many times as the person with two arrests.

Strictly speaking, medians, means, and standard deviations should be calculated only for interval and ratio data. There are, however, numerous "gray-area" situations in the calculation of averages.

---

nominal level of measurement A level of measurement that describes variables (such as gender or ethnicity) whose different attributes are categorical only, and can be described in terms of how many but not degree.

frequencies Head counts of how many cases there are in nominal categories.

ordinal level of measurement A level of measurement describing variables whose attributes may be rank-ordered according to degree. An example would be socioeconomic status as composed of the attributes high, medium, and low.

interval level of measurement A level of measurement that describes variables (such as IQ or Fahrenheit temperature) whose attributes are rank-ordered and have equal distances between adjacent attributes, but which do not have a true zero point.

ratio level of measurement A level of measurement that describes variables (such as age or number of children) whose attributes have all the qualities of interval measures and also are based on a true zero point.

Suppose, for example, that you were assessing client satisfaction with the services they received by asking them to rate those services on a four-point scale: 4 = very satisfied, 3 = satisfied, 2 = dissatisfied, and 1 = very dissatisfied. You should note that this would be an ordinal-level measurement because you would have no reason to believe that the distance from rating 1 (very dissatisfied) to rating 2 (dissatisfied) is the same as the distance between rating 2 and rating 3 (satisfied), and so on. Consequently, calculating the mean rating or the standard deviation for a large number of clients would be technically questionable because such calculations would treat these ordinal-level ratings as if they were real values.

Yet such technical violations are commonly found and still can be useful. A mean score across all clients may not have a precise mathematical meaning in regard to client satisfaction, but it could be useful in comparing large numbers of ratings across client subgroups. For example, suppose the mean rating from ethnic minority clients was 1.4, as compared to a mean rating of 3.2 from White clients. Despite its imprecise meaning, this comparison would provide a clear and useful indication that the two groups do not express the same levels of satisfaction and that you ought to assess and deal with the reasons for the difference. (We make similar comparisons all the time, by the way, when we discuss students' grade point averages!)

The key here is *utility*. If you find that a researcher's statistical calculations are useful in guiding practice, then you should be somewhat lenient in the application of statistical techniques to data that do not warrant them. The other edge of this sword, however, is the danger of being lulled into thinking that the results represent something truly precise. In the above case of client satisfaction ratings, for example, you might question the utility and appropriateness of carrying the means and standard deviations out to three decimal places.

17.4 RELATIONSHIPS AMONG VARIABLES

Univariate analysis looks at only one variable at a time; it does not look at relationships among variables. Sometimes we can look at more than one variable, but without looking at their relationship. That

would still be univariate analysis. For example, suppose we are describing our agency's caseload in terms of client age and country of origin. We might say that 50 percent of our clients are less than 20 years old and that 50 percent were born in the United States. Although we are quantifying two variables, we are saying nothing about their relationship. They may or may not be related. For example, all of the clients under age 20 may have been born in the United States, some of them may have been, or none of them may have been. If half of the clients under age 20 were born in the United States, and half were born elsewhere, there would be no relationship between the two variables: age and country of origin. At the other extreme, if all of the clients under age 20 were born in the United States, and all those over age 20 were born elsewhere, there would be an extremely strong (indeed, perfect) relationship between the two variables.

When we look at the relationship between two variables, we are conducting a bivariate analysis. Whereas univariate analyses of variables are primarily *descriptive* in purpose, bivariate analysis—in examining *relationships* between two variables—typically does so for *explanatory* purposes. For example, if we find that minority clients are more likely to refuse our services than are Caucasian clients, we may be wondering about deficiencies in our agency's cultural competence as a plausible *explanation*.

17.4a Interpreting Bivariate Tables

Explanatory bivariate tables can be read and interpreted by comparing the independent variable subgroups with one another in terms of a given attribute of the dependent variable. For example, Table 17.1 displays the relationship between ethnicity and service utilization in an imaginary agency. Ethnicity is the independent variable, because we wonder if it explains service refusal. Its categories are spread across the columns. The dependent variable, level of service utilization, is stacked at left in the labels for the rows. The raw numbers are in parentheses. The table shows percentages in the columns with each category of the independent variable summing to 100 percent in the Total row. That's because we want to compare the service refusal rate among Caucasians

Table 17.1 Bivariate Relationship between Ethnicity and Service Utilization in a Hypothetical Agency

SERVICE UTILIZATION	ETHNICITY	
	CAUCASIAN	MINORITY
Service Utilized	80% (80)	40% (80)
Service Refused	20% (20)	60% (120)
TOTAL	100% (100)	100% (200)

to the rate among other clients. We don't care that the number of clients of other ethnicities using the service (80) is the same as the number of Caucasians using the service. That's because the 80 others constitute only 40 percent of the 200 referred other cases, whereas the 80 Caucasians make up 80 percent of the 100 referred Caucasian cases. We do care about the percentages, however, because they take into account differences in the total number of cases in each column. Thus, we interpret the table by comparing the dependent variable rates (i.e., the service utilization and refusal rates) for each category of the independent variable.

17.4b Interpreting Multivariate Tables

Multivariate tables are constructed from several variables. They are constructed using the same logic that we just examined for bivariate tables. Instead of one independent variable and one dependent variable, however, we will have more than one

independent variable. Instead of explaining the dependent variable on the basis of a single independent variable, we'll seek an explanation through the use of more than one independent variable.

Consider our imaginary example of ethnicity and service refusal. Suppose we believed that the variable *country of origin* might affect the relationship between ethnicity and service refusal. Maybe it's not the difference in ethnicity that explains the different service refusal rates. Instead, maybe it's the fact that non-Caucasian referrals are more likely to be recent immigrants from another country. For example, if our imaginary agency is in south Florida or south Texas, a large proportion of our referrals may be recent immigrants from Cuba or Mexico. Perhaps the Cuban Americans or Mexican Americans who were born in the United States are no more likely to refuse services than are Caucasian Americans. If that is the case, then language or acculturation factors may have more to do with explaining the different refusal rates than the broader variable of *ethnicity*. Let's examine this possibility by interpreting the imaginary data in the multivariate Table 17.2.

At first glance, the seeming complexity of the multivariate table might overwhelm you. Where on earth to begin?! Let's simplify things. This table is nothing more than two bivariate tables side by side! If you understood how to interpret the bivariate table between ethnicity and service utilization, you should have no trouble interpreting this multivariate table. Just break the process down into two easy steps.

First, we examine the bivariate part of the table pertaining just to those cases born in the United States. There we see no difference whatsoever in

Table 17.2 Multivariate Relationship between Ethnicity and Service Refusal, Controlling for Country of Origin, in a Hypothetical Agency

	COUNTRY OF ORIGIN			
	UNITED STATES		OTHER COUNTRY	
	CAUCASIAN	MINORITY	CAUCASIAN	MINORITY
Service Utilized	88% (70)	88% (70)	50% (10)	8% (10)
Service Refused	12% (10)	12% (10)	50% (10)	92% (110)
TOTAL	100% (80)	100% (80)	100% (20)	100% (120)

the fictional data regarding service utilization and refusal rates for Caucasians and others. Each group had 80 cases born in the United States, with a 12 percent service refusal rate for each.

Next, we examine the bivariate part on the right side of the table—pertaining just to those cases born in another country. There we see a big difference in the fictional service utilization and refusal rates for Caucasians (50 percent refusal rate) and others (92 percent refusal rate). Now we are prepared to summarize the entire table. Here's what we might say (remember that these are fictional data for an imaginary agency):

> For referrals born in the United States, there is no difference in service utilization rates between Caucasians and others. However, for referrals who are born in another country, there is a big difference in service utilization rates between Caucasians and others—with other immigrants being much more likely to refuse services than Caucasian immigrants. Moreover, immigrants of either ethnicity are more likely to refuse services than people who were born in the United States. Thus, language and acculturation factors appear to have more to do with service refusal rates than ethnicity, but they appear to have a bigger impact on the service utilization rates of other immigrants than on Caucasian immigrants.

17.4c Interpreting Measures of Association

When we depict the difference in service utilization and refusal rates as "big," we are referring to the *strength of the association* between the variables of concern. Sometimes we can depict that strength merely by eyeballing different percentages in a table. However, it's not always easy to do that. Statistical procedures have been developed to facilitate and make more systematic the interpretation of how strongly variables are related to one another. These procedures can be called *measures of association, measures of relationship strength*, or *measures of effect size*.

Some commonly used measures of association yield values that range from zero, which signifies no relationship whatsoever, to 1.0, which signifies a perfect relationship. A value of −1.0 also would signify a perfect relationship. The minus sign in front of this type of relationship magnitude statistic does not mean the relationship is weaker than one with a plus sign. The minus sign means only that the variables are negatively (inversely) related: As one goes up, the other goes down. The closer the value is to zero, the less able we are to predict the relative value of one variable by knowing the other.

For example, if two groups had exactly the same service refusal rate, then knowing whether a particular case was in one group or the other would not affect our calculation of the odds that this case would refuse services. We might be able to predict the odds from the overall service refusal rate for cases in either group, but knowing what group the case was in would not influence our prediction one way or the other. Thus, the relationship magnitude would be zero.

On the other hand, if one group had a 0 percent service refusal rate and the other group had a 100 percent service refusal rate, then knowing which group a case was in would enable us to predict with 100 percent accuracy whether that case would refuse services. The relationship magnitude would be 1.0, a perfect relationship.

Table 17.3 illustrates one two-by-two table that shows a relationship magnitude of zero and two perfect relationships. The two-by-two table at the top shows no relationship, and the relationship magnitude therefore is zero, because the two groups have exactly the same service refusal rates. The fact that there are fewer service refusers than service utilizers (that is, the service refusal rate is 40 percent) may be an important descriptive finding. But because each group has the same 40 percent service refusal rate, knowing what group a case is in offers us nothing to help predict whether that case will refuse services, and therefore the relationship magnitude is zero.

In the second two-by-two table, the relationship magnitude is 1.0 because none of the U.S.-born cases refused services, whereas all of the immigrant cases did. Thus, knowing which group a case was in would be all we needed to know to predict with perfect accuracy whether the case will refuse services.

The same degree of predictability is evident in the third example, but this time there is a minus sign in front of the 1.0 because as one variable increases, the other decreases. The relationship magnitude is −1.0 because each additional session of treatment attended, without exception, reduces the number of

Table 17.3 Illustrations of Relationship Magnitudes of 0, 1.0, and −1.0

EXAMPLE OF A RELATIONSHIP MAGNITUDE OF 0

	U.S. BORN	IMMIGRANT
Service Refused	40	40
Service Utilized	60	60

EXAMPLE OF A RELATIONSHIP MAGNITUDE OF 1.0

	U.S. BORN	IMMIGRANT
Service Refused	0	100
Service Utilized	100	0

EXAMPLE OF A RELATIONSHIP MAGNITUDE OF −1.0

CASE NUMBER	NUMBER OF TREATMENT SESSIONS ATTENDED	NUMBER OF VERBAL ABUSE INCIDENTS
1	0	7
2	1	6
3	2	5
4	3	4
5	4	3
6	5	2
7	6	1
8	7	0

incidents of verbal abuse observed by the same amount each time. It is a perfect relationship because the number of sessions a client attends is all we need to know to predict with perfect accuracy the number of incidents of verbal abuse observed. The minus sign is not pejorative and does not signify a weaker relationship; it simply means that an increase in one variable is associated with a decrease in the other.

So far we have contrasted a perfect relationship (with a magnitude of 1.0 or −1.0) with no relationship (zero magnitude). But what about something in between—for example, a 40 percent service refusal rate for the U.S.-born group versus a 60 percent one for the immigrants? In that case, knowing that a referral was in the U.S.-born group would predispose us to predict service utilization, and knowing the referral was in the immigrant group would predispose us to predict service refusal. But if we predicted service refusal for every immigrant referral and service utilization for every U.S.-born referral, then we would be wrong 40 percent of the time. That's a lot of errors. But with an overall service

refusal rate of 50 percent (which would be the case with an equal number of referrals in the 40 percent and 60 percent groups), we would be wrong 50 percent of the time if we tried to predict recidivism for each referral without knowing which group each referral was in. Thus, knowing which group a referral was in would reduce our percentage of errors from 50 percent to 40 percent, or a proportional reduction in error of .20. (The .20 is derived from expressing the .10 reduction from .50 to .40 in proportional terms: .10 is 20 percent, or .20, of .50.)

In short, if there is some relationship between our variables, it means that knowing the value for one variable will reduce the number of errors we make in predicting the value for the other. And the stronger the relationship is, the more our prediction errors will be reduced.

Which measure of association should be used depends primarily on the level of measurement of your variables. Some of the most commonly used measures of association are *Pearson's product-moment correlation (r), lambda, Yule's Q, phi, Cramer's V, eta,* and the *point-biserial correlation coefficient.* (For more information about these measures, we encourage you to examine the statistical text listed in the Additional Readings section at the end of this chapter.) You may not remember for years to come all the measure of association labels we've just mentioned. That's okay. The important thing is not to get overwhelmed if you encounter them when reading research results. Instead, you can just remember what it basically means when an article says the correlation (or other measure of association) was .30, −.40, or whatever.

17.5 EFFECT SIZE

We mentioned above that a statistic that portrays the strength of association between variables is sometimes called an **effect size**. This term is used

---

effect size A term for various statistics that portray the strength of association between variables. Effect-size statistics might refer to the degree of correlation between variables (that is, between zero and plus or minus one) or to the difference between the means of two groups divided by the standard deviation.

especially in outcome research. Measures of association that range from zero to plus or minus one are all effect-size statistics. So are others that we haven't yet discussed but will address shortly. Effect-size statistics portray the strength of association found in any study, no matter what outcome measure is used, in terms that are comparable across studies. Thus, they enable us to compare the effects of different interventions across studies using different types of outcome measures.

To illustrate this function in outcome research, suppose two different studies are conducted, each an experimental evaluation of the effectiveness of a different approach to treating male batterers. The first evaluates a cognitive-behavioral approach and finds that the experimental group subjects who receive the tested treatment averaged two abusive incidents per subject during a posttreatment follow-up period, as compared to a mean of three physically abusive incidents for control subjects. The second study evaluates a psychosocial approach. Instead of using the ratio-level outcome measure of number of abusive incidents, it uses the nominal measure of whether any abuse occurred during the follow-up period. It finds that 40 percent of experimental subjects were abusive, as compared to 60 percent of control subjects.

How can we judge which of the two interventions had the stronger effects? Comparing their outcomes as just stated is a bit like comparing apples and oranges because they used different types of outcome indicators. Effect-size statistics help alleviate this problem. For example, the correlation coefficient for the first study can be compared to the correlation statistic for the second study. Although different correlation statistics might be used by different studies using outcome indicators that are at different levels of measurement, each has the same meaning. The intervention with the larger effect size is the one that had a greater effect on its dependent variable.

---

odds ratio An effect size statistic that shows how much more or less likely a certain dependent variable outcome is for the categories of the independent variable.

risk ratio An effect size statistic that divides the proportion of unsuccessful outcomes in one group by the risk of unsuccessful outcomes in the other group.

Not everyone who reports correlations refers to them as the "effect size." Some do, but many don't. For example, one author might say, "The effect size was substantial, because the correlation was .50," whereas another author might simply say, "The relationship was strong, because the correlation was .50." Among various other effect-size statistics three commonly used ones are odds ratios, risk ratios, and *Cohen's d*. Which one is used depends on the level of measurement of the variables.

17.5a Odds Ratios and Risk Ratios

When the independent and dependent variables are both dichotomous, in addition to reporting measures of association like *phi* or *Cramer's V*, one can report effect-size statistics called *odds ratios* and *risk ratios*. The **odds ratio** shows how much more or less likely a certain dependent variable outcome is for the categories of the independent variable. For example, suppose that 100 parents referred for child maltreatment receive innovative new Intervention A, and another 100 receive treatment as usual (TAU). Suppose further that only 20 (20%) of the 100 Intervention A recipient recidivate, as compared to 50 (50%) of the 100 TAU recipients. That would mean that the ratio of Intervention A recipients who had a *successful* outcome was 80/20, or 4 to 1 (or 4.0). In contrast, the ratio of TAU recipients with a successful outcome would be only 50/50, or 1 to 1 (or 1.0). Dividing the Intervention A ratio (4.0) by the TAU ratio (1.0) equals 4.0. The odds ratio regarding successful outcomes for Intervention A therefore would be 4.0, meaning that its odds of a successful outcome are 4.0 times greater than the odds of a successful outcome for TAU.

For some studies, it is preferable to calculate the risk ratio regarding unsuccessful outcomes. The risk ratio is calculated by dividing the proportion of unsuccessful outcomes in one group by the risk of unsuccessful outcomes in the other group. Using the previous example, the recidivism proportion for Intervention A is .20 (i.e., 20 divided by 100). The comparable proportion for TAU is .50 (i.e., 50 divided by 100). The **risk ratio**, therefore, would be .20 divided by .50, which equals .40. When a group's risk ratio is less than one, it means that that group has less risk than the other group. If it is greater than one, then it has more risk. If the risk ratio is exactly 1.0, then both groups have the same degree of risk. In this example, Intervention

A's .40 risk ratio is .60 less than 1.0; therefore, Intervention A reduced the degree of risk by 60% (i.e., 1.0 minus .40 is a .60 drop, and .60 is 60% of 1.0). Said another way, the recidivism rate of .20 for Intervention A was .30 less than the .50 recidivism rate of TAU, and a reduction of .30 is 60% of .50.

Cohen's d

Perhaps the most commonly used effect size statistic is *Cohen's d*. This statistic can be used when interval or ratio-level data permit dividing the difference between the means of the experimental and control groups by the standard deviation. Different approaches to calculating *Cohen's d* vary based upon whether the standard deviation that is used in the calculation is that of the control group, the pooled standard deviation of the two groups combined, or an estimate of the standard deviation of the population about which a study is attempting to generalize. To simplify our discussion, we'll just use the pooled standard deviation. In this approach, the *Cohen's d* formula is as follows:

$$ES(\textit{Cohen's d}) = \frac{(\text{experimental group mean}) - (\text{control group mean})}{(\text{pooled standard deviation})}$$

To illustrate the use of the preceding formula, let's return to the hypothetical example of two studies, each of which evaluates the effectiveness of a different approach to treating male batterers. This time, however, assume that each uses a ratio-level measure of outcome. Let's say that the first study assesses the mean number of physically abusive incidents and finds an experimental group mean of 2, a control group mean of 3, and a standard deviation of 1. Its effect size would be as follows:

$$\textit{Cohen's d} = \frac{2 - 3}{1} = -1.0 \rightarrow +1.0$$

When calculating *Cohen's d* this way, we interpret the plus or minus sign in the dividend according to whether a reduction in the outcome measure represents a desirable or undesirable effect. In the preceding example, it represents a desirable effect because we were seeking to reduce physical abuse. We would therefore report the *Cohen's d* as +1.0 (not −1.0), because the minus sign in reporting *Cohen's d* is used only to indicate undesirable effects (in the

opposite direction of what was sought). We would interpret this *Cohen's d* of +1.0 by observing that the experimental group's mean was one standard deviation better than the control group's mean.

Let's say that the second study in our hypothetical example assesses the mean number of verbally and physically abusive incidents combined (unlike the first study, which assessed only physical abuse) and has a longer posttreatment measurement period than did the first study. Suppose the second study finds an experimental group mean of 20, a control group mean of 26, and a standard deviation of 10. Its effect size would be as follows:

$$\textit{Cohen's d} = \frac{20 - 26}{10} = -.60 \rightarrow +.60$$

Although the two studies quantified outcome in different ways—one dealing with much larger numbers than the other—dividing by the standard deviation makes the results of the two studies comparable. The preceding results indicate that the cognitive-behavioral intervention evaluated in the first study had stronger effects on its outcome measure than the psychosocial intervention evaluated in the second study had on its outcome measure.

17.5b Strong, Medium, and Weak Effect Sizes

It is often useful to interpret our effect sizes in terms such as *weak*, *medium*, or *strong* so that they take on added meaning relative to other research findings and other explanations. But interpreting some effect sizes can be a tricky business.

We often have a reflexive tendency to attach the same meanings to correlations as we attach to our exam scores, seeing percentages above 70 or 80 percent as strong and anything much lower as weak. Although these benchmarks may be applicable to studies of measurement reliability, using them as general guideposts to distinguish strong and weak relationships is incorrect.

For example, suppose we conducted an experiment to evaluate the effectiveness of an intervention

---

Cohen's d   An effect size statistic that divides the difference between the experimental group mean and the control group mean by the pooled standard deviation of the two groups.

to prevent recidivism among parents referred for child abuse. Suppose our experiment found a 40 percent recidivism rate for 100 treated cases and a 60 percent recidivism rate for 100 untreated cases. We would find that the correlation for this relationship would equal .20. (You can examine a statistics book if you want to know how this is calculated; in this book we are only concerned with you understanding the meaning of this statistic.) Would we conclude that this was a weak relationship? Although we might not all give the same answer to that question, we probably would agree that there is no one mathematically correct answer to it. Although a correlation of .20 might seem weak at first glance, what about the fact that our intervention reduced the child abuse recidivism rate by 20 percent, which is a 33 percent reduction (20 percent is one-third of 60 percent)? Also, what if prior experimental research had found that alternative interventions had a weaker effect or even no impact on recidivism rates?

What if our hypothetical experiment were to find a 35 percent recidivism rate for treated cases versus a 65 percent recidivism rate for untreated cases? The *phi* statistic for that relationship would be .30. Although that may seem small in the context of an exam score or a reliability coefficient, the 65 percent recidivism rate for untreated cases would nearly double the 35 percent rate for treated cases.

In this connection, Cohen (1988) argues that a *Cohen's d* of approximately .5 should be considered to be of medium strength, noting that it pertains to the difference in average height if we compare 14- and 18-year-old girls and the difference in mean IQ between clerical and semiskilled workers. Cohen also argues that a *Cohen's d* of .8 should be considered strong, noting that this amount applies to the difference in the mean IQ between college graduates and persons with only a 50/50 chance of passing a high school academic curriculum.

Cohen deems a *Cohen's d* of about .2 to be weak. Yet Rosenthal and Rubin (1982) argue that the value of some interventions with "weak" effect

sizes is often underestimated. For example, a new intervention that improves a treatment success rate from 45 percent to 55 percent would have a correlation of only .10. An increase from .45 to .55 might be very important when the increase is in such outcome indicators as survival rates or cure rates.

Some researchers have developed empirical guidelines for interpreting the relative strength of relationship magnitude statistics, based on their reviews of hundreds of published research studies in the social sciences and helping professions. Their results have, by and large, been close to Cohen's guidelines for weak, medium, and strong relationships. These guidelines can provide approximate benchmarks that can be useful in interpreting effect sizes in future research.

But an intervention's effect size alone does not indicate its value. An intervention with a stronger effect size is not necessarily "better" than one with a weaker effect size. For example, an intervention that reduces the rate of child abuse or school dropout among high-risk individuals from 55 percent to 45 percent may be more valuable to society than an intervention that reduces the annual turnover rate among Big Brother or Big Sister volunteers from 60 percent to 40 percent. Or, returning to an example we used earlier, an intervention that reduces the rate of extreme physical abuse from 55 percent to 45 percent might be deemed more valuable than an intervention that reduces the rate of mild verbal abuse from 65 percent to 35 percent. Determining which intervention is "better" or more valuable requires considering the substantive significance of research findings, an issue we shall take up next.

17.6 SUBSTANTIVE SIGNIFICANCE

Measures of the strength of a relationship do not automatically indicate the **substantive significance** of that relationship. Some researchers might use the term *practical significance*, which is synonymous with substantive significance. In studies of the effectiveness of clinical interventions, the term **clinical significance** is likely to be used instead of the term *substantive significance*. Both terms mean the same thing. By the substantive significance of a relationship (or its practical or clinical significance), we mean its importance from a practical standpoint. No matter how strong a relationship may be—no

---

substantive significance (practical significance) The importance, or meaningfulness, of a finding from a practical standpoint.

clinical significance The *substantive significance* or meaningfulness of a finding in a study of the effectiveness of a clinical intervention.

matter how well it compares to an average effect size or how close to 1.0 it may be in a measure of association—we still can ask whether it constitutes a substantively important or trivial finding.

Let's consider this issue in connection to the child abuse example we used above. Suppose one intervention makes the difference between a 35 percent and a 65 percent recidivism rate. It is appropriate to ask, "How substantively significant is that finding?" In other words, how much practical importance does it have for the field? Suppose another experiment finds that a different intervention with the same target population makes a very substantial difference between a 20 percent recidivism rate and an 80 percent rate. Assuming that the two interventions were equal in terms of cost, time, and so on, determining which was the more substantively significant finding would seem to be a fairly straightforward process, and we would choose the one with the 20 percent recidivism rate. Because everything else but relationship magnitude was of equal importance, the stronger relationship would be the more substantively significant relationship.

But suppose a different experiment finds that, after five years of daily psychoanalysis costing $500 per week, 80 percent of treated abusive parents as compared to 20 percent of untreated parents say they agree with Freud's ideas. Which intervention would you find to be more valuable if you were providing services to that target population: the one that made a 30 percent difference in child abuse recidivism, or the one that made a 60 percent difference in agreement with Freud's ideas? We hope you would deem the weaker relationship involving the intervention that reduced child abuse by 30 percent to have more substantive significance than the stronger relationship pertaining to attitudes about a theory. (Not that there is anything wrong with psychoanalysis per se; we would say the same thing about any theory in this practical context.)

The preceding admittedly extreme hypothetical comparison illustrates that no automatic correspondence exists between the strength of a relationship and that relationship's substantive significance. It's important to know how strong a relationship is and how it compares to the findings of other comparable studies that used comparable variables. But not all studies are comparable in practical importance.

Therefore, after we have measured the strength of the association, we must make subjective value judgments to gauge the substantive significance of that relationship—value judgments that might consider such intangibles as the importance of the variables and problem studied, whether the benefits of implementing the study's implications are worth the costs of that implementation, and what prior knowledge we have about the problem studied and how to alleviate it. If we judge that the study addresses a trivial problem, assesses trivial variables, reports results that recommend actions whose costs far outweigh their benefits, or yields findings that add nothing to what is already known, then we might deem relationships to be trivial even if they are strong.

17.7 INFERENTIAL ANALYSIS

No matter how strongly two variables appear to be related in the data from our study, we have to consider the possibility that our results might be a fluke and that the two variables may not really be related in the population or in any theoretical sense. To illustrate this point, here is a silly hypothesis you can test before your next class session begins: "First-born or only-born children are more likely to have an odd number of letters in their last name than later-borns."

To test this hypothesis, ask all the students in the room whether they were their parents' first-born child and whether their last name has an odd or even number of letters in it. (If they are their parents' only child, count that as first-born.) Most likely, you'll find some relationship between the two variables. For example, maybe 6 of the 10 first-borns will have an odd number of letters in their last names, while 4 of 10 later-borns do.

Although that finding shows a 20 percent difference between the first- and later-borns, you would not interpret it to mean that first-borns are more likely than later-borns to have an odd number of letters in their last names. That would be ludicrous (as was our hypothesis in the first place), since siblings have the same last names! Yet almost every time we try this experiment in our research classes, we get a difference between first- and later-borns.

Sometimes a greater percentage of the first-borns in a classroom do have an odd number of letters in their last names, and sometimes the later-borns do. The point of this exercise is to illustrate that mere *chance*—also known as *sampling error*—can account for relationships that appear in our study data.

Here's another example. Suppose early in the 20th century a child psychologist who badly needed a vacation came up with the cockamamie idea that if a youth held his hand while reciting the Ten Commandments three times, the youth would grow up to be a humanitarian leader for world peace and social justice. Suppose he decided to test his goofy hypothesis by conducting an experiment in which he would randomly assign youths to either receive his intervention or a control group. As fate would have it, suppose only four youths agreed to participate in his experiment, and they appeared in this order: Mahatma Gandhi, Mother Teresa, Adolph Hitler, and Joseph Stalin.

Suppose that, as each youth arrived, the psychologist flipped a coin for the random assignment. If the coin toss resulted in a head, the youth received the intervention. Once two youths got assigned to one condition, the remaining ones automatically went to the other condition. Now, suppose the first two tosses were heads—so both Mahatma Gandhi and Mother Teresa received the intervention, while Hitler

and Stalin served as the control group. As time passed, the psychologist would find the strongest possible relationship in his data. With a 100 percent success rate for his experimental group, and a 0 percent success rate for his control group, his correlation would be the maximum possible: 1.0. But how rare is it to flip a coin and get two heads in a row? Not rare at all.

Likewise, it wouldn't have been unusual at all to get two tails in a row, resulting in Hitler and Stalin getting the intervention and therefore giving our psychologist great anguish years later when he saw the havoc he thought he'd wreaked on the world! We can see from this fictional illustration that the relationships we observe in our findings do not necessarily really exist in the population or in any theoretical sense. Rather than our independent variable (or intervention) being the cause or explanation for differences in our dependent variable, the real explanation may be mere chance—such as the luck of the coin toss or sampling error. (We discussed sampling error in Chapter 10.)

17.7a Refuting Chance

The foregoing examples illustrate the need to rule out chance (or sampling error) as the explanation for the relationships we observe in our quantitative data. The types of **descriptive statistics** discussed so far in this chapter won't enable us to rule out chance. For that, we need to use **inferential statistics**. There are many types of inferential statistics, some of which are mathematically complex and some of which are simpler. You can learn a lot about them in a statistics class or a little more about them in our more advanced text (Rubin & Babbie, 2011).

The inferential statistics pertinent to our current discussion are those that assess whether a relationship that we observe in our data has **statistical significance**. If the likelihood that a relationship can be attributed to chance is quite tiny, then that relationship will be deemed statistically significant. To determine what that likelihood is, a **test of statistical significance** is conducted. There are many types of statistical significance tests. Various considerations—including whether variables are at the nominal, ordinal, or ratio level of measurement—determine which statistical test is best suited for a particular relationship. Regardless of what type of significance test is used,

---

descriptive statistics Statistical computations that describe either the characteristics of a sample or the relationship among variables in a sample. Descriptive statistics merely summarize a set of sample observations, whereas inferential statistics move beyond the description of specific observations to make inferences about the larger population from which the sample observations were drawn.

inferential statistics The body of statistical computations that is relevant to making inferences from findings based on sample observations to some larger population.

statistical significance A general term that refers to the likelihood that relationships observed in a sample could be attributed to chance (sampling error) alone.

test of statistical significance A statistical procedure for calculating the probability that a relationship can be attributed to chance (sampling error).

however, the result of that test will be reported in terms of a probability level. That probability level will tell you the likelihood that the relationship can be attributed to chance (sampling error). The symbol for the term *probability* will be *p*. Thus, if you read a research report that tests a hypothesis and you see $p < .05$, that means that the probability (likelihood) that the results supporting that hypothesis can be attributed to chance is less than .05. (The symbol $<$ means "less than.")

Most research reports will call a relationship *statistically significant when* the *p* value is at or below .05. That's because .05 means that there is only a 1 in 20 chance (5 in 100 chance) that the relationship can be attributed to chance (such as the luck of the coin toss). Some studies with very small samples will use .10 as the cutoff point for determining whether a relationship is statistically significant. That's because it's mathematically harder to achieve statistical significance with small samples. You can study the math behind all this in a statistics course, but understanding that math is not necessary for you to understand what it means when you $p < .05$ or $p < .10$ read in a research report.

We hope this simplified chapter on quantitative data analysis enables you to comprehend the most relevant implications that you need to understand when you read a report with quantitative research findings. At the same time, we hope it spurs you to learn more about statistics.

17.8 MAIN POINTS

- Quantitative analysis requires the conversion of data items into numerical codes. These codes represent attributes comprising variables, which in turn are assigned locations within a data file.
- Frequency distributions show the number of times the various attributes of a variable are observed in a sample.
- Three measures of central tendency are the mean, median, and mode.
- Measures of dispersion give a summary indication of the distribution of cases around an average value.
- A descriptive statistic that portrays how far away from the mean individual scores on average are located is the standard deviation.

- In contrast to univariate analysis, bivariate analysis examines relationships between two variables and typically does so for explanatory purposes.
- Bivariate analysis is nothing more than a different interpretation of subgroup comparisons. The steps are as follows: (1) divide cases into subgroups in terms of their attributes on some independent variable, (2) describe each subgroup in terms of some dependent variable, (3) compare the dependent variable descriptions of the subgroups, and (4) interpret any observed differences as a statistical association between the independent and dependent variables.
- Multivariate analysis is a method of analyzing the simultaneous relationships among several variables; it may be used to more fully understand the relationship between two variables.
- Inferential statistics help rule out chance as a plausible explanation of our findings.
- Statistical significance testing identifies the probability that our findings can be attributed to chance.
- Measures of association such as correlation coefficients and analogous statistics assess a relationship's strength. The stronger the relationship, the closer the measure of association statistic will be to 1.0 or −1.0. The weaker the relationship, the closer it will be to zero.
- Statistics that portray the strength of association between variables are often referred to by the term *effect size*. Effect-size statistics might refer to the proportion of variation in the dependent variable that can be explained or to the difference between the means of two groups divided by the standard deviation.
- Three types of effect size statistics are Cohen's *d*, odds ratios, and risk ratios.
- Cohen's *d* divides the difference between the experimental group mean and the control group mean by the pooled standard deviation of the two groups.
- The odds ratio shows how much more or less likely a certain dependent variable outcome is for the categories of the independent variable.
- The risk ratio divides the proportion of unsuccessful outcomes in one group by the risk of

unsuccessful outcomes in the other group. Statistical significance, relationship strength, and substantive significance (also known as *clinical significance* or *practical significance*) must not be confused with one another. Statistically significant relationships are not necessarily strong or substantively meaningful.

17.9 PRACTICE-RELATED EXERCISES

1. You have provided a 15-session outpatient intervention for people who recently completed inpatient treatment for substance abuse. Of the 10 clients in the group, 2 attended all 15 sessions, 2 attended 14 sessions, 2 attended 13 sessions, 2 attended 12 sessions, and 2 attended just 1 session.

   a. Calculate the mean and the median number of sessions attended.
   b. Which measure of central tendency, the mean or the median, do you feel is more appropriate to use in portraying the average number of sessions attended for the above data? Why?

2. Discuss how you would interpret the following bivariate table for an imaginary study comparing the effectiveness of two interventions aimed at preventing students from dropping out of school. Also, explain why you'd want to employ inferential statistics to further analyze the data. The data in the table refer to the percentage (and number) of students receiving each intervention.

	TYPE OF INTERVENTION	
OUTCOME	INTERVENTION A	INTERVENTION B
Graduated	92%	82%
	(46)	(82)
Dropped	8%	18%
Out	(4)	(18)
TOTAL	100%	100%
	(50)	(100)

17.10 INTERNET EXERCISES

1. Using the search term *statistical significance*, find two articles on inferential data analysis issues discussed in this chapter. Write down the bibliographic reference information for each article and summarize its main points. Two articles worth looking for, both by Bruce Thompson, are the following:

   - "Improving Research Clarity and Usefulness with Effect Size Indices as Supplements to Statistical Significance Tests," *Exceptional Children*, Spring 1999.
   - "Why Encouraging Effect Size Reporting Is Not Working: The Etiology of Researcher Resistance to Changing Practices," *Journal of Psychology*, March 1999.

2. Go to the following website: www.socialresearch methods.net/OJtrial/ojhome.htm. Click on all of the prompts that appear on your screen, in order of appearance, to see how the O. J. Simpson trial illustrates inferential statistics concepts and effect size.

17.11 ADDITIONAL READING

Rubin, A. (2010). *Statistics for evidence-based practice and evaluation*, 2nd ed. Belmont, CA: Brooks/Cole. This introductory statistics text elaborates on the concepts overviewed in this chapter. It is written specifically for students in social work and other human service professions.

17.11a Competency Notes

EP 2.1.6b: Use research evidence to inform practice (p. 348): Understanding all of the concepts in this chapter will help social workers comprehend the statistical evidence supplied by quantitative research and thus use that evidence to inform their practice.

EP 2.1.10m: Critically analyze, monitor, and evaluate interventions (p. 348): Understanding all of the concepts in this chapter will help social workers analyze the results produced when monitoring and evaluating their interventions.

chapter 18

Qualitative Data Analysis

18.1 INTRODUCTION

EP 2.1.6b
EP 2.1.10m

Qualitative research methods involve a continuing interplay between data collection and theory. As a result, we've already talked about qualitative data analysis in our discussions of qualitative research and content analysis in Chapter 16. Although qualitative research is sometimes undertaken for purely descriptive purposes, this chapter focuses primarily on the search for explanatory patterns.

Regardless of which qualitative research methods you've employed, you will possess a mass of data—most typically in the form of textual materials—that you will need to analyze. Now what do you do? The first step is to process the data, which requires classifying or categorizing the individual pieces of data and being able to access them through some kind of retrieval system. Together, these classification and retrieval procedures allow you to access materials you may later be interested in. Processing a mass of qualitative data is as much art as science. There are no cut-and-dried steps that guarantee success. It's a lot like learning how to paint with watercolors or compose a symphony. Education in such activities is certainly possible, and university courses are offered in both. Each has its own conventions and techniques as well as tips you may find useful as you set out to create art or music. However, instruction can carry you only so far. The final product must come from you. Although far from a "how-to" manual, the ideas we'll examine for processing qualitative data give a useful starting point for finding order in the data.

18.2 CODING

The first step in processing qualitative data involves coding. Let's say you're chronicling the growth of a social reform movement. You recall writing up some notes about the details of the movement's earliest beginnings. Now you need that information. If all your notes have been catalogued by topic, retrieving those you need should be straightforward. As a simple format for coding and retrieval, you might have created a set of file folders labeled with various topics, such as "History." Data retrieval in this case means pulling out the "History" folder and rifling through the notes contained therein until you find what you need.

As you'll see later in this chapter, there are now some very sophisticated computer programs that allow for a faster, more certain, and more precise retrieval process. Rather than looking through a "History" file, you can go directly to notes dealing with the "Earliest History" or the "Founding" of the movement.

Coding requires a more refined system than a set of manila folders. The *concept* is the organizing principle for qualitative coding. For example, if you are conducting a content analysis of the documents of different social work agencies, the units of text appropriate for coding will vary within a given document. Agency "Size" might require only a few words per coding unit, whereas agency "Mission" might take a few pages. Or a lengthy description of a heated board meeting might be coded "Internal Dissent." Realize also that a given code category may be applied to text materials of quite different lengths. For example, some references to the agency's mission may be brief, others lengthy.

18.2a Coding as a Physical Act

Before continuing with the logic of coding, let's take a moment to see what it actually looks like. (In this section, we'll assume that you'll be doing your coding manually.) John and Lyn Lofland (1995) offer this description of manual filing:

> *Prior to the widespread availability of personal computers beginning in the late 1980s, coding frequently took the specific physical form of filing. The researcher established an expanding set of file folders with code names on the tabs and physically placed either the item of data itself or a note that located it in the appropriate file folder.... Before photocopying was easily available and cheap, some fieldworkers typed their field notes with carbon paper, wrote codes in the margins of the copies of the notes, and cut them up with scissors. They then placed the resulting slips of paper in corresponding file folders. (p. 188)*

As the Loflands point out, personal computers have greatly simplified this task. However, the image of slips of paper that contain text and that are put in folders representing code categories is useful for understanding the process of coding. In the next section, when we suggest that we code a textual passage with a certain code, imagine that we have the passage typed on a slip of paper and that we place it in a file folder bearing the name of the code. Whenever we assign two codes to a passage, imagine placing duplicate copies of the passage in two different folders representing the two codes.

18.2b Creating Codes

So, what should your code categories be? Glaser and Strauss (1967) allow for the possibility of coding data for the purpose of testing hypotheses that have been generated by prior theory (p. 101 f). In that case, then, the codes would be suggested by the theory, in the form of variables.

In this section, however, we're going to focus on the more common process of **open coding**. Strauss and Corbin (1990) define it as follows:

Open coding is the part of analysis that pertains specifically to the naming and categorizing of phenomena through close examination of data. Without this first basic analytical step, the rest of the analysi and communication that follows could not take place. During open coding the data are broken down into discrete parts, closely examined, compared for similarities and differences, and questions are asked about the phenomena as reflected in the data. Through this process, on'es own and others' assumptions about phenomena are questioned or explored, leading to new discoveries. (p. 2)

Here's a concrete example to illustrate how you might proceed. Suppose you are concerned about the problem of homophobia and want to do something to alleviate it. To begin, you interview some people who are opposed to homosexuality, and they cite a religious basis for their feelings. Specifically, they refer you to these passages in the Book of Leviticus (Revised Standard Version):

18:22 You shall not lie with a male as with a woman; it is an abomination.

20:13 If a man lies with a male as with a woman, both of them have committed an abomination; they shall be put to death, their blood is upon them.

Although the point of view expressed here seems unambiguous, you might decide to examine it in more depth. Perhaps a qualitative analysis of Leviticus can yield a fuller understanding of where these injunctions against homosexuality fit into the larger context of Judeo-Christian morality. By gaining this understanding, you hope to be better prepared to develop a social change strategy for combating homophobia.

Let's start our analysis by examining the two passages just quoted. We might begin by coding each passage with the label "Homosexuality." This is clearly a key concept in our analysis. Whenever we focus on the issue of homosexuality in our analysis of Leviticus, we want to consider these two passages.

Because homosexuality is such a key concept, let's look more closely into what it means within the data under study. We first notice the way *homosexuality* is identified: a man lying with a man "as with a woman." Although we can imagine a lawyer seeking admission to heaven saying, "But here's my point: if we didn't actually lie down...," it seems safe to assume the passage refers to having sex, though it is not clear what specific acts might or might not be included.

Notice, however, that the injunctions appear to concern *male* homosexuality only; lesbianism is not mentioned. In our analysis, then, each of these passages might also be coded "Male Homosexuality." This illustrates two more aspects of coding: (1) Each unit can have more than one code and (2) hierarchical codes (one included within another) can be used. Now each passage has two codes assigned to it.

An even more general code might be introduced at this point: "Prohibited Behavior." This is important for two reasons. First, homosexuality is not inherently wrong, from an analytical standpoint. The purpose of the study is to examine the way it's adjudged wrong by the religious texts in question. Second, our study of Leviticus may turn up other behaviors that are prohibited.

---

open coding A qualitative data processing method in which, instead of starting out with a list of code categories derived from theory, one develops code categories through close examination of qualitative data.

There are at least two more critical concepts in the passages: "Abomination" and "Put to Death." Notice that although these are clearly related to "Prohibited Behavior," they are hardly the same. Parking without putting money in the meter is prohibited, but few would call it an abomination and fewer still would demand the death penalty for that transgression. Let's assign these two new codes to our first two passages.

At this point, we want to branch out from the two key passages and examine the rest of Leviticus. We therefore examine and code each of the remaining chapters and verses. In our subsequent analyses, we'll use the codes we have already and add new ones as appropriate. When we do add new codes, it will be important to review the passages already coded to see whether the new codes apply to any of them.

Here are the passages we decide to code "Abomination." (We've boldfaced the abominations.)

7:18 If any of the flesh of the sacrifice of **his peace offering is eaten on the third day**, he who offers it shall not be accepted, neither shall it be credited to him; it shall be an abomination, and he who eats of it shall bear his iniquity.

7:21 And if any one **touches an unclean thing**, whether the uncleanness of man or an unclean beast or any unclean abomination, **and then eats of the flesh of the sacrifice** of the LORD's peace offerings, that person shall be cut off from his people.

11:10 But **anything in the seas or the rivers that has not fins and scales**, of the swarming creatures in the waters and of the living creatures that are in the waters, is an abomination to you.

11:11 They shall remain an abomination to you; **of their flesh you shall not eat, and their carcasses you shall have in abomination.**

11:12 **Everything in the waters that has not fins and scales** is an abomination to you.

11:13 And these you shall have in abomination among the birds, they **shall not be eaten**, they are an abomination: the **eagle**, the **vulture**, the **osprey**,

11:14 the **kite**, the **falcon** according to its kind,

11:15 every **raven** according to its kind,

11:16 the **ostrich**, the **nighthawk**, the **sea gull**, the **hawk** according to its kind,

11:17 the **owl**, the **cormorant**, the **ibis**,

11:18 the **water hen**, the **pelican**, the **carrion vulture**,

11:19 the **stork**, the **heron** according to its kind, the **hoopoe**, and the **bat**.

11:20 **All winged insects that go upon all fours** are an abomination to you.

11:41 **Every swarming thing** that swarms upon the earth is an abomination; it shall not be eaten.

11:42 Whatever goes on its belly, and whatever goes on all fours, or whatever has many feet, all the **swarming things** that swarm upon the earth, you shall not eat; for they are an abomination.

11:43 You shall not make yourselves abominable with **any swarming thing that swarms**; and you shall not defile yourselves with them, lest you become unclean.

18:22 You shall not **lie with a male as with a woman**; it is an abomination.

19:6 It shall be eaten the same day you offer it, or on the morrow; and anything left over until the third day shall be burned with fire.

19:7 **If it is eaten at all on the third day**, it is an abomination; it will not be accepted,

19:8 and every one who eats it shall bear his iniquity, because he has profaned a holy thing of the LORD; and that person shall be cut off from his people.

20:13 **If a man lies with a male as with a woman**, both of them have committed an abomination; they shall be put to death, their blood is upon them.

20:25 You shall therefore make a distinction between the clean beast and the unclean, and between the unclean bird and the clean; **you shall not make yourselves abominable by beast or by bird or by anything with which the ground teems** which I have set apart for you to hold unclean.

Male homosexuality, then, isn't the only abomination identified in Leviticus. As you compare these passages, looking for similarities and differences, it will become apparent that most of the abominations have to do with dietary rules—specifically those potential foods deemed "unclean." Other abominations flow from the mishandling of ritual sacrifices. "Dietary Rules" and "Ritual Sacrifices" thus represent additional concepts and codes to be used in our analysis.

Earlier, we mentioned the death penalty as another concept to be explored in our analysis. When we take this avenue, we discover that many behaviors besides male homosexuality warrant the death penalty. Among them are these:

20:2 Giving your children to Molech (human sacrifice)
20:9 Cursing your father or mother
20:10 Adultery with your neighbor's wife
20:11 Adultery with your father's wife
20:12 Adultery with your daughter-in-law
20:14 Taking a wife and her mother also
20:15 Men having sex with animals (the animals are to be killed, also)
20:16 Women having sex with animals
20:27 Being a medium or wizard
24:16 Blaspheming the name of the Lord
24:17 Killing a man

As you can see, the death penalty is broadly applied in Leviticus: everything from swearing to murder, including male homosexuality somewhere in between.

An extended analysis of prohibited behavior, short of abomination and death, also turns up a lengthy list. Among them are slander, vengeance, grudges, cursing the deaf, and putting stumbling blocks in front of blind people. In Chapter 19, verse 19, Leviticus quotes God as ordering, "You shall not let your cattle breed with a different kind; you shall not sow your field with two kinds of seed; nor shall there come upon you a garment of cloth made of two kinds of stuff." Shortly thereafter, he adds, "You shall not eat any flesh with the blood in it. You shall not practice augury or witchcraft. You shall not round off the hair on your temples or mar the edges of your beard." Tattoos were prohibited, though Leviticus is silent on body piercing. References to all of these practices would be coded "Prohibited Acts" and perhaps given additional codes as well (recall "Dietary Rules").

We hope this brief glimpse into a possible analysis will give you some idea of the process by which codes are generated and applied. You should also have begun to see how such coding would allow you to better understand the messages being put forward in a text and to retrieve data appropriately as you need them.

18.2c Memoing

In the grounded theory method (GTM), which we will discuss later, the coding process involves more than simply categorizing chunks of text. As you code data, you should also be using the technique of **memoing**—writing memos or notes to yourself and others involved in the project. Some of what you write during analysis may end up in your final report; much of it will at least stimulate what you write.

In GTM, these memos have a special significance. Strauss and Corbin (1990) distinguish three kinds of memos: *code notes, theoretical notes*, and *operational notes* (p. 197 f).

Code notes identify the code labels and their meanings. This is particularly important because, as in all social science research, most of the terms we use with technical meanings also have meanings in everyday language. It's essential, therefore, to write down a clear account of what you mean by the codes used in your analysis. In the Leviticus analysis, for example, you would want a code note regarding the meaning of *abomination* and how you've used that code in your analysis of text.

Theoretical notes cover a variety of topics: reflections and thoughts about the dimensions and deeper meanings of concepts, relationships among concepts, theoretical propositions, and so on. All of us have times of ruminating over the nature of something, of trying to think it out to make sense out of it. In qualitative data analysis, it's vital to write down these thoughts, even those you might later discard as useless. They will vary greatly in length, though you should limit them to a single main thought so that you can sort and organize them later. In the Leviticus analysis, one theoretical note might discuss the way that most of the

---

memoing A qualitative data analysis technique used at several stages of data processing to capture code meanings, theoretical ideas, preliminary conclusions, and other thoughts that will be useful during analysis.

injunctions implicitly address the behavior of *men*, with women being mostly incidental.

Operational notes deal primarily with methodological issues. Some will draw attention to data-collection circumstances that may be relevant to understanding the data later on. Others will consist of notes directing future data collection.

Writing these memos occurs throughout the data-collection and analysis process. Thoughts demanding memos will come to you as you reread notes or transcripts, code chunks of text, or discuss the project with others. It's a good idea to get in the habit of writing out your memos as soon as possible after the thoughts come to you.

John and Lyn Lofland (1995) speak of memoing somewhat differently, describing memos that come closer to the final writing stage (p. 93 f).

> *The elemental memo is a detailed analytic rendering of some relatively specific matter. Depending on the scale of the project, the worker may write from one to several dozen or more of these. Built out of selective codes and codings, these are the most basic prose cannon fodder, as it were, of the project. (p. 194)*

The *sorting memo* is based on several elemental memos and presents key themes in the analysis. Whereas we create elemental memos as they come to mind, with no particular rhyme or reason, we write sorting memos as an attempt to discover or create reason among the data being analyzed. A sorting memo will bring together a set of related elemental memos. A given project may see the creation of several sorting memos dealing with different aspects of the project.

Finally, the *integrating memo* ties together the several sorting memos to bring order to the whole project. It tells a coherent and comprehensive story, casting it in a theoretical context. In any real project, however, there are many different ways of bringing about this kind of closure. Hence, the data analysis may result in several integrating memos.

Notice that whereas we often think of writing as a linear process, starting at the beginning and moving through to the conclusion, memoing is very different. It might be characterized as a process of creating chaos and then finding order within it.

To explore this process further, refer to the works cited in this discussion and at the end of the chapter. You'll also find a good deal of information on the web. For Barney Glaser's rules on memoing, for example, you might go to http://gtm.vlsm.org/gnm-gtm3.html. Ultimately, the best education in this process comes from practice. Even if you don't have a research project underway, you can practice now on class notes. Or start a journal and code it.

18.3 DISCOVERING PATTERNS

Having completed your coding and memoing, you can begin seeking patterns in your data. John and Lyn Lofland (1995) suggest six different ways of looking for patterns in a particular research topic (pp. 127–145). Let's suppose you're interested in analyzing child abuse in a certain neighborhood. Here are some questions you might ask yourself to make sense out of your data.

1. Frequencies: How often does child abuse occur among families in the neighborhood under study? (Realize that there may be a difference between the actual frequency and what people are willing to tell you.)
2. Magnitudes: What are the levels of abuse? How brutal are they?
3. Structures: What are the different types of abuse: physical, verbal, emotional, sexual? Are they related in any particular manner?
4. Processes: Is there any order among the elements of structure? Do abusers begin with verbal abuse and move on to physical and sexual abuse, or does the order of elements vary?
5. Causes: What are the causes of child abuse? Is it more common in particular social classes or among different religious or ethnic groups? Does it occur more often during good times or bad?
6. Consequences: How does child abuse affect the victims, in both the short and the long term? What changes does it cause in the abusers?

For the most part, in examining your data you'll look for patterns appearing across several observations that typically represent different cases under study. Or you might attempt to understand a particular case fully. Next, you might turn to other subjects, looking into the full details of their lives as well but paying special note to the variables that seemed important in the first case. Some subsequent cases might closely parallel the first one in the apparent impact of particular variables. Other cases might bear no resemblance to the first. These latter cases may require the identification of other important variables, which might suggest exploring why some cases seem to exhibit one pattern while others exhibit another.

18.3a Grounded Theory Method

The method just described should sound somewhat familiar. In the discussion of grounded theory in Chapter 15, we saw how qualitative researchers sometimes attempt to establish theories on a purely inductive basis. This approach begins with observations rather than hypotheses and seeks to discover patterns and develop theories from the ground up, with no preconceptions, though some research may build and elaborate on earlier grounded theories.

The *grounded theory method (GTM)* employs the **constant comparative method**. As Glaser and Strauss originally described this method, it involved four stages (1967, pp. 105–113):

1. "Comparing incidents applicable to each category." Once a concept arises in the analysis of one case, researchers look for evidence of the same concept in other cases.
2. "Integrating categories and their properties." Here the researcher begins to note relationships among concepts.
3. "Delimiting the theory." Eventually, as the patterns of relationships among concepts become clearer, the researcher can ignore some of the concepts initially noted but evidently irrelevant to the inquiry. In addition to the number of categories being reduced, the theory itself may become simpler.
4. "Writing theory." Finally, the researcher must put his or her findings into words to be shared with others. As you may have already experienced for yourself, the act of communicating your understanding of something actually modifies and even improves your own grasp of the topic. In GTM, the writing stage is regarded as a part of the research process.

The selection of new cases is guided by theoretical sampling concepts in which new cases are selected that seem to be similar to those generated by previously detected concepts and hypotheses.

Once the researcher perceives that no new insights are being generated from the observation of similar cases, a different type of case is selected, and the same process is repeated. Additional cases similar to this new type of case are selected until no new insights are being generated. This cycle of exhausting similar cases and then seeking a different category of cases is repeated until the researcher believes that further seeking of new types of cases will not alter the findings.

GTM is only one analytical approach to qualitative data. In the remainder of this section, we'll take a look at some other specialized techniques.

18.3b Semiotics

Semiotics is commonly defined as the "science of signs" and has to do with symbols and meanings. It's commonly associated with content analysis, which was discussed in Chapter 16, though it can be applied in a variety of research contexts.

Signs are any things that are assigned special meanings. They can include such things as logos, animals, people, and consumer products. Sometimes the symbolism is subtle. A classic analysis can be found in Erving Goffman's *Gender Advertisements* (1979). Goffman focused on advertising pictures found in magazines and newspapers. The overt purpose of the ads, of course, was to sell specific products. But what else was communicated, Goffman asked. What in particular did the ads say about men and women?

Analyzing pictures containing both men and women, Goffman was struck by the fact that men were almost always bigger and taller than the

---

constant comparative method A qualitative data analysis method in which the researcher looks for patterns in inductive observations, develops concepts and working hypotheses based on those patterns, seeks out more cases and conducts more observations, and then compares those observations against the concepts and hypotheses developed from the earlier observations.

Semiotics The science of symbols and meanings, commonly associated with content analysis and based on language, that examines the agreements we have about the meanings associated with particular signs.

women accompanying them. (In many cases, in fact, the picture managed to convey the distinct impression that the women were merely accompanying the men.) Although the most obvious explanation is that men are, on average, heavier and taller than women, Goffman suggested the pattern had a different meaning: that size and placement implied *status*. Those larger and taller presumably had higher social standing—more power and authority (1979, p. 28). Goffman suggested that the ads communicated that men were more important than women.

In the spirit of Freud's comment that "sometimes a cigar is just a cigar" (he was a smoker), how would you decide whether the ads simply reflected the biological differences in the average sizes of men and women or whether they sent a message about social status? In part, Goffman's conclusion was based on an analysis of the exceptional cases: those in which the women appeared taller than the men. In these cases, the men were typically of a lower social status—the chef beside the society matron, for example. This confirmed Goffman's main point that size and height indicated social status.

The same conclusion was to be drawn from pictures with men of different heights. Those of higher status were taller, whether it was the gentleman speaking to a waiter or the boss guiding the work of his younger assistants. Where actual height was unclear, Goffman noted the placement of heads in the picture. The assistants were crouching down while the boss leaned over them. The servant's head was bowed so it was lower than that of the master.

The latent message conveyed by the ads, then, was that the higher a person's head appeared in the ad, the more important that person was. And in the great majority of ads containing men and women, the former were clearly portrayed as more important. The subliminal message in the ads, whether intended or not, was that men are more powerful and enjoy a higher status than do women.

---

conversation analysis (CA) A qualitative data analysis approach that aims to uncover the implicit assumptions and structures in social life through an extremely close scrutiny of the way we converse with one another.

Goffman examined several differences in the portrayal of men and women besides physical size. As another example, men were typically portrayed in active roles, women in passive ones. The (male) doctor examined the child while the (female) nurse or mother looked on, often admiringly. A man guided a woman's tennis stroke (all the while keeping his head higher than hers). A man gripped the reins of his galloping horse, while a woman rode behind him with her arms wrapped around his waist. A woman held the football, while a man kicked it. A man took a photo, which contained only women.

Goffman suggested that such pictorial patterns subtly perpetuated a host of gender stereotypes. Even as people spoke publicly about gender equality, these advertising photos established a quiet backdrop of men and women in the "proper roles."

18.3c Conversation Analysis

Conversation analysis (CA) aims to uncover the implicit assumptions and structures in social life through an extremely close scrutiny of the way we converse with one another. David Silverman (1993), reviewing the work of other CA theorists and researchers, speaks of three fundamental assumptions. First, conversation is a socially structured activity. Like other social structures, it has established rules of behavior. For example, we're expected to take turns, with only one person speaking at a time. In telephone conversations, the person answering the call is expected to speak first (e.g., "Hello"). You can verify the existence of this rule, incidentally, by picking up the phone without speaking.

Second, Silverman points out that conversations must be understood contextually. The same utterance will have totally different meanings in different contexts. For example, notice how the meaning of "Same to you!" varies if preceded by "I don't like your looks" or by "Have a nice day."

Third, CA aims to understand the structure and meaning of conversation through excruciatingly accurate transcripts of conversations. Not only are the exact words recorded, but all the "uhs," "ers," bad grammar, and pauses are also noted. Pauses, in fact, are recorded to the nearest tenth of a second.

The practical uses of this type of analysis are many. Ann Marie Kinnel and Douglas Maynard (1996), for example, analyzed conversations between staff and clients at an HIV testing clinic to examine how information about safe sex was communicated. Among other things, they found that the staff tended to provide standard information rather than trying to speak directly to a client's specific circumstances. Moreover, they seemed reluctant to give direct advice about safe sex, settling for information alone.

18.3d Concept Mapping

It should be clear by now that qualitative-data analysts spend a lot of time committing thoughts to paper (or to a computer file), but this process is not limited to text alone. Often, we can think out relationships among concepts more clearly by putting the concepts in a graphical format, a process called **concept mapping**. Some researchers find it useful to put all their major concepts on a single sheet of paper, while others spread their thoughts across several sheets of paper, blackboards, magnetic boards, computer pages, or other media. Figure 18.1 shows how we might think out some of the concepts of Goffman's examination of gender and advertising. (This image was created through the use of Inspiration, a concept-mapping computer program.)

FIGURE 18.1 An Example of Concept Mapping

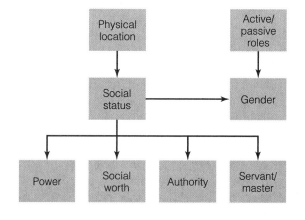

18.4 COMPUTER PROGRAMS FOR QUALITATIVE DATA

Although computers are commonly associated with quantitative research, they also are of use in qualitative research. Simple word-processing programs, for example, can be used for some data analysis. The "find" or "search" command will take you to passages containing key words. Or, going one step further, you can type code words alongside passages in your notes so that you can search for those key words later.

Database and spreadsheet programs can also be used for processing and analyzing qualitative data. Figure 18.2 is a simple illustration of how some of the verses from Leviticus might be manipulated within a spreadsheet. The three columns to the left represent three of the concepts we've discussed. An "x" means that the passage to the right contains that concept. As shown, the passages are sorted in such a way as to gather all those dealing with punishment by death. Another simple "sort" command would gather all those dealing with sex, with homosexuality, or any of the other concepts coded.

This brief illustration should give you some idea of the possibilities for using readily available programs as tools in qualitative data analysis. Happily, there are now a large number of programs created specifically for that purpose. One that is widely used is called NVivo. You can become more familiar with NVivo (and the computer analysis of qualitative data) by going to www.cengage.com/social_work/rubin, clicking on the link for this book, then clicking on the "Companion Site" link. At that site you can access a LEARNING GUIDE TO NViVO 1.2. Other programs are listed below. You can Google each to learn more about them.

> The Ethnograph
> HyperQual
> HyperResearch
> HyperSoft
> QUALPRO
> QUALOG
> Textbase Alpha
> SONAR
> Atlas-ti

concept mapping   A qualitative data analysis method in which relationships among concepts are examined and diagrammed in a graphical format.

FIGURE 18.2 Using a Spreadsheet for Qualitative Analysis

Sex	Homosex	Death	Verse	Passage
X	X	X	20:13	If a man lies with a male as with a woman, both of them have committed an abomination; they shall be put to death, their blood is upon them.
X		X	20:12	If a man lies with his daughter-in-law, both of them shall be put to death; they have committed incest, their blood is upon them.
X		X	20:15	If a man lies with a beast, he shall be put to death; and you shall kill the beast.
		X	20:09	For every one who curses his father or his mother shall be put to death; he has cursed his father or his mother, his blood is upon him.
		X	20:02	Any man of the people of Israel, or of the strangers that sojourn in Israel, who gives any of his children to Molech shall be put to death.
X	X		18:22	You shall not lie with a male as with a woman; it is an abomination.

18.5 IN CLOSING

We have finished the main part of this text. We hope it has inspired and enabled you to use quantitative as well as qualitative social work research to guide your practice throughout your career as a social worker. As we expressed in Chapter 1, the main reason to use research is compassion for our clients. To help them most effectively, we need scientific evidence about the effects of the services we are providing and of alternative services that might help them more. Perhaps more than ever before, social work research offers all social workers an opportunity to make a difference in the problems they confront.

18.6 MAIN POINTS

- Qualitative analysis is the non-numerical examination and interpretation of observations.
- Qualitative analysis involves a continual interplay between theory and analysis. In analyzing qualitative data, we seek to discover patterns such as changes over time or possible causal links between variables.
- Examples of approaches to the discovery and explanation of such patterns are the grounded theory method (GTM), semiotics, and conversation analysis.
- The processing of qualitative data is as much art as science. Three key tools for preparing data for analysis are coding, memoing, and concept mapping.
- In contrast to the standardized units used in coding for statistical analyses, the units to be coded in qualitative analyses may vary within a document. Although codes may be derived from the theory being explored, more often researchers use open coding, in which codes are suggested by the researchers' examination and questioning of the data.
- Memoing is appropriate at several stages of data processing to capture code meanings, theoretical ideas, preliminary conclusions, and other thoughts that will be useful during analysis.

- Concept mapping uses diagrams to explore relationships in the data graphically.
- Several computer programs, such as NVivo, are specifically designed to assist researchers in the analysis of qualitative data. In addition, researchers can take advantage of the capabilities of common software tools such as word processors, database programs, and spreadsheets.

18.7 PRACTICE-RELATED EXERCISES

1. Suppose you are conducting a qualitative analysis of how child welfare practitioners with different training and background characteristics emphasize protecting the child versus preserving families in their work. Identify the key concepts you might code in the following statements from two practitioners:

Practitioner #1: "When I did my honors thesis for my undergraduate psychology major, I found that there is no strong research evidence that family preservation programs are really effective. Sure, they can keep families together, but what happens to the child? The studies that I've seen all have serious methodological defects and all evaluate effectiveness in terms of whether there are fewer out-of-home placements in family preservation programs than in traditional child welfare approaches. But they do not assess whether the kids are really better off when the family is preserved. My emphasis is on protecting the child. Moreover, if neglectful or abusive parents are engaged in substance abuse, I think there is very little hope that the child can be adequately protected unless the child is placed in foster care. Despite what many think, I believe that most foster care placements are safer than the alternative when substance abuse is involved. I think this is particularly true if the parents are abusive, rather than neglectful, and if the child is quite young. And don't get me started if sexual abuse is involved. No way would I lean toward family preservation if that were the case. You also have to ask whether there has been just one abusive or neglectful incident or whether there have been multiple incidents. The way I look at it, the

more incidents, the harder it is to justify a family preservation emphasis."

Practitioner #2: "Research has shown that if children can be protected, they are better off emotionally if they can grow up with their biological parents and siblings. Moreover, in my MSW child welfare class I learned that research has also shown that many kids get abused in foster care, that foster care placements typically are unstable—with kids getting transferred to many different placements—and that this takes a terrible toll on their emotional well-being, especially regarding the likelihood of developing attachment disorders. I suppose this is particularly true the younger the child is when placed in foster care. Moreover, the research that I'm referring to is methodologically strong. I disagree with those who argue that all that family preservation programs can demonstrate is that they avoid out-of-home placements—especially when they minimize the value of such. When kids get placed in foster care, it means there is some serious abuse or neglect going on; it's not just a result of some practitioner's orientation. Thus, if family preservation programs have fewer out-of-home placements, it means that they are preventing future abuse or neglect, and that previously abused or neglected kids are really better off in them. Having said all that, however, I can understand the reluctance of some colleagues to preserve families in cases involving sexual abuse or severe forms of physical abuse, in cases where the abuse is repetitive, or in cases where the parents have a long history of addiction to drugs or alcohol."

2. Write one code note and one theoretical note for the above statements.

18.8 INTERNET EXERCISES

1. Using the key term *qualitative data analysis*, briefly describe the data analytic approaches used in two qualitative research studies you find.
2. Using the key term *concept mapping*, briefly describe a qualitative research study you find and how it used concept mapping.
3. Using the key term *grounded theory*, briefly describe a qualitative research study you find

that used the grounded theory method and summarize its data analysis approach.

4. Find a research report that uses conversation analysis. Summarize the main conclusions in your own words.

18.9 ADDITIONAL READINGS

Grbich, C. (2007). *Qualitative data analysis: An introduction*. London: Sage. This book provides a practical guide to a wide range of approaches to qualitative data analysis, and relates them to epistemological trends impacting the field of qualitative research.

Hutchby, I., & Wooffitt, R. (1998). *Conversation analysis: Principles, practices and applications*. Cambridge, England: Polity Press. An excellent overview of the conversation analysis method. The book examines the theory behind the technique, how to use it, and some possible applications.

Miles, M. B., & Huberman, A. M. (1994). *Qualitative data analysis* (2nd ed.). Thousand Oaks, CA: Sage. If you ever do a qualitative study and find yourself overwhelmed with masses of unstructured data and at sea as to how to analyze or report the data, this sourcebook will come in handy. It provides many practical illustrations of alternative ways to reduce, display, and draw verifiable conclusions from qualitative data.

Silverman, D. (1993). *Interpreting qualitative data*. Newbury Park, CA: Sage. This book brings together theoretical concerns, data collection techniques, and the process of making sense of what is observed.

Strauss, A., & Corbin, J. (1990). *Basics of qualitative research: Grounded theory, procedures and techniques*. Newbury Park, CA: Sage. This updated statement of grounded theory offers special guidance on coding and memoing.

18.9a Competency Notes

EP 2.1.6b: Use research evidence to inform practice (p. 364): Understanding all of the concepts in this chapter will help social workers comprehend the evidence supplied by qualitative research and thus use that evidence to inform their practice.

EP 2.1.10m: Critically analyze, monitor, and evaluate interventions (p. 364): Understanding all of the concepts in this chapter will help social workers analyze the results produced when using qualitative methods to monitor and evaluate their interventions.

Appendix A

Using the Library

EP 2.1.1e

We live in a world filled with social science research reports. Our daily newspapers, magazines, professional journals, alumni bulletins, club newsletters—virtually everything you pick up to read can carry reports that deal with a particular topic. For formal explorations of a topic, of course, the best place to start is still a good college or university library.

- **Getting help:** When you want to find something in the library, your best friends are the reference librarians, who are specially trained to find things in the library. Some libraries have specialized reference librarians: for social work, the social sciences, government documents, and so forth. Make an appointment with the librarian who specializes in what you need. Tell the librarian what you're interested in. He or she will probably put you in touch with some of the many available reference sources.
- **Using the stacks:** Today the most commonly used way to search for relevant books or articles is through an online computerized system. However, regardless of whether you use your computer or the card catalogues in your library, you may find additional useful references by using the library stacks, where most of the library's books and journals are stored. Once you've identified the call number for a particular book in your subject area, go to the stacks, find that book, and look over the other books on the shelves near it. Because the books are arranged by subject matter, this method will help you locate relevant books you didn't know about. Alternatively, you may want to go directly to the stacks and look at books in your subject area. In most libraries, books are arranged and numbered according to a subject matter classification system developed by the Library of Congress. (Some follow the Dewey Decimal System.)
- **Abstracts:** Some publications present summaries of books and articles that help them locate a great many references easily and effectively. These summaries,

called *abstracts*, are often prepared by the original authors. As you find relevant references, you can track down the original works and see the full details. In social work, the most relevant publication of these abstracts is *Social Work Abstracts*. Also useful are publications of abstracts in allied fields, such as *Psychological Abstracts* and *Sociological Abstracts*.

The first step in using *Social Work Abstracts* is to look at the subject index to find general subject headings related to your specific topic of interest. Then you should examine the subtopics listed under the relevant general headings, looking for topics that appear to be most directly related to your specific topic of interest. Beside each will be one or more numbers. Because the abstracts are presented in numerical order, you can use the listed numbers to locate the abstracts of potential interest to you. When you read the abstract, you will learn whether the study it summarizes is of sufficient relevance to warrant seeking out and reading the report in its entirety. If it is worth reading, the abstract will provide the reference information you'll need to find the full report, as well as where you can contact its author.

Let's walk through this process. Suppose you are searching the literature for a valid scale to assess the degree of acculturation of foreign-born Chinese Americans. In using *Social Work Abstracts* your first step will be to find a subject heading in the *Subject Index* that fits the focus of your search. If you look for the heading "Acculturation of Foreign-Born Chinese Americans," you won't find it—it's too specific. But if you look for the broader heading "Acculturation," you'll find it in the alphabetized Subject Index between the two headings: "Accountability" and "Activism," as follows:

Accountability
and Joint Reviews in England, 1083
and school choice, 1243

Acculturation
of Chinese Americans, 1081
of Hispanic middle school students, 1231

of Russian immigrants, 1430
of West Indians, 1387

Activism
judicial, 1366

Under the heading "Acculturation," you will find four subheadings. The first subheading, "of Chinese Americans," is the one you want. The number beside it refers to the number of the abstract you'll want to examine. Because each issue of *Social Work Abstracts* lists the abstracts it contains in numerical order, you can just flip pages until you find the page that contains abstract number 1081.

Many of the abstracts in *Social Work Abstracts* are referenced under multiple subject headings. Suppose that instead of the heading "Acculturation," you look for the heading "Chinese Americans." You will find it in the Subject Index between the headings "Children's services" and "Citizen participation," as follows:

Children's services
vouchers for, 1003

Chinese Americans
and acculturation, 1081
psychosocial issues in working with, 1426

Citizen participation
in advocacy for persons with disabilities, 1219

Under the heading "Chinese Americans," you will find two subheadings—the first subheading, "and acculturation," is the one you want, and again you will be referred to abstract number 1081. The abstract will give you the names of the article's coauthors, the title of the article, the journal in which it appeared, the volume and issue numbers of that journal, what pages the article appeared on, the date the article was published, a publication code number for that journal, an address for contacting the article's lead author, and a summary of the article.

Social Work Abstracts also provides an Author Index. Suppose you learn the name of an author who had studied the assessment of acculturation of foreign-born Chinese Americans. You can look up the author's name in the alphabetized Author Index and find the numbers of the abstracts of works written by that person appearing in the volume of *Social Work Abstracts* you happen to be examining. For example, if the author's name is R. Gupta, you will find abstract 1081 by examining the following section of the Author Index of the September 2002 issue of *Social Work Abstracts*:

Gumport, P.J., 1231
Gunther-Kellar, Y., 1003
Gupta, R., 1081

Gupta, R., 1398
Gurnack, A.M., 1122
Guzley, R.M., 1080

H
Hackworth, J., 1359

Gupta's name is listed twice—that's because Gupta authored two of the works abstracted in that issue of *Social Work Abstracts*. You'll want to examine all of the abstracts listed for a person you look up in the Author Index; perhaps all of them will be of interest to you.

ELECTRONICALLY ACCESSING LIBRARY MATERIALS

Increasingly, library materials are being catalogued electronically. Although there are different types of computerized library systems, here's a typical example of how they work. As you sit at a computer terminal in the library, at a computer lab, or at home, you can type the title of a book and in seconds see the catalogue card displayed on your computer screen. If you want to explore the book further, you can click on a link that will bring you to a brief note or description of the book and see an abstract of the book. Alternatively, you might type a subject name and see a listing of all the books and articles written on that topic. You could skim through the list and indicate which ones you want to see.

As discussed in Chapter 2, most college libraries today provide online access to periodicals, books, and other library materials. Your library's computerized system should allow you to see which materials are available online and whether paper copies of the materials you seek are available in your library. If your library holds those materials, the system may indicate their call numbers, whether the books you seek have been checked out, and, if so, the due date for their return.

ELECTRONICALLY ACCESSING INTERNET PROFESSIONAL DATABASES

To help you search for literature online, your university and local libraries may provide a variety of Internet professional literature database services that you can access at home through your personal computer. As mentioned in Chapter 2, there are many such literature databases, such as Social Services Abstracts and PsycINFO. Information on how to use these databases was provided in the section on searching for evidence in Chapter 2. If your school does not provide free remote access, one alternative is to inquire as to whether your city library provides access. (You might have to obtain a library card to access such services.) Also, as mentioned in Chapter 2, you can also use your personal computer (assuming you have Internet service) to access free online search engines such as MEDLINE and Google Scholar.

The process for electronically retrieving individual studies is similar for most professional literature databases. For example, they commonly involve entering search terms. However, there are some differences in their search rules and procedures; therefore, you may need to scan their search guidelines or talk to your librarian to make sure you are searching in the most efficient way.

One commonly used procedure is to use words like "AND," "OR," and "NOT" to connect different parts of your search term. Using "AND" narrows the list of links that come up to only those that contain all of the keywords in your search term. For example, if you want to find studies on Hispanic children who witness domestic violence, you could enter "Hispanic AND children AND domestic violence."

Some databases will provide different boxes for the different keywords. If you use PsycINFO, for example, you will see three rows of boxes in which to enter keywords. Beside the second and third boxes is a button with the option to choose "and," "or," or "not." We entered "domestic violence" in the top box, then selected "and" and entered "children" in the second box, and again selected "and" and entered "Hispanic" in the third box. Doing so limited the number of literature sources that came up to 44. PsycINFO also provides a prompt for adding more rows, which you can use if you want to add more keywords. We added a fourth row, again selected "and," and then entered "treatment" in the fourth box. Doing so reduced the number of sources that came up to 13.

To illustrate what happens when you use the connecting word "or" instead of "and," we repeated our search above, but switched from "and" to "or" beside the box in the second, third and fourth rows. Doing so resulted in 769,998 sources coming up! That's because using "or" meant that we got links to studies on children even if they had nothing to do with domestic violence, Hispanics, or treatment. Likewise, we got links to studies on Hispanics, even if they had nothing to do with domestic violence, and so on.

To illustrate what happens when you choose the connecting word "not," we went back to entering "domestic violence" in the top box, selecting "and" and entering "children" in the second box, and selecting "and" and entering "Hispanic" in the third box. But this time we selected "not" and then entered "treatment" in the fourth box. Doing so brought up 31 sources—13 fewer than the 44 that came up when we selected "and" with the search word "treatment." Thus, by selecting "not" we eliminated the 13 sources that covered treatment along with

the other keywords. (Those were the same 13 sources that came up when we selected "and" beside *treatment* in the fourth box.)

Google Scholar provides an alternative way to expand or narrow your search, without using connecting words like "and," "or," and "not." If you access Google Scholar, your search will probably be best facilitated by using its "Advanced Scholar Search Option." The screen that will come up for that option is presented in Figure A.1. To illustrate how to use Google Scholar, we entered the search terms "effective intervention with children who witness domestic violence" in the top text box labeled "with all of the words." That brought up links to 34,800 recent articles! That's because those words can appear anywhere in the article. Next, we attempted to reduce the number of links by adding the word "Hispanic" to the search, and tried again. This time, using the search terms "effective intervention with Hispanic children who witness domestic violence," 5,800 links were returned—still too many.

As mentioned above, some databases provide the option of using the connecting word "AND" to reduce the number of studies that will come up, and to increase the chances that those that do come up will be of interest to you. If you try that with Google Scholar, however, it will not shorten the list of links. Instead, you'll get the following message: "The 'AND' operator is unnecessary—we include all search terms by default." Thus, when we entered "effective interventions AND Hispanic children AND witness domestic violence" as our search terms, we got the above message along with 7,120 links (more than the 5,800 without using AND)!

An alternative way to get a more manageable list of article links is to use the text box in the second row of the Advanced Scholar Search screen, labeled "with the **exact phrase**." When we entered the search terms "effective intervention with Hispanic children who witness domestic violence" in that box, however, no links came up. So we deleted the word "Hispanic" from the search. Again, however, no links appeared. To increase our chances of finding some links, we broadened the search to "children who witness domestic violence" (eliminating the words "effective interventions with"). This time "only" 650 links came up. So we added the word "Hispanic" at the start of the search phrase, to narrow the search. But that led to no links. So, instead of adding the word "Hispanic" to the exact phrase text box, we entered it into the next text box, labeled "with **at least one** of the words." Thus, we had terms entered in two text boxes, as follows:

with the **exact phrase**	children who witness domestic violence
with **at least one** of the words	Hispanic

FIGURE A.1 Screen for Advanced Research Option in Google Scholar

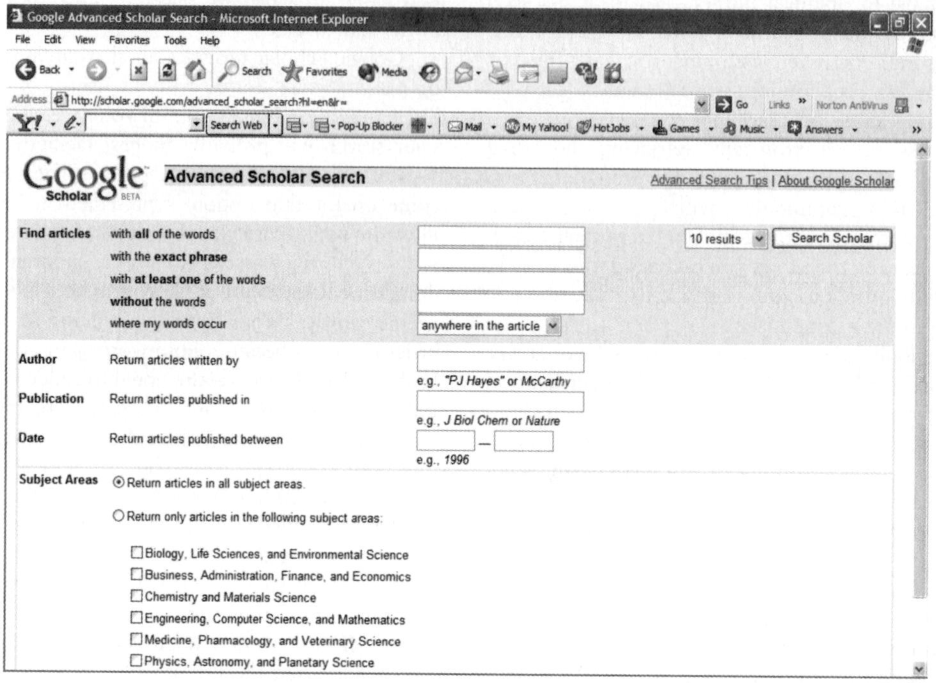

This time only 155 links came up. To limit the links to articles that mention interventions with such children, we added the term "intervention" to the top text box, so that the screen now contained the following:

with **all** of the words	intervention
with the **exact phrase**	children who witness domestic violence
with **at least one** of the words	Hispanic

That produced 146 links. Next, we added the word "effective" to the top box, so that the screen now appeared as follows:

with **all** of the words	effective intervention
with the **exact phrase**	children who witness domestic violence
with **at least one** of the words	Hispanic

That brought up links to 110 articles. That might still seem like a lot, but you can quickly reduce the number of references worth reading by clicking on the links and then reading the brief abstract that appears, eliminating those references that don't seem to be sufficiently pertinent to your focus. You might also be able to tell from the label of the link that the reference won't work for you. For example, it might be in a foreign language that you haven't learned. Or it might be on a topic so obscure that you don't need to read the abstract to know you can disregard the reference.

You may have noticed the drop-down box next to the phrase "where my words occur" in Figure A.1, and the fact that the term "anywhere in the article" appears in that drop-down box. If you click on the arrow, you will see that Google gives you only two options for that box: either "anywhere in the article" or "in the title of the article." As you might imagine, if you choose the "in the title of the article" option, your search will retrieve many fewer links. For example, when we entered the broad term "children who witness domestic violence" in the box "with the exact phrase" and then selected the "in the title of the article" option, only 33 links came up.

If you use databases other than PsycINFO or Google Scholar, you will encounter alternative ways to expand or limit the number of sources that come up. However, the foregoing examples ought to help you figure out how to make them work for you. If you have difficulty, your school's librarian, or perhaps its information technology specialist, will probably be happy to help you.

PROFESSIONAL JOURNALS

Despite the exciting advances occurring in computer-based systems and the great practical value of online database services and publications containing abstracts, you should not rely exclusively on them to locate journal articles that are pertinent to your interests. There is no guarantee that every reference of value to you will be identified in a computer search or a publication of abstracts. For example, there may be a time lag between the publication of an article and the appearance of its abstract in a publication of abstracts or a computerized system. You should therefore augment your search by examining the tables of contents in recent issues of professional journals that are the most relevant to your particular interest. For example, if you are searching for studies on interventions for abused children, two of the various journals you may want to examine are *Child Welfare* and *Children and Youth Services Review*.

Examining recent issues of journals is probably less time-consuming than you might imagine. These issues should be available in the section of your library that contains unbound current periodicals. Once you locate the recent issues of the relevant journals (the last two years or so ought to suffice), it should take only a few minutes to thumb through the tables of contents looking for titles that have some potential bearing on your topic. Once you spot a relevant title, turn to the page on which the article begins. There you will find an abstract of the article, and just like the abstracts that appear in publications of abstracts, this one should take only seconds to read and help you determine if the article is pertinent enough to warrant reading in greater detail.

Your examination of relevant journals can be expedited if your library's computerized system offers an online service listing the tables of contents of thousands of journals. It might also provide a list of *online journals—journals* whose entire contents can be downloaded and read online.

If you are uncertain about the professional journals that are pertinent to your topic, you might want to get help with this from your reference librarian. Just to start you thinking about some you might want to review, here's a list of some journals related to social work, by subject area:

Aging and the Aged
Abstracts in Social Gerontology
Canadian Journal on Aging
Clinical Gerontologist
International Journal of Aging and Human Development
Journal of Aging and Physical Activity
Journal of Aging & Social Policy
Journal of Aging Studies
Journal of Applied Gerontology
Journal of Elder Abuse & Neglect
Journal of Gerontological Social Work
Journal of Gerontology
Journal of Housing for the Elderly
Journal of Nutrition for the Elderly
Journal of Nutrition, Health and Aging
Journal of Social Work in Long-Term Care
Journal of Women & Aging
Psychology and Aging
Quality in Ageing: Policy, Practice and Research
The Gerontologist

Children and Adolescents
Adolescence (PubMed)
Child & Adolescent Social Work Journal
Children & Society
Child & Youth Services
Children and Youth Services Review
Children Today
International Journal of Adolescence and Youth
Journal of Adolescence
Journal of Adolescent Interpersonal Violence & Trauma
Journal of Child & Adolescent Trauma
Journal of Children & Poverty
Journal of Youth and Adolescence
Residential Treatment for Children & Youth

Child Welfare
Adoption & Fostering
Adoption Quarterly
Child Abuse & Neglect
Child Care Quarterly
Child Maltreatment
Child Welfare Journal
Family Preservation Journal
Journal of Child Abuse & the Law
Journal of Child Custody
Journal of Child Sexual Abuse
Journal of Public Child Welfare
The Child Survivor of Traumatic Stress

Cognitive or Behavioral Interventions
Behavior Modification
Behavior Research and Therapy
Behavior Therapy
Behavioral and Cognitive Psychotherapy
Child & Family Behavior Therapy
Cognitive and Behavioral Practice
Cognitive Therapy and Research
Journal of Applied Behavior Analysis

Communities

Community Development Journal
Journal of Community & Applied Social Psychology
Journal of Community Practice
Journal of Jewish Communal Service
Journal of Prevention & Intervention in the Community
Journal of Social Development in Africa

Crime and Delinquency

Canadian Journal of Criminology and Criminal Justice
Crime & Delinquency
Journal of Offender Rehabilitation
Journal of Research in Crime & Delinquency
Youth & Society
Youth Violence and Juvenile Justice

Cultural Diversity

Cultural Diversity & Ethnic Minority Psychology
Hispanic Journal of Behavioral Sciences
Journal of Black Studies
Journal of Ethnic & Cultural Diversity in Social Work
Journal of Ethnicity in Substance Abuse
Journal of Immigrant & Refugee Studies

Domestic Violence or Trauma

Family Violence & Sexual Assault Bulletin
Journal of Aggression, Maltreatment & Trauma
Journal of Child Sexual Abuse
Journal of Emotional Abuse
Journal of Family Violence
Journal of Interpersonal Violence
Journal of Threat Assessment
Journal of Trauma & Dissociation
Journal of Traumatic Stress
Sexual Abuse: A Journal of Research and Treatment
Stress, Trauma, and Crisis: An International Journal
Trauma, Violence, & Abuse
Traumatology
Violence Against Women
Violence and Victims

Families

American Journal of Family Therapy
Child & Family Social Work
Conflict Resolution Quarterly

Contemporary Family Therapy
Families in Society: The Journal of Contemporary Social Service
Family Process
Family Relations
Family Therapy
Family Therapy Networker
Journal of Child and Family Studies
Journal of Divorce & Remarriage
Journal of Family Issues
Journal of Family Psychology
Journal of Family Psychotherapy
Journal of Family Social Work
Journal of Family Therapy
Journal of Marital & Family Therapy
Journal of Marriage and Family
Journal of Sex & Marital Therapy
Marriage & Family Review

Gay, Lesbian, and Transgender Issues and Sexuality

Journal of Bisexuality
Journal of Gay & Lesbian Issues in Education
Journal of Gay & Lesbian Psychotherapy
Journal of Gay & Lesbian Social Services
Journal of Homosexuality
Journal of Lesbian Studies
Journal of Psychology & Human Sexuality
Sexuality Research and Social Policy

Group Work

Group Dynamics: Theory, Research, and Practice
Social Work with Groups
The Journal for Specialists in Group Work

Health

AIDS & Public Policy Journal
Health & Social Work
Home Health Care Management & Practice
Home Health Care Services Quarterly
Journal of Health and Social Behavior
Journal of Health & Social Policy
Journal of HIV/AIDS Prevention & Education for Adolescents & Children
Journal of HIV/AIDS & Social Services
Journal of Occupational Health Psychology
Journal of Psychosocial Oncology
Journal of Social Work in Disability & Rehabilitation
Journal of Social Work in End-of-Life & Palliative Care
Journal of Workplace Behavioral Health
Social Work in Health Care

Social Work in Public Health
The Hospice Journal The Journal of Behavioral
*   Health Services & Research*
The Journal of Nephrology Social Work

Mental Health
American Journal of Orthopsychiatry
American Journal of Psychotherapy
Archives of General Psychiatry
Clinical Social Work Journal
Community Mental Health
Evidence-Based Mental Health
Mental Health Services Research
NAMI Advocate
Psychiatric Rehabilitation Journal
Psychoanalytic Social Work
Psychotherapy Networker
Psychotherapy Research
Schizophrenia Bulletin
Social Work in Mental Health
The Journal of Psychotherapy Practice and
*   Research*

Mental Retardation
American Journal of Mental Deficiency
American Journal on Mental Retardation
Developmental Disabilities Research
*   Reviews* (formerly *Mental Retardation*
*   and Developmental Disabilities*
*   Research Reviews*)
Journal of Mental Deficiency Research

Program Evaluation
American Journal of Evaluation
Canadian Journal of Program Evaluation
Evaluation Review
Journal of Evaluation in Clinical Practice
New Directions for Evaluation

Qualitative Research
Grounded Theory Review: An International
*   Journal*
Qualitative Health Research
Qualitative Inquiry
Qualitative Research
Qualitative Social Work: Research and Practice
Qualitative Sociology

School Social Work
Children & Schools
Journal of School Violence
School Social Work Journal

Social Work Education: The International
*   Journal*

Social Policy
Analyses of Social Issues and Public Policy
Australian Social Policy
Critical Social Policy
Global Social Policy
International Journal of Social Welfare
Journal of Aging & Social Policy
Journal of Children & Poverty
Journal of European Social Policy
Journal of Health & Social Policy
Journal of Policy Analysis and Management
Journal of Policy Practice (formerly *The Social Policy*
*   Journal*)
Journal of Poverty
Journal of Social Distress and the Homeless
Journal of Social Policy and Social Work
Journal of Sociology and Social Welfare
Policy & Practice of Public Human Services
Public Welfare
Social Policy and Society
Social Policy Review
Social Work & Society
The Journal of Mental Health Policy and Economics
Urban Policy and Research

Social Work Research
Journal of Social Service Research
Journal of Social Work Research and Evaluation
Journal of the Society for Social Work and Research
Research on Social Work Practice
Social Work Research

Social Work (General)
Advances in Social Work
Australian Social Work
Canadian Social Work Review
Electronic Journal of Social Work
European Journal of Social Work
International Social Work
Irish Social Work
Journal of Evidence-Based Social Work
Journal of Social Work Practice
Smith College Studies in Social Work
Social Service Review
Social Work
Social Work Abstracts
The British Journal of Social Work
The Hong Kong Journal of Social Work
The Journal of Baccalaureate Social Work

Spirituality & Religion

Journal of Religion & Abuse
Journal of Religion & Spirituality in Social Work
Social Work & Christianity

Substance Abuse

Alcoholism Treatment Quarterly
International Journal of the Addictions
Journal of Addictions & Offender Counseling
Journal of Addictive Diseases (formerly
    Advances in Alcohol & Substance Abuse)
Journal of Chemical Dependency Treatment
*Journal of Child & Adolescent Substance
    Abuse*
Journal of Drug Education
Journal of Drug Issues
Journal of Ethnicity in Substance Abuse
Journal of Psychoactive Drugs
Journal of Social Work Practice in the Addictions
Journal of Studies on Alcohol
Journal of Substance Abuse Treatment
Substance Abuse
The American Journal of Drug and Alcohol Abuse

Women's Issues

Affilia
Archives of Women's Mental Health
Australian Feminist Studies
European Journal of Women's Studies
Feminism & Psychology
Feminist Theory
Gender & Society

Indian Journal of Gender Studies
Journal of Feminist Family Therapy
Violence Against Women
Women & Criminal Justice
Women & Trauma

Other

Administration in Social Work
Journal of Forensic Social Work
*Journal of Human Behavior in the Social
    Environment*
Journal of Progressive Human Services
Journal of Technology in Human Services
Nonprofit & Voluntary Sector Quarterly
Rural Social Work
Social Work & Social Sciences Review
The Journal of Applied Behavioral Science

No matter what approach you take to finding library materials, chances are there will be some documents you miss or that are not available in your library or online. If a document is not available at your particular library or via the Web, you can request an interlibrary loan, which is often free. Many libraries have loan agreements, but it might take some time before the document you need arrives at your library. If the document is located at another library nearby, you may want to go there yourself to get it directly. The key to a good library search is to become well informed, so remember what we said earlier: *When you want to find something in the library, your best friends are the reference librarians.* Don't be shy about seeking their assistance at various points in your search.

Appendix B

Writing Research Proposals

This appendix will provide guidelines for writing proposals to obtain funding for your research. The guidelines for writing a research proposal will vary depending on its purpose. At one extreme, a relatively lengthy and detailed proposal will be expected when you seek grants from federal government agencies, such as the National Institute of Mental Health (NIMH) or the National Institute on Drug Abuse (NIDA). The competition for grants from such sources is fierce. At the other extreme are sources that fund much smaller grants. These might include state or local government agencies seeking a limited evaluation of a program they fund, private foundations, or universities that offer small grants to encourage and facilitate research by faculty members. Although the proposal demands from these sources are likely to be less rigorous than from federal agencies, you should not underestimate them.

BEFORE YOU START WRITING THE PROPOSAL

Your chances of having your proposal funded will be enhanced if you take some preliminary steps before you start to write it. One such step is to learn about the expectations of the funding source before you prepare your proposal and then develop your proposal according to those expectations. You can learn about those expectations from the funding source's website or by obtaining its written materials.

In addition, you should try to develop a relationship with a staff member at the funding source whose role includes acting as a liaison to prospective grant applicants. Through that relationship you can learn of the funding source's potential interest in your research idea. If it is interested, the liaison can suggest how to develop or modify your idea and your proposal to fit the funding source's priorities and funding criteria. With some funding sources, it might be necessary to write a brief, preliminary letter summarizing your research idea before you

can begin to relate to any of their staff. If possible, however, it is best to develop a relationship prior to writing such a letter. Sometimes a liaison can guide you in writing even a preliminary letter and may perhaps advise you regarding the preparation of a brief concept paper, several pages long, summarizing your preliminary idea. In some instances the concept paper might be enclosed with the preliminary letter; in others, it should be submitted only after the funding source expresses a preliminary interest in your idea and encourages you to submit a concept paper. By developing and nurturing a relationship with a liaison from the funding source, and by following the liaison's advice, you not only increase the degree of fit between your proposal and the source's funding criteria, you increase the chances that the liaison will act as an advocate for your proposal. Another potentially helpful preliminary step is to examine some proposals that have previously been funded by the source you are considering. Doing so might provide further insights as to the funding source's expectations.

RESEARCH PROPOSAL COMPONENTS

The specific components of your proposal and the guidelines for writing those components will vary depending on the purpose of your research and the expectations of your funding source. Proposals for primarily qualitative investigations, for example, will differ from those for primarily quantitative studies. Proposals for small, preliminary pilot projects may not need to cover the following components as extensively or as rigorously as do more ambitious proposals. We'll present the following components on the assumption that you need to learn how to prepare an ideal proposal for a major piece of research. Learning how to do that should also prepare you to write less ambitious proposals, as well. In large part, these components will apply to both qualitative as well as quantitative research proposals. However, some of the material you are about to read will apply more to quantitative proposals than to qualitative ones. Moreover, preparing a proposal for a qualitative study can be more challenging than preparing one for a quantitative study. Therefore, after describing the following components we will discuss similarities and differences between quantitative and qualitative research proposals.

Cover Materials

Before reading your actual proposal, many funding sources will want to see some preliminary materials. A cover letter adapted to the source's expectations regarding cover letters is one rather obvious need. The source might also require a cover page that identifies the title of the proposal, the names and addresses of the people and organizations submitting the proposal, and other information such as the amount of money being requested, the duration of the project, and so on. An executive summary statement might also be required. The length of the executive summary will vary. Some sources might expect it to be no more than a paragraph that can fit on the cover page. Others might expect a longer summary that requires a separate page. The preliminary steps that we've discussed above will guide you in determining just how brief the summary should be. Typically it will supply a sentence or two on each of the proposal's components, highlighting the major features of each component.

Problem and Objectives

What exactly do you want to study? Why is it worth studying? Specify in precise terms the objectives of your proposed study. The objectives should be in the form of a brief list—for example, if you have two objectives, simply indent and number each of them, with a sentence or two after each number. Your objectives likely will be in the form of seeking answers to the research questions of your study and should reflect the attributes of well-posed research questions. They need to be narrow and specific, answerable by observable evidence, and feasible to investigate and answer. Most important, you need to explain how the answers to your research questions have significance for practice and policy.

When discussing the importance of the study, cite facts. For instance, if you are proposing to study homelessness, then you might want to cite figures from prior studies that assessed the number of homeless individuals in the nation or in a particular city or state. Or you might describe concrete examples taken from previous case studies so that the subject of your study and its purpose are not vague abstractions. When discussing significant implications for policy or practice, be specific. For example, if you are proposing to study factors that influence school dropout, don't just make vague statements such as, "By identifying why some children drop out of school and others do not, we can develop new policies and programs to deal with this problem." Spell out in detail how certain kinds of findings would imply specific policy or program alternatives. Thus, you might say something like: "If we find that the absence of positive male role models is an important factor that contributes to the dropout problem among males of a particular ethnic group, then this may imply the need to hire more male teachers of that ethnicity or to create a special alternative program in which such male role models work exclusively with boys on academic material as well as on issues such as what it means to be a man...."

As we noted earlier, you should know the funding source's priorities before you prepare or submit your proposal. Try to find a funding source whose priorities come closest to the problem you want to study and to your study's potential significant implications, then word your problem statement in a manner that emphasizes the degree of fit between your proposed study and the funding source's priorities.

Writing the Literature Review

In Chapter 2 and Appendix A we discussed how to conduct a literature review. Here we will focus on how to write about it as a section of your research proposal. You should show how your study will relate to, yet go beyond, the previous studies. How has the prior work influenced

EP 2.1.3c

your proposed or completed study? Do not cite monotonous, minute details about every relevant study that has ever been done—especially if the body of existing literature is extensive. If the literature is extensive, concentrate on the most recent findings, while also including "classic" studies. Your literature review should be thorough in informing readers about the study's topic, yet not so long and detailed that it becomes tedious. Focus only on those studies that have direct relevance to your study. And even when you focus on the most relevant literature, you should report only the most relevant aspects of those studies.

Stick to major themes and succinctly sum up groups of related studies, connecting them to a major theme. If multiple studies have had similar findings, rather than discuss each study separately, you might simply identify the general finding(s) they agreed on, followed by a citation of the authorship and date of each study in parentheses. For instance, you might say something like this (we'll use fictitious references): "Prior studies on the effectiveness of case management with the severely mentally ill have had inconsistent findings. Four studies (Rubin, 1998; Babbie, 1999; Rubin and Babbie, 2000; Babbie, Rubin, and Freud, 2001) found that it is effective. Three studies (Nietzsche, 1998; Scrooge, 1999; Fischer, 2000) found that it is ineffective. The four studies with positive outcomes all used 'days hospitalized' as the dependent variable, whereas the three studies with negative outcomes all used 'quality of life' as the dependent variable...." On the other hand, if you have difficulty finding prior studies that are directly relevant to your proposed research, then you should cite studies that are relevant in an indirect way.

The importance of avoiding excessive detail in your literature review does not mean that you can safely skip mentioning any relevant studies, especially if the literature is not extensive. Funding source review committees are likely to evaluate your expertise in the topic and your competence as an investigator based on the thoroughness and adequacy of your literature review. They may, for example, ask an expert in your topic to provide an external review of your proposal. That expert might know the literature on your topic as well as or better than you do. If your review has omitted any relevant studies, your chances of being funded can be significantly diminished, particularly if the reviewer thinks the omitted studies are important. Although you don't want to be tedious in reporting the details of each study, you should cite all the relevant ones and be sure to give adequate attention to those that are most relevant to your line of inquiry.

You should also avoid writing your literature review in a perfunctory fashion, as if it were just a ritualistic list of studies that you are required to provide in a superficial manner without thoughtful organization. Rather than merely provide a summary listing of what other studies have reported, your literature review should show why you chose your particular line of inquiry and why you conceptualized it the way you did. When reviewers read your research questions and hypotheses, they should not

perceive them as coming out of thin air. Having read your literature review, they should see where your hypotheses and variables came from. For example, a common mistake students make when proposing studies to evaluate an intervention is to review the literature on the problem the intervention is aimed at alleviating without showing how the literature led them to choose the particular intervention they want to evaluate instead of other alternative possibilities. Figure B.1 lists criteria for critically appraising the literature review section of research proposals.

Conceptual Framework

In the conceptual framework section of your proposal, you clearly specify and provide rationales for your research questions, hypotheses, variables, and operational definitions. You should justify why and how you chose each of these facets of your proposal. Your explanation should flow in part from your literature review. It also should show the logic of your own thinking about the inquiry, as well as how your study goes beyond and builds upon the prior literature. For example, if none of the previous studies supporting an intervention to prevent child abuse included Mexican Americans in their sample, you could refer to those studies (which were in your literature review), and the absence of Mexican Americans in their samples, as the rationale for your point of departure. Suppose all of the previous studies only looked at the reduction of out-of-home placement of children as the sole indicator of success, and none assessed whether the children who were kept in their homes were actually better off than those placed elsewhere. Even if this issue has not been raised in the previous literature, you can raise it yourself in presenting your conceptual framework and explaining your reasoning. You would thus show how your study improves on the methods of prior studies in this regard,

EP 2.1.6b

FIGURE B.1 Criteria for Critically Appraising Literature Review Sections in Research Proposals

- Is the review thorough and up to date?
- Does it point out any general agreements or disagreements among previous researchers?
- Does it cover relevant theoretical literature?
- Does it consider whether any of the previous studies are flawed?
- Does it show how the current or proposed study will relate to, yet go beyond, the previous studies?
- Is it thorough in summarizing the existing literature without becoming so lengthy and detailed that it becomes tedious?
- Does it avoid going off on tangential studies of the broad topic area that are not really relevant to the specific focus of the current or proposed study?
- Does it succinctly sum up groups of related studies, offering the citations for each but without repetitively reporting the details of each?
- Does it read as a cohesive synthesis rather than as a list of prior studies?
- Does it help the reader understand why the particular line of inquiry was chosen and the rationale for how it was conceptualized?

as well as explain to your readers why you chose your particular variables and why you chose to operationally define them the way you did.

Measurement

In the section on measurement you elaborate on how you will measure the variables that you have identified and operationally defined in your conceptual framework. This section should flow smoothly from the operational definitions in your conceptual framework, and you should make sure that you are not too redundant and repetitive regarding the specifying of your operational definitions and your measurement procedures. For example, if you plan to operationally define child well-being as a score on a validated instrument for assessing the well-being of children in families at risk for abuse, avoid repeating the detail about that scale in both the conceptual framework and measurement sections of your proposal. Instead, you might simply mention that scores on the scale will be your operational definition, and then later, in your measurement section, go into detail about the nature of the scale, how it is scored, what subscales it contains, and its reliability and validity. Regardless of whether you are using existing scales or measurement instruments you may have developed yourself, you should include a copy of each in an appendix to your proposal. If you are using an instrument that has had its reliability and validity tested, you should not just cite studies that have tested them; you should report specific reliability and validity data. For example, you might say that the five studies that have tested the internal consistency reliability of a scale have found coefficient alphas ranging from .87 to .94, all indicating good to excellent internal consistency reliability. In many studies the investigator can choose from more than one validated instrument to measure a particular construct. There are various validated scales, for example, to measure constructs like depression, self-esteem, and so on. If this is true for your study, provide a rationale for your choice of scale. You might also choose to measure a particular variable in more than one way. Earlier in this book we discussed the value of doing this, in connection to the principle of triangulation. Review committees are likely to be favorably impressed by proposals that incorporate triangulation in their measurement procedures.

Study Participants (Sampling)

Who or what will you study to collect data? Identify any inclusion or exclusion criteria you will use. Will it be appropriate to select a sample? If so, how will you do

that? If you will be conducting an exploratory, qualitative study, you will need to use your judgment in identifying and observing variations (such as age, ethnicity, class) among participants as you go along—ensuring that you have tapped into the range of those variations. If your aim is to conduct a survey for purposes of estimating frequencies of characteristics in the population (for instance, determining the unemployment rate), then you will need to select a probability sample. If you must use nonprobability sampling procedures, you will need to justify that, including attention to the chances that your sample will be biased and unrepresentative of your target population. What efforts will you make to try to offset or avoid those potential biases? Regardless of whether you use probability or nonprobability sampling procedures, you will need to address issues associated with sample attrition and refusal to participate. What special efforts will you make to enhance recruitment and retention of participants?

You will also need to justify the projected size of your sample. This often requires conducting a statistical power analysis, which shows whether your sample size is large enough to give you a good chance of supporting your hypothesis if that hypothesis is indeed true. You'll probably need help from a statistician to conduct your statistical power analysis. You can learn more about this concept in our more advanced text (Rubin and Babbie, 2008).

You should include your statistical power analysis in the sampling section (and perhaps also in the data analysis plans section) of your proposal. You should also tell reviewers why you think it will be feasible for you to obtain the needed sample size. For example, if you are proposing to evaluate an intervention to prevent child abuse, provide evidence that the child welfare agencies you'll need to supply participants for your study will indeed do so in sufficiently large numbers. Such evidence might be letters of support from the agencies as well as data showing how many clients who would be eligible for your study have been served by those agencies in recent years.

Design and Data-Collection Methods

How will you actually collect the data for your study? Will you conduct an experiment or a survey? Will you use qualitative observation methods, conduct a historical study, or focus on reanalyzing statistics already created by others? Regardless of which design you employ, be sure to address the key methodological issues that we discussed previously in the chapter on the design you employ. (For example, if a survey, see Chapters 10 and 11, if an experiment, see Chapter 12, and so on.) Regardless of which design you use, describe when, where, and by whom your data will be collected with each instrument. What expertise and experience qualifications will you seek in your data collectors? How will you recruit and train them? What will be done to avoid or minimize bias among them? What about feasibility issues, such as agency cooperation with your proposed procedures or the amount of time it will take for respondents to complete your instruments or interviews?

Data Analysis

Spell out the kind of analysis you plan to conduct. If you anticipate the use of specific statistical analytic techniques, identify, describe, and justify your choice. Perhaps your intention is to conduct a qualitative data analysis. Describe how you will do that. As we noted earlier, different funding sources will have different expectations regarding the length and detail of this section of your proposal. If you are not sure of those expectations, the safe thing to do is to develop this section in detail—providing a detailed rationale for the selection of each data analysis procedure. If you must use procedures in which you lack sufficient expertise, it is advisable to engage a statistician as a collaborator in your research and in writing this section of your proposal.

Schedule

It is often appropriate to provide a schedule for the various stages of research. Even if you don't do this for the proposal, do it for yourself. Unless you have a time line for accomplishing the several stages of research—and keep in touch with how you're doing—you may end up in trouble. Your proposed time line in your proposal should be reasonable. If you project too little or too much time for specific stages of the research, reviewers might question how well prepared you are to carry out the research successfully.

Budget

If you are asking someone to give you money to pay the costs of your research, then you will need to provide a budget that specifies where the money will go. Large, expensive projects include budgetary categories such as personnel, equipment, supplies, and expenses such as telephones and postage. Even for a more modest project that you will pay for yourself, it is a good idea to spend time anticipating expenses: office supplies, photocopying, computer disks, telephone calls, transportation, and so on. The costs you specify in your budget should be reasonable, and you should justify each. You can hurt your chances of being funded by overestimating the costs or by underestimating them. If you overestimate them, funders may fear being "ripped off" or may deem the benefits of the study to be not worth the costs. If you underestimate the costs, you may convey the impression of an inexperienced investigator who does not yet "know the ropes." You may need technical assistance to calculate some expenses, such as pay rates and fringe benefits for personnel. You should inquire as to whether there is a staff member at your school or agency who provides such technical assistance in the preparation of grant applications.

Additional Components

Most funding sources will require additional proposal components, perhaps attached as appendices. For example, you'll probably have to supply materials showing that your proposed study has been approved by an institutional review board regarding its ethics and protection of human subjects. Chapter 4 discussed this process. You may also need to supply attachments that provide evidence of the proposed project's feasibility and your preparedness to carry it out successfully. These attachments might include (1) your resume or a biographical sketch and perhaps the resumes and biographical sketches of your co-investigators showing how your prior experiences have prepared you to carry out the research successfully; (2) letters of support from administrators of the agencies that will supply you with data or research participants; (3) statements supplying additional evidence as to the potential feasibility of the study regarding recruiting and retaining a sufficient sample and collecting sufficient data in an appropriate manner; and (4) plans for disseminating the results of your research, such as through publication in professional journals and newsletters and through presentations at professional conferences or agency meetings attended by those whose practice or research can be guided by your findings.

The degree of difficulty you will encounter in preparing a proposal is likely to vary depending on the type of study you plan to conduct. Preparing a proposal for a qualitative study that you will submit for funding is likely to be particularly challenging, as is discussed in the box titled "Similarities and Differences between Quantitative and Qualitative Research Proposals."

You should not get too discouraged if your first proposal is not funded. Learn from the process. If the funding source provides feedback about the reasons your proposal was not funded, you might revise the proposal and resubmit it, perhaps to the same or a different funding source. With some federal funding sources, for example, researchers often resubmit improved versions of their proposals several times before eventually being funded.

Similarities and Differences Between Quantitative and Qualitative Research Proposals

The elements of research proposals that we've identified in this book are fairly common, irrespective of the type of research being proposed. Whether you are proposing a quantitative or qualitative study (or perhaps a blending of the two), you will probably need to begin with a statement of the problem or objective and follow that with a literature review, a description of your research methods, and so on. Regardless of which type of study you propose to do, you will have to make a persuasive case as to the importance of the research question and the value of the study. The criteria for a good literature review will also be similar in both types of proposals. Other similarities include the need for a schedule with a realistic time line, a section covering human subjects review approval, a reasonable budget that anticipates all of the various costs you will encounter, and a neat professional appearance that reflects clear and interesting writing.

Although certain criteria for proposal preparation such as those mentioned above commonly apply to all research proposals, qualitative methodologists have been identifying ways in which proposals for qualitative studies differ from those for quantitative studies. Qualitative proposals are generally agreed to be more difficult to write than quantitative proposals, mainly because of the greater degree of structure and preplanning involved in designing quantitative research. Sandelowski, Holditch-Davis, and Harris (1989:77), for example, see the preparation of the proposal for a qualitative study as requiring the negotiation of "the paradox of planning what should not be planned in advance." Likewise, Morse (1994) notes the relatively unstructured, unpredictable nature of qualitative research and the difficulty this presents for writing a proposal that promises exciting results or is even specific about the types of alternative conclusions the study is likely to generate. These authors point out that the design of qualitative research tends to be in the form of an open-ended starting point from which methods and truth will emerge through encountering subjects in their natural environment. This is unlike quantitative research, in which the methods and specific alternative findings can be planned and spelled out in detail in advance.

The dilemma for the qualitative researcher, then, is figuring out how to put enough detail about the plan in the proposal to enable potential funders to evaluate the proposal's merits, while remaining true to the unstructured, flexible, inductive qualitative approach. In the words of Sandelowski and her colleagues, "The most difficult task in preparing the proposal ... is delineating the method when the investigator can have no definitive method prior to initiating inquiry" (p. 78). This task is even more challenging to the extent that the merits of the proposal will be judged by reviewers who are likely to be more oriented to quantitative research and who expect the precise planning that goes into proposals for quantitative research studies.

One suggestion for those preparing proposals for qualitative studies is to go ahead and describe a plan for sampling and data collection and analysis, but indicate that it is only a tentative and initial direction that is open to change as the study proceeds and new insights emerge. Also, the proposal can specify the type of qualitative approach being employed and then describe the general ideas underlying that approach. Although you will not be able to say in advance exactly what you will do or find, you can convey to reviewers the general principles you will follow in conducting your flexible, emergent inquiry.

The same general idea applies to other qualitative proposal sections that, in a quantitative proposal, would contain a much greater degree of operational specificity. For example, when you discuss sampling, you may not be able to anticipate with the precision of a quantitative proposal the exact number of subjects who will participate in the study and their characteristics. But you can discuss the variety of types of subjects you tentatively think are likely to participate and who you think are likely to supply the most relevant data. You can also describe the general ideas and rationale that underlie the qualitative sampling methods you expect to employ.

Although you may find these suggestions helpful, they won't change the fact that qualitative proposals are more difficult to write and may be reviewed by people who are more accustomed to reading proposals for quantitative research and to judging proposals according to the canons of quantitative research design. Because they may be apt to react to your qualitative proposal with puzzlement, it is particularly important that your proposal demonstrate your expertise about qualitative research and your ability to carry it out. Make sure that every section of your proposal is well written and that your literature review is adequate. (The literature review in qualitative proposals should perhaps be more extensive than in quantitative proposals to demonstrate the investigator's expertise, because it may appear as though the funders are being told "Trust me" in qualitative studies more than in quantitative ones.)

Along these lines, it may be helpful to conduct a pilot study on the topic addressed in your proposal and then describe that pilot study in your proposal and submit it as an appendix to the proposal. This will show your commitment and competence. It can also demonstrate how you might go about analyzing the data that might emerge in the proposed study. Of course, being able to refer to previously completed pilot studies will also help your prospects for funding in submitting a proposal for quantitative research, and the two types of proposals are similar in this respect.

Although we do not want to understate the similarities between the two types of proposals or overstate their differences, anyone planning to prepare a proposal for qualitative research should be aware of the special dilemma they face. Reviewers and board members of funding sources also should understand this dilemma and apply different criteria when reviewing the two types of proposals.

Appendix C

Writing Social Work Research Reports

By the time you are ready to write the report of your completed study, you will have invested a great deal in your research. But, unless your research is properly communicated, all the efforts devoted to the various procedures discussed throughout this book will go for naught. This means, first and foremost, that good research reporting requires good English (or Spanish or whatever language you use). Whenever we ask the figures "to speak for themselves," they tend to remain mute. Whenever we use unduly complex terminology or construction, communication is reduced.

Our first advice to you is to read and reread (at approximately three-month intervals) an excellent small book by William Strunk, Jr., and E. B. White, *The Elements of Style.** If you do this faithfully, and if even 10 percent of the contents rub off, you stand a good chance of making yourself understood and your findings appreciated.

Scientific reporting has several functions. First, your report should communicate a body of specific data and ideas. You should provide those specifics clearly and with sufficient detail to permit an informed evaluation by others. Second, you should view your report as a contribution to the general body of scientific knowledge. While remaining appropriately humble, you should always regard your research report as an addition to what we know about social behavior. Finally, the report should stimulate and direct further inquiry.

SOME BASIC CONSIDERATIONS

Despite these general guidelines, different reports serve different purposes. A report appropriate for one purpose

*4th ed. (New York: Macmillan, 1999). Here's another useful reference on writing: R. W. Birchfield, *The New Fowler's Modern English Usage*, 3rd ed. (New York: Oxford University Press, 1998).

might be wholly inappropriate for another. This section deals with some of the basic considerations in this regard.

Audience

Before drafting your report, ask yourself who you hope will read it. Normally you should make a distinction between professional colleagues and general readers. If the report is written for the former, you may make certain assumptions about their existing knowledge and therefore summarize certain points rather than explain them in detail. Similarly, you may use more technical language than would be appropriate for a general audience.

At the same time, remain aware that social work, like other professions, is diverse. Terms, assumptions, and special techniques familiar to some of your colleagues may only confuse others. If you report a study on cognitive-behavioral interventions to an audience of colleagues who are not familiar with those interventions, for example, you should explain previous findings in more detail than would be necessary if you were addressing an audience of social workers who specialize in cognitive-behavioral interventions.

Likewise, you should communicate differently depending on the research expertise and professional roles of the colleagues in your intended audience. For example, how you describe the logic of your research design or your data analysis procedures should vary depending on whether your intended audience consists primarily of researchers, administrators, or direct-service practitioners. If your target audience consists primarily of researchers, you'll have less need to explain or avoid using technical research terminology. If your target audience consists primarily of administrators or other practitioners with relatively little advanced technical experience in research, you should keep the terminology as simple as possible and be sure to explain any unavoidable technical terms that they may not yet understand. Also keep in mind that administrators and other practitioners will be far more attentive to executive summaries, visual representations via simple charts and graphs, and implications for practice than to the technical details of your research methodology.

Form and Length of the Report

Often researchers must prepare reports for the sponsors of their research. These reports may vary greatly in length. In preparing such a report, you should bear in mind its audience—professional or lay—and their reasons for sponsoring the project in the first place.

Aim of the Report

Earlier in this book, we considered the different purposes of social work research projects. In preparing your report, you should keep these different purposes in mind.

Some reports may focus primarily on the *exploration* of a topic. As such, their conclusions are tentative and incomplete. You should clearly indicate to your audience the exploratory aim of the study and point to the shortcomings of the particular project. An exploratory report serves to point the way to more refined research on the topic.

Most research reports have a *descriptive* element reflecting the descriptive purpose of the studies they document. Carefully distinguish those descriptions that apply only to the sample and those that apply to the population. Give your audience some indication of the probable range of error in any inferential descriptions you make.

Many reports have an *explanatory* aim: pointing to causal relationships among variables. Depending on your probable audience, carefully delineate the rules of explanation that lie behind your computations and conclusions. Also, as in the case of description, give your readers some guide to the relative certainty of your conclusions.

Regardless of your research purpose, all social work research projects should have the overarching aim of providing information that will be useful in guiding practice or policy. Thus, your report probably will propose implications for action. Be sure that the recommendations you propose are warranted by your data. Thus, you should be especially careful to spell out the logic by which you move from empirical data to proposed action.

Avoiding Plagiarism

Whenever you're reporting on the work of others, you must be clear about who said what. That is, you must avoid *plagiarism*: the theft of another's words and/or ideas—whether intentional or accidental—and the presentation of those words and ideas as your own. Because this is a common and sometimes unclear problem for students, let's examine it. Here are the ground rules regarding plagiarism:

> *You cannot use another writer's exact words without using quotation marks and giving a complete citation,*

which indicates the source of the quotation such that your reader could locate that quotation in its original context. As a general rule, taking a passage of eight or more words without citation is a violation of federal copyright laws.

It's also not acceptable to edit or paraphrase another's words and present the revised version as your own work. Finally, it's not even acceptable to present another's ideas as your own—even if you use totally different words to express those ideas.

The following examples should clarify what is or is not acceptable in the use of another's work.

The Original Work

Laws of Growth

> *Systems are like babies: once you get one, you have it. They don't go away. On the contrary, they display the most remarkable persistence. They not only persist; they grow. And as they grow, they encroach. The growth potential of systems was explored in a tentative, preliminary way by Parkinson, who concluded that administrative systems maintain an average growth of 5 to 6 percent per annum regardless of the work to be done. Parkinson was right so far as he goes, and we must give him full honors for initiating the serious study of this important topic. But what Parkinson failed to perceive, we now enunciate—the general systems analogue of Parkinson's Law.*
>
> *The System Itself Tends to Grow at 5 to 6 Percent Per Annum*
>
> *Again, this Law is but the preliminary to the most general possible formulation, the Big-Bang Theorem of Systems Cosmology.*
>
> *Systems Tend To Expand To Fill the Known Universe.*
>
> *(Gall, 1975: 12–14)*

Now let's look at some of the *acceptable* ways you might make use of Gall's work in a term paper.

> *Acceptable:* John Gall, in his work *Systemantics*, draws a humorous parallel between systems and infants: "Systems are like babies: once you get one, you have it. They don't go away. On the contrary, they display the most remarkable persistence. They not only persist; they grow."*
>
> *Acceptable:* John Gall warns that systems are like babies. Create a system and it sticks around.

---

*John Gall, *Systemantics How Systems Work and Especially How They Fail* (New York: Quadrangle, 1975), 12–14.

Worse yet, Gall notes, systems keep growing larger and larger.*

Acceptable: It has also been suggested that systems have a natural tendency to persist, even grow and encroach (Gall, 1975:12).

Note that the last format requires that you give a complete citation in your bibliography, as we do in this book. Complete footnotes or endnotes work as well. See the publication manuals of various organizations such as the NASW, as well as the *Chicago Manual of Style,* for appropriate citation formats.

Here now are some *unacceptable* uses of the same material, reflecting some common errors.

Unacceptable: In this paper, I want to look at some of the characteristics of the social systems we create in our organizations. First, systems are like babies: once you get one, you have it. They don't go away. On the contrary, they display the most remarkable persistence. They not only persist; they grow. [It is unacceptable to directly quote someone else's materials without using quotation marks and giving a full citation.]

Unacceptable: In this paper, I want to look at some of the characteristics of the social systems we create in our organizations. First, systems are a lot like children: once you get one, it's yours. They don't go away; they persist. They not only persist, in fact: they grow. [It is unacceptable to edit another's work and present it as your own.]

Unacceptable: In this paper, I want to look at some of the characteristics of the social systems we create in our organizations. One thing I've noticed is that once you create a system, it never seems to go away. Just the opposite, in fact: they have a tendency to grow. You might say systems are a lot like children in that respect. [It is unacceptable to paraphrase someone else's ideas and present them as your own.]

Each of the preceding unacceptable examples is an example of plagiarism and represents a serious offense. Admittedly, there are some "gray areas." Some ideas are more or less in the public domain, not "belonging" to any one person. Or you may reach an idea on your own that someone else has already put in writing. If you have a question about a specific situation, discuss it with your instructor in advance.

We've discussed this topic in some detail because, although you must place your research in the context of what others have done and said, the improper use of their materials is a serious offense. Learning to avoid plagiarism is a part of your "coming of age" as a scholar.

---

*John Gall, *Systemantics How Systems Work and Especially How They Fail* (New York: Quadrangle, 1975), 12.

ORGANIZATION OF THE REPORT

Although the organization of reports differs somewhat in terms of form and purpose, a general format for presenting research data can be helpful. The following comments apply most directly to a journal article, but with some modification they apply to most forms of research reports as well.

Title

Your title should closely reflect the main point of your research. Deciding on the best title, however, is not always easy. You should try to give readers enough information without making it too wordy. If it is more than about a dozen words, it probably needs to be shortened. If it has a subtitle, however, it can be a bit longer. Still, it should be as terse as possible. If possible, you may want to devise a title that is likely to pique the interest of potential readers.

Although a catchy title may be a good idea, be careful not to go overboard. You don't want your audience to think you are hyping your report in a misleading manner.

The intended audience for your report should influence your choice of a title. To be on the safe side, you may want to devise several alternative tentative titles and then seek feedback from your colleagues, or any coauthors you may have, as to their reactions to the various titles.

Abstract

Immediately after the title page, reports will include a separate page containing an abstract that briefly summarizes the study. Most abstracts are somewhere between 75 and 150 words long. Abstracts typically begin with a sentence identifying the purpose of the research. Next usually comes a sentence or two summarizing the main features of the research design and methodology. The main findings are then highlighted in a sentence or two, followed by a brief mention of any major implications. Here is an illustrative abstract:

A randomized experiment tested the effectiveness of adding a psychoeducational group therapy intervention to standard inpatient chemical dependency services for clients dually diagnosed with mental and substance dependence disorders. One hundred clients were randomly assigned to an experimental group and a control group. Outcome variables included drug and alcohol use, incarceration days, psychiatric symptoms, and psychiatric inpatient admissions. No significant treatment effects were found on any of the outcome variables. The tested intervention did not add to the effects of standard treatments for dually diagnosed clients. Practitioners should continue to develop and evaluate alternative treatment approaches that might prove to be more effective than the one tested in this study.

Introduction and Literature Review

The main narrative of your report should begin with an introduction that provides a background to the problem you have investigated. This section of your report should share some of the same features as the problems and objectives and literature review sections of your research proposal. It should, for example, convey the scope of the problem, the objectives and rationale for the study, and the study's importance. It should summarize the previous research as briefly as possible, yet provide enough detail to give readers an adequate overview of the topic and to show them how your study is connected to and builds on the prior literature. The entire introductory part of your report—including your problem statement, literature review, objectives, and hypotheses—might appear under one subheading, called "Introduction." Or it might be broken up under one or more additional subheadings, such as "Literature Review," "Hypotheses," and so on. More important than how many subheadings you use is whether your introductory material makes clear to the reader the objectives of your research and their rationale, why your study is timely and important, and how your study connects to and builds on the prior literature.

Your review of the literature should bring the reader up to date on the previous research in the area, and should point out any general agreements or disagreements among the previous researchers. What theories address your topic and what do they say? What research has been done previously? Are there consistent findings, or do past studies disagree? Are there flaws in the body of existing research? If you wish to challenge previously accepted ideas, carefully review the studies that have led to the acceptance of those ideas, then indicate the factors that have not been previously considered or the logical fallacies present in the previous research. When you're concerned with resolving a disagreement among previous researchers, you should summarize the research supporting one view, then summarize the research supporting the other, and finally suggest the reasons for the disagreement.

As is the case with research proposals, you should do the following:

- Show how your study will relate to, yet go beyond, the previous studies
- Show how the prior works have influenced your study
- Avoid citing monotonous, minute details about every relevant study that has ever been done—especially if the body of existing literature is extensive. If the literature is extensive, concentrate on the most recent findings, while also including "classic" studies.
- Be thorough in informing readers about the study's topic, but not so long and detailed that the review becomes tedious.

- If multiple studies have had similar findings, rather than discuss each study separately, you might simply identify the general finding(s) they agreed upon, followed by a citation of the authorship and date of each study in parentheses.

If you have difficulty finding prior studies that are directly relevant to your proposed research, then you should cite studies that are relevant in an indirect way. Thus, if you find no studies on the effectiveness of case management with the mentally ill, then you might look for studies that evaluate its effectiveness with other populations, such as the physically or developmentally disabled.

Methods

The worth of the findings of a study depends on the validity of the study's design and data-collection procedures. Informed readers will want to read the details of your study's methodological design and execution so they can judge the value of your findings and decide whether to be guided by them. Readers need to be provided with sufficient detail to enable them to know precisely what was done and to replicate your study.

For some studies this section will begin with a specification of your hypotheses and variables. For other studies you might provide that information in the preceding section, showing how your conceptual framework flows from the prior literature. In either case, your methods section should describe in detail how you measured each variable, and should give readers enough information to ascertain whether your measurement procedures were reliable and valid. The same sort of detail is needed regarding your data-collection procedures, the logical arrangements for drawing causal inferences (if that was your study's purpose), and your sampling procedures.

Results

Having set the study in the perspective of previous research and having described the design and execution of it, you should then present your data. The presentation of data analyses should provide a maximum of detail without being cluttered. You can accomplish this best by continually examining your report to see whether it achieves the following aims.

If you're using quantitative data, present them so the reader can recompute them. Provide details. If you're doing a qualitative analysis, you must provide enough detail that your reader has a sense of having made the observations with you. Presenting only those data that support your interpretations is not sufficient; you must also share those data that conflict with the way you've made sense of things. Ultimately, you should provide enough information that the reader might reach a different conclusion than you did, though you can hope your interpretation will make the most sense. The reader, in fact, should be in position to replicate the entire study independently, whether it involves participant observation of people who are homeless, an experiment evaluating the effectiveness of an intervention for abused children, or any other kind of study. Recall that replicability is an essential norm of science. A single study does not prove a point; only a series of studies can begin to do so. And unless studies can be replicated, there can be no meaningful series of studies.

Tables, charts, and figures, if any, can be integrated into the text of the report—appearing near that portion of the text discussing them—or they can be placed in an appendix. Either way, as a general rule, it is best to (1) describe the purpose for presenting the table, (2) present it, and (3) review and interpret it.

It is often best to wait until you reach your Discussion section, which follows the Results section, to present your interpretations of the implications of your results. Interpretations in the Results section are usually limited to explaining what the data mean in a technical, factual sense. For example, suppose your study finds that an intervention for spouse abusers appears to be effective according to the self-reports of the perpetrators, but ineffective according to the reports of their spouses. You would factually report each of those findings in your Results, but might want to delay trying to explain the discrepancy until your Discussion section. On the other hand, your report might be more readable if you integrated the presentation of data, the manipulations of those data, and your interpretations into a logical whole. That is, you would do that all in one section, called Findings, instead of having separate Results and Discussion sections. In your Findings section, you could present your rationale for each particular analysis, present the data relevant to it, interpret the results, and then indicate where that result leads next.

Discussion and Conclusions

The narrative part of your report should conclude with a section that develops explicit conclusions, draws practical implications based on those conclusions, discusses the methodological limitations of your study, and draws implications for future research.

Many studies have findings that can be interpreted in alternative ways. Reasonable people may disagree about the most appropriate interpretations and conclusions to be drawn. You should acknowledge all of the alternative interpretations that may reasonably be made of your data. Then you should identify which interpretations seem the most warranted and explain why. This is not to imply, however, that you should merely editorialize. The conclusions you draw should be warranted by your data. You should carefully note the specific basis for each conclusion. Otherwise you may lead your reader into accepting unwarranted

conclusions. Point to any qualifications or conditions warranted in the evaluation of conclusions, including the methodological limitations bearing on each conclusion. Typically, you know best the shortcomings and tentativeness of your conclusions, and you should give the reader the advantage of that knowledge.

Based on your conclusions, you should draw implications for social work practice or social welfare policy. Some studies may yield implications for social work education. You should also develop implications for future research, based on new questions emerging from your findings and perhaps also based on any unanticipated practical or methodological pitfalls you encountered in conducting your study. You should review the particular shortcomings of your own study and suggest ways by which those shortcomings might be avoided.

At the end of your report you may want to tell your readers what you told them. In summarizing your research report, you should avoid reviewing every specific finding, but you should review all the significant ones, pointing once more to their general significance.

References and Appendices

Immediately following the conclusion of the narrative portion of your report should be a list of all the references you cited in the report. Typically, each citation will be indicated in the narrative by putting the authors' last names and the year of publication in parentheses.

Your list of references at the end of your report should display each full citation in the alphabetical order of the first author's last name. An alternative method is to just number each citation in the text as follows:[1]. Then you would list each full citation in your reference list by number, in the order that they appear in the text.

Your decision as to which reference format to use should be based on the expectations of those to whom you will be submitting your report. In lieu of such expectations, it's probably best to use the alphabetical method because it is used more widely. If you have any tables, figures, or graphs that you opted not to integrate into the text of your report, these should be placed immediately after your list of references, followed by any other appendices you may have.

ADDITIONAL CONSIDERATIONS WHEN WRITING QUALITATIVE REPORTS

Most of our foregoing comments about writing research reports apply to both quantitative and qualitative studies. We have, however, cited some of the ways in which reports of qualitative research may differ from reports of quantitative research. Let's now look at some additional considerations that apply only to qualitative reports—considerations suggested by Neuman (2000).

Because qualitative studies collect data that are harder to condense than the statistics in quantitative studies, and because qualitative studies often seek to provide a deeper, empathic understanding of phenomena, qualitative reports tend to be lengthier than quantitative reports. For example, instead of providing summary statistics, qualitative reports may need to present lengthy quotes. They may need to present photographs and very detailed descriptions of the people and circumstances that have been observed. Descriptions of and justifications for less structured, less standardized, and sometimes idiosyncratic data-collection methods often need to be longer in qualitative reports than in quantitative ones. More space might also be needed to explain the development of new concepts and new theory that may emerge from a qualitative study. In historical and comparative studies, many detailed footnotes may be needed to describe the sources and evidence for each conclusion. In light of all of these factors, it may be difficult to meet the page limitations of many journals that are more accustomed to publishing reports of quantitative studies. Authors of lengthy qualitative reports may need to submit their studies to journals that specialize in qualitative research, such as those with the term *Qualitative* in their journal's title. Such authors also commonly report their research in book-length form.

Whereas quantitative reports typically are written in a formal and succinct style, qualitative reports are more likely to use more creative and varied literary styles in order to convey to readers a deeper, more empathic, more subjective understanding of what it is like to walk in the shoes of the people being portrayed in the report. This is not to imply that anything goes. As we noted earlier, the conclusions being drawn in a qualitative report should be well supported by a wealth of data. Although qualitative researchers have more leeway regarding the style and organization of their reports, each conclusion they draw should be accompanied by sufficient supportive evidence collected in a plausible manner.

We will conclude with a point we mentioned earlier. Research reports should be written in the best possible style. Writing lucidly is easier for some people than for others, and it is always harder than writing poorly. You are again referred to the Strunk and White book. Every researcher would do well to adhere to the following procedure: Write. Read Strunk and White. Revise. Reread Strunk and White. Revise again. After you are satisfied with your report, ask your colleagues to read it and criticize it. Based on their criticism, revise yet again. This will be a difficult and time-consuming endeavor, but so is science.

A perfectly designed, carefully executed, and brilliantly analyzed study will be altogether worthless unless you can communicate your findings to others. We have attempted to provide some guidelines toward that end. The best guides are logic, clarity, and honesty. Ultimately, there is no substitute for practice.

ADDITIONAL READINGS

Birchfield, R. W. 1998. *The New Fowler's Modern English Usage*, 3rd ed. New York: Oxford University Press. H. W. Fowler's concise and witty *Modern English Usage* has been the chief resource and final word on "proper" English since it was first published in 1926. The third edition ensures the advice is "modern."

Strunk, William, Jr., and E. B. White. 1999. *The Elements of Style*, 4th ed. New York: Macmillan. This marvelous little book provides specific guidance as to grammar and spelling, but its primary power is its ability to *inspire* good writing.

Walker, Janice R., and Todd Taylor. 1998. *The Columbia Guide to Online Style*. New York: Columbia University Press. A guide to citing web materials in a scholarly report.

Appendix D

Random Numbers

10480	15011	01536	02011	81647	91646	69179	14194	62590	36207	20969	99570	91291	90700
22368	46573	25595	85393	30995	89198	27982	53402	93965	34095	52666	19174	39615	99505
24130	48360	22527	97265	76393	64809	15179	24830	49340	32081	30680	19655	63348	58629
42167	93093	06243	61680	07856	16376	39440	53537	71341	57004	00849	74917	97758	16379
37570	39975	81837	16656	06121	91782	60468	81305	49684	60672	14110	06927	01263	54613
77921	06907	11008	42751	27756	53498	18602	70659	90655	15053	21916	81825	44394	42880
99562	72905	56420	69994	98872	31016	71194	18738	44013	48840	63213	21069	10634	12952
96301	91977	05463	07972	18876	20922	94595	56869	69014	60045	18425	84903	42508	32307
89579	14342	63661	10281	17453	18103	57740	84378	25331	12566	58678	44947	05585	56941
85475	36857	53342	53988	53060	59533	38867	62300	08158	17983	16439	11458	18593	64952
28918	69578	88231	33276	70997	79936	56865	05859	90106	31595	01547	85590	91610	78188
63553	40961	48235	03427	49626	69445	18663	72695	52180	20847	12234	90511	33703	90322
09429	93969	52636	92737	88974	33488	36320	17617	30015	08272	84115	27156	30613	74952
10365	61129	87529	85689	48237	52267	67689	93394	01511	26358	85104	20285	29975	89868
07119	97336	71048	08178	77233	13916	47564	81056	97735	85977	29372	74461	28551	90707
51085	12765	51821	51259	77452	16308	60756	92144	49442	53900	70960	63990	75601	40719
02368	21382	52404	60268	89368	19885	55322	44819	01188	65255	64835	44919	05944	55157
01011	54092	33362	94904	31273	04146	18594	29852	71585	85030	51132	01915	92747	64951
52162	53916	46369	58586	23216	14513	83149	98736	23495	64350	94738	17752	35156	35749
07056	97628	33787	09998	42698	06691	76988	13602	51851	46104	88916	19509	25625	58104
48663	91245	85828	14346	09172	30168	90229	04734	59193	22178	30421	61666	99904	32812
54164	58492	22421	74103	47070	25306	76468	26384	58151	06646	21524	15227	96909	44592
32639	32363	05597	24200	13363	38005	94342	28728	35806	06912	17012	64161	18296	22851
29334	27001	87637	87308	58731	00256	45834	15398	46557	41135	10367	07684	36188	18510
02488	33062	28834	07351	19731	92420	60952	61280	50001	67658	32586	86679	50720	94953
81525	72295	04839	96423	24878	82651	66566	14778	76797	14780	13300	87074	79666	95725
29676	20591	68086	26432	46901	20849	89768	81536	86645	12659	92259	57102	80428	25280
00742	57392	39064	66432	84673	40027	32832	61362	98947	96067	64760	64584	96096	98253
05366	04213	25669	26422	44407	44048	37937	63904	45766	66134	75470	66520	34693	90449
91921	26418	64117	94305	26766	25940	39972	22209	71500	64568	91402	42416	07844	69618
00582	04711	87917	77341	42206	35126	74087	99547	81817	42607	43808	76655	62028	76630
00725	69884	62797	56170	86324	88072	76222	36086	84637	93161	76038	65855	77919	88006
69011	65795	95876	55293	18988	27354	26575	08625	40801	59920	29841	80150	12777	48501

25976	57948	29888	88604	67917	48708	18912	82271	65424	69774	33611	54262	85963	03547
09763	83473	73577	12908	30883	18317	28290	35797	05998	41688	34952	37888	38917	88050
91567	42595	27958	30134	04024	86385	29880	99730	55536	84855	29080	09250	79656	73211
17955	56349	90999	49127	20044	59931	06115	20542	18059	02008	73708	83517	36103	42791
46503	18584	18845	49618	02304	51038	20655	58727	28168	15475	56942	53389	20562	87338
92157	89634	94824	78171	84610	82834	09922	25417	44137	48413	25555	21246	35509	20468
14577	62765	35605	81263	39667	47358	56873	56307	61607	49518	89656	20103	77490	18062
98427	07523	33362	64270	01638	92477	66969	98420	04880	45585	46565	04102	46880	45709
34914	63976	88720	82765	34476	17032	87589	40836	32427	70002	70663	88863	77775	69348
70060	28277	39475	46473	23219	53416	94970	25832	69975	94884	19661	72828	00102	66794
53976	54914	06990	67245	68350	82948	11398	42878	80287	88267	47363	46634	06541	97809
76072	29515	40980	07391	58745	25774	22987	80059	39911	96189	41151	14222	60697	59583
90725	52210	83974	29992	65831	38857	50490	83765	55657	14361	31720	57375	56228	41546
64364	67412	33339	31926	14883	24413	59744	92351	97473	89286	35931	04110	23726	51900
08962	00358	31662	25388	61642	34072	81249	35648	56891	69352	48373	45578	78547	81788
95012	68379	93526	70765	10592	04542	76463	54328	02349	17247	28865	14777	62730	92277
15664	10493	20492	38391	91132	21999	59516	81652	27195	48223	46751	22923	32261	85653
16408	81899	04153	53381	79401	21438	83035	92350	36693	31238	59649	91754	72772	02338
18629	81953	05520	91962	04739	13092	97662	24822	94730	06496	35090	04822	86774	98289
73115	35101	47498	87637	99016	71060	88824	71013	18735	20286	23153	72924	35165	43040
57491	16703	23167	49323	45021	33132	12544	41035	80780	45393	44812	12515	98931	91202
30405	83946	23792	14422	15059	45799	22716	19792	09983	74353	68668	30429	70735	25499
16631	35006	85900	98275	32388	52390	16815	69298	82732	38480	73817	32523	41961	44437
96773	20206	42559	78985	05300	22164	24369	54224	35083	19687	11052	91491	60383	19746
38935	64202	14349	82674	66523	44133	00697	35552	35970	19124	63318	29686	03387	59846
31624	76384	17403	53363	44167	64486	64758	75366	76554	31601	12614	33072	60332	92325
78919	19474	23632	27889	47914	02584	37680	20801	72152	39339	34806	08930	85001	87820
03931	33309	57047	74211	63445	17361	62825	39908	05607	91284	68833	25570	38818	46920
74426	33278	43972	10119	89917	15665	52872	73823	73144	88662	88970	74492	51805	99378
09066	00903	20795	95452	92648	45454	09552	88815	16553	51125	79375	97596	16296	66092
42238	12426	87025	14267	20979	04508	64535	31355	86064	29472	47689	05974	52468	16834
16153	08002	26504	41744	81959	65642	74240	56302	00033	67107	77510	70625	28725	34191
21457	40742	29820	96783	29400	21840	15035	34537	33310	06116	95240	15957	16572	06004
21581	57802	02050	89728	17937	37621	47075	42080	97403	48626	68995	43805	33386	21597
55612	78095	83197	33732	05810	24813	86902	60397	16489	03264	88525	42786	05269	92532
44657	66999	99324	51281	84463	60563	79312	93454	68876	25471	93911	25650	12682	73572
91340	84979	46949	81973	37949	61023	43997	15263	80644	43942	89203	71795	99533	50501
91227	21199	31935	27022	84067	05462	35216	14486	29891	68607	41867	14951	91696	85065
50001	38140	66321	19924	72163	09538	12151	06878	91903	18749	34405	56087	82790	70925
65390	05224	72958	28609	81406	39147	25549	48542	42627	45233	57202	94617	23772	07896
27504	96131	83944	41575	10573	08619	64482	73923	36152	05184	94142	25299	84387	34925
37169	94851	39117	89632	00959	16487	65536	49071	39782	17095	02330	74301	00275	48280
11508	70225	51111	38351	19444	66499	71945	05422	13442	78675	84081	66938	93654	59894
37449	30362	06694	54690	04052	53115	62757	95348	78662	11163	81651	50245	34971	52924
46515	70331	85922	38329	57015	15765	97161	17869	45349	61796	66345	81073	49106	79860

30986	81223	42416	58353	21532	30502	32305	86482	05174	07901	54339	58861	74818	46942
63798	64995	46583	09785	44160	78128	83991	42865	92520	83531	80377	35909	81250	54238
82486	84846	99254	67632	43218	50076	21361	64816	51202	88124	41870	52689	51275	83556
21885	32906	92431	09060	64297	51674	64126	62570	26123	05155	59194	52799	28225	85762
60336	98782	07408	53458	13564	59089	26445	29789	85205	41001	12535	12133	14645	23541
43937	46891	24010	25560	86355	33941	25786	54990	71899	15475	95434	98227	21824	19585
97656	63175	89303	16275	07100	92063	21942	18611	47348	20203	18534	03862	78095	50136
03299	01221	05418	38982	55758	92237	26759	86367	21216	98442	08303	56613	91511	75928
79626	06486	03574	17668	07785	76020	79924	25651	83325	88428	85076	72811	22717	50585
85636	68335	47539	03129	65651	11977	02510	26113	99447	68645	34327	15152	55230	93448
18039	14367	61337	06177	12143	46609	32989	74014	64708	00533	35398	58408	13261	47908
08362	15656	60627	36478	65648	16764	53412	09013	07832	41574	17639	82163	60859	75567
79556	29068	04142	16268	15387	12856	66227	38358	22478	73373	88732	09443	82558	05250
92608	82674	27072	32534	17075	27698	98204	63863	11951	34648	88022	56148	34925	57031
23982	25835	40055	67006	12293	02753	14827	23235	35071	99704	37543	11601	35503	85171
09915	96306	05908	97901	28395	14186	00821	80703	70426	75647	76310	88717	37890	40129
59037	33300	26695	62247	69927	76123	50842	43834	86654	70959	79725	93872	28117	19233
42488	78077	69882	61657	34136	79180	97526	43092	04098	73571	80799	76536	71255	64239
46764	86273	63003	93017	31204	36692	40202	35275	57306	55543	53203	18098	47625	88684
03237	45430	55417	63282	90816	17349	88298	90183	36600	78406	06216	95787	42579	90730
86591	81482	52667	61582	14972	90053	89534	76036	49199	43716	97548	04379	46370	28672
38534	01715	94964	87288	65680	43772	39560	12918	86537	62738	19636	51132	25739	56947

Abridged from *Handbook of Tables for Probability and Statistics*, Second Edition, edited by William H. Beyer (Cleveland: The Chemical Rubber Company, 1968). Used by permission of The Chemical Rubber Company.

Appendix E

Using Effect Sizes to Bridge the Gap Between Research and Practice

As we mentioned in several parts of this book, it is usually difficult to carry out well-controlled, rigorous outcome evaluations in agency practice settings. Program evaluations, therefore, often must be limited to preexperimental designs without control groups. In this appendix, we'll look at how calculating within-group effect size statistics can enhance the value of preexperimental outcome findings for the evaluated programs. We'll also discuss how those effect size statistics might be used to advance evidence-based practice to a new level by reducing the gap between agency realities and the findings of well-controlled experimental evaluations of intervention effectiveness. Let's begin by looking at the gap between research and practice.

THE RESEARCH PRACTICE GAP

As discussed in Chapter 2, one incentive practitioners have for engaging in the evidence-based practice process is to have the best research evidence inform their decision about what intervention to implement. However, several barriers commonly complicate their ability to employ the intervention that has the best evidence in an ideal and effective fashion. In most of the rigorous experimental research studies the evaluated intervention is provided under relatively ideal conditions. For example, the practitioners in those studies are likely to have low caseload sizes, a homogeneous clientele without multiple and severe co-occurring disorders, and many fewer problems with client attendance and premature termination. Those practitioners commonly receive training and supervision in the intervention from the best experts in the intervention—a level of training and supervision that typically is unobtainable for practitioners in non-research settings because of the steep costs of the training and supervision.

Consequently, when practitioners attempt to adapt research-supported interventions (RSIs) in non-research settings (typically service delivery agencies) the results can be disappointing (Embry & Biglan, 2008; Weisz, Ugueto, Herren, Afienko, & Rutt, 2011). This implies the need for studies that examine the factors associated with more successful adaptations of RSIs in non-research settings. For example, each study could assess the way in which a particular non-research setting modifies and adapts a particular RSI and the corresponding outcomes that clients achieve. However, the term *non-research* implies that well-controlled experimental or quasi-experimental outcome studies are unlikely to be feasible in such settings. Instead, studies in these settings will usually be limited to using preexperimental designs.

As discussed in Chapter 12, such designs have extremely limited internal validity and therefore do not rule out the plausibility of alternative explanations (other than the intervention) as the cause of improvements in client outcome. In this appendix we will show how the use of effect size statistics—combined with advances in evidence-based practice—can enhance the value of using preexperimental designs to assess the client outcomes when the adapted intervention is an RSI. The particular type of statistics that we will focus on will be *within-group* effect sizes.

USING WITHIN-GROUP EFFECT SIZES TO REDUCE THE GAP

As you may recall from Chapter 17, the effect sizes traditionally reported in outcome studies—such as *Cohen's d*, odds ratios, and risk ratios—pertain to differences in outcome between the experimental group and the control group. Thus, they are between-group effect sizes. You may also recall that *Cohen's d* involves dividing the difference between the two group means by the pooled standard deviation of the two groups. Without a control group, however, there would be a standard deviation for the intervention recipients, only. However, if there is a pretest mean and a posttest mean, the difference between them can be divided by the pretest standard deviation—or by the pooled standard deviation of both the pretest and posttest scores—to produce a within-group effect size. That within-group effect size could then be compared to the within-group effect sizes in the experimental studies that provided the strong research support for the intervention adapted by the agency.

To make the above comparison, however, the within-group effect sizes in the experimental studies would have to be calculated because typically only the between-group effect sizes are reported in the published results of those studies. Doing so requires examining the pretest and posttest means and standard deviations reported for each group in those studies and calculating the mean within-group effect sizes per group across the studies that support a particular intervention.

One example of such a study is discussed by Rubin (2014) regarding a preexperimental study of an agency's adaptation of an RSI called *problem-solving tools therapy* in treating low-income, African American women at risk for postpartum depression (Sampson, Villarreal, & Rubin, 2014). That study found a within-group effect size of 1.24. To enhance the value of that finding, mean within-group effect sizes were calculated in the experimental studies included in the meta-analysis that provided the strong research support for the RSI. Those mean within-group effect sizes were 1.81 for the treatment groups and 0.11 for the wait-list control groups. Rubin reasoned that although the 1.24 within-group effect size is less than 1.81, it is encouraging because it is far above 0.11. Moreover, service provision realities required that the intervention be provided in half as many sessions (4) as recommended in the treatment manual (8) for the adapted RSI. Rubin (p. 71) concluded that although this comparison does not provide as strong a basis for causal inferences as do randomized experiments, "it helps bridge the gap between research and practice by giving agencies a better empirical basis than has heretofore been available to them for deciding whether to continue providing their adaption of an [RSI], modify the approach, or choose a different treatment approach altogether."

In connection to this reasoning, you may recall the section near the end of Chapter 14 on the utility of preexperimental designs in program evaluation. There we discussed this reasoning in connection to effect sizes for nominal data and noted that if the mean annual rehospitalization rate in experimental studies of an RSI is 10 percent for experimental groups and 30 percent for control groups, and if an agency adapting that RSI had an annual rehospitalization rate at about 15 percent, that would reflect positively on how well the agency was implementing the RSI. We also reasoned that although threats to internal validity cannot be ruled out as potential alternate explanations for the agency's outcome, the fact that its outcome was so much better than the mean outcome for the control groups in the experiments would enhance the plausibility of the notion that perhaps the adapted RSI really was the cause of the reduced rehospitalization rate.

ADVANCING EVIDENCE-BASED PRACTICE

So far we have focused on the value of these studies to the agency. If a large number of these studies are completed on a particular RSI, however, meta-analyses can be conducted on them to ascertain what service provision characteristics and intervention adaptation approaches are associated with better client outcomes. For example, recall the study on problem-solving tools therapy mentioned above with low-income, African American women at risk for postpartum depression that obtained promising results with only half as many as sessions (4) as were recommended in that intervention's treatment manual. Suppose several additional preexperimental studies of that RSI with only half of the recommended sessions obtained similar results in treating low-income, African American women at risk for postpartum depression. Next, imagine that your clinical caseload includes one or more low-income, African American women at risk for postpartum depression. Suppose further that in your setting, providing more than 4 sessions for these women is not feasible and that the experimental studies that provided the strong research support for that intervention all used at least 8 sessions and had no low-income African American participants. Had the additional preexperimental studies using 4 sessions with that target population not been conducted, you might be predisposed to think that problem-solving tools therapy, despite its strong research support, was not applicable to your setting or client(s). Consequently, you might try some alternative approach—perhaps one with less research support. But if these additional studies were published and found by you, one of the major problems of the evidence-based practice process would be overcome—the gap between the service provision characteristics in the experimental research settings and the realities of non-research practice settings. You could proceed with the problem-solving tools therapy intervention knowing that it was a good choice and had strong research support applicable to your clients and setting.

CONCLUSION

The ever-increasing number of meta-analyses supporting a growing list of RSIs for various target problems of concern to social workers and allied professionals provides the basis for the approach recommended in this appendix. Our reasoning is that because these meta-analyses are reporting enough internally valid experiments to support the effectiveness of RSIs, the value of the preexperimental studies regarding causality is enhanced even though they would not completely rule out the plausibility of threats to internal validity. In addition, the preexperimental studies could describe the service provision conditions under which better client outcomes are attained. In this connection, an important caveat is that our discussion of the value of using within-group effect sizes to enhance the value of preexperimental designs pertains only to situations in which the intervention in question is an RSI—that is, an intervention with an already strong evidence-base of internally valid experimental studies showing that it, and not some threat to internal validity (such as history, passage of time, and so on), is the most plausible explanation for client outcomes. Thus, we do not recommend this approach for interventions that lack such an evidence base. Moreover, we have provided this appendix not with the intent of diminishing the importance of attempting to conduct outcome studies with the most rigorous designs possible. Rather, our intent is to show that when practice realities prevent practitioners or agencies from implementing or evaluating in an ideal manner adaptations of the interventions that have the best research evidence, there are ways to enhance the value of what is feasible for them to do.

Glossary

AB design The simplest single-case evaluation design, which includes one baseline phase (A) and one intervention phase (B). This is a popular design among practitioner/researchers because it involves only one baseline phase and therefore poses the least conflict with service delivery priorities, but it has less control for history than most alternative single-case evaluation designs. See Chapter 13.

ABAB withdrawal/reversal design A single-case evaluation design, which adds a second baseline phase (A) and a second intervention phase (B). This design assumes that if the intervention caused the improvement in the target problem during the first intervention period, then the target problem will reverse toward its original baseline level during the second baseline. When the intervention is reintroduced, the target problem should start improving again. The basic inferential principle here is that if shifts in the trend or level of the target problem occur successively each time the intervention is introduced or withdrawn, then it is not plausible that history explains the change. See Chapter 13.

accidental sampling See *availability sampling*.

acculturation The process in which a group or individual changes after coming into contact with a majority culture, taking on the language, values, attitudes, and lifestyle preferences of the majority culture. See Chapter 6.

acquiescent response set A source of measurement error in which people agree or disagree with most or all statements regardless of their content. See Chapter 8.

agency tracking Asking service providers or other community agencies whether they have been in recent contact with research participants—particularly those who are transient or homeless—whom you are unable to locate and whom you need to contact for further sessions or interviews. See Chapter 6.

alternative treatment design with pretest An experiment that compares the effectiveness of two alternative treatments. Participants are assigned randomly to two experimental groups, each of which receives a different intervention being evaluated, or to a control group that

does not receive any intervention. Each group is tested on the dependent variable before and after the experimental groups receive the intervention. See Chapter 12.

anchor points Pieces of information about the various places you may be able to find particular research participants—particularly transient or homeless participants—for future follow-up sessions or interviews. See Chapter 6.

anonymity An arrangement that makes it impossible for a researcher to link any research data with a given research participant. Distinguished from confidentiality, in which the researcher is able to identify a given person's responses but essentially promises not to do so publicly. See Chapters 4 and 5.

anonymous enrollment A method of recruiting members of hidden and oppressed populations to participate in research studies; it emphasizes techniques that enable prospective participants to feel safer in responding to recruitment efforts and participating in studies. See Chapter 6.

assent form A brief informed consent form that a child can understand and sign before participating in a study and that uses simpler language than consent forms for adults about the features of the study that might affect their decision about whether they want to participate in it. See *consent form* and Chapter 5.

attributes Characteristics of persons or things. See *variables* and Chapter 7.

attrition A threat to the validity of an experiment that occurs when participants drop out of an experiment before it is completed. Also called *experimental mortality*. See Chapter 12.

auditing A strategy for improving the trustworthiness of qualitative research findings in which the researcher leaves a paper trail of field notes, transcripts of interviews, journals, and memos documenting decisions made along the way, and so on. This enables an impartial and qualitatively adept investigator who is not part of the study to scrutinize what was done to determine if efforts to control for biases and reactivity were thorough, if the procedures used were justifiable, and if the interpretations fit the data that were collected. See Chapter 15.

availability sampling A sampling method that selects elements simply because of their ready availability and convenience. Frequently used in social work because it is usually less expensive than other methods and because other methods may not be feasible for a particular type of study or population. See also *accidental sampling, convenience sampling*, and Chapter 11.

available records A source of data for a study in which the information of concern already has been gathered by others. For example, an evaluation of a statewide dropout prevention program may use available school records on dropout rates. See Chapters 7, 8, and 16.

average An ambiguous term that generally suggests "typical" or "normal." *Mean, median*, and *mode* are specific examples of mathematical averages. See Chapter 17.

back-translation A method used when translating instruments from one language into another, which begins with a bilingual person translating the instrument and its instructions to a target language, then having another bilingual person translate from the target language back to the original language (without seeing the original version of the instrument), then comparing the original instrument to the back-translated version, and modifying further any items with discrepancies. See Chapter 6.

baseline The phase of a single-case evaluation design that consists of repeated measures before a new intervention or policy is introduced. See Chapter 13.

bias That quality of a measurement device that tends to result in a misrepresentation of what is being measured in a particular direction. See Chapter 8.

bivariate analysis The analysis of two variables simultaneously to determine the relationship between them. See Chapter 17.

case-control design A design for evaluating interventions that relies on multivariate statistical procedures and that compares groups of cases that have had contrasting outcomes and then collects retrospective data about past differences that might explain the difference in outcomes. See Chapter 12.

case study An examination of a single individual, family, group, organization, community, or society using a full variety of evidence regarding that case. See Chapter 15.

clinical significance The term used for substantive significance or meaningfulness in clinical outcome studies. See *substantive significance* and Chapter 17.

closed-ended questions Unlike in open-ended questions, the respondent is asked to select an answer from among a list provided by the researcher. See Chapter 17.

cluster sample A sample drawn using cluster sampling procedures. See Chapter 11.

cluster sampling A multistage sampling procedure in which natural groups (clusters) are sampled initially, with the members of each selected group being sub-sampled afterward. For example, we might select a sample of U.S. colleges and universities from a directory, get lists of the students at all the selected schools, and then draw samples of students from each. This procedure is discussed in Chapter 11.

coding The process whereby raw data are transformed into a standardized form that is suitable for machine processing and analysis. See Chapters 17 and 18.

coefficient alpha A statistic for depicting the internal consistency reliability of an instrument that represents the average of the correlations between the subscores of all possible subsets of half of the items on the instrument. See Chapter 8.

community forum An approach to needs assessment that involves holding a meeting where concerned members of the community can express their views and interact freely about their needs. See Chapter 10.

compensatory equalization A threat to the validity of an evaluation of an intervention's effectiveness that occurs when practitioners in the comparison, routine treatment condition compensate for the differences in treatment between their group and the experimental group by providing enhanced services that go beyond the routine treatment regimen for their clients, thus potentially blurring the true effects of the tested intervention. See Chapter 12.

compensatory rivalry A threat to the validity of an evaluation of an intervention's effectiveness that occurs when practitioners in the comparison, routine treatment condition decide to compete with the therapists in the other unit. They may start reading more, attending more continuing education workshops, and increasing their therapeutic contact with clients. Their extra efforts might improve their effectiveness and thus blur the true effects of the tested intervention. See Chapter 12.

computer-assisted telephone interviewing (CATI) Interviewing over the phone by reading questions from a computer screen and immediately entering responses into the computer. See Chapter 10.

concept A mental image that symbolizes an idea, an object, an event, or a person. See Chapter 7.

concept mapping A qualitative data analysis method in which relationships among concepts are examined and diagrammed in a graphical format. See Chapter 18.

conceptual equivalence Instruments and observed behaviors having the same meanings across cultures. See Chapter 6.

conceptualization The mental process whereby fuzzy and imprecise notions (concepts) are made more specific and precise. See Chapter 7.

concurrent validity A form of criterion validity examining a measure's correspondence to a criterion that is known concurrently. See Chapter 8.

confidentiality A promise by the researcher not to publicly identify a given research participant's data. Distinguished from *anonymity*, which makes it impossible for a researcher to link any research data with a given research participant. See Chapters 4 and 5.

consent form A form that human subjects sign before participating in a study and that provides full information about the features of the study that might affect their decision about whether they want to participate in it—particularly regarding the procedures of the study, potential harm, and *anonymity* and *confidentiality*. See Chapter 5.

constant comparative method A qualitative data analysis method in which the researcher looks for patterns in inductive observations, develops concepts and working hypotheses based on those patterns, seeks out more cases and conducts more observations, and then compares those observations against the concepts and hypotheses developed from the earlier observations. The selection of new cases is guided by theoretical sampling concepts in which new cases are selected that seem to be similar to those generated by previously detected concepts and hypotheses. Once the researcher perceives that no new insights are being generated from the observation of similar cases, a different type of case is selected, and the same process is repeated. Additional cases similar to this new type of case are selected until no new insights are being generated. This cycle of exhausting similar cases and then seeking a different category of cases is repeated until the researcher believes that seeking further new types of cases will not alter the findings. See also *constant comparisons method* and Chapter 18.

constant comparisons method A grounded theory method in which, as researchers detect patterns in their inductive observations, they develop concepts and working hypotheses based on those patterns, then seek out more cases, conduct more observations, and compare those observations against the concepts and hypotheses developed from the earlier observations. See *constant comparative method* and Chapter 15.

construct validity The degree to which a measure relates to other variables as expected within a system of theoretical relationships and as reflected by the degree of its *convergent validity* and *discriminant validity*. See also *convergent validity*, *discriminant validity*, and Chapter 8.

contemporary positivism A paradigm that emphasizes the pursuit of objectivity in our quest to observe and understand reality. See Chapter 4.

content analysis A research method for studying virtually any form of communication, consisting primarily of coding and tabulating the occurrences of certain forms of content that are being communicated. See Chapter 16.

content validity The degree to which a measure covers the range of meanings included within the concept. See Chapter 8.

contingency question A survey question that is to be asked only of some respondents, depending on their responses to some other question. See Chapter 9.

control group In experimentation, a group of participants who do not receive the intervention being evaluated and who should resemble the experimental group in all other respects. The comparison of the control group and the experimental group at the end of the experiment points to the effect of the tested intervention. See Chapter 12.

control variable A variable that is held constant in an attempt to further clarify the relationship between two other variables. Having discovered a relationship between education and prejudice, for example, we might hold gender constant by examining the relationship between education and prejudice among men only and then among women only. In this example, "gender" would be the control variable. See Chapter 7.

convenience sampling See *availability sampling*.

convergent parallel mixed methods design With this design quantitative and qualitative data are collected concurrently and then analyzed separately. The results of the separate analyses are then compared to see if they confirm each other. See Chapter 3.

convergent validity The degree to which scores on a measure correspond to scores on other measures of the same construct. See also *construct validity*, *discriminant validity*, and Chapter 7.

conversation analysis (CA) A qualitative data analysis approach that aims to uncover the implicit assumptions and structures in social life through an extremely close scrutiny of the way we converse with one another. See Chapter 18.

criterion-related validity The degree to which a measure correlates with some external criterion. For example, the validity of college entrance exams is shown in their ability to predict the college success of students. See *known groups validity*, *concurrent validity*, *predictive validity*, and Chapter 8.

critical social science A paradigm distinguished by its focus on oppression and its commitment to using research procedures to empower oppressed groups. See Chapter 4.

cross-sectional study A study based on observations that represent a single point in time. Contrasted with a *longitudinal study*. See Chapters 4 and 12.

cultural bias A source of measurement or sampling error stemming from researcher ignorance or insensitivity regarding how cultural differences can influence measurement or generalizations made to the entire population when certain minority groups are inadequately represented in the sample. A measurement procedure is culturally biased when it is administered to a minority culture without adjusting for the ways in which the minority culture's unique values, attitudes, lifestyles, or limited opportunities alter the accuracy or meaning of what is really being measured. See Chapters 4, 6, and 8.

cultural competence A researcher's ability to obtain and provide information that is relevant, useful, and valid for minority and oppressed populations. Cultural competence involves knowledge about the minority culture's historical experiences, traditions, values, family systems, socioeconomic issues, and attitudes about social services and social policies; awareness of how one's own attitudes are connected to one's cultural background and how they may differ from the worldview of members of the minority culture; and skills in communicating effectively both verbally and nonverbally with members of the minority culture and establishing rapport with them. See Chapters 4 and 6.

culturally competent research Being aware of and appropriately responding to the ways in which cultural factors and cultural differences should influence what we investigate, how we investigate, and how we interpret our findings—thus resulting in studies that are useful and valid for minority and oppressed populations. See Chapters 4 and 6.

curvilinear relationship A relationship between two variables that changes in nature at different values of the variables. For example, a curvilinear relationship might exist between amount of social work practice experience and practice effectiveness, particularly if we assume that practitioners with a moderate amount of experience are more effective than those with none and at least as effective as those nearing retirement. See Chapter 7.

deductive method The logical model in which specific expectations of hypotheses are developed on the basis of general principles. Starting from the general principle that all deans are meanies, you might anticipate that this one won't let you change courses. That anticipation would be the result of deduction. See also *inductive method* and Chapter 4.

dependent variable That variable that is assumed to depend on or be caused by another (called the independent variable). If you find that income is partly a function of amount of formal education, then income is being treated as a dependent variable. See Chapter 7.

descriptive statistics Statistical computations that describe either the characteristics of a sample or the relationship among variables in a sample. Descriptive statistics merely summarize a set of sample observations, whereas inferential statistics move beyond the description of specific observations to make inferences about the larger population from which the sample observations were drawn. See Chapter 17.

deviant case sampling A type of nonprobability sampling in which cases selected for observation are those that are not thought to fit the regular pattern. For example, the deviant cases might exhibit a much greater or lesser extent of something. See Chapter 11.

diffusion or imitation of treatments A threat to the validity of an evaluation of an intervention's effectiveness that occurs when practitioners who are supposed to provide routine services to a comparison group implement aspects of the experimental group's intervention in ways that tend to diminish the planned differences in the interventions received by the groups being compared. See Chapter 12.

direct behavioral observation A source of data, or type of data collection, in which researchers watch what people do rather than rely on what they say about themselves or what others say about them. See Chapters 7, 8, and 13.

direct observation A way to operationally define variables based on observing actual behavior. See also *direct behavioral observation* and Chapters 7 and 8.

discriminant validity The degree to which scores on an instrument correspond more highly to measures of the same construct than they do to scores on measures of other constructs. See also *convergent validity*, *construct validity*, and Chapter 8.

dismantling studies Experiments designed to test not only whether an intervention is effective but also which components of the intervention may or may not be necessary to achieve its effects. Participants are assigned randomly to groups that receive the entire intervention package, separate components of it, or a control condition and are tested on a dependent variable before and after the intervention components are provided. See Chapter 12.

dispersion The distribution of values around some central value, such as an *average*. The range is a simple example of a measure of dispersion. Thus, we may report that the *mean* age of a group is 37.9, and the *range* is from 12 to 89. See Chapter 17.

disproportionate stratified sampling A sampling method aimed at ensuring that enough cases of certain minority groups are selected to allow for subgroup comparisons within each of those minority groups. See Chapter 11.

double-barreled question Asking for a single answer to a question that really contains multiple questions, such as "Should taxes be raised so welfare funding can be increased?" See Chapter 9.

effect size (ES) A statistic that portrays the strength of association between variables, thus enabling us to compare the effects of different interventions across studies using different types of outcome measures. Effect-size statistics might refer to the difference between the means of two groups divided by the standard deviation. See Chapter 17 and Appendix E.

element That unit in a sample about which information is collected and that provides the basis of analysis. Typically, in survey research, elements are people or certain types of people. See Chapter 11.

emic perspective Trying to adopt the beliefs, attitudes, and other points of view shared by the members of the culture being studied. See Chapter 15.

empirical support Observations that are consistent with what we expect to experience if a theory is correct or an intervention is effective. See Chapters 1 and 2.

ES See *effect size.*

ethnography A qualitative research approach that focuses on providing a detailed and accurate description of a culture from the viewpoint of an insider rather than the way the researcher understands things. See Chapter 15.

etic perspective Maintaining objectivity as an outsider and raising questions about the culture being observed that wouldn't occur to members of that culture. See Chapter 6.

evidence-based practice A process in which the best scientific evidence available pertinent to a particular practice decision is an important part of the information practitioners consider when making that practice decision. See Chapters 1, 2, and Appendix E.

existing statistics analysis Research involving the analysis of statistical information in official government or agency documents and reports. See Chapter 16.

experimental demand characteristics Research participants learn what experimenters want them to say or do, and then cooperate with those "demands" or expectations. See Chapter 12.

experimental design A research method that attempts to provide maximum control for threats to internal validity

by (1) randomly assigning individuals to experimental and control groups, (2) introducing the independent variable (which typically is a program or intervention method) to the experimental group while withholding it from the control group, and (3) comparing the amount of experimental and control group change on the dependent variable. See Chapter 12.

experimental group The group of individuals in an experiment who receive the intervention or program being evaluated. See Chapter 12.

experimental mortality A threat to the validity of an experiment that occurs when participants drop out of an experiment before it is completed. Also called *attrition.* See Chapter 12.

experimenter expectancies Research participants learn what experimenters want them to say or do, and then cooperate with those "demands" or expectations. See Chapter 12.

explanatory sequential mixed methods design This design is thought to appeal to researchers who are more quantitatively oriented. The quantitative data are collected first, followed by qualitative data collection aimed at developing a better understanding of the quantitative data. See Chapter 3.

exploratory sequential mixed methods design With this design the qualitative data are collected first, to provide a basis for formulating the quantitative phase. One aim of this design could be to see if the insights generated from a small sample of people in the qualitative phase can be generalized to a larger, more representative sample of the population in the quantitative phase. Another aim might be to use the qualitative data as a basis for developing a good quantitative data collection instrument. See Chapter 3.

external evaluators Program evaluators who do not work for the agency being evaluated, but instead work for external agencies such as government or regulating agencies, private research consultation firms, or universities. See Chapter 14.

external validity The extent to which we can generalize the findings of a study to settings and populations beyond the study conditions. See Chapter 12.

extraneous variable See *control variable.*

face validity That quality of an indicator that makes it seem a reasonable measure of some variable. That the frequency of church attendance is some indication of a person's religiosity seems to make sense without a lot of explanation—it has face validity. See Chapter 8.

feminist paradigm A research paradigm, like the critical social science paradigm, distinguished by its commitment to using research procedures to address issues of concern to women and to empower women. See Chapter 4.

field tracking Talking with people on the streets about where to find research participants—particularly those who are homeless—to secure their participation in future sessions or interviews. See Chapter 6.

focus groups An approach to needs assessment in which a small group of people is brought together to engage in a guided discussion of a specified topic. See Chapter 15.

formative evaluation A type of program evaluation not concerned with testing the success of a program, but focusing instead on obtaining information that is helpful in planning the program and in improving its implementation and performance. See Chapter 14.

frequencies The numbers of cases in each category of a variable. See Chapter 17.

frequency distribution A description of the number of times the various attributes of a variable are observed in a sample. See Chapter 17.

gender bias The unwarranted generalization of research findings to the population as a whole when one gender is not adequately represented in the research sample. See Chapter 11.

generalizability That quality of a research finding that justifies the inference that it represents something more than the specific observations on which it was based. See Chapter 15.

generalization of effects A rival explanation in a multiple-baseline design that occurs when an intervention that is intended to apply to only one behavior or setting affects other behaviors or settings that are still in baseline. See Chapter 13.

generalize To infer that the findings of a particular study represent causal processes or apply to settings or populations beyond the study conditions. See Chapter 12.

grounded theory A qualitative research approach that begins with observations and looks for patterns, themes, or common categories. See Chapters 15 and 18.

hermeneutics A qualitative research approach in which the researcher tries to mentally take on the circumstances, views, and feelings of those being studied to interpret their actions appropriately. See Chapter 16.

historical and comparative research A research method that traces the development of social forms over time and compares those developmental processes across cultures, seeking to discover common patterns that recur in different times and places. See Chapter 16.

history A threat to internal validity referring to extraneous events that coincide in time with the manipulation of the independent variable. See Chapter 12.

hypothesis A tentative and testable prediction about how changes in one thing are expected to explain and be accompanied by changes in something else. It's a statement of something that ought to be observed in the real world if a theory is correct. See Chapter 7.

independent variable A variable whose values are not problematical in an analysis but are taken as simply given. An independent variable is presumed to cause or explain a dependent variable. If we discover that religiosity is partly a function of gender—women are more religious than men—"gender" is the independent variable and "religiosity" is the dependent variable. Note that any given variable might be treated as independent in one part of an analysis and dependent in another part of the analysis. "Religiosity" might become an independent variable in the explanation of crime. See Chapter 7.

inductive method The logical model in which general principles are developed from specific observations. See also *deductive method* and Chapter 4.

inferential statistics The body of statistical computations that is relevant to making inferences from findings based on sample observations to some larger population. See also *descriptive statistics* and Chapter 17.

informal conversational interview An unplanned and unanticipated interaction between an interviewer and a respondent that occurs naturally during the course of fieldwork observation. It is the most open-ended form of interviewing with the interviewee perhaps not thinking of the interaction as an interview. Flexibility to pursue relevant information in whatever direction seems appropriate is emphasized, and questions should be generated naturally and spontaneously from what is observed at a particular point in a particular setting or from what individuals in that setting happen to say. See Chapter 9.

in-house evaluators Program evaluators who work for the agency being evaluated and who therefore may be under pressure to produce biased studies or results that portray the agency favorably. See Chapter 14.

institutional review board (IRB) An independent panel of professionals that is required to approve the ethics of research involving human subjects. See Chapters 4 and 5.

intensity sampling A qualitative sampling technique like deviant case sampling, in which cases are selected that are more or less intense than usual, but not so unusual that they would be called deviant. See Chapter 11.

internal consistency reliability A practical and commonly used approach to assessing reliability that examines the homogeneity of a measurement instrument by dividing the instrument into equivalent halves and then calculating the correlation of the scores of the two halves. See Chapter 8.

internal validity The degree to which an effect observed in an experiment was actually produced by the experimental stimulus and was not the result of other factors. See *external validity* and Chapter 12.

interobserver reliability See *interrater reliability*.

interpretivism An approach to social research that focuses on gaining an empathic understanding of how people feel, seeking to interpret individuals' everyday experiences, deeper meanings and feelings, and idiosyncratic reasons for their behaviors. See Chapter 4.

interrater reliability The extent of consistency among different observers in their judgments, as reflected in the percentage of agreement or degree of correlation in their independent ratings. See Chapter 8.

interval level of measurement A level of measurement that describes a variable whose attributes are rank-ordered and have equal distances between adjacent attributes. See Chapter 17.

intervention fidelity The degree to which an intervention being evaluated is actually delivered to clients as intended. See Chapter 12.

intervention mixed methods design A qualitative inquiry is merged with a quantitative evaluation of an intervention's outcome to get a better handle on the meaning of the results. See Chapter 3.

interview A data collection encounter in which one person (an interviewer) asks questions of another (a respondent). Interviews may be conducted face-to-face or by telephone. See Chapters 9, 10, and 15.

interview guide approach A semistructured form of qualitative interviewing that lists in outline form the topics and issues that the interviewer should cover in the interview, but allows the interviewer to adapt the sequencing and wording of questions to each particular interview. See Chapter 9.

inverse relationship See *negative relationship*.

IRB See *institutional review board*.

judgmental sample A type of nonprobability sample in which we select the units to be observed on the basis of our own judgment about which ones will be the most useful or representative. Another name for this is *purposive sample*. See Chapter 11.

key informants An approach to needs assessment that is based on obtaining expert opinions from individuals who are presumed to have special knowledge about the target population's problems and needs, as well as about current gaps in service delivery to that population. See Chapters 6 and 10.

known groups validity A form of *criterion validity* that pertains to the degree to which an instrument accurately differentiates between groups that are known to differ in respect to the variable being measured. See Chapter 8.

latent content As used in connection with content analysis, the underlying meaning of communications as distinguished from their *manifest content*. See Chapter 16.

level of significance In the context of tests of statistical significance, the degree of likelihood that an observed, empirical relationship could be attributable to sampling error. A relationship is significant at the .05 level if the likelihood of its being only a function of sampling error is no greater than 5 out of 100. See Chapter 17.

life history (or life story or oral history interviews) A qualitative research method in which researchers ask open-ended questions to discover how the participants in a study understand the significant events and meanings in their own lives. See Chapter 15.

life story See *life history*.

Likert scale A type of composite measure developed by Rensis Likert in an attempt to improve the levels of measurement in social research through the use of standardized response categories in survey questionnaires. Likert items use such response categories as strongly agree, agree, disagree, and strongly disagree. Such items may be used in the construction of true Likert scales and also be used in the construction of other types of composite measures. See Chapter 9.

linguistic equivalence (or translation equivalence) The result of a successful translation and back-translation of an instrument originally developed for the majority language, but which will be used with research participants who don't speak the majority language. See Chapter 6.

logic model A graphic portrayal that depicts the essential components of a program, shows how those components are linked to short-term process objectives, specifies measurable indicators of success in achieving short-term objectives, conveys how those short-term objectives lead to long-term program outcomes, and identifies measurable indicators of success in achieving long-term outcomes.

longitudinal study A study design that involves the collection of data at different points in time, as contrasted with a *cross-sectional study*. See Chapter 4.

mail tracking A method of locating and contacting research participants by mailing reminder notices about impending interviews or about the need to call in to update any changes in how they can be contacted. Mail tracking also might include sending birthday cards, holiday greetings, and certificates of appreciation for participation. See Chapter 6.

managed care A variety of arrangements that try to control the costs of health and human services by having a large organization that pays for the cost of services for many people contract with care providers who agree to provide that care at reduced costs. Managed care is thought to have contributed to the growth of program evaluation. See Chapter 14.

manifest content In connection with content analysis, the concrete terms contained in a communication, as distinguished from *latent content*. See Chapter 16.

maturation A threat to internal validity referring to aging effects or developmental changes that influence the dependent variable. See Chapter 12.

mean An average, computed by summing the values of several observations and dividing by the number of observations. See Chapter 17.

measurement equivalence The degree to which instruments or observed behaviors have the same meaning across cultures, relate to referent theoretical constructs in the same way across cultures, and have the same causal linkages across cultures. See Chapter 6.

median An average that represents the value of the "middle" case in a rank-ordered set of observations. If the ages of five men are 16, 17, 20, 54, and 88, then the median would be 20 (the mean would be 39). See Chapter 17.

mediating variable (intervening variable) The mechanism by which an independent variable affects a dependent variable. See Chapter 7.

member checking A strategy for improving the trustworthiness of qualitative research findings in which researchers ask the participants in their research to confirm or disconfirm the accuracy of the research observations and interpretations. Do the reported observations and interpretations ring true to the participants? See Chapter 15.

memoing A qualitative data analysis technique used at several stages of data processing to capture code meanings, theoretical ideas, preliminary conclusions, and other thoughts that will be useful during analysis. See Chapter 18.

meta-analysis A type of systematic review that pools the statistical results across studies of particular interventions and generates conclusions about which interventions have the strongest impacts on treatment outcome. See Chapter 2.

metric equivalence (also known as psychometric equivalence or scalar equivalence) Scores on a measure being comparable across cultures. See Chapter 6.

mixed methods research A stand-alone research design in which a single study not only collects both qualitative and quantitative data, but also integrates both sources of data at one or more stages of the research process so as to improve the understanding of the phenomenon being investigated. See Chapter 3.

mode A type of average that represents the most frequently observed value or attribute. See Chapter 17.

moderating variable A variable that influences the strength or direction of a relationship between independent and dependent variables. See Chapter 7.

multiphase mixed methods design This design is distinguished by the use of several mixed methods projects that are implemented in multiple phases over time in a longitudinal study in which the multiple projects focus on a common objective. See Chapter 3.

multiple-baseline design A type of single-case evaluation design that attempts to control for extraneous variables by having more than one baseline and intervention phase. See Chapter 13.

multiple-component designs Single-case evaluation designs that attempt to determine which parts of an intervention package really account for the change in the target problem. See Chapter 13.

multivariate analysis The analysis of the simultaneous relationships among several variables. Examining simultaneously the effects of age, sex, and social class on religiosity would be an example of multivariate analysis. See Chapter 17.

needs assessment Systematically researching diagnostic questions for program planning purposes. For example, community residents might be surveyed to assess their need for new child care services. See Chapters 10 and 14.

negative case analysis A strategy for improving the trustworthiness of qualitative research findings in which researchers show they have searched thoroughly for disconfirming evidence—looking for deviant cases that do not fit the researcher's interpretations. See Chapter 15.

negative, or inverse, relationship A relationship between two variables in which one variable increases in value as the other variable decreases. For example, we might expect to find a negative relationship between the level of utilization of community-based aftercare services and rehospitalization rates. See Chapter 7.

nominal definition A dictionary-like definition that uses a set of words to help us understand what a term means but that does not tell us what indicators to use in observing the term in a research study. See Chapter 7.

nominal level of measurement A level of measurement that describes a variable in terms of the number of cases in each category of that variable. See Chapter 17.

nonequivalent comparison group design A quasi-experimental design in which the researcher finds two existing groups that appear to be similar and measures change on a dependent variable before and after an intervention is introduced to one of the groups. See Chapter 12.

nonprobability sampling Selecting a sample with procedures that do not involve random selection. Examples include availability, judgmental (purposive), quota, and snowball sampling. See Chapter 11.

non-response bias A threat to the representativeness of survey findings, the seriousness of which depends upon the extent to which survey respondents differ from non-respondents in important ways relevant to the research question. See Chapter 10.

novelty and disruption effects A form of research reactivity in experiments in which the sense of excitement, energy, and enthusiasm among recipients of an evaluated intervention—and not the intervention itself—causes the desired change in their behavior. See Chapter 12.

observations What we experience in the real world that helps us build a theory or verify whether that theory is correct when testing hypotheses. See Chapter 2.

obtrusive observation This occurs when the participant is keenly aware of being observed and thus may be predisposed to behave in socially desirable ways and in ways that meet experimenter expectancies. See Chapters 12 and 16.

odds ratio An effect size statistic that shows how much more or less likely a certain dependent variable outcome is for the categories of the independent variable.

one-group pretest–posttest design A preexperimental design, with low internal validity, that assesses a dependent variable before and after an intervention or another type of stimulus is introduced but does not attempt to control for alternative explanations of any changes in scores that are observed. See Chapter 12.

one-shot case study A preexperimental research design, with low internal validity, that simply measures a single group of participants on a dependent variable at one point in time after they have been exposed to an intervention or another type of stimulus. See Chapter 12.

online surveys Surveys conducted via the Internet—either by e-mail or through a website. See Chapter 10.

open coding A qualitative data processing method in which, instead of starting out with a list of code categories derived from theory, one develops code categories through close examination of qualitative data. During open coding the data are broken down into discrete parts, closely examined, and compared for similarities and differences; questions are then asked about the phenomena

as reflected in the data. Through this process, one's own and others' assumptions about phenomena are questioned or explored, leading to new discoveries. See Chapter 18.

open-ended questions Unlike closed-ended questions, respondents are asked to provide their own answer without selecting from among a list of possible responses provided by the researcher. See Chapter 9.

operational definition The concrete and specific definition of something in terms of the operations by which observations are to be categorized. See Chapter 7.

oral history interviews See *life history*.

ordinal level of measurement A level of measurement describing a variable whose attributes may be rank-ordered along some dimension. An example would be socioeconomic status as composed of the attributes "high," "medium," and "low." See also *nominal measure, interval measure, ratio measure,* and Chapter 17.

paradigm A set of philosophical assumptions about the nature of reality—a fundamental model or scheme that organizes our view of some things. See Chapters 4 and 15.

parallel-forms reliability Consistency of measurement between two equivalent measurement instruments. See Chapter 8.

parameter A summary statistic describing a given variable in a population, such as the mean income of all families in a city or the age distribution of the city's population. See Chapter 11.

participatory action research A qualitative research paradigm in which the researcher's function is to serve as a resource to those being studied—typically, disadvantaged groups—as an opportunity for them to act effectively in their own interest. The disadvantaged participants define their problems, define the remedies desired, and take the lead in designing the research that will help them realize their aims. See Chapter 15.

passage of time A threat to internal validity referring to changes in a dependent variable that occur naturally as time passes and not because of the independent variable. See Chapter 12.

Pearson product-moment correlation (*r*) A parametric measure of association, ranging from -1.0 to $+1.0$, used when both the independent and dependent variables are at the *interval or ratio level* of measurement. See Chapter 17.

peer debriefing and support A strategy for improving the trustworthiness of qualitative research findings in which teams of investigators meet regularly to give each other feedback, emotional support, alternative perspectives, and new ideas about how they are collecting data or about problems and meanings in the data already collected. See Chapter 15.

phone tracking A method of locating and contacting research participants—particularly those who are transient or homeless—to secure their participation in future sessions or interviews. This method involves repeated telephoning of *anchor points* in advance to schedule an interview and providing participants a toll-free number where they can leave messages about appointment changes or changes in how to locate them, incentives for leaving such messages, and a card that lists appointment times and the research project's address and telephone number. See Chapter 6.

placebo control group design An experimental design that controls for placebo effects by randomly assigning subjects to an experimental group and two control groups and exposing one of the control groups to a stimulus that is designed to resemble the special attention received by subjects in the experimental group. See *placebo effects* and Chapter 12.

placebo effects Changes in a dependent variable that are caused by the power of suggestion among participants in an experimental group that they are receiving something special that is expected to help them. These changes would not occur if they received the experimental intervention without that awareness. See Chapter 12.

plagiarism Presenting someone else's words or thoughts as though they were your own, constituting intellectual theft. See Appendix C.

population The group or collection that a researcher is interested in generalizing about. More formally, it is the theoretically specified aggregation of study elements. See Chapter 11.

positive relationship A relationship between two variables in which one variable increases in value as the other variable also increases in value (or one decreases as the other decreases). For example, we might expect to find a positive relationship between rate of unemployment and extent of homelessness. See Chapter 7.

positivism A paradigm that emphasizes the pursuit of objectivity in our quest to observe and understand reality. See Chapter 4.

postmodernism An extreme form of *social constructivism* that rejects the notion of an objective social reality. See Chapter 4.

posttest-only control group design A variation of the classical experimental design that avoids the possible testing effects associated with pretesting by testing only after the experimental group receives the intervention, based on the assumption that the process of random assignment provides for equivalence between the experimental and control groups on the dependent variable before the exposure to the intervention. See also *pretest–posttest control group design*. See Chapter 12.

posttest-only design with nonequivalent groups A preexperimental design that involves two groups that may not be comparable, in which the dependent variable is assessed after the independent variable is introduced for one of the groups. See Chapter 12.

practice models Guides to help us organize our views about social work practice that may reflect a synthesis of existing theories. See Chapter 4.

predictive validity A form of *criterion validity* involving a measure's ability to predict a criterion that will occur in the future. See Chapter 7.

preexperimental designs Pilot study designs for evaluating the effectiveness of interventions that do not control for threats to internal validity. See Chapter 12.

pretesting Testing out a scale or questionnaire in a dry run to see if the target population will understand it and not find it too unwieldy and to identify any needed modifications. See Chapters 6 and 9.

pretest–posttest control group design The classical experimental design in which participants are assigned randomly to an experimental group that receives an intervention being evaluated or to a control group that does not receive it. Each group is tested on the dependent variable before and after the experimental group receives the intervention. See Chapter 12.

probability sampling The general term for sampling performed in accord with probability theory, typically involving some random-selection mechanism. See Chapter 11.

probe A technique employed in interviewing to solicit a more complete answer to a question, this nondirective phrase or question is used to encourage a respondent to elaborate on an answer. Examples include "Anything more?" and "How is that?" See Chapters 10 and 15.

prolonged engagement A strategy for improving the trustworthiness of qualitative research findings that attempts to reduce the impact of reactivity and respondent bias by forming a long and trusting relationship with respondents and by conducting lengthy interviews or a series of follow-up interviews with the same respondent, thus increasing the likelihood that the respondent ultimately will disclose socially undesirable truths and improving the researcher's ability to detect distortion. See Chapter 15.

pseudoscience Fake science about an area of inquiry or practice that has the surface appearance of being scientific, but upon careful inspection can be seen to violate one or more principles of the scientific method or to contain fallacies against which the scientific method attempts to guard. See Chapter 1.

psychometric equivalence See *metric equivalence* and Chapter 6.

purposive sample See *judgmental sample* and Chapters 6 and 11.

purposive sampling Selecting a sample of observations that the researcher believes will yield the most comprehensive understanding of the subject of study, based on the researcher's intuitive feel for the subject, which comes from extended observation and reflection. See Chapter 11.

qualitative analysis The nonnumerical examination and interpretation of observations for the purpose of discovering underlying meanings and patterns of relationships in qualitative research. See Chapters 15 and 18.

qualitative interview An interaction between an interviewer and a respondent in which the interviewer usually has a general plan of inquiry but not a specific set of questions that must be asked in particular words and in a particular order. Ideally, the respondent does most of the talking. See Chapters 9 and 15.

qualitative research methods Researcher methods that emphasize depth of understanding and the deeper meanings of human experience and that aim to generate theoretically richer, albeit more tentative, observations. Commonly used qualitative methods include participant observation, direct observation, and unstructured or intensive interviewing. See Chapters 3, 15 and 18.

quantitative analysis The numerical representation and manipulation of observations for the purpose of describing and explaining the phenomena that those observations reflect. See Chapter 17.

quantitative research methods Research methods that emphasize precise, objective, and generalizable findings. See Chapter 3.

quasi-experimental designs Designs that attempt to control for threats to internal validity and thus permit causal inferences but that are distinguished from true experiments primarily by the lack of random assignment of participants. See Chapter 12.

questionnaire A document that contains questions and other types of items that are designed to solicit information appropriate to analysis. Questionnaires are used primarily in survey research and also in experiments, field research, and other modes of observation. See Chapter 9.

quota sampling A type of nonprobability sample in which units are selected into the sample on the basis of prespecified characteristics, so that the total sample will have the same distribution of characteristics as are assumed to exist in the population being studied. See Chapter 11.

random error A measurement error that has no consistent pattern of effects and that reduces the reliability of measurement. For example, asking questions that respondents do not understand will yield inconsistent (random) answers. See Chapter 8.

random sampling A precise, scientific procedure for selecting from research populations elements for a sample that guarantees an equal probability of selection of each element when substantial samples are selected from large populations. See Chapter 11.

random selection A probability sampling procedure in which each element has an equal chance of selection independent of any other event in the selection process. See Chapter 11.

randomization A technique for assigning experimental participants to experimental and control groups—randomly. See Chapter 12.

range A measure of dispersion that is composed of the highest and lowest values of a variable in some set of observations. See Chapter 17.

rates under treatment An approach to needs assessment based on the number and characteristics of clients already using a service in a similar community. See Chapter 10.

ratio level of measurement A level of measurement that describes variables (such as number of children) whose attributes have all the qualities of interval measures and also are based on a true zero point. See Chapter 17.

reactivity A process in which change in a dependent variable is induced by research procedures. See Chapters 12 and 13.

recall bias A common limitation in case-control designs that occurs when a person's current recollections of the quality and value of past experiences are influenced either positively or negatively by knowing whether things did or did not work out for them later in life. See Chapter 7.

relationship Variables changing together in a consistent, predictable fashion.

reliability That quality of measurement that suggests that the same data would have been collected each time in repeated observations of the same phenomenon. In the context of a survey, we would expect that the question

"Did you attend church last week?" would have higher reliability than the question "About how many times have you attended church in your life?" This is not to be confused with *validity*. See Chapter 8.

reminder calls Telephoning research participants to remind them of their scheduled treatment or assessment sessions in a study. See Chapter 6.

replication The duplication of a study to expose or reduce error or the reintroduction or withdrawal of an intervention to increase the internal validity of a quasi-experiment or single-case design evaluation. See Chapters 2 and 13.

representativeness That quality of a sample of having the same distribution of characteristics as the population from which it was selected. By implication, descriptions and explanations derived from an analysis of the sample may be assumed to represent similar ones in the population. Representativeness is enhanced by *probability sampling* and provides for generalizability and the use of inferential statistics. See Chapter 11.

research reactivity Changes in outcome data that are caused by researchers or research procedures rather than the independent variable. See Chapter 12.

resentful demoralization A threat to the validity of an evaluation of an intervention's effectiveness that occurs when practitioners or clients in the comparison, routine treatment condition become resentful and demoralized because they did not receive the special training or the special treatment. Consequently, their confidence or motivation may decline and may explain their inferior performance on outcome measures. See Chapter 12.

respondent A person who provides data for analysis by responding to a survey questionnaire. See Chapter 10.

response rate The number of persons who participate in a survey divided by the number selected in the sample, in the form of a percentage. This is also called the completion rate or, in self-administered surveys, the return rate—the percentage of questionnaires sent out that are returned. See Chapter 10.

retrospective baseline A type of pre-intervention single-case evaluation design phase that consists of chronologically ordered data points that are reconstructed from past data. See Chapter 13.

risk ratio An effect size statistic regarding unsuccessful outcomes that is calculated by dividing the proportion of unsuccessful outcomes in one group by the risk of unsuccessful outcomes in the other group.

sampling error The degree of error to be expected for a given sample design, as estimated according to probability theory. See Chapter 11.

sampling frame That list or quasi-list of units that make up a population from which a sample is selected. If the sample is to be representative of the population, then it's essential that the sampling frame include all (or nearly all) members of the population. See Chapter 11.

sampling interval The standard distance between elements selected from a population for a sample. See Chapter 11.

sampling ratio The proportion of elements in the population that are selected to be in a sample. See Chapter 11.

sampling unit That element or set of elements considered for selection in some stage of sampling. See Chapter 11.

scalar equivalence See *metric equivalence* and Chapter 6.

scale A type of composite measure composed of several items that have a logical or empirical structure among them. See Chapter 9.

scientific method An approach to inquiry that attempts to safeguard against errors commonly made in casual human inquiry. Chief features include viewing all knowledge as provisional and subject to refutation, searching for evidence based on systematic and comprehensive observation, pursuing objectivity in observation, and replication. See Chapter 1.

secondary analysis A form of research in which the data collected and processed by one researcher are reanalyzed—often for a different purpose—by another. See Chapter 16.

selection bias A threat to internal validity referring to the assignment of research participants to groups in a way that does not maximize their comparability regarding the dependent variable. See Chapter 12.

self-mailing questionnaire A mailed questionnaire that requires no return envelope: When the questionnaire is folded a particular way, the return address appears on the outside. The respondent therefore doesn't have to worry about losing the envelope. See Chapter 10.

self-report scales A source of data in which all research participants respond in writing to the same list of written questions or statements that has been devised to measure a particular construct. For example, a self-report scale to measure marital satisfaction might ask how often one is annoyed with one's spouse, is proud of the spouse, has fun with the spouse, and so on. See Chapters 7 and 8.

self-reports A way to operationally define variables according to what people say about their own thoughts, views, or behaviors. See Chapters 7 and 8.

semiotics The science of symbols and meanings, commonly associated with content analysis and based on language, which examines the agreements we have about the meanings associated with particular signs. See Chapter 18.

sensitivity The ability of an instrument to detect subtle differences. See Chapter 8.

significance level The probability level that is selected in advance to serve as a cut-off point to separate findings that will and will not be attributed to chance. Findings at or below the selected probability level are deemed to be statistically significant. See Chapter 17.

simple random sampling A type of probability sampling in which the units that make up a population are assigned numbers. A set of random numbers is then generated, and the units having those numbers are included in the sample. Although probability theory and the calculations it provides assume this basic sampling method, it's seldom used for practical reasons. An equivalent alternative is *systematic sampling* (with a random start). See Chapter 11.

single-case evaluation design A time-series design used to evaluate the impact of an intervention or a policy change on individual cases or systems. See Chapter 13.

snowball sample A nonprobability sample generated by asking each person interviewed to suggest additional people for interviewing. See Chapters 6 and 11.

social constructivism A paradigm that emphasizes multiple subjective realities and the impossibility of being completely objective. See Chapters 4 and 15.

social desirability bias A source of systematic measurement error involving the tendency of people to say or do things that will make them or their reference group look good. See Chapter 8.

social indicators An approach to needs assessment based on aggregated statistics that reflect conditions of an entire population. See Chapter 10.

social justice mixed methods design. This design is distinguished by the use of various methods that are based on a social justice theory and is aimed at collecting data that will yield a call for action to improve the plight of vulnerable, marginalized, or oppressed groups. See Chapter 3.

Solomon four-group design An experimental design that assesses testing effects by randomly assigning participants to four groups, introducing the intervention being evaluated to two of them, conducting both pretesting and posttesting on one group that receives the intervention and one group that does not, and conducting posttesting only on the other two groups. See Chapter 12.

spurious relationship A relationship between two *variables* that are no longer related once a third variable is controlled. See Chapter 7.

standard deviation A descriptive statistic that portrays the dispersion of values around the mean. It's the square root of the averaged squared differences between each value and the mean. See Chapter 17.

standardized open-ended interviews The most highly structured form of qualitative interviews. These are conducted in a consistent, thorough manner. Questions are written out in advance exactly the way they are to be asked in the interview, reducing the chances that variations in responses are being caused by changes in the way interviews are conducted. See Chapter 9.

static-group comparison design A cross-sectional design for comparing different groups on a dependent variable at one point in time. The validity of this design will be influenced by the extent to which it contains multivariate controls for alternative explanations for differences among the groups. See Chapter 12.

statistical regression A threat to internal validity referring to the tendency for extreme scores at pretest to become less extreme at posttest. See Chapter 12.

statistical significance A general term for the unlikelihood that relationships observed in a sample could be attributed to sampling error alone. See *tests of statistical significance* and Chapter 17.

stratification The grouping of the units that make up a population into homogeneous groups (or strata) before sampling. This procedure, which may be used in conjunction with simple random, systematic, or cluster sampling, improves the representativeness of a sample, at least in terms of the stratification variables. See Chapter 11.

stratified sampling A probability sampling procedure that uses stratification to ensure that appropriate numbers of elements are drawn from homogeneous subsets of the target population. See *stratification* and Chapter 11.

study population The aggregation of elements from which the sample is actually selected. See Chapter 11.

substantive significance (practical significance) The importance, or meaningfulness, of a finding from a practical standpoint. See Chapter 17.

summative evaluation A type of program evaluation focusing on the ultimate success of a program and decisions about whether it should be continued or chosen from among alternative options. See Chapter 14.

switching replications A procedure to assess whether posttest differences in a nonequivalent comparison groups design are due to a selection bias.

systematic error An error in measurement with a consistent pattern of effects. For example, when child welfare workers ask abusive parents whether they have been abusing their children, they may get biased answers that are consistently untrue because parents do not want to admit to abusive behavior. Contrast this to *random error*, which has no consistent pattern of effects. See Chapter 8.

systematic review A report of a comprehensive search for unpublished as well as published studies that address a particular research question. See Chapter 2.

systematic sampling A type of probability sampling in which every *k*th unit in a list is selected for inclusion in the sample—for example, every 25th student in the college directory of students. We compute *k* by dividing the size of the population by the desired sample size; the result is called the *sampling interval*. Within certain constraints, systematic sampling is a functional equivalent of *simple random sampling* and usually easier to do. Typically, the first unit is selected at random. See Chapter 11.

test–retest reliability Consistency, or stability, of measurement over time. See Chapter 8.

tests of statistical significance A class of statistical computations that indicate the likelihood that the relationship observed between variables in a sample can be attributed to sampling error only. See *inferential statistics* and Chapter 17.

theoretical sampling A sampling method associated with the grounded theory paradigm of qualitative research, in which new cases are selected that seem to be similar to those that generated previously detected concepts and hypotheses, but once the researcher perceives that no new insights are being generated from observing similar cases, a different type of case is selected, and the same process is repeated until the observation of different types of cases seems to be generating no new insights. See Chapter 11.

theory A systematic set of interrelated statements intended to explain some aspect of social life or enrich our sense of how people conduct and find meaning in their daily lives. See Chapter 4.

time-series designs A set of quasi-experimental designs in which multiple observations of a dependent variable are conducted before and after an intervention is introduced. See Chapter 12.

translation equivalence See *linguistic equivalence, translation validity*, and Chapter 6.

translation validity Successful translation of a measure into the language of respondents who are not fluent in the majority language, thus attaining *linguistic equivalence*. See Chapter 6.

trend studies Longitudinal studies that monitor a given characteristic of some population over time. See Chapter 4.

triangulation The use of more than one imperfect data collection alternative in which each option is vulnerable to different potential sources of error. For example, instead of relying exclusively on a client's self-report of how often a particular target behavior occurred during a specified period, a significant other (teacher, cottage parent, and so on) is asked to monitor the behavior as well. See Chapters 8 and 15.

univariate analysis The analysis of a single variable for purposes of description. Frequency distributions, averages, and measures of dispersion would be examples of univariate analysis, as distinguished from *bivariate* and *multivariate analysis*. See Chapter 17.

unobtrusive observation Unlike obtrusive observation, the participant does not notice the observation and is therefore less influenced to behave in socially desirable ways and ways that meet experimenter expectancies. See Chapters 12 and 16.

validity The degree to which a measure accurately reflects the concept that it's intended to measure. For example, your IQ would seem a more valid measure of your intelligence than would the number of hours you spend in the library. See Chapter 8.

variables Logical groupings of attributes. The variable "gender" contains the attributes "male" and "female." See Chapter 7.

verstehen The German word meaning "understanding," used in qualitative research in connection to hermeneutics, in which the researcher tries to take on, mentally, the circumstances, views, and feelings of those being studied to interpret their actions appropriately. See Chapter 16.

visual significance A pattern in single-case design graphs in which shifts in the level or trend of the target problem tend to coincide only with shifts in the independent variable. See Chapter 13.

weighting A procedure employed in connection with sampling whereby units selected with unequal probabilities are assigned weights in such a manner as to make the sample statistically representative of the population from which it was selected. See Chapter 11.

withdrawal/reversal design A type of single-case evaluation design that adds a second baseline phase and a second intervention phase after the conclusion of the first baseline and intervention phases. See Chapter 13.

Bibliography

Adler, Patricia A., and Peter Adler. 1994. "Observational Techniques," pp. 377–392 in Norman K. Denzin and Yvonna S. Lincoln (eds.), *Handbook of Qualitative Research*. Thousand Oaks, CA: Sage.

Allen, James, and James A. Walsh. 2000. "A Construct-Based Approach to Equivalence: Methodologies for Cross-Cultural/Multicultural Personality Assessment Research," pp. 63–85 in Richard Dana (ed.), *Handbook of Cross-Cultural Personality Assessment*. Mahwah, NJ: Erlbaum.

Altheide, David L., and John M. Johnson. 1994. "Criteria for Assessing Interpretive Validity in Qualitative Research," pp. 485–499 in Norman K. Denzin and Yvonna S. Lincoln (eds.), *Handbook of Qualitative Research*. Thousand Oaks, CA: Sage.

Alvidrez, Jennifer, Francisca Azocar, and Jeanne Miranda. 1996. "Demystifying the Concept of Ethnicity for Psychotherapy Researchers," *Journal of Consulting and Clinical Psychology*, 64(5), 903–908.

Aneshenshel, Carol S., Rosina M. Becerra, Eve P. Fiedler, and Roberleigh A. Schuler. 1989. "Participation of Mexican American Female Adolescents in a Longitudinal Panel Survey," *Public Opinion Quarterly*, 53 (Winter), 548–562.

Areán, Patricia A., and Dolores Gallagher-Thompson. 1996. "Issues and Recommendations for the Recruitment and Retention of Older Ethnic Minority Adults into Clinical Research," *Journal of Consulting and Clinical Psychology*, 64(5), 875–880.

Baxter, Ellen, and Kim Hopper. 1982. "The New Mendicancy: Homeless in New York City," *American Journal of Orthopsychiatry*, 52(3), 393–407.

Berg, Bruce. 1998. *Qualitative Research Methods for the Social Sciences*, 3rd ed. Boston: Allyn & Bacon.

Black, Donald. 1970. "Production of Crime Rates," *American Sociological Review*, 35 (August), 733–748.

Bloom, Martin, Joel Fischer, and John G. Orme. 2009. *Evaluating Practice: Guidelines for the Accountable Professional*, 6th ed. Boston: Allyn & Bacon.

Buckingham, R., S. Lack, L. Mount, J. MacLean, and J. Collins. 1976. "Living with the Dying," *Canadian Medical Association Journal*, 115, 1211–1215.

Burnette, Denise. 1998. "Conceptual and Methodological Considerations in Research with Non-White Ethnic Elders," pp. 71–91 in Miriam Potocky and Antoinette Y. Rodgers-Farmer (eds.), *Social Work Research with Minority and Oppressed Populations: Methodological Issues and Innovations*. New York: Haworth Press.

Campbell, Patricia B. 1983. "The Impact of Societal Biases on Research Methods," pp. 197–213 in Barbara L. Richardson and Jeana Wirtenberg (eds.), *Sex Role Research*. New York: Praeger.

Carmines, Edward G., and Richard A. Zeller. 1979. *Reliability and Validity Assessment*. Beverly Hills, CA: Sage.

Cauce, Ana Mari, Nora Coronado, and Jennifer Watson. 1998. "Conceptual, Methodological, and Statistical Issues in Culturally Competent Research," pp. 305–329 in Mario Hernandez and Mareasa R. Isaacs (eds.), *Promoting Cultural Competence in Children's Mental Health Services*. Baltimore, MD: Paul H. Brookes, 1998.

Census Bureau. See U.S. Bureau of the Census.

Cohen, Jacob. 1988. *Statistical Power Analysis for the Behavioral Sciences*, 2nd ed. New York: Lawrence Erlbaum Associates.

Coleman, James. 1966. *Equality of Educational Opportunity*. Washington, DC: U.S. Government Printing Office.

Corcoran, Kevin, and Wallace J. Gingrich. 1994. "Practice Evaluation in the Context of Managed Care: Case-Recording Methods for Quality Assurance Reviews," *Research on Social Work Practice*, 4(3), 326–337.

Coulton, Claudia, Shanta Pandey, and Julia Chow. 1990. "Concentration of Poverty and the Changing Ecology of Low-Income, Urban Neighborhoods: An Analysis of the Cleveland Area," *Social Work Research and Abstracts*, 26(4), 5–16.

Couper, Mick P. 2001. "Web Surveys: A Review of Issues and Approaches," *Public Opinion Quarterly*, 64(4), 464–494.

Cournoyer, B., and G. T. Powers. 2002. "Evidence-Based Social Work: The Quiet Revolution Continues," pp. 798–807 in Albert R. Roberts and

Gilbert J. Greene (eds.), *Social Workers' Desk Reference*. New York: Oxford University Press.

Creswell, J. (2014a). *A Concise Introduction to Mixed Methods Research*. Thousand Oaks, CA: Sage.

Creswell, J. (2014b). *Research Design: Qualitative, Quantitative, and Mixed Methods Approaches*. Thousand Oaks, CA: Sage.

Cuéllar, Israel, and Freddy A. Paniagua, eds. 2000. *Handbook of Multicultural Mental Health: Assessment and Treatment of Diverse Populations*. San Diego, CA: Academic Press.

Dana, Richard, ed. 2000. *Handbook of Cross-Cultural Personality Assessment*. Mahwah, NJ: Erlbaum.

Davis, Fred. 1973. "The Martian and the Convert: Ontological Polarities in Social Research," *Urban Life*, 2(3), 333–343.

Denzin, Norman K., and Yvonna S. Lincoln. 2000. *Handbook of Qualitative Research*, 2nd ed. Thousand Oaks, CA: Sage.

Dillman, Don A. 1978. *Mail and Telephone Surveys: The Total Design Method*. New York: Wiley.

_____. 2000. *Mail and Internet Surveys: The Tailored Design Method*. New York: Wiley.

Draguns, Juris G. 2000. "Multicultural and Cross-Cultural Assessment: Dilemmas and Decisions," pp. 37–84 in Gargi Roysircar Sodowsky and James C. Impara (eds.), *Multicultural Assessment in Counseling and Clinical Psychology*. Lincoln, NE: Buros Institute of Mental Measurements.

DuBois, B. 1983. "Passionate Scholarship: Notes on Values, Knowing and Method in Feminist Social Science," pp. 105–116 in G. Bowles and R. Duelli-Klein (eds.), *Theories of Women's Studies*. London: Routledge & Kegan Paul.

Duelli-Klein, R. 1983. "How to Do What We Want to Do: Thoughts about Feminist Methodology," pp. 88–104 in G. Bowles and R. Duelli-Klein (eds.), *Theories in Women's Studies*. London: Routledge & Kegan Paul.

Eichler, Margrit. 1988. *Nonsexist Research Methods*. Boston: Allen & Unwin.

Einstein, Albert. 1940. "The Fundamentals of Theoretical Physics," *Science* (May 24), 487.

Embry, D. D., and Biglan, A. 2008. Evidence-based kernels: Fundamental units of behavioral influence. *Clinical Child and Family Psychology Review*, 11, 75–113.

England, Suzanne E. 1994. "Modeling Theory from Fiction and Autobiography," pp. 190–213 in Catherine K. Reissman (ed.), *Qualitative Studies in Social Work Research*. Thousand Oaks, CA: Sage.

Epstein, W. M. 2004. "Confirmational Response Bias and the Quality of the Editorial Processes among American Social Work Journals," *Research on Social Work Practice*, 14(6), 450–458.

Fairbanks, E. (2008). Wiki Woman: The battle to define Hilary online. *The New Republic*, April 9, 2008, retrieved online at http://www.tnr.com/article/wiki-woman

Federal Communications Commission (FCC), Truth About Wireless Phones and the National Do-Not-Call List, May 24, 2011, online at http://www.fcc.gov/guides/truth-about-wireless-phones-and-national-do-not-call-list AAPOR Cell Phone Task Force, NEW CONSIDERATIONS FOR SURVEY RESEARCHERS WHEN PLANNING AND CONDUCTING RDD TELEPHONE SURVEYS IN THE U.S. WITH RESPONDENTS REACHED VIA CELL PHONE NUMBERS, 2010, online at http://www.aapor.org/AM/Template.cfm?Section= Cell_Phone_Task_Force_Report&Template=/CM/ContentDisplay.cfm&ContentID=3179#.UrCkt5Fe3PQ

Finckenauer, James. 1979. *Evaluation of Juvenile Awareness Project: Reports 1 and 2*. Newark, NJ: Rutgers School of Criminal Justice.

Fischer, Joel. 1973. "Is social work effective: A review," *Social Work*, 18(1), 5–20.

Fischer, Joel. 1990. "Problems and Issues in Meta-Analysis," pp. 297–325 in Lynn Videka-Sherman and William J. Reid (eds.), *Advances in Clinical Social Work Research*. Silver Spring, MD: NASW Press.

Gall, John. 1975. *Systemantics: How Systems Work and Especially How They Fail*. NewYork: Quadrangle.

Gambrill, E. 1999. "Evidence-Based Practice: An Alternative to Authority-Based Practice," *Families in Society*, 80, 341–350.

_____. 2001. "Educational Policy and Accreditation Standards: Do They Work for Clients?" *Journal of Social Work Education*, 37, 226–239.

Gaventa, J. 1991. "Towards a Knowledge Democracy: Viewpoints on Participatory Research in North America," pp. 121–131 in O. Fals-Borda and M. A. Rahman (eds.), *Action and Knowledge: Breaking the Monopoly with Participatory Action-Research*. New York: Apex Press.

Gibbs, Leonard, and Eileen Gambrill. 1999. *Critical Thinking for Social Workers: Exercises for the Helping Professions*. Thousand Oaks, CA: Pine Forge Press.

Gilgun, Jane. 1991. "Hand into Glove: The Grounded Theory Approach and Social Work Practice Research." Paper presented at the Research Conference on Qualitative Methods in Social Work Practice Research, Nelson A. Rockefeller Institute of Government, State University of New York at Albany, August 24.

_____, Kerry Daly, and Gerald Handel, eds. 1992. *Qualitative Methods in Family Research*. Thousand Oaks, CA: Sage.

Glaser, Barney, and Anselm Strauss. 1967. *The Discovery of Grounded Theory*. Chicago: Aldine.

Glock, Charles Y., Benjamin B. Ringer, and Earl R. Babbie. 1967. *To Comfort and to Challenge*. Berkeley: University of California Press.

Goffman, Erving. 1961. *Asylums: Essays on the Social Situation of Mental Patients and Other Inmates.* Chicago: Aldine.

_____. 1963. *Stigma: Notes on the Management of a Spoiled Identity.* Englewood Cliffs, NJ: Prentice Hall.

_____. 1974. *Frame Analysis.* Cambridge, MA: Harvard University Press.

_____. 1979. *Gender Advertisements.* New York: Harper & Row.

Goyder, John. 1985. "Face-to-Face Interviews and Mailed Questionnaires: The Net Difference in Response Rate," *Public Opinion Quarterly,* 49, 234–252.

Grinnell, R. M., Jr. 1997. *Social Work Research & Evaluation: Quantitative and Qualitative Approaches.* Itasca, IL: Peacock.

Guba, E. G. 1981. "Criteria for Assessing the Trustworthiness of Naturalistic Inquiries," *Educational Resources Information Center Annual Review Paper,* 29, 75–91.

Hanson, W. E., Creswell, J. W., Plano Cark, V. L., Petska, K. S., and Creswell, J. D. 2005. "Mixed Methods Research Designs in Counseling Psychology," *Journal of Counseling Psychology,* 52(2), 224–235.

Hepworth, D. H., R. Rooney, and J. A. Larsen. 2002. *Direct Social Work Practice: Theory and Skills,* 6th ed. Belmont, CA: Wadsworth.

Herman, Daniel B., Exra S. Susser, Elmer L. Struening, and Bruce L. Link. 1997. "Adverse Childhood Experiences: Are They Risk Factors for Adult Homelessness?" *American Journal of Public Health,* 87, 249–255.

Hernandez, Mario, and Mareasa R. Isaacs, eds. 1998. *Promoting Cultural Competence in Children's Mental Health Services.* Baltimore, MD: Paul H. Brookes.

Higginbotham, A. Leon, Jr. 1978. *In the Matter of Color: Race and the American Legal Process.* New York: Oxford University Press.

Hogarty, G. 1979. "Aftercare Treatment of Schizophrenia: Current Status and Future Direction," pp. 19–36 in H. M. Pragg (ed.), *Management of Schizophrenia.* Assen: Van Gorcum.

Hohmann, Ann A., and Delores L. Parron. 1996. "How the NIH Guidelines on Inclusion of Women and Minorities Apply: Efficacy Trials, Effectiveness Trials, and Validity," *Journal of Consulting and Clinical Psychology,* 64(5), 851–855.

Hough, Richard L., Henry Tarke, Virginia Renker, Patricia Shields, and Jeff Glatstein. 1996. "Recruitment and Retention of Homeless Mentally Ill Participants in Research," *Journal of Consulting and Clinical Psychology,* 64(5), 881–891.

Hudson, Walter W. 1982. *The Clinical Measurement Package.* Homewood, IL: Dorsey Press.

_____. 1997. "Assessment Tools as Outcomes Measures in Social Work," pp. 68–80 in Edward J. Mullen and Jennifer L. Magnabosco (eds.), *Outcomes Measurement in the Human Services: Cross-Cutting Issues and Methods.* Washington, DC: NASW Press.

Jackman, Mary R., and Mary Scheuer Senter. 1980. "Images of Social Groups: Categorical or Qualified?" *Public Opinion Quarterly,* 44, 340–361.

Jackson, Aurora P., and Andre Ivanoff. 1999. "Reduction of Low Response Rates in Interview Surveys of Poor African-American Families," *Journal of Social Service Research,* 25(1–2), 41–60.

Jayaratne, Srinika, Tony Tripodi, and Eugene Talsma. 1988. "The Comparative Analysis and Aggregation of Single Case Data," *Journal of Applied Behavioral Science,* 1(24), 119–128.

Jensen, Arthur. 1969. "How Much Can We Boost IQ and Scholastic Achievement?" *Harvard Educational Review,* 39, 273–274.

Johnson, Jeffrey C. 1990. *Selecting Ethnographic Informants.* Newbury Park, CA: Sage.

Jones, James H. 1981. *Bad Blood.* New York: Free Press.

Kaplowitz, Michael D., Timothy D. Hadlock, and Ralph Levine. 2004. "A Comparison of Web and Mail Survey Response Rates," *Public Opinion Quarterly,* 68(1), 94–101.

Keeter, Scott. 2006. "The Impact of Cell Phone Non-coverage Bias on Polling in the 2004 Presidential Election," *Public Opinion Quarterly,* 70(no. 1, Spring), 88–98.

Keeter, Scott, Michael Dimock, Leah Christian, and Courtney Kennedy. 2008. "The Impact of 'Cell-Onlys' on Public Opinion Polls: Ways of Coping with a Growing Population Segment," Pew Research Center Publications; online at http://pewresearch.org/pubs/714/the-impact-of-cell-onlys-on-public-opinion-polls; posted January 31.

Kinnel, Ann Marie, and Douglas W. Maynard. 1996. "The Delivery and Receipt of Safer Sex Advice in Pretest Counseling Sessions for HIV and AIDS," *Journal of Contemporary Ethnography,* 24, 405–437.

Krefting, Laura. 1991. "Rigor in Qualitative Research: The Assessment of Trustworthiness," *American Journal of Occupational Therapy,* 45(3), 214–222.

Kronick, Jane C. 1989. "Toward a Formal Methodology of Document Analysis in the Interpretive Tradition." Paper presented at the meeting of the Eastern Sociological Society, Baltimore, MD.

Kvale, Steinar. 1996. *InterViews: An Introduction to Qualitative Research Interviewing.* Thousand Oaks, CA: Sage.

Lincoln, Y. S., and E. A. Guba. 1985. *Naturalistic Inquiry.* Beverly Hills, CA: Sage.

Lofland, John. 1995. "Analytic Ethnography: Features, Failings, and Futures," *Journal of Contemporary Ethnography,* 24(1), 30–67.

_____, and Lyn H. Lofland. 1995. *Analyzing Social Settings,* 3rd ed. Belmont, CA: Wadsworth.

Marsden, Gerald. 1971. "Content Analysis Studies of Psychotherapy: 1954 through 1968," in Allen E. Bergin and Sol L. Garfield (eds.), *Handbook of Psychotherapy and Behavior Change: An Empirical Analysis*. New York: Wiley.

McRoy, Ruth G. 1981. *A Comparative Study of the Self-Concept of Transracially and Intraracially Adopted Black Children*. Dissertation, University of Texas at Austin.

_____, Harold D. Grotevant, Susan Ayers Lopez, and Ann Furuta. 1990. "Adoption Revelation and Communication Issues: Implications for Practice," *Families in Society* 71(9), 550–557.

Mercer, Susan, and Rosalie A. Kane. 1979. "Helplessness and Hopelessness Among the Institutionalized Aged," *Health and Social Work*, 4(1), 91–116.

Milgram, Stanley. 1963. "Behavioral Study of Obedience," *Journal of Abnormal and Social Psychology*, 67, 371–378.

_____. 1965. "Some Conditions of Obedience and Disobedience to Authority," *Human Relations*, 18, 57–76.

Millar, M.M., and D.A. Dillman. 2012. "Encouraging Survey Response via Smartphones: Effects on Respondents' Use of Mobile Devices and Survey Response Rates," *Survey Practice*, 5(3). www.surveypractice.org

Miranda, Jeanne. 1996. "Introduction to the Special Section of Recruiting and Retaining Minorities in Psychotherapy Research," *Journal of Consulting and Clinical Psychology*, 64(5), 848–850.

Mitchell, Richard G., Jr. 1991. "Secrecy and Disclosure in Field Work," pp. 97–108 in William B. Shaffir and Robert A. Stebbins (eds.), *Experiencing Fieldwork: An Inside View of Qualitative Research*. Newbury Park, CA: Sage.

Monette, Duane R., Thomas J. Sullivan, and Cornell R. DeJong. 1994. *Applied Social Research: Tool for the Human Services*, 5th ed. Orlando, FL: Harcourt Inc.

Moreland, Kevin L. 1996. "Persistent Issues in Multicultural Assessment of Social and Emotional Functioning," pp. 51–76 in Lisa Suzuki, Paul J. Meller, and Joseph G. Ponterotto (eds.), *Handbook of Multicultural Assessment*. San Francisco, CA: Jossey-Bass.

Morgan, David L. 1993. *Successful Focus Groups: Advancing the State of the Art*. Newbury Park, CA: Sage.

Morrissey, J., and H. Goldman. 1984. "Cycles of Reform in the Care of the Chronically Mentally Ill," *Hospital and Community Psychiatry*, 35(8), 785–793.

Morse, Janice M. 1994. "Designing Funded Qualitative Research," in Norman K. Denzin and Yvonna S. Lincoln (eds.), *Handbook of Qualitative Research*. Thousand Oaks, CA: Sage.

Moskowitz, Milt. 1981. "The Drugs that Doctors Order," *San Francisco Chronicle* (May 23), 33.

Mowbray, Carol T., Lisa C. Jordan, Kurt M. Ribisl, Angelina Kewalramani, Douglas Luke, Sandra Herman, and Deborah Bybee. 1999. "Analysis of Post-Discharge Change in a Dual Diagnosis Population," *Health & Social Work*, 4(2), 91–101.

Moynihan, Daniel. 1965. *The Negro Family: The Case for National Action*. Washington, DC: U.S. Government Printing Office.

Mullen, Edward, and Jennifer Magnabosco, eds. 1997. *Outcomes Measurement in the Human Services: Cross-Cutting Issues and Methods*. Washington, DC: NASW Press.

Mullen, E. J., and Dumpson, J. R., eds. 1972. *Evaluation of social intervention*. San Francisco: Jossey-Bass.

Murray, Charles, and Richard J. Herrnstein. 1994. *The Bell Curve*. New York: Free Press.

Myrdal, Gunnar. 1944. *An American Dilemma*. New York: Harper & Row.

Neuman, W. Lawrence. 2000. *Social Research Methods: Qualitative and Quantitative Approaches*, 4th ed. Needham Heights, MA: Allyn & Bacon.

New York Times. 1988. "Test of Journals is Criticized as Unethical," September 27, 21, 25.

Nicholls, William L., II, Reginald P. Baker, and Jean Martin. 1996. "The Effect of New Data Collection Technologies on Survey Data Quality," in L. Lyberg, P. Biemer, M. Collins, E. de Leeuw, C. Dippo, N. Schwarz, and D. Trewin (eds.), *Survey Measurement and Process Quality*. New York: Wiley.

Nichols, David S., Jesus Padilla, and Emilia Lucio Gomez-Maqueo. 2000. "Issues in the Cross-Cultural Adaptation and Use of the MMPI-2," pp. 247–266 in Richard Dana (ed.), *Handbook of Cross-Cultural Personality Assessment*. Mahwah, NJ: Erlbaum.

Norton, Ilena M., and Spero M. Manson. 1996. "Research in American Indian and Alaska Native Communities: Navigating the Cultural Universe of Values and Process," *Journal of Consulting and Clinical Psychology*, 64(5), 856–860.

Nugent, William R. 1991. "An Experimental and Qualitative Analysis of a Cognitive-Behavioral Intervention for Anger," *Social Work Research and Abstracts*, 27(3), 3–8.

Ortega, Debora M., and Cheryl A. Richey. 1998. "Methodological Issues in Social Work Research with Depressed Women of Color," pp. 47–70 in Miriam Potocky and Antoinette Y. Rodgers-Farmer (eds.), *Social Work Research with Minority and Oppressed Populations: Methodological Issues and Innovations*. New York: Haworth Press.

Padgett, Deborah K. 1998. *Qualitative Methods in Social Work Research*. Thousand Oaks, CA: Sage.

_____. 1998. "Does the Glove Really Fit? Qualitative Research and Clinical Social Work Practice," *Social Work*, 43(4), 373–381.

Padilla, Amado M., and Antonio Medina. 1996. "Cross-Cultural Sensitivity in Assessment," pp. 3–28 in Lisa Suzuki, Paul J. Meller, and Joseph G. Ponterotto (eds.), *Handbook of Multicultural Assessment*. San Francisco, CA: Jossey-Bass.

Patton, Michael Quinn. 1990. *Qualitative Evaluation and Research Methods*, 2nd ed. Newbury Park, CA: Sage.

Petersen, Larry R., and Judy L. Maynard. 1981. "Income, Equity, and Wives' Housekeeping Role Expectations," *Pacific Sociological Review* (January), 87–105.

Petrolia, Daniel R., and Sanjoy Bhattacharjee. 2009. "Revisiting Incentive Effects: Evidence from a Random-Sample Mail Survey on Consumer Preferences for Fuel Ethanol," *Public Opinion Quarterly*, 73, 537–550.

Popper, Karl. 2002. *The Logic of Scientific Discovery*. New York: Routledge Classics, [1934].

Posavac, Emil J., and Raymond G. Carey. 1985. *Program Evaluation: Methods and Case Studies*. Englewood Cliffs, NJ: Prentice Hall.

Quoss, Bernita, Margaret Cooney, and Terri Longhurst. 2000. "Academics and Advocates: Using Participatory Action Research to Influence Welfare Policy," *Journal of Consumer Affairs*, 34(1), 47.

Rank, Mark. 1992. "The Blending of Qualitative and Quantitative Methods in Understanding Childbearing among Welfare Recipients," pp. 281–300 in Jane Gilgun, Kerry Daly, and Gerald Handel (eds.), *Qualitative Methods in Family Research*. Thousand Oaks, CA: Sage.

Reinharz, Shulamit. 1992. *Feminist Methods in Social Research*. New York: Oxford University Press.

Reissman, Catherine, ed. 1994. *Qualitative Studies in Social Work Research*. Thousand Oaks, CA: Sage.

Rhodes, B. B., and E. L. Marks. 2011. "Using facebook to locate sample members," *Survey Practice*, 4, 5.

Robinson, Robin A. 1994. "Private Pain and Public Behaviors: Sexual Abuse and Delinquent Girls," pp. 73–94 in Catherine Reissman (ed.), *Qualitative Studies in Social Work Research*. Thousand Oaks, CA: Sage.

Rodwell, Mary K. 1998. *Social Constructivist Research*. New York: Garland.

Roffman, R. A., L. Downey, B. Beadnell, J. R. Gordon, J. N. Craver, and R. S. Stephens. 1997. "Cognitive-Behavioral Group Counseling to Prevent HIV Transmission in Gay and Bisexual Men: Factors Contributing to Successful Risk Reduction," *Research on Social Work Practice*, 7, 165–186.

_____, Joseph Picciano, Lauren Wickizer, Marc Bolan, and Rosemary Ryan. 1998. "Anonymous Enrollment in AIDS Prevention Telephone Group Counseling: Facilitating the Participation of Gay and Bisexual Men in Intervention and Research," pp. 5–22 in Miriam Potocky and Antoinette Y. Rodgers-Farmer (eds.), *Social Work Research with Minority and Oppressed Populations: Methodological Issues and Innovations*. New York: Haworth Press.

Rogler, Lloyd H. 1989. "The Meaning of Culturally Sensitive Research in Mental Health," *American Journal of Psychiatry*, 146(3), 296–303.

_____, and A. B. Hollingshead. 1985. *Trapped: Puerto Rican Families and Schizophrenia* Maplewood, NJ: Waterfront Press.

Rosenhan, D. L. 1973. "On Being Sane in Insane Places," *Science*, 179, 240–248.

Rosenthal, Richard N. 2006. "Overview of Evidence-Based Practice," pp. 67–80 in A. R. Roberts and K. Yeager (eds.), *Foundations of Evidence-Based Social Work Practice*. New York: Oxford University Press.

Rosenthal, Robert, and Donald Rubin. 1982. "A Simple, General Purpose Display of Magnitude of Experimental Effect," *Journal of Educational Psychology*, 74(2), 166–169.

Rossi, Peter H., and Howard E. Freeman. 1993. *Evaluation: A Systematic Approach*, 5th ed. Newbury Park, CA: Sage.

Rothman, Ellen K. 1981. "The Written Record," *Journal of Family History (Spring)*, 47–56.

Royse, David. 1991. *Research Methods in Social Work*. Chicago: Nelson-Hall.

Rubin, A. (2010). Teaching EBP in social work: retrospective and prospective. *Journal of Social Work*, 11, 1, 64–79.

Rubin, Allen, and Earl Babbie. 2011. *Research Methods for Social Work*, 7th ed. Belmont, CA: Brooks/Cole.

Rubin, A. 2014. "An Alternative Paradigm for Social Workers Seeking to Do Intervention Research," *Social Work Research*, 38, 69–71.

Sackett, D. L., W. S. Richardson, W. Rosenberg, and R. B. Haynes. (1997). *Evidence-Based Medicine: How to Practice and Teach EBM*. New York: Churchill Livingstone.

Sales, Esther, Sara Lichtenwalter, and Antonio Fevola. 2006. "Secondary Analysis in Social Work Research Education: Past, Present, and Future Promise," *Journal of Social Work Education*, 42(3), 543–558.

Saletan, William, and Nancy Watzman. 1989. "Marcus Welby, J.D.," *New Republic*, 200(16), 22.

Sampson, M., Villarreal, Y., and Rubin, A. 2014. An Adaptation of a Problem Solving Tools Intervention for Low-Income, African American Women at Risk for Postpartum Depression: A Pilot Study. Manuscript submitted for publication.

Sandelowski, M., D. H. Holditch-Davis, and B. G. Harris. 1989. "Artful Design: Writing the Proposal for Research in the Naturalistic Paradigm," *Research in Nursing and Health*, 12, 77–84.

Schuerman, John. 1989. "Editorial," *Social Service Review*, 63(1), 3.

Shadish, William R., Thomas D. Cook, and Laura C. Leviton. 1991. *Foundations of Program Evaluation.* Newbury Park, CA: Sage.

_____, Thomas D. Cook, and Donald T. Campbell. 2001. *Experimental and Quasi-Experimental Designs for Generalized Causal Inference.* New York: Houghton Mifflin.

Shanks, J. Merrill, and Robert D. Tortora. 1985. "Beyond CATI: Generalized and Distributed Systems for Computer-Assisted Surveys." Prepared for the Bureau of the Census, First Annual Research Conference, Reston, VA, March 20–23.

Shlonsky, A., and Gibbs, L. 2004. Will the Real Evidence-Based Practice Please Stand Up? Teaching the Process of Evidence-Based Practice to the Helping Professions. *Brief Treatment and Crisis Intervention*, 4(2), 137–153.

Silverman, David. 1993. *Interpreting Qualitative Data: Methods for Analyzing Talk, Text, and Interaction.* Newbury Park, CA: Sage.

Singer, Eleanor, Robert M. Groves, and Amy D. Corning. 1999. "Differential Incentives: Beliefs about Practices, Perceptions of Equity, and Effects on Survey Participation," *Public Opinion Quarterly*, 63, 251–260.

Snow, David A., and Leon Anderson. 1987. "Identity Work among the Homeless: The Verbal Construction and Avowal of Personal Identities," *Journal of Sociology*, 96(6), 1336–1371.

Sodowsky, Gargi Roysircar, and James C. Impara, eds. 1996. *Multicultural Assessment in Counseling and Clinical Psychology.* Lincoln, NE: Buros Institute of Mental Measurements.

Solomon, Phyllis, and Robert I. Paulson. 1995. "Issues in Designing and Conducting Randomized Human Service Trials." Paper presented at the National Conference of the Society for Social Work and Research, Washington, DC.

Strauss, Anselm, and Juliet Corbin. 1990. *Basics of Qualitative Research: Grounded Theory Procedures and Techniques.* Newbury Park, CA: Sage.

Stuart, Paul. 1981. "Historical Research," pp. 316–332 in Richard M. Grinnell (ed.), *Social Work Research and Evaluation.* Itasca, IL: Peacock.

Suzuki, Lisa A., Paul J. Meller, and Joseph G. Ponterotto, eds. 1996. *Handbook of Multicultural Assessment.* San Francisco, CA: Jossey-Bass.

Tan, Alexis S. 1980. "Mass Media Use, Issue Knowledge and Political Involvement," *Public Opinion Quarterly*, 44, 241–248.

Thompson, Estina E., Harold W. Neighbors, Cheryl Munday, and James S. Jackson. 1996. "Recruitment and Retention of African American Patients for Clinical Research: An Exploration of Response Rates in an Urban Psychiatric Hospital," *Journal of Consulting and Clinical Psychology*, 64(5), 861–867.

Thyer, Bruce. 2001. "Evidence-Based Approaches to Community Practice," pp. 54–65 in Harold E. Briggs and Kevin Corcoran (eds.), *Social Work Practice: Treating Common Client Problems.* Chicago: Lyceum Books.

_____. 2002. "Principles of Evidence-Based Practice and Treatment Development," pp. 738–742 in Albert R. Roberts and Gilbert J. Greene (eds.), *Social Workers' Desk Reference.* New York: Oxford University Press.

U.S. Bureau of the Census. 1979. *Statistical Abstract of the United States.* Washington, DC: U.S. Government Printing Office.

_____. 1992. *Statistical Abstract of the United States.* Washington, DC: U.S. Government Printing Office.

_____. 1995. *Statistical Abstract of the United States.* Washington, DC: U.S. Government Printing Office.

_____. 1996. *Statistical Abstract of the United States.* Washington, DC: U.S. Government Printing Office.

_____. 2006. *Statistical Abstract of the United States 2006: The National Data Book.* Washington, DC: U.S. Government Printing Office.

U.S. Department of Health and Human Services. 1992. *Survey Measurement of Drug Use.* Washington, DC: U.S. Government Printing Office.

U.S. Department of Labor (Bureau of Labor Statistics). 1978. *The Consumer Price Index: Concepts and Content over the Years.* Report 517. Washington, DC: U.S. Government Printing Office.

Vonk, M. Elizabeth. 2001. "Cultural Competence for Transracial Adoptive Parents," *Social Work*, 46(3), 246–255.

Wallace, Walter. (1971). *The Logic of Science in Sociology.* Chicago: Aldine-Atherton

Weber, Max. 1925. "Science as a Vocation," in Hans Gerth and C. Wright Mills (trans., eds.), *Essays in Sociology.* New York: Oxford University Press, 1946.

Weisz, J. R., Ugueto, A. M., Herren, J., Afienko, S. R., and Rutt. 2011. "Kernels vs. Ears and Other Questions for a Science of Treatment Dissemination," *Clinical Psychology: Science and Practice*, 18, 41–46.

Weitzman, Eben, and Matthew Miles. 1995. *Computer Programs for Qualitative Data Analysis.* Newbury Park, CA: Sage.

Whyte, William Foote, D. J. Greenwood, and P. Lazes. 1991. "Participatory Action Research: Through Practice to Science in Social Research," pp. 19–55 in W. F. Whyte (ed.), *Participatory Action Research.* New York: Sage.

Wood, K. M. (1978). "Casework Effectiveness: A New Look at the Research Evidence," *Social Work*, 23(6), 437–458.

Yoshihama, Mieko. 2002. "Breaking the Web of Abuse and Silence: Voices of Battered Women in Japan," *Social Work*, 47(4), 389–400.

Index